Teach Yourself® the iMac™

Teach Yourself® the iMac™

Jennifer Watson

IDG Books Worldwide, Inc.
An International Data Group Company

Foster City, CA • Chicago, IL • Indianapolis, IN • New York, NY

Teach Yourself® the iMac™

Published by
IDG Books Worldwide, Inc.
An International Data Group Company
919 E. Hillsdale Blvd., Suite 400
Foster City, CA 94404
www.idgbooks.com (IDG Books Worldwide Web site)

ISBN: 0-7645-3396-7

Printed in the United States of America

10 9 8 7 6 5 4 3 2 1

1P/RW/RS/ZZ/IN

Distributed in the United States by IDG Books Worldwide, Inc.

Distributed by CDG Books Canada Inc. for Canada; by Transworld Publishers Limited in the United Kingdom; by IDG Norge Books for Norway; by IDG Sweden Books for Sweden; by IDG Books Australia Publishing Corporation Pty. Ltd. for Australia and New Zealand; by TransQuest Publishers Pte Ltd. for Singapore, Malaysia, Thailand, Indonesia, and Hong Kong; by Gotop Information Inc. for Taiwan; by ICG Muse, Inc. for Japan; by Intersoft for South Africa; by Eyrolles for France; by International Thomson Publishing for Germany, Austria and Switzerland; by Distribuidora Cuspide for Argentina; by LR International for Brazil; by Galileo Libros for Chile; by Ediciones ZETA S.C.R. Ltda. for Peru; by WS Computer Publishing Corporation, Inc., for the Philippines; by Contemporanea de Ediciones for Venezuela; by Express Computer Distributors for the Caribbean and West Indies; by Micronesia Media Distributor, Inc. for Micronesia; by Chips Computadoras S.A. de C.V. for Mexico; by Editorial Norma de Panama S.A. for Panama; by American Bookshops for Finland.

For general information on IDG Books Worldwide's books in the U.S., please call our Consumer Customer Service department at 800-762-2974. For reseller information, including discounts and premium sales, please call our Reseller Customer Service department at 800-434-3422.

For information on where to purchase IDG Books Worldwide's books outside the U.S., please contact our International Sales department at 317-596-5530 or fax 317-596-5692.

For consumer information on foreign language translations, please contact our Customer Service department at 800-434-3422, fax 317-596-5692, or e-mail rights@idgbooks.com.

For information on licensing foreign or domestic rights, please phone +1-650-655-3109.

For sales inquiries and special prices for bulk quantities, please contact our Sales department at 650-655-3200 or write to the address above.

For information on using IDG Books Worldwide's books in the classroom or for ordering examination copies, please contact our Educational Sales department at 800-434-2086 or fax 317-596-5499.

For press review copies, author interviews, or other publicity information, please contact our Public Relations department at 650-655-3000 or fax 650-655-3299.

For authorization to photocopy items for corporate, personal, or educational use, please contact Copyright Clearance Center, 222 Rosewood Drive, Danvers, MA 01923, or fax 978-750-4470.

Library of Congress Cataloging-in-Publication Data

Watson, Jennifer.
Teach Yourself the iMac / Jennifer Watson.
p. cm.
ISBN 0-7645-3396-7 (alk. paper)
1. iMac (Computer). I. Title.
QA76.8.I52 W37 1999
004.165--dc21 99–048100
CIP

ABOUT IDG BOOKS WORLDWIDE

Welcome to the world of IDG Books Worldwide.

IDG Books Worldwide, Inc., is a subsidiary of International Data Group, the world's largest publisher of computer-related information and the leading global provider of information services on information technology. IDG was founded more than 30 years ago by Patrick J. McGovern and now employs more than 9,000 people worldwide. IDG publishes more than 290 computer publications in over 75 countries. More than 90 million people read one or more IDG publications each month.

Launched in 1990, IDG Books Worldwide is today the #1 publisher of best-selling computer books in the United States. We are proud to have received eight awards from the Computer Press Association in recognition of editorial excellence and three from Computer Currents' First Annual Readers' Choice Awards. Our best-selling *...For Dummies®* series has more than 50 million copies in print with translations in 31 languages. IDG Books Worldwide, through a joint venture with IDG's Hi-Tech Beijing, became the first U.S. publisher to publish a computer book in the People's Republic of China. In record time, IDG Books Worldwide has become the first choice for millions of readers around the world who want to learn how to better manage their businesses.

Our mission is simple: Every one of our books is designed to bring extra value and skill-building instructions to the reader. Our books are written by experts who understand and care about our readers. The knowledge base of our editorial staff comes from years of experience in publishing, education, and journalism — experience we use to produce books to carry us into the new millennium. In short, we care about books, so we attract the best people. We devote special attention to details such as audience, interior design, use of icons, and illustrations. And because we use an efficient process of authoring, editing, and desktop publishing our books electronically, we can spend more time ensuring superior content and less time on the technicalities of making books.

You can count on our commitment to deliver high-quality books at competitive prices on topics you want to read about. At IDG Books Worldwide, we continue in the IDG tradition of delivering quality for more than 30 years. You'll find no better book on a subject than one from IDG Books Worldwide.

John Kilcullen
Chairman and CEO
IDG Books Worldwide, Inc.

Steven Berkowitz
President and Publisher
IDG Books Worldwide, Inc.

Eighth Annual Computer Press Awards 1992

Ninth Annual Computer Press Awards 1993

X
WINNER

Tenth Annual Computer Press Awards 1994

Eleventh Annual Computer Press Awards 1995

IDG is the world's leading IT media, research and exposition company. Founded in 1964, IDG had 1997 revenues of $2.05 billion and has more than 9,000 employees worldwide. IDG offers the widest range of media options that reach IT buyers in 75 countries representing 95% of worldwide IT spending. IDG's diverse product and services portfolio spans six key areas including print publishing, online publishing, expositions and conferences, market research, education and training, and global marketing services. More than 90 million people read one or more of IDG's 290 magazines and newspapers, including IDG's leading global brands — Computerworld, PC World, Network World, Macworld and the Channel World family of publications. IDG Books Worldwide is one of the fastest-growing computer book publishers in the world, with more than 700 titles in 36 languages. The "...For Dummies®" series alone has more than 50 million copies in print. IDG offers online users the largest network of technology-specific Web sites around the world through IDG.net (http://www.idg.net), which comprises more than 225 targeted Web sites in 55 countries worldwide. International Data Corporation (IDC) is the world's largest provider of information technology data, analysis and consulting, with research centers in over 41 countries and more than 400 research analysts worldwide. IDG World Expo is a leading producer of more than 168 globally branded conferences and expositions in 35 countries including E3 (Electronic Entertainment Expo), Macworld Expo, ComNet, Windows World Expo, ICE (Internet Commerce Expo), Agenda, DEMO, and Spotlight. IDG's training subsidiary, ExecuTrain, is the world's largest computer training company, with more than 230 locations worldwide and 785 training courses. IDG Marketing Services helps industry-leading IT companies build international brand recognition by developing global integrated marketing programs via IDG's print, online and exposition products worldwide. Further information about the company can be found at www.idg.com.

1/24/99

Credits

Acquisitions Editor
Michael Roney

Development Editor
Katharine Dvorak

Technical Editor
Dennis Cohen

Copy Editors
Sally Davis Neuman
Ami Knox

Project Coordinator
Regina Snyder

Book Designers
Daniel Ziegler Design, Cátálin Dulfu, Kurt Krames

Proofreading and Indexing
York Production Services

About the Author

Jennifer Watson is the author of *Cliffs Notes on Using Your First iMac* and ten other popular and best-selling books on computers and the Internet. As an early adopter of the Macintosh, Jennifer has run the gamut of the Mac experience from absolute virgin and obsessed beginner to fanatical power user and guru. She was hooked from the moment she learned the Mac during her first day on a new job, mastering in hours what her coworkers had missed for months. From there she went on to help form and lead one of the first Macintosh user groups in Kyoto, Japan. She has also edited and published the newsletter of the Ann Arbor MacTechnics user group. Jennifer has been around the world to Mac trade shows, from Tokyo to Boston to San Francisco. Jennifer earned her undergraduate degree from the University of Michigan at Ann Arbor, and still makes her home there, in the city that boasts of having more Macintoshes per capita than any other city in the world. You can reach Jennifer at jennifer@jenuine.net.

To Dave Marx, my personal Mac student, and to George Louie, my personal Mac guru. May the circle of learning continue indefinitely.

Welcome to Teach Yourself

Welcome to *Teach Yourself*, a series read and trusted by millions for nearly a decade. Although you may have seen the *Teach Yourself* name on other books, ours is the original. In addition, no *Teach Yourself* series has ever delivered more on the promise of its name than this series. That's because IDG Books Worldwide recently transformed *Teach Yourself* into a new cutting-edge format that gives you all the information you need to learn quickly and easily.

Readers told us that they want to learn by doing and that they want to learn as much as they can in as short a time as possible. We listened to you and believe that our new task-by-task format and suite of learning tools deliver the book you need to successfully teach yourself any technology topic. Features such as our Personal Workbook, which lets you practice and reinforce the skills you've just learned, help ensure that you get full value out of the time you invest in your learning. Handy cross-references to related topics and online sites broaden your knowledge and give you control over the kind of information you want, when you want it.

More Answers . . .

In designing the latest incarnation of this series, we started with the premise that people like you, who are beginning to intermediate computer users, want to take control of their own learning. To do this, you need the proper tools to find answers to questions so you can solve problems now.

In designing a series of books that provide such tools, we created a unique and concise visual format. The added bonus: *Teach Yourself* books actually pack more information into their pages than other books written on the same subjects. Skill for skill, you typically get much more information in a *Teach Yourself* book. In fact, *Teach Yourself* books, on average, cover twice the skills covered by other computer books — as many as 125 skills per book — so they're more likely to address your specific needs.

Welcome to Teach Yourself

. . . In Less Time

We know you don't want to spend twice the time to get all this great information, so we provide lots of time-saving features:

- ▶ A modular task-by-task organization of information: Any task you want to perform is easy to find and includes simple-to-follow steps
- ▶ A larger size than standard makes the book easy to read and convenient to use at a computer workstation. The large format also enables us to include many more illustrations — 500 screen illustrations show you how to get everything done!
- ▶ A Personal Workbook at the end of each chapter reinforces learning with extra practice, real-world applications for your learning, and questions and answers to test your knowledge
- ▶ Cross-references appearing at the bottom of each task page refer you to related information, providing a path through the book for learning particular aspects of the software thoroughly
- ▶ A Find It Online feature offers valuable ideas on where to go on the Internet to get more information or to download useful files
- ▶ Take Note sidebars provide added-value information from our expert authors for more in-depth learning
- ▶ An attractive, consistent organization of information helps you quickly find and learn the skills you need

These *Teach Yourself* features are designed to help you learn the essential skills about a technology in the least amount of time, with the most benefit. We've placed these features consistently throughout the book, so you quickly learn where to go to find just the information you need — whether you work through the book from cover to cover or use it later to solve a new problem.

You will find a *Teach Yourself* book on almost any technology subject — from the Internet to Windows to Microsoft Office. Take control of your learning today, with IDG Books Worldwide's *Teach Yourself* series.

Teach Yourself

More Answers in Less Time

Search through the task headings to find the topic you want right away. To learn a new skill, search the contents, chapter opener, or the extensive index to find what you need. Then find — at a glance — the clear task heading that matches it.

Setting Application Preferences

Taking a cue from the iMac, most large applications — and even many small ones — offer the ability to set preferences. Some applications may call it Customize, while others use Settings. Most applications stick with good old reliable Preferences. The most likely place to find an application's preferences are under the File menu, though I've also seen them under Edit, Tools, and Help.

While all application preferences differ a bit from one another, most of them work in similar ways. So let's explore Adobe Acrobat Reader's preferences, as they are particularly good. In fact, Adobe Acrobat Reader mostly displays (and prints) special instructional and informational files. Thus, setting your preferences is one of the few things you can actually *do* in Adobe Acrobat Reader besides open and print files.

Begin by opening Adobe Acrobat Reader and selecting the Preferences submenu under the File menu. You have four sets of preferences: General, Notes, Full Screen, and Weblink. Choose General and take a look at the staggering array of available options. Most of this stuff just isn't going to make much sense until you've learned to use the application. For now, my recommendation is to stick with all these default values and preferences. The software manufacturer set each option with new users in mind.

Note the different ways you can choose your settings in Adobe Acrobat Reader. Drop-down menus let you choose from a list of options. Text entry fields let you type in specific values. Check boxes allow you to enable a particular setting. You'll encounter these methods in other applications' preferences, too.

Save your preferences by clicking the OK button (or click the Apply button, if it is available). If you set

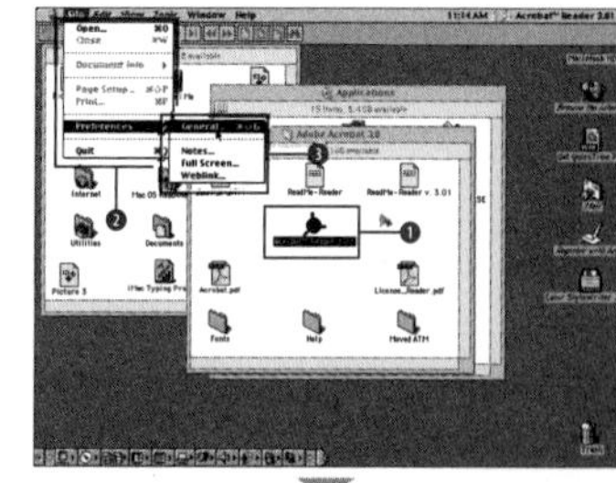

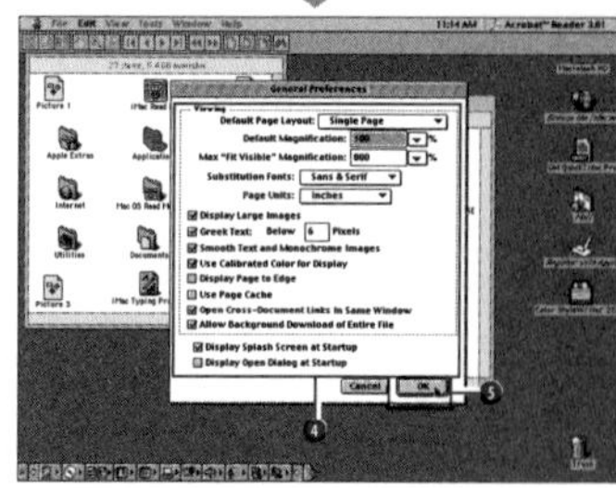

❶ *Double-click Adobe Acrobat Reader to run the application.*

❷ *Pull down the File menu and display the Preferences submenu.*

❸ *Choose the General preferences.*

❹ *Set your general preferences, if you wish.*

▶ *Optional: Click the Cancel button if you want to discard any changes you made.*

❺ *Click OK.*

❻ *Open your Weblink preferences from the File menu.*

CROSS-REFERENCE

See "Setting Your Preferences" in Chapter 2 for advice on deciding which preferences to use.

152

Learn the concepts behind the task at hand and, more important, learn how the task is relevant in the real world. Time-saving suggestions and advice show you how to make the most of each skill.

After you learn the task at hand, you may have more questions, or you may want to read about other tasks related to the topic. Use the cross-references to find different tasks to make your learning more efficient.

Ultimately, people learn by doing. Follow the clear, illustrated steps presented with every task to complete a procedure. The detailed callouts for each step show you exactly where to go and what to do to complete the task.

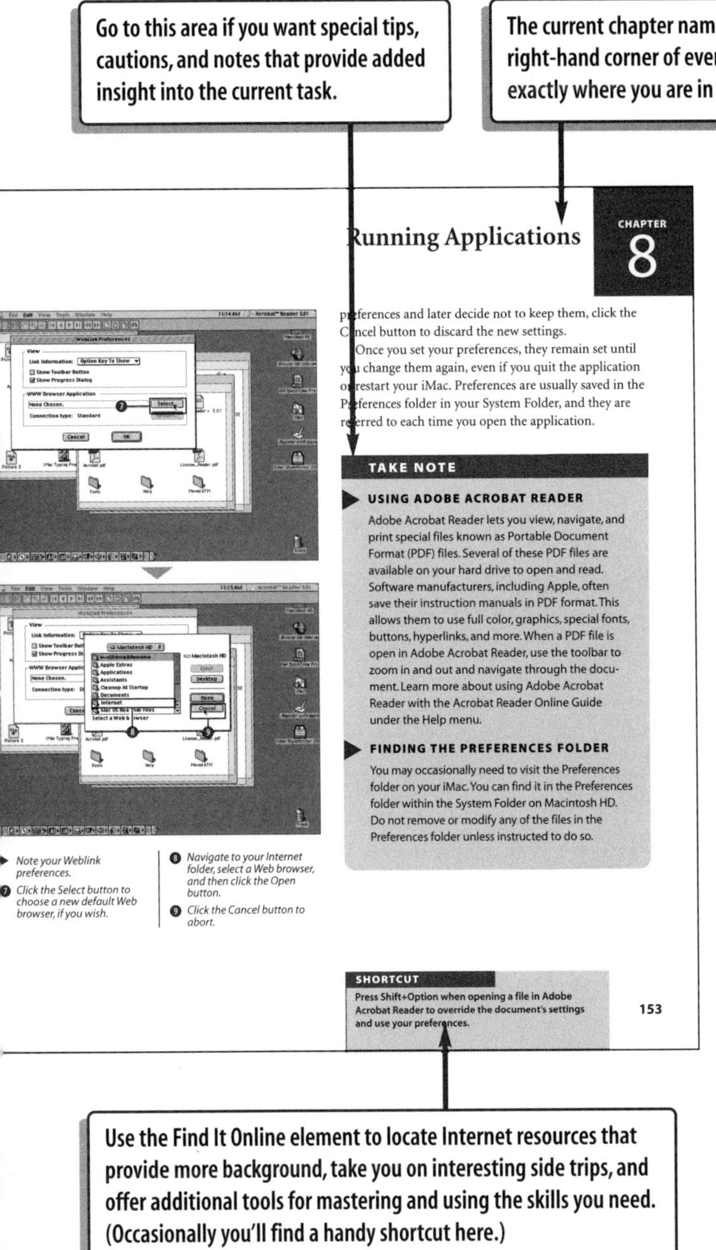

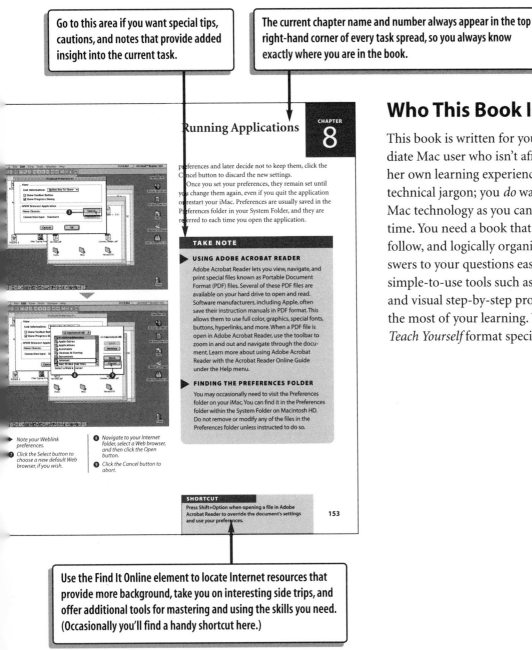

Who This Book Is For

This book is written for you, a beginning to intermediate Mac user who isn't afraid to take charge of his or her own learning experience. You don't want a lot of technical jargon; you *do* want to learn as much about Mac technology as you can in a limited amount of time. You need a book that is straightforward, easy to follow, and logically organized, so you can find answers to your questions easily. And, you appreciate simple-to-use tools such as handy cross-references and visual step-by-step procedures that help you make the most of your learning. We have created the unique *Teach Yourself* format specifically to meet your needs.

Personal Workbook

It's a well-known fact that much of what we learn is lost soon after we learn it if we don't reinforce our newly acquired skills with practice and repetition. That's why each *Teach Yourself* chapter ends with your own Personal Workbook. Here's where you can get extra practice, test your knowledge, and discover ideas for using what you've learned in the real world. There's even a Visual Quiz to help you remember your way around the topic's software environment.

Feedback

Please let us know what you think about this book, and whether you have any suggestions for improvements. You can send questions and comments to the *Teach Yourself* editors on the IDG Books Worldwide Web site at **www.idgbooks.com**.

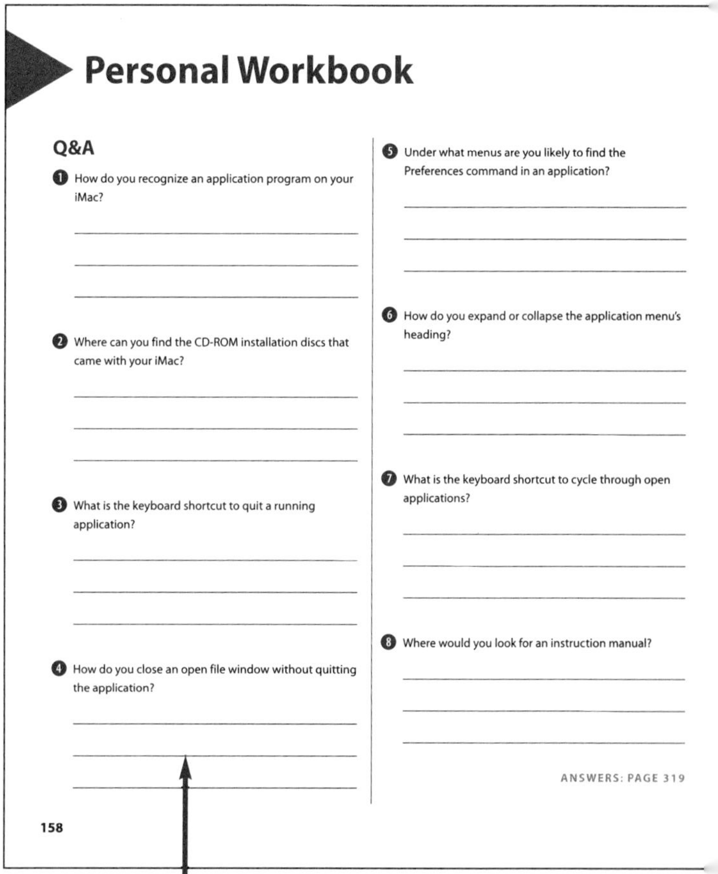

Personal Workbook

Q&A

1. How do you recognize an application program on your iMac?
2. Where can you find the CD-ROM installation discs that came with your iMac?
3. What is the keyboard shortcut to quit a running application?
4. How do you close an open file window without quitting the application?
5. Under what menus are you likely to find the Preferences command in an application?
6. How do you expand or collapse the application menu's heading?
7. What is the keyboard shortcut to cycle through open applications?
8. Where would you look for an instruction manual?

ANSWERS: PAGE 319

158

After working through the tasks in each chapter, you can test your progress and reinforce your learning by answering the questions in the Q&A section. Then check your answers in the Personal Workbook Answers appendix at the back of the book.

Another practical way to reinforce your skills is to do additional exercises on the same skills you just learned without the benefit of the chapter's visual steps. If you struggle with any of these exercises, it's a good idea to refer to the chapter's tasks to be sure you've mastered them.

Running Applications

CHAPTER 8

Read the list of Real-World Applications to get ideas on how you can use the skills you've just learned in your everyday life. Understanding a process can be simple; knowing how to use that process to make you more productive is the key to successful learning.

EXTRA PRACTICE

1. Find and open the Calculator application that came installed on your iMac. Leave it running.
2. Install a program from a CD-ROM (skip if you've already installed it). Find all the places on your iMac you can go to run the application.
3. Run AppleWorks from its folder in the Applications folder. Use it to open a document you find in the Adobe Acrobat 3.0 folder.
4. Find the Preferences for AppleWorks. See if there are any settings you'd like to change and change them. When you're finished, change them back to their original settings.
5. Switch to the Calculator using the Application menu. Switch back to AppleWorks by clicking an open AppleWorks window.

REAL-WORLD APPLICATIONS

✔ You're positive you installed an application on your computer, but you can't find its icon on the iMac desktop. You use Sherlock to search your hard drive, find the application, and open it. You also create an alias for the program and place it on your Desktop.

✔ You buy a new application program for your children on CD-ROM. As they look on skeptically, you pop the CD-ROM into the iMac and install the program as if you've been doing it for years. In minutes they're playing (and learning), and you're a hero!

✔ Your children complain that their new application is hard to use. Knowing that many educational programs can be adjusted for a child's age and skill level, you search for a Preferences menu. You find it in the File menu and start tweaking.

Visual Quiz

How do you get this window and what can you do there?

159

Take the Visual Quiz to see how well you're learning your way around the technology. Learning about computers is often as much about how to find a button or menu as it is about memorizing definitions. Our Visual Quiz helps you find your way.

Acknowledgments

I gratefully acknowledge the many wonderful people who helped bring this book to life.

A huge thank you to Dave Marx, who happily read every word, tried out the tasks on the iMac, returned invaluable feedback, and offered suggestions and comments. Dave is also the Master of Introductions for this book, helping me introduce a chapter in a fun, friendly, informative way. All this, and he isn't even a Mac fanatic!

Many thanks to George Louie, who knows virtually everything about Macs. He answered each one of my calls (even the ones in the wee hours of the morning) with patience and a genuine desire to help.

A special thank you to Glenn White, who also knows virtually everything about Macs. Your colorful sidebars on feng shui, iMac color considerations, and iMac name ideas really brighten up the book!

Thank you to Ben Foxworth, who introduced me to the art of using America Online on the Mac years ago and continues to dazzle me with his Mac knowledge.

Thank you to Kim and Chad Larner and Dan, Jeannie, Kayleigh, Melanie, and Nina Marx, each of whom were my reader stand-ins when I needed to visualize my audience. May your love and respect for Macs continue to grow!

Thank you also to my family and friends who provided much needed breaks during the writing process: Carolyn Tody, Tom Anderson, Jeanne and David Beroza, Fred and Adele Marx, Tracy DeGarmo, and Bradley Zimmer.

A warm thank you to the incredibly professional folks at IDG Books Worldwide: Andy Cummings, Mike Roney, Katharine Dvorak, Dennis Cohen, Sally Neuman, Ami Knox, and the many people in production I don't get the pleasure of meeting. Without you none of this would be possible!

Finally my thanks to you, my readers, for your faith in my writing, this series, and the wonderfully different, technicolor iMac.

Contents

Contents

Contents

Contents

Teach Yourself® the iMac™

PART I

Discovering Your iMac

Do you have a large, square box sitting in your living room? Does it shout, "Open me, open me, *please* open me"? If it does, you're a rare iMac owner. An unopened iMac carton is as rare as an unwrapped present on the day after Christmas.

If you've already opened and set up your iMac, I'll forgive you. After all, the colorful, oh-so-nifty iMac is awfully hard to resist. Even I, who have had close, loving relationships with nearly a dozen different Macintosh computers, was as excited as a kid who inherited a candy store when my iMac arrived.

Still, an author can always hope that she can get her readers started off on the right foot, and this is definitely the place to get started. So let's play make-believe for a little while, and pretend you haven't already set up and turned on your iMac. We'll start at the very beginning, and very soon, our step-by-step, visual exploration of your new iMac will teach you things you never knew, and it will also create a firm foundation for everything that follows.

CHAPTER 1

MASTER THESE SKILLS

- Identifying Your iMac Components
- Setting Up and Plugging In Your iMac
- Turning On Your iMac
- Moving the Mouse
- Viewing the Menus
- Opening Windows
- Understanding Icons
- Setting Your Apple Menu Options
- Closing Your Windows
- Ending Your Session

Getting Started

The folks at Apple set out to make the iMac the easiest Macintosh ever, and they've succeeded. This is no small feat: the Macintosh has always set the pace for ease of use in the computer world. What's more, the iMac is one of the most visually exciting computers ever made. I dare anyone to walk past an iMac without stopping to marvel at its colorful, curvy, see-through case and its compact, all-in-one design. Under the hood, it performs like a sports car, zipping through demanding tasks like a seasoned professional. It's quite a computer!

Of course, if you're reading this book, you're already sold. But just in case you weren't itching to open up your iMac and get started, the last paragraph should have set your heart racing. Fortunately, this is the chapter that shouts, "On your mark, get set, go!"

You're going to get off to a fast start. The iMac's design lets us dash through the setup, plug-in, and startup lessons in record time. You won't even break a sweat. Who can blame you if you want to jump right in and learn how to use the mouse?

The Macintosh has a Graphical User Interface (or GUI, pronounced as *gooey*). That's computer geek-speak for the iMac's equivalent of a steering wheel, a gear shift, the gas and brake pedals, a speedometer, a windshield, a rear view mirror, and a gas gauge. Yes, this is the first part of your driving lesson, so you'll learn how to start up your iMac, recognize what you see on the screen, and get a feel for the controls.

One of the keys to the Mac's ease of use is consistency — no matter what computer programs you'll someday use on your iMac, they all depend on that common user interface. Once you learn the basics of maneuvering your mouse, viewing menus, opening and manipulating windows, understanding icons, and setting options, you can apply that knowledge to any task you can accomplish with your iMac. You'll learn these basics in this first chapter, preparing you for your adventures ahead.

So fuel up on those carbonated beverages and fasten down your mouse pads. Your iMac is going to take you for the ride of your life!

Identifying Your iMac Components

Your iMac comes neatly packed in a large, pumpkin-orange box. It may remind you of Halloween, but resist the temptation to immediately dive in for the goodies. Check the box first for punctures and corner cave-ins that could indicate hidden damage or poor handling. If your iMac will be delivered, read the carrier's forms carefully before you sign them — you may be waiving your right to damage recovery. Everything you need for your iMac comes in one box. If you ordered a peripheral such as a printer or external floppy drive, verify that those boxes are also included. Also, check the flavor label on top of the box to verify that your iMac is the color you ordered.

When you're ready to open the box, lift the box by the two handholds cut into the sides and move it to a spacious, well-lighted area. Carefully cut the tape on top of the box and open the flaps. The Accessory Kit is the first item in the box — the photo on the lid looks like lollipops if you squint a bit (they're actually iMac mice). Open the Accessory Kit and note its three compartments: one for documentation and software, one for cables and the mouse, and one for the keyboard. Make a beeline for the Welcome To Your iMac reference card, which should be on top of the documentation pile. It illustrates the six steps required to set up your iMac — complete with photographs.

Begin identifying your iMac components, referring to the Welcome card as a reference if you're not sure what something should look like. In the cable compartment of the Accessory box, look for the power cord. It may be color-matched to your iMac (mine reminded me of a lime candy stick), with a three-prong plug on one end and a three-prong receptacle on the other. Locate the telephone line cord, which is generally translucent and has two standard RJ-11 phone plugs on each end. The

CROSS-REFERENCE

Chapter 3 covers removable media drives (if you purchased an external floppy or Zip drive), and Chapter 6 covers printers (if you purchased a printer).

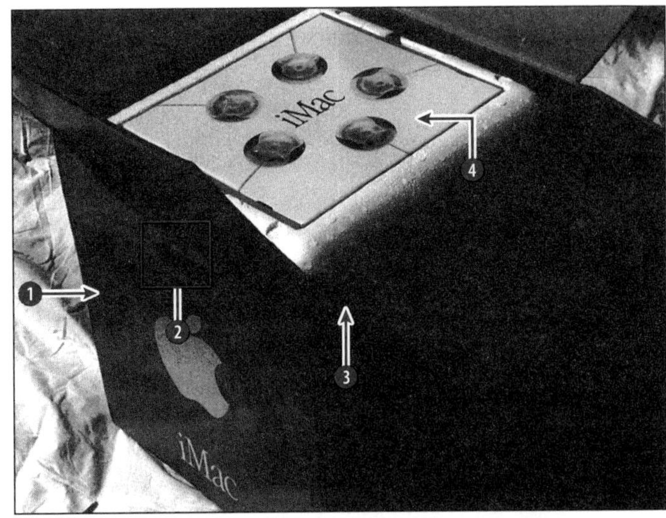

1. *Check your iMac box for damage.*
2. *Lift and carry your iMac box with the handholds.*
3. *Open your iMac box by cutting the tape.*
4. *Open the lid of your iMac Accessory Kit and check for your documentation, cables, and accessories.*
5. *Unpack the power cord, identified by the three-prong plug on one end.*
6. *Unpack the telephone phone line cord, identified by the standard phone plugs on both ends.*
7. *Unpack your mouse.*
8. *Unpack your keyboard.*

What's Your Flavor?

If you haven't yet purchased your iMac, take some time to carefully consider which flavor (color) you want. At press time, the iMac comes in six delicious flavors: tangerine (orange), grape (purple), lime (green), blueberry (blue), strawberry (red), and for the iMac Special Edition, graphite (gray). You're going to be putting this computer somewhere in your home or office, so it probably ought to fit in with the rest of your stuff. Your iMac might become a part of your daily routine and you'll probably be looking at it a lot. For some of us, looking at a tangerine iMac the first thing in the morning might not be appealing. On the other hand, for others, tangerine might be just what we need to thrust ourselves headlong into the splendors and thrills of a new day.

When you purchase your iMac, keep in mind that it is a lot like furrnu. It should match the rest of your stuff, to some degree, or it should provide contrast if that's your style. Your iMac flavor should say something about you! Some people can tell what kind of person you are by knowing the color of your iMac. Most of all, your iMac flavor should make you happy! My lime iMac makes me smile.

Don't worry if you already have your iMac and it doesn't match your décor. You'll love it just as much. As with people, iMac beauty is only skin-deep. It's what's on the inside that counts.

last thing in the cable compartment should be the mouse (it looks like a lollipop). The iMac mouse is round with an attached cable, colored to match your iMac. The keyboard is hard to miss in its own separate compartment and, like the mouse, has an attached, color-matched cable and distinguished-looking black keys.

Once you've verified that each of these components is in your Accessory Kit, lift the kit and the foam packing material immediately beneath it out of the box. Your all-in-one iMac is nestled snugly in the bottom of the box. It looks for all the world like a huge gumdrop. Halloween was never this good!

TAKE NOTE

CONSIDER A SURGE SUPPRESSOR

While you can plug your iMac directly into the wall, you may want to purchase a quality *surge protector*. A surge protector provides some protection from power surges. Lightning storms, among other things, produce power fluctuations and surges that may damage your iMac. A surge protector also offers outlets for other equipment, such as printers and scanners. You can get a surge protector at an office supply or computer store.

FIND IT ONLINE

Apple provides an overview of the iMac at **http://www.info.apple.com/info.apple.com/te/training/overviewimac/Overview/index.html.**

Setting Up and Plugging In Your iMac

Before you remove your iMac from its box, decide where it will go. Your iMac needs space for the computer itself (about 18" by 18" by 18"), the keyboard (about 5" deep and 15" wide), and the mouse (a minimum of 6" by 6" of desk space). Pick a flat surface where the keyboard won't be higher than your elbows. It should also be within easy distance of a wall outlet.

Once your iMac's new living quarters are ready, lift it out of the box using the built-in handle on the top. Support the bottom of the iMac as well, once you can reach it (just don't use the foot stand or the handle-like object on the bottom as handles — neither will support the iMac's weight). As you set your iMac down, you can then choose to flip its foot stand down to adjust the viewing angle.

Take a moment to look your iMac over. Outrageous, isn't it? It's even better plugged in! Note the access door on the right side and the recessed power socket even further back.

Locate your power cord and plug the receptacle end into the socket. Now plug the other end of the power cord into a three-prong wall outlet or a surge suppressor (you'll need to plug the surge suppressor into a wall outlet, too).

Next, set your keyboard on the desk in front of your iMac and find the end of its attached cable. Open the iMac's access door (place your finger in the big hole and pull downward) and locate the two small rectangular Universal Serial Bus (USB) sockets, or *ports,* inside. You can identify the USB ports by matching the symbol on the end of the keyboard cable to the symbols on the ports (the symbol looks a bit like a trident or a pitchfork). Plug the keyboard cable into either one of the ports symbol-side up.

CROSS-REFERENCE

Chapter 3 and Chapter 6 cover attaching other peripherals such as floppy drives and printers to your iMac.

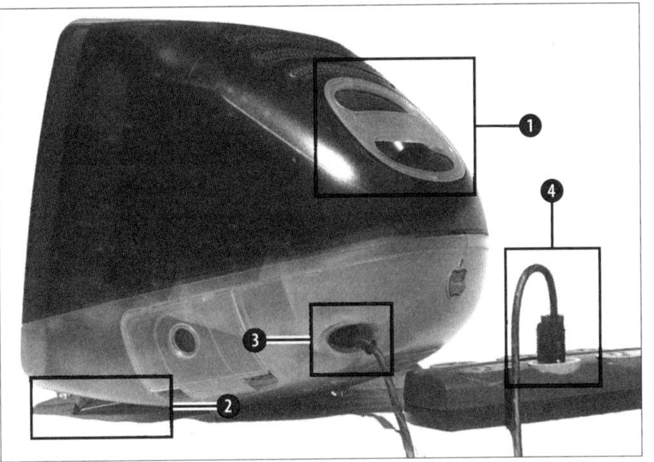

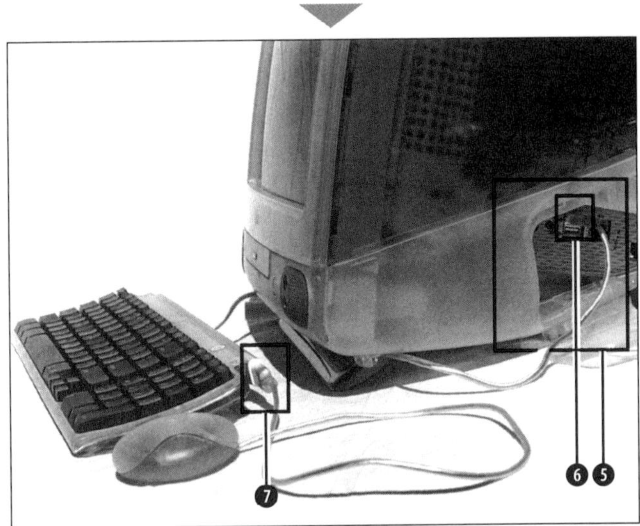

1. *Carry your iMac by the handle while you also support the bottom.*
2. *(Optional) Swing the foot stand out before you set your iMac down.*
3. *Plug the receptacle end of the power cord into the recessed socket in the back of your iMac.*
4. *Plug the power cord into the wall outlet or a plugged-in surge suppressor.*
5. *Open the access door by it pulling downward.*
6. *Plug the keyboard cable into one of the USB ports behind the access door.*
7. *Plug the mouse cable into one of the USB ports on the keyboard.*

Feng Shui of the iMac

Where will you put your iMac? The Chinese have an art, called *Feng Shui,* of placing things such that the energies flow well, bringing good luck and fortune. While I'm no Feng Shui expert, I do have suggestions on iMac placement. Don't get a desk that just barely fits your iMac; you'll need space around it for books, papers, a telephone, sushi, and so on. Use a chair that you can spend hours in. Your iMac likes comfortable temperatures and good lighting, and so will you. Locate your iMac where you'd like to spend your time. I prefer Florida.

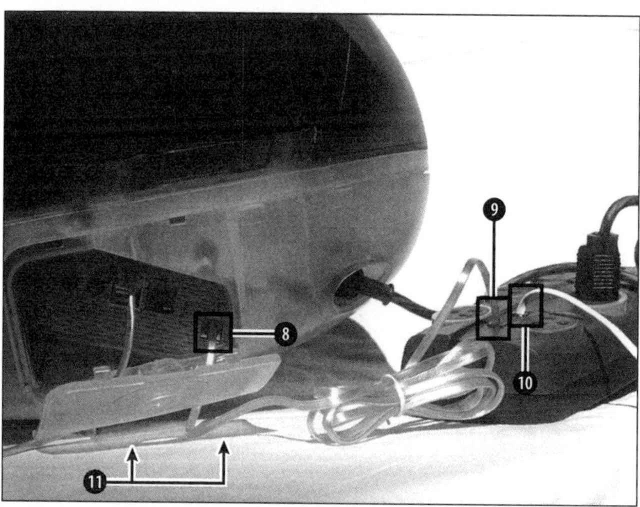

8 *Plug one end of the telephone cable into the modem jack.*

9 *Plug the other end into a wall jack or a surge suppressor.*

10 *If you have a surge suppressor, run another telephone cable from the surge suppressor to the wall jack.*

11 *Let your cables snake out through the two bottom corners of the access door, and then close the access door.*

Set the mouse on the desk next to the keyboard and find the end of its attached cable. Plug the mouse cable into one of the two USB ports located on either side of the keyboard. Use the port on the left if you're left-handed; otherwise, you'll probably want to use the port on the right side.

If you intend to use the Internet or an online service, locate the telephone line cable. Plug one end (it doesn't matter which one) into the modem jack in the lower right corner behind the access door on the right side of the computer. Plug the other end into a telephone wall jack or into the surge protector if it has a phone port (you'll need to run another phone line cable from the surge protector to the wall jack, too). Close the access door.

TAKE NOTE

THREADING YOUR CABLES

Wondering how you can close the access door with all those cables in the way? If you're like me, you might try to thread the cables through the large finger hole in the door. But if you look closely, you'll see the bottom corners of the door are missing — the cables snake out through those corners and leave the finger hole unobstructed.

FIND IT ONLINE

More information on USB ports is available at **http://www.info.apple.com/info.apple.com/te/training/overviewimac/Overview/overview3.html.**

Turning On Your iMac

It's time to flip the switch, or — in the case of your iMac — to push its button! Every iMac has one power button on the front of the computer (below the screen). Newer iMacs also have a power button on the top right of the keyboard. Both are round and have a symbol that looks like a circle with a line through it. Push either button (but not both) to turn on your iMac.

If all goes well, you'll hear a musical chord from your iMac and the power button on the computer (but not the button on the keyboard) will light up. If nothing happens when you push the power button, double-check that the power cord is plugged in to both the iMac and the wall outlet (or surge suppressor) and push the power button again.

Your iMac needs a minute or so to start up. Watch the screen as it does. A small Mac with a happy face first greets you, quickly followed by the Apple logo and the words, "Welcome to Mac OS." You may see "Mac OS 9" if you have a more recent iMac. Mac OS (pronounced *Oh Es*) stands for Operating System, which is the software that runs your iMac. Your iMac comes with the Mac OS already installed.

As the iMac continues to start up, you'll notice about 15 small pictures — or icons — march along the bottom of the screen. These icons represent special pieces of software being loaded by the Mac OS. The puzzle-like shapes you see are a good indication of how they enhance the Mac OS. You don't need to worry about these icons now, however.

Following the icon march, your iMac completes its start-up process and displays its *Desktop* on the screen. The Desktop (which is also called the Finder) is your home base on the iMac — the place you begin and end virtually every session. It fills the screen with a *menu bar* along the top, icons representing the *hard drive* and

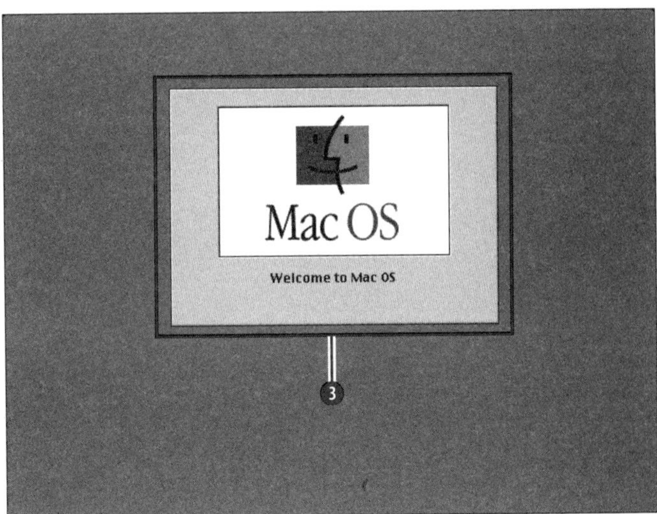

1. *Press the power button on your computer to start your iMac.*
2. *Alternatively, press the keyboard's power button (if you have one).*

▶ *Note that the power button on your computer lights up as your iMac starts up.*

3. *The iMac welcomes you to the Mac Operating System.*

CROSS-REFERENCE

If your iMac doesn't start, see "Resolving a Startup Problem" in Chapter 17.

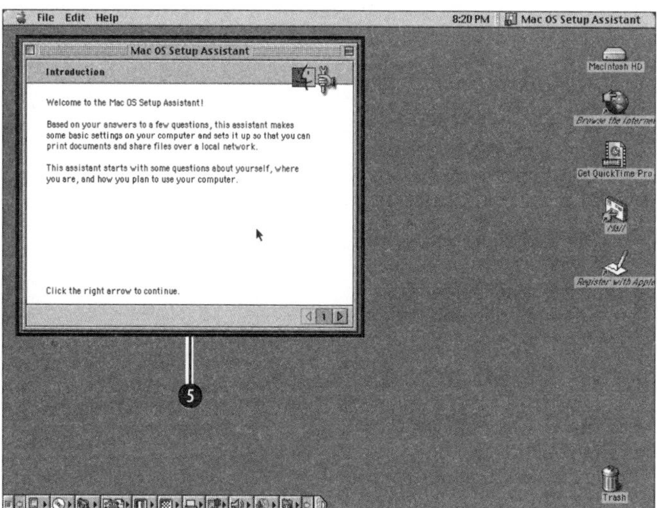

❹ *Observe the icon march along the bottom of the screen as the iMac completes its startup.*

- *The iMac displays the Desktop upon successful startup.*
- *The menu bar at the top gives you access to commands and settings.*
- *The icons along the right side represent the hard drive and some files.*

❺ *Close the Mac OS Setup Assistant window on the Desktop if it is open.*

various *files* along the right side, a *window* (or two or three) in the middle, a *control strip* in the lower left, and a *trash can* in the lower right. Don't worry if you don't recognize these terms yet — I'll explain them as we go along.

TAKE NOTE

SETTING UP

If this is the first time you've started your iMac, the Mac OS Setup Assistant window opens and welcomes you. The Setup Assistant can walk you through various settings for your iMac. You do not have to use the Assistant now, however — it is available at any time. Let's remove (close) that window for now: press and hold the Command key (the key with the Apple logo on it) on the bottom row of the keyboard and press the W key at the same time. Release both keys. A small message appears asking if you're sure you want to quit. Tap the Return key on the keyboard once (it is toward the right side) and the message will go away.

SHORTCUT

You only need to press one of the two power buttons to start your iMac. Pressing one right after the other may turn your computer off again.

Moving the Mouse

Remember the mouse, that lollipop-like thing on the desk beside the keyboard? At least, that is where the mouse should be, along with some space to move it about. You can place the mouse directly on the desk or on a *mouse pad* (a rectangle of plastic or heavy material that gives the mouse better traction). Make sure the mouse sits flat with the *tail* (cord) pointed away from you.

Get a good grip on the mouse by placing your hand over the mouse, resting your thumb and ring fingers on its colored sections, and grasping firmly. Now lightly rest your index finger on the large button situated between the Apple logo and the cord.

Keeping your hand on the mouse and the mouse flat on its surface, push the mouse a bit to the right and the left, and then up and down. You should see the two-toned ball inside the mouse's translucent case roll about as you push it. Now watch the screen as you push the mouse around. Do you see a small black arrow moving around the screen? This arrow is the *mouse pointer* (or a *cursor*). Your mouse controls the position of the pointer. When you push the mouse, you're moving the mouse pointer on the screen.

Practice moving the pointer. It may take some time to get the feel of it. Try to position the pointer over various items on the screen. Once you feel confident moving the mouse where you want it to go, practice positioning the very tip of the pointer's arrow in a particular spot. The tip of the arrow is the only part that really matters.

You could just move the pointer around, but it doesn't do much by itself. You also need to *click* the button on the mouse by lightly pressing the button (you'll hear a click) and then releasing it (another click). You'll hear just one click if you press and release too fast. Try clicking the mouse in various places around the screen,

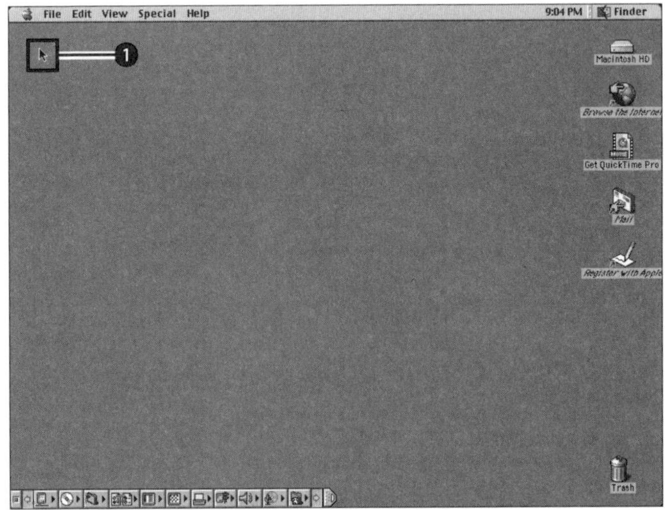

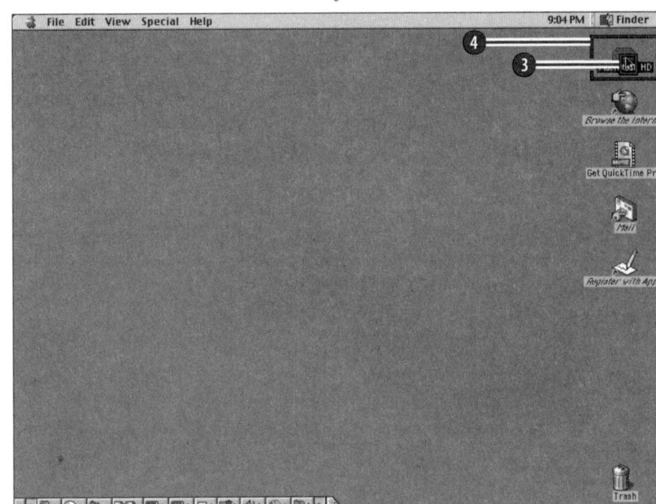

1. *Locate the mouse pointer (black arrow) on the screen.*
2. *Practice moving the mouse on your desk and watch the pointer move on the screen.*
3. *Position the mouse pointer over an icon on the Desktop.*
4. *Select the icon once by clicking once with the mouse button. Notice that the icon changes color when it is selected.*

CROSS-REFERENCE

If you find the mouse too slow or too fast for your tastes, Chapter 14 shows you how to set your mouse preferences.

Making More Room

If you reach the edge of the mouse pad before you reach the edge of the screen, just raise the mouse up a bit, put it back down anywhere on the pad, and continue moving the mouse. Notice that the mouse pointer stayed where it was when you picked up and repositioned the mouse. The mouse only works when it is flat on a surface. If you're in the middle of a press-and-drag action when you reach the edge of the mouse pad, just keep your finger pressed on the button as you pick it up and set it down.

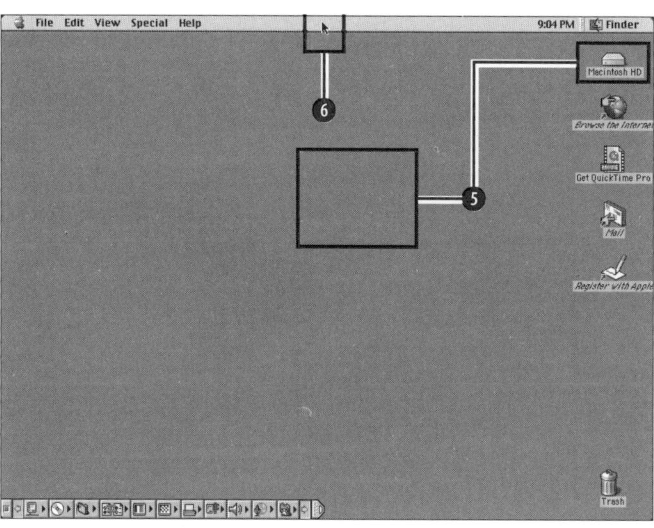

❺ *Click once on an empty area of the Desktop to deselect the icon. Notice that the icon returns to normal.*

❻ *Practice positioning the mouse pointer on other areas of the Desktop, such as on the menu bar at the top of the screen.*

such as on an icon or the menu bar. Click only once (a *single-click*) at this point. You may also see single-clicking referred to as *selecting*. A selected item changes colors. You can *deselect* an item you selected by clicking on an empty area of the iMac Desktop.

TAKE NOTE

CLICKING INTO PLACE

You can click the mouse in three more ways: *double-clicks* (two clicks in rapid succession), *clicks and drags* (a single click followed by moving the mouse), and *press and drags* (moving the mouse while pressing the button). To double-click, position the pointer and click the mouse button twice very quickly (press and release, press and release). It is important to keep the mouse very still as you double-click. To click and drag, position the mouse pointer, click the mouse button once (press and release), and then move the mouse. Be careful not to move the mouse while you're clicking. To press and drag, position the pointer, click and hold the mouse button (press), and then move the mouse. Release the mouse button when you're finished dragging.

SHORTCUT

You can lock the iMac's mouse ball. Insert a paper clip into the hole on the inner ring on the underside and press down while you turn the ring clockwise until it stops.

Viewing Your Menus

What's the first thing you do at a restaurant? Look at the menu, right? That's often the first thing you'll do on your iMac, too. Only you don't get your iMac menus from a host or hostess; you get them from the *menu bar*. The menu bar is the light gray strip across the very top of the screen. The multi-colored apple logo is on the far left, immediately followed by words like File, Edit, and so on. Both the time and the active application (program) name are shown on the far right side of the menu bar. The menu bar is virtually always visible, but the menu will change as you run different programs.

Each item in the menu bar is the title of a *menu*, a list of commands that make your iMac do something. To *pull down* (open) a menu, move the mouse pointer to a word or an icon on the menu bar and single-click it. Instantly, a menu drops down revealing your options. Acquaint yourself with the menus and options available from your iMac's Finder (you may recall from an earlier lesson that Finder is another name for Desktop). How do you know you're in the Finder? The application menu on the far right of the menu bar should read Finder and show the Mac OS logo. If it doesn't, that's okay, too.

To choose an item from a menu, start by pulling down the menu with the mouse pointer using a single-click. Now slide the pointer down to the item that interests you. Notice that as you pass the pointer over other menu items, your iMac highlights them. A highlighted item is a selected item. Single-click a selected item to execute that command. Only execute a command if you're sure what it does (unless you want some adventure in your life). To close a menu, click an empty area outside the menu, or wait a bit and the Finder will close the menu on its own.

CROSS-REFERENCE

The first section in Chapter 2, "Using Menus," explains the purpose of many menu commands on the Desktop.

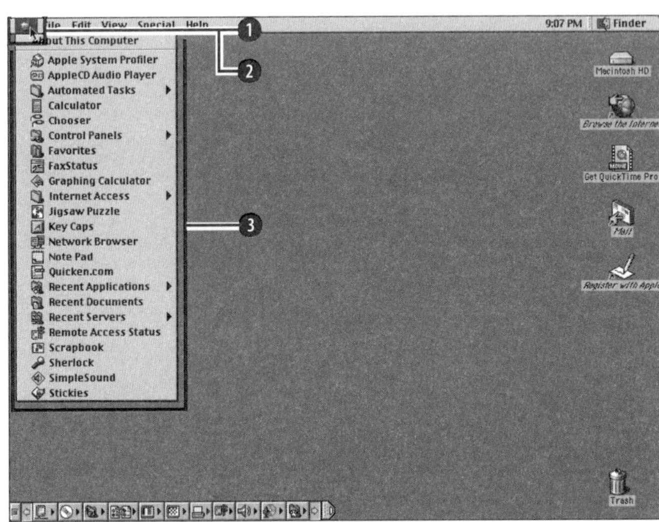

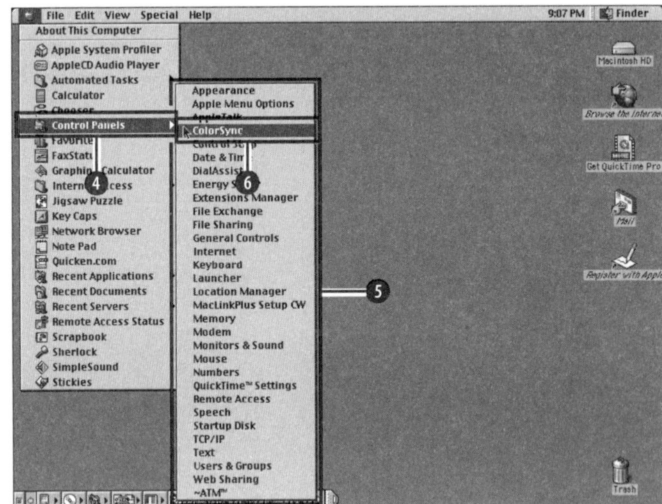

1. *Position the mouse pointer over the Apple menu on the far left side of the menu bar.*
2. *Single-click the mouse to pull down the Apple menu.*
3. *Examine the items in the menu carefully.*
4. *Slide the mouse down so the pointer is directly over the Control Panels item.*
5. *Notice that the Control Panels submenu opens.*
6. *Slide the pointer horizontally across to the submenu, being careful not to select the item above or below it.*
7. *Slide the mouse pointer up and down the Control Panels submenu and observe how the iMac highlights selected items on the menu.*

The Case of the Disappearing Menus

You may notice that the menus automatically close if you take a while to make a choice. In fact, you have about 15 seconds from the time you pull down the menu to execute an item. If you need more time, keep the mouse in motion within the menu. Or, open a menu by pressing and dragging, releasing the mouse button only when you are ready to execute a selected command or want to close the menu. Your iMac can keep the menu open as long as you can keep the mouse button pressed down.

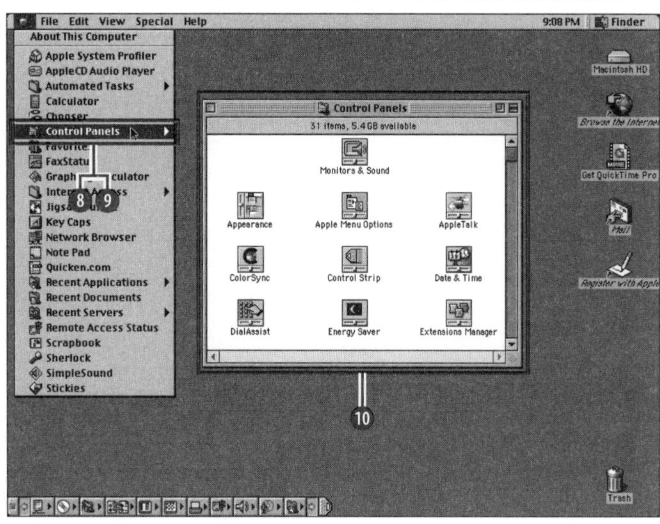

8. *Slide the mouse pointer back to the Apple menu and select Control Panels, keeping the pointer in the main menu.*
9. *Execute the Control Panels command by single-clicking it once with the mouse.*
10. *Observe as the command executes, opening the Control Panels window on the Desktop.*

TAKE NOTE

WASHING OUT THE GRAY

You may be wondering why some menu items are black while others are gray. Black indicates those items that are available to be selected and executed. Any item that is currently unavailable is gray.

USING SUBMENUS

Have you noticed the arrows to the right of some menu items? Those indicate a *submenu*, or hierarchical menu. Move the pointer over a menu item with an arrow and another menu appears immediately to its right. Getting the mouse pointer to that submenu is a little tricky at first — keep the pointer steady and move it sideways to the submenu. If the submenu disappears, it was probably because the mouse pointer touched a neighboring menu item while you were moving it. Just try again and you'll get the hang of it. Items in submenus can be selected just like those in regular menus. You may even find submenus in your submenus!

SHORTCUT

Once you've single-clicked a menu on the menu bar, you can slide the mouse pointer along the menu bar and watch the contents of each menu drop down in turn.

Opening Windows

You may have heard other computer systems make a big deal about their Windows, but they were all inspired by those on the Mac. Your iMac *windows* (we use lowercase w in the Macintosh world) look much like the word implies — a framed, white rectangle that can be opened and closed. You'll want to get comfortable with windows, because they are everywhere on your iMac, including the Desktop.

Chances are you've already opened windows, and you may even have one open now. If you don't see an open window on the screen, move the pointer to the Apple menu on the far left side of the menu bar and select Control Panels (don't worry about the submenu). Now, single-click Control Panels and watch as your iMac opens a window on the screen.

To move a window, position the tip of the pointer in the top bar of the window (called a *title bar*) or on its gray borders, avoiding the small boxes in either corner and the bars along the bottom and right side for the moment. Now press and drag. As you move the mouse pointer, the window's outline follows along so you can see exactly where the window is going. When the outline is where you want it, release the mouse button and the window moves to that spot.

You can often *scroll* the windows, too. Scrolling is a lot like it sounds. Imagine rolling the two ends of an ancient scroll; the paper at the top rolls up as the paper at the bottom unrolls. Windows with more information than can be displayed at once can be scrolled, using *scroll bars* on the right and the bottom of the window. An active scroll bar is gray with black arrows on each end and a small box within it, while an inactive scroll bar is simply white.

To scroll a window, single-click one of the arrows on the scroll bar. The small box in the scroll bar moves to

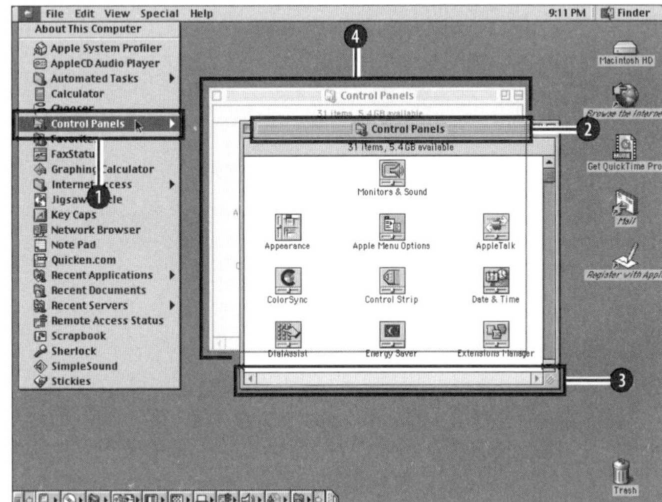

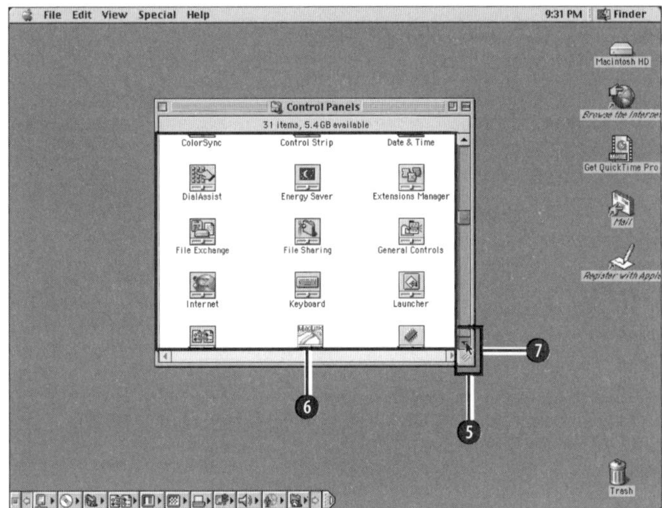

1. *Select and click Control Panels from the Apple menu to open a window.*
2. *Position the mouse pointer in the title bar, avoiding the small boxes.*
3. *Alternatively, position the mouse pointer along one of the edges of the window.*
4. *Press and drag the window until the outline is in the position you want, and then release the mouse button.*
5. *Single-click the down arrow below the scroll bar.*
6. *Notice how the view of the window's contents change.*
7. *Press and hold the down-arrow key to scroll the window quickly.*

CROSS-REFERENCE

The section "Closing Windows," later in this chapter, provides more information on manipulating windows.

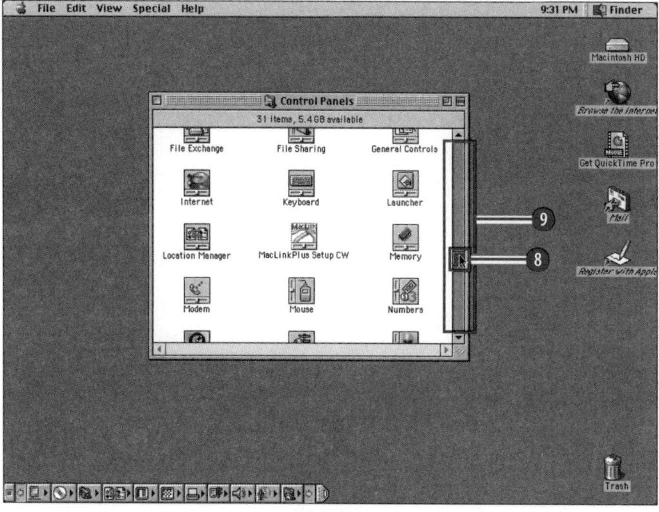

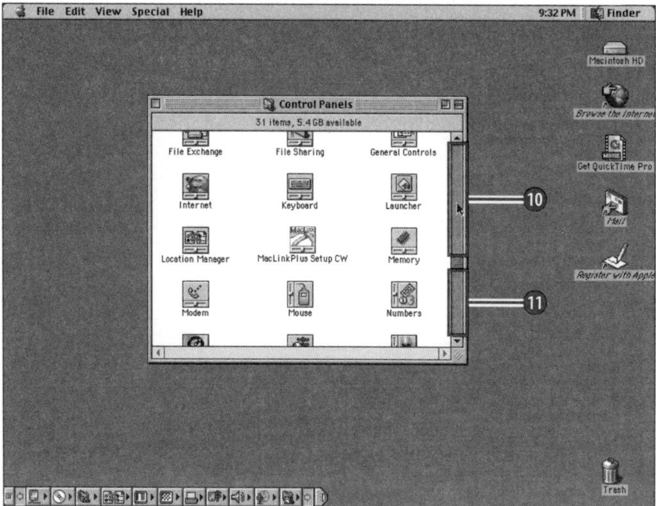

8 *Position the tip of the mouse pointer on the small box in the scroll bar.*

9 *Press and drag the small box anywhere along the scroll bar.*

10 *Single-click anywhere along the scroll bar, above or below the small box, to quickly scroll the window.*

11 *Press and hold the mouse pointer anywhere along the scroll box to scroll the window even faster.*

show which section of the window's contents are being displayed (top or bottom, left or right, or somewhere in between). Your view of the window's contents changes accordingly. If this method of scrolling doesn't feel precise or fast enough, just place the tip of the pointer over the small box, press and drag to a new spot on the scroll bar, and release — the window scrolls while you drag.

TAKE NOTE

RESIZING WINDOWS

You can change the size of the windows, or *resize* them, at any time. Position the tip of the pointer in the lower right corner of a window where you see three diagonal lines — this is the *size box*. Press and drag the size box until the window outline is the size you want and release the mouse button. Another way to resize a window is to use the *Zoom box*, the box with small square within it, located on the right size of a window's title bar. Single-click the Zoom box once and the window is automatically resized larger or smaller (depending on its original size).

SHORTCUT

Scroll a window quickly by single-clicking anywhere on an active scroll bar. The scroll box (and the window's contents) move toward the mouse pointer.

Understanding Icons

Icons are also characteristically Mac. The small pictures you see on the Desktop and in the windows are all icons, representing information, programs, or equipment in your computer. The first icons you'll probably notice are those along the right side of the Desktop. The top icon always represents the *hard drive*, the place where all your computer's information is stored. If you look closely at the icon, you'll notice the small picture looks like a box — this is what your hard drive might look like if you could see inside the computer. An icon's picture provides a visual clue to the kind of information it represents. Below the icon is the label, in this case Macintosh HD (the HD stands for Hard Disk). Most icons you'll encounter follow this same format: small pictures and labels.

Icons are similar to menus. As with menus, you can select and activate items represented by icons. You select an icon by positioning the tip of the pointer over it and single-clicking. The icon changes color (is highlighted) once it is selected. To activate an icon, just double-click it. Remember, a double-click is two single-clicks in rapid succession. Activating an icon may open a window, perform a command, or run a program. Like menu items, it is a good idea to know what an icon does before you activate it.

Once you've double-clicked an icon and activated it, the icon changes yet again. This time, the small picture changes to an outline filled with small dots (although the icon may be hidden by a newly opened window). When you see an icon that looks like this, you'll know you've already activated it. You can double-click an activated icon again to bring it to forward on the screen.

As you open a new window, it may overlap or cover previously opened windows. Click a window in back to bring it to the front. You can resize and move windows

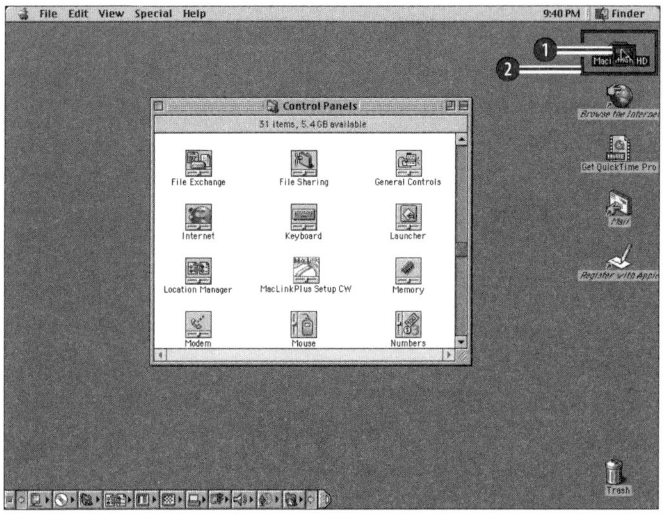

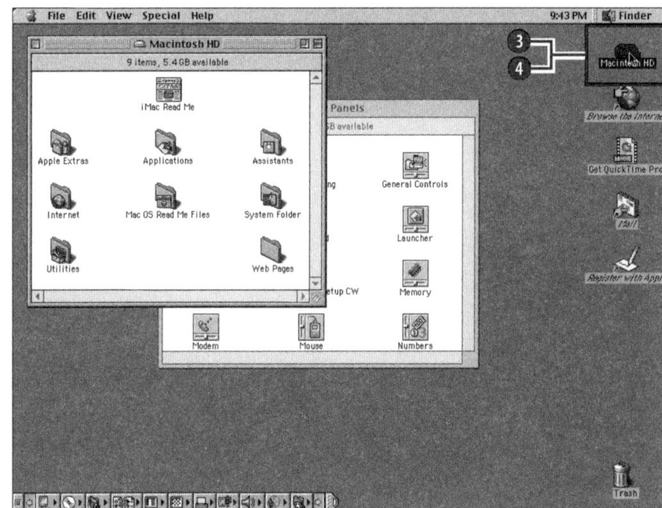

1. *Position the tip of the mouse pointer over the Macintosh HD icon.*
2. *Single-click the icon to select it. Notice that it changes color.*
3. *Keep the tip of the pointer over the Macintosh HD icon (or position it there again if you moved it).*
4. *Double-click the icon (click twice very quickly).*

▶ *The Macintosh HD window opens, displaying icons within the window.*

CROSS-REFERENCE

Chapter 2 explains how to do more things with icons (and the files they represent), including creating, naming, copying, and deleting.

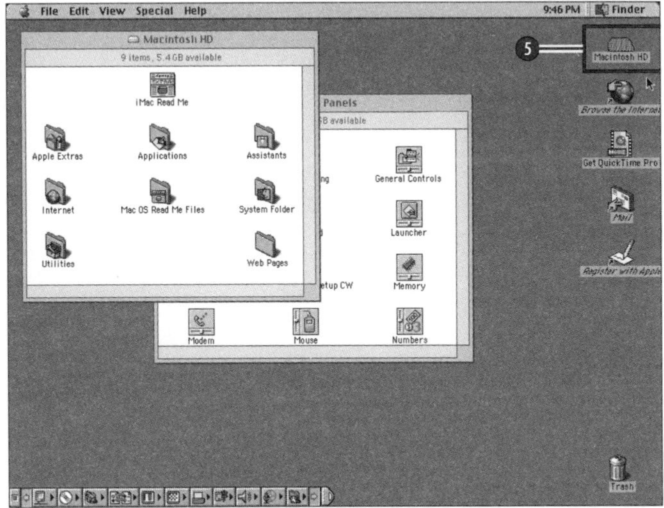

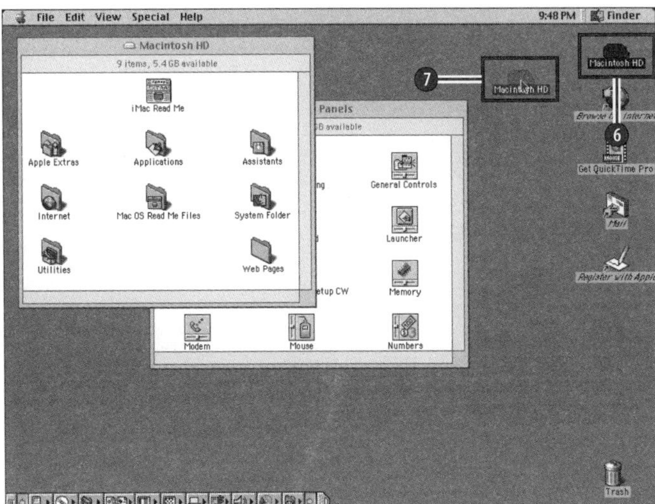

5 *Notice how the icon appears gray on the Desktop after it has been double-clicked.*

6 *Position the tip of the pointer over the Macintosh HD icon again.*

7 *Press and drag the icon to a new location. Release the mouse button when the icon is where you want it.*

so they aren't hidden by other open windows, but as you open more and more windows, the overlap gets worse. This is to be expected, and you will learn more ways to deal with overlapped windows later.

TAKE NOTE

USING ICONS AND MENUS TOGETHER

Icons and menus work hand-in-hand. You can often select an icon (single-click), and then apply a menu command. For example, you can activate (or open) an icon by first selecting the icon, clicking the File menu on the menu bar, and then selecting and single-clicking Open. The Open command does the same thing as double-clicking an icon.

MOVING ICONS

Just as windows overlap one another, they may overlap icons, too. While it is usually more efficient to simply move the window out of the way, you can move the icon instead. To move an icon, position the tip of the mouse pointer over the icon and press and drag its outline to a new location, releasing the button to actually move it.

SHORTCUT

You can also activate (open) an icon by first selecting it with the mouse pointer and then pressing the Return key on the keyboard.

Setting Your Apple Menu Options

You've been dancing around the Apple menu for a while, so it's time to cut in and go for a whirl! The Apple menu is found on the far left side of the menu bar, under the multi-colored Apple logo. You'll always find it here, no matter what other menus may come and go on the menu bar. You could think of the Apple menu as the iMac menu since it is always available (and always first on the menu bar), and it lets you change settings that affect your iMac as a whole. One of the joys of owning a Mac is the freedom to customize the way your iMac looks and behaves. I'll start you on that journey by customizing the Apple menu itself!

To change the way the Apple menu appears, pull down the Apple menu, select Control Panels, and then select and single-click Apple Menu Options from the Control Panels submenu. A window titled Apple Menu Options appears on the screen. Note that this window has no scroll bar or resize box, unlike those discussed in the previous lesson. You can still move the window to another location on the screen if you wish, however.

The first Apple menu option is for submenus — you can keep them on or turn them off. I recommend you keep them turned on; submenus are quite convenient. If you want to turn the submenus off, position the mouse pointer over the small round button next to the word Off and single-click it. Turning submenus off generally means you'll have to do a lot more clicking to get where you're going.

You also can set your iMac to remember recently used items, which comes in handy as you start using your iMac in earnest. If there is a check mark in the box next to Remember recently used items, you know the option is enabled (or *turned on*). If the box is empty, position the mouse pointer over the box and single-click; a small check mark appears in the box to show

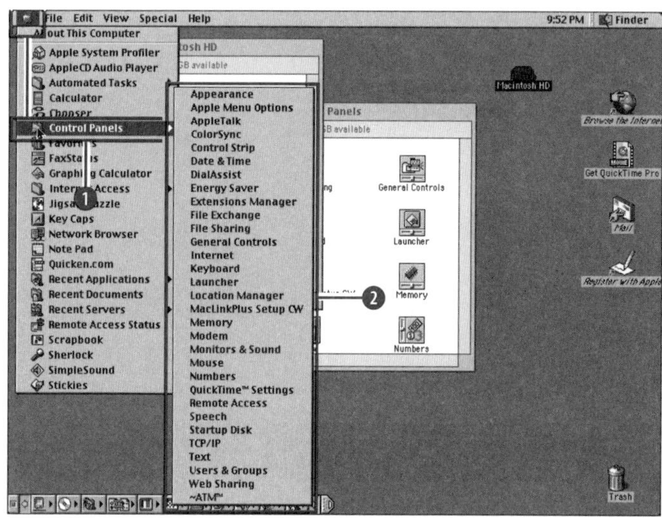

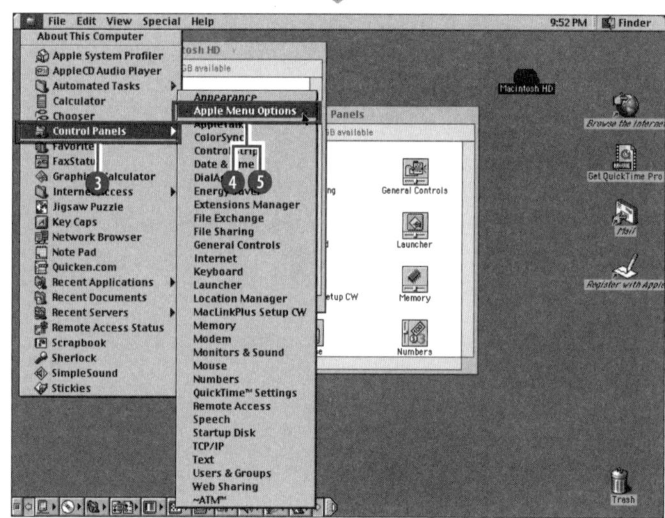

1. *Pull down the Apple menu by positioning the mouse pointer over the Apple logo and single-clicking.*
2. *Select Controls Panels and watch its submenu appear to the right of it.*
3. *Slide the pointer horizontally over to the submenu.*
4. *Highlight Apple Menu Options on the submenu.*
5. *Single-click Apple Menu Options.*

CROSS-REFERENCE

Learn how to return to recently used applications via the Apple menu in Chapter 8, "Running Applications."

Understanding Control Panels

Your iMac provides plenty of ways to customize it to your liking, one of which is using *Control Panels*. Essentially small programs, Control Panels contain settings for various aspects of your iMac. The Apple Menu Options window is a Control Panel, as is every other option in the Control Panels submenu. You can use Control Panels to change the Desktop appearance and more. Just like the Apple menu, Control Panels are always accessible. You will learn more about how specific Control Panels work later in the book.

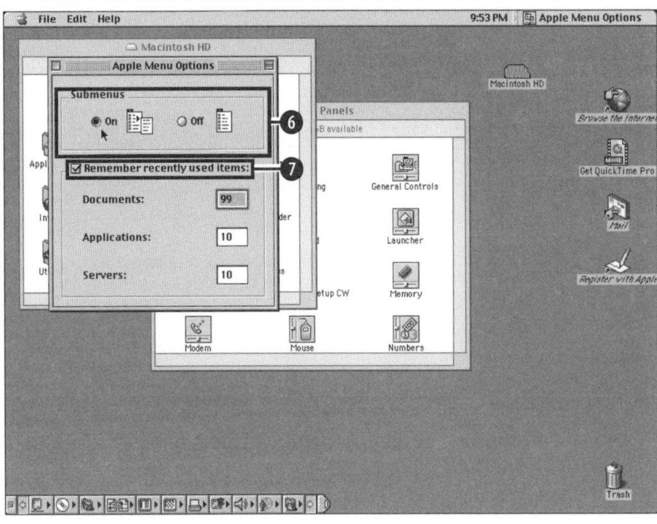

6 *Turn submenus on or off by single-clicking one of the two radio buttons.*

7 *Verify that there is a check mark in the box next to the option to remember recently used items. If not, single-click once in the box.*

that it is now enabled. The set of numbers below the box indicate the number of items your iMac will remember. You can change these too, though I'll explain how they work later.

TAKE NOTE

PUSHING THE BUTTONS

You may see the pushbuttons next to the submenu settings referred to as *radio buttons*. They get that name from the fact that only one radio button in a set can — and must — be on at any one time, much like the pushbuttons on an old-fashioned car radio. Radio buttons always appear in sets of two or more and always indicate a choice of some kind.

CHECKING IT ON AND OFF

Check boxes (literally, boxes that can be checked) are another common item on your iMac. Unlike radio buttons, check boxes come alone, as well as in sets, and you can check as many or as few boxes as you like. A single-click in a box *selects* it or *unselects* it — that is, it toggles it on or off.

SHORTCUT

The Apple menu is a shortcut in itself, because all the items here are found elsewhere. It pays to be familiar with the Apple menu.

Closing Your Windows

How many times did you hear your parents say, "If you open a window, close it!" I have good news. The iMac isn't your parents' computer (well, hey, maybe it is, but that's okay, too). If you want, you *can* leave windows open with gleeful abandon. After a while, though, the desktop is going to get very cluttered — you'll *want* to close some windows. Luckily, closing a window on your iMac is a lot easier than lowering that dormer window you left open during last week's storm.

Take a closer look at a window's title bar. Remember those other mysterious little boxes? The box on the upper-left corner is called the *close box*. It may remind you of the check boxes you saw in the last lesson, until you notice the close box looks a little concave. If you single-click the close box, the window instantly *closes*, or disappears, from the screen. Closing a window just closes, or puts away, the window; it generally does not delete it from the computer.

You won't always want to close a window, however. If you just want to get a window out of the way temporarily, you can *minimize* or *collapse* it. The small box on the far right of a window's title bar is called the *collapse box*. The collapse box looks like it has a bar through it. A single-click of the collapse box reduces the window to just its title bar, which takes a lot less space on the screen. You can move this title bar around on the screen if it also is in the way. Of course, windows that are just title bars aren't generally very useful, so you can expand the window again when you're ready to see it all. Just single-click the collapse box again and it opens the window to its original size.

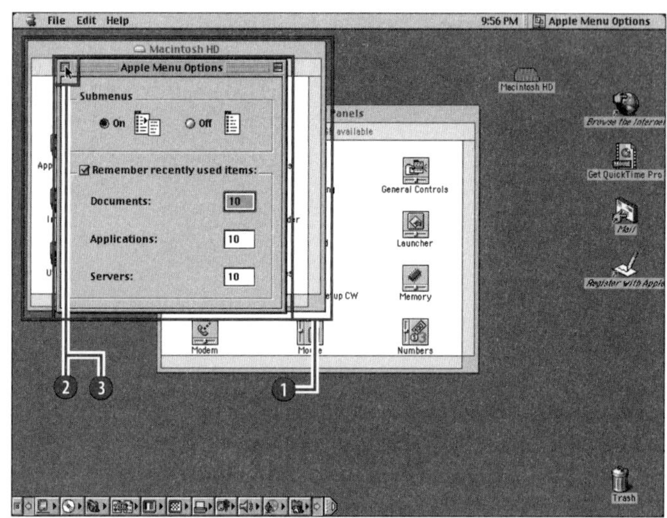

1. *Note the positions of the Macintosh HD and Apple Menu Options windows.*

▶ *The Macintosh HD window in the back has no visible close box or collapse box.*

2. *Position the tip of the mouse pointer in the close box of the Apple Menu Options window.*
3. *Single-click the close box, watching the window disappear from the screen.*
4. *Notice the Macintosh HD window now has a close box and a collapse box, as well as its racing stripes.*
5. *Position the tip of the pointer in the collapse box.*
6. *Single-click the collapse box and watch the window roll up so only its title bar is visible.*

CROSS-REFERENCE

To learn how to collapse windows with a double-click, see "Changing Your iMac's Appearance" in Chapter 14.

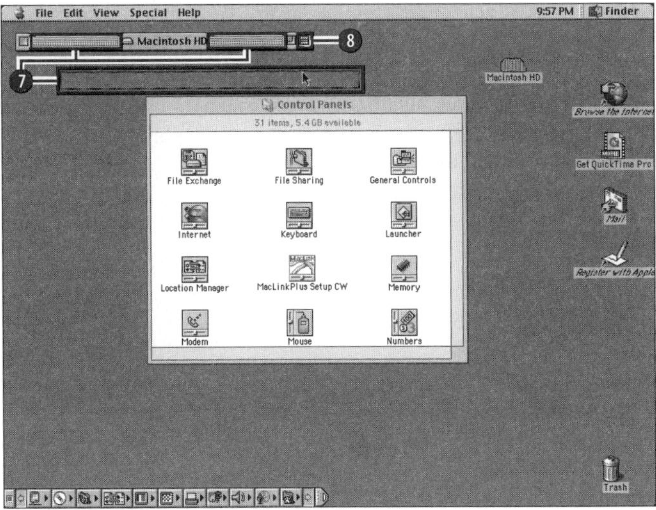

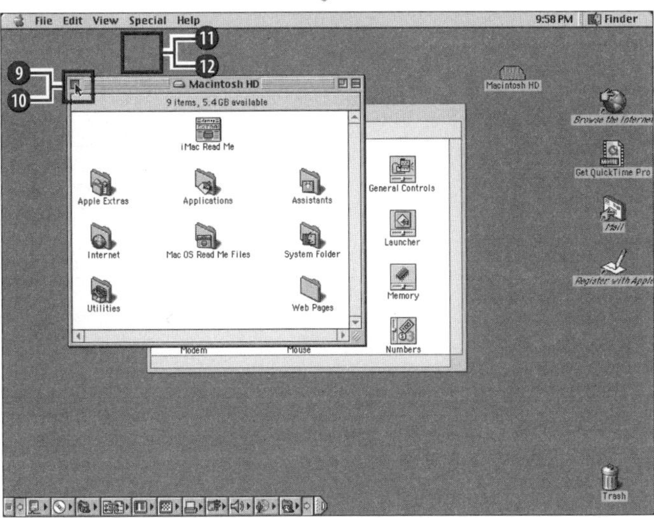

7. *Position and press the pointer on the racing stripes in the title bar and move it around the screen.*
8. *Single-click the collapse box again and watch the window expand to its original size.*
9. *Position the pointer in the close box.*
10. *Press and hold the mouse button. Notice that the close box darkens when pressed.*
11. *Move the pointer outside the close box, keeping the mouse button depressed. The close box lightens again.*
12. *Release the mouse button outside the close box. The window stays open.*

TAKE NOTE

GETTING IN FRONT

You may have noticed that not all window title bars have close boxes and collapse boxes. In fact, nearly all windows do have these boxes, but you can't always see them. If a window is behind another window on the screen, the window's title bar takes on a light gray cast, the racing stripes to either side of the title disappear, and the boxes become invisible. You can bring a window forward on the screen (and get the boxes back) with a single-click on its title bar.

BACKING OUT OF A CLICK

What if you click the close box and then change your mind about closing the window? If the window is already closed, you can always open it again. If you haven't finished clicking the close box, there is time to back out. Remember, a single-click requires that you depress *and* release the mouse button. If you've only depressed the button but not yet released it, move the mouse pointer out of the box before releasing it, cancelling the click.

SHORTCUT

Close all the open windows on the screen by holding down the Option key on the keyboard as you click in any one window's close box.

Ending Your Session

You've taught yourself the basics. You can turn on your iMac, use the mouse, open menus and windows, change some settings, and clean up the desktop. Now you can turn off your iMac and take a well-deserved break. Wait, how do you turn off the iMac? Ah, one basic but very essential skill remains.

First, I must warn you: don't try to turn off your iMac by simply unplugging it from the wall or by toggling the switch on the surge suppressor. You could resort to this only when it is absolutely necessary, because you can cause real harm to your iMac. Your iMac is designed to shut itself down in an orderly manner.

The most obvious way to turn off your iMac is using the power button either on the computer or on the keyboard (if you have a power button there). If you press the computer's power button once, your computer shuts down immediately. But if you press the keyboard's power button once, a *dialog box* (a special sort of window that asks a question and prompts you for a response) appears on the screen. If you are sure that you want to shut down your computer, go ahead and single-click the Shut Down button (or press the Return key on the keyboard). If you've changed your mind, click Cancel. The Restart button turns your iMac off and back on again immediately. The Sleep button turns off your iMac screen, but not the rest of the computer (you can wake it up by pressing a key on the keyboard later). If you take more than a few seconds to make your decision, your iMac will literally ask the question again — aloud this time! Yes, your iMac does sometimes talk back. You can interrupt the speaking at anytime by making a choice in the dialog box.

You also can turn off your iMac using a menu option. Pull down the Special menu, select Shut Down from the bottom of the menu, and single-click it. There won't be

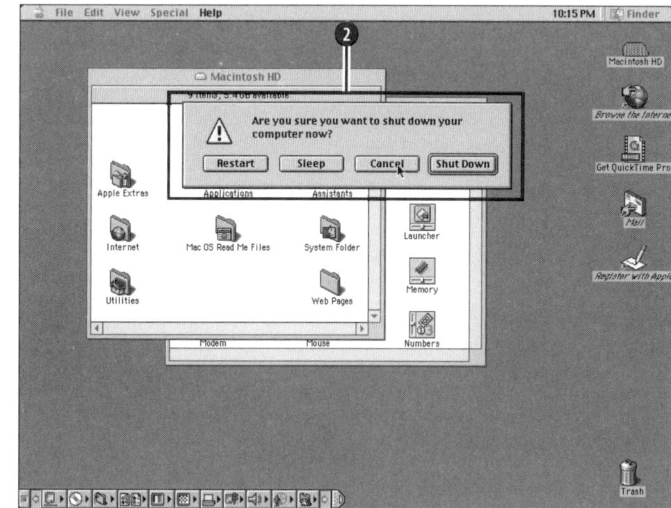

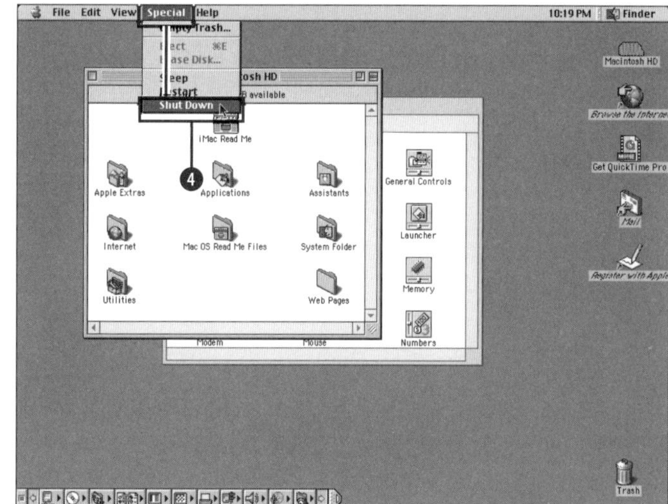

1. *Press the power button on the keyboard or the computer.*
2. *Read the dialog box that appears on the screen and click Cancel.*
3. *Alternatively, you could click Shut Down, Restart, or Sleep if you wanted to perform one of those functions.*
4. *Pull down the Special Menu, highlight Shut Down, and single-click it.*
5. *Alternatively, press the power button on your computer.*

CROSS-REFERENCE

If your iMac doesn't respond when you attempt to shut it down, refer to "Surviving a Freeze or Crash" in Chapter 17.

Leaving Your iMac Unattended

As much as you might enjoy your iMac, I doubt you can spend every moment guarding it from marauders and joyriders. If you use your iMac where other people can access it, shut it down when it is not in use to discourage others from snooping. Even better, install a security program that adds password protection at startup. When you leave for extended periods, shut down and then unplug the power cord (or surge suppressor).

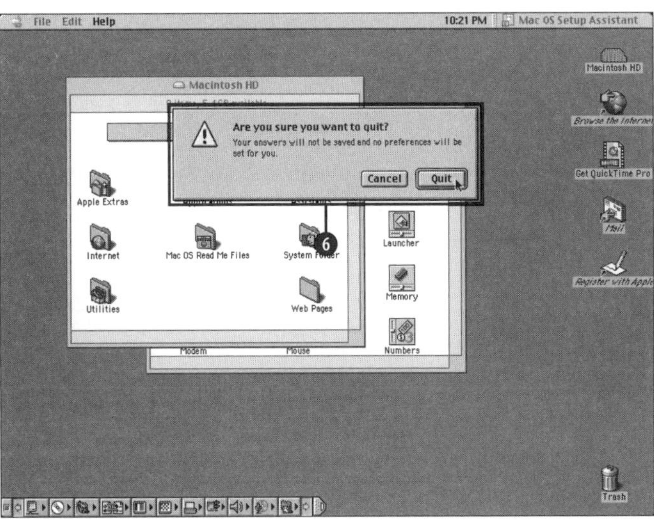

❻ *Your iMac closes any open programs (prompting you to save any unsaved items) and then turns off the computer.*

a dialog box this time, since it assumes you know what you're doing. Your iMac blinks out immediately.

TAKE NOTE

DECIDING WHEN TO SHUT DOWN

You may be wondering when to shut down your iMac, when to restart it, and when to let it sleep. Shut down is selected when you finish using your computer and won't be returning for many hours.

RESTARTING

Restarts are useful when you want to wipe the computer slate clean, so to speak. Restart the iMac after you install new software, or when your iMac begins to run sluggishly.

SLEEPING

Sleep mode is a good option when you aren't actively using the computer and want to conserve power, and when you also know you'll be returning to it soon. In fact, your iMac is set to automatically go to sleep if it is inactive for 30 minutes. Read the instructions in the dialog box and click Specify Settings to change the sleep time settings. Refer to Chapter 14 for more details on Energy Saver.

FIND IT ONLINE

Security programs for your iMac are available at **http://www.symantec.com/disklock/index.html** and **http://www.citadel.com/products/ntwatch.html.**

Personal Workbook

Q&A

1. What can a surge suppressor do for you?

2. Where do the cables go when you close the access door?

3. What is the Finder and what is another term for it?

4. What does a gray menu item indicate?

5. What are the two ways to open (activate) an icon on the Desktop?

6. What are submenus, how do you use them, and how do you enable or disable them?

7. What is the difference between collapsing a window and closing it?

8. What are the two ways to shut down your iMac?

ANSWERS: PAGE 313

EXTRA PRACTICE

1. Single-click the Apple logo to pull down the Apple Menu and single-click the Jigsaw Puzzle option. What happens?
2. Examine the new menus that appear when you open the Jigsaw Puzzle. Choose the menu option that lets you start a new puzzle. What happens?
3. Use the radio buttons to choose the jigsaw puzzle piece size. Click OK after you've made your selection. What happens?
4. Press and drag the jigsaw puzzle pieces to the appropriate location in the puzzle window, releasing the mouse button when they are in place. What happens when you drag a piece to the correct location in the puzzle? What happens when you drag a piece anywhere else?

REAL-WORLD APPLICATIONS

- ✔ When you purchased your iMac, you also purchased an optional external floppy drive and a printer. Each piece of hardware has its own power cord, making a total of three. The wall outlet has only two sockets. You purchase a surge suppressor, plug it into the wall outlet, and plug the three power cords into it.
- ✔ While practicing your mouse skills, you accidentally single-click one of the icons on the Desktop. To keep from opening the unfamiliar icon, you move the mouse pointer and single-click on an empty area of the Desktop.
- ✔ Your inquisitive child accidentally pushes the power button on the keyboard just before you place the last piece in the jigsaw puzzle. You click Cancel to stop your iMac from shutting down.

Visual Quiz

What is missing from this Apple menu? How would you get it back?

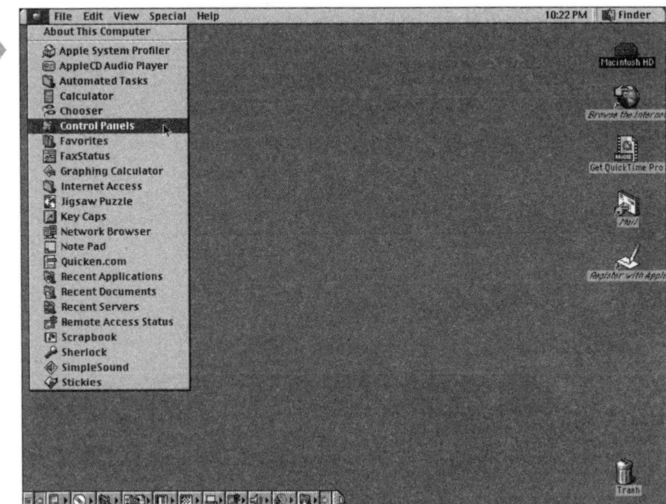

CHAPTER 2

MASTER THESE SKILLS

- Using Menus
- Viewing Your Desktop and Windows
- Creating and Naming Folders
- Moving Files
- Copying Files
- Aliasing Files
- Trashing and Deleting Files
- Finding Files
- Setting Your Preferences

Exploring Your Desktop

The Desktop is a special place on your iMac. It is the first thing you see after your computer finishes its startup. It is also your home base on the iMac, where you will return again and again at the beginning, middle, and end of a computing session. It is even the place to visit when you want to perform disk functions, organize files, and find stuff on your iMac. Yet, there is something else that's special about your Desktop. It's your iMac's face, as recognizable as the colorful plastic shell encasing it (if not more so).

Desktop isn't just a cute name. The iMac Desktop is the center of your computing activities, no less than the top of that real desk in your office or home. Oh, it may get buried in work, but behind it all, your Desktop is still there — a solid foundation for your activities.

On your Desktop you can find all the basic tools and supplies you need to be productive, from "filing cabinets" to a "trash can." Depending on your work habits, your Desktop may become cluttered with folders and files, or it may be organized just so. Yet, unlike a real desk, even the most disorganized Desktop can be straightened up with a few clicks of the mouse. You can even rummage in the trash if your cleanup efforts were a bit too enthusiastic.

Where do menus and windows fit in to a Desktop? The menu selections across the top of the iMac Desktop are a cross between a multi-drawer organizer and a whiz-bang control panel, crammed with useful gadgets and essential functions. When it's actually time to get down to business, you have to open some windows on the Desktop. That's how you view the contents of folders and display documents, and it's also where you work (or play) with your applications.

Your Desktop even comes equipped with a helpful assistant — Sherlock — who ferrets out information. Sherlock is the perfect helper. He never complains about the mess, or he never takes too long of a lunch break.

Now, in case you're wondering about that face thing, yes, your Desktop has personality. Although all Desktops look the same on the first day, you're free to organize your work area to suit your style and decorate it to express your individuality.

Well, so much for introductions! It's time to take your seat and get comfy at your new desk.

Using Menus

Menus are always a good place to begin. Let's take a quick tour of the menus available on your Desktop to get briefly acquainted with them. We'll go into more depth on menu options when appropriate throughout this book. Note that some menu options are gray rather than black, meaning they're not currently available. When those options are needed, they become available. Also remember that menus are virtually always available whether you're in the Finder or another program, but those menus and menu options change, depending on your current task.

The Apple menu offers programs and links to programs that need to be readily available. These include common desk accessories, utilities, and recently used items. The option at the top of the menu always gives you information on the program you're currently running. If you're in the Finder, you can get information about your computer, as well.

The File menu offers commands to manipulate files on your Desktop. Files can be opened, printed, closed, and much more. Programs always offer a File menu, though the options differ from one program to another.

The Edit menu offers commands to manipulate information and actions. Your preferences for the Desktop are located on the bottom of this menu. Every program offers an Edit menu, though the options will differ between programs.

The View menu offers commands to manipulate how items look on the Desktop. You probably have your view set to "as Icons" by default (the check mark in the menu indicates your current setting) and thus, you see items on your Desktop as icons. We delve into this menu in more detail in the next task.

The Special menu offers commands to perform various disk- and computer-related functions. Empty Trash

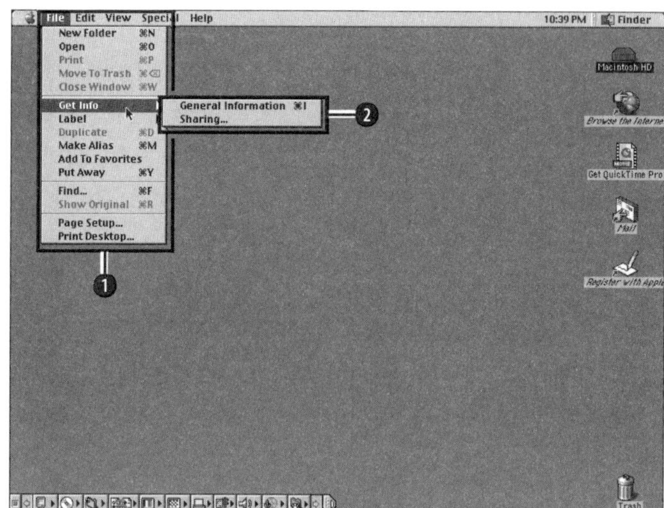

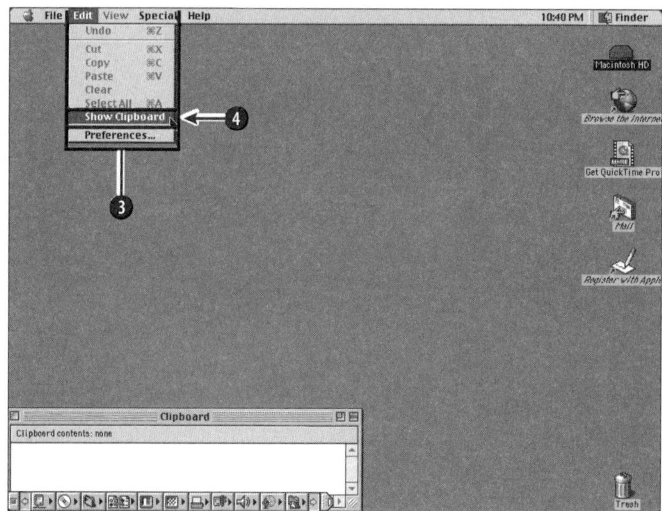

1. *Pull down the File menu and examine your options.*

▶ *Available menu items are black, while unavailable menu items are gray.*

2. *Explore your submenus.*

▶ *Items with ellipses (...) indicate that more options will appear in a dialog before the command is executed.*

3. *Pull down the Edit menu.*

▶ *Note the keyboard shortcut characters to the right of many of the menu items.*

4. *Click Show Clipboard.*

▶ *The window that appears is your Clipboard, which holds items you've cut or copied while editing.*

CROSS-REFERENCE

Explore the Edit menu options in more depth in Chapter 4, "Working With Text."

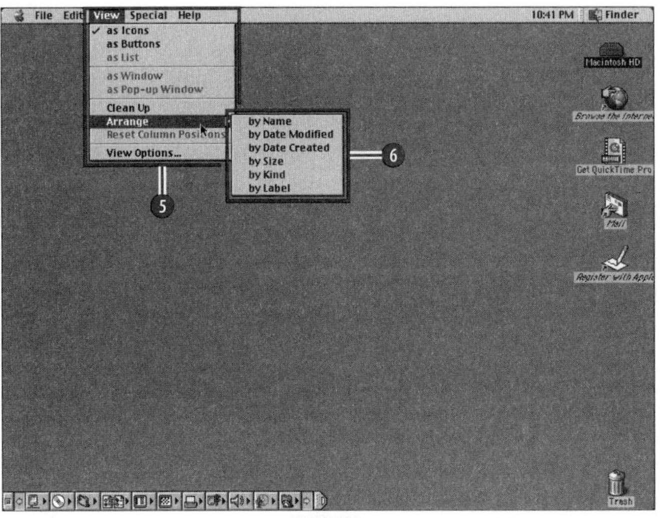

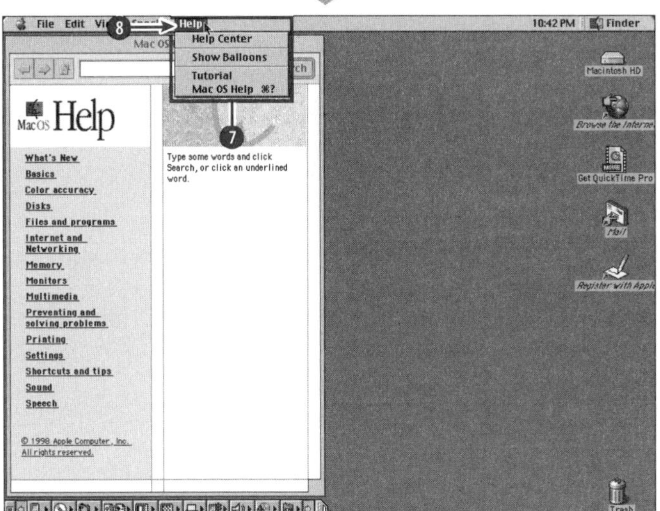

5. *Slide your mouse pointer to the View menu.*
6. *Explore your Arrange submenu items.*
7. *Click the Help menu. Notice the keyboard shortcut.*
8. *Click Help on the menu bar again to close it.*
9. *Press and hold the Command and ? keys. Release both keys.*

▶ *The Mac OS Help window opens.*

deletes files earmarked for removal, Eject spits out a CD-ROM disc or removable media disk (if you have an optional external floppy or Zip drive from which to read them), and Erase Disk permanently removes data from a disk (don't use this one yet).

The Help menu offers commands that help you use your iMac. Help Center contains a collection of information about your iMac. Show Balloons displays helpful hints when the mouse pointer hovers over some items. The Tutorial and Mac OS Help offer information on basic Mac skills. Most applications also offer a Help menu.

The Application menu (the menu on the far right side of your menu bar) offers the ability to switch between open programs. A check mark next to an item indicates the active program. If no programs are currently open, only the Finder is available. The Application menu is always available.

TAKE NOTE

USING KEYBOARD SHORTCUTS

Take a close look at one of your menus again. Do you see the small cloverleaf symbol and the letter located to the right of many of your menu options? These are *keyboard shortcuts* for your menu options. You can use them to execute menu commands without using the mouse. To use one, press and hold the Command key (the key displaying that same cloverleaf symbol, to the left of your spacebar) and press the letter indicated next to the menu option.

SHORTCUT

You can use keyboard shortcuts at any time, though shortcuts may differ from program to program.

Viewing Your Desktop and Windows

Customization is one of the cornerstones of the Mac OS. Your ability to change aspects of your iMac environment according to your needs and whims is both powerful and useful. It was this power to change the Desktop and its windows that first drew me in. What fun I had! You, too, can change views, sort windows, and more, all using the View menu.

Let's begin with your Desktop view. Once you've made sure your Desktop (Finder) is the active program (check the Application menu), examine your View menu. The first two options, "as Icons" and "as Buttons", affect the appearance of files on the Desktop itself. The Clean Up command rearranges the icons (or buttons) on your Desktop in an orderly manner. The Arrange submenu lets you designate the order in which items on your Desktop appear. The View Options command offers several more viewing options. The option Icon Arrangement allows you to set a default arrangement for your Desktop. The default arrangement is None, but you can select "Always snap to grid" to keep items in straight rows and columns or "Keep arranged" to lock-in your current arrangement. Icon Size toggles between small or large (default) icons or buttons. If you make changes and later decide you want to return to the system-wide view, click the Set to Standard Views button on the bottom of the dialog box.

The View menu also affects items in windows on your Desktop. Open the Macintosh HD window (make sure it is in the foreground with its "racing stripes" visible), and examine the View menu again. A couple of new menu options are now available. In addition to the "as Icons" and "as Buttons" views, you also can select the "as List" view — a powerful option that displays item names and other useful information in a columnar style. Once a window is in List view, the Sort List submenu

CROSS-REFERENCE

Learn more about choosing Desktop preferences in the last task of this chapter, "Setting Your Preferences."

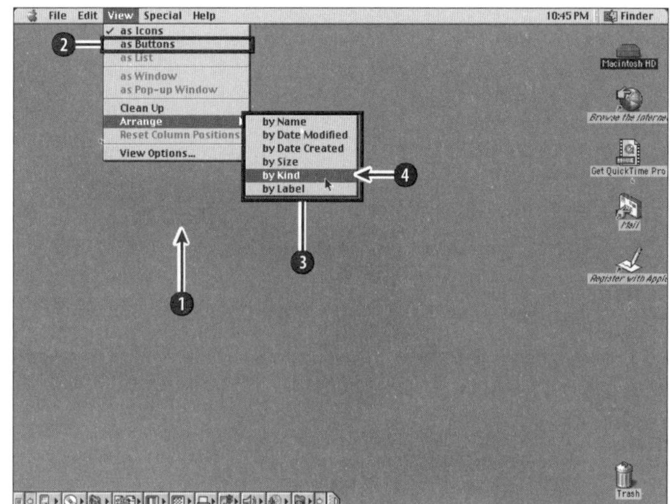

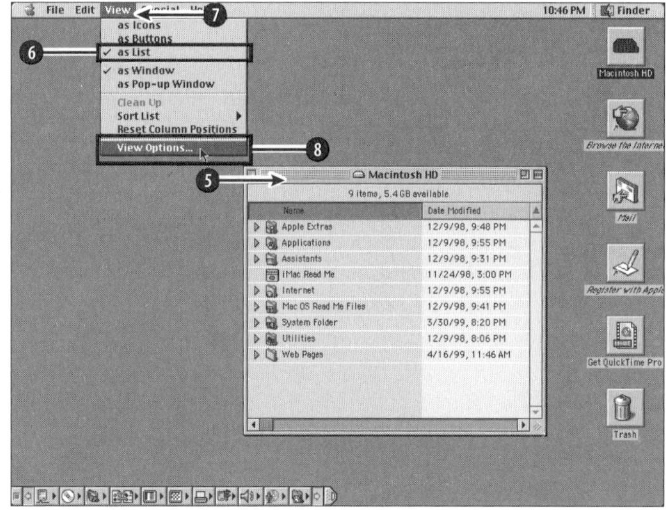

1. *Click your Desktop once to ensure it is the active element.*
2. *Choose "as Buttons" from the View menu.*
3. *Select the Arrange submenu.*
4. *Choose any one of the arrangement options and note the changes.*
5. *Select your Macintosh HD window, or open it if closed.*
6. *Choose "as List" from the View menu.*
7. *Pull down the View menu again to see the new options.*
8. *Choose View Options from the View menu.*

Customizing Window Columns

With a window open in List view, return to View Options. Choose the information you'd like to see in a window from the Show Columns list. Kind refers to the file type, while Label refers to colors designated in the File menu. If you add more columns, information may scroll off the right edge of the window; use the bottom scroll bar to view the hidden text. You could also maximize the window or change the column size.

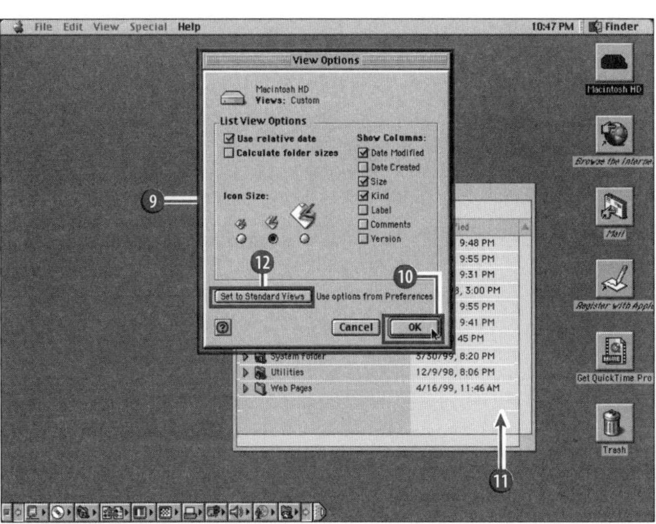

- 9 *Explore your View Options and select those that interest you.*
- 10 *Click OK to activate your View options.*
- 11 *Experiment with different options.*
- 12 *Click the Set to Standard Views button to restore your window view.*

becomes available on the View menu. This works much like the Arrange submenu in Icon or Button view. The "as Window" (default) and "as Pop-up Window" options let you change the appearance of your window frames. A pop-up window displays a tab at the top that can be used to minimize (drop down) or maximize (pop up) the window. When minimized, the tab appears on the bottom of your screen. If a window tab is obscured by the Control Strip (the long, thin bar with small icons on it on the bottom of your Desktop), just double-click the pull-tab at the end of the Control Strip to minimize it. Click once on a window tab to pop up the window.

TAKE NOTE

LISTING YOUR WINDOWS

More options are available for window contents when they are in List view. First, make sure a window is active, and then set it to List view and select the View Options command from the View menu. Select Use Relative Date if you want dates displayed as Today or Tomorrow rather than displaying as April 11 or April 12, for example. Calculate Folder Sizes shows you the size of a folder and its contents; select this option with care because it can slow down window display on your iMac.

SHORTCUT

Set views for all your windows at once. Choose Preferences from the Edit menu, click the Views tab, and then make your selections.

Creating and Naming Folders

Your iMac has a Desktop and windows with great views. It probably comes as no surprise to you that there are file folders on the Desktop, too. Just like real file folders, your iMac folders are containers that hold items such as files and even other folders. They organize items in your iMac and on your Desktop. Your iMac comes with lots of folders. Your Macintosh HD window has many folders in it, for example. You also can manually create folders to organize, reorganize, clean up, mess up, and even just decorate your Desktop!

Before you create a folder, decide where you want it to go. Folders can be created directly on the Desktop, in the Macintosh HD window (your hard disk's top level), or in any pre-existing folder. Once you've decided where you want to place a folder, make that place the active element on your screen. To make the Desktop the active element, click once in an empty area. To make your Macintosh HD window active, click once on its title bar, or open it (double-click) if it is closed. To make any other folder active, open it with a double-click.

Once you've chosen a spot for your new folder, choose New Folder from the File menu. A new folder instantly appears in the active window (or on your Desktop). You can't see it? Look for the small picture (icon) of a darkened file folder named "untitled folder." Notice that the folder's name is surrounded by a border, indicating that it is waiting to be given a name. Just start typing. You can type up to 31 letters, numbers, or punctuation characters. The only character you can't use is the colon (:). When you're finished typing the new folder name, click once on an empty space on the Desktop or in the window. The folder's icon returns to a normal color and the border disappears, leaving behind the new folder name.

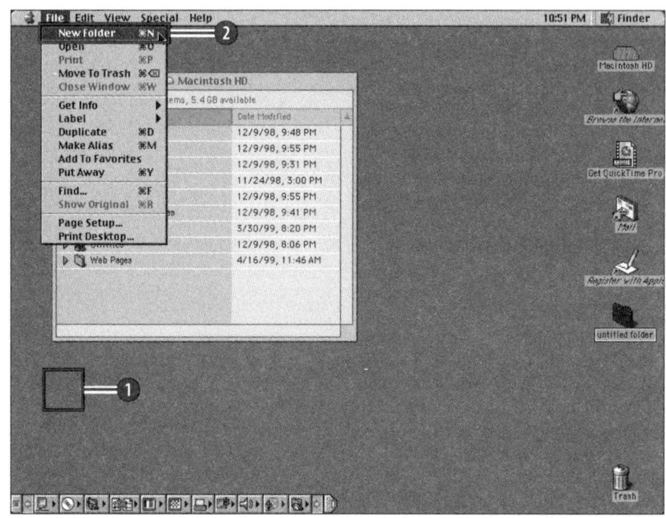

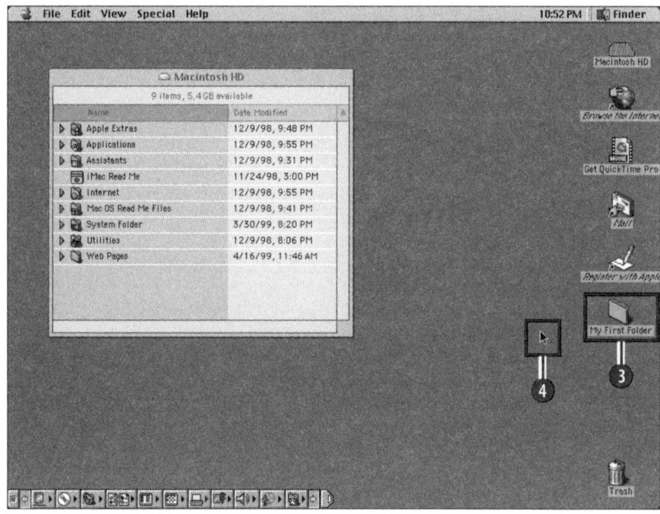

1. *Click an empty spot on your Desktop to make the Desktop active.*
2. *Pull down the File menu and choose New Folder.*

▶ *A new folder instantly appears on your Desktop. Notice the darkened icon and border around the name.*

3. *Type **My First Folder**.*
4. *Click once on the Desktop.*

CROSS-REFERENCE

Learn more about editing your typing in Chapter 4, "Working with Text."

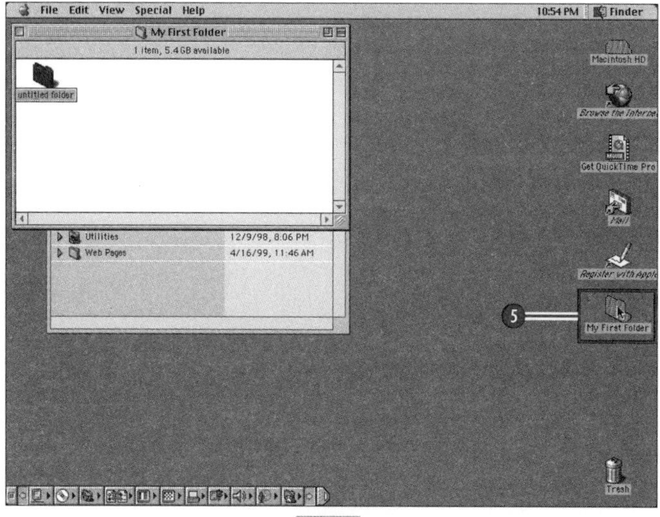

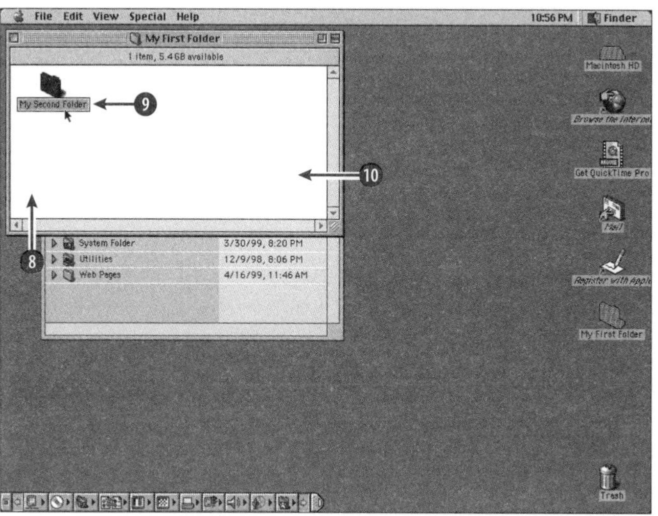

5 *Open (double-click) your new folder.*

▶ *The folder's name appears in the title bar.*

6 *Press and hold the Command key and press the N key.*

▶ *Another new folder appears in the window.*

7 *Type **My Second Folder**.*

8 *Click once on an empty spot in the window.*

9 *Click the second folder's name.*

10 *Type a new name and click an empty part of the window.*

If your new folder doesn't have a border, or you already named it, but you want to change it, click once on the folder's name. The border reappears and you can start typing. If you make a mistake while typing, it is easiest to click once outside the name, click the folder's name again, and then retype the name.

TAKE NOTE

NAMING AND ORGANIZING FOLDERS

Are you wondering what to name a new folder? It really depends on how you intend to use your iMac and the way in which you work best. There are no hard and fast rules, though it does help to be more — rather than less — specific. Good spelling also makes it easier to find things later on. Think about how you prefer to organize things outside your computer, and consider applying that theme to the folder organization of your iMac. I like to make a folder for each project, person, trip, and so on. I keep a few on my Desktop, but most are organized within other folders. Your folder organization will develop as you begin using your iMac. If it doesn't, you may wish it had.

SHORTCUT

You also can use the keyboard shortcut Command+N to create a new folder.

Moving Files

Now that you can create folders, what are you going to put in them? You could file your folders with folders, more folders, and nothing but folders, but that's a bit like buying books you don't read (which I'll bet isn't your style). Folders primarily hold files, or hold folders with files, or hold folders with folders with files, or any combination thereof — you get the idea.

If you're not familiar with the term *file*, this is an all-encompassing word for a unit of data on your iMac. Most files are either *applications* (program files) or *documents* (files created by those applications). If you see an icon that doesn't look like a folder, it could be a file of some sort (but not always).

To really make folders work, you need to put files in them. Generally, you can do this either by moving a file into a folder, or by creating a file and saving it in a folder. We'll get to creating files later in Chapter 4. For now, let's focus on how to move files.

To move a file to another spot on the Desktop or in the same window, press and drag the file's icon to that spot (notice a gray, ghostly icon follows your pointer as you drag), and let go of the mouse button. Be careful not to double-click (open) the file.

To move a file into something else, like a folder or your hard disk's top level, press and drag the icon directly into the hard disk's or the folder's window (find an empty spot) and let go of the mouse button. If the hard disk or folder isn't open, press and drag the icon directly on top of the icon representing the hard disk or folder; when the hard disk/folder icon darkens (highlights), let go of the mouse button.

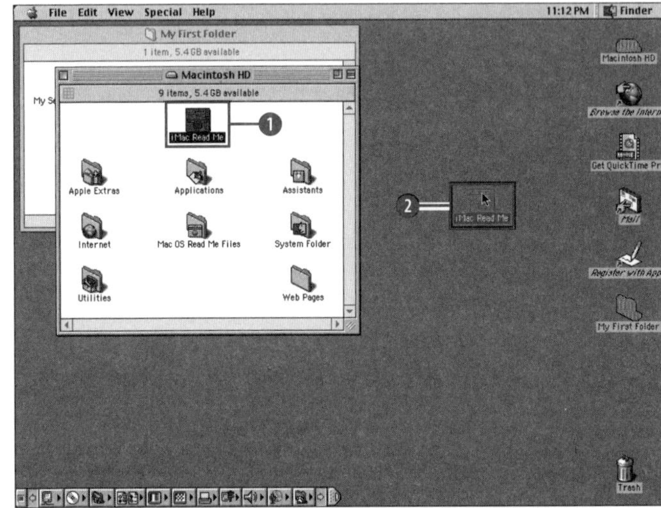

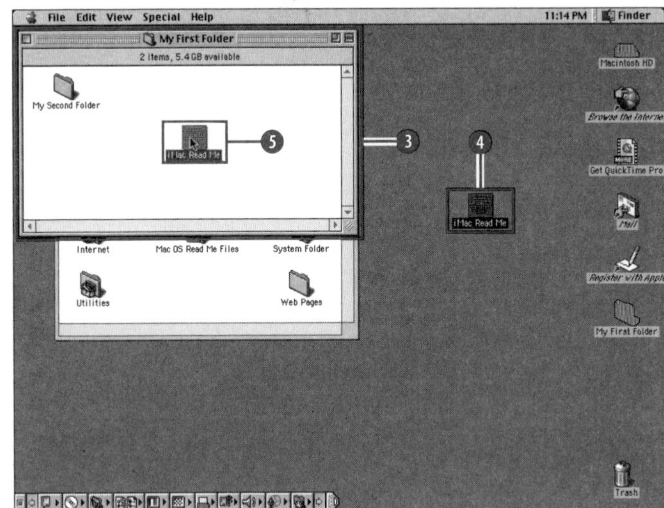

1. Press and drag the iMac Read Me icon in the Macintosh HD window.
   - ▶ *A gray icon ghost follows your mouse pointer.*
2. Position your pointer on an empty spot of the Desktop and release the mouse button.
   - ▶ *The icon reappears on your Desktop.*
3. Locate the My First Folder window on your Desktop.
4. Press and drag the iMac Read Me file icon.
5. Drag the file icon into a blank spot in the new folder window.
   - ▶ *The icon reappears in the window.*

CROSS-REFERENCE

Learn how to save documents in folders in "Saving Your Work" in Chapter 4.

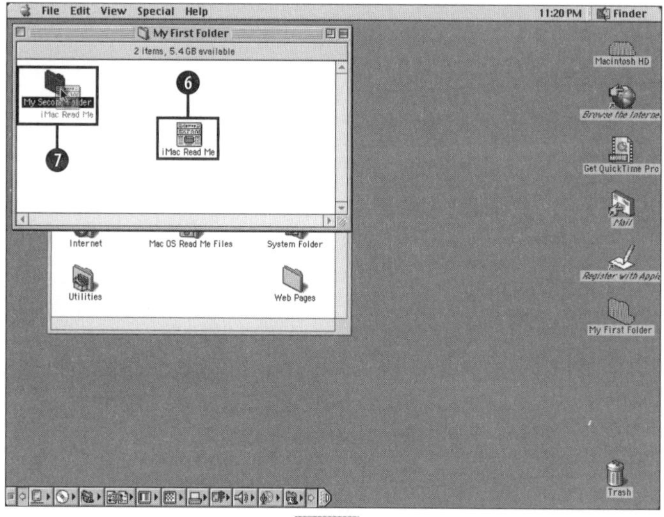

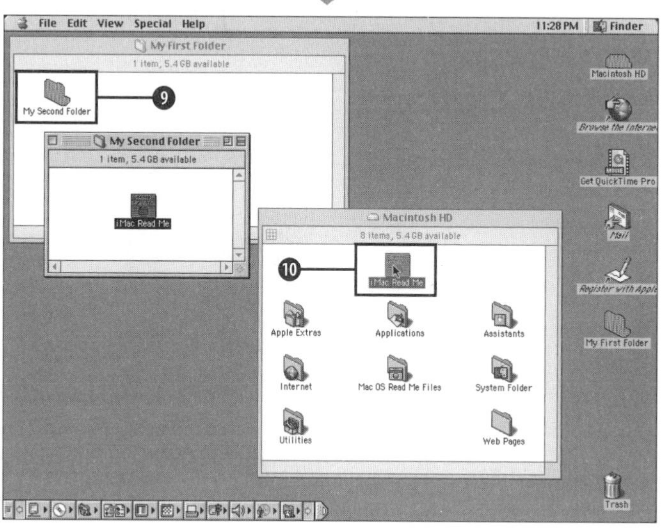

6. *Press and drag the iMac Read Me icon.*
7. *Drag the icon on top of the second new folder you created.*

▶ *The folder icon darkens (highlights) when the file icon hovers over it.*

8. *Release the mouse button.*
9. *Double-click the second new folder icon to open it.*

▶ *The iMac Read Me icon appears in the folder window.*

10. *Press and drag the iMac Read Me icon back to the Macintosh HD window.*

▶ *The icon reappears in the Macintosh HD window.*

TAKE NOTE

USING SPRING-LOADED FOLDERS

You may have noticed that if you let your mouse pointer hover over a hard disk/folder icon for a moment while pressing and dragging, the window automatically opens. These are called *spring-loaded folders*, which your iMac provides by default. If you want to turn this feature off (it can be a bit distracting), choose Preferences from the Edit menu, click the General tab at the top, and then click the check box next to "Spring-loaded folders." While there, you also can adjust the delay time so that the folder doesn't open so quickly. Just press and drag the small indicator arrow along the slider bar, letting go of the mouse button when the arrow is at the desired point.

MOVING FOLDERS

You can move folders in the same way you move files — by pressing and dragging them to a new location (or into something else). But what if the folder you want to move is already open? Rather than close the window, press and drag the small icon to the left of the folder's name in the title bar. The folder moves, but the folder's window remains open and in the same spot as it was when you started.

SHORTCUT

If you turn off the "Spring-loaded folders" option, you can still spring-load a folder when desired. Just press the spacebar as you press and drag the folder.

Copying Files

Everyone knows it isn't nice to copy. One thing that makes the iMac so captivating is its innovation — a fresh idea in a marketplace stale with copycats and clones. So what's all this about copying files? It's often helpful — and sometimes even necessary — to copy some files on your iMac.

To copy a file or a folder, first select it with your mouse. Remember that a selected item becomes highlighted (darkens). Now, choose Duplicate from the File menu. A copy of the item you duplicated appears, offset slightly from the original item. Note that the original item remains highlighted (so you can copy it again if you wish) and the duplicate has the word "copy" at the end of its name. If you were to repeat the process, another copy would appear, again offset slightly from both the original and the first copy. It also would have the word "copy" at the end of its name — you can't have two identically named files within a folder — along with a number to differentiate it from the others. The copies are exact duplicates (with the exception of the names) and include everything contained in the original. This means that if you copy a folder, everything in the folder is copied, as well!

Another way to copy files is using the Option key. Try this: hold down the Option key, press and drag an item to a blank spot on the Desktop or in its window, and then release the mouse button. A copy is automatically created in the exact spot where you released the mouse button.

What if you want to create a copy in a new location? Keep in mind that if you drag an item out of a folder and put it into another, you're moving the original. To copy something to another folder, to the same window, or to the Desktop, hold down the Option key and then press and drag the item to a new location. The iMac

CROSS-REFERENCE

Consider using an alias in lieu of creating a copy. See the next task, "Aliasing Files," for details.

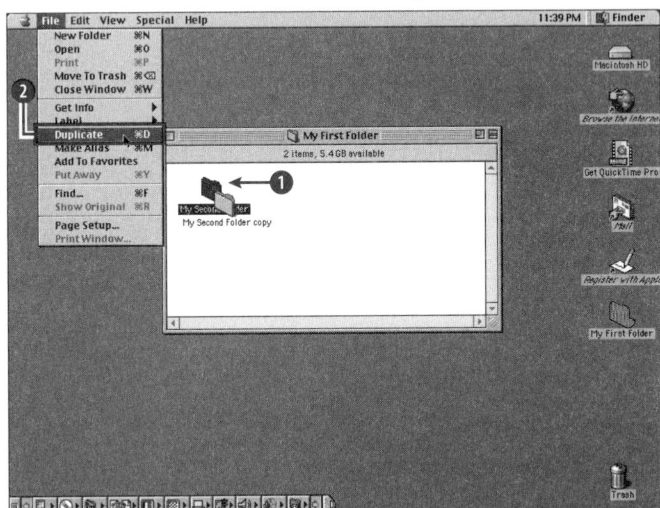

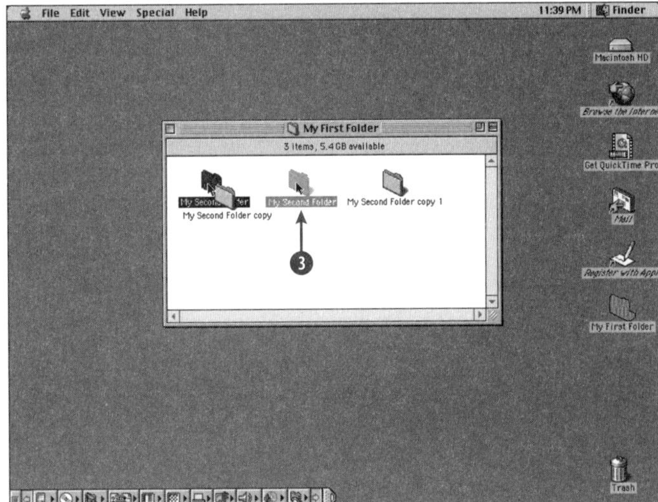

1. *Select the second new folder you created. Note that it is highlighted.*
2. *Choose Duplicate from the File menu.*

- *Alternatively, you could press Command+D.*
- *A copy appears offset from the original.*
- *Hold down the Option key*

3. *Press and drag the original icon to a new location, and then release the mouse button.*

- *Another copy of the folder appears in the spot where you released the mouse button.*

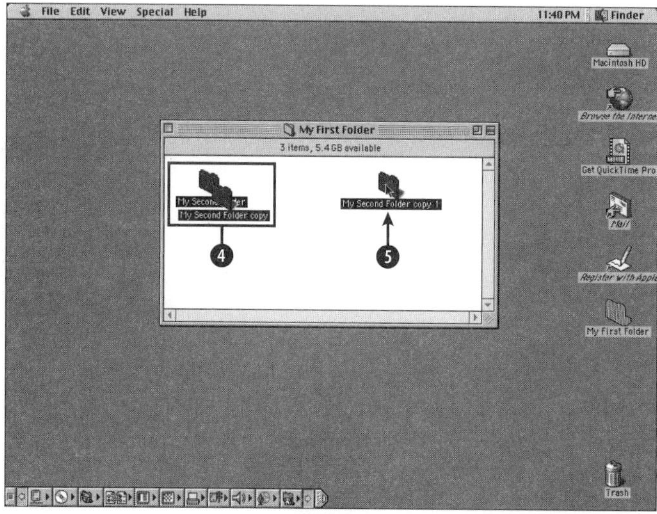

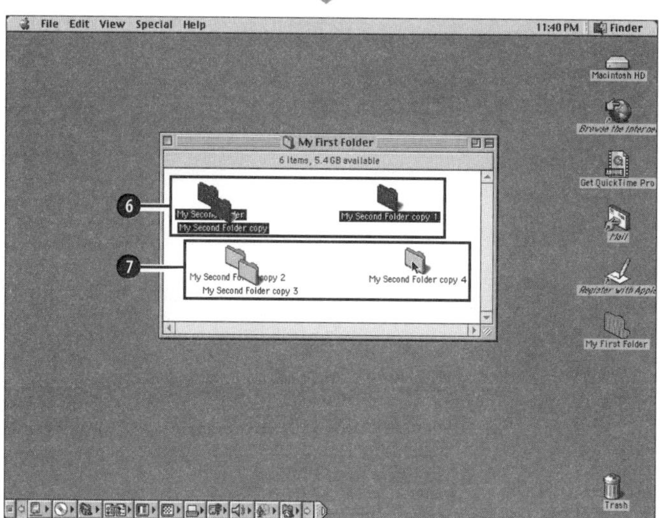

4. *Hold the Shift key down and select all three folders.*
   - *Alternatively, press Command+A to select all items.*
5. *Position the mouse pointer over one of the folders.*
6. *Hold the Option key down, and then press and drag the folders to a new location.*
   - *The other selected folders follow along.*
7. *Release the mouse button and note that the new copies appear.*
   - *All folder copies bear their original names.*

automatically creates a copy in that new location, also with "copy" appended to the name.

TAKE NOTE

COPYING GROUPS

You can copy more than one item at a time. Select all the items you want to copy by holding down the Shift key as you individually click each item. If you accidentally click one you didn't want to copy, just click it again (keeping the Shift key depressed). Release the Shift key and select Duplicate from the File menu, or hold the Option key down, click one of the selected items, drag the items as a group, and then release the mouse button.

KEEPING TABS ON A COPY

You may notice that a small box pops up as you copy an item or group of items. This is a copy progress dialog box. A progress meter fills up as your copies are created, visually showing you how many items have been copied and how many items remain. If your copy is taking a long time, click the small arrow on the window to show more information about the copies in progress.

SHORTCUT

Use the keyboard shortcuts Command+D to duplicate items and Command+A to select all items in a window.

Aliasing Files

Copying files only gets you so far. Sometimes it isn't practical or appropriate to copy an entire file or folder. Copies take space, after all. Too many copies on your hard disk can become confusing, and the wrong copy may be modified. If you want quick access to a file or folder in more than one location, and you also want to be sure you have only one version of a file or folder, you need to create an alias to it instead.

An alias is a small file that points to the original file, creating a shortcut to it. For example, if you use a program every day, and every day you have to navigate through several folders to get to it, you're just wasting time and energy (and wearing down the mouse pad). You could move the program to your Desktop, but then the program might not work (programs generally need to stay in the folder they started out in). You can copy the contents of program's folder to your Desktop, but it still may not work and your Desktop would get cluttered. Instead, make an alias to the program and place the alias on your Desktop. When you open the alias, the original program opens for you.

To create an alias, simply select it (highlight it) and choose Make Alias from the File menu. You also can use the keyboard shortcut Command+M. The new alias appears slightly offset from the original and looks a lot like it, but with two notable differences. First, a small arrow appears in the lower left corner of the icon to identify it as an alias. (If you don't see this arrow, it only means you're using an older version of the Mac OS.) Second, the name appears in italics (slanted type) and the word "alias" is added to the end. You can remove the word "alias" if you like (the name remains in italics), and you can even change the entire name (click once on the name and start typing, just as you did earlier when you renamed a folder).

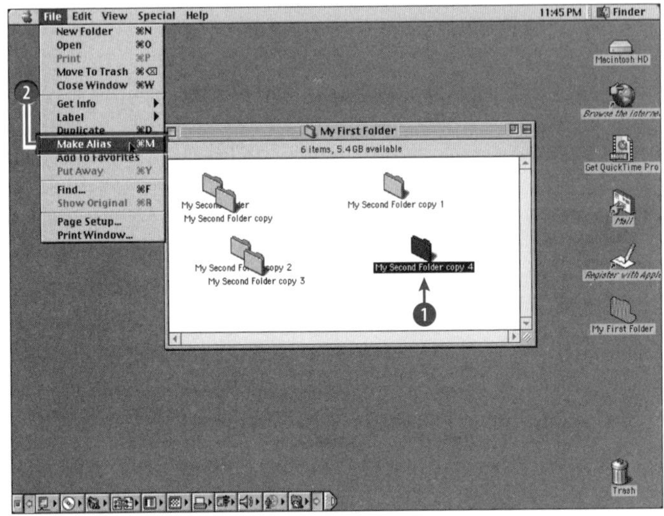

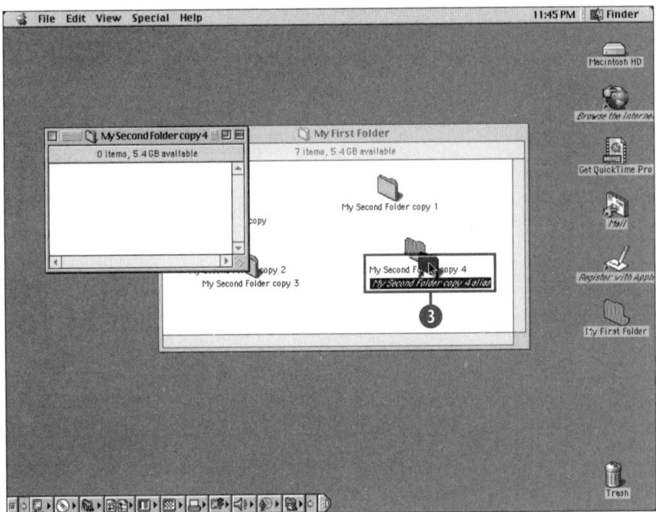

❶ *Select (highlight) one of the folders (or folder copies) you created.*

❷ *Choose Make Alias from the File menu.*

▶ *An alias file appears, offset from the original. Note the arrow, italic type, and word "alias" at the end.*

❸ *Double-click the alias.*

▶ *The original folder opens. Note the original folder icon is gray, verifying that it is open.*

CROSS-REFERENCE

Learn how to add aliases to your Apple menu in "Making the Most of Your Apple Menu" in Chapter 14.

The Get Info Window

Good things come in small packages, and the little Get Info window is no exception. Beyond locating the original program or file for an alias, you can learn and do all sorts of interesting things. You can look up the dates that a file was created and last modified, add to the label, change the color of the icon to set a priority level, and even type in a comment for you or others to read. We'll revisit the Get Info box several times again in this book. Take a moment now to learn the keyboard shortcut to quickly access the Get Info window (Command+I).

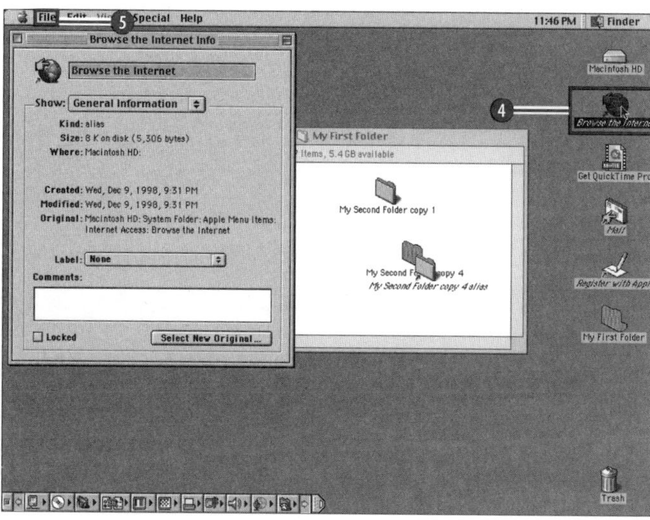

❹ *Select the Browse the Internet icon on your Desktop.*

❺ *Choose Get Info from the File menu.*

▶ *Note the original file's location in the file information window.*

You can make as many aliases as you like. Remember, they aren't copies — they're only pointers to the original files or folders. You also can put aliases anywhere you like — on your Desktop, in folders, in your Apple menu, and so on.

TAKE NOTE

▶ **FINDING THE ORIGINAL**

Aliases are a bit like speed dial buttons on a telephone. It is as easy to forget the location of the original file or program as it is to forget a telephone number once you've added it to the speed dial list. To view the folder with the original file, select the alias in question and choose Show Original from the File menu (or press Command+R). If you only want to see the original folder's location and not actually open the folder, select the alias and choose Get Info from the File menu. The window that appears lists lots of file information (name, kind, size, location, and so on.) Note the "Original" line toward the bottom of the window. This is the location of the original file or program.

SHORTCUT

Hold down both the Option and Command keys as you press and drag a file or folder to automatically create an alias.

Trashing and Deleting Files

Have you noticed how messy your Desktop has become with all these folders, copies of folders, and aliases? If you're anything like me, you've been eyeing that trash can icon in the lower right corner of your screen. It's time to use it!

Cleaning up your Desktop or windows is a two-part process. First, you move the items to the trash can, and then you empty the trash. Sound familiar?

To move something to the trash, first select it (highlight it) and then choose Move to Trash from the File menu. Alternatively, you can press and drag the item to the trash can, releasing the mouse button when the item is on top of the Trash icon. You can actually see the item move to the Trash icon and then disappear from the screen. The Trash icon even changes to indicate something is in it (the lid comes off and you can see papers sticking out of the can). Time to empty the trash!

To empty the Trash, choose Empty Trash from the Special menu. A small window appears to inform you of the number of items in the Trash and the amount of disk space the items use. You are then asked if you want to permanently remove the items. Click OK (or press the Return key) if you want to permanently delete the items, or click Cancel if you change your mind. Deleted items cannot be retrieved by conventional means, so be careful before you empty the trash. If you get tired of being asked if you really want to empty the trash, you can disable this dialog box. Just select the Trash icon, press Command+I for the Get Info window, and clear the "Warn before emptying" check box at the bottom of the Get Info window.

Keep in mind that items dragged to the trash aren't really deleted until you empty the trash. This means you can retrieve them at any time before you empty the trash (just double-click the Trash icon and press and

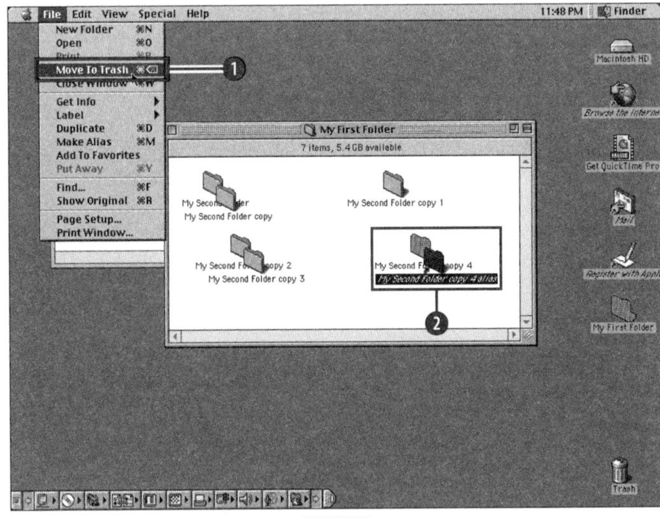

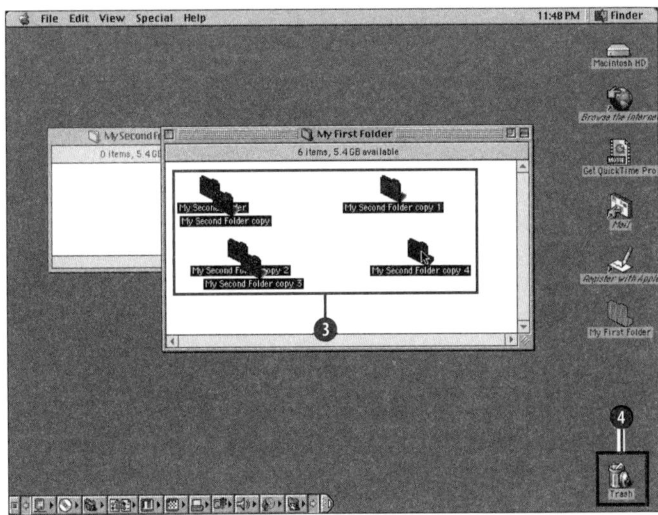

1. Select the folder alias you created earlier.
2. Choose Move to Trash from the File menu.

▶ Note that when you delete an alias, you only delete the shortcut and not the item the shortcut points to.

▶ Notice that the Trash icon changes and that the item you moved to the Trash has disappeared.

3. Shift-click to select several folders.
4. Press and drag them on top of the Trash icon and release the mouse button.

CROSS-REFERENCE

Learn more about hard disk space in Chapter 3, "Using Discs and Drives."

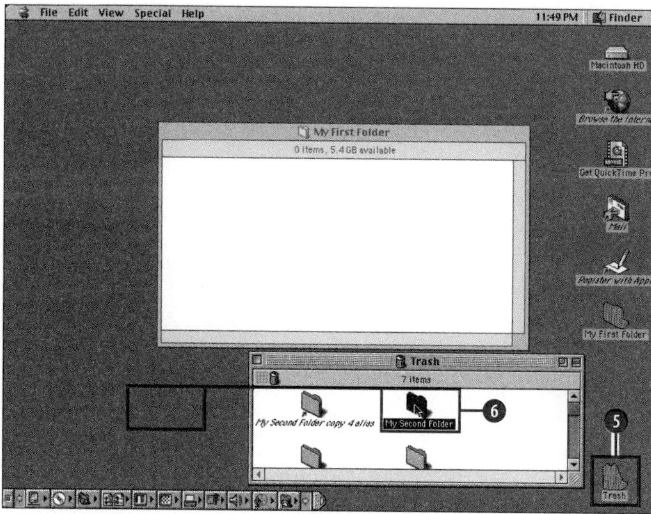

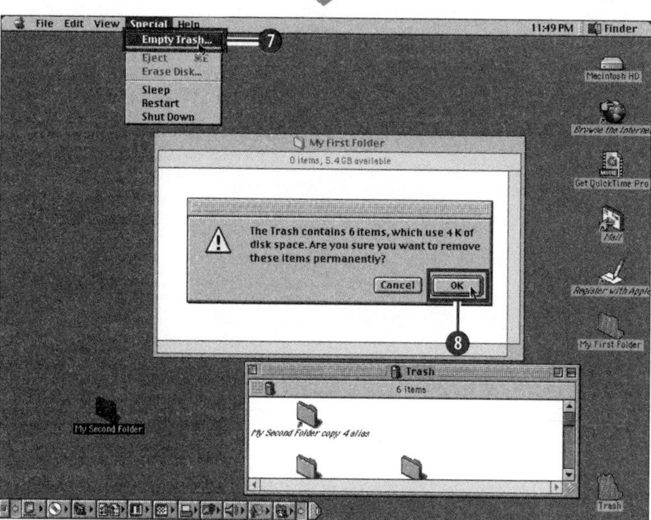

5 *Open (double-click) the Trash icon.*

▶ *Use the scroll bars to view all the items in the Trash window.*

6 *Press and drag an item from the Trash to the Desktop.*

▶ *Check everything else in the Trash before proceeding.*

7 *Choose Empty Trash from the Special menu.*

8 *Click OK when prompted, or click Cancel if you change your mind.*

drag the item somewhere else). It also means that you won't free up any room on your hard disk until the trash has been emptied.

TAKE NOTE

USING CONTEXT MENUS

If you get tired of all the pressing and dragging about the Desktop, consider using *context menus* instead. You have context menus available all over your Desktop and even in other programs. What are they? Context menus are pop-up menus that appear when you hold down the Control key while you click items such as icons or windows. For example, if you Control-click an icon on your Desktop (or in a window), a small menu pops up with a number of options, including Move to Trash, Get Info, Duplicate, and Make Alias. To choose a context menu item, slide your pointer to the appropriate item and click it once. Context menus may have submenus, too. Windows, folders, and icons (including the Trash icon) all have context menus. How many context menus can you find?

SHORTCUT

Hold down the Command key and press the Delete key to move an item to the Trash.

Finding Files

Folders are a boon for organization, but let's face it: nested folders (folders within other folders) can make it tough to find things. Sure, you can open all your folders one by one. Do you have time for that? I don't. Luckily, your iMac offers a better, faster way to find things. Enter Sherlock, a savvy program integrated into your Desktop that can search for files on your entire hard drive (or even the Internet). Sherlock looks a bit different with the Mac OS 9 software (which you may be using if you have a newer iMac)—in fact, it is called "Sherlock 2" on Mac OS 9. Sherlock 2 also works a little differently, though basic operation is much the same—I'll call out any significant differences for you as we go.

To find an item, begin by choosing Find from the File menu. You also can choose Sherlock (or Sherlock 2) from the Apple menu (which is always accessible, regardless of what you are doing on your iMac). Either menu command opens the Sherlock program. As soon as it appears, the Sherlock window is ready to accept your search word or phrase; you can start typing at any time. The blinking insertion point in the box is your visual clue that it accepts typing. Press the Return key (or click the Find or magnifying glass icon) and Sherlock begins searching for your word or phrase.

If Sherlock finds no items, it informs you of this with a dialog box. If on the other hand Sherlock matches your word or phrase, your new items are displayed in either a new window (Mac OS 8) or in the top half of the same window (Mac OS 9). Click any name once to get a hierarchical view of that item's location on your hard drive. You can now double-click to open any item displayed in the window. If you want to open the folder an item resides in, double-click the folder itself in the hierarchical view (you can open any other folder you see there, too).

CROSS-REFERENCE

Learn how to search the Internet with Sherlock in "Finding Information on the Internet" in Chapter 11.

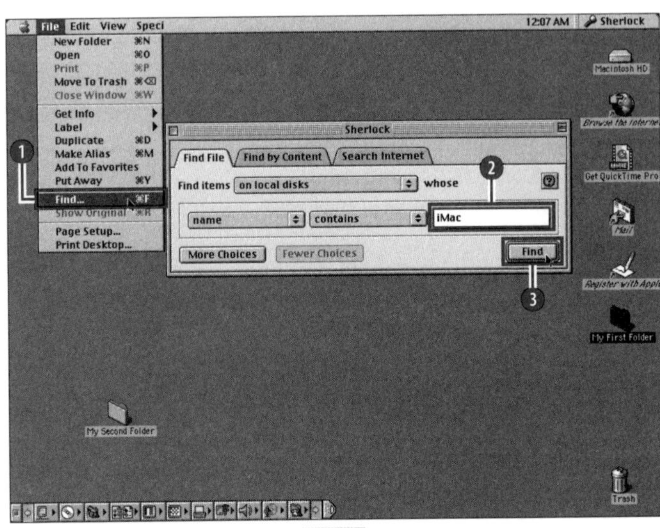

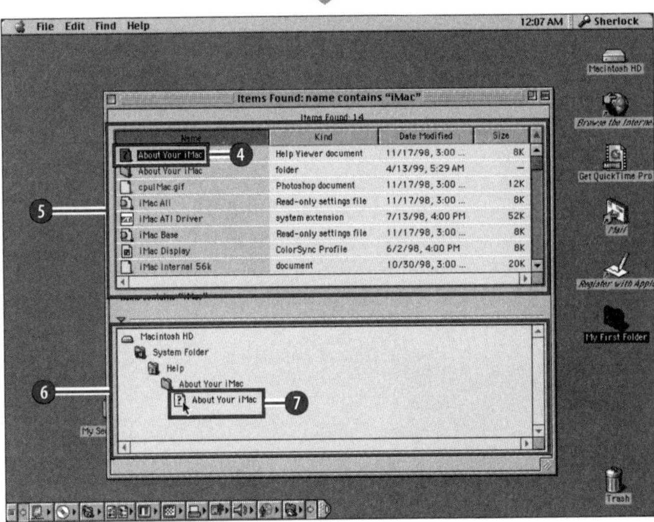

1. Choose Find from the File menu.

▶ Alternatively, choose Sherlock or Sherlock 2 from the Apple menu.

2. Type ***iMac*** and watch it appear as you type.
3. Click Find or press the Return key. Alternatively, click Find or the magnifying glass.
4. Examine the list of results.
5. Click About Your iMac at the top of the list.
6. Sherlock visually displays the file's location.
7. Double-click the file to open it now, if you wish.

Searching Inside Your Files

Sherlock can peer inside some of your files to find matches to words or phrases. Begin by opening Sherlock and click the Find by Content tab (Mac OS8) or the contents radio button (Mac OS 9). You need to index your hard drive first, so click Index Volumes from the Find menu, select your hard drive in the list, and then click Create Index. Once the indexing is complete, close the Index Volumes window and return to Sherlock. Now, type any word or phrase into the window, click the check box beside your hard drive, and then click Find.

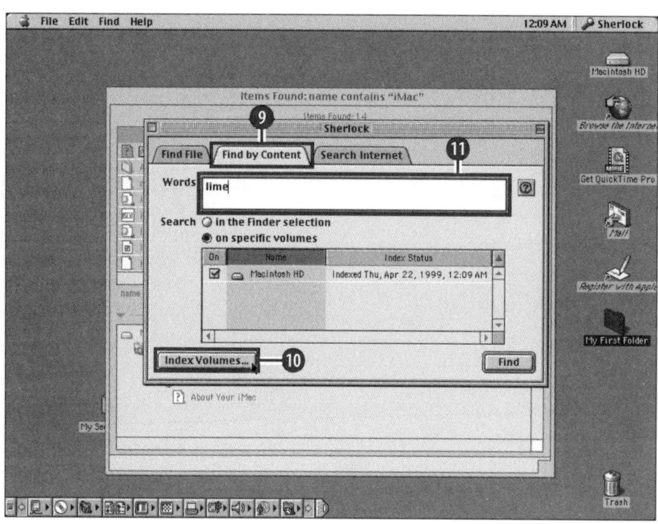

8 *Return to the Finder and press Command+F.*

9 *Click the Find by Content tab or the contents radio button.*

10 *Click Index Volumes and complete the indexing.*

11 *Return to Sherlock, type a word or phrase, and press Return.*

TAKE NOTE

NARROWING YOUR SEARCH

You've probably noticed the other buttons and menus in Sherlock's window. They all offer ways to fine-tune your search. You can tell Sherlock where to look on your hard drive using the drop-down menu (Mac OS 8) or by clicking the checkboxes next to your hard drive or CD-ROM discs (Mac OS 9). On Mac OS 8, additional drop-down menus let you tell Sherlock what attributes to search for — such as name, size, or kind — and how they should be matched (contains, starts with, ends with, and so forth). The More Choices button at the bottom of the Mac OS 8 dialog box adds another set of drop-down buttons to the window to refine your search. On Mac OS 9, you click the Edit button to set the attributes and further refine your search.

READING YOUR RESULTS

Sherlock displays its search results alphabetically, which isn't always helpful if it found a lot of stuff. To change the order of the list, just click one of the column labels near the top of the window, such as Kind, Date Modified, or Size. The list rearranges itself by your chosen parameter. You can even reverse the order by clicking the arrow in the upper-right corner of the results window. If you want to jump to a specific word in the list, type the first few letters of that word. These navigational tips can be used for other windows with similar lists, as well.

SHORTCUT

To open an item's folder from Sherlock, just select the file and press Command+E.

Setting Your Preferences

Now that you know how your Desktop works, you can set your Desktop preferences with confidence. To view your options, choose Preferences from the Edit menu. Note the three tabs at the top of the resulting window: General, Views, and Labels.

Under the General tab, your first option is for a Simple Finder. Check the box beside it if you feel distracted by the many menu options available in the Finder. Otherwise, I recommend you leave it unchecked. Spring-loaded folders automatically open when you press and drag a file or folder onto them. Clear the check box next to this option if having folders suddenly pop open bothers you. If you like the option, keep it checked and adjust the delay before opening time. Grid Spacing lets you choose how your icons line up on the Desktop: choose Tight if you want to fit more, or keep Wide if you want your icons in neat, generous columns.

Under the Views tab, you can set standard view options for windows in Icon, Button, and List views. Select the view you want to modify from the drop-down menu and then click to adjust the options. Icon view offers icon arrangement and icon size options. Button view offers the same arrangement and size options, for buttons. List view offers Use relative date (on by default), Calculate folder sizes (off by default), Icon Size, and Show Columns options.

Under the Labels tab, you can designate colors and categories for your icons. Your iMac provides seven levels, which you can use to organize icons in any manner you like. The most important thing to remember is that when you choose to sort a list by label, the label order shown in your Preferences window determines the order of the sort. That is, the label at the top (orange and Essential, by default) is considered the most important

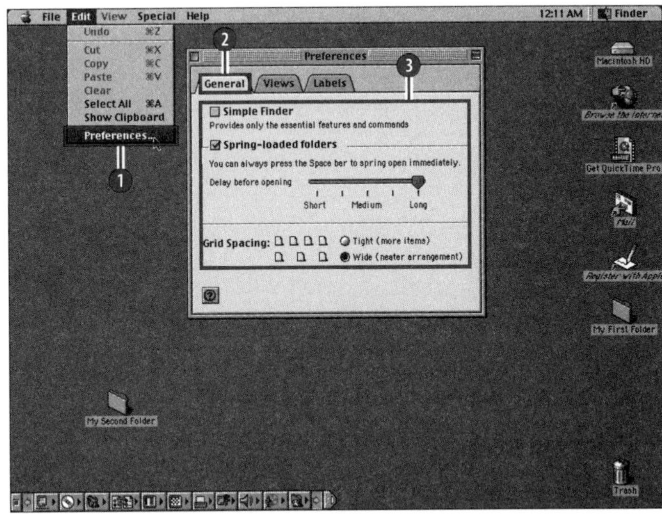

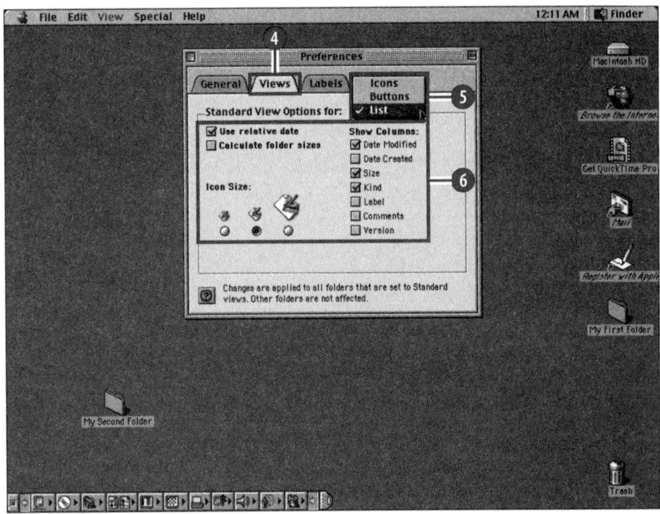

1. *Choose Preferences from the Edit menu.*
2. *Click the General tab on top if it isn't active.*
3. *Select your preferences.*
4. *Click the Views tab.*
5. *Click the double arrow to drop down the menu and choose a view option.*

▶ *Notice that the available options differ according to view.*

6. *Select your preferences.*

CROSS-REFERENCE

Learn how to customize the background of your Desktop in "Changing Your iMac's Appearance" in Chapter 14.

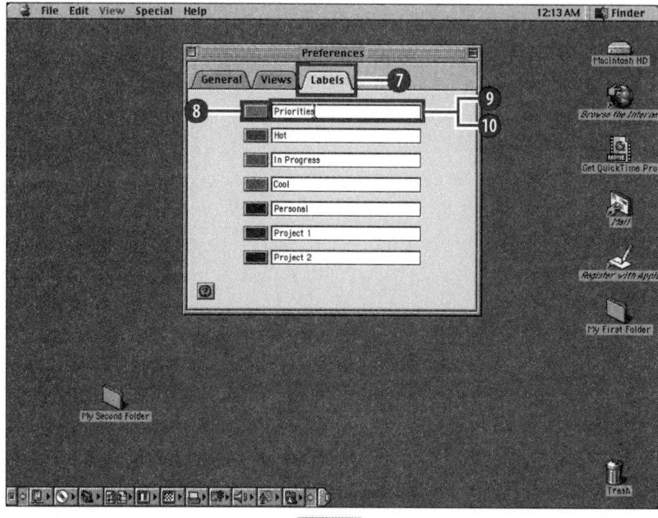

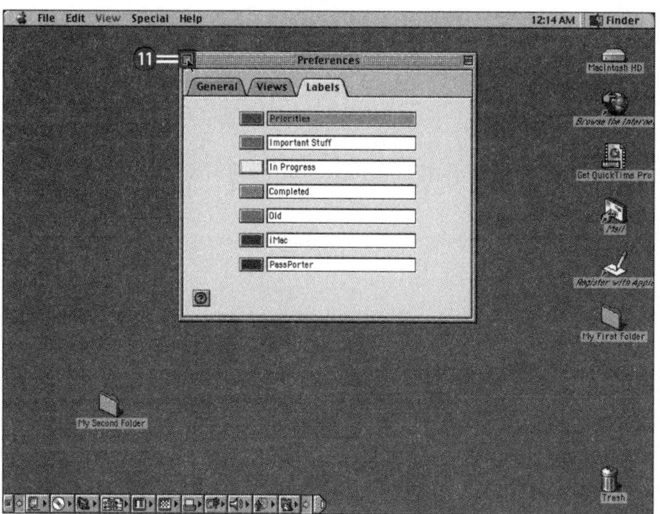

7 *Click the Labels tab.*

8 *Click a color button to change a label color.*

9 *Click a label name and repeatedly press the Delete key to remove a name.*

10 *Type a new name.*

11 *Close your Preferences window using the close box in the upper left.*

▶ *New preferences take effect when you close the window.*

and shows up first, red and Hot is second, pink and In Progess is third, and so on down the line. You can take advantage of these priority levels, or you can simply color-code your icons. You can use the colors provided, or you can click the color button next to a label to access the Color Picker window and choose a new color. To change a label, just click a label, press the delete key until you've completely removed the existing label name, and then type a new name.

TAKE NOTE

DECIDING WHICH PREFERENCES TO USE

You're going to see your Desktop every time you turn on your iMac, so it pays to set your preferences well. But if you're new to the iMac, you may not be sure what will and will not work. Here's what I suggest: try using the iMac's default preferences for a week or so to see how you like them. Revisit your Desktop preferences to make minor changes as necessary and live with the changes for a while. Always give yourself some time to adjust to a change, but don't wait too long to change something back if doesn't work for you, either. Avoid drastic, across-the-board changes unless you know exactly what you want. This philosophy applies to preferences throughout your iMac and in other applications, as well.

SHORTCUT

Press the help button on your keyboard at any time to get more information about anything.

Personal Workbook

Q&A

1. What is the Application menu and how does it work?

2. How do you view the items in a window as a list?

3. How do you change the name of a folder?

4. How do you move a file from one folder to another?

5. How do you copy a file or folder without selecting Duplicate from the File menu?

6. How can you tell the difference between an alias and an original?

7. How do you remove an item from the Trash?

8. How do you find a file on your hard drive without opening a single folder?

ANSWERS: PAGE 314

EXTRA PRACTICE

1. Select your Macintosh HD window and choose "as List" from the View menu. What happens to the icons in your window?
2. Display the Macintosh HD window in list view and click the arrow button to the right of the column labels. In what way does the list order change?
3. Create a new folder in the Macintosh HD window, name it "My Test Folder," and press the Return key. What happens to the folder after you rename it?
4. Hold down the Shift key, select all the other test folders you created earlier, and then press and drag them into the My Test Folder.
5. Select My Test Folder and press Command+D. Open the original and the copy and compare them.

REAL-WORLD APPLICATIONS

- ✔ A friend comes over and tries out your iMac's programs. You're left with layers of open windows and no sign of the Desktop. You pull down the Application menu on the far right end of your menu bar and select Finder to return to the Desktop. You then select Hide Others to hide the other program's open windows.
- ✔ You open a window that has over 50 icons scattered in it and you can't open it large enough to see them all. You choose "as List" from the View menu to view the items more clearly.
- ✔ You want to keep your Desktop clean. You notice that three of the icons that came on your iMac desktop are aliases, not actual programs, so you move those three to the Trash. The fourth item isn't an alias, so you press and drag it to the Macintosh HD window.

Visual Quiz

What kind of menu is this, and how do you access it?

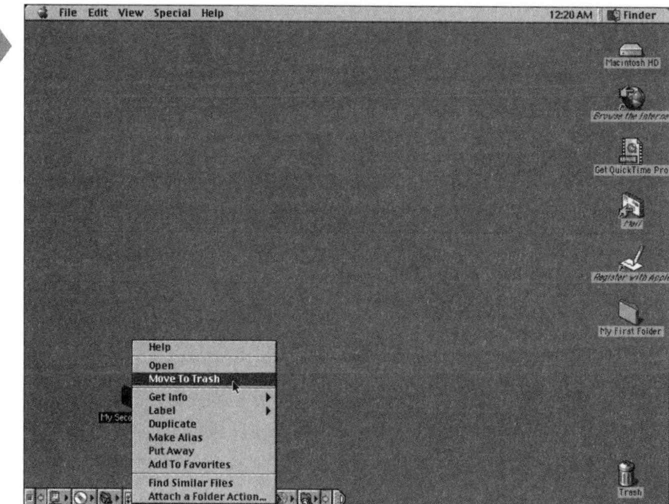

CHAPTER 3

MASTER THESE SKILLS

- Understanding Bytes
- Reading from a CD-ROM Disc
- Installing New Software
- Using Other Removable Media

Using Discs and Drives

Your hard drive (also called a hard disk) is the storage warehouse of your iMac. Incredible amounts of information can be recorded (written) to and retrieved (read) from the hard drive. It certainly seems that way when your iMac is new and the drive is mostly empty. The hard drive holds the Mac OS, without which your iMac would be a colorful doorstop. When you install programs onto your computer, the hard drive is where they're kept. And when it's time to save your work, you'll be saving it on your hard drive.

The hard drive is hidden away inside your iMac. Its incredibly fragile, magnetically coated platter spins many thousands of times per minute and is permanently sealed away from dust and minor vibrations. It's a marvel that hard drives can work flawlessly for years on end. But they are mechanical devices with motors and other moving parts, which means they're far more likely to break down than the solid-state chips that make up much of the rest of your iMac.

Hard drives, CD-ROM discs, and removable media are also the cold storage warehouses of your iMac. Information stored on a disk survives when the power is off, or when the computer crashes. Removable media and CD-ROM discs can even be stored offsite to protect your information in case of fire, theft, or other disasters.

On the other hand, information stored only in RAM is lost forever if the power fails. *RAM* (which stands for Random Access Memory) is your iMac's short-term memory. Information moves in and out of RAM at least 10 times faster than that on a hard drive, but RAM is about 60 times more expensive than an equivalent amount of hard drive space.

Your hard drive is where your programs and files live (you can think of it as their home), while your RAM is where they run or work (think of it as their office). Like most of us, an iMac's home is bigger than its office. Following this analogy, the CD-ROM drive in your iMac is your local public library where you can read information from it, but you can't write new information to it. Removable media drives are the self-storage warehouses of the neighborhood. You only rent (or buy) one if you really need it, and you're most likely to store and retrieve information from it on an occasional basis.

Understanding Bytes

We measure our homes and offices in square footage, while the iMac uses bytes. A byte is the smallest unit you'll come across on your iMac. Yet because it is so small, people usually don't measure things in bytes. That would be like measuring your body weight in ounces rather than pounds. Ouch! Instead, we use the terms kilobyte, megabyte, and gigabyte.

A kilobyte is 1024 bytes. A typical document is between 10K and 100K (K is short for kilobytes, and is pronounced *kay*). For example, "The iMac Read Me document is 24K." A megabyte is 1024K. A typical application program uses between 5MB and 50MB (MB is short for megabytes) of disk space. Megabytes are also used to measure RAM (32MB, 64MB, or 128MB on your iMac). Usually, folks shorten megabytes to the terms *meg* or *megs* when speaking about them. For example, they might say "Quicken 98 is about 42 megs," or "My iMac has 32 megs of RAM."

A gigabyte is 1024MB. Your iMac's hard drive might be 4GB, 6GB, 10GB, or 13GB (GB is short for gigabytes). Most folks shorten gigabytes to the terms gig or gigs when referring to them. For example, they might say, "My iMac has a 6-gig hard drive."

You might be wondering, "What about bits?" Every byte is composed of 8 binary digits (bits), but the iMac doesn't nibble bits one at a time — it takes larger bytes. Since it takes a full byte to represent one character of text, bytes are a much more useful unit of measure.

Why 1024 and Not 1000?

You may be wondering why a kilobyte is 1024 bytes and not 1000 bytes, as one would rightly assume. 1024 is the power of 2 (2^{10} to be specific), and powers of 2 are important to computers. You will come across other numbers and limits as you use your iMac, such as 16, 32, 64, 128, 256, and so on. Like the 32MB of RAM in most iMac computers, you can expand that to 256MB. Understanding this should make you feel more comfortable around these funky numbers, or at least help you make educated decisions about memory.

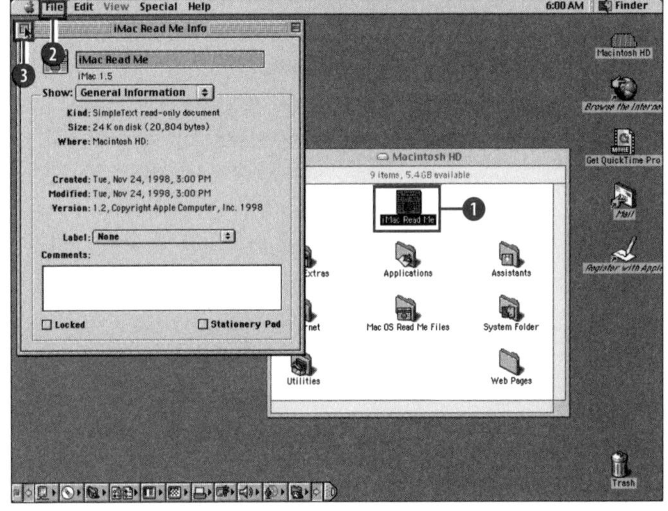

1. Select the iMac Read Me icon.
2. Choose Get Info from the File menu.

▶ The iMac Read Me Info window displays the file's size in kilobytes and bytes.

3. Close the window.

CROSS-REFERENCE

Learn more about removable media capacities in "Using Removable Media" at the end of this chapter.

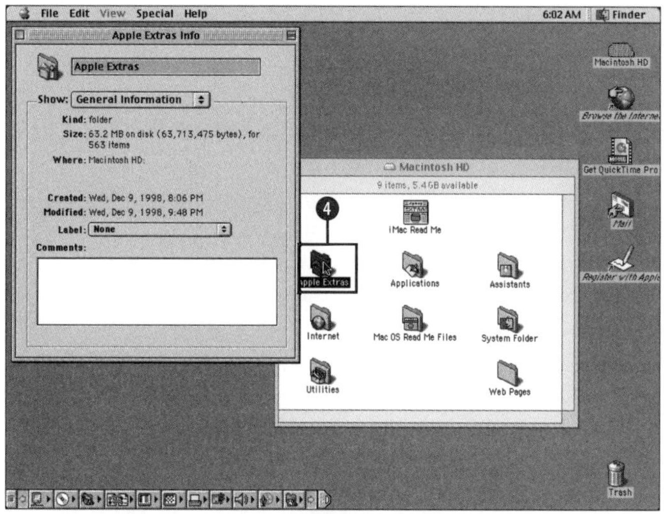

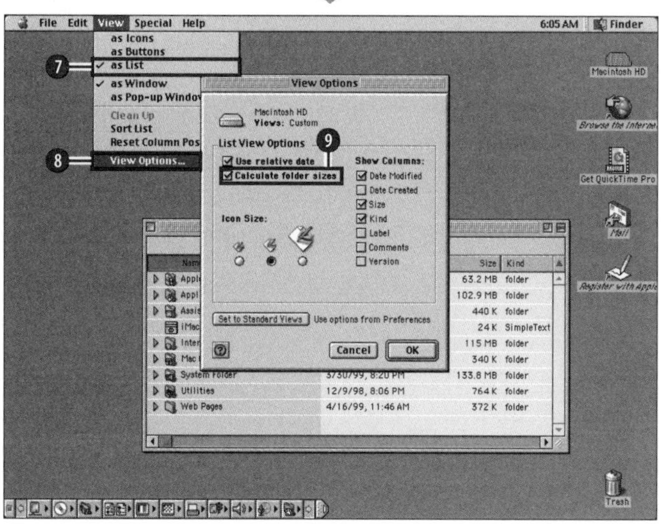

4 *Select the Apple Extras icon.*

5 *Press Command+I.*

▶ *The Info window displays the folder's size in megs and bytes, and includes the number of items.*

6 *Press Command+W.*

7 *Choose "as List" from the View menu.*

8 *Choose View Options.*

9 *Enable Calculate folder sizes.*

▶ *The window displays folder and file sizes and the available space on the hard disk.*

TAKE NOTE

DETERMINING THE SIZE OF FILES AND FOLDERS

How can you tell how much space a file or folder uses? The easiest way is to select the item in question and press Command+I to access Get Info. The Size line shows you the number of K (kilobytes), MB (megabytes), or even GB (gigabytes). Another way to measure size is with the Calculate folder sizes option. First, open a window containing the item in question, change it to list view, enable the Calculate folder sizes option in the View Options window, and then give your iMac a few moments to do its math. Check your window again and you'll see a Size column listing the size of every item in the window (you may need to widen or scroll your window to see it).

DETERMINING SIZE OF DRIVES AND DISKS

You also can check a hard drive or CD-ROM disc to view its capacity, generally measured in MB or GB. Just select its icon on the Desktop and press Command+I. The Capacity line shows the total capacity, the Available line shows how much space you have left, and the Used line shows how much space is currently in use for files and folders.

DETERMINING AMOUNT OF RAM

Choose About This Computer from the Apple Menu while you're in the Finder. The Built-In Memory line tells you how much total RAM is installed in your iMac (measured in megabytes).

SHORTCUT

Check the amount of available space on your hard drive in its window on the Desktop, which displays the available space just below the window's title bar.

Reading from a CD-ROM Disc

Now that you know your iMac has a whopping 4- 6-, 10-, or 13-gig hard drive, what can you do with it? My first thought was, "Wow, what can I put on it?" Apple anticipated your question. Your iMac comes with a folder of CD-ROM discs: some contain your Mac OS software, while the others are various programs that come bundled with your iMac. You can read the discs with your iMac's built-in CD-ROM reader. CD-ROM stands for compact disc – read only memory, which means that it stores information that can be read, but it cannot be recorded to.

Mounting a CD-ROM disc is different for newer and older iMacs. With newer iMacs, you simply put the disc into the CD-ROM slot on the front of your iMac (I'll explain how to do that later). Older iMacs have a CD-ROM tray that you need to open—just push the colored, oblong button directly below the word iMac on the front of your computer. The tray pops out for you, but not all the way. Gently pull the tray toward you until it stops.

Now, remove a CD-ROM disc from its protective sleeve or case. Be careful not to touch the underside of the disc; fingerprints and dust can confuse the CD-ROM reader. Instead, hold the disc by the edges with the label up and the shiny side down. On a newer iMac, insert the disc into the slot on the front of your computer and gently push it in. On an older iMac, place the disc in the tray you opened earlier, press the center of the disc down until it snaps onto the spindle, and gently push the tray back into your computer. You will hear a whirring noise as the disc spins up.

If all goes well, the icon for the CD-ROM disc appears on your Desktop. Usually, the icon opens by itself and a window appears on your Desktop. If it doesn't or you can't see the window, just double-click the disc icon (it often resembles a round disc, but not always). Now,

CROSS-REFERENCE

Learn how to install software from a CD-ROM disc in the next task in this chapter.

Playing a Music CD

Your iMac's CD-ROM player can play music CDs, too! Just insert a music disc the same way you do a computer disc. Your iMac recognizes the music data and begins playing the first track. Double-click the audio CD icon that appears on the Desktop to view the tracks. Double-clicking a track icon will open the AppleCD Audio Player and begin playing that track. Use the Audio Player to pause, fast-forward, reverse, and so on. Adjust the volume with the slider on the right, or plug earphones into the jack on the front of your iMac to hear the CD music.

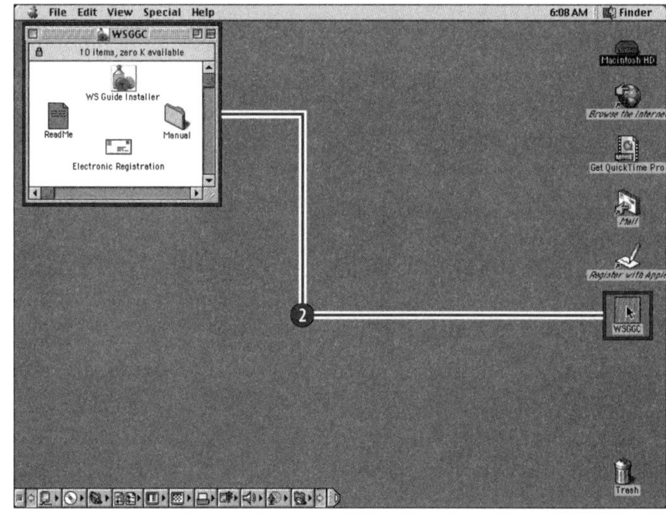

1. *Open your CD tray and place a disc in the tray.*
- *The disc icon appears on your Desktop.*
2. *Double-click the disc icon to open its window if it isn't already open.*

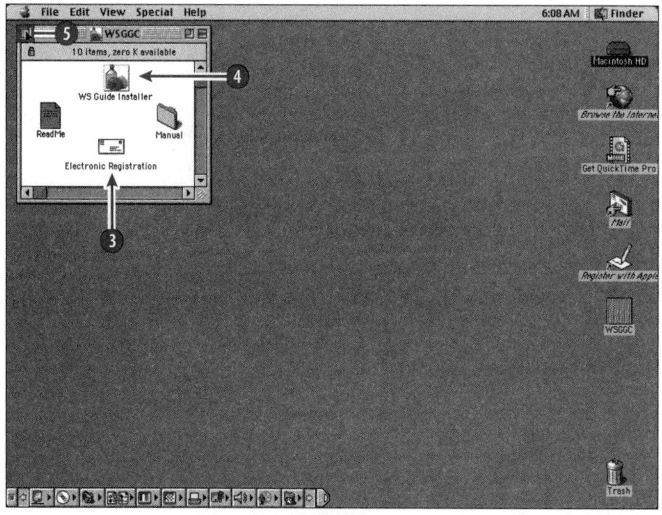

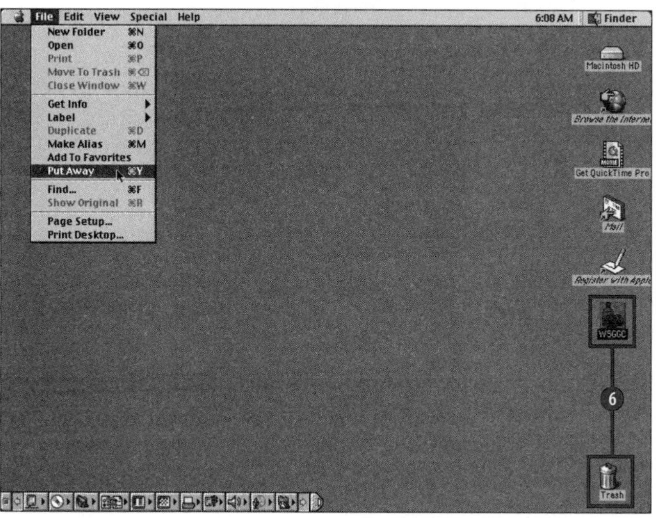

3. *Explore your disc's window(s).*
   - ▶ *The padlock icon indicates that the disc is locked and the disc cannot be written to.*
4. *Read files or run programs, if you wish.*
5. *Close the disc's window and any running programs.*
6. *Press and drag the icon onto the Trash to eject the disc.*
   - ▶ *Alternatively, select the icon and choose Put Away from the File menu.*
   - ▶ *Or choose Eject from the Special menu.*

all the data on the CD-ROM is available to read, run, install, and so on. Just double-click the appropriate item in the disc window as you would any window on the Desktop. Note the small padlock and the crossed-out pencil symbols in the upper-left corner of the disc's window. These symbols indicate that the disc is locked and can only be read from, not written to.

To dismount a CD-ROM disc, first close all open files and programs on it. Now, press and drag the disc icon to the Trash. Don't worry — this won't remove any data from the disc. Remember, you can only read from a CD, not write to it. You also can choose Eject from the Special menu or Put Away from the File menu. On a newer iMac, your CD-ROM disc will pop out of the slot; remove it by placing your fingers along the disc's edges and pulling towards you gently. On an older iMac, your CD tray will pop open again; remove it by placing your fingers along the disc's edges and pull up gently. Put the disc back into its sleeve or case to protect it.

TAKE NOTE

UNSTICKING A STUCK DISC

Occasionally a disc won't eject, no matter how many ways you try. If this happens, restart your iMac and hold down your mouse button. Keep it down until the Desktop appears. If that doesn't eject your disc, you'll have to resort to more forceful measures. Find a paper clip, straighten it out, and insert it into the small pinhole on your CD slot or tray (to the right of the oblong button). The tray's eject mechanism is behind this hole, and when it is pushed firmly, the tray pops out.

SHORTCUT

You can remove a disc from your computer by pressing Command+E or Command+Y.

Installing New Software

So you can mount and read a CD-ROM, but how do you get that nifty software onto your iMac? Begin by installing your new software, not just copying it onto your hard drive. Installing is an automated process that puts all the right files in all the right places for you. Most new software comes with a special installer program, usually labeled Installer. The Installer is usually located in a prominent location on the disc.

To install new software, simply double-click the Installer icon. Follow the directions on the screen — they will differ from program to program — and answer any necessary questions. Installations usually go more smoothly if there are no other programs running while you're installing. If you need to quit any open programs, you'll be given the opportunity to do so before continuing. Once the installation process begins, a progress meter keeps you up-to-date on the installation progress. After installing the software, your iMac may prompt you to restart the computer. This is a good habit to get into, even when it isn't required.

After successfully installing the new software and returning to the Desktop, you should see an open window containing your new software. You can now double-click the main application icon to run your software. Some programs (such as Kai's Photo Soap, which comes with older iMacs) are copied in their entirety to your hard drive; you might never use the CD-ROM disc again unless a problem occurs and you have to reinstall the program. Other programs (such as the Williams-Sonoma Guide, which also comes with older iMacs) only copy a few files to your hard drive; you will need to insert the disc each time you run the program. Still other programs like Quicken Deluxe have extra goodies on the CD-ROM disc which are not copied to your hard drive, but they are not crucial to running the program.

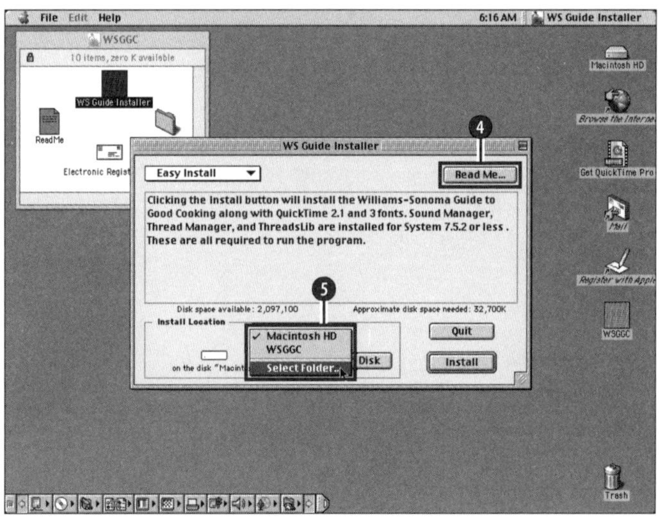

1. Insert the Williams-Sonoma Guide to Good Cooking disc.
2. Double-click the WS Guide Installer icon.
3. Click the various Continue buttons on the resulting windows.
4. Click the Read Me button to learn about this installation.

▶ Note the space available and space needed.

5. Choose Select Folder from the Macintosh HD drop-down menu.

CROSS-REFERENCE

Learn more about using your new software in Chapter 8,"Running Applications."

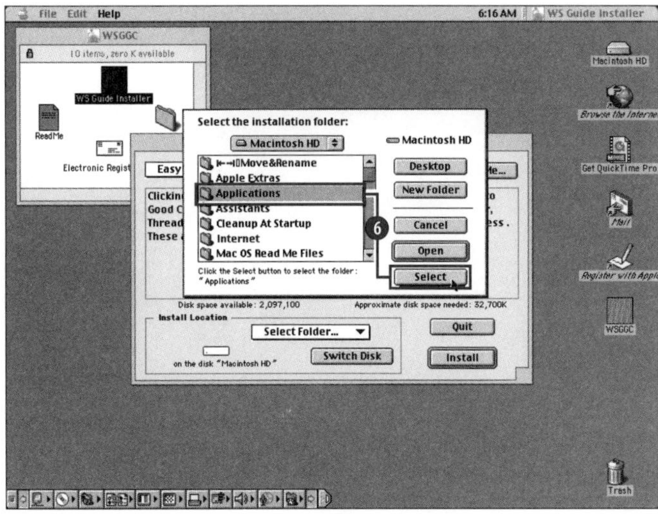

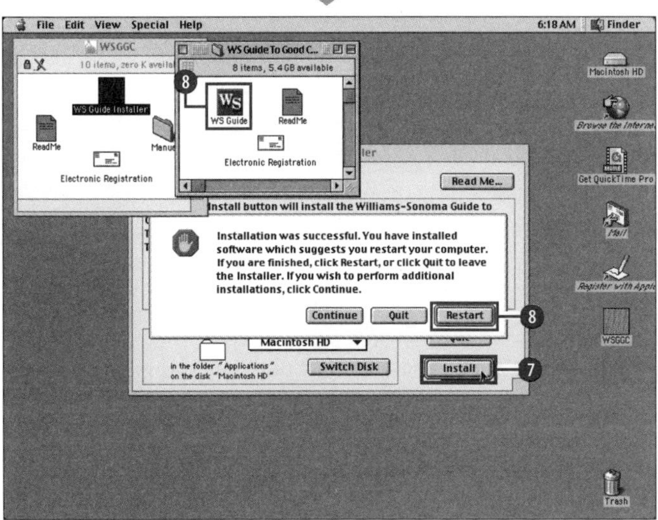

❻ *Select the Applications folder and click Select (or press the Return key).*

▶ *Alternatively, click New Folder to create a different folder.*

❼ *Click the Install button (or press the Return key) to begin the installation.*

❽ *When the installation is finished, restart your computer, and double-click the WS Guide program icon in the new window.*

TAKE NOTE

CHOOSING AN INSTALLATION LOCATION

The main Installer window (where you actually click the Install button) allows you to pick a location for your new software to be installed. Use either the hard drive drop-down menu or the Switch Disk button. To choose a specific folder on the hard drive (strongly recommended), choose Select Folder from the drop-down menu, select a folder in the dialog box, and then click Select. The Applications folder is a good bet for new software, though you can create a new folder using the New Folder button, too.

REMOVING SOFTWARE

From time to time, you will want to remove software you installed on your iMac. Resist the temptation to drag the program file and its folder to the Trash. Most programs install files in other areas on your hard drive and you may not be able to find them all. Instead, run the installer again, but this time, look for a remove or uninstall feature.

RESOLVING A PROBLEM

If you encounter a problem installing new software (as I did when I installed the Williams-Sonoma application), flip ahead to Chapter 17 for help.

SHORTCUT

Pressing the Return key in a dialog box activates the button with the double border around it.

Using Other Removable Media

You may have noticed something missing from your iMac. A floppy disk drive! Indeed, a standard iMac comes without a floppy drive. Frankly, you probably won't ever need one. I use my G3 Mac (a predecessor to my iMac) all day every day and I used a floppy disk only a few times in the last year. Even then, it was only because I needed a file on a floppy. Virtually all software comes on CD-ROM discs or off the Internet these days, and the Internet works better for exchanging files with friends and coworkers, too.

Even so, for a few people, floppy disks do have their purpose. SuperDisks, Zip disks, and Jaz disks are other forms of removable media. These are even more popular because they hold a reasonable amount of data (from 100MB to 2GB). I use a Jaz drive myself, both as an extra hard disk and for backups. You can purchase an external floppy, SuperDisk, Zip, or Jaz drive for your iMac. Just be sure you get the USB-compatible version.

If you do break down and buy a removable media drive, you'll need to know how to use it. First, like CD-ROM discs, you need to keep your disks safe. Store the media in the case or sleeve they came with and keep them away from magnets. Unlike CD-ROM discs, however, you don't need to be as careful about how you hold the disk; the outer plastic shells protect the disc or platter inside.

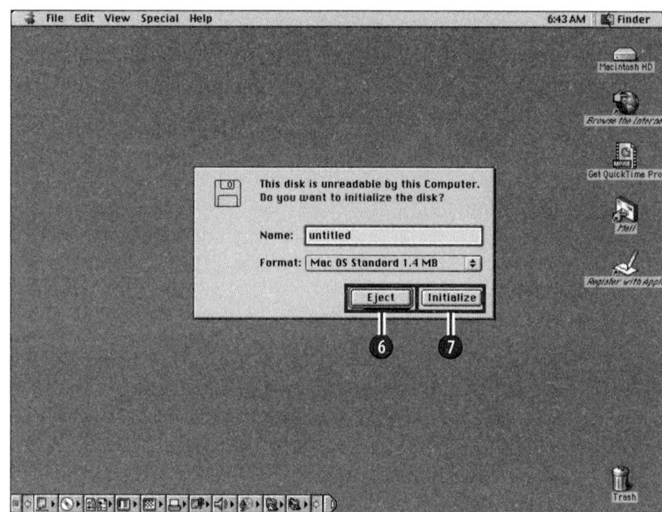

1. *Purchase a removable media drive and read the installation instructions.*
2. *Plug the drive's cable into the second USB port.*
3. *Plug the drive's power cord into a surge suppressor or a wall outlet.*
4. *Power it on following the directions.*
5. *Insert a disk into the drive slot.*

▶ *If the disk is new, you are asked to Initialize it.*

6. *Type a name and press Initialize if your disk is new.*
7. *Alternatively, click Eject if your disk is not new.*

CROSS-REFERENCE

Learn more about backing up your files onto removable media in "Backing Up Your Data" in Chapter 13.

Using Discs and Drives

CHAPTER 3

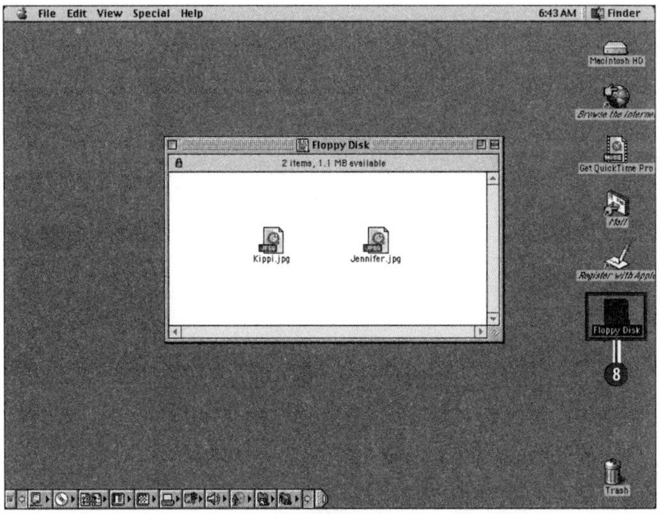

- ▶ *The disk's icon appears on your Desktop.*
- ❽ *Double-click the disk's icon.*
- ▶ *The window displays the disk's available space and files (if any).*
- ▶ *If you see the padlock icon, your disk is locked.*
- ❾ *Quit any programs you may have running from the disk.*
- ❿ *Press and drag the disk's icon to the Trash.*
- ▶ *Alternatively, select the icon and press Command+Y.*
- ▶ *Or select the icon and press Command+E.*

Insert a removable media disk into its drive slot, metal side first and label side up. Push the disk in until it clicks or becomes flush with the slot. If your disk is formatted (ready to use), its icon appears on your Desktop much like a CD-ROM disc. If the disk is brand new, you'll be asked if you want to initialize it. Go ahead and click the Initialize button if the disk really is brand new. Otherwise, eject it and take it back to the source (such as the person or company you received it from) because there might be a problem with the disk.

You can use the data on your disks just like the data on your hard drive, though you may notice that it is much slower. You may want to copy data onto your hard drive to speed things up. Unlike CD-ROM discs, you can write to removable media provided the disk is not locked.

TAKE NOTE

EJECTING MEDIA

You can eject most removable media in the same way you eject CD-ROM discs: drag the icon to the Trash, use the Put Away command from the File menu, or use the Eject command from the Special menu. The disk automatically pops out of the drive. Gently remove it and place it back in its case or sleeve for protection. Some disks prefer to be stored one way or another, so be sure to read any documentation that accompanies your disk drive.

FIND IT ONLINE

Visit **http://www.superdisk.com** for more information on SuperDisk drives, and **http://www.iomega.com** for more information on Zip and Jaz drives.

Personal Workbook

Q&A

1. What is the difference between a hard drive and RAM?

2. How many bytes is a kilobyte? A megabyte? A gigabyte?

3. How do you determine the size of a file or folder?

4. How do you mount a CD-ROM disc? How do you dismount it?

5. How do you play a music CD on your iMac?

6. How do you tell your iMac where you want it to install a new piece of software?

7. What is the best way to remove installed software from your iMac?

8. What is the difference between a CD-ROM disc and a removable media disks?

ANSWERS: PAGE 315

Using Discs and Drives

CHAPTER 3

EXTRA PRACTICE

1. Select your hard drive icon and choose Get Info. How many items are in it? How much available space does it have? What is its capacity? How much space is used?
2. Mount one of the CD-ROM discs that came with your iMac and run the installer program on the disc. Select the Application folder, and then create a new folder within it to store the software.
3. After installation, eject the CD-ROM disc. Double-click the icon for the installed software. Does it ask for you to insert the CD-ROM disc, or does it run independently?
4. If you have a removable media drive, insert a disk. Initialize it if necessary. How much available space does it have?

REAL-WORLD APPLICATIONS

✔ Your friend admires your iMac and asks how much memory it has. You ask if your friend means hard drive capacity or the amount of RAM. Your friend replies, "Both." You reply proudly, "My iMac has 6 gigs of hard drive space and 32 megs of RAM."

✔ You purchase a new game on a CD-ROM disc from the computer superstore. You mount the disc, install the software successfully, eject the disc, and restart your iMac. When you try to play the game, you discover that it requires the disc during play. You remount the disc and play the game.

✔ You later discover that your new game is too addictive. You mounti the disc again and remove the game software using the software's Installer program.

Visual Quiz

What does this dialog box mean and why would you see it?

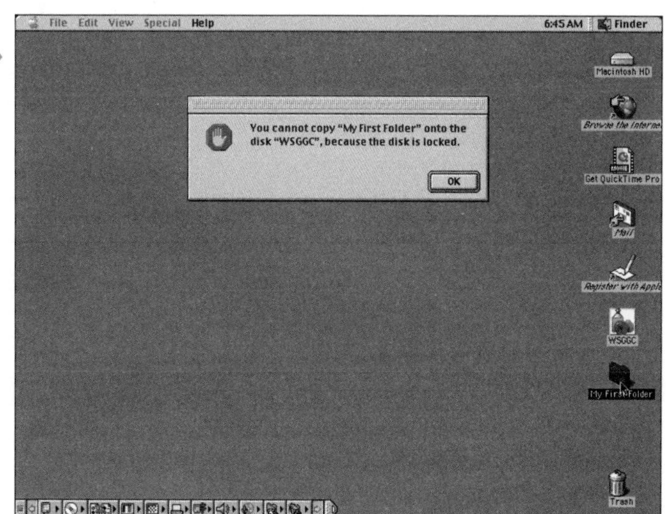

PART II

Applying Your iMac

You've got a mighty handsome-looking iMac sitting over there on your desk. If you're like one family I know, you may have even repainted your family room to match your computer! But after all, you did buy your iMac so you could *do* something with it, right? What say we start to put it to work?

Even though, way down deep in its guts, a computer relates to everything as numbers, we're going to start with writin' rather than 'rithmetic. Writing is fundamental, and most of us (especially authors like me) will be writing with our iMacs far more than we'll be figurin'. In no time at all, you'll be able to create and print great-looking documents!

Since any work you do with a computer requires application programs, you'll learn how to use some of the other applications that came installed on your iMac, too. Before this section is done, you *will* also know how to do that 'rithmetic with a spreadsheet, organize information into a database, find and use other pre-installed applications, and even have some fun with sound and video!

So, roll up your sleeves. We've got some words to process!

File Edit View Special Help

CHAPTER 4

MASTER THESE SKILLS

- Opening Applications
- Typing with Your Keyboard
- Selecting Text
- Moving Text
- Copying Text
- Pasting Text
- Deleting Text
- Backing Up a Step
- Saving Your Work

Working with Text

As the author, there's one thing I can tell you with absolute certainty. Despite the stereotypes, I am not sitting at an old-fashioned portable or manual typewriter, pounding the keyboard with two fingers to make the letters fly up, and strike a carbon ribbon, making a mark upon a sheet of paper. The noisy clacking and thumping — and the frustration of retyping an entire page from scratch — has never been a part of my life, and I owe it all to my Mac!

Who better to teach you how to use your iMac to work with text than a computer book author? It's what we do, all day and all night (especially when we're pushing a deadline!) Oh, the things I can teach you! Come on over here and sit beside me.

Of course, before you can start writing and editing the Great American Novel (or a shopping list), you'll have to know how to open a word processing program (application). It's a good lesson, since all iMac applications are opened in the same manner. From there, we'll take a look at the keyboard. You can't learn to edit text until you have a bit of text to edit.

Computers — even your wonderful iMac — are pretty dumb. You have to tell them exactly what text you want to edit before you can do a thing to it. Selecting text is what it's called, and I'll tell you exactly how to do it. From there, we'll cover all the fundamentals that go into moving, copying, pasting, and deleting entire words, sentences, paragraphs, and even chapters. Oops! Did you make a mistake? You'll learn how to undo the changes you made, too.

Finally — and in some ways, most importantly — you'll learn how to save your hard work. Like opening an application and working with text, this is one of those bottom-line computing skills that apply to nearly everything you'll do with your iMac.

Before we start, let me take a second to encourage you to learn how to touch-type. As those who touch-type already know, it's hard to speak through your keyboard when you're staring down at the keyboard searching for the next character to type. With all the applications out there that can teach you how to type by touch, in the comfort of your own iMac, I hope you give this some serious thought.

Now, let's type!

Opening Applications

If you've been following along in the book up to this point, I have some good news for you. You've already opened an application — several, in fact. An application is just a program, small or large, that lets you accomplish something. You can do something simple like listen to a CD, or something complicated like write the Great American Novel.

You may not be aware that you have opened applications before, so let me tell you how it works. First, double-clicking virtually any icon opens an application, even if the icon represents a document or an alias. Of course, you can double-click an application's icon to open the application directly, as well. Application icons usually bear the name of the application itself and have fancy logos to represent what the application is. The Williams-Sonoma Guide to Good Cooking application is a good example.

As I mentioned, you can double-click an icon to open it *and* the application that created it (or an application that is able to read it). Document icons often look like pieces of paper or newspapers, sometimes with a turned down corner. The iMac Read Me file is an example of a document.

You also can double-click an alias to open the original application or file. Remember, aliases are shortcuts to other files or programs, so unless the alias goes to a folder, you're probably opening an application. The Browse the Internet alias on your Desktop is a good example.

An alternative to double-clicking any icon is to select it (highlight it) and choose Open from the File menu. You could even get fancy and click and drag a document icon on top of the application icon that created it, but in most cases that's just a lot of extra work, since a simple double-click does the same thing.

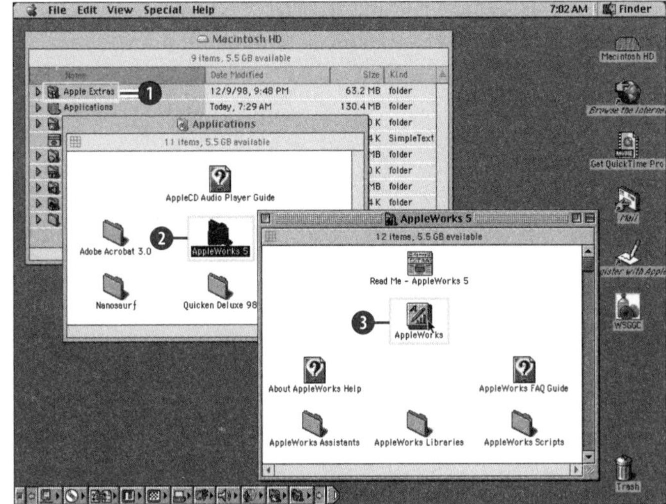

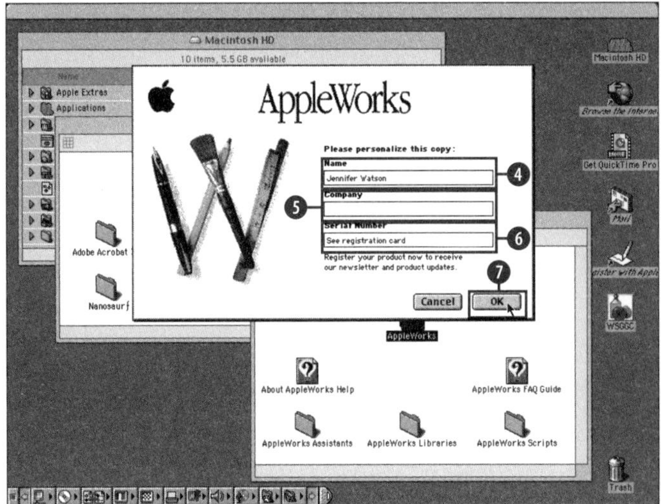

1. *Open the Applications folder in your Macintosh HD window.*
2. *Open the AppleWorks5 folder.*
- ▶ *Note the various document icons.*
3. *Double-click the AppleWorks icon.*
4. *Type your first and last name.*
5. *Type your company name (or your school or organization name).*
6. *Write down your serial number (located on the back of your iMac).*
7. *Type your serial number and click OK.*

CROSS-REFERENCE

Learn how to add Apple Menu shortcuts to applications in "Making the Most of Your Apple Menu" in Chapter 5.

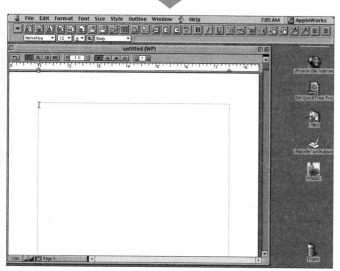

8 *Select Word Processing from the list on the left if it is not already selected.*

9 *Click the Create New Document radio button (if it is not already selected).*

10 *Click OK.*

- *AppleWorks displays its own set of menus, though the familiar Apple, File, Edit, Help, and Application menus are also here.*
- *An untitled window is open and ready for input. Note the familiar Close box, Zoom box, Minimize box, and scroll bars.*

Another way to open an application is through the Apple menu. Many applications have shortcuts listed in the Apple menu, such as the Apple System Profiler. The Recent Applications submenu lists all the recent applications you've visited, too. You may be surprised to see how many places you've gone. To return to any one of them, simply choose it from the submenu.

TAKE NOTE

OPENING AN APPLICATION FOR THE FIRST TIME

Some applications ask you for information the first time you open them, such as AppleWorks. They will want to know your name, your company's name, and your serial number or registration code. These numbers and codes are unique and are generally used to provide support and updates after registration. You usually can find the serial numbers and registration codes accompanying your software's documentation (if you purchased it separately) or with the papers that came with your iMac (for example, the World Book Macintosh Edition). AppleWorks is an exception to this rule: when it asks for the serial number, it really means the computer's serial number. You can find your iMac's serial number on your computer. Look inside the panel on the side of your iMac for a label containing the number.

SHORTCUT

Press Command+O to open any selected (highlighted) icon on your Desktop.

Typing with Your Keyboard

AppleWorks is a *word processing* program, among other things. Word processors are great for typing letters, reports, and even entire books. It doesn't type for you, however. That's your job. If you're not an accomplished typist, don't worry. Your iMac keyboard is as friendly as they come. Even if you are a touch typist, read this section anyway. It explains how things work on the iMac's keyboard, and it lays the groundwork for the rest of the chapter.

Take a good look at your keyboard now. The largest group of keys is where you'll do almost all your typing, especially in a word processor. The letter and number keys are in the center, with special function keys like Command, Shift, and so on arranged around the outside. The smaller group of keys on the right is the *numeric keypad*, and you use it much like a calculator.

When it comes to word processing, several keys are particularly useful. Starting in the upper-left corner of the keyboard, the Tab key works much like a typewriter's tab key, shifting the insertion point across the page in preset increments — usually one-half inch. The Caps Lock key turns all letters you type into capital letters, but it does not affect the numbers and punctuation marks; it simply lights up when it is enabled. The Shift key also makes capital letters and selects the secondary (upper) characters on the number and punctuation keys: hold it down and then press a letter, number, or punctuation key at the same time. The Control, Option, and Command keys perform special operations and keyboard shortcuts. The spacebar (the long bar without a name on it) inserts a blank space. The arrow keys in the

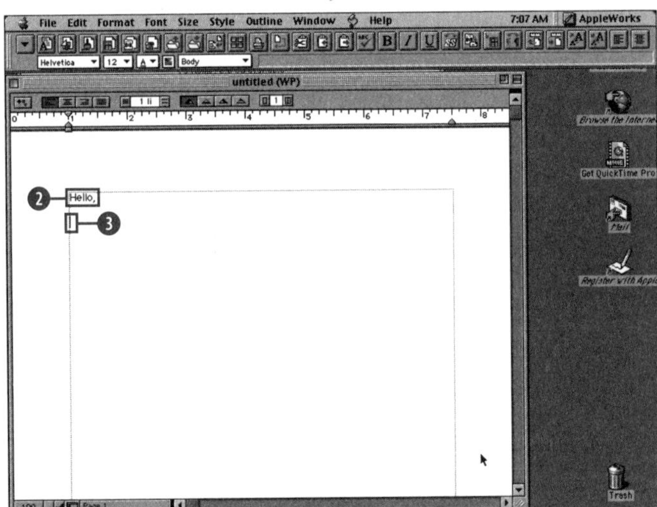

❶ *Open a new word processing document in AppleWorks (if one isn't open already) using New under the File menu.*

▶ *Alternatively, click the button with the letter A and a document icon.*

▶ *Note the location of your blinking text insertion point.*

❷ *Type "Hello," (without the quotation marks). Hold down the Shift key and press H to produce a capital H.*

▶ *Observe that the letters appear in the document as you type them.*

❸ *Press Return twice to move down two lines.*

CROSS-REFERENCE

Learn how to set your keyboard preferences in "Customizing your Keyboard and Monitor" in Chapter 14.

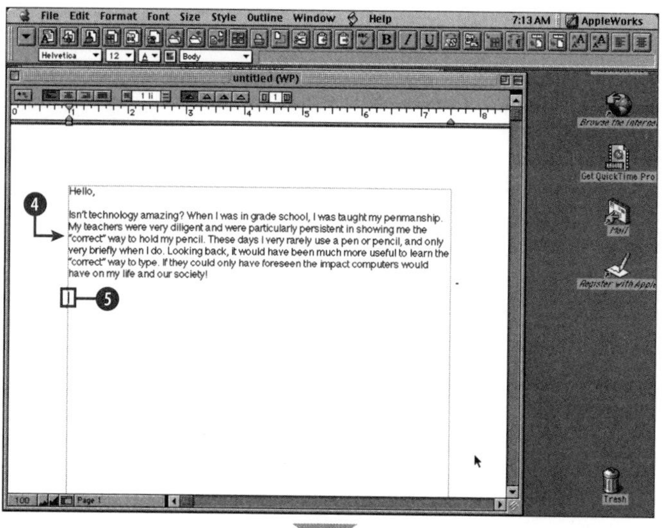

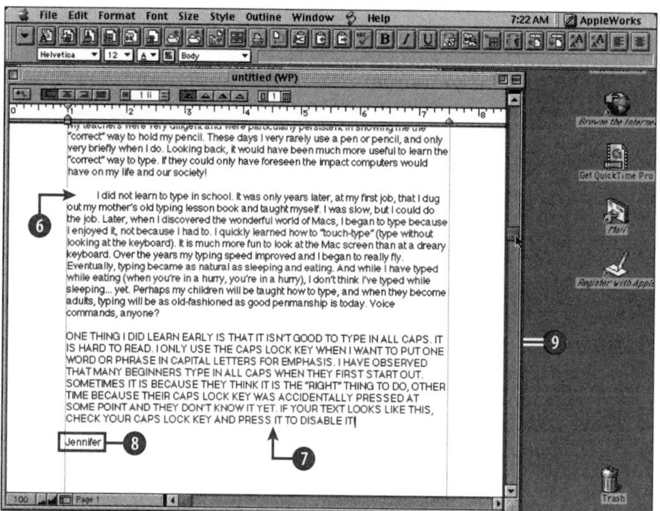

4 *Type several sentences, pressing the spacebar once after each word and period.*

▶ *Notice that your text wraps to the next line automatically as you type.*

5 *Press Return twice to start a new paragraph.*

6 *Press the Tab key and type another paragraph.*

7 *Press the Caps Lock key and type another paragraph.*

8 *Press the Caps Lock key again and type your name.*

9 *Use the scroll bar to move back to the top.*

lower-right corner move the insertion point up, down, left, and right. The Return key inserts a hard return when you want it, like at the end of a paragraph. The Delete key backspaces over your text and erases it at the same time. You'll get a chance to practice using each of these keys later in this chapter.

To begin typing, start by opening an application. Many applications begin with a new, blank document for you. If this doesn't happen, you can choose New from the File menu in most applications. Your text insertion point — the blinking vertical line — appears in the upper-left corner of a new document. This is where your text displays as you type. You can begin typing as soon as this insertion point appears. Just place your hands on the keyboard in a natural position. If you have to look at the keyboard as you type, don't worry — no one is looking!

TAKE NOTE

UNDERSTANDING WORD WRAP

If you're used to a typewriter, it may seem logical to hit the Return key when you reach the right edge of your document. Don't do this on your iMac. Instead, just keep typing — your text will automatically wrap down to the next line. This is called *word wrap*, and you'll find it almost everywhere on your iMac. You can (and should) use the Return key when you reach the end of a paragraph. You also can press the Return key when you want to force text down to the next line.

SHORTCUT

To type an entire word in capital letters, press the Caps Lock key rather than hold down the Shift key.

Selecting Text

If you were starting to think your iMac was just a glorified typewriter, think again. Typewriters proceed in a linear fashion. You type and the words appear, one after the other. That's about the extent of it. If you want to make significant changes, you have to retype the page on a typewriter. On the iMac, you could type this way if you wanted, but it isn't required. You can type a paragraph, go back and change a word in the first sentence, remove a word in the second, and even clear an entire line of text if you wish. You can do a lot more than this, too, and I'll show you how later in the chapter.

The first step in each of these tricks is to position the mouse pointer and select text. First, move the mouse pointer over your text (don't press the mouse button yet, though). Did you notice that it changed? It is now a funky-looking I, called an *I-beam*. If you were to move the mouse pointer out of the text area, it would change back to an arrow. For now, move the I-beam pointer back over your text and position it in a specific point in your text. Press the mouse button and the insertion point moves to wherever you just clicked. Now if you begin typing, your text appears exactly where you clicked. This is how you can go back and add a letter or a word to the text you already typed.

To select text, just position the I-beam over a point in your text and press and drag the mouse to a new point in the text. You can select a letter, a set of letters, or a word, phrase, or paragraph — as much or as little text as you like. As you select text, it highlights it (the screen

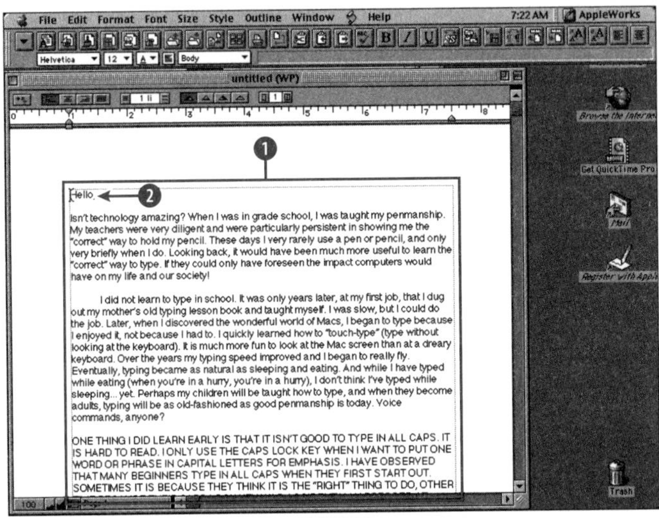

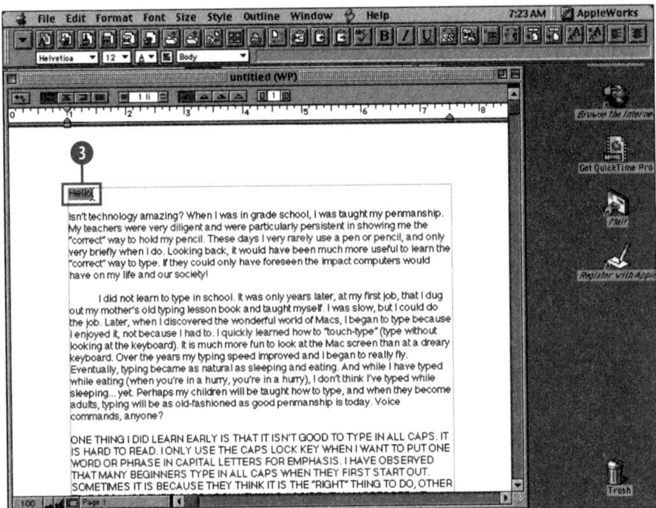

1. *Move the mouse pointer over your text and watch it change to an I-beam.*
2. *Position the I-beam to the left of the word Hello.*
3. *Click and drag the I-beam right across the word "Hello," releasing the mouse before you reach the comma.*

▶ *Observe how the word "Hello" is now highlighted.*

CROSS-REFERENCE

Learn how to change the highlight color in "Changing Your iMac's Appearance" in Chapter 14.

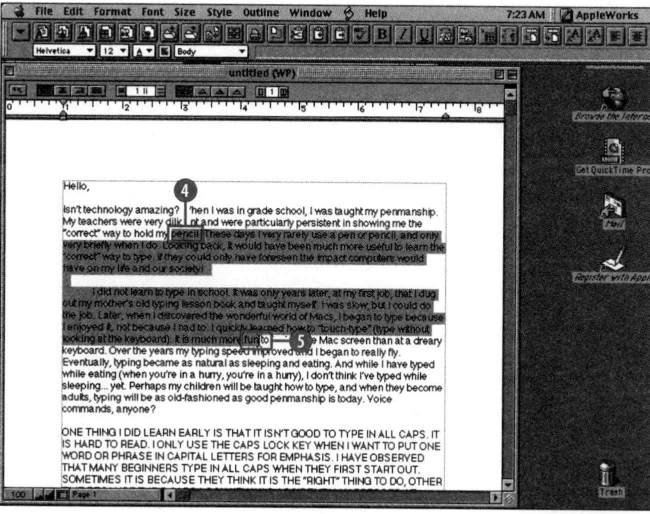

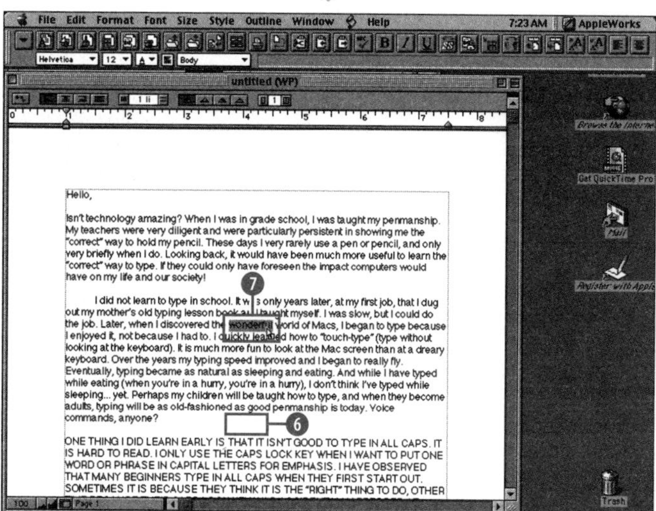

4 *Position the I-beam over a word in the first paragraph.*

5 *Click and drag the word to another point in the second paragraph and release.*

▶ *Note the selected text in the two paragraphs.*

6 *Position the I-beam between two paragraphs and click to deselect the text.*

7 *Position the I-beam over a word and double-click.*

▶ *Your cursor changes to an arrow and a small box.*

behind the text it changes color). The trick is to position the I-beam at one end of the text you want to select and then click and drag to the other end.

To select an entire word, position the I-beam directly over it and double-click. To select an entire line, position the I-beam over it and triple-click. (In AppleWorks, this triple-click action selects the line as it appears on the screen, not necessarily a full sentence.) To select an entire paragraph, position the I-beam over the paragraph and quadruple-click. When you move the mouse pointer over a text selection, it changes to an arrow and a small box, indicating that you can move the selection somewhere else (which I discuss in the next task).

TAKE NOTE

USING THE SHIFT KEY TO SELECT

When you want to select a bunch of text that isn't a contiguous single line or paragraph, the Shift key can help. Position the I-beam at one end of the text you want to select, click your mouse button once, hold down the Shift key, position the I-beam at the other end, click again, and then release the Shift key. You also can use this method to add text to a selection — just hold down the Shift key before you click and everything between the selected text and the I-beam is added to the selection. This also works in reverse if you accidentally select more text than you wanted to select.

SHORTCUT

To select all text in a document, use the keyboard shortcut Command+A.

Moving Text

For those used to typewriters, moving text usually meant two things: scissors and tape. While you can cut (like scissors) and paste (like tape) on the iMac, you don't need to resort to that. You can move entire blocks of text in a word processing document without any cutting and pasting — real or electronic.

First, begin by selecting the text you want to move. Once the text is highlighted, move the mouse pointer over the highlighted text — the mouse pointer changes to an empty arrow with a small box beneath it. Once you see this pointer, click and drag to another location in the text. As you drag, an outline of the selection follows you as the text insertion point moves to the next available position. When the text insertion point is at the position you want the text to move to, let go of the mouse button. The text disappears from its previous location and reappears in the new location.

When you move a character or a portion of a word or words, the spaces go along for the ride. If you move an entire word or sentence, the word processor is smart enough to handle the spaces that appear before and after it for you. Just double-click to select a word (and no spaces) and then click and drag the word to a new location. The word reappears in the sentence with a space before and after it. This technique, called smart cut and paste, works with multiple words and sentences, too.

Moving text works best for entire sentences and paragraphs. In fact, as I write this chapter, I've moved several sentences around before I settled on the arrangement that made the most sense.

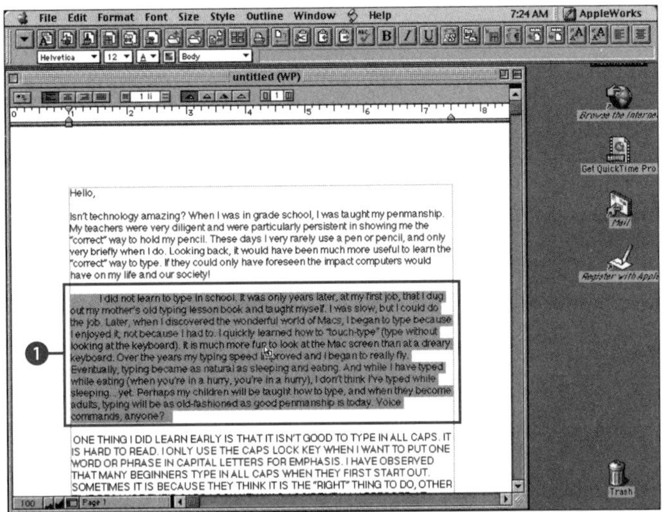

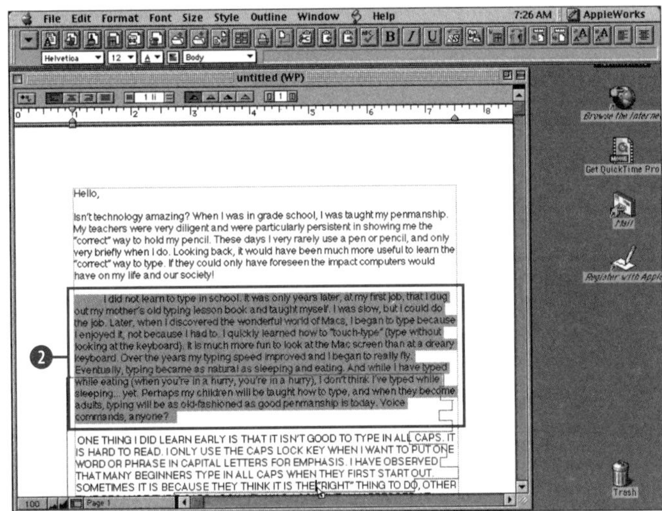

1. *Position the I-beam over a paragraph and quadruple-click.*

- *Your iMac highlights the entire paragraph and the pointer changes.*

2. *Click and drag the selection to the bottom of the window.*

- *An outline follows the mouse, and the insertion point moves down as you go.*
- *If necessary, the page scrolls automatically when the pointer reaches the bottom of the window.*

CROSS-REFERENCE

Slow down or speed up the blinking rate of the insertion point in "Setting Your General Controls" in Chapter 14.

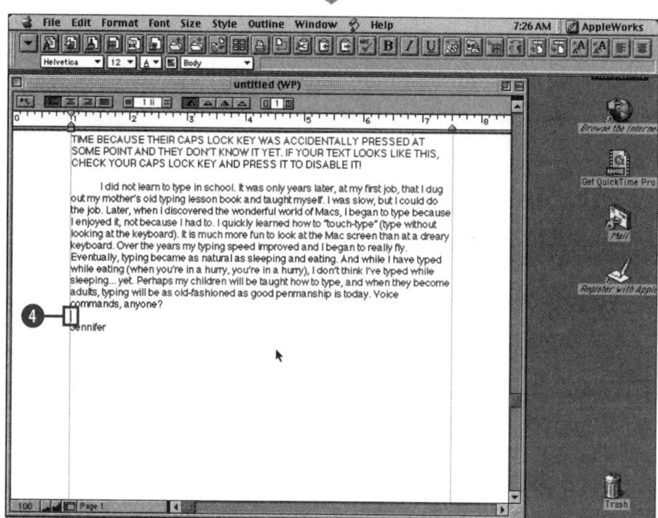

❸ *Release the mouse button when the insertion point is where you want it.*

▶ *The selection reappears in the new location.*

❹ *Press the right-arrow key until the insertion point is where you want it.*

❺ *Resume typing.*

TAKE NOTE

GETTING BACK TO TYPING

To continue typing after selecting and moving text, position the I-beam at the end of the document (you may need to use the scroll bar) and click once. Your text insertion point moves to the location you clicked. Move the I-beam out of the way and begin typing. Remember, your text appears at the insertion point, not at the position of the I-beam.

MOVING THROUGH YOUR DOCUMENT

While the trusty scroll bars work great for navigating through your document, you do have alternatives. The arrow keys can move you through your document character by character, line by line. You can even use these keys to select text — just hold down the Shift key and press the arrow keys until you've selected the text. Another way to move through a document is with the Page Up (labeled pg up) and Page Down (labeled pg dn) keys above the numeric keypad. A page, in this case, is the equivalent of how much you can see at one time in the window. You also can click the Page button at the bottom of the document window to choose another page. In this case, a page is what you would see on one sheet of paper if you printed the document.

SHORTCUT

To copy a text selection, hold down the Option key as you click and drag it to a new location.

Copying Text

Do you remember how we discussed copying files on the Desktop in Chapter 2? You can copy text on your iMac, too. It works a little differently than copying files, but it is also easier and more versatile.

To copy text, first select it. Now choose Copy from the Edit menu. That's it! You've copied the text. If you're wondering where it went, it is stored in a *buffer*— an invisible holding area for text, pictures, and so on (the buffer is also called the Clipboard). Unlike the Duplicate command for files on the Desktop, the Copy command only records the selected information— it doesn't actually make a copy of it yet. That comes later (in our next task).

If you want to remove something but keep a copy of it to place somewhere else later, you can use the Cut command (also on the Edit menu). Cut removes the selected text, and it also stores a copy for you in the buffer. Cut works best when you want to do some more typing before you place the copy somewhere else. Otherwise, it's just easier to move it.

You need to know that the buffer holds only one item at a time. If you copy something, and you then copy something else, the first thing you copied disappears from the buffer, so that only the last item you copied is then in the buffer. Some applications do allow for multiple copies to be stored, but it isn't standard and you won't find it in AppleWorks. Also, if you restart your computer, the buffer is cleared. Thus, it is a good idea to do something with your copy before anything happens to it. The next task shows you how to paste that information into your document.

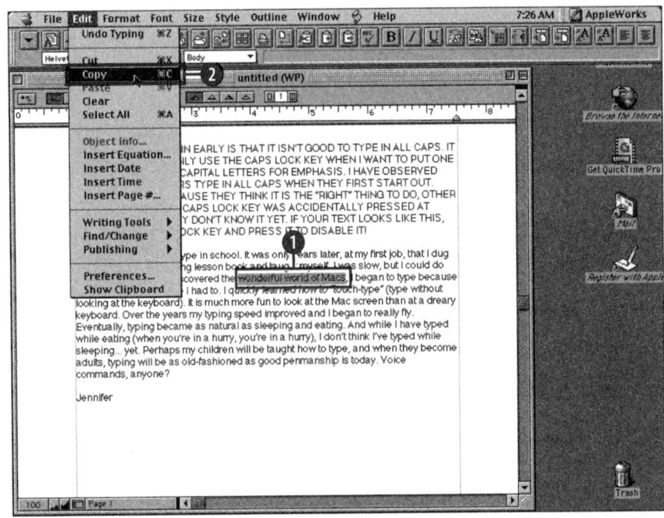

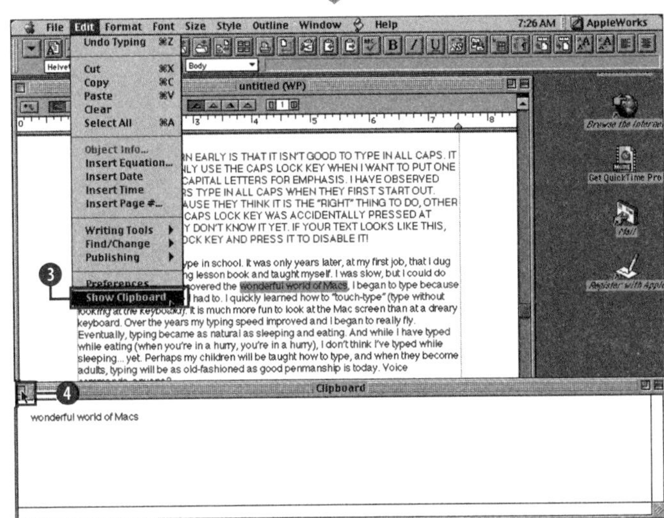

❶ *Select some text in your document.*

❷ *Choose Copy from the Edit menu.*

▶ *Alternatively, press Command+C or click the Copy button.*

▶ *Note the Paste command is not available yet.*

❸ *Select Show Clipboard from the Edit menu.*

▶ *Note that the Paste command is now available.*

▶ *Your text appears in the Clipboard window.*

❹ *Close the Clipboard.*

CROSS-REFERENCE

Learn about copying information in databases and spreadsheets in Chapter 7.

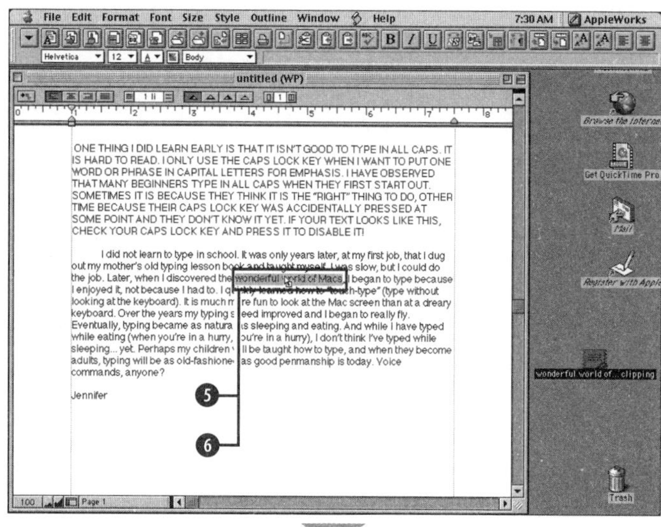

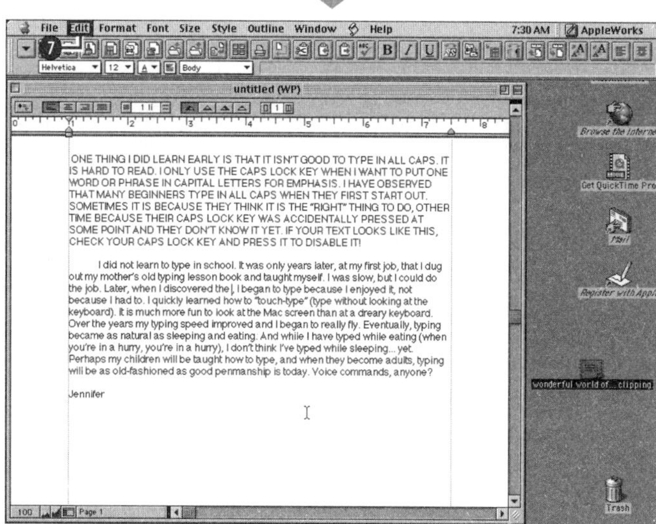

❺ *Position the pointer over the selected text.*

❻ *Click and drag the text to the Desktop, which is visible in the background.*

▶ *A clipping of your text appears on the Desktop.*

❼ *Choose Cut from the Edit menu.*

▶ *Alternatively, press Command+X or click the Cut button.*

▶ *Your selection disappears, but it is now stored in the Clipboard.*

TAKE NOTE

CHECKING THE CLIPBOARD

If you're ever unsure that you actually copied something, there are two ways to tell. Check to see if the Paste command is now available under the File menu (this only works if you didn't copy anything in the previous session). You also can check the Clipboard. Just choose Show Clipboard from the Edit menu. If the resulting window is empty or contains something other than what you just tried to copy, your copy was unsuccessful. Otherwise, you should see whatever is in the buffer (such as text or a picture) in the Clipboard window. Keep in mind that you can't edit the information in the Clipboard. Also, not all applications have a Show Clipboard command, but you can always use the one under the Edit menu in Finder.

CLIPPING TEXT

If you want to permanently copy and store text, select the text and then click and drag it to your Desktop (you'll need to be able to see the Desktop in the background). This creates a *clipping file* on your Desktop, which you can later open and use in any way you like.

SHORTCUT

Use the keyboard shortcuts Command+C to copy and Command+X to cut.

Pasting Text

What do you do with the text you copied or cut from your document? Paste it somewhere else!

To paste something you've copied, begin by moving the insertion point to the place you'd like it to appear. Just move the mouse pointer until the I-beam is in the right spot and then click. Now, select Paste from the Edit menu. Whatever you copied previously to the Clipboard appears at the insertion point.

You can use the paste feature to replace text in a document with the text on the Clipboard, too. Just select the text to replace and, while that text is still highlighted, paste it into your next text.

Pasting something does not remove it from the Clipboard. You can paste it over and over again to your heart's content, until you either copy something new (thereby overwriting whatever was in the Clipboard) or you restart your computer.

If you want to copy something else and also store whatever is in the Clipboard for later use, you can. Choose Scrapbook from the Apple menu and paste it in. You can close the Scrapbook — you can even restart your iMac — and your item stays in there. To retrieve it, just open the Scrapbook again, copy it (or use the scrollbar along the bottom to find it and then copy it), and then return to your document and paste it. Clippings you may have saved to your Desktop work much the same way — double-click to open them, copy the information, return to your application, and then paste it.

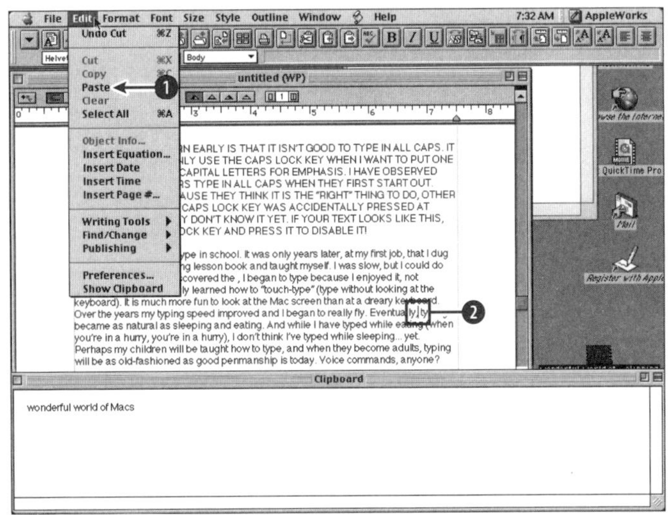

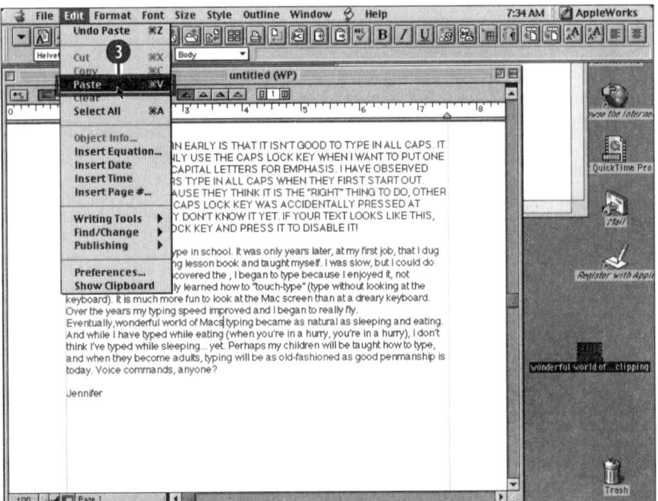

1. *Verify you have something to paste by checking that the Paste command in the Edit menu is available.*
   - *Alternatively, you can choose Show Clipboard from the Edit menu.*
2. *Position the insertion point in the spot where you want to paste your text.*
3. *Choose Paste from the Edit menu.*
   - *Alternatively, press Command+V or press the Paste button on the toolbar.*
   - *The text appears at the insertion point.*

CROSS-REFERENCE

Learn how to find and replace (paste) text automatically in "Finding and Replacing Text" in Chapter 5.

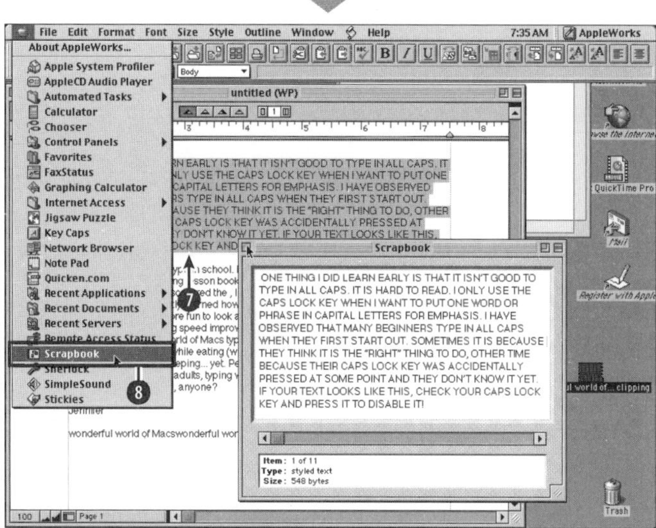

❹ *Position the insertion point at the bottom of the page.*

❺ *Paste the text.*

❻ *Paste the text again.*

❼ *Select new text and copy it.*

❽ *Select Scrapbook from the Apple menu.*

❾ *Press Command+V.*

▶ *The Scrapbook records your text for you to retrieve later.*

Pasting something you copied from one application into another can be tricky. Copying and pasting text is simple and works in virtually all applications. You will encounter problems, however, when you try to paste a spreadsheet, a picture, or another complicated item into an application other than the application it was created in. Sometimes it works, but more often, it won't. Feel free to try, however. If it isn't possible, your iMac either tells you so or nothing at all happens.

TAKE NOTE

▶ USE KEYBOARD SHORTCUTS

Copying and pasting is much quicker once you master your keyboard shortcuts. Of course, remembering what they are when you need them (without having to stop and look them up) is the real trick. The keyboard shortcut for pasting is Command+V. Try thinking of the V as an arrow pointing to the place you want to insert something. Command+C (for copy) is easy to remember. Command+X is another tricky one; try thinking of the X as a cross (to cross something out). Another way to remember these shortcuts is to look at their placement on the keyboard: X, C, and V are all next to one another on the bottom row. They are also right above the Command key for easy, one-handed operation. If you accidentally press the X key when you meant to press the C key (Cut instead of Copy), just paste it right back in with the V key. I confess that I have to do this all the time.

SHORTCUT

You also can paste using the button in the AppleWorks toolbar (a clipboard with an arrow pointing outward).

Deleting Text

With all this moving, copying, cutting, and pasting you're doing, you may also need to get rid of the extra stuff accumulating in your document. You could select it and cut it out, but that could replace the contents of the Clipboard. Instead, use the special key on your keyboard: the Delete key.

To delete text one character at a time, position the insertion point at the end (to the right) of the text to be deleted and press the Delete key. Each time you press Delete, you backspace over the character preceding the insertion point. You can continue pressing the Delete key until you've deleted all your text. Alternatively, you can hold down the Delete key to put the process into lawnmower mode (it mows down all your letters very quickly). I don't recommend this method if you're deleting an entire sentence or more. Use one of the methods explained later instead.

Another way to delete text is to first select the text you want to delete and then press the Delete key. This is much faster than deleting text character by character. You also could select your text, and then either cut it (remove it), type right over it (replace it), or click and drag it to the Trash (if it is visible in the background). Use the cut method if you think you might want to use the text later in another part of your document. Remember, however, that the cut method will replace anything you may have stored in the Clipboard — use it with care. The Delete and Clear functions do not affect

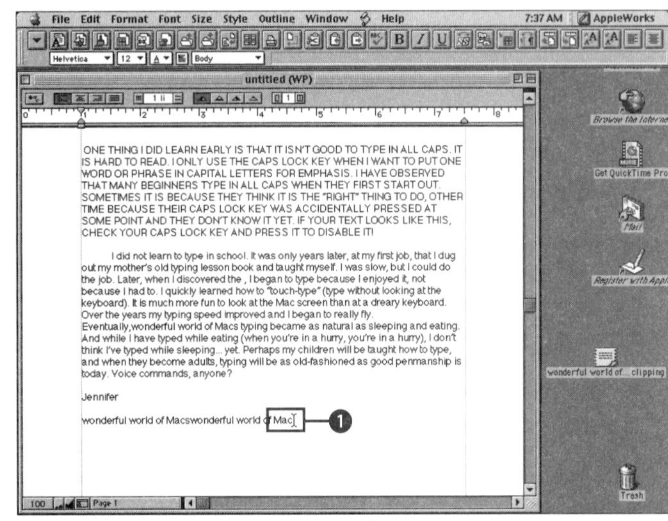

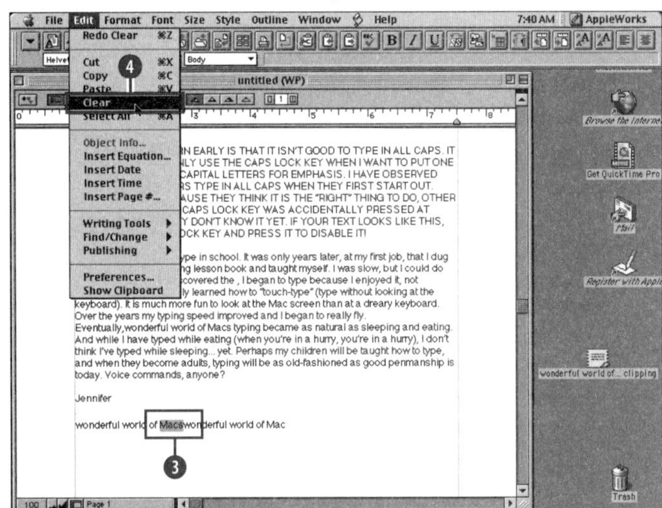

1. *Position the I-beam at the end of your document and click.*
2. *Press the Delete key once.*

▶ *Your iMac removes one character to the left of the insertion point.*

3. *Select an entire word (double-click).*
4. *Choose Clear from the Edit menu.*

▶ *Alternatively, press the Clear key.*

▶ *Your iMac removes the word.*

CROSS-REFERENCE

Learn how to save important documents from a run-in with the Delete key in "Backing Up Your Data" in Chapter 13.

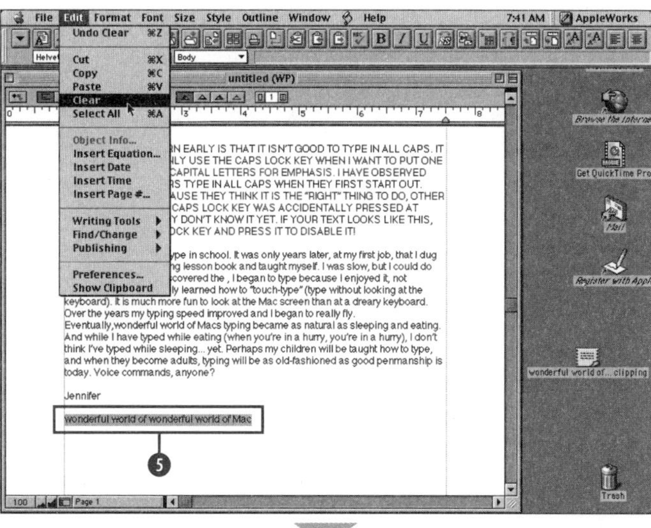

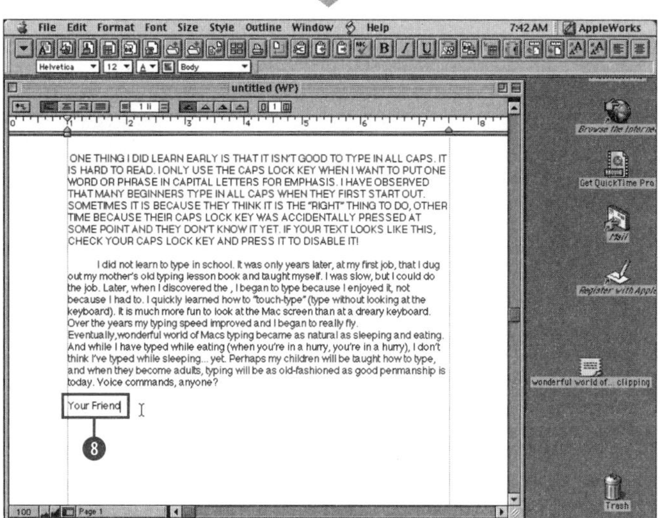

❺ *Select an entire line (triple-click).*

❻ *Press the Delete key once.*

▶ *Alternatively, choose Clear from the Edit menu.*

▶ *Your iMac removes the entire line.*

❼ *Select your name (double-click or triple-click).*

❽ *Type "Your Friend."*

▶ *Your iMac removes the selected text and replaces it with the text you type.*

the Clipboard in any way, so anything you may have stored there is safe while you are deleting or clearing elsewhere.

The Clear command (on the Edit menu) also deletes things. To use it, select the text you want to delete and choose Clear from the Edit menu. You may also have noticed a Clear key above your numeric keypad. It works the same way as the Clear menu command, but it is much faster. Clear — both the menu command and the key — is particularly good for deleting other things such as cells in a spreadsheet.

The Delete and Clear functions are potent. They have the ability to wipe out hours of work in one fell swoop. Use them with caution. If you accidentally delete something you didn't intend to, flip ahead to the next task to learn how to undo it.

TAKE NOTE

FIXING MISTAKES

We all make mistakes. And the Delete key stands ready to erase our goofs and remove our whoops. When you need to fix a typo, for example, just position the I-beam to the right of the offending character, click, press the Delete key once (or as many times as needed), and then retype as necessary. Once you get more adept at working with text, try this: select only the wrong characters and retype them correctly. Any text you type replaces any text you selected — no Delete key needed!

SHORTCUT

To delete all the text in a document, press Command+A and then press the Delete key.

Backing Up a Step

If you flipped to this task because you made a mistake, welcome! If you haven't made a mistake yet, can I have your autograph? Seriously though, you often can recover from a mistake on your iMac. I can't promise that it is always an available option, but more often than not, it is.

If you make a mistake or do something you didn't intend to do, the first thing to do is stop what you're doing. You'll be stuck with your goof if you continue to work. It isn't a matter of time, but of actions. The key here is to back up and *undo* the action you just did, thereby erasing the mistake. To do this, make a beeline for the Edit menu and select Undo at the very top. If the Edit menu reads "Can't Undo," that means you can't undo whatever you just did. But if it is present, you're in luck; everything should reset itself to its previous state.

If you undo something and then decide you really did want to do it, don't worry. Just revisit the Edit menu again before you do anything else and you should see a *Redo* option. Some applications (not AppleWorks) even offer Redo (or Repeat) as a separate option from Undo. The keyboard shortcut for Redo is Command+Y. Multiple Undo's and Redo's are available in some applications, too. This means you could step back through your actions, systematically undoing or redoing them.

What if your application doesn't allow multiple Undo's and you just realized you made a mistake several steps ago? Another option may be available. If you already

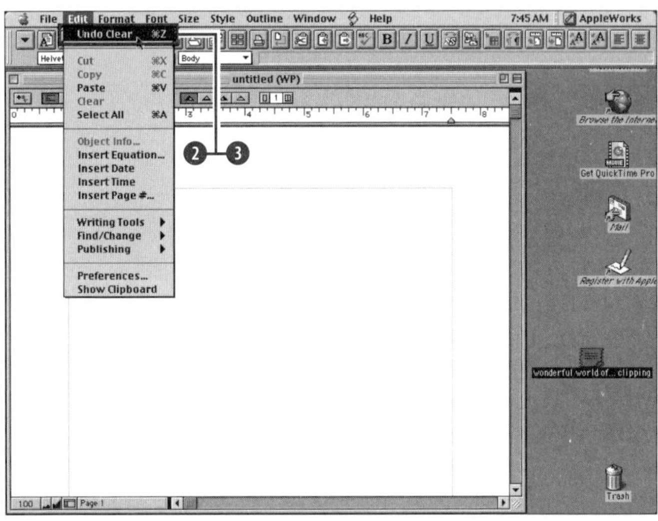

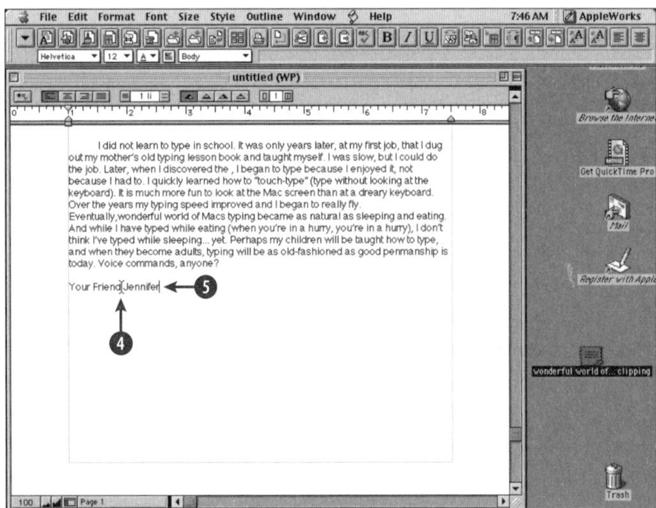

1. *Press Command+A and then press Clear.*
2. *Pull down the Edit menu.*
- ▶ *The Undo Clear command is available.*
3. *Choose Undo Clear.*
- ▶ *The text you just removed returns to the window.*
4. *Position your insertion point at the end of your document and click once.*
5. *Type a word without pressing Delete or repositioning the insertion point.*
6. *Press Command+Z.*

CROSS-REFERENCE

Learn how to lock down a file to prevent any changes in "Locking Your Files and Folders" in Chapter 13.

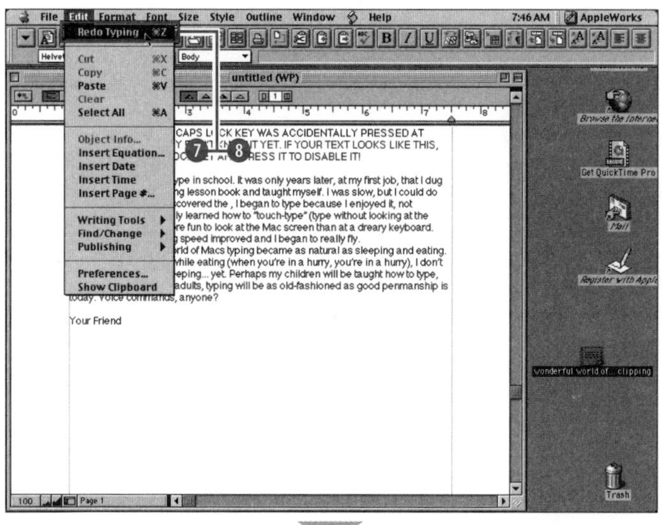

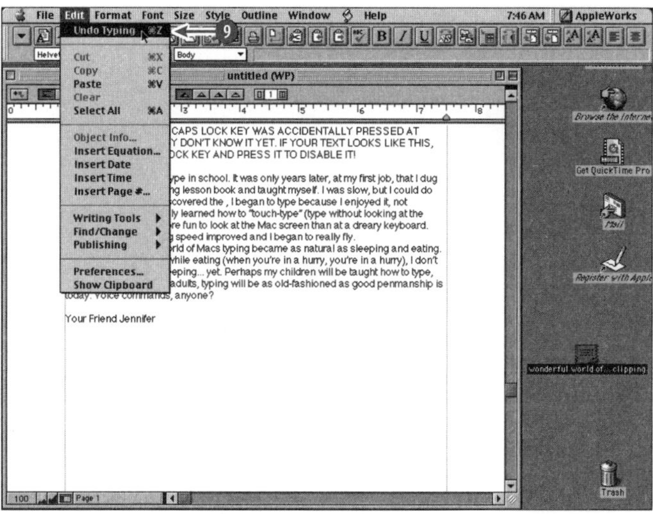

- The iMac clears your typing.
- ❼ Pull down the Edit menu.
- The Redo Typing command is now available.
- ❽ Choose Redo Typing from the Edit menu.
- Your typing reappears.
- ❾ Pull down the Edit menu.
- Note that you can Undo your action yet again.

saved your document (I'll discuss how to do this in the next task), the Revert command under the File menu becomes available. Revert lets you back up to the last saved version of your document. Think very carefully before you do this. Revert causes you to lose any changes you may have made since the last time you saved the document. If fixing your mistake is more important than the time spent to bring your document up-to-speed, Revert is for you.

TAKE NOTE

EDITING WITH THE TOOLBAR

AppleWorks, like many other applications, displays a *toolbar* at the top of the screen, just beneath the menu bar. On it are lots of buttons and drop-down menus. Though I've mentioned the editing buttons on the toolbar in passing throughout the chapter, I wouldn't want you to miss them. To use them, just move the mouse pointer up to the toolbar and hover it over a button. The toolbar displays the button's purpose in the lower portion of the toolbar, just in case you can't decipher the tiny picture on the button. Three of the buttons I've mentioned are here — cut, copy, and paste — along with a new button, undo (a small document with an arrow pointing left). You might find these tools useful if you use your mouse a lot.

SHORTCUT

Use the keyboard shortcut Command+Z to quickly undo an action.

Saving Your Work

I've saved the most important task for last: saving your work. Your iMac holds all unsaved data in temporary memory (RAM), which means you could lose it in the blink of an eye. To protect your data, you must *save*, storing your data on your hard drive in permanent memory.

To save a file, select Save from the File menu. A dialog box pops up and asks for some information. You can click the Save button (or press Return) right away if you're in a hurry. Better yet, take the time to choose a good name and a good location.

Choosing a name for your file is important. Your filename can be as long as 31 characters, but it must be different from other names in the folder to which you want to save it. If you try to save something with the same name as another file in that location, you are asked if you want to replace it. Be as specific as possible when you name your files, like "Letter to Dave - 4/21/99" or "Chapter 4 of iMac Book." Good spelling counts, too. When you can't find your file and you then use Sherlock (discussed in Chapter 2)to search for it, generic words and misspellings make life difficult. Note that a default filename (usually something like Untitled) appears in the dialog box. Unless you click somewhere else first, the default filename is highlighted and you only need to start typing to replace it.

Pick a location for your file from the list in the Save dialog box. You can double-click one of the folders and stop there, or you can continue double-clicking to navigate to another folder. The name on the drop-down

Exercising Your Options

Depending on the application, you may have other options for your saved file, too. In AppleWorks, you can select a file format from the Save As drop-down menu. The file format you choose determines what other applications can open the file. If you open your file in AppleWorks, keep AppleWorks as your file format. Otherwise, select a format such as Text from the drop-down menu. Another option is to save a file as stationery, which means that when you open the file again the future, a copy of the file is automatically created for you.

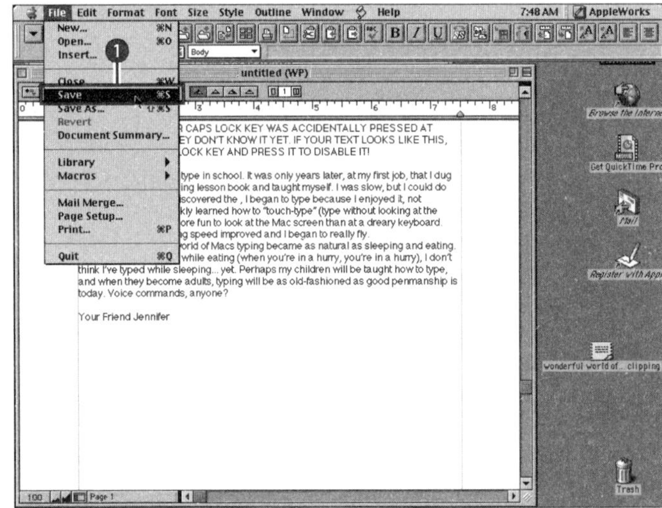

- Note by the name in the title bar that the file is unsaved.
- ❶ Select Save from the File menu.
- Alternatively, press Command+S or click the Save button.
- Note the Save As command is also an option.

CROSS-REFERENCE

See "Creating Stationery" in Chapter 5 for more details on this Save option.

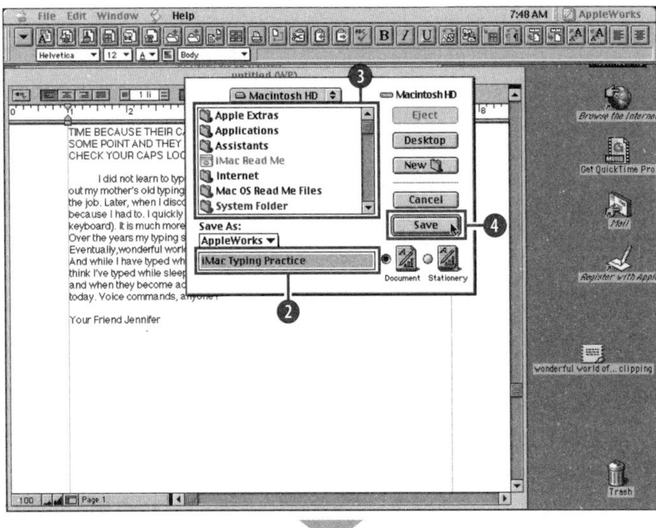

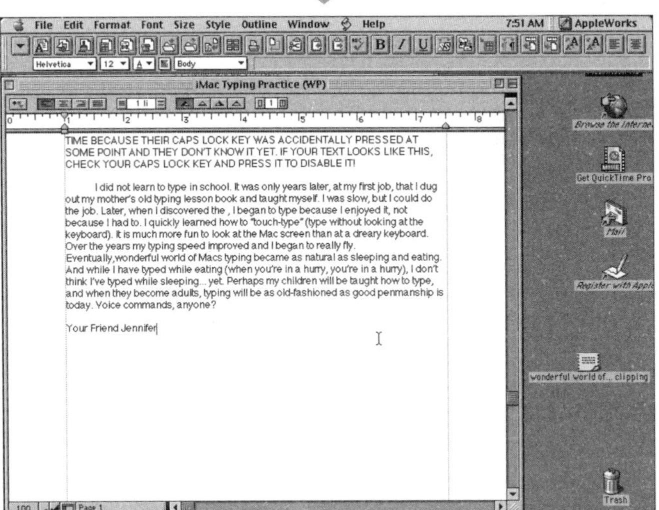

❷ *Type a new name to replace the default name.*

❸ *Double-click a folder to select another location.*

▶ *Alternatively, use the drop-down menu to navigate to a folder or create a new folder.*

❹ *Click Save (or press Return).*

▶ *Note the new filename in the title bar. The phrase (WP) is displayed by AppleWorks to indicate it is a word processing document and not part of the filename.*

menu at the top of the dialog box indicates the location that is currently selected. Click this menu to back up one level. Note that you can back up all the way to the Desktop using either the drop-down menu or the Desktop button on the right of the dialog box. You can save a file on your Desktop, although it will get cluttered and use valuable resources if you do this too often.

Most importantly, save your work. Do it early and often! Trust me.

TAKE NOTE

CREATE A DOCUMENTS FOLDER

Looking for a good place to save your files? You can create a special Documents folder to store your files. Go to the Apple menu, select Control Panels, choose General Controls, and select the Documents folder radio button in the lower right of the dialog box. This creates a special Documents folder at the top level of your hard drive. Even better, your Documents folder then becomes the default location for all saved files.

USING THE SAVE AS COMMAND

Save As in the File menu lets you save another copy of an open file, rather than saving to the original file. Use this command to save a different version of the file and keep the original (the one you previously saved) unharmed.

SHORTCUT

Use the keyboard shortcut Command+S to save your file often while you work.

Personal Workbook

Q&A

1. How do you open a document file?

2. What is the difference between the Caps Lock key and the Shift key?

3. What is an I-beam and what is its significance?

4. What is the quickest way to move a block of text from one part of a document to another?

5. What is the Clipboard? How do you view it?

6. What is the difference between the Delete key and the Caps Lock key?

7. What is the keyboard shortcut for Undo?

8. Why is it important to save early and often?

ANSWERS: PAGE 316

EXTRA PRACTICE

1. Open a new word processing document in AppleWorks. Type a letter to a friend about the iMac. Save it after the first sentence, and then save it again when you finish typing.
2. Edit the letter by moving one selection of text to another part of the document. Save it again.
3. Select the entire letter and copy it. Paste the letter in your Scrapbook.
4. Return to AppleWorks and edit the letter by adding a reference to this book. Save it again.
5. Address the same letter to another friend. Choose Save As from the File menu and give it a different name.

REAL-WORLD APPLICATIONS

- ✔ As you type the first letter, you notice that all your letters are capitalized, and you aren't pressing the Shift key. You look down at the keyboard and notice that the Caps Lock light is on. You press the Caps Lock key to disable it. Now when you type, your letters are all lowercase unless you hold down the Shift key.
- ✔ You write a particularly witty statement in a letter and want to record it for posterity. You select the quote and then click and drag it to the Desktop to create a clipping file.
- ✔ You selected an entire letter to copy to the Clipboard. Instead of copying it, however, you accidentally cleared it. You select Undo from the Edit menu to back up a step and restore your text.

Visual Quiz

Why would you see this dialog box? When would you click Cancel? When would you click Replace?

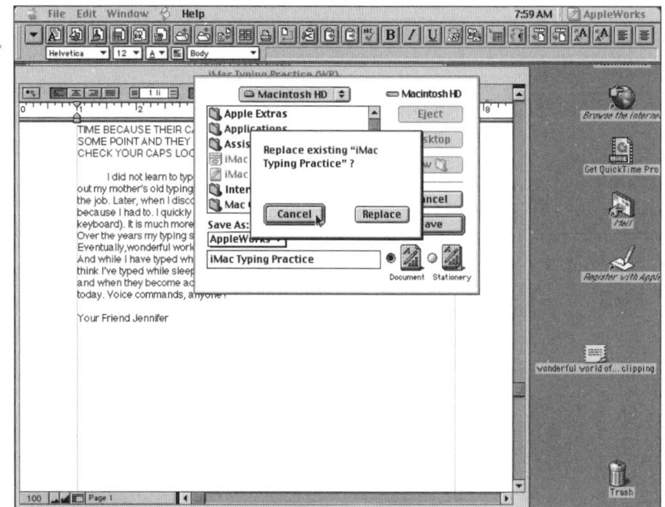

CHAPTER 5

MASTER THESE SKILLS

- Applying Fonts
- Installing New Fonts
- Formatting with Sizes and Styles
- Choosing Fonts and Styles Wisely
- Finding and Replacing Text
- Navigating Documents
- Creating Stationery

Using Fonts and Formatting

Fonts and formatting are two of the more delightful and creative aspects of your iMac. With them, you can make appealing, eye-catching documents that are indistinguishable from the work of professional print shops. Properly formatted, a document becomes much easier to read, and carefully used fonts add a dimension of personality that sets it apart from the crowd.

One of the niftiest aspects of your iMac is that what you see on your screen is what you'll get on your printed paper. This feature is called "WYSIWYG" (pronounced "wizzy wig," which literally means *What You See Is What You Get*). Although today's computer users take WYSIWYG for granted, it was a revolutionary concept when the Macintosh was introduced that quickly changed everyone's expectations of what a personal computer could do. Today, whether you're preparing a simple business letter or an entire book, you can do it right on your iMac and it will look the same onscreen as it does when the printer runs off a million copies.

Although computers are reducing the need to print on paper, you probably want and need to have a printer connected to your iMac. Again, thanks to the Macintosh revolution, you can buy inexpensive printers capable of amazing things. The black text of a laser printer rivals that of a fine printing press, and color inkjet printers produce vibrant documents and render illustrations with amazing fidelity.

Electronic fonts have replaced the cast-metal letters used in old-fashioned printing presses. A *font*, is an electronic file that defines a particular style of type with which you can display and print your text. Your iMac comes with about 40 fonts already installed and ready to use, and you're free to install lots more. Unlike with the cast-metal variety, you are free to change the size of your fonts at will, and even change some aspects of their appearance.

There is a small catch (isn't there always a catch?): the fonts you see on your screen (and that print on your printer) may not be present on your friend's computer, and vice versa. If you exchange a document and they don't have the same fonts, their computers will substitute a similar font. If appearance is critical, be sure you both have the same fonts.

You're probably itching to start fonting and formatting. Believe me, you're going to have a ball!

Applying Fonts

The best way to learn about fonts is to jump right in and experiment! Don't be afraid to try fonts on for size. You won't hurt anything. More important, you won't offend your iMac if you choose a weird font (though I can't speak for others).

You can apply fonts to your text using the Font menu. Many applications, including AppleWorks, have a Font menu that lists all available fonts installed on your iMac. If you don't see a distinct Font menu, look for a Format or Style menu that may offer a Font submenu. The Font menu or submenu lists all available fonts in alphabetical order. A black, downward-pointing arrow at the bottom of the menu indicates there are more fonts than can be displayed. Move the mouse pointer down to the arrow to scroll the menu and see more font names. To see the fonts at the beginning of the menu again, move the mouse pointer to the arrow at the top. A checkmark next to a font menu item indicates the currently selected font in your document.

To tell your iMac which font to use, just choose a specific font from the menu. From that point on, all the text you type displays itself in your chosen font until you choose another font. Any text you may have already typed remains in the font that was active when your text was originally typed.

If you want to change text you have already typed to a new font, first select that text and then select the new font. Your text instantly changes to the new font. To change all the text in a document to a particular font, press Command+A (or choose Select All from the Edit menu) and then choose your new font.

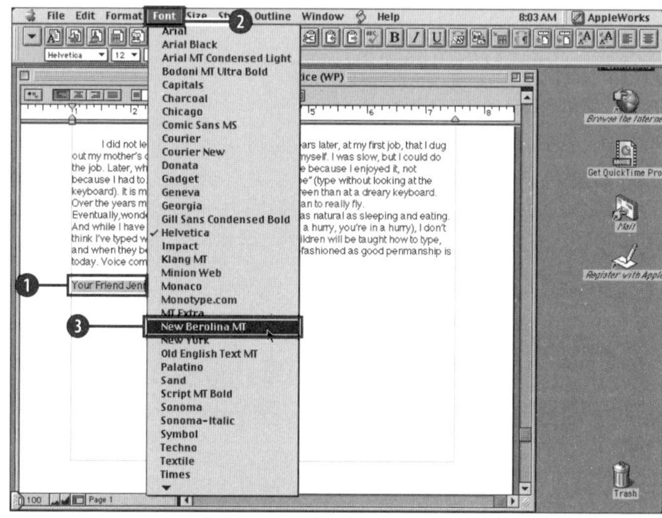

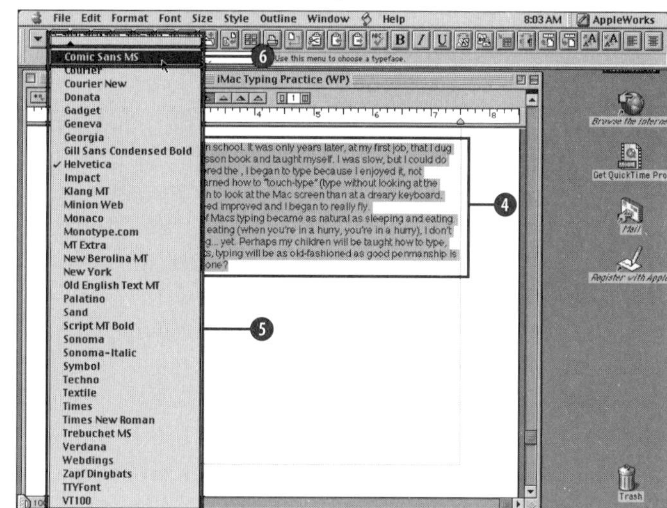

1. *Select the text you want to change.*
2. *Pull down the Font menu.*
3. *Choose an appropriate font.*

▶ *Note the toolbar's Font menu.*

4. *Select the text you want to change.*
5. *Pull down the toolbar's Font menu.*
6. *Choose an appropriate font.*

CROSS-REFERENCE

Learn how to pick the best fonts for your document in "Choosing Fonts and Styles Wisely," later in this chapter.

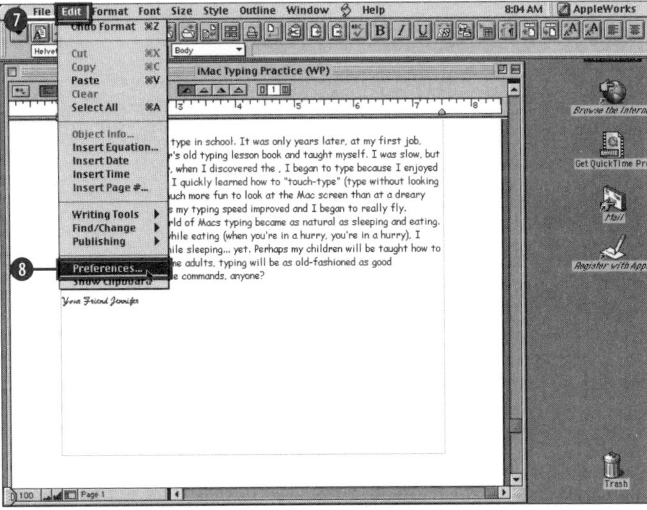

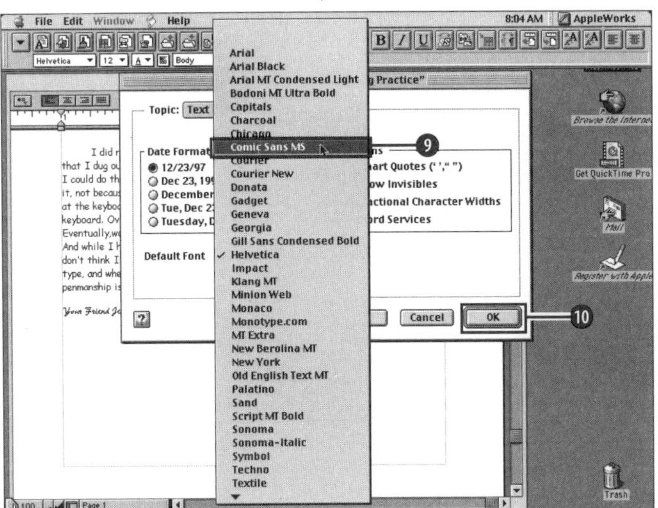

- Note that AppleWorks now displays your text in the font you chose.

7. Pull down the Edit menu.
8. Choose Preferences.
9. Select a new default font from the drop-down menu if you wish.
10. Click OK to save your preferences.

- Any text you haven't specified a font for is now changed to the new default font.

By the way, you should know that you don't have to choose a font before you begin typing in a new document. A font has already been designated as the default font, and it will be used if you don't specifically choose another font. You can change the default font for most applications in the Preferences dialog box (under the Edit menu).

TAKE NOTE

SNEAKING A PEEK AT A FONT

How do you know what a font looks like before you apply it? While there are several ways to sneak a peek at a font, I find that just changing my text to a new font is the best way to judge a font. If you must know what a font looks like before you try it, go to the Apple menu and select Key Caps. Now choose the font you want from the Font menu and notice that the letters on the keyboard buttons change. Type a few characters to see the font in action.

USING THE TOOLBAR

Some applications — including AppleWorks — provide a second Font menu on the toolbar. Not only is this a quick way to change fonts, but it also tells you at a glance which font is currently selected.

FIND IT ONLINE

Adobe Type Manager Deluxe (**http://www.adobe.com/prodindex/atm/**) is commercial software that lets you preview and manage your fonts.

Installing New Fonts

Once you get a taste for fonts, you might decide you want more, just like I did. I've been collecting fonts since the days of my very first Mac back in the '80s, and I still get inordinately excited when I discover a new and unique font. Fonts are the spice of Mac.

When you purchase or find a new font, the font files are usually installed in a *font suitcase* (the icon looks like a suitcase with the letter *A* on it). If you were to double-click the font suitcase and peek inside, you would see the installed font files. Some fonts need only one file, while other fonts work better with a collection of files — it usually depends on the font type and style. (I don't recommend that you add files to or remove files from a font suitcase unless you know what you are doing.)

To install a font, click and drag the font suitcase (or font files, if there is no font suitcase) on top of your System Folder icon. Once you release the mouse button, your iMac informs you that the items need to be stored in the Fonts folder. Just click the OK button to authorize the iMac to place them where they belong. If you have an application program running when you do this, you will need to quit and re-open it before the new font will be available to that application.

To remove a font, first quit all running applications, and then locate the Fonts folder inside your System folder on your hard drive. Drag the font suitcase (or the font files) you want to remove to your Desktop, to another folder, or to the Trash. Only remove fonts if you are quite sure you will not need them. Note that you cannot remove certain fonts, such as Charcoal and Geneva, because they are required for your iMac.

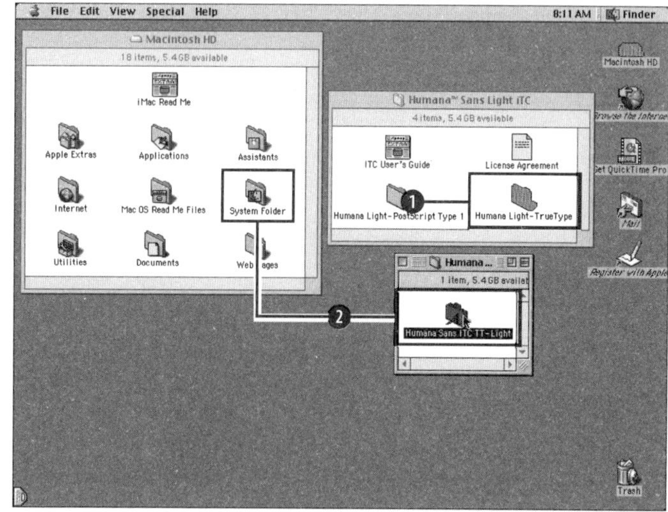

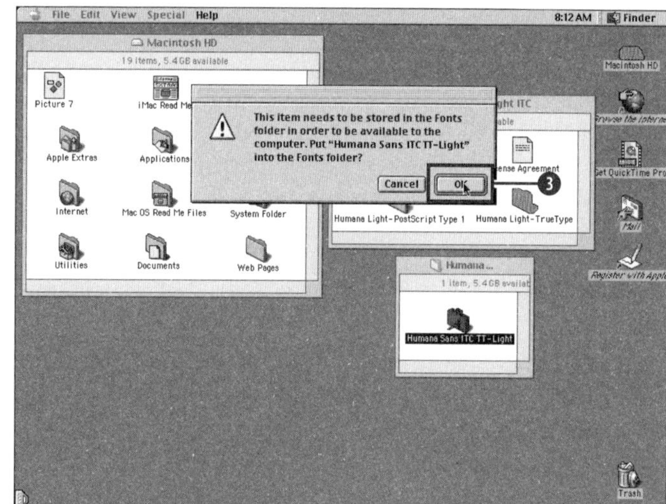

- *A folder containing a typical font and its documentation.*
- *Note the Postscript and True Type folders.*

1. *Open either folder for a font suitcase.*
2. *Click and drag the font suitcase on top of the System folder icon.*

- *A dialog box informs you that your fonts will be stored in the Fonts folder.*

3. *Click OK.*
4. *Click OK on the confirming dialog box informing you that fonts will not be available until you quit all open applications.*

CROSS-REFERENCE

To learn more about utilities that help you organize and control your fonts, see Chapter 14.

Using Fonts and Formatting

CHAPTER 5

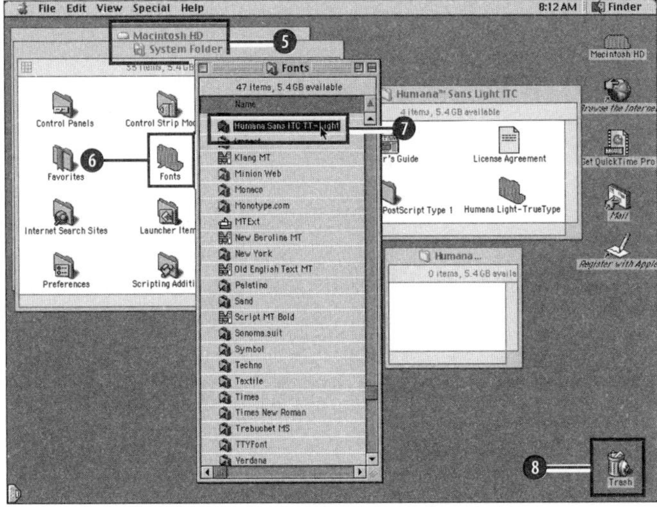

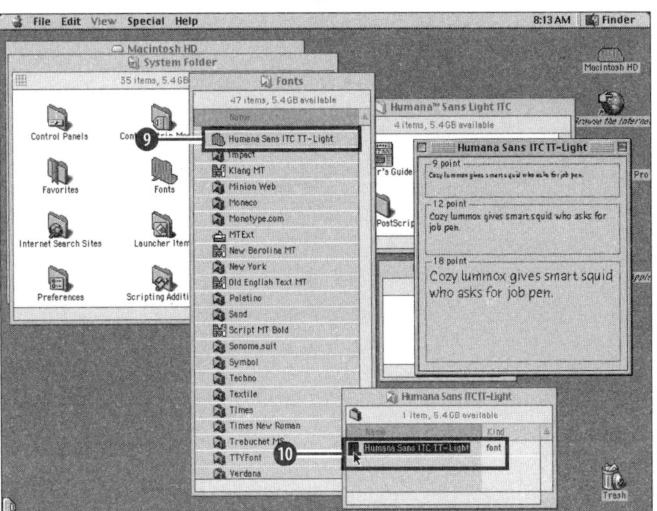

5 *Open your hard drive (Macintosh HD) and then open the System folder.*

6 *Double-click the Fonts folder to open it.*

7 *The font you just installed is listed.*

8 *Drag a font to the Trash to remove it.*

9 *Double-click a Font Suitcase.*

▶ *The font suitcase window opens.*

10 *Double-click an item in the Font Suitcase.*

▶ *A window displays a sample of the font.*

Be cautious of installing too many fonts on your iMac. Fonts take up memory (RAM). Your Font menu will also become too long if you have too many fonts, making it difficult to pick and choose the font you want. Your iMac also has a limit to the number of files that can be open at any one time, and each font you install is the equivalent of an open file.

TAKE NOTE

FINDING NEW FONTS

Fonts are everywhere these days. You can purchase professional, high-quality fonts from type companies such as ITC and Image Club. You can purchase CD-ROM collections of fonts from computer stores and mail-order catalogs. You may find new fonts included with other application programs you buy, as well. You also can download free and low-cost fonts from online services and sites on the Internet.

UNDERSTANDING FONT TECHNOLOGIES

Fonts come in two basic formats: TrueType and Postscript Type 1. You can mix and match font technologies on your iMac and in your documents. TrueType fonts are very iMac-friendly and are very easy to work with. Most of the pre-installed fonts on your iMac are TrueType fonts. Postscript Type 1 fonts are preferable if you are doing high-level design work (and if you are, you probably don't need me telling you how fonts work).

FIND IT ONLINE

Go to **http://www.shareware.com** on the Internet for free and low-cost fonts.

Formatting with Sizes and Styles

Fonts are only the beginning of your control over the look and feel of your text. You can change the size of your text if it is too small or if it is taking up too much space in a document. You can change text styles to emphasize or differentiate it from the surrounding text. You can change alignment of your text to align with the edges of the document. You can even change the color of your text to call attention to it — or just to add some pizzazz.

To change the size of your text in AppleWorks, pull down the Size menu and choose an appropriate size. The default size is usually 12 points. Note that in AppleWorks, you also can use keyboard shortcuts to increase the font size (Shift+Command+>) or decrease the font size (Shift+Command+<), or to choose another size altogether (Shift+Command+O). Use the Other command to choose a size lower than 9 and higher than 72 points.

To change text styles in AppleWorks, pull down the Style menu and choose an appropriate style, such as bold or italic. The menu previews each style as it will appear in your document to help you choose. Most styles are self-explanatory, though a few can initially appear mysterious. Condense makes your text narrower so you can fit more letters onto a line of a document. Conversely, Extend makes your text wider. Superscript shifts text up, while Subscript shifts text down. Superior makes text smaller and shifts it up, while Inferior makes text smaller and shifts it down. These last four styles are most useful for mathematical equations and footnote references.

To change text alignment in AppleWorks, click one of the alignment buttons on the toolbar (the buttons look like sets of lines aligned in four different styles). Left alignment moves text flush against the left margin.

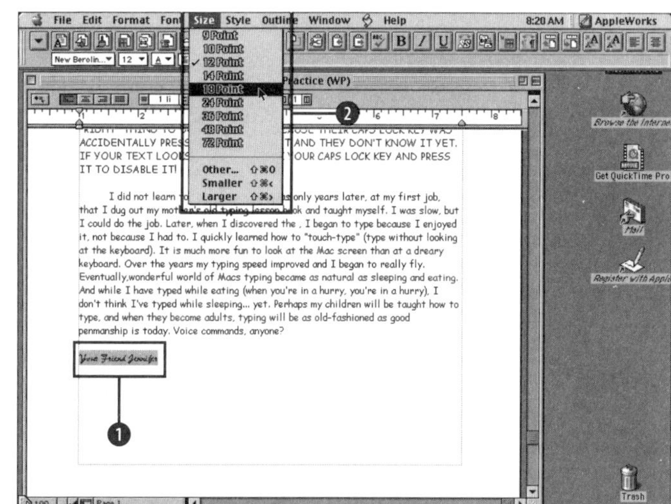

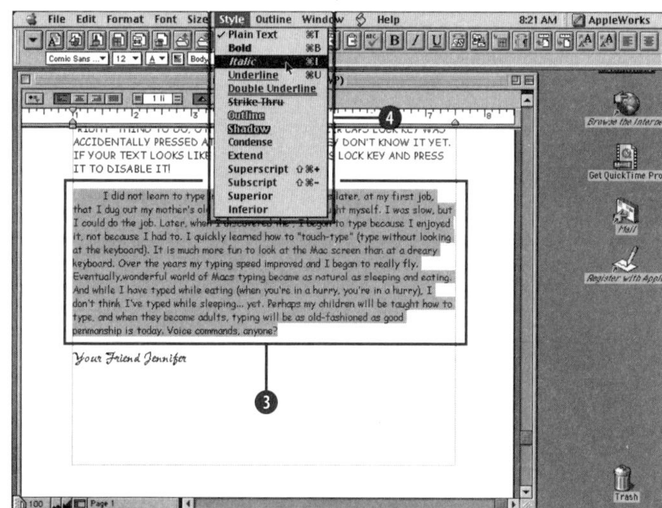

1. Select the text you want to change.
2. Pull down the Size menu and choose a new size.

- Alternatively, use the size menu on the toolbar.
- Optional: Use the Smaller or Larger commands at the bottom of the menu.
- Note that the size of your text has changed.

3. Select another block of text to change.
4. Pull down the Style menu and select a new style.

- Alternatively, use the style buttons on the toolbar.

CROSS-REFERENCE

Did you accidentally apply the wrong size or style? Learn how to back up a step in Chapter 4.

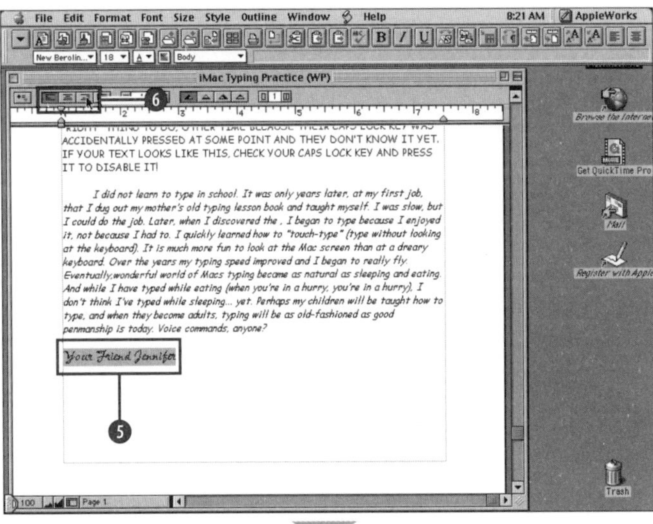

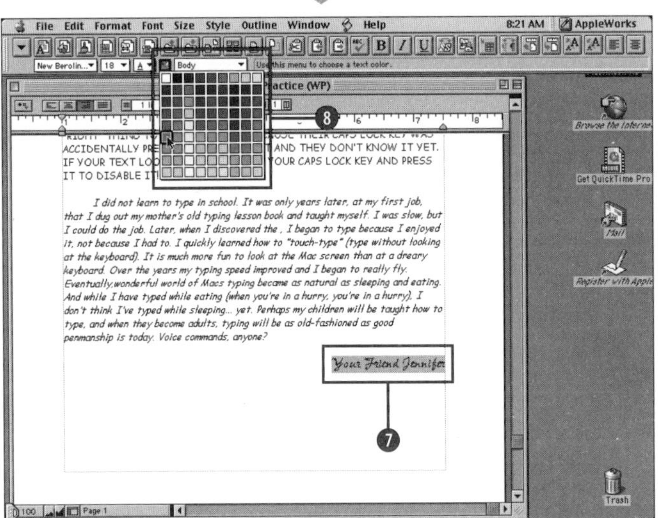

- Note that the style of your text has changed.
- ❺ Select another block of text to change.
- ❻ Click an alignment button at the top of the document window.
- Alternatively, use the alignment buttons on the toolbar.
- Note that your text alignment has changed.
- ❼ Keep the same block of text selected.
- ❽ Choose a new color from the color button on the toolbar.
- Note that your text changes color.

Center alignment centers text in the middle of the page. Right alignment moves text flush against the right margin. Justified alignment makes all your lines the same width on both margins. You also can change alignment with the Paragraph command under the Format menu in AppleWorks.

To change the text color, click the color button on the toolbar (the button with a prism of color on it) and choose a color from the grid.

TAKE NOTE

CONTROLLING LINE SPACING

In addition to changing the size of your text, you can change the spacing between lines of text so they occupy more or less space in your document. Select Paragraph from the Format menu and change the Line Spacing (or use the increase/ decrease line spacing buttons at the top of a document's window).

CHANGING MARGINS

You also can change the width of your document. Choose Document from the Format menu, change the number of inches in the Margins section, and then click OK. You also can click and drag the arrows along the ruler at the top of the document window to modify the paragraph indentation.

SHORTCUT

Use the keyboard shortcuts indicated in menus to change the size, style, and alignment of your text.

Choosing Fonts and Styles Wisely

I still remember the first letter I typed on my iMac. I used a simple, down-to-earth font for the introductory paragraph; a bold, friendly font for the second paragraph; and, a curly script font for my name at the bottom. I put some of the words I wanted to emphasize in bold, while others were italicized. I underlined and double-underlined important sentences. I reduced the size of my name at the bottom (I'm really very shy). For the crowning touch, I changed the color of all the text to fire-engine red (my favorite color). I thought it was a masterpiece. It was really a monstrosity.

The first rule in choosing the right fonts and styles is moderation. The tendency to overdo it is common when you're just getting acquainted with the iMac's fun features. Keep your documents simple. Try not to use more than two fonts, two styles, two colors, and two sizes in any one document.

Keep your readers in mind when you choose fonts and styles. Readability is important. The Times font is one of the most readable fonts ever created — you can't go wrong with it. Other good choices for large blocks of text include Arial, Helvetica, and New Century Schoolbook.

Use special fonts sparingly. Fonts like Impact, New Berolina, Old English Text, and Sand are visually interesting, but hard to read in large quantities. You can use them to add a dash of spice to a headline sized above 12 points.

Be consistent with styles. If you emphasize one word by making it bold, emphasize any other important words in the same manner. Documents with too many styles are confusing. Reserve complicated styles like Outline and Shadow for headlines; even then they should be used only when appropriate.

CROSS-REFERENCE

Learn more about using color in documents and about printing documents in color in Chapter 6.

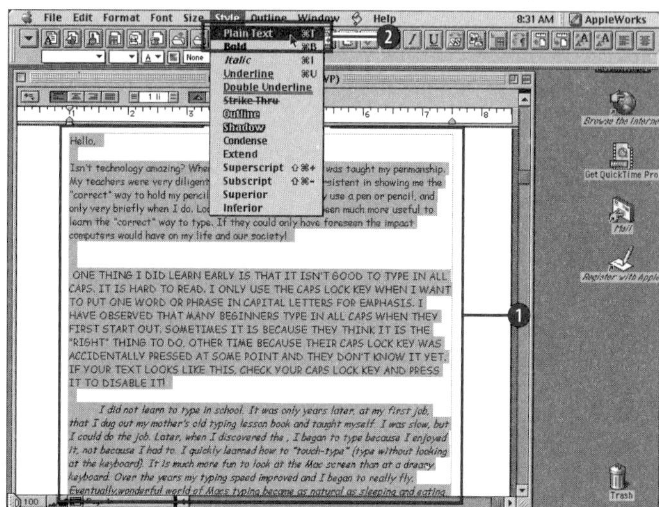

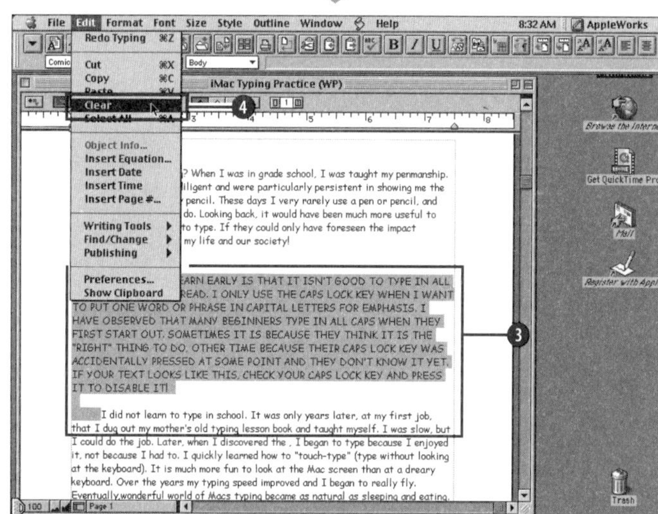

1. Select all the text in a document.
   - ▶ Alternatively, choose Select All from the Edit menu.
2. Choose Plain Text from the Style menu to remove extraneous styles.
   - ▶ Alternatively, press Command+T to remove styles.
3. Select any extraneous text.
4. Choose Clear from the Edit menu to remove it.
   - ▶ Alternatively, press the Delete key once to remove the text.

Using Fonts and Formatting

CHAPTER 5

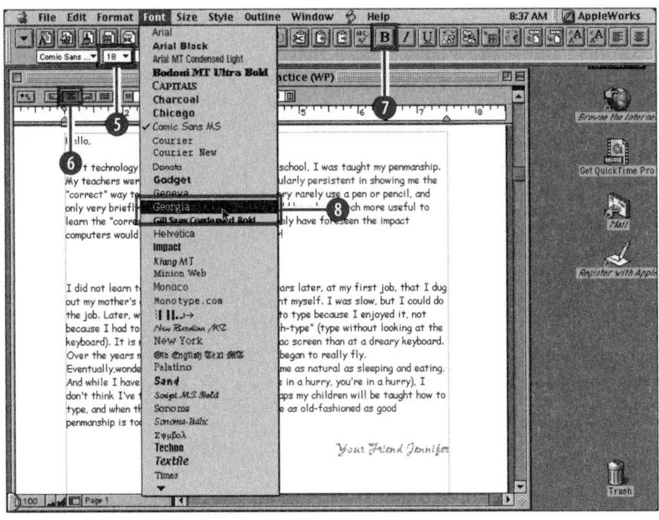

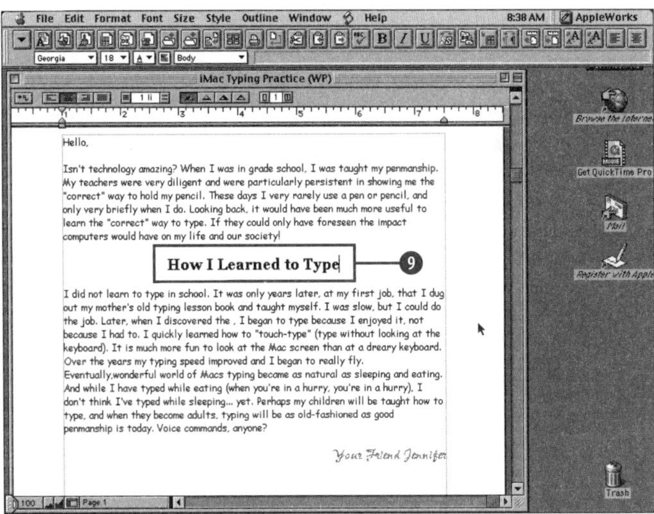

5 *Choose a size that is appropriate for a headline.*

6 *Choose an alignment for a headline.*

7 *Choose a style for a headline.*

8 *Choose a font for a headline.*

9 *Type your headline.*

▶ *Note how easy to read your headline is and how it helps the reader organize the page better.*

Size does matter. If your text is too small, only the very young or very determined will be able to read it. A safe choice for paragraph text is 12 points, while 18 points works well for headlines.

Black text is always safe. Don't use color in your documents just because you can. When color does seem appropriate, be sure your colored text is legible. Colors always seem lighter when applied to text. (Note that you need a color printer to print your color documents.)

TAKE NOTE

USING TWO FONTS TOGETHER

If you opt to use more than one font in a document, choosing two fonts that look good together can be a challenge. One way around this is to use just one font, but to use two different styles — such as plain and bold, plain and italic, or even plain and bold/italic. Another idea is to choose one serif font and one sans serif font. A *serif* font has small lines or other embellishments on the tips of the letters (like the font of the text to the left). A *sans serif* font has no extra lines or embellishments (like the font you are reading now). It is easier to match serif and sans serif fonts because they are less likely to clash with one another.

FIND IT ONLINE

Visit **http://www.will-harris.com/use-type.htm** for a tutorial by Daniel-Will Harrison choosing and using type.

Finding and Replacing Text

Let's say you wrote a chatty letter to Aunt Mary. Now you want to send the same letter to Aunt Matilda. You could go through your document, select every occurrence of "Mary" and change it to "Matilda," but this is time-consuming and tedious. To save time and trouble, you can use the find and replace tools available in most all word processing applications, including AppleWorks. This technique also helps you prevent missing an occurrence of a word and thus incurring the wrath of Aunt Matilda.

In AppleWorks, begin by pulling down the Edit menu. Select the Find/Change submenu, and choose Find/Change (or just type Command+F). Type the word or phrase you'd like to find in the first box (be sure to spell it as you did in your document). In the second box, type the new word or phrase to which you want to change the original word. Enable the Whole Word option if you want an exact word match (so "Mary" finds only occurrences of the word "mary" and not words like "amaryllis" or "rosemary"). Enable the Case sensitive option if you want to find exact case matches (to find "Mary" and not "mary"). Click Change All to find and change all occurrences. If the idea of changing all occurrences in one batch makes you nervous, click the Find Next button instead. Find Next locates the first occurrence, and it then stops and waits for your decision. You can change just that occurrence, change it and find the next occurrence, or just find the next occurrence without changing it.

Find and replace also works for deleting all occurrences of a word or phrase, with no replacement at all. Just press Command+F, type the word to delete in the first box, and leave the second box blank. This technique can leave two spaces where the deleted word used to be.

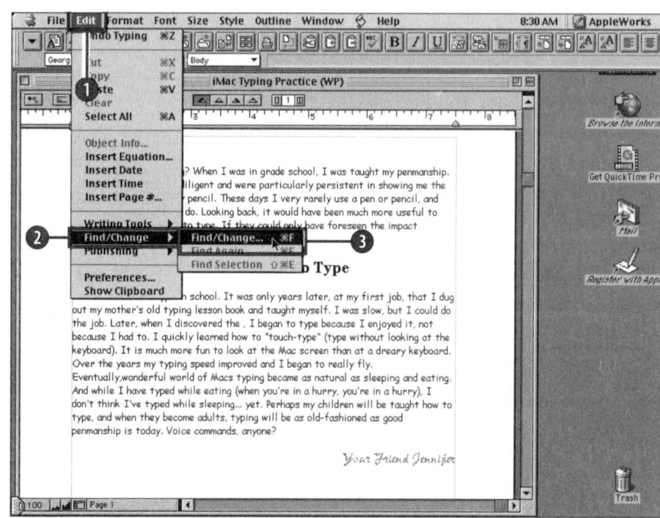

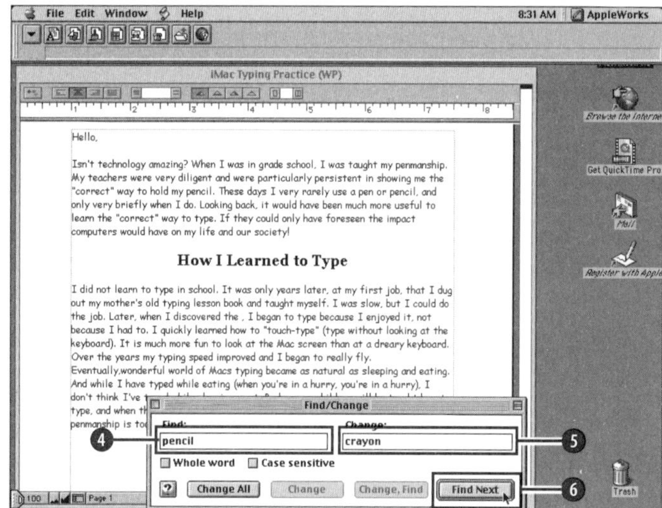

1. *Pull down the Edit menu.*
2. *Select Find/Change to display the submenu.*
3. *Choose Find/Change.*
- *Alternatively, press Command+F.*
4. *Type the word you want to find.*
5. *Type the word you want to replace it with.*
- *Check one of these boxes, if desired.*
6. *Click Find Next (or press Return).*

CROSS-REFERENCE

Learn how to find specific words in many documents using Sherlock, which is described in Chapter 2.

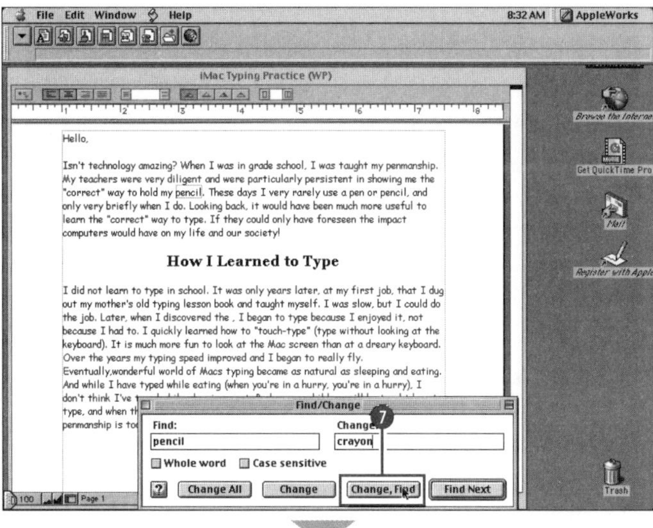

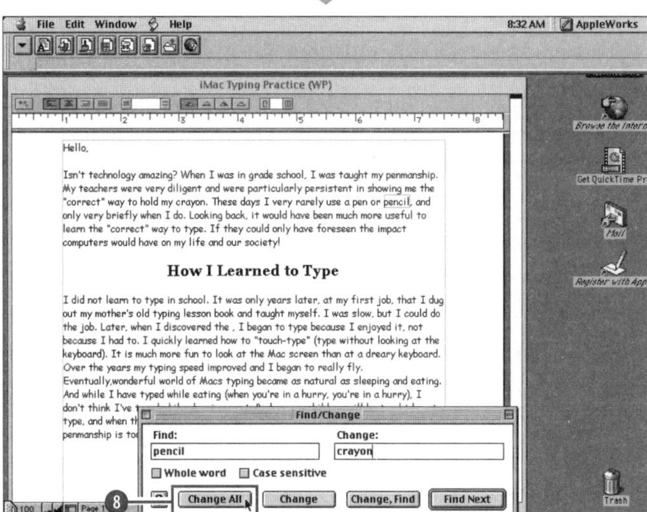

▶ AppleWorks highlights the first occurrence it finds.

7 Click Change, Find to change the word and find the next occurrence.

▶ Optional: Click Find Next (or press Return) if you don't want to change this occurrence.

▶ The word changed.

▶ AppleWorks highlights the next occurrence it finds.

8 Click Change All to change every occurrence of the word to the end of the document.

You also can use find and replace for those double spaces, and replace them with a single space.

You can initiate a find and replace operation at the beginning, middle, or end of a document and still search through the entire document.

TAKE NOTE

FINDING WITHOUT CHANGING

You can search your document for a specific word or phrase without making any changes. Just type the word to find in the first box of the Find/Change window and leave the second box empty. An even faster way to search with AppleWorks is to select the word or phrase and then choose Find Selection from the Find/Change submenu on the Edit menu. You can bypass the menu altogether by using Shift+Command+F.

FINDING FONTS AND STYLES

Some applications also give you the option to find words and phrases in particular fonts, styles, colors, and so on. This is a quick and easy way to change all those underlined words to bold. Look for a Format, Styles, or More button, menu, or toggle in an application's Find/Change window.

SHORTCUT

Use Command+E to find the next occurrence of a word or phrase after you've initiated a find command.

Navigating Documents

As you've seen, your iMac is much more flexible and versatile than even the fanciest typewriter. Once you begin taking advantage of the iMac's editing features and jump around your document to make changes, additions, and deletions, you may begin to wonder if this flexibility is such a good thing. You can put a lot of miles on your mouse just moving through a document. Find and replace tools help a bit, but not in all cases. The solution is to learn and use the various navigation techniques and shortcuts.

To move up and down through a document, use your arrow keys (beneath the Shift key) for small, one- or two-line moves. Use the scroll bar for short jumps. The Page button at the bottom of the document window in AppleWorks is great for moves between pages — just double-click it to go to another page. (If you don't see the Page button, choose Page View from the Window menu.) Use the Home key (above your numeric keypad on the right side of your keyboard) to return to the top of your document at any time. The Page Up and Page Down keys also work great for single page navigation.

If you find you're moving between pages too often, try viewing more of your document on the screen. One way to do this is by reducing the scale of your page view. In AppleWorks, click the 100 button on the bottom-left of your document window to choose another scale view. To the immediate right of the scale button are two more buttons: the decrease and increase scale buttons (they look like mountains); use these buttons to expand or shrink your page view.

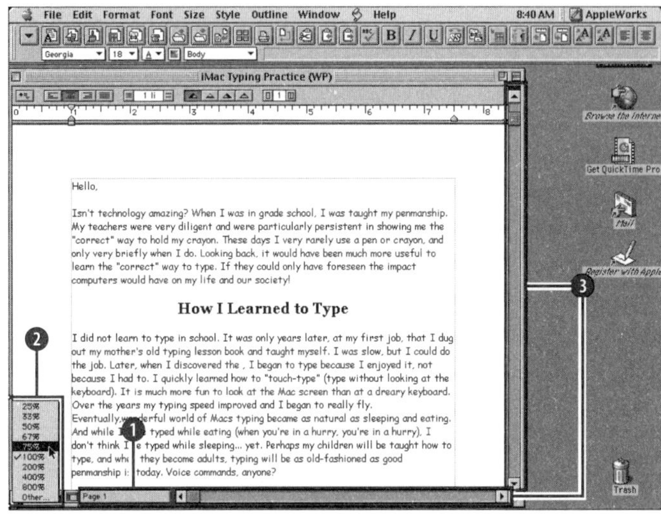

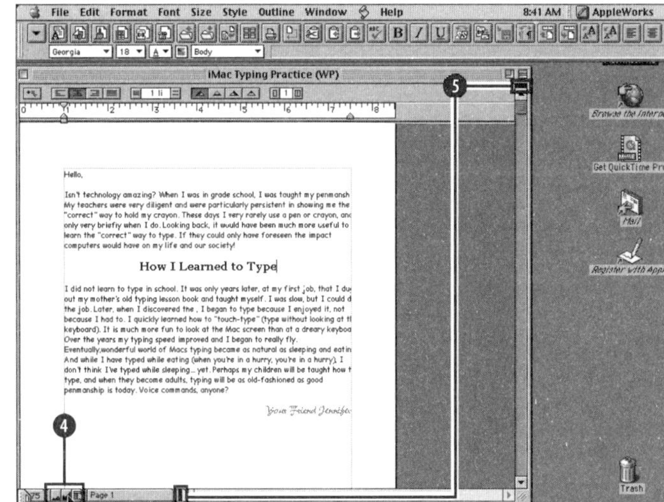

1. Double-click the Page button to go to a specific page.
2. Choose a new view from the scale menu.
3. Use the scroll bars to move through the document.

▶ Note your view changes.

4. Click one of the Decrease or Increase Scale buttons, if desired.
5. Click and drag these bars to split your window.

CROSS-REFERENCE

See "Moving Text" in Chapter 4 for more tips on document navigation.

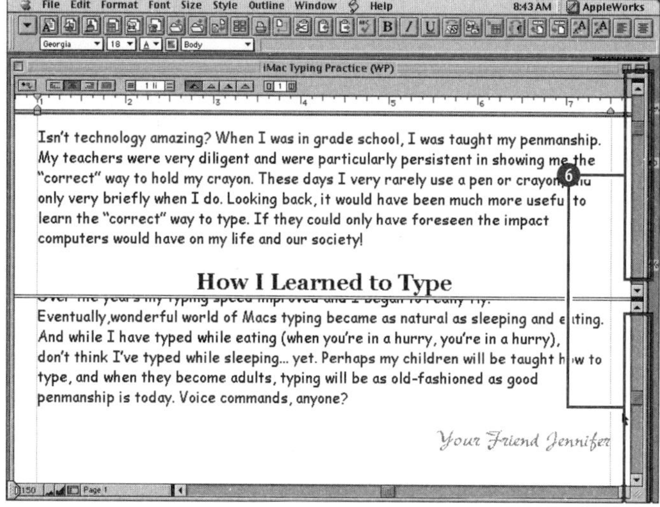

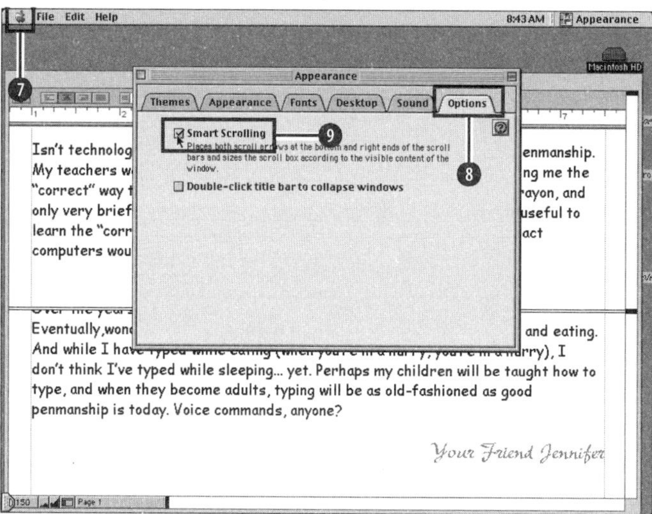

▶ AppleWorks splits your window into two panes.

6 Use the two scroll bars to independently scroll through the panes.

7 Pull down the Apple menu, select Control Panels, and choose Appearance.

8 Click the Options tab.

9 Click once on the check box to enable Smart Scrolling.

Another technique is to split your document window so you can see two parts of your document at one time and thus move around less. To do this in AppleWorks, click and drag the black bar beside either scroll bar to create a split. Now you can move the scroll bars (and use other navigational techniques) in each window independently of one another. Split windows are also useful for comparing two parts of your document, and for copying and pasting between them.

TAKE NOTE

USING SMART SCROLLING

If you get tired of moving your mouse along the entire length of the scrollbar just to reach the up or down scroll arrow, enable the iMac's *smart scrolling* feature. Smart scrolling places both scroll arrows at the bottom and right ends of the scrollbars, respectively, so you have far less distance to move. To enable smart scrolling, go to the Apple menu, select the Control Panels submenu, and then choose Appearance. Click the Options tab at the top of the dialog box and enable the Smart Scrolling check box.

INCREASING MOUSE SPEED

Also consider increasing the tracking speed of your mouse to move the mouse pointer around the screen faster. You can increase tracking speed in the Mouse control panel. Double-click speed is also set here.

SHORTCUT

Hold down the Command key and press an arrow key to move to the top, bottom, far left, or far right of your document.

Creating Stationery

Now that you know how to use fonts and styles, you also know how time-consuming it can be to apply them. If you find yourself repeatedly applying the same formatting, consider creating *stationery* instead. With stationery, you can create a document layout once, and then use it over and over again to save time and effort.

To create stationery, begin by opening a new document, adding the text, and configuring the fonts and styles you want to use. For example, you could create a letterhead with your name, address, and telephone number. You could just as easily create a business form.

Once you have the document set up the way you want it, choose Save As from the File menu. Click the radio button next to Stationery in the lower-right corner of the resulting dialog box. Now, give the file a name, choose a location to store it (the AppleWorks Stationery folder is a good place), and then click Save. Type a title, an author name, a version number, any keywords, a category name, and a description for your new stationery. If you want to protect the stationary from prying eyes, click the Set Password button at the bottom of the dialog box and type in a password. Click the OK button to complete the process. That's all there is to it!

To use your new stationery, locate the stationery file you just saved. You can use the AppleWorks Open command, or you can double-click the file in the Finder. AppleWorks displays a preview of the document, which comes in handy when you're not sure which file you want to use. Opening your stationery file actually opens a *copy* of the file rather than the original. You can add to, delete from, and change anything in the file, and you

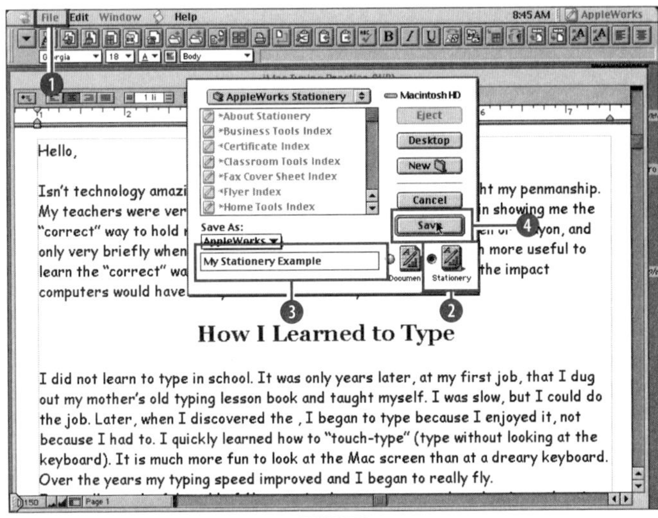

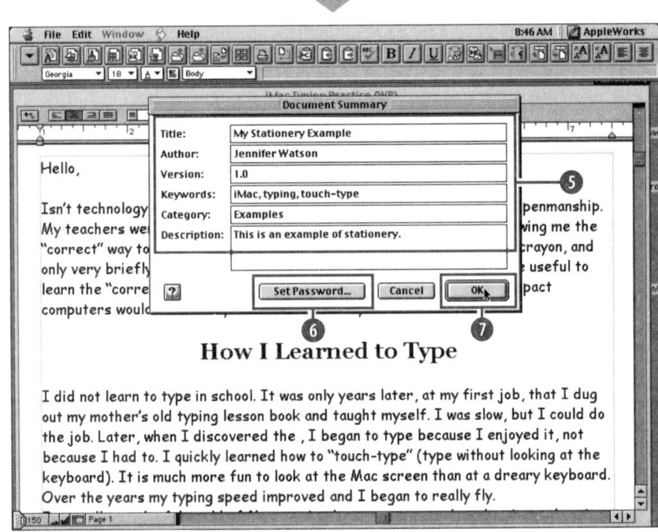

1. *Choose Save As from the File menu.*
2. *Click the Stationery radio button.*
3. *Type a name for your new stationery.*
4. *Click Save (or press Return).*
5. *Optional: Type your stationery information.*
6. *Optional: Click Set Password and type in a password of your choice.*
7. *Click OK (or press Return).*

CROSS-REFERENCE

Learn how to use the Save As command as an alternative to creating stationery in Chapter 4.

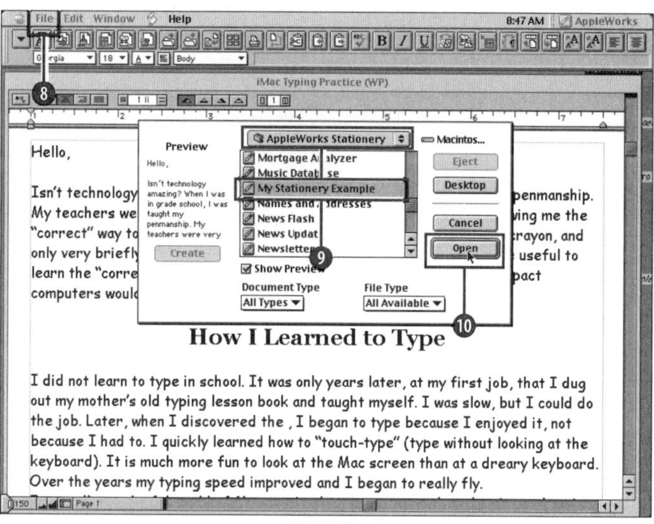

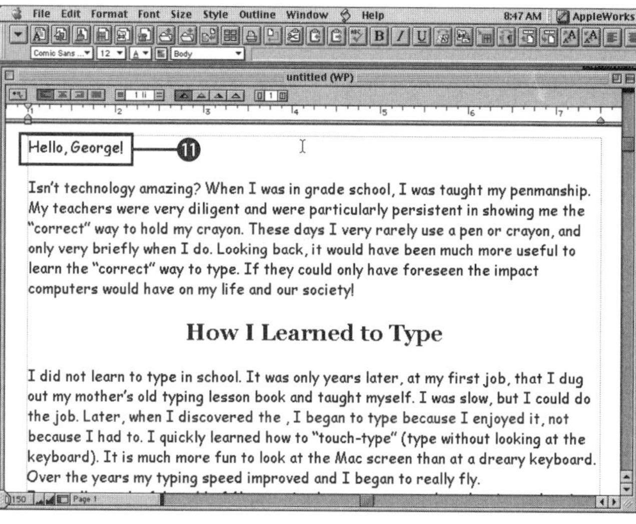

8. *Choose Open from the File menu.*
9. *Navigate to the AppleWorks Stationery folder and select your new stationery file.*

▶ *AppleWorks displays a preview of the file.*

10. *Click Open (or press Return).*

▶ *AppleWorks opens a copy of your stationery file.*

▶ *Note that the file is untitled until you save it.*

11. *Change the new file in any way without modifying the original stationery file.*

can then save the new file without affecting your stationery. Your original stationery remains as pristine as the day you saved it. Just be sure you give your new stationery a different filename than your original stationery (or save it in a different location if you must use the same name).

Of course, if your original stationery is protected from changes, you may wonder how you can make changes to the stationery file yourself. To change your stationery, open it to create a copy, modify the copy as you like, and then save the copy as a stationery with the same name as your original stationery, overwriting the old stationery with the new one.

TAKE NOTE

USING STATIONERY TEMPLATES

AppleWorks comes with several ready-to-use stationery templates you can use as is or to customize to your needs. These templates are stored in the AppleWorks Stationery folder. To see an overview of the templates, open one of the Stationery Index files, such as the Letter, Letterhead Index, and Memo Index templates. The thumbnails (small pictures) in the Index give you a sneak peek at the available template designs. Click the blue, underlined link below a thumbnail to open a stationery template so you can modify it. To create a new stationery file from one of these templates, just save the modified file in stationery format.

SHORTCUT

Change the file type to AppleWorks Stationery in the Open File window to find only stationery files.

Personal Workbook

Q&A

1. In addition to the Font menu, where else might you find a menu of available fonts?

2. How do you install a new font on your iMac?

3. What is the difference between the Superscript and Subscript styles?

4. Ideally, what is the maximum number of fonts and/or styles you should use in a single document?

5. How do you find a specific word or phrase in a document? How do you replace it?

6. How do you zoom in (enlarge your view) or zoom out (shrink your view)?

7. What is smart scrolling and how do you enable it on your iMac?

8. Where can you find a collection of stationery template files for AppleWorks?

ANSWERS: PAGE 316

Using Fonts and Formatting

CHAPTER 5

EXTRA PRACTICE

1. Write a brief note to a friend to tell him or her about your cool, new iMac and to demonstrate all the fun things you have learned about selecting fonts. Be tasteful!
2. Quit any running applications. Search the Fonts folder in your iMac's system folder for several fonts you've never used, and move them from the Fonts folder to your iMac desktop. Check the Fonts folder again to be sure they've been uninstalled.
3. Reinstall the fonts you removed in the previous exercise and create a practice document using those fonts.
4. Open the note you wrote in the first exercise and modify the note so that it demonstrates font sizes and styles, as well as font selection.

REAL-WORLD APPLICATIONS

- ✔ You prepare a new resume highlighting your newly found computing skills for a company that is looking for experienced salespeople capable of preparing their own sales materials. Your ability to prepare an exciting, yet tasteful, resume helps convince them that you're the right person for the job.
- ✔ Your new boss agrees that you can work part of the time from home where you can prepare those sales materials in peace and quiet. The company buys you the fonts you need so your documents conform to the company's carefully groomed image. You easily install them on your iMac.
- ✔ With some peace, quiet, skill, and imagination, you design a 12-page sales presentation. Your boss says it looks as good as the work done by their ad agency. You grin and accept the compliment.

Visual Quiz

Where would you find this file on your hard drive? What can you do with it?

____

____

____

____

____

____

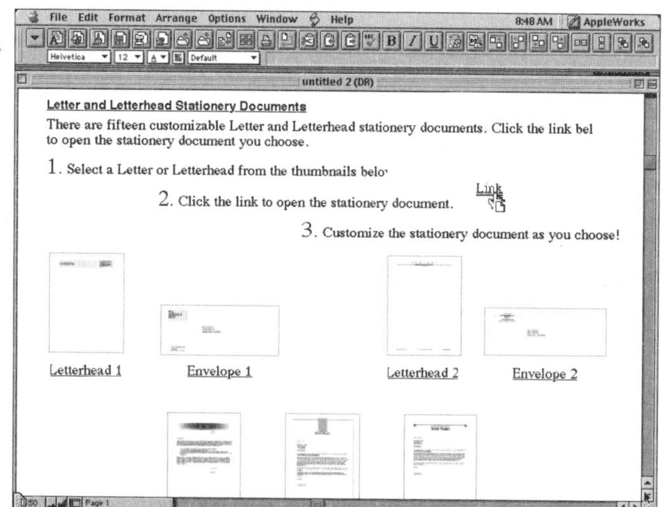

File Edit View Special Help

CHAPTER 6

MASTER THESE SKILLS

- Choosing and Installing a Printer
- Servicing a Printer
- Setting Up a Page
- Setting Printing Options
- Previewing a Page
- Printing a Page
- Printing in the Background (Print Monitor)
- Printing from the Desktop

Printing Documents

Life with your iMac isn't nearly as much fun (or as useful) as it can be with a printer is attached to it. You can design iron-on transfers and make T-shirts for the family reunion, print shipping labels for the packages containing the T-shirts, create customized maps and travel instructions for everyone attending, and include a picture of Great-Aunt Martha, all in brilliant color. And of course, how can you run a business and not print letters, invoices, envelopes, and shipping labels?

The concept of What You See Is What You Get (WYSIWYG) holds true for iMac printers, too. iMac printers are *graphics printers.* They treat everything — whether it's text or artwork — as a picture made up of tiny dots. Printer manufacturers are in a constant competition to make those dots smaller (the more dots per inch, the merrier!) so you can print in ever greater clarity and detail.

The laser printer helped start the Mac revolution 15 years ago. For the first time, an affordable printer created documents that looked like they came from a print shop. Laser printers are still your best bet if what you need most is top-notch, permanent black text and speedy output.

Inkjet printers spray ink onto the page through many incredibly small nozzles. For a long time, the quality of inkjets couldn't quite match that of laser printers. Even inexpensive inkjet printers are now so good, however, that only a professional can tell the two apart. Inkjet printers are generally slower than laser printers. Unlike laser printers, the ink from inkjet printers must dry after documents leave the printer, and the print may smudge or run if the page gets wet.

Not many years ago, there were few color printers available for personal computers, and either they weren't quite good enough, or they were fabulously expensive. Now, a $150 inkjet printer is good enough to duplicate a common photograph. All you need to achieve the best result is the right printer and special glossy paper. I use my color inkjet constantly, for everything from letterhead livened-up with a splash of yellow to small quantities of glossy, full-color brochures.

You also can connect more than one printer to your iMac at a time. If it makes sense (or if you can't make up your mind), you can own both a laser printer and a color inkjet and have the best of both worlds, like me.

Choosing a Printer

Not all printers are the same. When you make the decision to purchase a printer for your iMac, it pays to carefully consider your choice. Price, quality, and type of printer are important factors. Two essential points to keep in mind: your printer must be Mac-compatible, and it must be able to connect to your iMac with either Ethernet or USB connectors. If you want to use an Ethernet printer, you will need either a special *crossover* cable or a *hub*—inquire when you purchase your iMac. Most printers come with the right cable for your iMac, but make sure before you leave the store. Check the length, too. You may need to purchase a longer cable, depending on where you want to locate the printer.

When you get your new printer home, find the unpacking and installation instructions and follow them carefully. There will be pieces of packing tape and packing materials hidden in the darndest places. Failure to remove them may cause serious problems.

Your printer comes with software for your iMac, usually on an accompanying CD-ROM disc. If your printer software came on floppy disks, contact the manufacturer for a CD-ROM (unless you purchased and installed an optional floppy disk drive). Install the printer software on your iMac according to instructions, and then restart your iMac.

Once everything is installed and turned on, your next task is to tell your iMac what printer you want to use. You must do this even if you only have one printer attached. Go to the Apple menu and select Chooser. Click your printer's icon in the box on the left to select it. You should recognize your printer by name—if you don't, check your printer's documentation to see which printer to select. When you click the printer icon, the printer's name appears in the box on the right, indicating that it

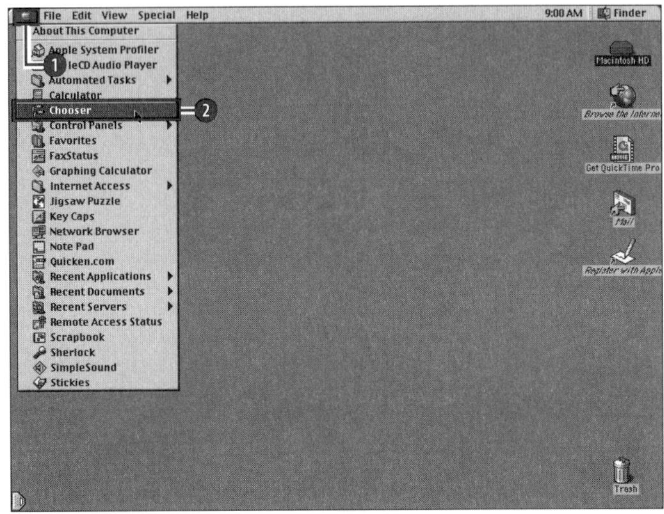

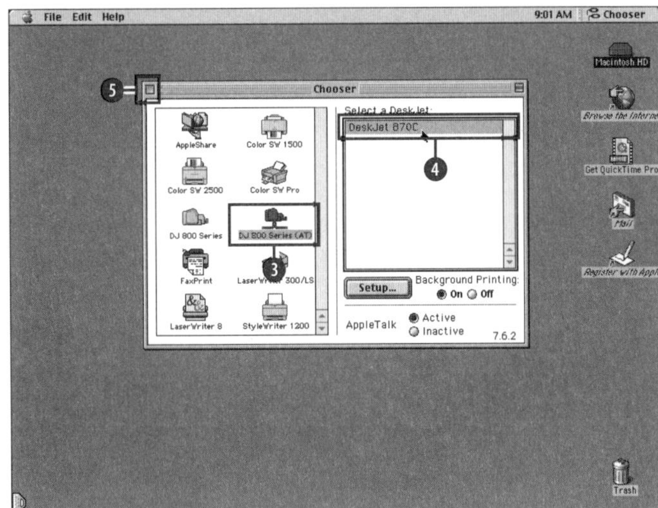

1. *Pull down the Apple menu.*
2. *Select the Chooser.*

▶ *The Chooser displays various printer icons.*

3. *Click the printer icon that matches your printer name.*
4. *Click the printer or port name in the list box to make it active.*
5. *Close the window.*

CROSS-REFERENCE

Learn more about Ethernet networking in Chapter 12, "Networking and File Sharing."

Types of Printers

Printers you can use with the iMac come in three general styles: laser, inkjet, and dot-matrix. Laser printers are generally the most expensive, use the same technology as Xerox copy machines, and usually offer the highest print quality. Inkjet printers are the most affordable, and the quality is nearly as good as laser. Inkjet printers spray ink onto the paper, and these days, they are nearly always color printers. Dot-matrix printers use an inked ribbon, just like a typewriter does. They aren't very common these days; inkjet printers are now cheaper and offer much better print quality. If you need to print multi-part forms (carbon-interleaved or carbonless), dot-matrix printers are still the only available choice.

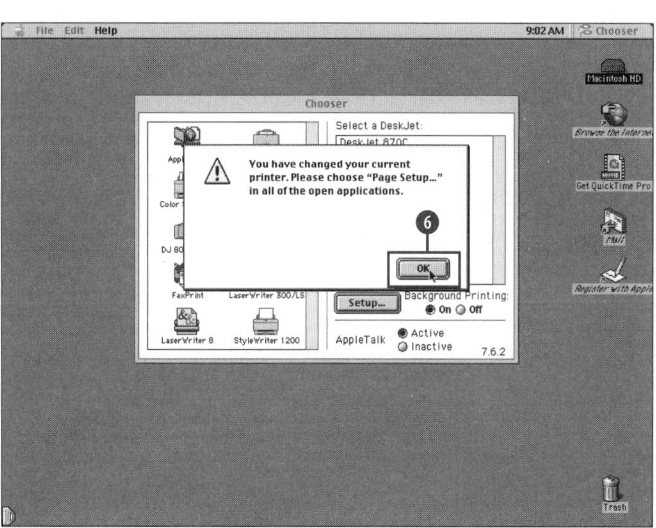

❻ *Click OK.*

is ready and waiting. If you see <Printer Port> and <Modem Port> appear instead, select <Printer Port>. Now close the Chooser and click OK in the resulting confirming dialog box.

Note that your printer software may do this for you during installation, too.

TAKE NOTE

UNDERSTANDING PRINTER DRIVERS

Printers drivers are programs that give your iMac details about a how a particular printer functions. Usually your printer software places the appropriate printer driver on your iMac during the installation process. If you need to install the printer driver yourself, click and drag it to the System folder icon and then drop the driver to install it.

CONNECTING AN APPLETALK PRINTER

If you already own an older Mac printer, chances are it uses AppleTalk or LocalTalk, rather than USB or Ethernet. If this is the case, you may still be able to use it with your iMac. One workaround is to purchase a special adapter. Farallon Communications, Inc. (**http://www.farallon.com**) offers adapters for AppleTalk printers and some Apple StyleWriters. Another option for those of you who use an Ethernet network is to purchase a *bridge* and install it between your network hub and your printer.

SHORTCUT

Click the printer icon in the Control Strip (the strip of icons at the bottom of your screen) to select and change printers quickly.

Servicing a Printer

Newly installed printers often need a bit more tweaking before they are ready to use. Even if you've had your printer for a while, you may still want to service your printer first. Printers, in particular, deserve some attention when you move them, when you connect them to a new computer, or when you replace the toner cartridge, ink cartridge, or ink ribbon.

Laser printers are usually serviced through the Chooser. Look for a Setup button when you select your laser printer icon in the Chooser. Clicking Setup offers a number of service options that vary according to which printer driver you installed. I recommend you click the Auto Setup button for any newly installed printer. Other options may include selecting the PPD (Postscript Printer Description) file, displaying and updating Printer Info, and configuring your printer. Refer to your printer manual for specific directions on how to service your laser printer.

Servicing an inkjet printer tends to be more hands-on. No, you don't need to get out your toolkit and disassemble the inkjet printer (nor do I recommend it), but you will probably need to print out a few test pages. To begin, choose Page Setup from the File menu and look for a Service, Utilities, or Options button — in that order. If you don't see these menu options, choose Print on the File menu and check there for the button. Service options range from cleaning the ink cartridge before printing to aligning the ink cartridges. It is a good idea to perform each of these service functions before you use your printer, because they ensure that you get the best possible image from your inkjet. Just start a service process and follow the directions on the screen to complete it.

One more important — but often overlooked — task: turn your printer on! Your printer should be turned on

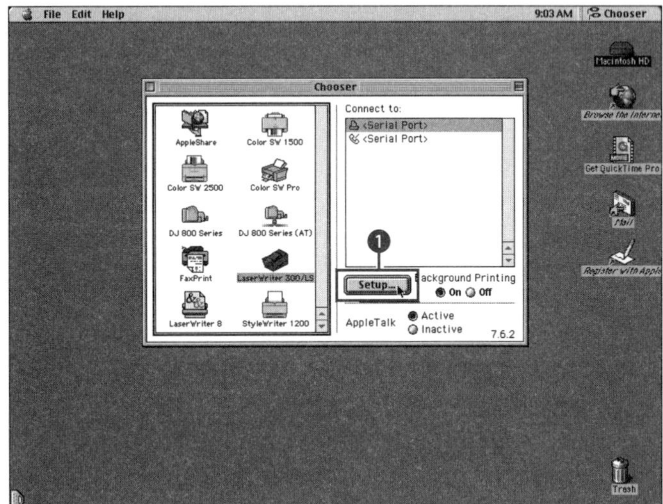

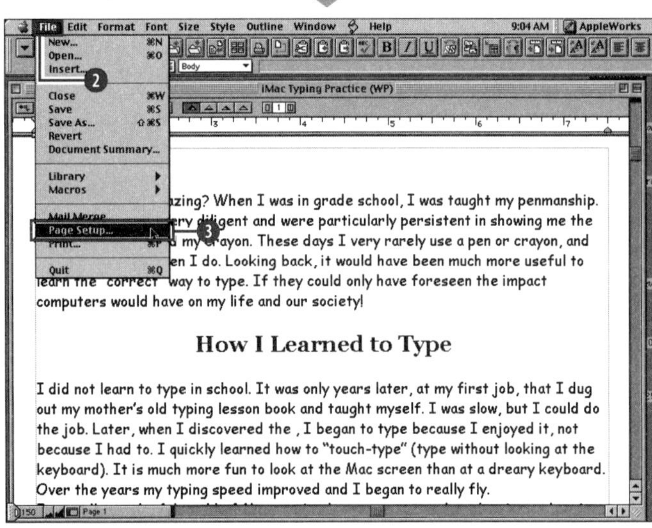

❶ *To service a laser printer, open the Chooser, select your printer, and click Setup.*

❷ *To service an inkjet printer, pull down the File menu in an application.*

❸ *Choose Page Setup.*

CROSS-REFERENCE

If you encounter problems with your printer, refer to "Fixing a Printing Problem" in Chapter 17.

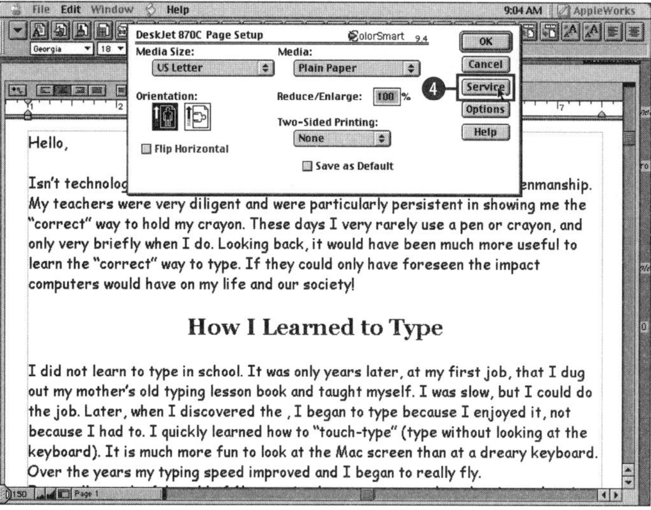

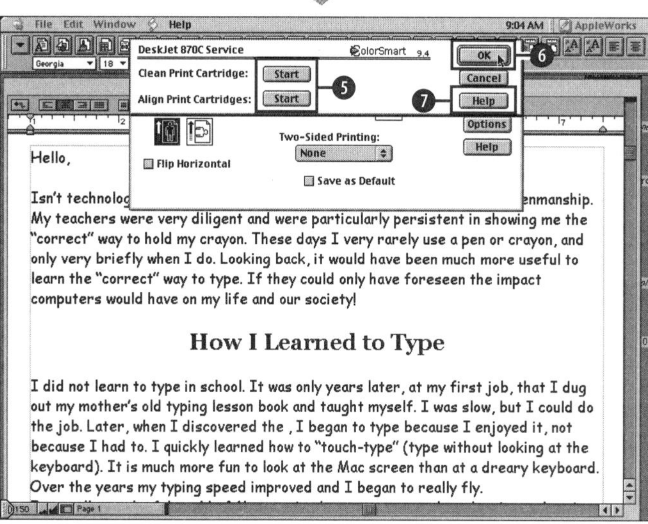

4 *Click Service.*

5 *Click one of the Start buttons to service your printer.*

6 *Click OK when finished.*

7 *Optional: Click Help for more information.*

before you attempt to select it in the Chooser, before you service it, and before you print to it.

TAKE NOTE

ALIGNING INKJET CARTRIDGES

I can't overemphasize how important it is to align your inkjet cartridges before you begin printing. If your cartridges aren't aligned, everything you print might be offset a bit on the page. What's more serious is that the black and colored inks can also become offset from one another, giving everything a funky light/dark shadow. If your printer doesn't do it for you automatically, always align your ink cartridges when you install a new printer and when you replace ink cartridges. Note that inkjet printers with only one ink cartridge do not generally need to be aligned (though there are some exceptions — check your documentation).

GETTING SERVICE HELP

The first time I attempted to service my printer, I was left utterly confused. I hadn't even realized it was necessary! So if my brief explanations above don't do your particular printer justice, look for a Help button (as you should in any application that has you stumped) and check your documentation. You should find more detailed information on how to set up and prepare your printer.

SHORTCUT

Any time you need more help, just press the Help key above the numeric keypad on your keyboard.

Setting Up a Page

Connecting your printer, installing your printer software, and selecting your printer in the Chooser are only the first steps. Now turn your attention to *what* you want to print. Your iMac lets you print many different things — AppleWorks documents and Desktop windows are just two examples. Before you click that Print button, you must make sure your document, page, or window is set up properly for printing.

In AppleWorks, begin by choosing Page Setup from the File menu. The Page Setup window differs based on the type of printer you're using, but some elements remain the same for all printers, such as page size, layout, scale, and orientation. AppleWorks documents default to US Letter page size (8.5" x 11"). If you want another paper size, such as legal size, select it from the page size drop-down menu. The Layout option, if available, lets you print several pages of a document onto a single piece of paper. The scale option allows you to increase or decrease the size of your document when it prints. Keep in mind that increasing the size of a document to fill a sheet of paper — especially when it contains a graphic — can decrease the print quality. The orientation option determines whether your document is printed or displayed in the default portrait (vertical) view or in landscape (horizontal) view. Set your options and click OK to save them for your document.

Now take a good look at the page you want to print. Are the margins wide enough? Good margins are generally ¾" to 1" wide (they probably should be no less than ½", because your printer may not be able to print that close to the edge of the paper). Do you want page numbering or footnotes at the bottom of your page? Choose Document from the Format menu to set up page numbering and footnotes before you print. Are you using

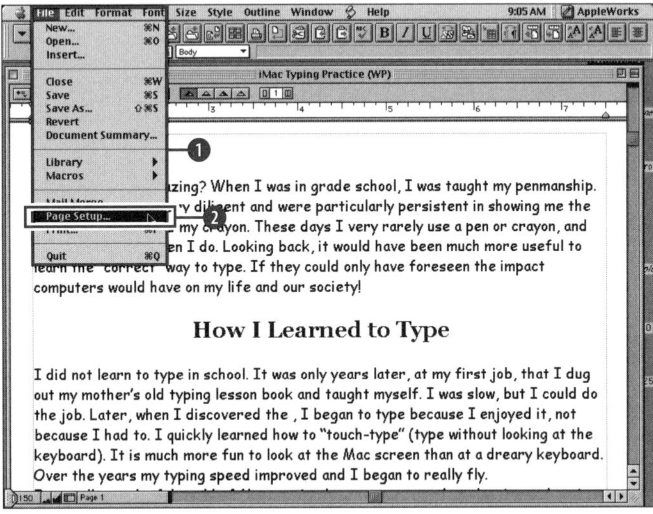

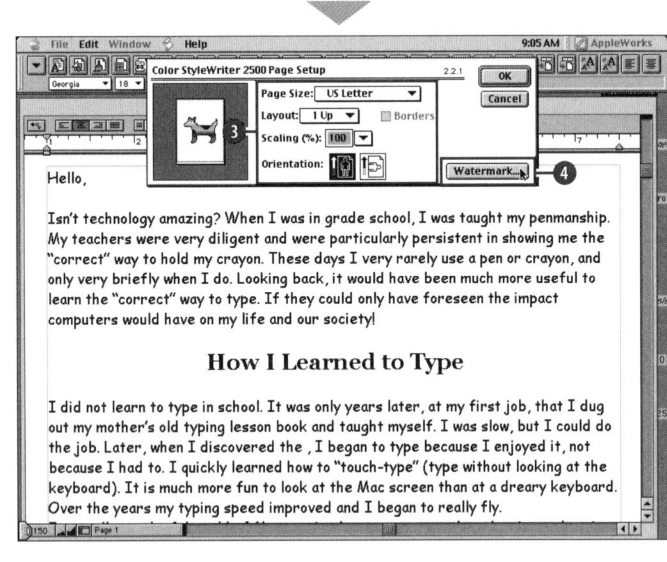

1. *Pull down the File menu.*
2. *Choose Page Setup.*
3. *Choose your Page Setup options.*
4. *Optional: Click Watermark, if available.*

CROSS-REFERENCE

Instructions on how to change page margins are offered in "Formatting with Sizes and Styles" in Chapter 5.

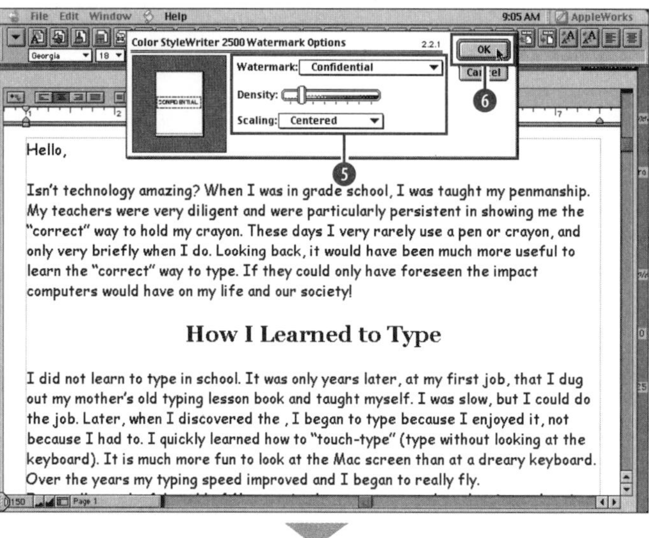

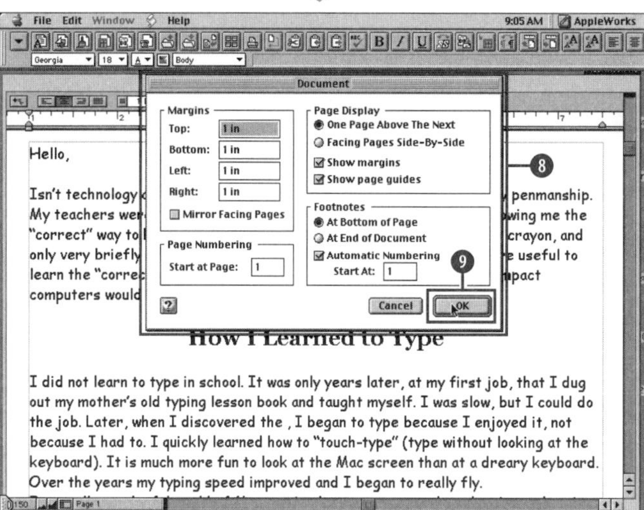

5. *Optional: Set your Watermark options.*
6. *Click OK when finished.*
7. *Choose Document from the Format menu.*
8. *Optional: Set your margins, page numbering, page display, and footnote options.*
9. *Click OK to save your changes.*

color in your document but printing to a single color printer? If so, you may want to change your colors to black (or gray) to ensure they print out as crisp and clear as possible.

TAKE NOTE

WATERMARKING A DOCUMENT

Some printers offer the option to *watermark* a document, meaning it will print a special message in light gray on your page. For example, you can place the word Draft or Confidential centered at the top of the page, aligned at the top left margin, or stretched to fit across the top of your page. If the watermark option is available for your printer, you'll most likely find it in the Page Setup window.

SETTING UP IN OTHER APPLICATIONS

Some applications and utilities may refer to Page Setup as Document Setup, while others may offer various setup options in different places within the application. If in doubt, check your Help menu for setup assistance.

SHORTCUT

Use the Tab key to move from field to field in the Page Setup window (and other similar windows).

Setting Printing Options

With the printer and page setup, you're ready to execute the Print command. As soon as you choose Print, a new window pops up with a whole bunch of new printing options. Are you surprised? After all, you need to tell your iMac and your printer *how* you want your page or document printed.

Like the Page Setup window, the Printing Options window varies based on the printer and the printer drivers you've installed and selected. Also like Page Setup, many of the options are the same, regardless of which printer you use.

Your first option is usually the number of copies to print (the default is 1). Increase this number as appropriate, but I don't recommend you print too many at once until you've printed at least one as a test.

Another option is page range, which is used for those documents having more than one page. The default is all pages, but you can choose to print only the first page or only pages 4-14 (enter 4 in the From: box and 14 in the To: box). Some printing options provide a line to enter a range such as "4-14" or a noncontiguous range such as "4, 11, 14." You also might have the option to print all odd or even pages, or all left or right pages (when your document is set up like a book).

The Quality option also could be called a Speed option. Low quality (such as Draft or Econofast) is generally much faster than medium quality (such as Normal). When you want your document to look its best, choose Best quality.

Set the Paper Type option for the best possible image. Paper type is important in printers, because different kinds of paper absorb ink (or toner) in different ways.

Some sort of Collate option is generally available. You may have the choice to print Back to Front (so your

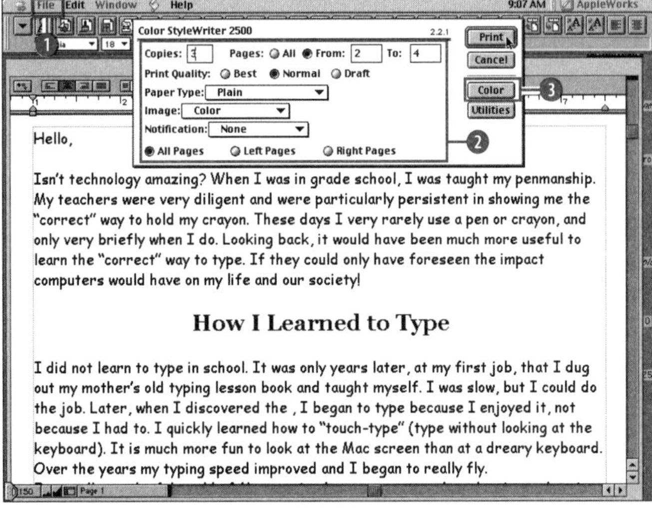

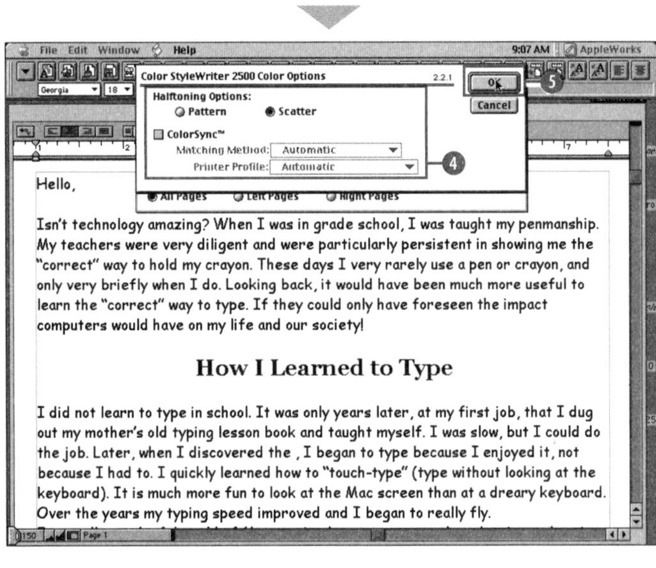

1. *Choose Print from the File menu.*
2. *Set your printing options.*
3. *Optional: Click Color, if available.*
4. *Set your color printing options.*
5. *Click OK to save your changes.*

CROSS-REFERENCE

See "Setting Your Preferences" in Chapter 2 for details on how to set options of this type.

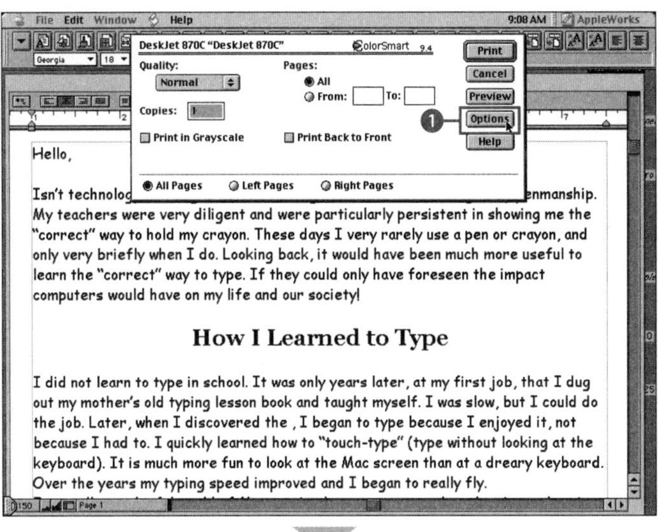

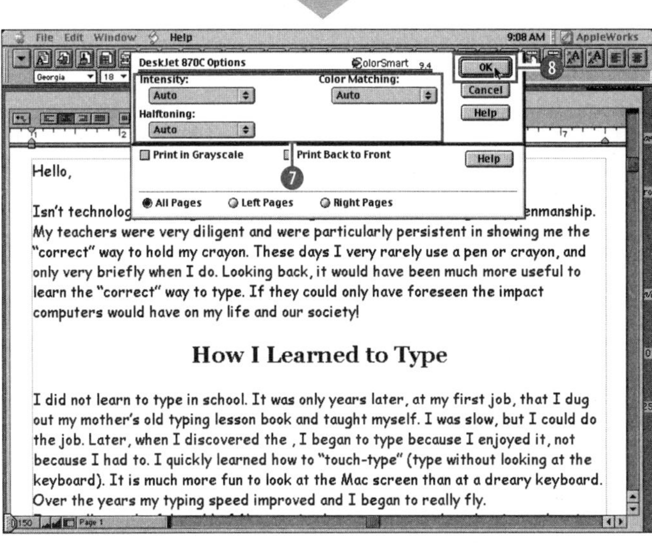

- *Notice the different printing options available for another printer.*

6. *Click Options.*
7. *Set your printing options.*
8. *Click OK to save your changes.*

printed document is in the correct order right out of the printer) or just a check box for Collated copies.

Additional settings like intensity (darkness of ink or toner), color matching, and halftoning (for photographs or illustrations with shading) also may be available under an Options or Graphics button.

TAKE NOTE

PRINTING COLOR DOCUMENTS IN GRAYSCALE

To preserve ink or prepare a printed document for reproduction, color printers usually offer the option to print in color, grayscale, or black-and-white. A separate Color button may lead to another set of color-only options, too.

DESIGNATING A PAPER TRAY

Many printers allow for both tray feed (the tray is where you store the paper in the printer) and manual feed (usually a special slot above the tray). If you want to manually feed your paper (a good idea for odd paper sizes, envelopes, or heavier stock), select the Manual option.

SHORTCUT

If you find yourself setting the same options each time you print, save them as the default settings.

Previewing a Page

If you're like me, you want to know how your page is going to print *before* it actually prints. Who wants to waste good paper and ink or toner on a mistake? On most printers, it is possible to preview your page before it prints, and I heartily recommend it.

To preview a page, just click the Preview button in the print options window (the window you get right after you choose Print from the File menu). If you don't have a Preview button, you may have a Print Preview command on the File menu instead (AppleWorks does not).

Once you choose Print Preview, your iMac processes the information in your file and then displays it onscreen for you. The onscreen image looks nearly identical to what your printer can print for you. Do note, however, that just because Print Preview displays something does not necessarily mean that your printer can print it. A black-and-white printer can't print in color, even though Print Preview may show color.

Buttons along the bottom of the Preview window help you navigate through the pages (if you have more than one) with the left and right arrows, or you can type in the number of a particular page. Use the zoom buttons (the mountain-like buttons) to fit more of the page in the window or get up close to it.

Carefully check over your document for possible problems. Make sure pages are breaking (continuing on to the next page) in the appropriate places, that the headers and footers show up correctly, and that the margins aren't too narrow or too wide.

When you're satisfied with the preview, you can click the Print button to print one copy of the page you're currently viewing in Preview mode. You may also prefer to click Cancel, choose Print again, select your options, and then print.

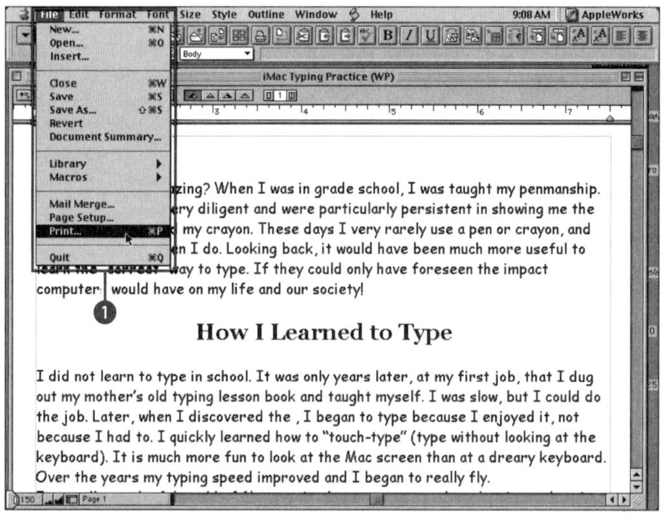

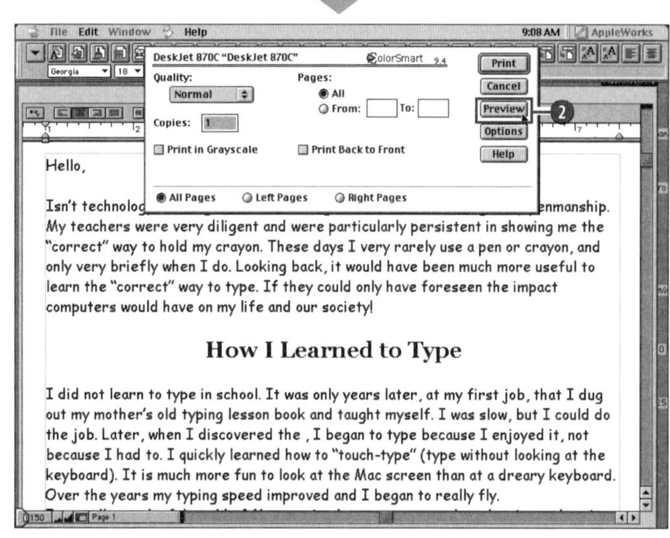

1. *Choose Print from the File menu.*

▶ *Alternatively, look under the File menu or Window menu for a Print Preview option.*

2. *Click Preview.*

CROSS-REFERENCE

Refer to Chapter 4 for details on how to select text and correct mistakes in a document.

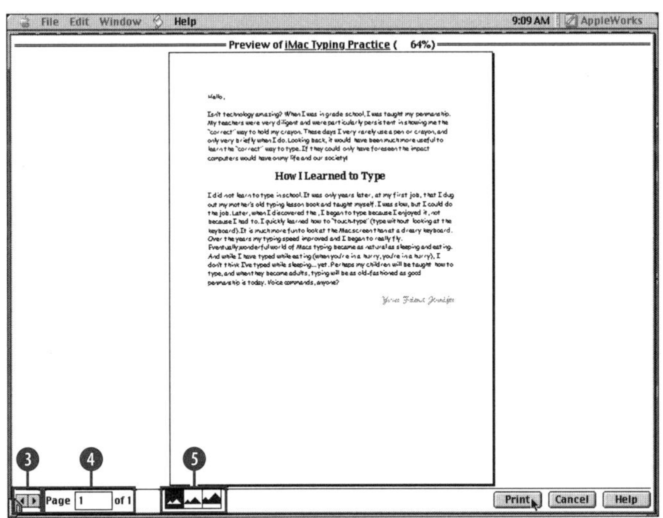

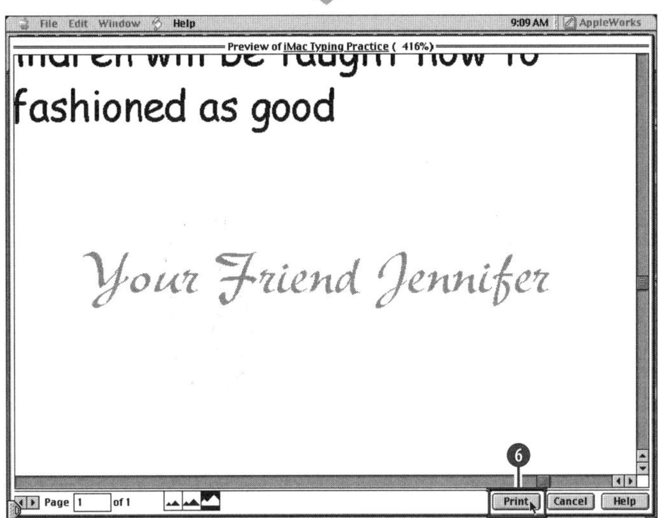

- *Note the preview of your page.*

3. *Click the arrow buttons to move a back or forward a page in Preview mode.*
4. *Type a number to go directly to that page.*
5. *Increase or decrease your view.*

- *Note your view changes.*

6. *Click Print to print this page.*
7. *Optional: Press Option while clicking Print to print all pages in the document.*

TAKE NOTE

CORRECTING MISTAKES

Print Preview is often the place where you'll notice mistakes in a document. Unfortunately, Preview isn't the place to correct them. If you try selecting anything in Print Preview, nothing will happen — the preview image will not be editable. To correct mistakes or make other changes, click Cancel in Preview mode to return to your document. Now you can make as many changes as you like. You can always preview a page again, just to be sure your changes didn't introduce new mistakes.

SIMULATING A PREVIEW

Not all printers and applications have the ability to preview a page. If this happens, try a small utility called Print2PICT by Baudouin Raoult. This program allows you to print a page to an image file or to the clipboard, giving you the ability to preview the page. Print2PICT is a shareware product (shareware means you're allowed to try it out for free, and then pay a reasonable fee if you decide to continue using it). This utility is available online at **http://thaigate.rd.nacsis.ac.jp/ftp/upload/krit/thaigfx/Graphics/Print2Pict.html**.

SHORTCUT

To print all pages from the Preview window, hold down the Option key when you click the Print button.

Printing a Page

At last! It's time to print a page! But don't despair if it seems like it has taken a long time to get to this point. In the future, you'll whiz through the setup and options — they'll take you no more than a few seconds, in most cases.

If you've opened the print options window on your screen, all you need to do is click the Print button. If you've already dismissed this window (or tried Print Preview first), just select Print from the File menu. You also can click the Print button on the toolbar (the button with the picture of a boxy-looking printer with a piece of paper sticking out of it). Better yet, use the keyboard shortcut: Command+P.

Immediately upon executing a print command, your iMac prepares the data for your printer and begins sending it. If you tried Print Preview, it looks very similar. A small box (or two) pops up to keep you informed of the process. If you want to cancel a print job while the data is being sent to the printer, click the Cancel button (if available) or press Command+. (period). Command+. works in a lot of other places on your iMac, too — try it out the next time you want to cancel or stop something. Note that you may need to press Command+. several times, and that it often takes some time for a response.

If your document is particularly long or graphic-intensive, it may take some time to send it to your printer. Watch your screen carefully at this point. If there is a problem sending your document to the printer, you are informed onscreen and may be given directions on what to do (i.e., load more paper if your printer is out).

Once your printer receives enough of the data to begin printing, you'll hear it whir and chug as it applies the image to the paper. Keep an eye on your printed pages as

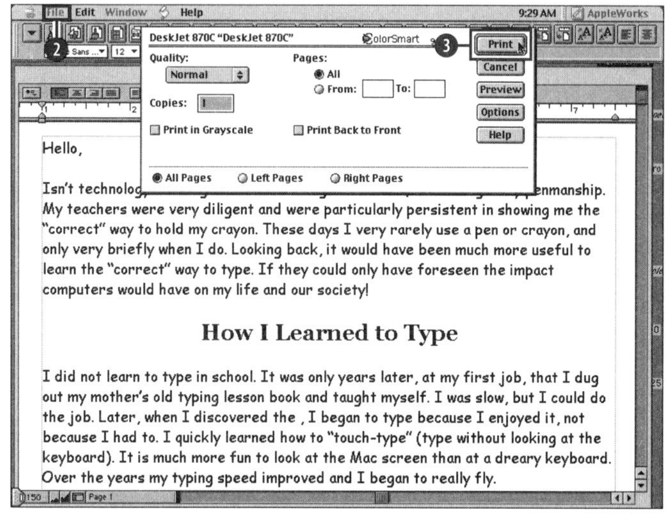

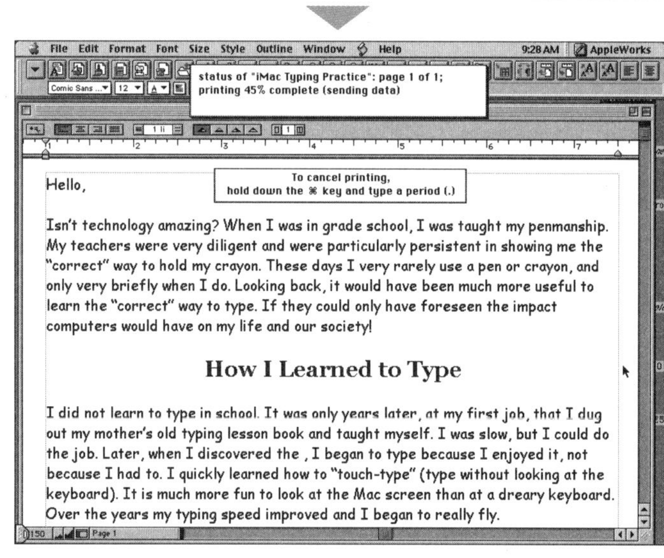

1. *Check your printer to be sure it has enough paper.*
2. *Choose Print from the File menu, if necessary.*
3. *Click the Print button (or press Return).*

- *Your iMac announces the status of the printing.*
- *Note you can press Command+. to cancel at any time.*

CROSS-REFERENCE

You can print checks with Quicken Deluxe, too! See Chapter 8 for more details on Quicken Deluxe.

Printing Envelopes

Most printers are capable of printing envelopes, though it can often be a challenge. Not only are envelopes odd sizes, but you have to be sure you're printing the addresses on the right side and in the right orientation. Most printers' instruction manuals will explain exactly how to insert the envelope, as well as make recommendations for setting up your page before you print. You can use AppleWorks for envelope printing — be sure to select the envelope type you're using in the paper size drop-down menu of the Page Setup window. Be prepared to test a few times before you get envelope printing just right, too!

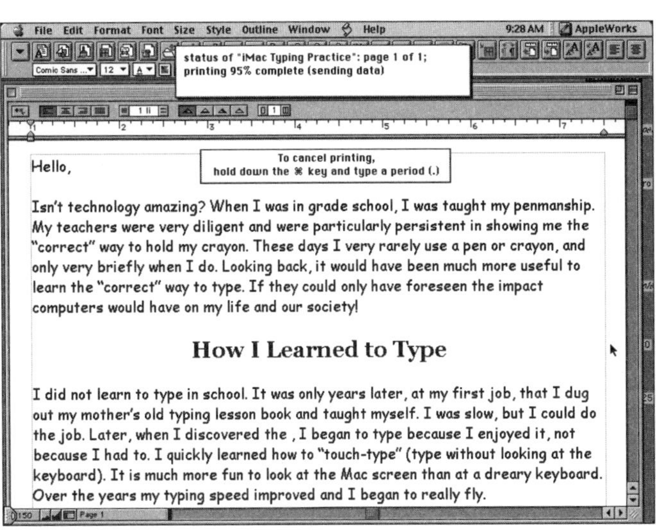

▶ *Your iMac continues to keep you up-to-date on the progress of the printing.*

4 *Check your printer for the finished copies.*

they come out of your printer, too. If you notice mistakes you didn't catch in Print Preview, cancel it with the trusty Command+. trick.

TAKE NOTE

PRINTING ON INKJET PRINTERS

Prints from an inkjet printer may need time for the ink to dry. Either leave the pages in the printer for a few minutes, or set them carefully aside to dry.

PRINTING ON BOTH SIDES OF THE PAPER

You can print on both sides of a piece of paper (often called *double-sided* printing). First print one side, let it dry (if using an inkjet), reinsert the same piece of paper into the paper tray, and print the other side. Refer to your printer documentation to verify the orientation of the paper in the tray to ensure it will print on the correct side of the paper.

SHORTCUT

To print one copy of a document in a hurry, just press Command+P and press the Return key.

Printing in the Background

Now that you're a printing pro, you probably have better things to do than watch your iMac send data to your printer. Frankly, it's as exciting as watching paint dry. And when you have a long document, who wants to tie up their iMac for an hour or more while it prints? Thankfully, the iMac comes with a feature known as *background printing* ,which lets you execute the Print command and then get on with things!

Background printing generally comes enabled on the iMac, though it may differ from printer to printer. To verify that you have background printing turned on, open the Chooser (remember, it is under the Apple menu) and select your printer icon on the left. Now look on the right side for the Background Printing radio buttons. If the option is off, I recommend you turn it on. If you can't find the Background Printing option for your printer in the Chooser, check the Print options dialog box (the window that pops up when you press Command+P). Look for a Background Printing button or menu, or a small icon of a document with a clock on it.

With background printing enabled, your iMac sends the data to a file on your hard drive, which is then sent on to your printer as needed. This releases your application and lets you continue working, if you like. Your iMac may work a bit slower during background printing, but it seems like a small price to pay for such convenience.

Not all printers support background printing, while others require certain setup steps to activate it. Check your printer's documentation for details.

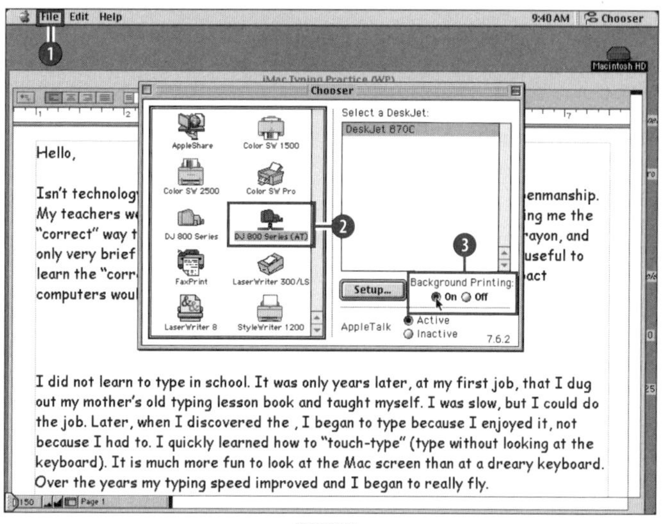

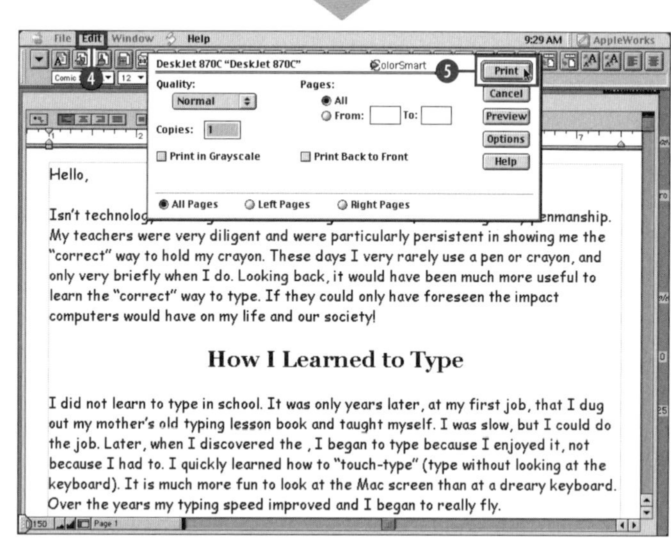

1. *Choose the Chooser from the Apple menu.*
2. *Select your printer icon.*
3. *Enable Background Printing.*
4. *Choose Print from the File menu (or press Command+P).*
5. *Click Print (or press Return).*

CROSS-REFERENCE

Read "Moving Between Applications" in Chapter 8 to learn how to move to another application during background printing.

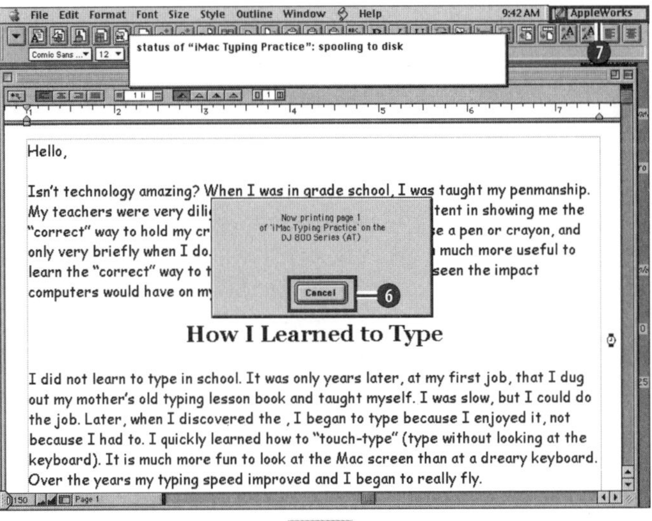

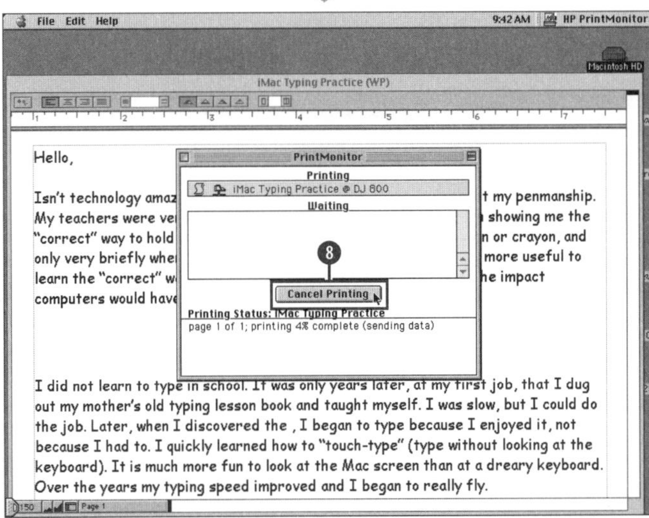

- *Your iMac announces the status of the printing.*
- ❻ *Click Cancel if you wish to abort.*
- ❼ *Optional: Pull down the Applications menu to look for Print Monitor, if available.*
- *PrintMonitor keeps you up-to-date on the progress of your print job.*
- ❽ *Click Cancel Printing if you wish to abort.*
- ❾ *Return to work while your document prints.*

TAKE NOTE

MONITORING BACKGROUND PRINTING

With background printing, you don't get the progress boxes that keep you up-to-date on the status of your document. If you'd like to monitor your printing anyway, you can usually do so in one of two ways. First, go to your Application menu in the upper-right corner and look for something called PrintMonitor. If you find it, open it to get a list of the files queued for printing and their status. Alternatively, you can check on your Desktop for an icon with the same name as your printer. Double-click it to get the same information as given in the PrintMonitor. These are also the places to go when you need to cancel a background print job. Select the print job you want to cancel and then click the Cancel button or the small Trash icon.

DOING STUFF DURING BACKGROUND PRINTING

You can do pretty much anything while a document is printing in the background. You can even send another document to the printer — it is automatically queued to print. The only thing you want to avoid is selecting a different printer in the Chooser during background printing. This can cause an error and you may need to send your document to the printer again.

SHORTCUT

Click the printer icon in the Control Strip (the strip of icons at the bottom of your screen) to quickly select and change printers.

Printing from the Desktop

Remember that icon of your printer on the Desktop? You can do a lot more with it than just monitor a background print job. You can print files with it, schedule print jobs, start and stop printing, and more!

To print with your desktop printer icon, locate the saved file you want to print (you did save your file, right?), click and drag it over to the printer icon, and release it when the printer icon becomes darker. Some folks would say you *dragged and dropped* the file onto the printer icon. The print options dialog box pops up for you to make selections and then to click the Print button, just as if you'd selected Print from within your application. Everything else works the same as regular printing.

Desktop printing works well for those who have more than one printer connected to their iMac or on a network. Instead of going to the Chooser or Control Strip to change to a new printer, you just drag the file over the printer icon you wish to print to. If you don't see your printer icons on the Desktop, go to the Chooser and select them first. This should create a printer icon and place it on the Desktop for you.

To schedule a print job, first send the job to the printer through an application or with the desktop printer icon. Now, double-click the printer icon to open the monitoring window and see the list of current print jobs. Select the job and click the clock button. The pause button temporarily stops a particularly document from printing, the arrow button starts a document printing again, and the trash can button cancels a print job. You also can reorder the print jobs in the queue if you want a particular job to print earlier or later. Just click and drag a job up or down the list, and then release the

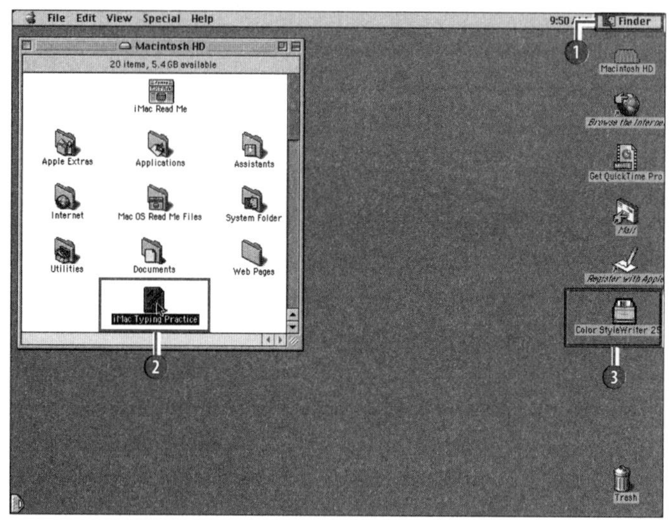

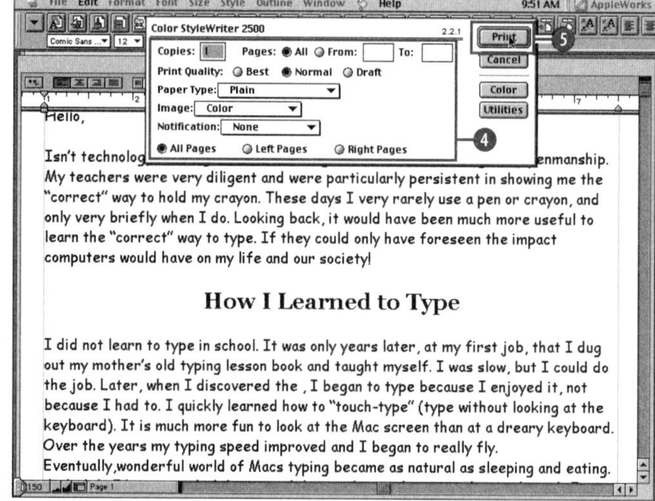

1. *Go to your Desktop (choose Finder on the Applications menu).*
2. *Locate the file you want to print.*
3. *Click and drag the file onto the printer icon on the Desktop.*

▶ *The application that created the file automatically opens for you.*

4. *Choose your print options.*
5. *Click Print.*
6. *Choose Finder from the Applications menu again.*

CROSS-REFERENCE

Learn how to organize your Desktop so you can find your desktop printer icons easily in Chapter 2.

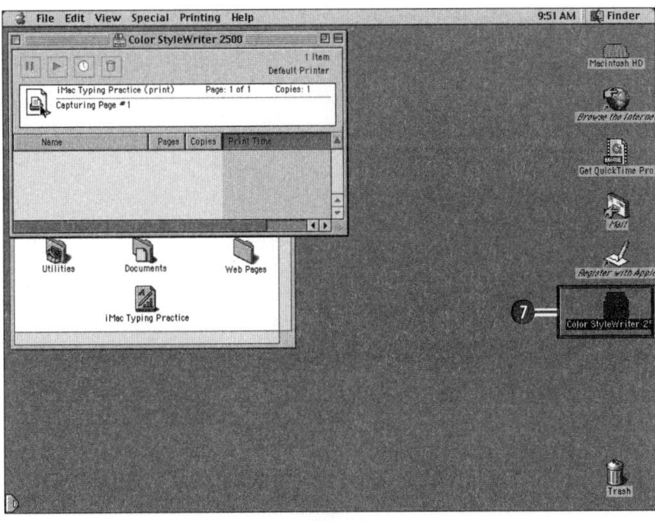

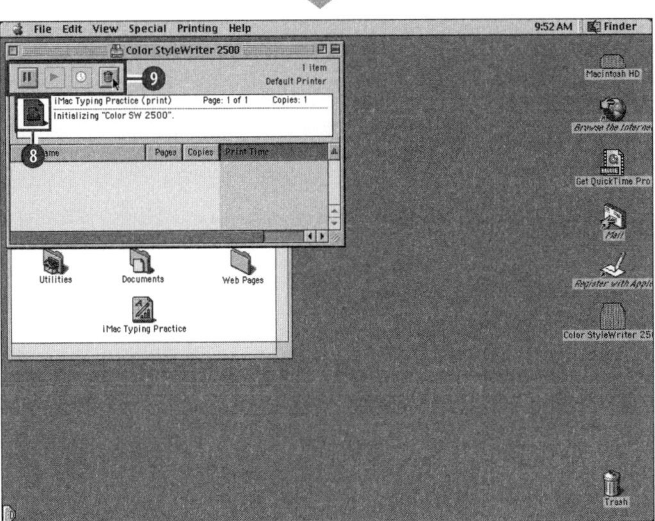

7 *Double-click the printer icon on the Desktop.*

▶ *The printer windows shows you the status of your print job.*

8 *Optional: Click the icon to select the document being printed.*

9 *Optional: Click one of the buttons to pause, schedule, or delete the print job.*

button, or use the clock button to set a print job to Urgent and move it to the top of the list.

To stop printing altogether, choose Stop Printing from the Printing menu. Choose Start Printing when you're ready to resume.

TAKE NOTE

REMOVING DESKTOP PRINTER ICONS

If you don't use the desktop printer icons much and don't have multiple printers, you might want to remove these icons from your desktop. It'll save you hard disk space and memory, too. To remove a printer icon, first pull down the Apple menu, select the Control Panels submenu, and then choose the Extensions Manager. Select the printer icon you want to remove (they should have Desktop Printing or Desktop Printer in their names), and then disable them. Now restart your iMac. When your Desktop reappears, you can throw away the disabled printer icons (those with an X on the icon).

RECOGNIZING ACTIVE PRINTER ICONS

Have you noticed that one of your printer icons has a thick border around it? This border indicates the default printer.

SHORTCUT

Click and drag a group of files to a desktop printer icon to queue each of them to print.

Personal Workbook

Q&A

1. Where do you find the Chooser?

2. Why is it necessary to align ink cartridges in an inkjet printer?

3. What is the difference between portrait and landscape view? How does this relate to page setup?

4. How do you tell your iMac that you want to print a range of pages in a document?

5. How do you print while previewing a page?

6. What is the keyboard shortcut for printing?

7. How do you enable background printing?

8. How do you schedule a print job for four hours from now?

ANSWERS: PAGE 317

Printing Documents

EXTRA PRACTICE

1. Using AppleWorks, create a one-page document, "The Top 10 Reasons Why I Love My iMac." Lay out and print the page in Landscape mode.
2. Reformat the document so that it occupies two pages, preview the page, make adjustments in the formatting until you're satisfied with the results, and then print the whole document from Preview mode.
3. Reformat the document again so that it occupies two pages in portrait mode. Preview the document, background print it, and immediately start working on Task 4.
4. Background print two copies of page two of the same document.

REAL-WORLD APPLICATIONS

✔ You've created a colorful one-page brochure that includes a photograph. You decide to use expensive glossy paper and print ten copies. Before printing, you make sure that your color inkjet printer has been set to print on glossy paper and that you have checked the document in Preview mode to be sure you won't waste that expensive paper when you start to print. Satisfied, you print one copy, examine the results (which are brilliant), and background print the other nine pages.

✔ While those nine pages are printing on your inkjet printer, you type a memo to the staff regarding the upcoming softball game. When you're done, you print 25 copies on your laser printer (which is also connected to your iMac).

Visual Quiz

What does this window do? How would you access it?

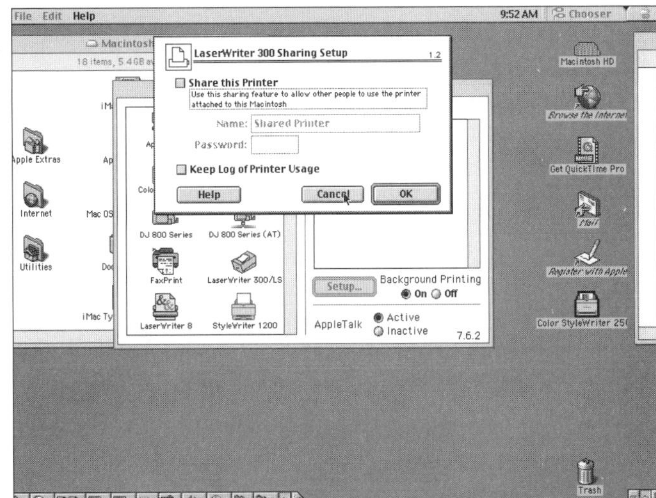

CHAPTER 7

MASTER THESE SKILLS

- Creating a Basic Database
- Adding Records
- Generating a List of Records
- Creating a Basic Spreadsheet
- Entering Data
- Adding a Formula

Using Databases and Spreadsheets

Spreadsheet and *database* are two words that can strike fear into the heart of typical computer user, and send some computing professionals into fits of ecstasy. Why the fear, and why the joy?

A database is an organized system for saving, searching, sorting, and arranging information — any information. Your Rolodex is a database, and so is your checkbook, your clothes closet, your accounts payable ledger, and that tray full of slides from your trip to Italy. As with anything you save, the information you store in a computer database must be carefully organized so that you can find what you want, when you want to find it.

"Who, in the State of Michigan, bought more than 2,000 units of our Model 32 Widget between April 1 and April 12, 1999? Of those purchasers, which were new clients, and when did we last pay them a sales call?" These questions are the bread and butter of corporate database users. Someone else may be keeping track of phone numbers, kissing techniques, and spending habits of every date they've ever gone out with so that when a phone number appears on their caller ID, they'll automatically get all the scoop.

Databases are one of the oldest applications available for computers, and they are still one of the most important. Although modern database programs make it simple to create a database, without careful thought about how the information will be used and how it might be used in the future, a beginner's database may create more frustration than joy. Think carefully about what information you'll need, create a place for everything, and be sure when you enter information in the database that everything is in its proper place.

Spreadsheets are a specialized kind of database, created for accountants and organized in the horizontal rows and vertical columns like those on an accountant's ledger paper. Spreadsheets excel at math. Once you've told the spreadsheet how you want things done, you can change one number and every subtotal and total will automatically be updated. This makes it simple to play "What if?" games when you need to project future results. Due to their highly visual row-and-column layout, many people find spreadsheets easier to use than database programs. While spreadsheets are fine for many simple kinds of databases, they do have their limitations. Learn how to use both, and use the right tool for the job.

Creating a Basic Database

By now, you know that AppleWorks does a pretty darn good job of word processing. But did you also know that it can create databases and spreadsheets, too? That's why they call it Apple*Works*, after all!

Begin by opening AppleWorks (if it is not open) and choose Database when you are prompted to create a new document. If AppleWorks is already open, just choose New from the file menu, or click the Database button on the toolbar (the one with little rolodex in front of a document).

Upon creating a new database, the Define Database Fields dialog box pops up on your screen. Here's where you define the *fields* (the kinds of information) in your database. Let's say you want to create a birthday database (with the birthdays of all your friends and family members). One field might be the first name of the birthday boy or girl. So you would type "First Name" in the Field Name box, and then click Create to add the field to the list. Create a "Last Name" field, too. It is always a good idea to separate first and last names so that you can properly sort the names later.

Continue creating the information fields you think are important for your birthday database, such as a Comments field for the sorts of gifts the birthday person prefers. Eventually, you will want to add a "Birthdate" field using a date format. The Field Type drop-down menu to the right of the Field Name box offers a date format, along with several other choices. Choose Date for a birthdate. When you want to add another text field, be sure you change the Field Type back to Text. (In AppleWorks, text is also the best Field Type for zip

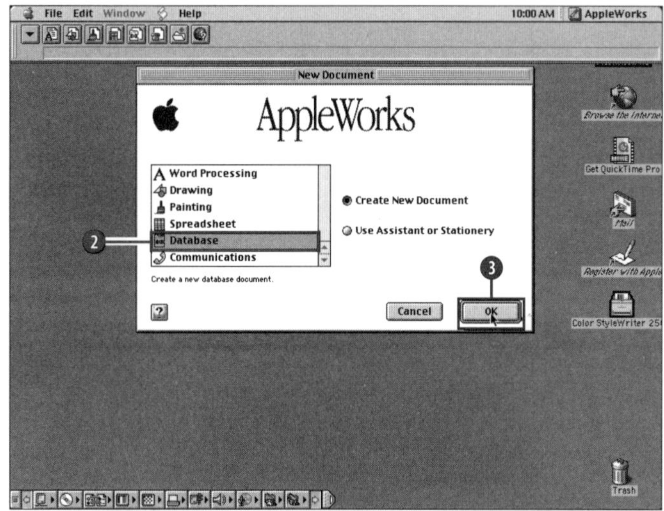

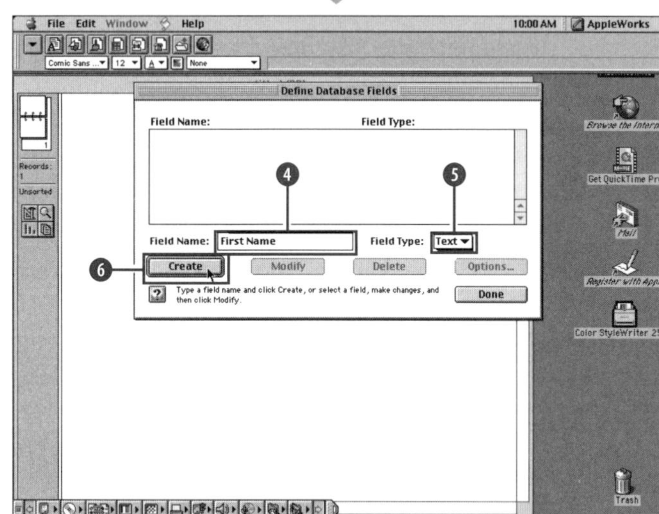

1. *Open AppleWorks (if it isn't already open).*
   - ▶ *Alternatively, choose New from the File menu (if AppleWorks is already open).*
2. *Select Database.*
3. *Click OK.*
4. *Type a field name.*
5. *Choose a type from the Field Type drop-down menu.*
6. *Click Create.*

CROSS-REFERENCE

Refer to the first task in Chapter 4 to learn how to open AppleWorks if it is not currently open.

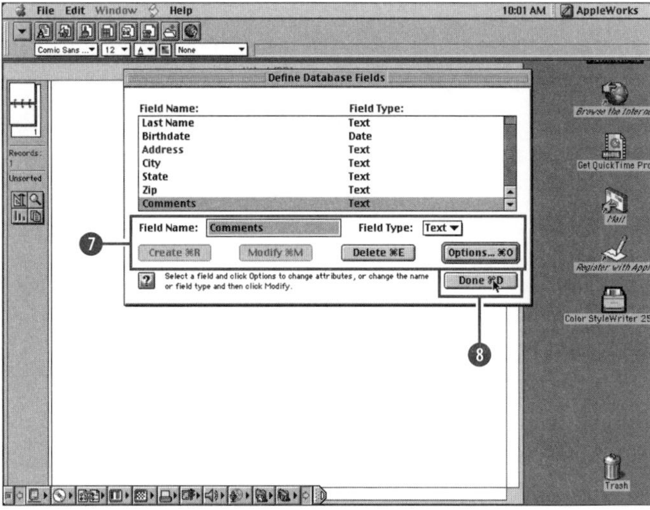

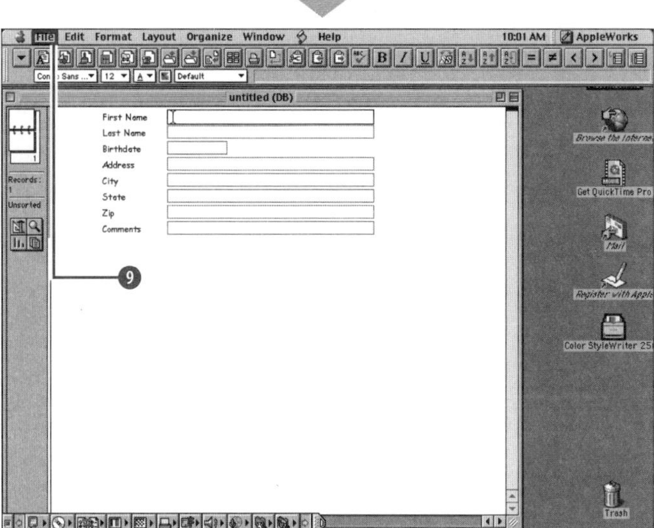

- AppleWorks adds your new field to the list above.

7. *Continue adding fields.*
8. *Click Done when you are finished.*

- AppleWorks creates and displays your new database.

9. *Choose Save from the File menu before you continue.*

codes, telephone numbers, part numbers and the like. If you input zip codes using a Number field format, the program will eliminate the leading zero from zip codes such as 07601.) Click Done when you've created all the fields you need for your database. Before you do anything else, choose Save from the File menu (or press Command+S) and give your database a name.

TAKE NOTE

MODIFYING A FIELD

If you make a mistake while creating your fields, don't worry — you're not stuck with it. Begin by selecting the field you want to change in the list. Now type a new name in the Field Name box and select a different Field Type, if necessary. Then, click Modify.

APPLYING FIELD OPTIONS

The Options button in the Define Database Fields dialog box allows you to set preferences for individual fields. The Cannot Be Empty option means that there must always be data in this field — this is a good option for the birthdate field. The Must Be Unique field means that data entered cannot match data that already exists in the database. The Default Text field lets you designate text to be automatically inserted in your database.

SHORTCUT

Press Shift+Command+D to add, delete, or change fields after you've initially created them.

Adding Records

A database is useless without data. The next step is to enter data (type your information) into the database. Each set of data in a database is known as a *record*, and your database can have thousands of records. If you think of an old-fashioned card file, the information you write on the card is the data and each card is a record.

To begin entering data, click in the first field at the top of the database window. The outline of the field box changes from gray to black, and the insertion point appears in the box and begins flashing. If you don't see the field box or the insertion point, press the Tab key once. With the insertion point in the top field (the First Name field), type your information. To move to the next field, you could move your pointer and click in the box, but it is easier to press the Tab key. Continue through each field, adding information to each one as you go. If you don't have information for a field, it is fine to skip it so long as you didn't enable the Cannot Be Empty option.

Now that you've created your first record, how do you make more records? Choose New Record from the Edit menu, press Command+R, or click the Create Record button on the toolbar (a form with an arrow beside it). This inserts a new record below the first record (or the record you're currently on). You can type information into the new record fields in the same way you did with the first record.

You can navigate through your records with the scrollbars, but that gets tedious as your database grows. Use the miniature picture of a Rolodex on the left side of the database window to move between records. You can even go directly to a specific record by clicking the

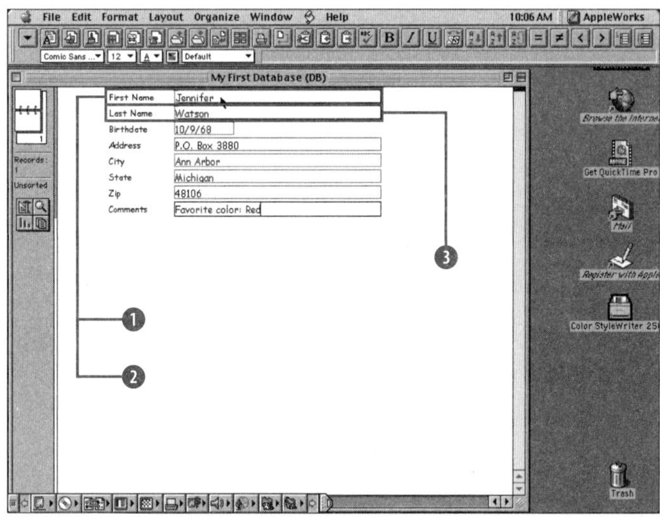

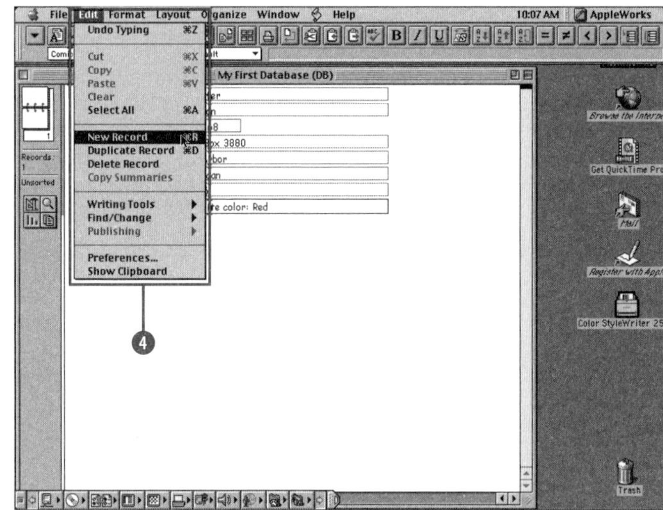

1. *Click in the first field.*
2. *Type your data.*
3. *Press Tab to move to the next field.*
4. *Choose New Record from the Edit menu.*

CROSS-REFERENCE

Refer to Chapter 4 for details on how to select text (which also applies to information in a database).

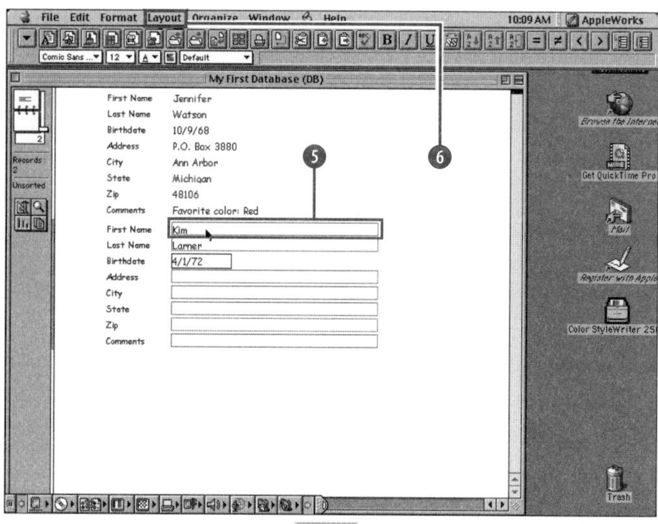

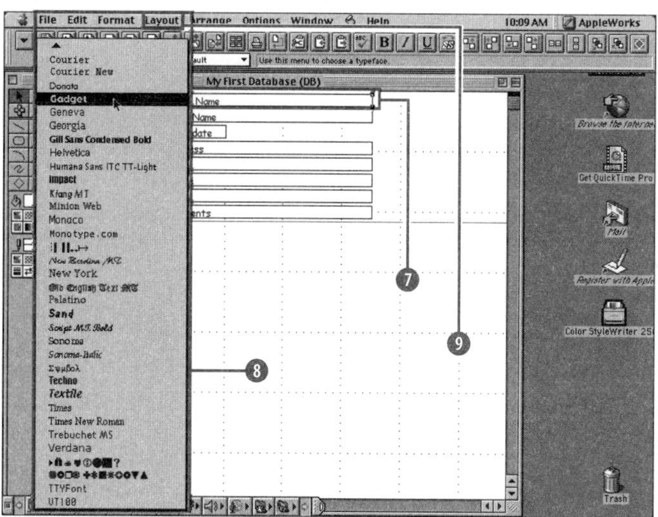

- A new record is inserted below your first record.
- ⑤ Type your data.
- ⑥ Choose Layout from the Layout menu.
- ⑦ Select a field.
- ⑧ Use the menus on the toolbar to format your field.
- ⑨ Choose Browse from the Layout menu to resume entering data.

number below the Rolodex, typing in a new number, and pressing the Return key. You also can press Command+G to move to a particular record.

Save your database often! Data is precious and you may not miss it until it's gone.

TAKE NOTE

FORMATTING YOUR FIELDS

AppleWorks offers font, style, size, and alignment control over the information in your database. To format the data in only one record, just select the text and change it as you would in a word processor. To change the format of a field so the field information in all records displays in the same way, choose Layout from the Layout menu (or press Shift+Command+L), select the field boxes you want to format, and choose your format from the Format menu or the toolbar. You also can change the format of the titles for each field by selecting the titles and then formatting them. When you are finished, choose Browse from the Layout menu (or click Shift+Command+B) to enter more data.

SHORTCUT

Quickly create a new record by pressing Command+D to duplicate a similar record. Now, change anything in the new record that differs from the original.

Generating a List of Records

One of the benefits of a database is the ability to sort and list the information within it. You could have entered similar information into a word processing document, but you couldn't reorder it by last name without actually moving the text around in your document. Yuck!

To view your data in list form, select List from the Layout menu (or press Shift+Command+L). AppleWorks displays your data in neat little columns and rows. If a column is too narrow or too wide, just click the line between two of the column headings and click and drag it to a new position. This works for row depth, as well. You also can rearrange the columns by clicking and dragging the column headings to the left or the right.

To sort your data, choose Sort Records from the Organize menu (or press Command+J). Select the field you want to sort by in the list on the left (such as Last Name or Birthdate) and click the Move button. The field name appears in the list on the right, indicating that the data will be sorted alphabetically or numerically, based on the information in that field. If you have a lot of names in your database with the same last name or same birthdate, you may want to add a second field to the Sort Order list for additional sorting. For example, if your sort order is by Last Name first and First Name second, Jennifer Watson would appear before Kippi Watson. You also can change the sort order from ascending (A to Z) to descending (Z to A), if you wish. If you add a field to the Sort Order window and later decide not to sort on that field, just select it from the Sort Order list and click Move again. You can sort data in either Browse or List layout modes.

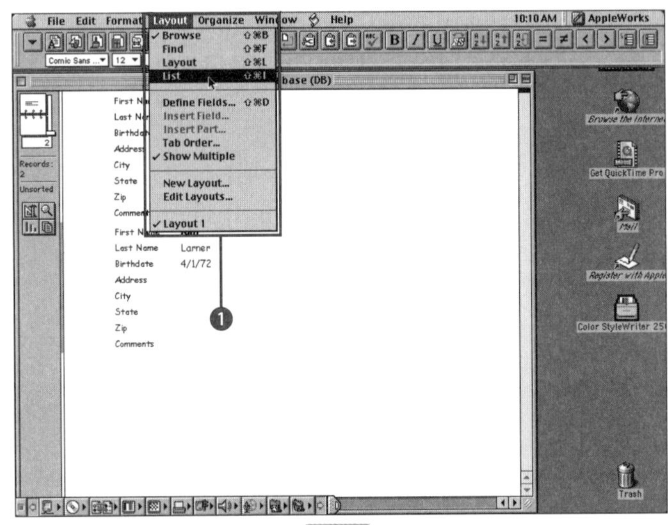

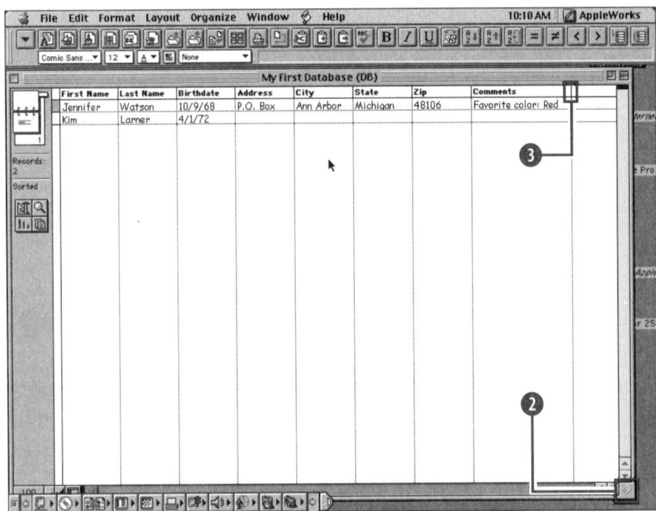

1 *Choose List from the Layout menu (or press Shift+Command+L).*

▶ *AppleWorks displays your database records in list format.*

2 *Expand your window if you cannot see enough of the data.*

3 *Alternatively, expand your columns by clicking and dragging the vertical line between the column headings.*

CROSS-REFERENCE

Refer to Chapter 6 for more information on printing from your iMac.

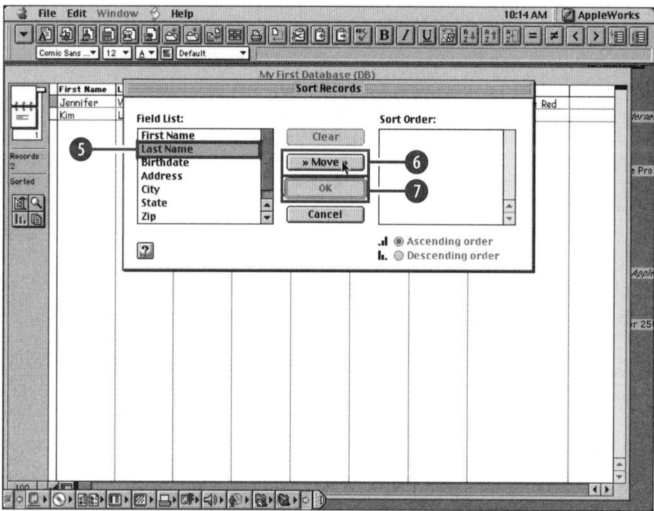

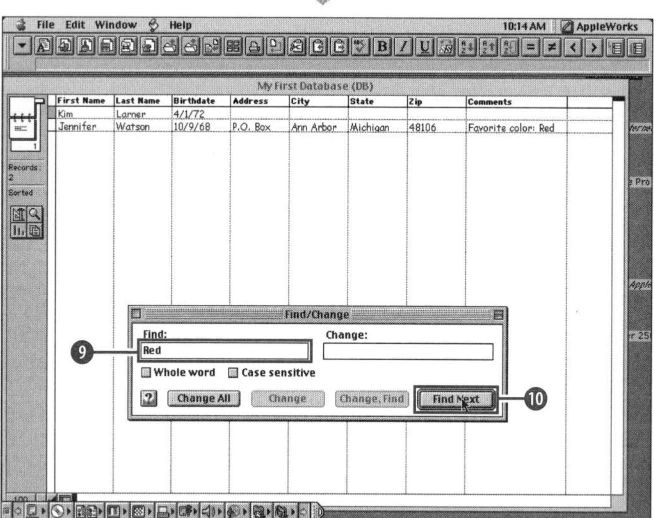

4 *Choose Sort Records from the Organize menu (or press Command+J).*

5 *Select a field name on the left.*

6 *Click the Move button.*

7 *Click OK (or press Return).*

▶ *AppleWorks sorts your database as you requested.*

8 *Press Command+F.*

9 *Type a search word.*

10 *Click Find Next.*

TAKE NOTE

SEARCHING YOUR DATA

Choose Find on the Layout menu (or press Shift+Command+F) to bring up what looks like a blank database record. Type the data you want to search for in the appropriate field. For example, you would type a last name in the Last Name field and a birthdate in the Birthdate field. You can type information into more than one field. Now, press Return or click the Find button on the left side of the window. AppleWorks then displays all the matching records in the window. If your search returns too many records, choose Find again, provide more specific information in a field, and then choose to search only the Visible records (click the Visible radio button on the left). If you want to see all the records again after a search, choose Show All Records on the Organize menu.

PRINTING YOUR DATA

First prepare your data for printing by searching for the information you want to print and then changing to Browse or List layout view. You can now print as you normally would.

SHORTCUT

Move backward through fields by holding down the Shift key as you press the Tab key.

Creating a Basic Spreadsheet

Where databases are good with data, spreadsheets are good with numbers. This is a good thing, because I'm not so good with numbers. Even if you are, spreadsheets can be a huge help when it comes to storing and calculating numbers.

If AppleWorks is still open on your iMac, choose New from the file menu or click the Spreadsheet button on the toolbar (the one with the little ledger in front of a document). If AppleWorks is not running, open it and choose Spreadsheet when you are prompted to create a new document. A new spreadsheet that looks like a document with grid lines then appears on your screen.

Spreadsheets are organized along a grid. Columns with alphabetic headings appear across the top and rows with numeric headings appear down the left side. The columns and rows form small boxes, called *cells,* that are identified by the column letter and row number. For example, the box in column A and row 1 shows cell A1.

To type data into a spreadsheet, begin by selecting a cell. You don't have to start with cell A1 if you don't want to. Now, type your data. Note that the information goes into the entry bar at the top of the spreadsheet, rather than directly into the cell. When you've typed all the information for a particular cell, press the Enter key or just select another cell to complete the entry.

When a cell contains a lot of information, the spreadsheet displays it in the cell itself, as well as spread over one or more adjacent cells (assuming that the adjacent cells are empty). Yet, if you select an adjacent cell with run-over information, the entry bar at the top of the spreadsheet is blank, indicating that the cell is empty. When information runs over into other cells like this,

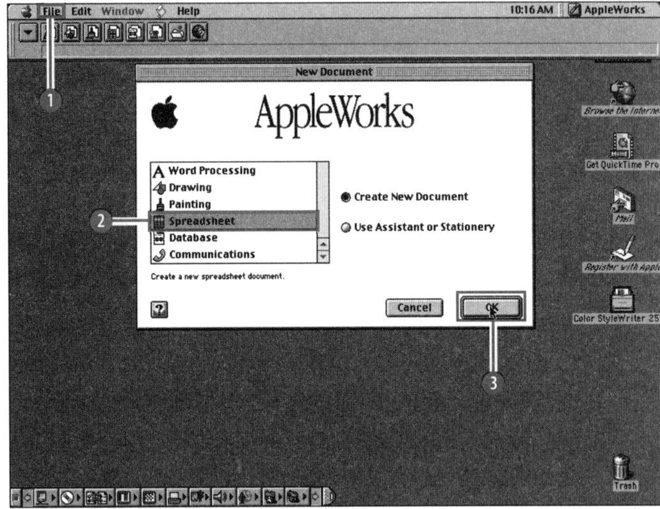

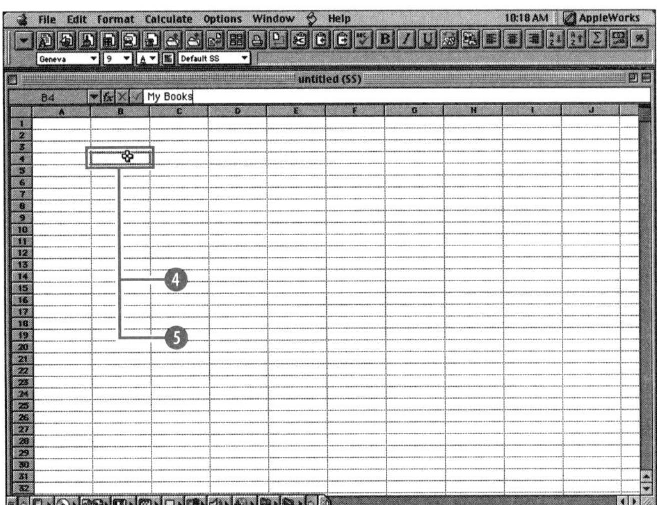

1. *Choose New from the File menu (if AppleWorks is already open).*
▶ *Alternatively, open AppleWorks (if it isn't already open).*
2. *Select Spreadsheet.*
3. *Click OK.*
4. *Select any cell in the spreadsheet.*
5. *Type your data.*
▶ *Your data appears in the entry bar above the spreadsheet grid.*

CROSS-REFERENCE

Refer to Chapter 5 for information on how to format text.

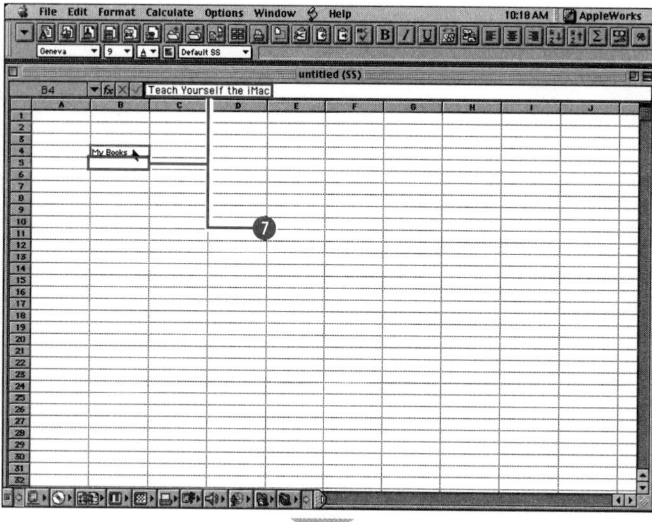

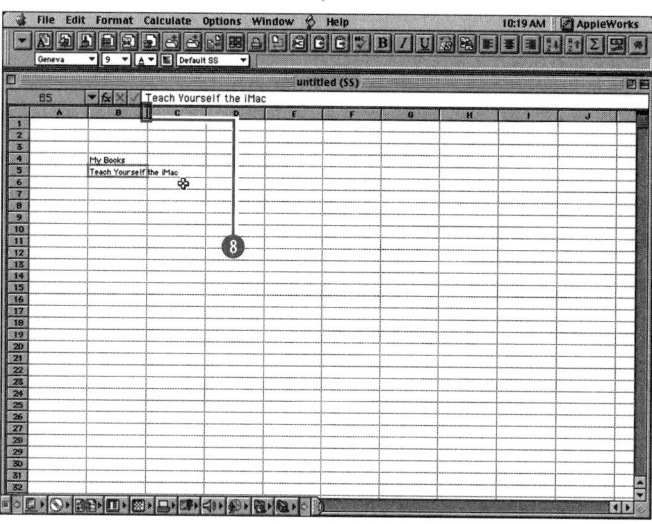

6. Press Enter.

▶ Your data appears in the selected cell.

7. Select another cell and type a long string of data.

▶ Your data appears in the selected cell and runs over into one or more adjacent cells.

8. Optional: Increase the width of the column by clicking and dragging the line between the column headings.

trace the stream of data back toward the left of the spreadsheet to find the actual cell. You also might want to increase the width of the column to accommodate the cell's data. Just move the mouse pointer to the vertical line between the two column headings, and then click and drag to the left or right to resize the column. This technique also works for increasing the row height.

TAKE NOTE

FORMATTING CELLS

Like word processing documents and databases, you can format information in spreadsheets to your liking. Just click once in a cell to select it and choose fonts, sizes, styles, colors, and alignments from the Format menu. If you increase the text size, you also might need to increase the width of the column and row.

SELECTING CELLS

Spreadsheets make it particularly easy to select groups of cells. Just click a cell and then drag the mouse pointer to another cell; everything in between is then selected. If you look closely, you'll see that all the cells you selected are highlighted, with the exception of the first cell; it still has the selection border around it. Don't worry; the first cell is still highlighted.

SHORTCUT

Press the Tab key to move to the next cell. Press Shift+Tab to move to the previous cell.

Entering Numbers

By now you're probably shouting, "Show me the numbers!" After all, what is a spreadsheet without numbers? Actually, you could create a spreadsheet with text (and even graphics) and absolutely no numbers if you wanted. I'm sure that someone, somewhere, has a use for such a beast. Let's turn our attention to inputting numbers into a spreadsheet, however.

First, you should know that numbers can be typed into a cell in the same way as any other information. Just select the cell, type in your number, and press Enter. You can type whole numbers, decimals, dollar amounts, percentages — you name it, you can probably enter it. Note that unlike text, large numbers won't run over into an adjacent cell when they are too long. Instead, they display a series of ####### symbols, meaning the column width is too small to show the result. It might even display a funky exponential equation. If this happens, widen the column.

You may notice as you enter numbers that a particular number format changes after you enter them. For example, if you type in $386.10, the dollar sign disappears and the number is abbreviated to 386.1. To tell AppleWorks to display your number in the appropriate format, select the cell in question and choose Number on the Format menu. Select the number style from the choices on the left (choose Currency for dollar amounts). If you aren't working with dollar amounts, but you still want your cell to display a number with one or two or more places after the decimal point, change the Precision number to correspond to the number of decimal places. Conversely, if you are working with dollar amounts and want the spreadsheet to display the

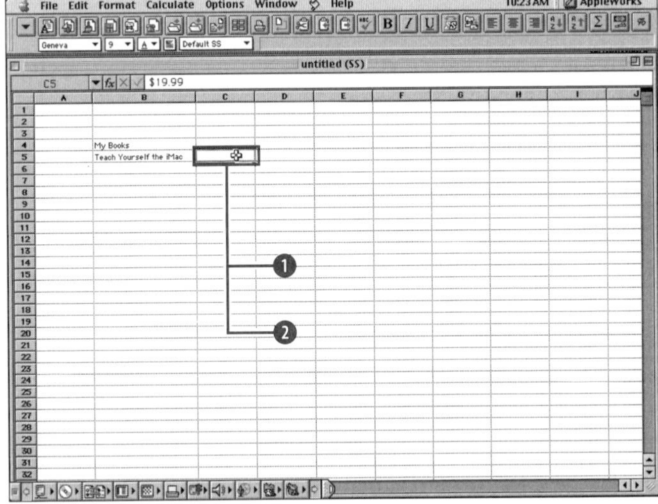

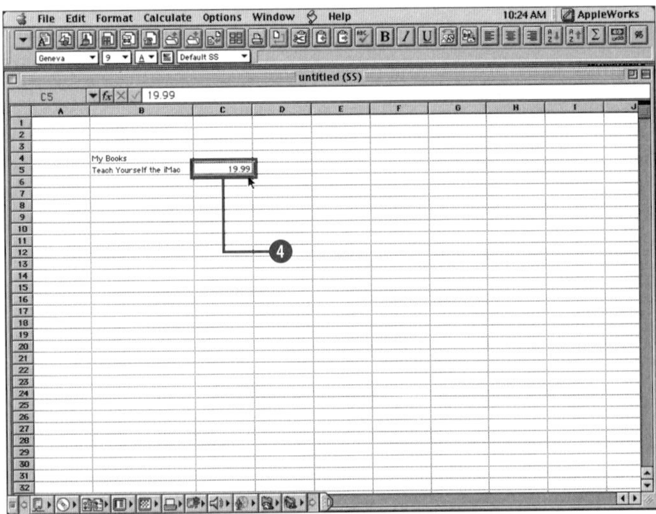

1. *Select a cell.*
2. *Type a dollar amount into it.*
▶ *Your number appears in the entry bar at the top of the spreadsheet.*
3. *Press Enter.*
▶ *Your number appears in the cell without the dollar sign.*
4. *Double-click the cell.*

CROSS-REFERENCE

Refer to Chapter 4 for details on how to copy and paste, which works for spreadsheet cells, too.

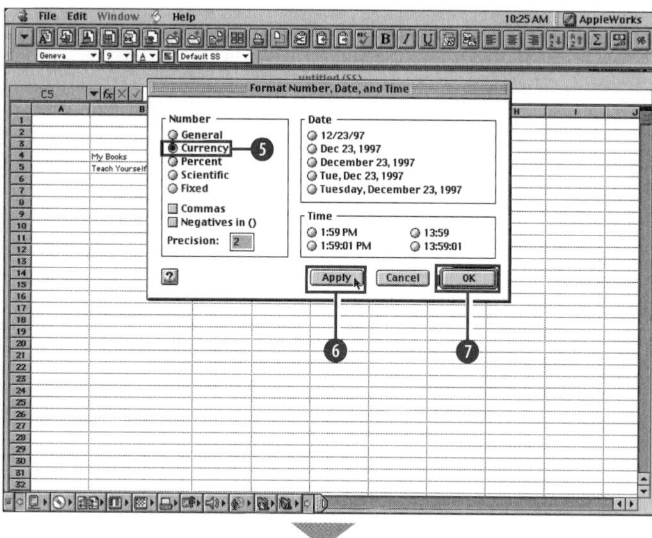

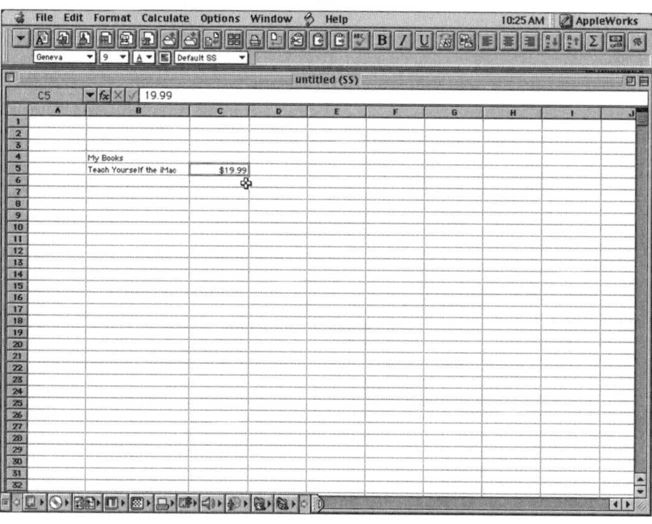

5 *Select Currency.*

6 *Click Apply.*

7 *Press Return (or click OK).*

▶ *Your number appears in the cell with the dollar sign.*

amounts in whole dollars, set the Precision amount to 0 (zero). Date and time formats for numbers also can be set; these formats are self-explanatory.

If you want to format a group of cells, select the rows or columns and press Shift+Command+N. Choose the appropriate formats, click OK, and all the selected will then cells become formatted.

TAKE NOTE

CHARTING THE NUMBERS

AppleWorks lets you chart groups of numbers in a variety of ways. Just select a group of cells, choose Make Chart on the Options menu, and select a chart format. AppleWorks then creates the chart for you and pastes it into your spreadsheet. Click and drag the chart to a new location in your spreadsheet, if desired. You can fine-tune the look of your chart by double-clicking the chart and the chart key.

CHANGING THE BORDERS

While the gridlines in the spreadsheet are good for most work, you may prefer to hide them. Choose Display from the Options menu and deselect the Cell grid check box. You also can remove the column and row headings, if you wish. Note that removing cell grids and headings is an all-or-nothing proposition: you cannot remove grids for only a group of cells.

SHORTCUT

You can quickly edit the number format of a cell by double-clicking the cell contents.

Adding a Formula

Spreadsheets don't just store numbers, they crunch numbers, too! You can manipulate, speculate, and calculate to your heart's content. AppleWorks provides a bunch of predefined formulas for number functions, and you also can create your own.

To use a predefined formula, begin by selecting the cell in which you would like to display the results. Now, choose Paste Function on the Edit menu, select SUM(number1, number2,) from the list, and click OK. AppleWorks inserts the SUM formula (which performs a simple addition) into the entry bar at the top of the spreadsheet. Select and delete everything in between the parentheses in your formula — these are the formula *arguments*, and you need to specify them for your particular purposes. Now, with the insertion point between the two parentheses in your formula, click the first cell in which you want to add to your formula. Notice that AppleWorks adds the cell name B18 to your formula. Continue clicking each cell in which you want to add to your formula. (Alternatively, you can click and drag a range of cells.) If you make a mistake, just press the red X to the left of the entry bar to undo it. When you're finished, press the Enter key. Presto! AppleWorks adds the amounts in the cells you selected, and then displays the total in the formula cell.

While AppleWorks has a lot of ready-made formulas, it can't anticipate everything you might need to do. For example, if you are selling a product, you might want to create a formula to subtract the discount from the list price and then calculate the tax. To do this, type an equal (=) sign in the entry bar. The equal sign lets AppleWorks know that what follows is a formula. Now,

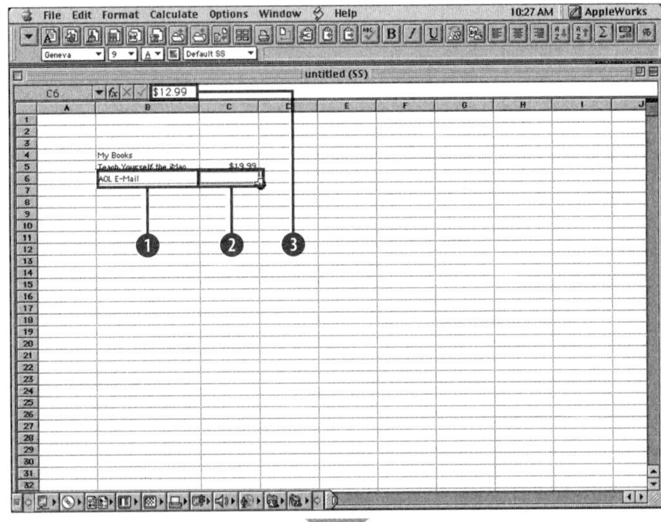

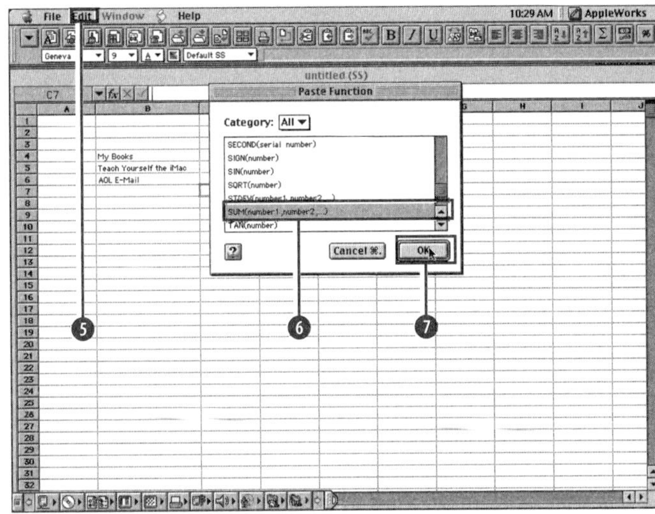

1. *Select another cell and type your data.*
2. *Press Tab.*
3. *Type a dollar amount.*
4. *Press Return.*
5. *Choose Paste Function on the Edit menu.*
6. *Select SUM (number1,number2) from the list.*
7. *Click OK.*

CROSS-REFERENCE

Learn more about Quicken Deluxe, which performs many other financial functions, in Chapter 8.

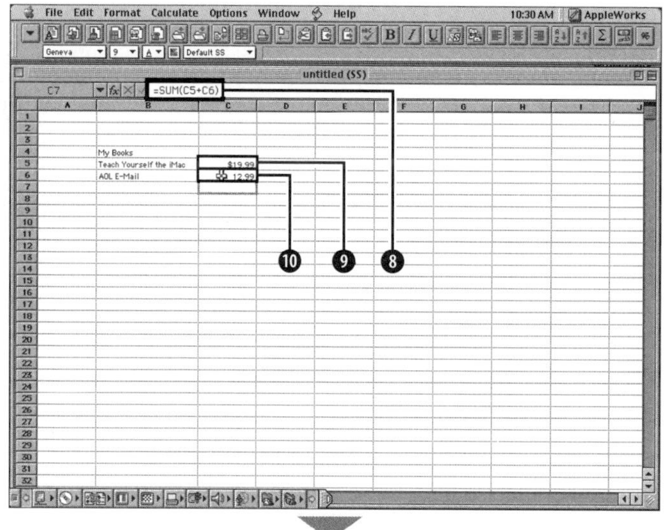

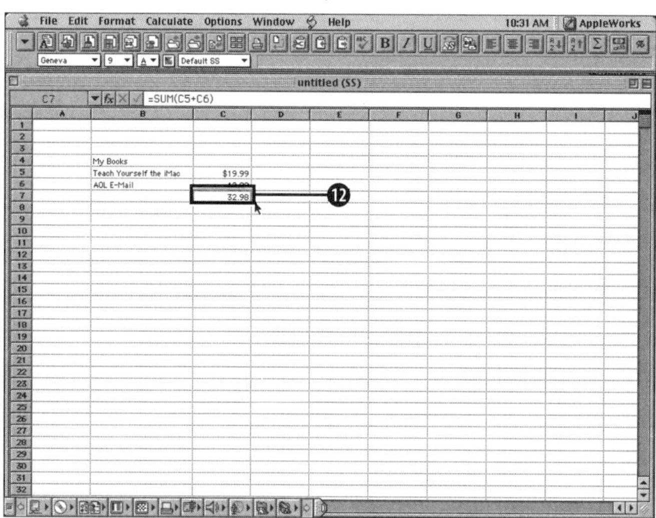

8 *Select everything between the parentheses in the entry bar.*

9 *Click your first cell with a dollar amount once.*

10 *Click your second cell with a dollar amount once.*

11 *Press Enter.*

▶ *AppleWorks calculates the total of the two cells and displays it.*

12 *Double-click the cell to change it to a currency format.*

click the first cell for your formula (the selling price cell), type a minus (-) sign, and click the second cell (the discount). This tells AppleWorks to subtract the second cell from the first cell (subtract the discount from the selling price). To manipulate this number, add parentheses around the two cells, like this: (C12-C13). Position the insertion point at the end of the formula and type an asterisk (*), which tells AppleWorks to multiply the amount in parentheses by the amount that follows. Click the third cell (the tax percentage) to add it to the formula. Finally, press Enter and let AppleWorks do its thing! You can then use this formula in another formula, such as to add the amount of tax to a discounted price to get the total price.

If you get confused or want to try something more complicated, take a look at the AppleWorks Help Index for details on creating and using formulas.

TAKE NOTE

CHANGING CELL NUMBERS

Once you have typed your formula, you can change the amounts in the cells included in the formula for a new total. Just press the Enter key after typing a new number to get the new total. This is where you see the real strength in spreadsheets!

SHORTCUT

Use the buttons next to the entry bar to add a ready-made formula (fx), undo something (X), or complete a formula (check mark).

Personal Workbook

Q&A

1. Why is it a good idea to use separate First Name and Last Name fields in a database?

2. What constitutes a record in a database?

3. How do you create a new record?

4. How do you view the information in your database as a list?

5. How do you increase or decrease the size of a column or row?

6. How do you format a cell in a spreadsheet so it shows a full dollar amount?

7. How do you add two cells together in a spreadsheet?

8. What symbol do you type first when you create your own formula?

ANSWERS: PAGE 318

Using Databases and Spreadsheets

CHAPTER 7

EXTRA PRACTICE

1. Create a new database to be used as an inventory of the contents of your home. Create fields for item description, date acquired, serial number, purchase cost, replacement cost, and current market value. Set the field types to Text, Date, or Currency, as appropriate.
2. Create at least five records for that database, starting with your iMac. Include your printer and any other extra peripherals you may have.
3. Display your inventory as a list and change the width of the item description field so that all descriptions are fully visible. Sort the list alphabetically using the item description field, and then print the list (if you have a printer).

REAL-WORLD APPLICATIONS

✔ You've volunteered to publish a newsletter for your favorite local charity and create and maintain a mailing list for that newsletter. The newsletter will be mailed to all donors for two years following a donation. The President of the organization also wants you to give her a report listing all donors who haven't made a donation in 18 months. You go home, open AppleWorks, and create a database of charity's donor information. From the database you easily extract a list of people who haven't donated in the last 18 months.

✔ Some weeks later the President asks you to start keeping track of phone numbers as well so they can use your list for a telephone tree. You add new fields to the database, update each record, sort and format the list, and then send the President the results.

Visual Quiz

Where would you see this window? What is its purpose?

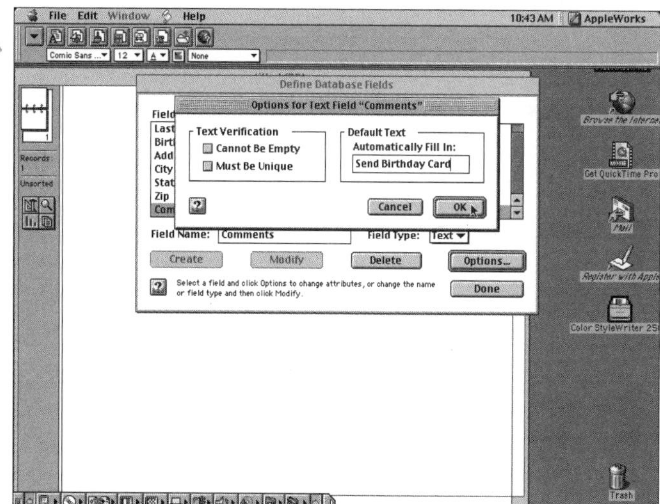

CHAPTER 8

MASTER THESE SKILLS

- Finding Applications
- Installing Your Bundled Applications
- Running Applications
- Opening Files from Within Applications
- Setting Application Preferences
- Switching Between Applications
- Making the Most of Applications

Running Applications

Just what are running applications? Are they entry forms for the Boston Marathon? Maybe those entry forms are fleeing down the street? No, that can't be it. Perhaps we should ask, "What *is* running applications?" Causing an application to operate? We're getting warmer. What about the definition of an *application*? Application is short for application program, which is a computer program (a series of instructions to a computer) that can be applied to a particular task. In other words, when we run applications, we're trying to accomplish something.

The beauty of computers is that there are so many application programs that are capable of doing so many things. Some applications came bundled with your iMac. You'll have to acquire other applications on your own. Since computers themselves are so complicated, there are scads of applications that help you use your computer. Still other applications are available to help you work and play.

This chapter builds on earlier lessons in recognizing the applications that come pre-installed on your iMac: installing additional applications, starting up and shutting down applications, and running — using — more than one application at a time.

Using more than one application at a time is pretty impressive when you think about it. Think about your iMac as if it were a kitchen: You can have the oven baking one item, the stove simmering another, the freezer holding a few more items, and all the while, the blender can be churning away at a final item. Let's just hope that with all this activity, nothing crashes to the floor.

In many cases, running an application is a pointless exercise unless you can open the information files the program is designed to work with. I'll show you how to open a file or two once the application is up and running.

Running an application can also be pointless unless you know *how* to use it. While some of you may like to fly by the seat of your pants, I'll also show the rest of you where to look for the instructions, tutorials, and other learning aids that come with the applications to speed you on your way.

Applications are fairly accommodating things, usually giving you the freedom to adjust the way they go about their business. I'll show you where to look to find these preference settings.

Altogether, by the time we're done, you'll be in a position to apply all sorts of new knowledge about applications to your tasks.

Finding Applications

You can find applications almost everywhere. Many are already on your iMac in various places, while others are somewhere out there, waiting for you to find them.

The first place to look for applications on your iMac is the Applications folder on your hard drive. Many of the applications that came with your iMac are here, as are other applications you or someone else may have installed. I'll explore most of the applications that came with your iMac in this chapter, but a brief rundown now may be helpful to you.

The AppleCD Audio Player controls the play of audio CDs. SimpleText is a basic word processing program. Adobe Acrobat reads and prints documents created in the PDF file format (such as instructions or forms). AppleWorks is the multifunctional program suite. FAXstf lets you send and receive faxes through your iMac's modem. Quicken Deluxe is a personal finance program. QuickTime displays pictures and plays movies. Nanosaur is a way cool arcade-style game. Network Browser is covered briefly in Chapter 12. Newer iMacs also come with iMovie (which lets you edit, title, and add sound to digital movies), Palmtop Desktop (a personal information manager), and Bugdom (another very cool 3D game based on popular animated movie, "A Bug's Life"). Older iMacs come with WS Guide to Good Cooking (electronic cookbook).

Many applications on your iMac also can be found on your Apple menu (though with Mac OS 9 most applications are in your Applications folder). Your Apple menu items — *Apple System Profiler* (obtains information about your iMac and operating system), *Graphing Calculator* (graphs equations), the *Jigsaw Puzzle, Key Caps, Note Pad, Scrapbook, Sherlock,* and *Stickies* — are all applications. If you've used Macs before, you may

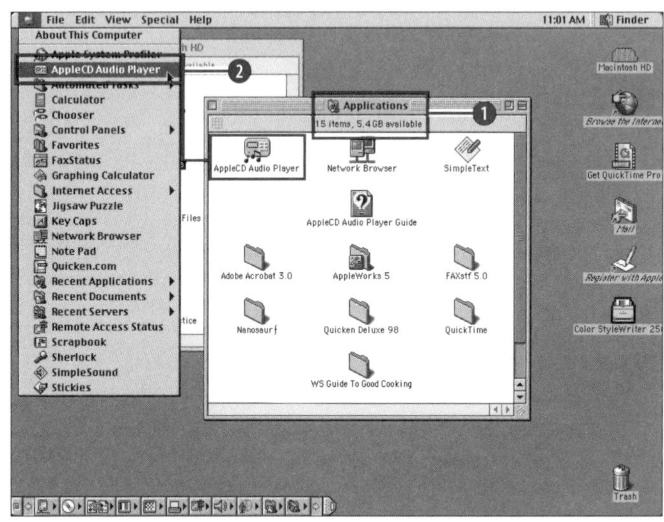

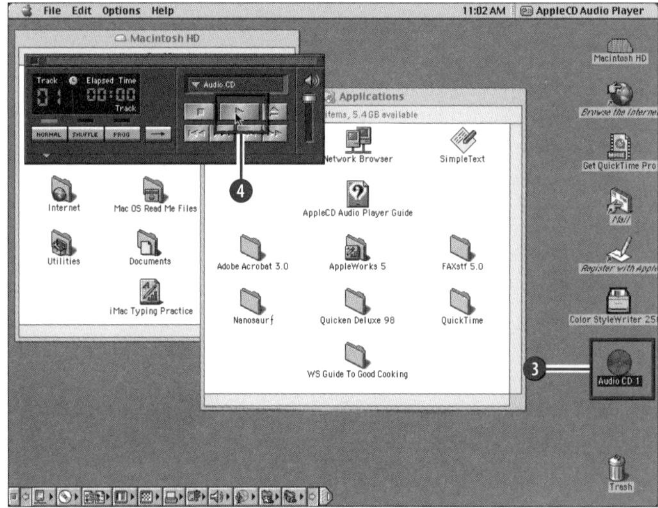

1. *Open the Applications folder to find applications.*
- *Alternatively, pull down the Apple menu to look for more applications.*
2. *Open the AppleCD Audio Player.*
3. *Insert an Audio CD into your iMac.*
4. *Click the Play button.*

CROSS-REFERENCE

Refer to "Finding Files" in Chapter 2 for help using Sherlock.

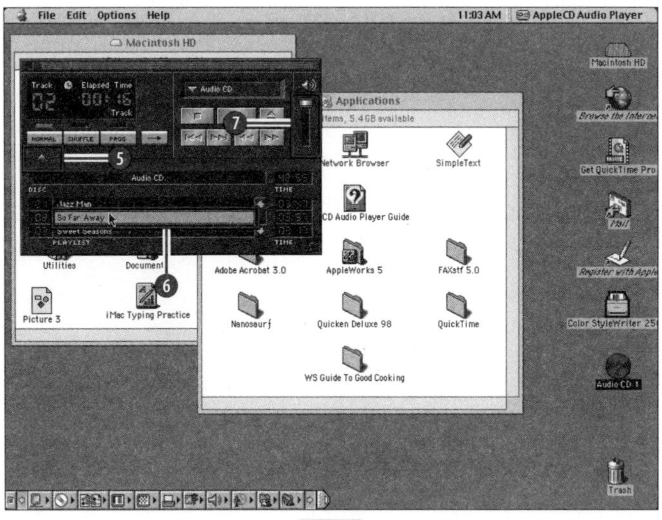

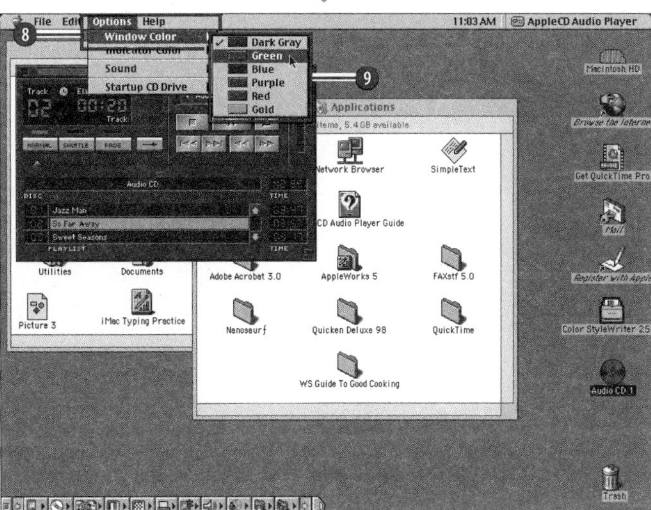

5 Click the small arrow to see the track list.

6 Click one of the track names to type a new name.

7 Adjust your volume.

8 Pull down the Options menu and display the Window Colors submenu.

9 Choose a new color for your AppleCD Audio Player window.

recognize these applications as desk accessories (DAs), as they used to be called. You also may find applications at the top level of, or in the folders on, your hard drive or your Desktop. It all depends on where you choose to install an application.

Some of the applications that came with your iMac haven't been installed yet, such as Adobe PageMill (a World Wide Web page creator), and on older iMacs, Kai's Photo Soap (a photo manipulation program), and World Book (an encyclopedia). You must install these programs before you can use them, which I explain in the next chapter.

Of course, you can purchase new applications at a computer store or through a mail-order house. You also can find applications on the Internet and on America Online (discussed in Chapter 11). Other people may give you applications to install on your computer, too. Before you install applications you obtained from the Internet or someone else, seriously consider using a virus protection program (discussed in Chapter 13).

TAKE NOTE

RECOGNIZING APPLICATIONS

You usually can tell if a file is an application program by selecting it and pressing Command+I. The Info window displays the file's type near the top of the window. If it says application program, you have a winner. If it says alias, it also could be pointing to an application program. If it says folder, open the folder (even if it doesn't look like a typical folder); it may contain an application inside. Alternatively, you can change your window to List view and check the Kind column for applications.

SHORTCUT

Use Sherlock (Command+F) to find all kinds of application files on your iMac.

Installing Your Bundled Applications

Actually, this task is a refresher. I introduced you to the basic concept of installing new software in Chapter 3. Yet, I would be remiss if I didn't show you the in's and out's of installing the applications that came on the CD-ROM accompanying your iMac.

To install Adobe PageMill (or any other software that comes on a CD-ROM), begin by quitting any running applications and ejecting any other CD-ROM disc that may be in your drive. Now locate the Adobe PageMill CD-ROM in the CD case that came in your iMac accessory kit and place the CD-ROM in the drive. Once the CD-ROM tray is closed, you can double-click the Adobe PageMill icon that appears on your Desktop. Now, click the Install PageMill icon to begin installing the program. After answering some questions and accepting the license agreement, you are prompted to select an installation location, and then to click the Install button (or press Return). At the end of the installation process, you will be asked to type in your contact information. Be sure to click the check box if you don't want your information shared with other companies. Continue answering the questions through to the end, where you can elect to send in your registration information by Internet e-mail, fax, or mail (your iMac's phone/modem connection or printer connection needs to be established before you register). When the installation is complete, you will need to restart your iMac. The Adobe PageMill window will remain open when your Desktop reappears. Simply eject the CD-ROM disc (if you aren't familiar with ejecting CD-ROMs, see Chapter 3 for details).

To install Kai's Photo Soap, insert the CD-ROM, double-click the icon that appears, double-click the English icon in the resulting window, and then double-click the Installer icon. The Installer window looks a bit different from how both Williams-Sonoma and

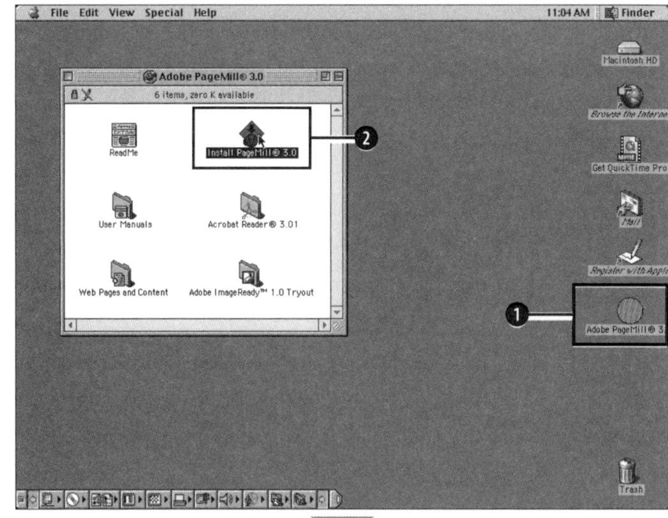

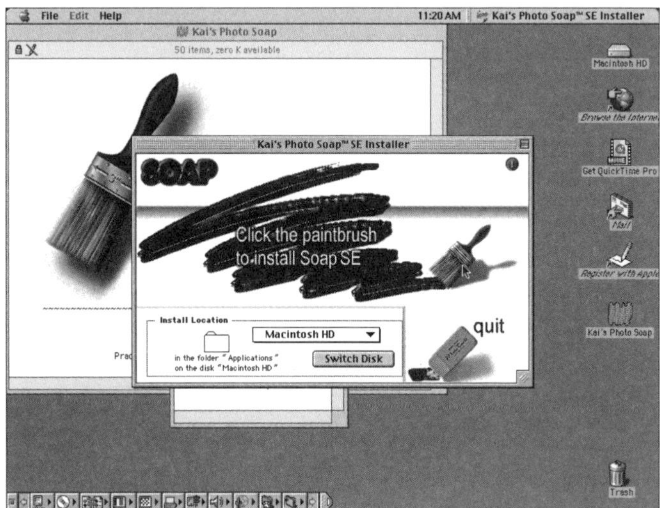

1. *Double-click the CD-ROM icon to open it.*
2. *Double-click the Installer icon.*

- *When installing Kai's Photo Soap, click here to select an install location.*
- *Click the paintbrush icon to begin installation.*

CROSS-REFERENCE

Refer to "Installing New Software" in Chapter 3 for details on using installer programs and selecting install locations.

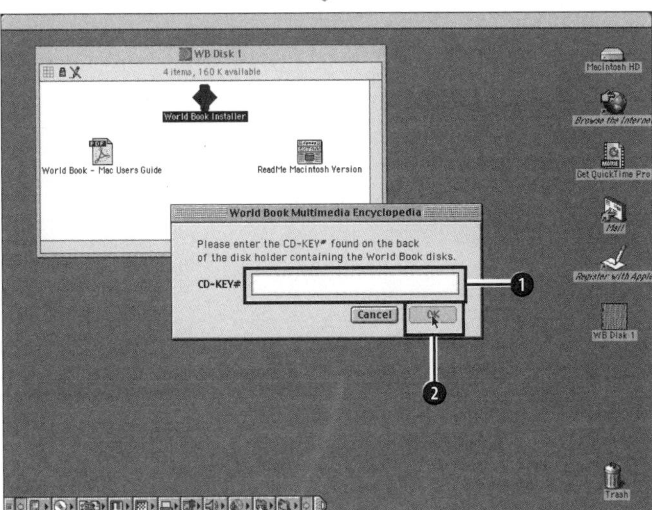

- *The installer shows you some of the application's features while you wait.*
- *The installation's progress is displayed.*
- *Click the Stop button if you want to abort the installation.*
- *When you install World Book Encyclopedia, type your CD-KEY here.*
- *Click the OK button to continue installation.*

Adobe PageMill looked, but it functions in the same way. Choose an installation location, and then single-click the paintbrush icon. The installer program showcases the application's features while it installs. When the installation is complete, restart your iMac. Eject the CD-ROM when you are finished. The folder for Kai's Photo Soap is located wherever you installed it — usually in the Applications folder.

To install World Book Multimedia Encyclopedia, insert the CD-ROM (Disc 1), double-click the icon that appears, and then double-click the World Book Installer icon in the resulting window. After accepting the license agreement, you are prompted to enter the CD-KEY number. The installer program claims the number is on the back of the disk holder; don't believe it. You'll find the number listed on a separate sheet of paper titled World Book Macintosh Quick Start in your iMac Accessory Kit. After you type in your CD-KEY, the installer window pops up. Click the Install button, and then choose a location for the application in the resulting window. You don't need to restart your iMac, though I recommend it anyway. You will need to have the one of the two CD-ROM discs in your iMac to use the application. Eject the CD-ROM disc when you are finished.

TAKE NOTE

REGISTERING APPLICATIONS

Many newly installed applications require registration, and they may also require typing a registration number. For assistance, check the list of installation directions and registration numbers in your iMac Accessory Kit.

SHORTCUT

Press Command+. to cancel an installation while it is in progress.

Running Applications

Now that you've identified your applications, what do you do with them? First things first: open them. Not all at one time, of course. Generally, you only want to open one application at a time. While your iMac certainly lets you have more than one application open and running at the same time, I wouldn't recommend having more than seven or so open all at once. Applications require memory (RAM); if too much memory is being used, your iMac can slow down considerably.

Applications are generally opened either by double-clicking their icon, or by selecting their icons and choosing Open from the File menu (or pressing Command+O). Apple Menu applications are opened by choosing them from the menu.

Some applications, like AppleWorks, may prompt you for information when you open them. Others, like World Book and Williams-Sonoma Guide to Good Cooking, require that the program's CD-ROM disc be inserted into your iMac before the program can be opened.

Applications like the AppleCD Audio Player open easily, but they don't do much on their own otherwise. You'll need to insert an audio CD into your iMac's CD-ROM drive to take advantage of the Audio Player. Once the disc spins up, click the Play button (it looks just like it would on a standard CD player). Use the slider control on the right to increase or decrease the volume. You can shuffle, program, and loop the CD tracks, and you can also move forward and in reverse. Click the small arrow in the lower-left corner for the track list and times. You can even name the tracks by clicking a track number and typing a name. Your iMac saves the track names for the next time you listen to the CD, too. Explore the Options menu if you want to change colors or listen to specific channels. You can eject

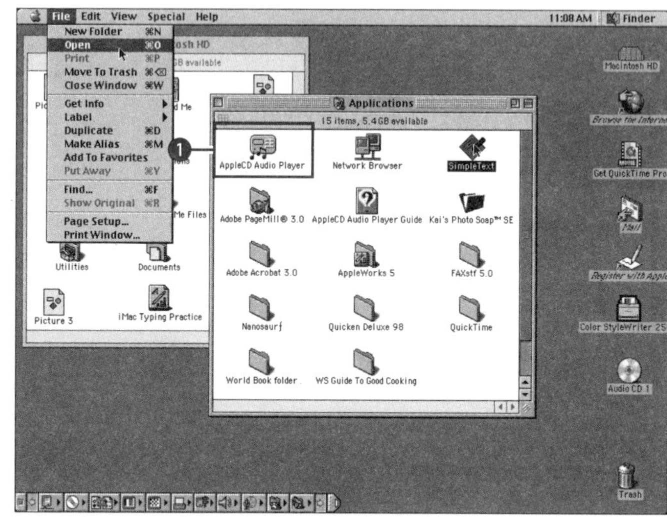

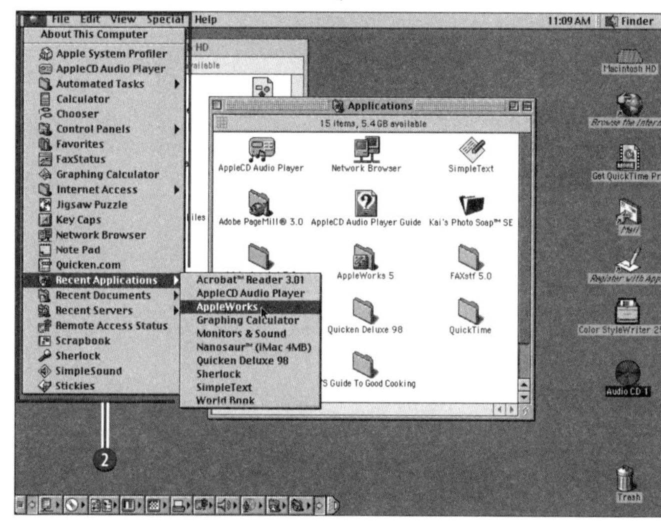

❶ *Double-click an application to run it.*

▶ *Alternatively, select the icon and choose Open from the File menu.*

❷ *Choose an application from the Apple menu to run it.*

▶ *The Recent Applications submenu contains many applications, as well.*

CROSS-REFERENCE

Refer to "Opening Files from Within Applications" for more detailed explanations of opening applications.

Running Applications From Sherlock

Yes, your trusty sidekick Sherlock takes on yet another task. This time, Sherlock can retrieve applications, and it allows you to open them without going back to the Desktop. The trick to opening an application from within Sherlock is first to locate it, and then to double-click its icon in the results window. Use the Kind column to help you spot applications (and documents) to open from within Sherlock.

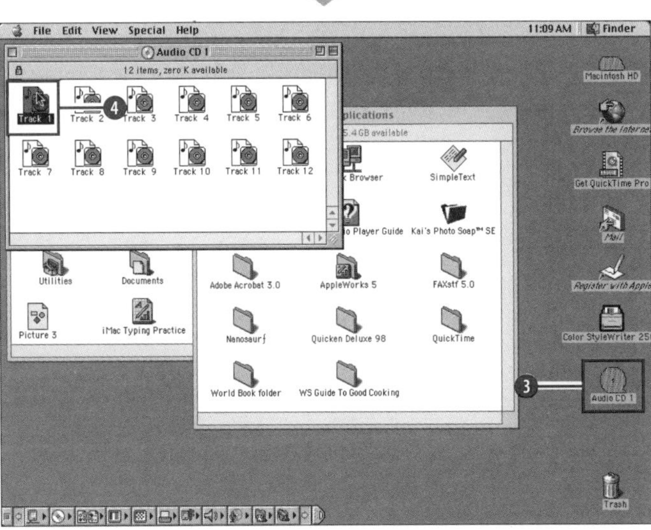

3. *Double-click an audio CD to displays its tracks.*
4. *Double-click a track file to open the AppleCD Audio Player.*

the CD-ROM disc (just drag its icon to the Trash) to make way for a new one.

TAKE NOTE

RUNNING APPLICATIONS FROM FILES

Another way to open and run an application is to open one of its files. For example, if you insert an audio CD before you open the AppleCD Audio Player, you can double-click the CD icon to open it, and then double-click one of the track files to open the Audio Player application. Not all files can be opened outside of their associated applications, however. The AppleCD Audio Player Guide, for example, won't open if you double-click it, but you can open it by choosing AppleCD Audio Player Guide from the Help menu while the application is running.

QUITTING APPLICATIONS

All this talk of opening and running applications, and I haven't really explained how to quit (or exit) from one. When you're inside a running application, choose Quit from the bottom of the File menu. Better yet, press Command+Q. Be sure you saved your work before you quit (though most applications will prompt you to save if you haven't already done so).

SHORTCUT

You can quickly adjust the speaker volume using the speaker button in the Control Strip.

Opening Files from Within Applications

Applications are a lot like workbenches. A workbench may be wonderfully organized and chock full of great tools, but it isn't going to do much on its own. You need things to work on at the workbench. Along the same lines, you need files to use in or with your applications.

To open a file from within an application, first open the application itself and then choose Open from the File menu. The File Open dialog box appears so you can navigate to, select, and open a file. Most applications are smart enough to show you only the files that the application can open. If the list is empty, there are no available files in that particular location. Change to another folder by selecting one from the drop-down menu at the top of the dialog box. You also might want to click the Desktop button to go up to the Desktop level. Some applications offer a preview feature to help you choose which file to open. If you decide you don't want to open a file after all, click the Cancel button. Otherwise, select your file and click the Open button (or just double-click it).

Let's take a closer look at opening files from within the SimpleText application. Open SimpleText and then choose Open from the File menu. Examine your list of files and then use the drop-down menu at the top of the dialog box to move up to the Macintosh HD level. You should see at least one file you can open: the iMac Read Me file. Double-click the file and it opens within SimpleText. Voila!

Most applications let you open more than one file within them. This is very useful when comparing files or transferring data between two files. In fact, some applications — like AppleWorks — have a special Window menu where you can tile or stack your open file windows on top of or beside one another. The Window menu also may keep a list of all your open windows.

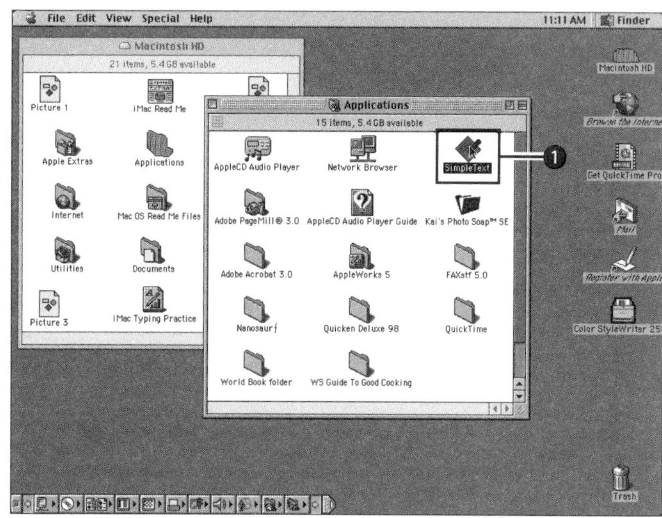

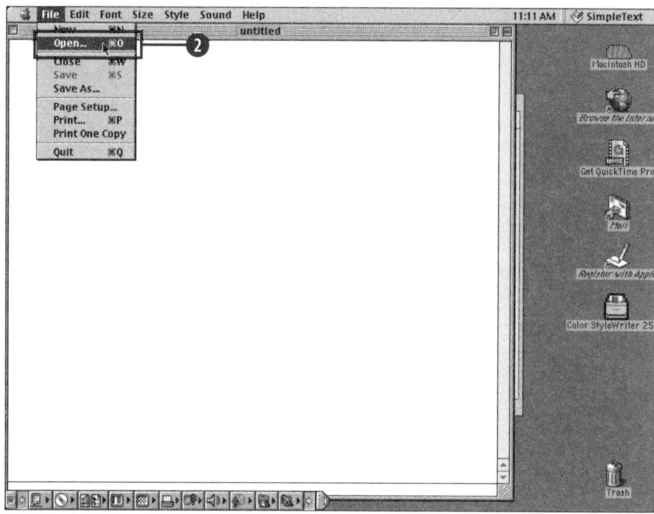

1 *Double-click SimpleText to run the application.*

2 *Choose Open from the File menu.*

▶ *Alternatively, press Command+O.*

CROSS-REFERENCE

Refer to "Closing Your Windows" in Chapter 1 for details on how to zoom open a file window.

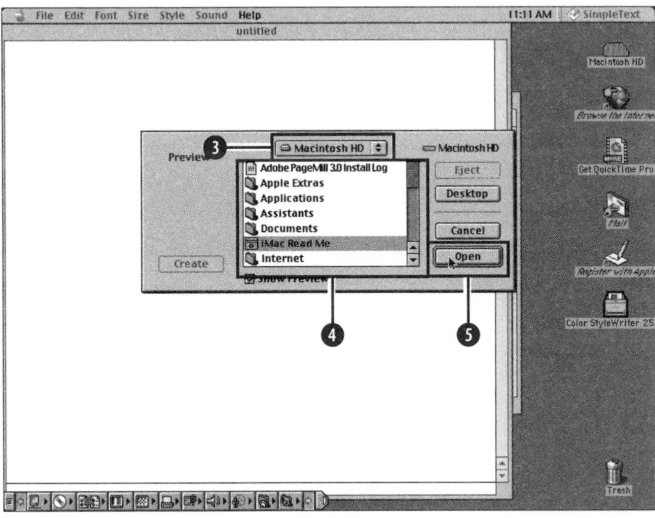

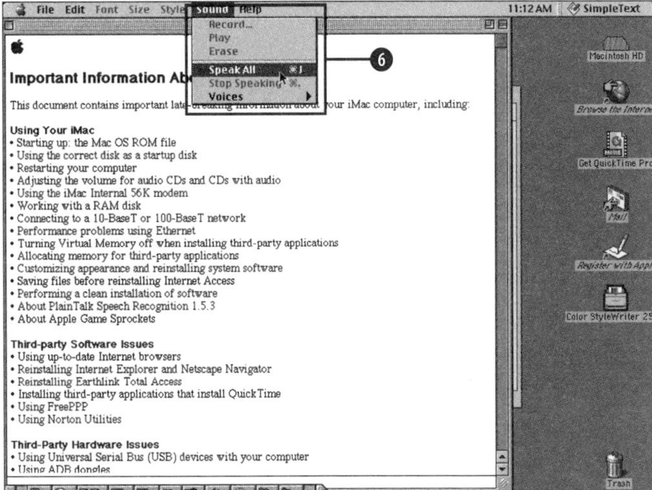

3. *Navigate to the Macintosh HD level.*
4. *Select the iMac Read Me file.*
5. *Click the Open button (or press Return).*

▶ *SimpleText displays the iMac Read Me file.*

6. *Choose Speak All from the Sound menu to have SimpleText read the document to you.*

To close an open file without quitting the application altogether, choose Close from the File menu. You also can click the close box in the upper-right corner of the window.

TAKE NOTE

USING SIMPLETEXT

SimpleText is an amazingly versatile application. Besides opening various types of text and formatted documents, it can open PICT (the standard Mac graphics format) and QuickDraw 3D graphics, and QuickTime movies. You also can have SimpleText *read* text aloud to you. You can create documents with SimpleText and include text, sounds, and graphics. To learn more about using SimpleText, choose SimpleText Guide from the Help menu and click the Topics button.

COLLAPSING FILE WINDOWS

Remember you can *collapse* (or minimize) your open file windows within an application to see what's behind them or just to make more room. Just click the box in the upper-right corner of a file window to minimize it. See "Changing Your iMac's Appearance" in Chapter 14 to collapse a window just by double-clicking its title bar.

SHORTCUT

Press Command+O to open a file within an application, and Command+W to close a file.

Setting Application Preferences

Taking a cue from the iMac, most large applications — and even many small ones — offer the ability to set preferences. Some applications may call it Customize, while others use Settings. Most applications stick with good old reliable Preferences. The most likely place to find an application's preferences are under the File menu, though I've also seen them under Edit, Tools, and Help.

While all application preferences differ a bit from one another, most of them work in similar ways. So let's explore Adobe Acrobat Reader's preferences, as they are particularly good. In fact, Adobe Acrobat Reader mostly displays (and prints) special instructional and informational files. Thus, setting your preferences is one of the few things you can actually *do* in Adobe Acrobat Reader besides open and print files.

Begin by opening Adobe Acrobat Reader and selecting the Preferences submenu under the File menu. You have four sets of preferences: General, Notes, Full Screen, and Weblink. Choose General and take a look at the staggering array of available options. Most of this stuff just isn't going to make much sense until you've learned to use the application. For now, my recommendation is to stick with all these default values and preferences. The software manufacturer set each option with new users in mind.

Note the different ways you can choose your settings in Adobe Acrobat Reader. Drop-down menus let you choose from a list of options. Text entry fields let you type in specific values. Check boxes allow you to enable a particular setting. You'll encounter these methods in other applications' preferences, too.

Save your preferences by clicking the OK button (or click the Apply button, if it is available). If you set

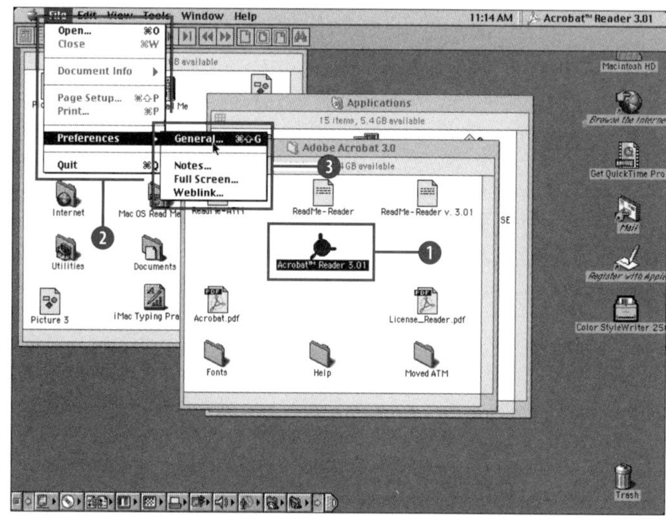

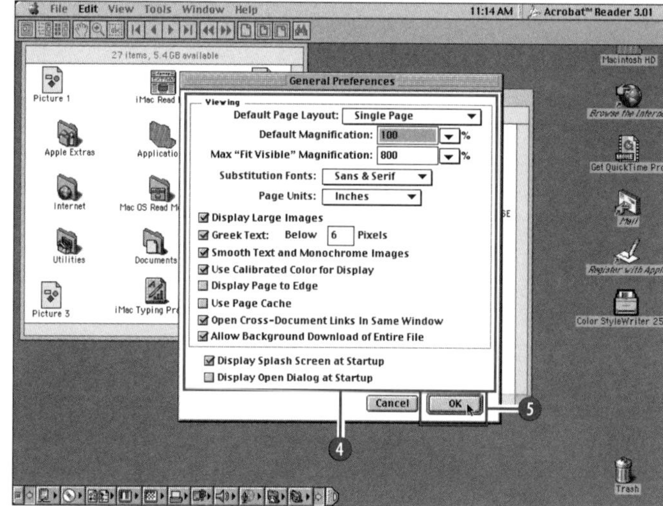

1. *Double-click Adobe Acrobat Reader to run the application.*
2. *Pull down the File menu and display the Preferences submenu.*
3. *Choose the General preferences.*
4. *Set your general preferences, if you wish.*

▶ *Optional: Click the Cancel button if you want to discard any changes you made.*

5. *Click OK.*
6. *Open your Weblink preferences from the File menu.*

CROSS-REFERENCE

See "Setting Your Preferences" in Chapter 2 for advice on deciding which preferences to use.

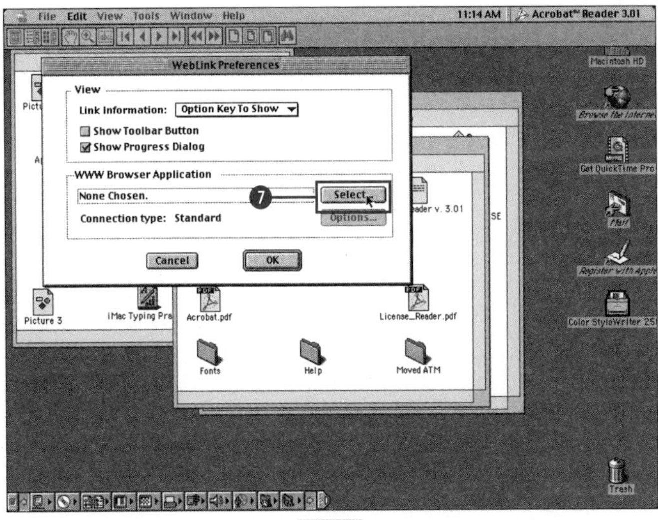

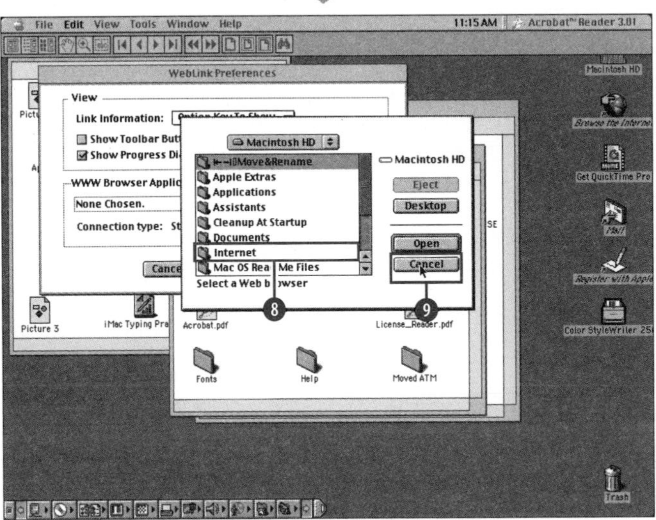

- ▶ *Note your Weblink preferences.*
- 7 *Click the Select button to choose a new default Web browser, if you wish.*
- 8 *Navigate to your Internet folder, select a Web browser, and then click the Open button.*
- 9 *Click the Cancel button to abort.*

preferences and later decide not to keep them, click the Cancel button to discard the new settings.

Once you set your preferences, they remain set until you change them again, even if you quit the application or restart your iMac. Preferences are usually saved in the Preferences folder in your System Folder, and they are referred to each time you open the application.

TAKE NOTE

USING ADOBE ACROBAT READER

Adobe Acrobat Reader lets you view, navigate, and print special files known as Portable Document Format (PDF) files. Several of these PDF files are available on your hard drive to open and read. Software manufacturers, including Apple, often save their instruction manuals in PDF format. This allows them to use full color, graphics, special fonts, buttons, hyperlinks, and more. When a PDF file is open in Adobe Acrobat Reader, use the toolbar to zoom in and out and navigate through the document. Learn more about using Adobe Acrobat Reader with the Acrobat Reader Online Guide under the Help menu.

FINDING THE PREFERENCES FOLDER

You may occasionally need to visit the Preferences folder on your iMac. You can find it in the Preferences folder within the System Folder on Macintosh HD. Do not remove or modify any of the files in the Preferences folder unless instructed to do so.

SHORTCUT

Press Shift+Option when opening a file in Adobe Acrobat Reader to override the document's settings and use your preferences.

Switching Between Applications

Unless you've been diligently closing applications behind yourself, I'll bet you have a lot of applications running right now. Do you know how many? And — more importantly — do you know how to switch between them?

The quickest and easiest way to find out how many applications you have running is to check your Application menu on the far right edge of your menu bar. You will always see the Finder (Desktop) on the list — any other items listed there are running applications. Tip: Expand or collapse the heading of the application menu by clicking and dragging the dotted bar to the left of it.

Another way to get a list of your running applications is to go to your Finder (click the Desktop in the background, assuming you can see it), and then choose About This Computer from the Apple menu. You'll always see Mac OS listed (this is your operating system). Any other items are running applications. The bars on the right indicate how much memory (RAM) each application is using. Hmm. Maybe you should close some of them!

To switch to another application, just choose it from the Application menu. This isn't the only way, but it is usually the most reliable. If you can see the window of another application in the background, clicking it moves that application to the front of the pack.

Alas, the Application menu doesn't work for all applications. Nanosaur, a cool arcade game that comes on your iMac, is a good example. It actually hides the menu bar (which means no menus at all). I suppose Nanosaur does this to give you a more realistic game setting, but it is a bit annoying. The only way to move to another application from Nanosaur is to quit (press Command+Q at any time) and then use the Application menu. Thankfully, Nanosaur is one of the few exceptions to the rule.

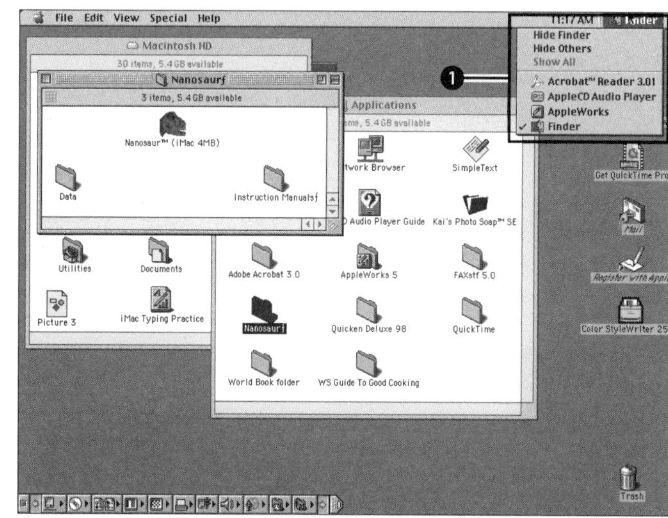

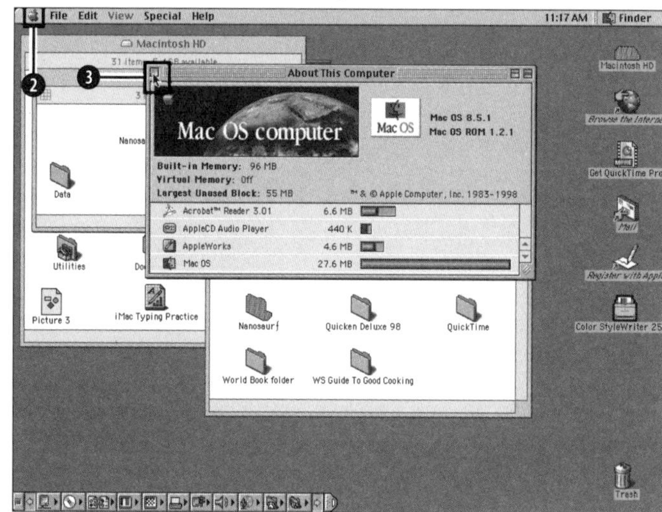

1. *Pull down the Application menu to view your running applications.*
2. *Choose About This Computer from the Apple menu.*
3. *Click the close box when finished.*

CROSS-REFERENCE

Refer to the "Running Applications" task earlier in this chapter for more details on how to quit applications.

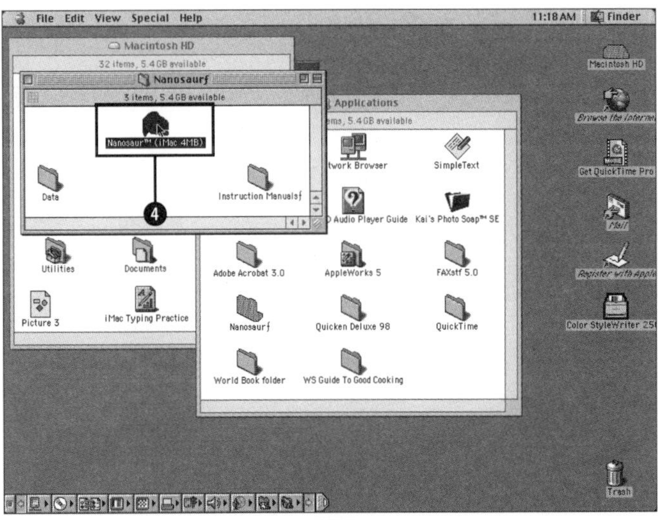

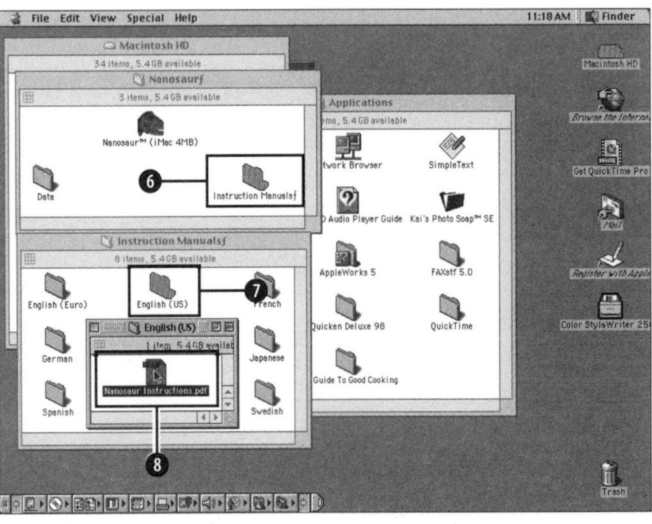

4. *Double-click Nanosaur to play.*
5. *Press Command+Q when you want to quit.*
6. *Double-click the Instructions Manual folder to open it.*
7. *Double-click the English US folder to open it.*
8. *Double-click the Nanosaur Instructions.pdf file to open Adobe Acrobat Reader and display the file.*

TAKE NOTE

PLAYING NANOSAUR

Nanosaur is a very fun, shoot-em-up game created to take advantage of some of the iMac's more powerful features (and it's included with your iMac to show them off!). Double-click the icon to open the application and press the spacebar to move through the introductory screens. If the sound is too loud, press the - key to decrease the volume (the + key increases it if you can't hear it). Keep hitting the spacebar until you get to the screen with the Nanosaur and the falling, blue-speckled eggs. Press the right- or left-arrow keys to cycle through the various options: play (Nanosaur), high scores, exit, help (question mark), and options (checkmark). The object of the game is to collect five different dinosaur eggs and transport them back to the future before the giant asteroid hits and destroys all life. Use the arrow keys to move your Nanosaur left, right, forward, and backward through the jungle to hunt for the eggs. And if you see any dinosaurs come at you, press the spacebar to shoot 'em! Press Esc to pause the game. Read the instructions in the Instruction Manuals folder to learn more.

SHORTCUT

Press Command+Tab to cycle through each open application until you reach the one you want.

Making the Most of Applications

Your applications are what you make of them. Explore each of your applications in detail, look in all their nooks and crannies, and get to know them better. You may come to love some applications and treat them as best friends. Others you may visit only occasionally, like good acquaintances. A few you may totally ignore like, well, never mind. This is how it works for most people, including me.

To make the most of your applications, begin by reading the instructions! Most applications come with a Read Me file, which you should always read. Don't stop there, though. Look for a separate instruction manual, either in the application's folder or within the application itself. Don't neglect the packaging your application came with, either. Explore the Help menu inside the application, and look under the Apple menu for an About command. All of these pieces will help you to form a larger picture of an application.

Some applications are small and unsophisticated, so there may not be a lot to get to know. Even so, it pays to explore it carefully and not to let its size fool you. It was many years before I discovered that I could copy and paste totals from the Calculator, for example. On the other hand, larger applications can seem daunting. Indeed, it may take a lot of exploration and practice before you really know all the features of a large, complicated program.

Quicken Deluxe, a personal financial program, is a good example of a sophisticated application with lots of room for discovery. In fact, when you run Quicken Deluxe for the first time, you can get a special new user tutorial to help you get started with Quicken (which I strongly recommend). Other applications have tutorials like this that walk you through a setup process step-by-step — check under the Help menu for it. Once you complete the tutorial, choose the Quicken Deluxe

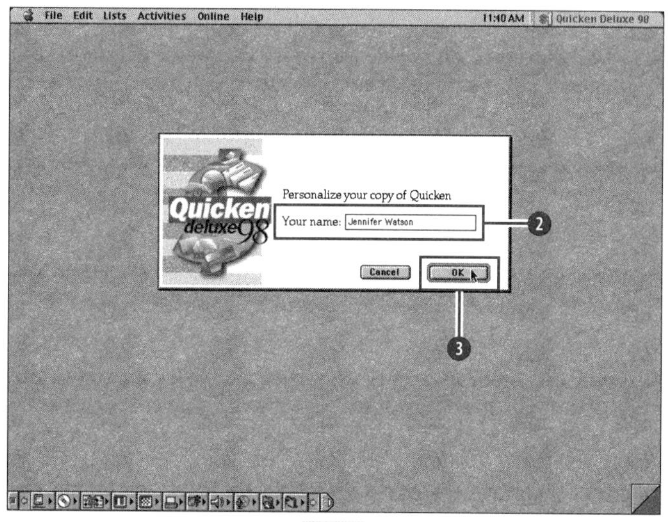

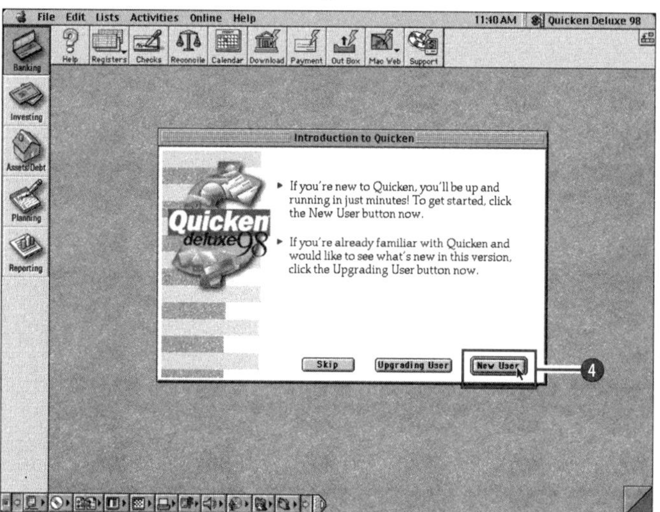

1. *Double-click the Quicken Deluxe icon to run the application.*
2. *Type your name.*
3. *Click the OK button to continue.*
4. *When you are prompted, click the New User button.*

▶ *Alternatively, click the Upgrading User button if you've used Quicken before.*

CROSS-REFERENCE

Refer to Chapter 7 if you want to create your own customized database and/or spreadsheet.

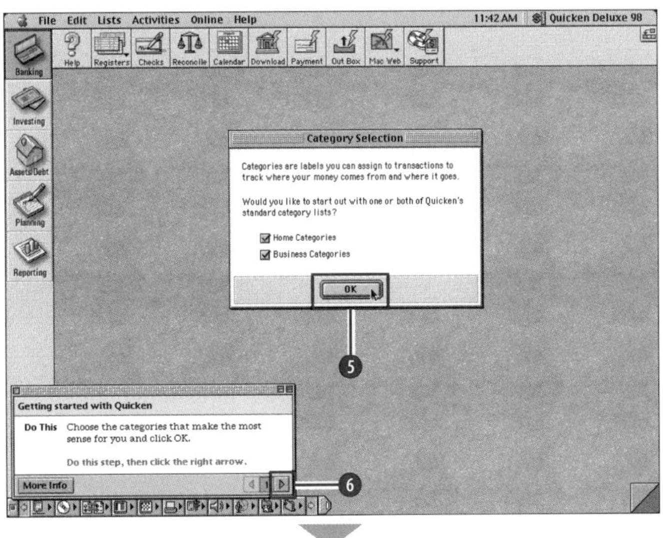

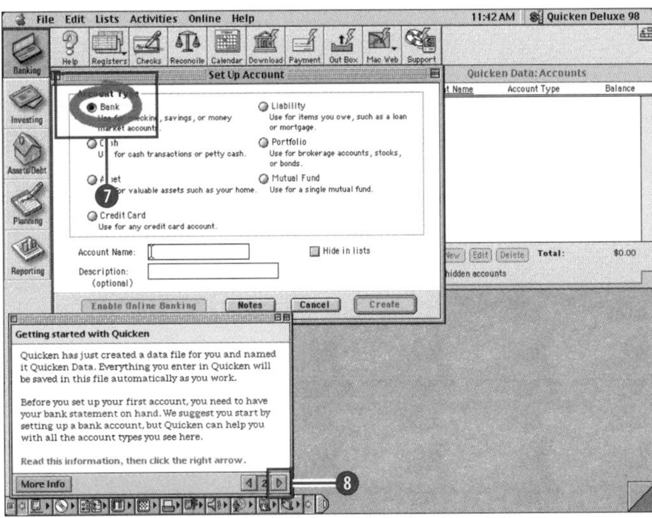

5 *Follow the tutorial directions and click OK.*

6 *Click this arrow to continue in the tutorial.*

7 *Watch for these marks to guide you along.*

8 *Click this arrow to continue.*

option from the Apple menu. The About box offers a different tip at the bottom each time you open it. Just click the Tell me more! button to get details. Quicken Deluxe's Help menu offers Help, Tips & Shortcuts, Basics, and a User's Manual, too.

Even if you don't want to read everything about an application, you can still learn a lot just by using it. In fact, I know some Mac users who brag about never cracking open a manual or reading a help file. Get to know your applications your way!

TAKE NOTE

USING QUICKEN DELUXE

Quicken is a wonderfully useful program that helps you keep track of bank accounts, cash transactions, assets and liabilities, credit card balances, loans, stock portfolios, and mutual funds. Even if you don't need all those capabilities, it does a darn good job of keeping track of your checkbook. In fact, you can write checks with Quicken, have it automatically balance your checkbook with each check, and then print out the checks on your printer. You can even set up Quicken to pay your bills electronically through the Internet or even via a local access number.

SHORTCUT

Click the blue triangle in the lower-right corner to go to the Desktop at any time in Quicken.

Personal Workbook

Q&A

1. How do you recognize an application program on your iMac?

2. Where can you find the CD-ROM installation discs that came with your iMac?

3. What is the keyboard shortcut to quit a running application?

4. How do you close an open file window without quitting the application?

5. Under what menus are you likely to find the Preferences command in an application?

6. How do you expand or collapse the application menu's heading?

7. What is the keyboard shortcut to cycle through open applications?

8. Where would you look for an instruction manual?

ANSWERS: PAGE 319

EXTRA PRACTICE

1. Find and open the Calculator application that came installed on your iMac. Leave it running.
2. Install a program from a CD-ROM (skip if you've already installed it). Find all the places on your iMac you can go to run the application.
3. Run AppleWorks from its folder in the Applications folder. Use it to open a document you find in the Adobe Acrobat 3.0 folder.
4. Find the Preferences for AppleWorks. See if there are any settings you'd like to change and change them. When you're finished, change them back to their original settings.
5. Switch to the Calculator using the Application menu. Switch back to AppleWorks by clicking an open AppleWorks window.

REAL-WORLD APPLICATIONS

✔ You're positive you installed an application on your computer, but you can't find its icon on the iMac desktop. You use Sherlock to search your hard drive, find the application, and open it. You also create an alias for the program and place it on your Desktop.

✔ You buy a new application program for your children on CD-ROM. As they look on skeptically, you pop the CD-ROM into the iMac and install the program as if you've been doing it for years. In minutes they're playing (and learning), and you're a hero!

✔ Your children complain that their new application is hard to use. Knowing that many educational programs can be adjusted for a child's age and skill level, you search for a Preferences menu. You find it in the File menu and start tweaking.

Visual Quiz

How do you get this window and what can you do there?

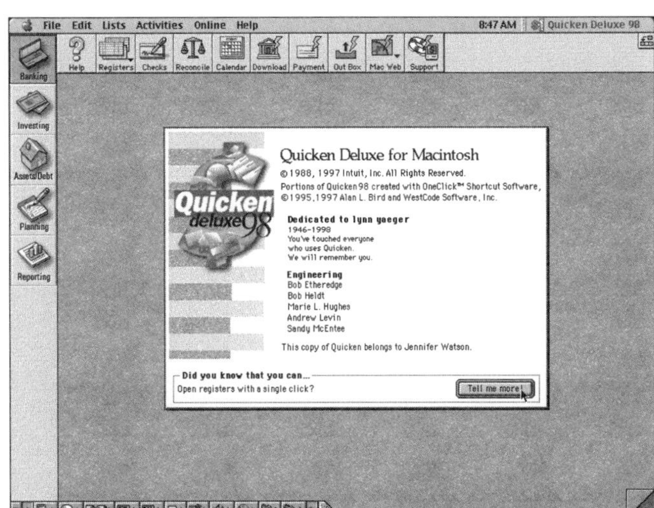

CHAPTER 9

MASTER THESE SKILLS

- Configuring Your Sound
- Listening to Music
- Playing and Setting Sounds
- Recording Sounds
- Converting Text to Speech
- Using QuickTime

Using Sound and Video

Everyone's been talking about the great looks of the iMac — its sleek, flowing design, the choice of vibrant colors and, as always, the elegant appearance of the Macintosh graphical user interface (GUI). We spend so much time looking at our iMac screens that we forget an iMac can be a treat for our ears, as well as our eyes.

For that matter, we may also forget that iMacs are multimedia computers. Not only can they display simple text and graphics, but they can play sounds, movies, and videos, too. These built-in sound and video capabilities are essential to the enjoyment of computer games and — more importantly — the multimedia educational CD-ROMs that make computers such valuable learning machines.

Most of the time, we take the iMac sound system for granted, whether it's the glorious chord that announces the successful startup of your iMac every day, or the little clicks and dings that accompany your everyday activities. For that matter, when your iMac has something really important to tell you, it even speaks out loud to tell you what's on its mind! Granted, some of these sounds may seem annoying because they may be warning you that you did something wrong. Still, these sound effects engage another of your senses in the computing experience, and that leads to greater productivity and enjoyment.

Built into every iMac are a CD player (remember, there's a CD in CD-ROM), a pair of stereo speakers (newer iMacs have fancy Harman/Kardon Odyssey audio systems), headphone jacks, a sound recording system, and a microphone. With these tools and a little imagination, there's no end to the fun you can have. The built-in CD player is perfect for setting the right mood as you work on your iMac, but what can you do with the sound recording features? Due to the location of the sound recording controls, one might assume that they're intended only for recording customized alert sounds. However, once a sound has been recorded, you can use it in almost any way that makes sense to you, from leaving a voice message for the kids on the iMac desktop to exchanging funny sound effects with your friends online.

Configuring Your Sound

To configure your iMac sound, begin by pulling down the Apple menu and choosing Monitors & Sound (Mac OS 8) or Sound (Mac OS 9) from the Controls Panels submenu. On Mac OS 8, you must also click the Sound button at the top of the resulting window to display the iMac sound countrols. On Mac OS 9, use the menu on the left of the resulting window to switch between different sets of controls, starting with the Output controls.

Most of the time, you'll visit this control panel to change the speaker volume. The first box on the left side allows you to adjust the speaker volume with a slider control. Click and drag the sliding box to the right to increase volume or to the left to decrease volume. When the slider is in the position you want it, release the mouse button — your iMac beeps to indicate its new volume level. When you simply want to turn off the sound, click the Mute check box rather than slide the volume control all the way to the left. Now when you're ready to hear your iMac make noise again, just uncheck the Mute check box and the sound will resume at its previous level.

You can also adjust the speaker balance, just like you can on standard stereo systems. Just slide the Computer System Balance control to the left or right as needed, though you'll probably want to keep it right in the center most of the time.

The Sound Output (and Sound Output Quality) controls only become selectable when you attach external speakers. Without external speakers, your iMac is set to use the built-in speakers (on older iMacs your setting will be 44.100 kHz).

The Sound Monitoring Source defaults to CD (for playing audio CDs), but you can select other options from the drop-down menu.

CROSS-REFERENCE

Learn more about sound monitoring sources in Recording Sounds later in this chapter.

Finding Sound Sources

The best way to adjust the volume is when you're actually listening to something! If the default iMac beep doesn't cut it for you, try the WorldBook Encyclopedia (remember to insert CD-ROM disc #1 into the drive before you open the application). Click the Media button (or Browse Media), click All Disc 1, and then look for items with a speaker icon. Click them to hear various sounds and music clips. If you see a camcorder icon, click it for a video clip that usually includes sound. Use the speaker icon in the lower-left corner of the video window to adjust the volume.

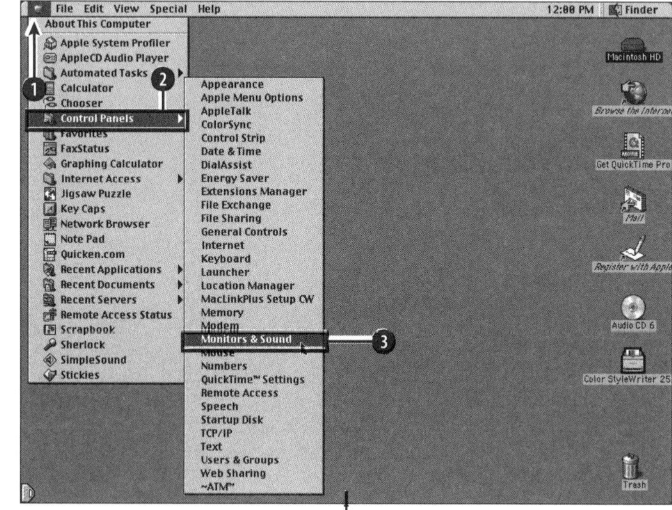

1. *Pull down the Apple menu.*
2. *Display the Control Panels submenu.*
3. *Choose Monitors & Sound, or Sound on Mac OS 9..*

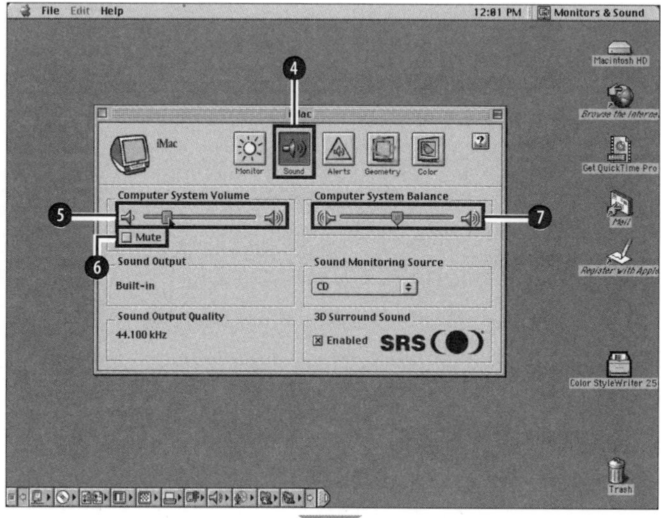

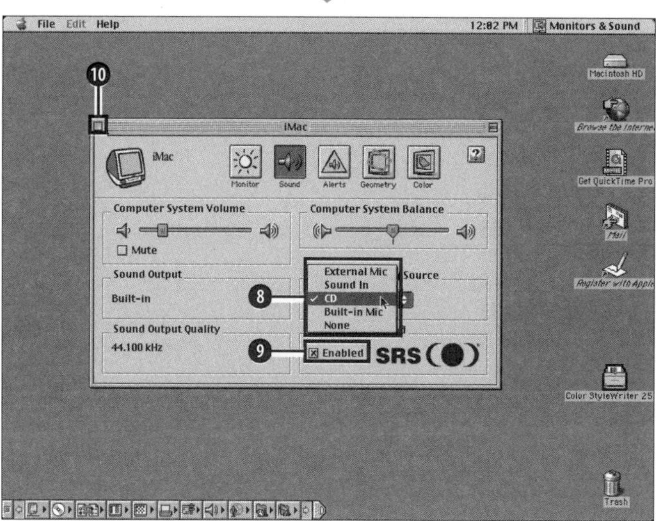

4. *Click the Sound button.*
5. *Optional: Adjust your computer system volume.*
6. *Optional: Click the Mute check box if you want to turn off the sound.*
7. *Optional: Adjust your computer system balance.*
8. *Optional: Choose a monitoring source from the drop-down menu.*
9. *Optional: Disable 3D Surround Sound (though I recommend you leave it enabled).*
10. *Close the window.*

If you want to record sounds with a microphone or attach an external CD player or cassette player, be sure to select an appropriate option from the menu.

3D Surround Sound is enabled by default, which I recommend. It really does make a difference. If you don't believe me, experiment with it yourself.

You also can adjust the volume of the alerts only— the beeps you hear when you do something wrong or when your iMac needs attention. Click the Alerts button (or option) at the top of the Monitors & Sound (or Sound) control panel and adjust the slider control.

TAKE NOTE

HEARING THE SOUND

If you aren't hearing any sounds, check your Monitor & Sounds (or Sounds) control panel to ensure the Mute button isn't checked under Alerts, and the system volume slide control isn't all the way to the left. Also check your Sound Monitoring Source; CD should be selected if you're playing an audio CD, while Sound In is your best bet if you've attached an external CD player or cassette player. If you're still not hearing any sound, make sure you don't have headphones plugged in to your iMac (we'll talk about these in the next section). Finally, if you don't have any external sound input devices, make sure your sound input port behind the access panel on your iMac is empty.

SHORTCUT

Use the speaker option on your Control Strip to quickly adjust the sound volume.

Listening to Music

Beyond the beeps, squawks, and chords of your iMac, audio CDs are the most common sources of sound. You already know that you can play and hear audio CDs on your iMac. If you've experimented with this, you'll likely want to know more about how it works and how you can fine-tune your listening experience. Let's delve deeper into the art and science of listening to music on your iMac.

The AppleCD Audio Player offers advanced features for those who are serious about their music. The display panel in the upper-left corner of the AppleCD Audio Player windows shows the track number and the elapsed time of play. If you prefer to see the track time remaining, the disc elapsed time, or the disc remaining time, click the small clock icon and select that option from the drop-down menu.

The buttons below the display panel let you play your audio CD in normal mode (sequentially), in Shuffle mode (random shuffle), or in Prog (program) mode. Clicking the Prog button initiates a program you've set up. To design a program, click the Prog button, click the toggle arrow below the Normal button, and then click and drag the track names or numbers from the track list in the left column to the play list in the right column in the order you'd like to hear them. Now click the Play button to listen to your programmed tracks.

If you want to loop your music endlessly (or until you shut down your iMac), click the arrow button next to the Prog button and it changes to a looped arrow.

The traditional fast forward and reverse buttons work when you want to change tracks, but it is easier to choose a track from the drop-down menu above them (click Audio CD or the CD's name, if you've named it).

CROSS-REFERENCE

The AppleCD Audio Player is introduced in Running Applications in Chapter 8.

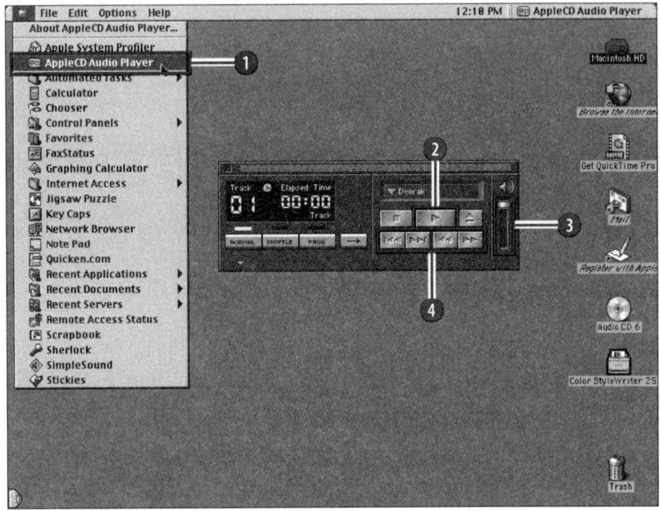

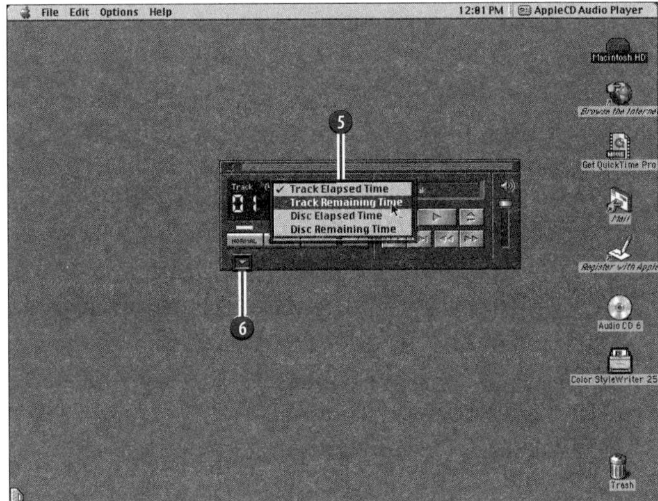

1. Open the AppleCD Audio Player.
2. Click the Play button to hear music.
3. Optional: Adjust your volume.
4. Optional: Forward and reverse through the tracks on the CD.
5. Optional: Click the clock icon to change the display.
6. Click the small arrow to display the track information.

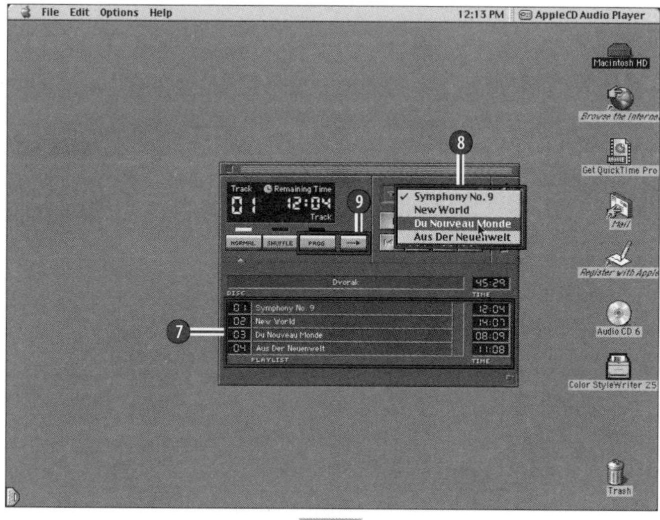

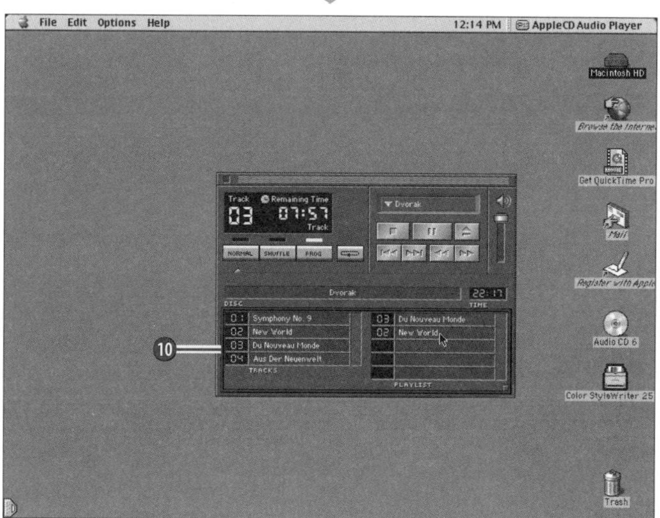

- *Note that the display changes if you selected a new display type.*

7. *Optional: Name your tracks.*
8. *Optional: Change to a new track using the drop-down menu.*
9. *Click the Loop button, and then click the Prog button.*

- *Note that the CD is now on loop mode.*

10. *Optional: Add tracks to your program list by clicking and dragging them from the left column to the right column.*

TAKE NOTE

USING EXTERNAL SPEAKERS

Newer iMacs are capable of rich, booming sound using the cool, built-in Harmon/Kardon speakers. Older iMacs are also capable of producing great sound using special computer speakers that can be connected to the speaker jack behind your iMac's access panel.If this interests you, look for self-powered, shielded speakers at a computer store. After plugging the power supply into a wall outlet and plugging the speaker jack into your iMac, revisit your Monitors & Sound control panel and select External speakers from the Sound Output menu (which should now be available). Note that you may need to adjust the volume on the speakers themselves, as well as in the control panel.

USING HEADPHONES

Your iMac has not one, but two, headphone jacks right on the front of the computer. Why two? So that two can listen to music or play a game without disturbing the rest of the household, of course! Actually, headphones offer all the rich sound features of external speakers, so you may want to use headphones even if you're alone. I often use headphones while I'm writing. For example, the piece I'm listening to now is Dvorák's *Symphony No. 9*, which you might see in the figures to the left if you squint.

FIND IT ONLINE

Computerized music makes for good listening, too. Go to **http://www.midi.com/** for downloads and links.

Playing and Setting Sounds

The iMac's repertoire isn't limited to music and sound clips. Your iMac also uses sound effects to request your attention and enhance your experience.

The most common sound effect is the *system alert.* This is the beep you hear when you click in the wrong spot or when your iMac needs your attention. You can change the system alert in the Alerts section of the Monitors & Sounds (or Sounds) control panel. Your iMac comes with six (Mac OS 8) or thirteen (Mac OS 9) different alert sounds, with the default as the Simple Beep sound. To use a different alert sound, simply select it from the list. You'll hear the sound when you select it. The sound's name in italics is the one you were previously using.

Besides the system alert, your iMac also has a *soundtrack* option. A soundtrack is a set of sound effects played when you do certain things, like open a window or trash a file. To turn on the soundtrack, pull down the Apple Menu and choose Appearance from the Control Panels submenu. Click the Sound tab near the top of the window, and then select a soundtrack from the drop-down menu (you probably only have one available soundtrack). Once you've selected a soundtrack, you can disable sound effects using the check boxes, should you want to. You may enjoy your iMac soundtrack (as I do), or you may go batty hearing all the clicks and clangs. Try it for a little while to find out.

Finally, sounds also come in sound files. You can usually spot these by their icon, which looks like a speaker. If you double-click the icon itself, one of two things happens. If the sound is brief, your iMac plays it for you. If the sound is longer than one or two seconds, your iMac displays a slider control with which you can play the sound and adjust the volume.

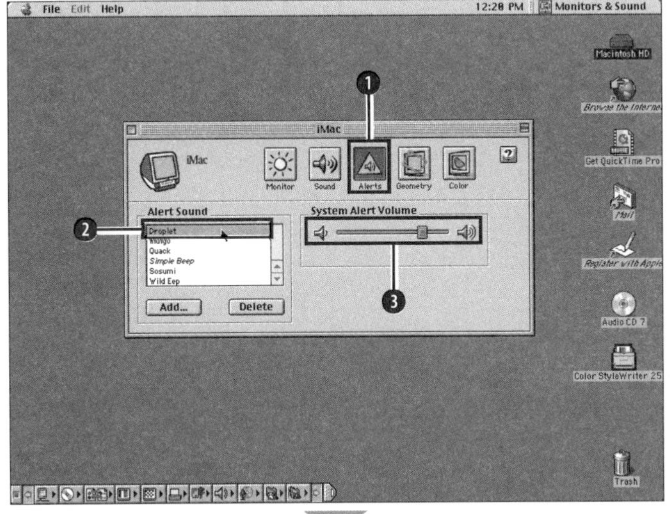

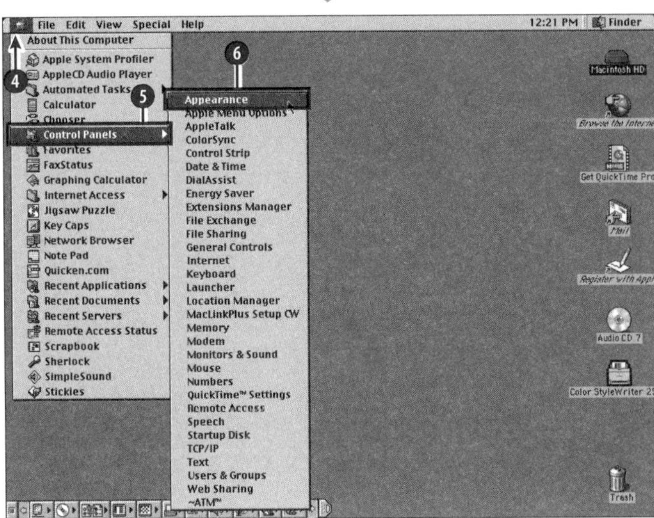

1. *Open the Monitors & Sound (or Sound) control panel again and choose Alerts.*
   - ▶ *Note your current alert in italics.*
2. *Optional: Select a new alert.*
3. *Optional: Adjust the alert volume.*
4. *Pull down the Apple menu.*
5. *Display the Control Panels submenu.*
6. *Choose Appearance.*

CROSS-REFERENCE

See Chapter 11 to learn how to access the Internet and America Online.

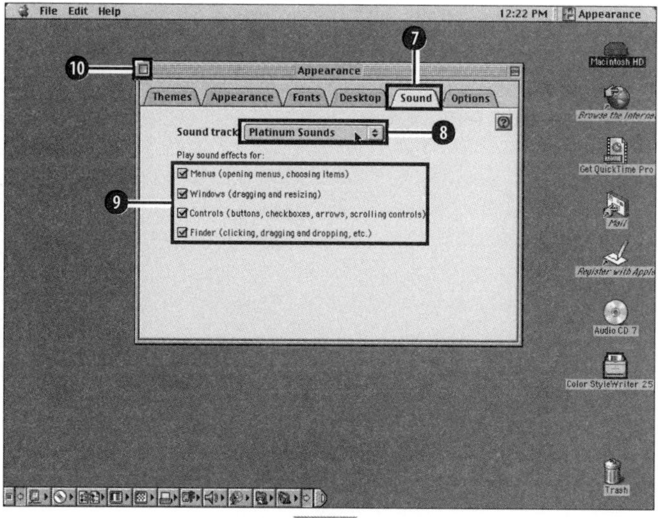

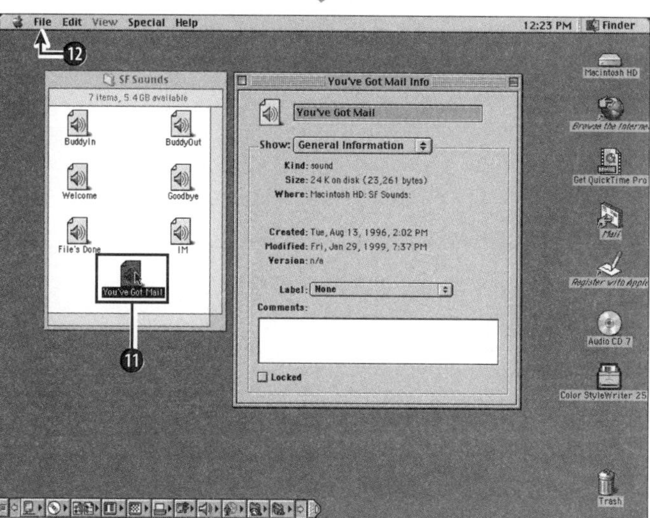

7 *Click the Sound tab.*

8 *Optional: Select a sound track.*

9 *Optional: Disable sound effects.*

10 *Close the window.*

11 *Double-click a sound file icon to hear its sound.*

12 *Choose Get Info from the File menu (or press Command+I).*

▶ *Note the kind of sound file.*

TAKE NOTE

ADDING SYSTEM ALERT SOUNDS

If you get tired of the Simple Beep and Wild Eep alert sounds, you can use other sounds instead. If you find (or have) a sound file that you want to use as your system alert, click and drag it to the System Folder. If it is the right format (SND, or sound type), you are asked if you want to put the file in the System file. Go ahead and click the OK button. Now, return to your Monitors & Sound (or Sound) control panel, click Alerts, and your sound then appears in the list. Select it and you've got a new system alert sound.

CONVERTING SOUNDS

If a friend with a PC sends you a sound, it may be in WAV format. To convert it to a Mac sound format, you can use a shareware program called Balthazar by Craig Marciniak. Search for it by name on America Online (keyword: FILE SEARCH) or the Internet (try Lycos at **http://www.lycos.com**). America Online also can play WAV sounds without conversion.

FIND IT ONLINE

Find sounds on America Online at keyword: MMS and on the Internet with a search engine such as Lycos (**http://www.lycos.com**).

Recording Sounds

If you can't find the right sound for your iMac, create it yourself! Your iMac even comes with a microphone for this purpose. Before you return your iMac to where you purchased it because you can't find the microphone, you should know that your iMac has a built-in microphone — the small rectangle above your screen is a microphone. Bet you didn't notice it until now. (I had my iMac two months before I discovered it.)

You also have a built-in sound recorder in the Monitor & Sound (or Sound) control panel. Open the control panel again, click the Sound button (in Mac OS 8) or click Input (in Mac OS 9), and then choose Built-in Mic from the drop-down Sound Monitoring Source or Input Source menu. Now, click Alerts, and then click the Add button in the lower-left corner. The resulting window is the sound recorder.

Before you begin recording, reduce background noise as much as possible. Your iMac's microphone is very sensitive and will pick up more than you think it will. When you're ready, click the Record button and begin speaking (or making your sound). You should see the *waves* of sound radiate out from the little picture of the speaker in the window, indicating that it is picking up the sound. Click the Stop button as soon as you're done. To hear what you just recorded, click the Play button. If the volume is too low or too high, use the Control Strip to increase or decrease it without closing the recording window. If you don't like the sound, click the Record button and try again, or click the Cancel button if you don't want it at all. If you do like it, click the Save button and type an appropriate name.

Once you record and save your sound, it appears selected in the list box with your other alert sounds. Deselect it if you don't want to hear it every time you take a misstep. If you later decide you don't want it, you can return to this window to delete it with the Delete button.

CROSS-REFERENCE

See the first task in this chapter for information on how to change your iMac's speaker volume.

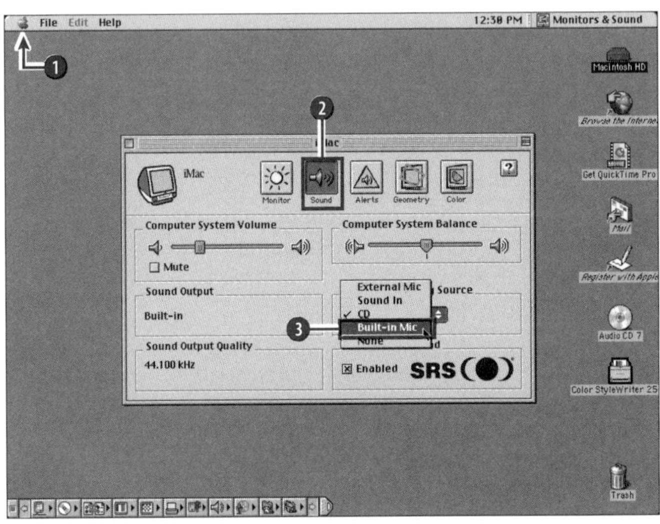

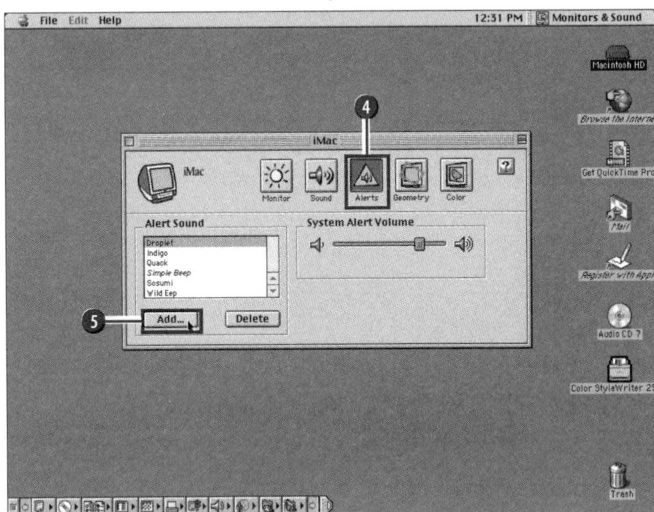

1. *1 Choose Monitors & Sound (or Sound) again.*
2. *2 Click the Sound button (in Mac OS 8) or the Input menu item (in Mac OS 9)*
3. *3 Select Built-In Mic from the Sound Monitoring Source or Input Source menu.*
4. *Click Alerts.*
5. *Click Add.*

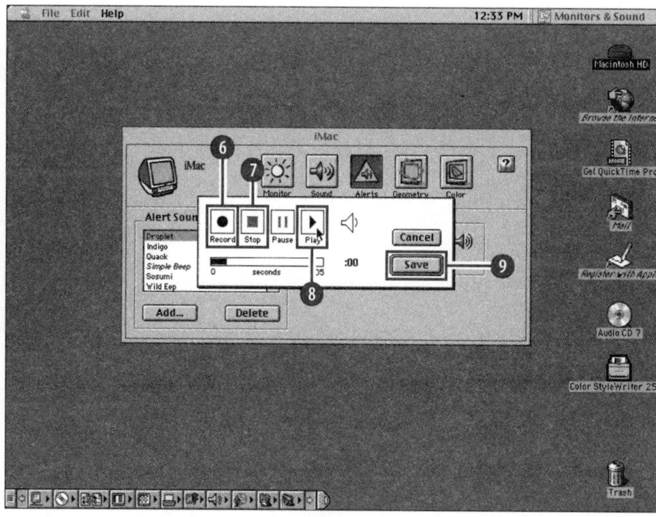

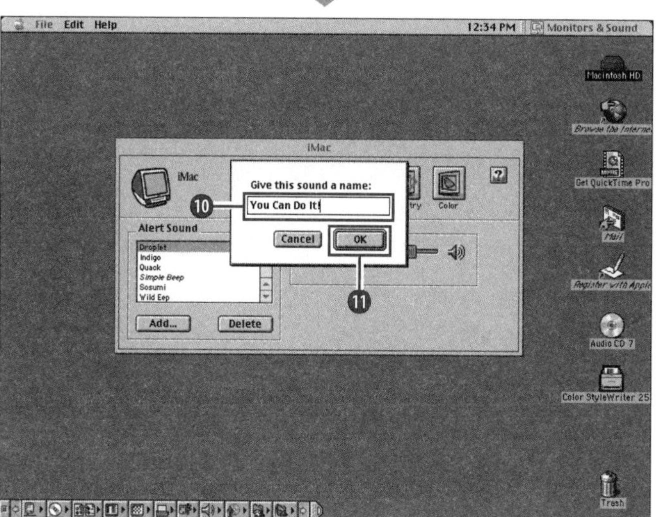

6 *Click the Record button and begin speaking.*

7 *Click the Stop button when you are finished.*

8 *Optional: Click the Play button to hear what you recorded.*

9 *Click the Save button to keep your recording.*

10 *Name your new sound.*

11 *Click the OK button (or press Return).*

▶ *Your new sound appears in the list.*

TAKE NOTE

RECORDING SOUNDS FROM CDS

Your iMac can record sounds from the built-in CD player, too! Just insert an audio CD into your CD player, queue it almost up to the point you'd like to record and let it continue playing. Now open your Monitors & Sounds (or sound) control panel, click Alerts, click Add, and then click the Record button when the CD plays the portion you want to record. Click the Stop button when appropriate, and then click the Save button. Now you've got a great alert or sound effect!

SHARING SOUNDS WITH FRIENDS

Your new sound is saved in a sound file. To find the file, open the System Folder, and then open the System file and locate your sound file. Hold down the Option key and click and drag the file to your Desktop to make a copy of it. Anyone else with a Mac can play your sound file. Use Balthazar (mentioned in the previous task) to convert it to WAV format before sending it to a PC user.

FIND IT ONLINE

Apple also offers information for musicians and sound designers on its Web site at http://www.apple.com/publishing/music.

Converting Text to Speech

You've probably already heard your iMac's tendency towards verbosity. Remember the last time a dialog box was up on your screen and you didn't click the OK or Cancel buttons right away? Your iMac, worried you weren't paying attention, began to *read* the text of the dialog box out loud. That always gets my attention!

Your iMac's speaking abilities extend beyond the garden-variety dialog box. Try opening the iMac Read Me file which should still be on your Macintosh HD. Double-click the icon to open SimpleText. Now select Speak All from the Sound menu and sit back and listen. Adjust the volume on your Control Strip, if necessary. Choose Stop Speaking from the Sound menu again to shut it up. You can do something similar in America Online, as well.

If you didn't like the tone of your iMac's voice, or really prefer a more manly tenor, you can give your iMac a new voice. Open the Speech control panel to access your settings. The Options drop-down menu at the top toggles between Voice and Talking Alerts (those dialog box readings). Begin with Voice, and then select a voice from the drop-down menu. After choosing a voice, click the speaker icon to the right for a voice sample. These samples are really quite amusing. My favorite is Deranged. Too slow? Turn your iMac into a fast-talker with the Rate slider adjustment — move it to the right to speed up the voice rate, and to the left to slow it down.

The Talking Alerts options let you specify how your dialog boxes are read (if at all). You can choose to have your iMac speak a phrase before it begins reading your dialog box. Alert! is the default, but other options such as "It's not my fault!" and "Excuse me!" are also possibilities. Select Random from the list for a different alert phrase each time. You can even create your own alert

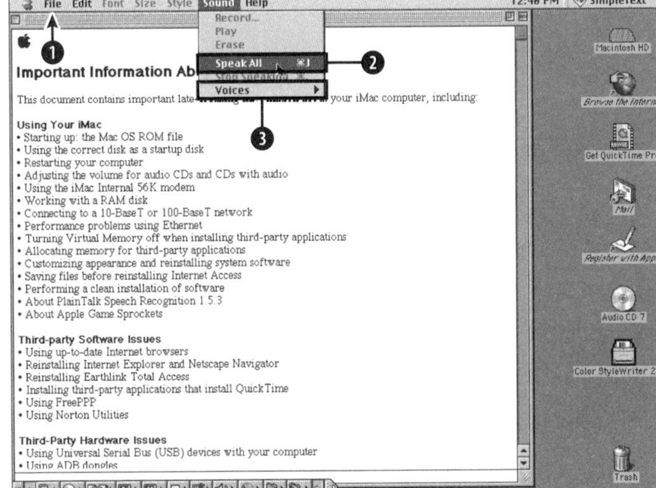

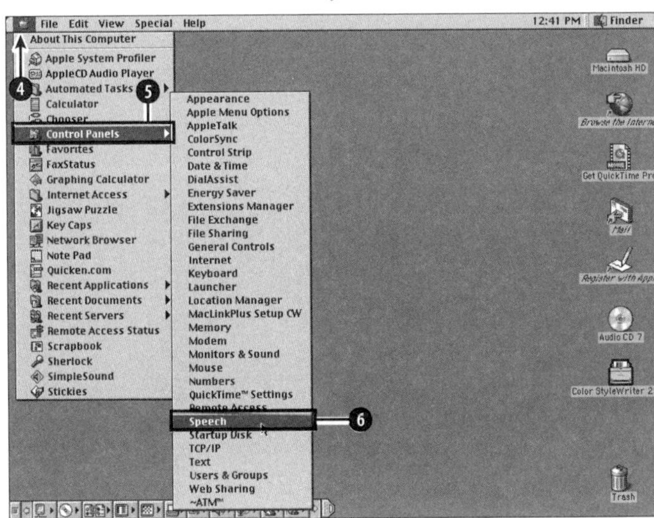

1. *Open SimpleText, and then open a file from the File menu.*
2. *Choose Speak All from the Sound menu.*
3. *Optional: Choose Voices to change your iMac's voice.*

▶ *Press Command+. to stop speaking.*

4. *Pull down the Apple menu.*
5. *Display the Control Panels submenu.*
6. *Choose Speech.*

CROSS-REFERENCE

See Chapter 15 for more information about your iMac's memory resources.

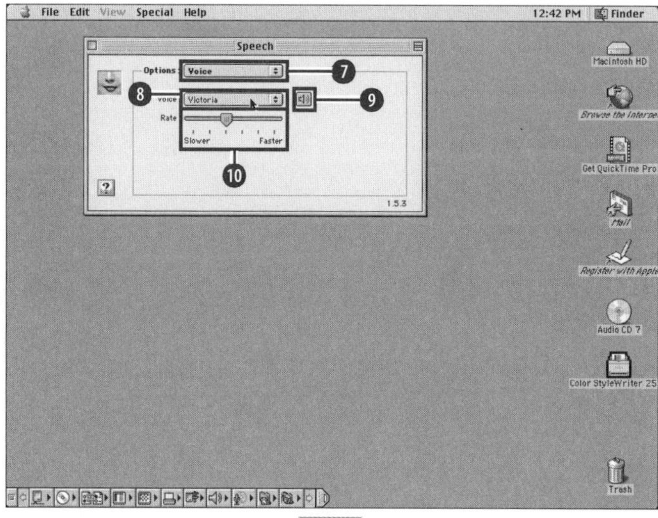

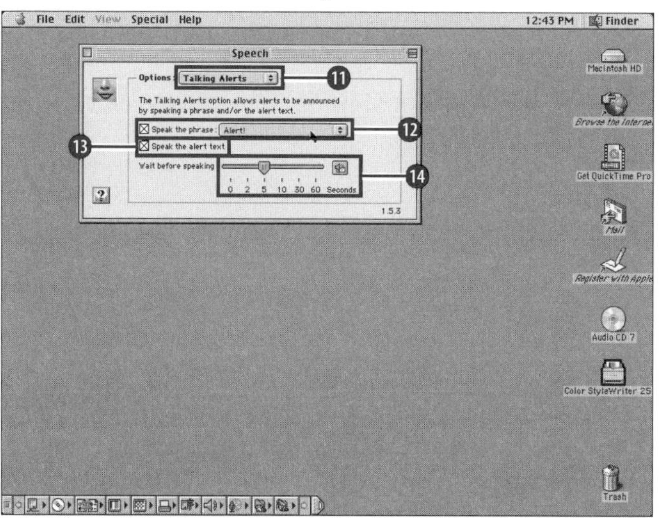

7 *Choose Voice from the drop-down menu.*

8 *Optional: Select a new voice.*

9 *Optional: Click the speaker button to hear a voice sample.*

10 *Optional: Adjust the voice rate.*

11 *Choose Talking Alerts from the drop-down menu.*

12 *Optional: Deselect "Speak the phrase," or choose a new alert phrase.*

13 *Optional: Deselect "Speak the alert text."*

14 *Optional: Adjust the number of seconds before your iMac begins speaking the alert.*

phrase. I had fun with "Jennifer, pay attention!" Of course, you can deselect this option if you'd rather not have an alert phrase. Deselect "Speak the alert text" option if you don't want talking alerts at all. Modify the "Wait before speaking" slider control to hear your talking alerts earlier or later.

TAKE NOTE

CHOOSING VOICES

Your iMac's default voice is Victoria, which is about as good as they come. Agnes and Bruce are also easy voices to comprehend. You may be tempted to change to the high-quality version of these voices, but keep in mind that doing so will take more memory (RAM), meaning that less RAM will be available for other applications.

USING SPEECH RECOGNITION

Speech recognition, a computer's ability to understand and obey spoken voice commands, isn't possible on the iMac yet. Apple's speech recognition software requires that commands be recorded at 22 kHz, and the iMac only records at 44 kHz. I hear Apple is working on this, however.

SHORTCUT

Press Command+. to stop your iMac speaking at any time, including the dialog box Talking Alerts.

Using QuickTime

The iMac does more than tickle your eardrum — it can stimulate your visual cortex, too! Your iMac does this with QuickTime, a set of tools that let you play, edit, and create multimedia presentations. With it, your iMac is capable of video — even virtual reality.

To view a video, begin by opening the MoviePlayer application inside the QuickTime folder, which is inside the Applications folder. Now locate a movie and double-click to open it. Look for the Sample Movie file in the QuickTime folder. Once opened, the iMac displays the first frame of the video. Controls along the bottom of the window let you change the volume (speaker button), start the video (play button), move to a specific frame in the video (slider control), rewind, and fast forward.

Another amazing capability of QuickTime is *virtual reality.* While I'm not sure it's virtually real, virtual reality, in this context, means the ability to look around at all vantage points of an object or setting, and even move through them, in some cases. To see what I mean, insert your iMac Software Install CD-ROM, and then open the Apple Tour.mov file from within MoviePlayer (you'll find it in the QuickTime Samples folder within the CD Extras folder on the CD-ROM). Click and hold anywhere on the picture with your mouse pointer (it changes to an omni-directional set of arrows). Now, move the mouse pointer in the direction you want to turn. Pretty realistic, huh? Locate the building's front doors and click them to go inside the virtual building. You can actually go out to the quad and look around. Hot spots around the picture give a brief description when you move over them. Use the arrow and question mark button at the bottom of the window to find the hot spots. Use the magnifying glass icons at the bottom to zoom in and out. Click and drag the resize button in the lower-right corner to increase or decrease the size of the picture.

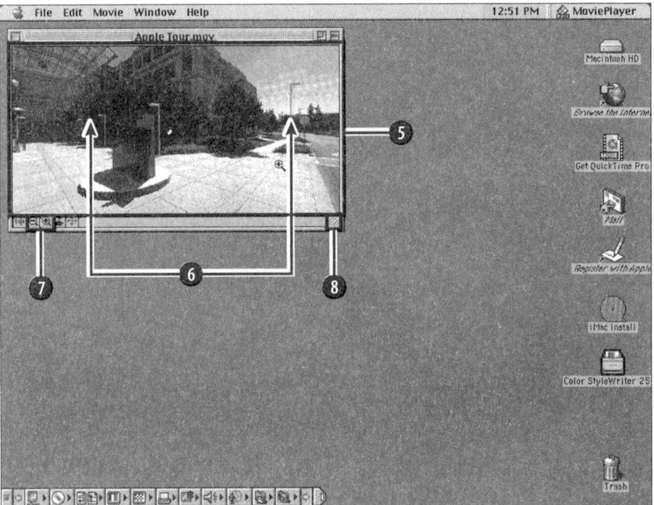

1. *Open a QuickTime video.*
2. *Optional: Adjust the sound volume.*
3. *Click the Play button, or use the slider to move through the video.*
4. *Optional: Reverse or fast forward.*
5. *Open a QuickTime VR movie.*
6. *Click and drag in the image to change your view.*
7. *Optional: Click the magnifying glass buttons to zoom in and out.*
8. *Optional: Resize the window.*

CROSS-REFERENCE

If you want to print a video or movie image, refer to Chapter 6 for information on printing.

Using Sound and Video

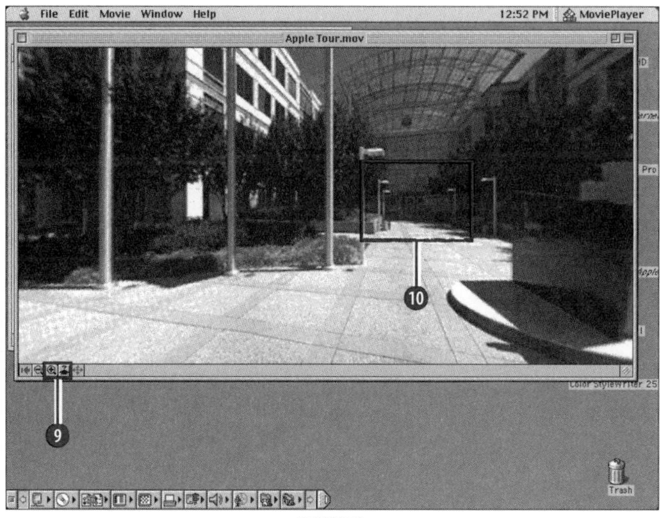

9 *Optional: Click the Hot Spots button to see the places you can click.*

10 *Click the doors to enter the virtual building (go to a new view).*

11 *Click the doors to go to the quad area.*

12 *Close the window when you are finished exploring.*

QuickTime supports many multimedia formats, including those used by Windows. If you double-click a multimedia file and QuickTime doesn't open, try opening it from within MoviePlayer or click and drag the file on top of the MoviePlayer icon.

TAKE NOTE

FINDING VIDEOS AND VR MOVIES

Like sounds, your best bet for finding videos and movies is online. Your iMac Software Install CD-ROM offers a few movies in the QuickTime 3 Effects folder (personally, I like the Splash movie). Apple also offers some movies for download on its Web site at **http://www.apple.com**. You also can find a list of travel sites offering virtual tours of scenic destinations at **http://dir.lycos.com/Recreation/Travel/Virtual/**.

GETTING QUICKTIME PRO

The first time you open MoviePlayer, you are asked if you want to upgrade to QuickTime Pro. You don't need to upgrade to watch a movie, but you do if you want to make changes or access advanced features. Upgrading to QuickTime Pro costs about $30. Once you upgrade, the video editing features of QuickTime become available. You can even convert sounds with QuickTime Pro.

USING IMOVIE

Newer iMacs come with iMovie, a digital video enhancement program. To learn more about iMovie, visit http://www.apple.com/imovie/.

SHORTCUT

Press and hold the Command key to zoom in or the Control key to zoom out.

Personal Workbook

Q&A

1. How do you adjust the volume of only your system alerts?

2. How do you set an audio CD to endlessly play or loop?

3. Where are your iMac's headphone jacks? How many are there?

4. How do you turn on your iMac's soundtrack?

5. Where is your built-in microphone and how do you turn it on?

6. How do you give your iMac a new voice?

7. How do you turn off the Talking Alerts you hear when you don't dismiss a dialog box right away?

8. What is the difference between a QuickTime video and a QuickTime virtual reality movie?

ANSWERS: PAGE 320

EXTRA PRACTICE

1. If you have an older iMac, purchase and install new external speakers for your iMac. Use the Monitors & Sound (or Sound) control panel to select your sound output through your new speakers. Experiment with volumes and balance to find the right sound.

2. Find new alert sounds on the Internet. Double-click each sound file to hear it. If it doesn't open, convert the sound file as needed. Drag your favorite sound file to your System Folder to install it into your system. Select it in your Monitors & Sound (or Sound) control panel.

3. Create a new alert sound from an audio CD. Make two versions — one very short (a second or two) and one very long (ten seconds or so). Try using both as alert sounds to see which one works best.

REAL-WORLD APPLICATIONS

✔ Your brother is always playing with your iMac and you really wish he'd stop. Thanks to the iMac's built-in microphone and the Add Alert sound feature in the Monitors & Sound (or Sound) control panel, your iMac now says (in your own voice), "I'm telling Mom!" every time your brother messes up.

✔ You and your brother keep fighting over which CD to play on the stereo. Right now he wants to play Metallica, and you want to hear Schubert's Trout Quintet. You make a deal with him: He can listen to Metallica now, but he'll have to give you that ice cream cone. You plug a pair of headphones into your iMac, pop the Schubert CD into the iMac's CD-ROM drive, and start licking that ice cream cone. Mmmm!

Visual Quiz

When would you see these windows? What do they accomplish?

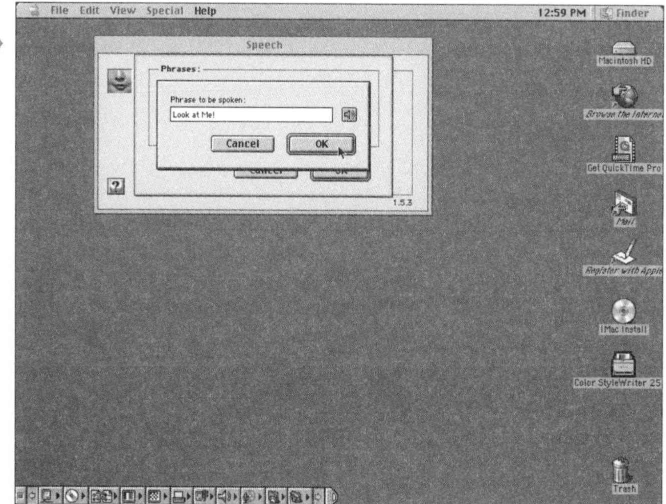

PART III

Working With Your iMac

The folks at Apple Computer tell us that the "i" in iMac doesn't refer to me, myself, and I, even if it *is* a personal computer. "A" is for *Apple*, and "i" is for *Internet*!

Your iMac wasn't built to stand on a desk, all alone. Fresh out of the box, it's ready and waiting to be connected to that world-wide network of computers and computer users known as the Internet. Whether you choose the bundled America Online or EarthLink online services, or you choose another service altogether, your iMac makes it very easy to plug into the vast world of online information.

iMacs also come ready-made to send and receive faxes, and to connect to office computer networks. In fact, if you own two Macintosh computers, all you may need is one cable (and maybe an adapter) to hook them up and begin sharing information at the speed of light.

Of course, a stay-at-home computer is much safer than one that is off gallivanting around the world. But no matter how you use your iMac, there's a lot you can do to keep it safe from disaster, so we'll end this section with lessons on keeping your iMac safe and secure.

CHAPTER 10

MASTER THESE SKILLS

- Configuring Your Modem
- Using Your Fax Software
- Sending a Fax
- Receiving a Fax

Connecting to the World

Once upon a time, when dinosaurs ruled the Earth, a Brontosaurus in Belize had no way of speaking to a Pterodactyl in Tehran. Millions of years later, that was still true of your Great-Great-Aunt Myrna in Minnesota and Great-Great-Uncle Felix in Florida. Then, about 125 years ago, Alexander Graham Bell summoned Mr. Watson from the adjoining room, and telephone bells started ringing the world over.

There was also a time when most personal computers just sat on a desk with no connection at all to the outside world. People used them to write letters, just as Great-Great-Aunt Myrna and Great-Great-Uncle Felix did, which they sent via U.S. Mail. Then, seemingly overnight, personal computers started talking to each other over the telephone. The *modem* that made it possible for a computer to use a telephone line went from an expensive computer accessory to built-in standard equipment within a few short years.

Today, that modem is the gateway to all sorts of incredible communications, from the e-mail and Web browsing of the Internet to the seemingly simple task of sending and receiving a fax. All it takes, for the most part, is the right software, a telephone cable, and a handy telephone line. You don't even need a separate fax machine! As you probably already know, your iMac comes with everything but that telephone line, and the process of connecting the phone line and configuring your iMac to make use of it is amazingly simple.

Of course, in our hooked-in, hurry-up world, we all feel the need for speed. The maximum communication speed available to you via modem is quickly becoming as outmoded as the dinosaurs, since the Internet has become the conduit for incredibly bulky data like music and television. The answer to these speed limitations are new telephone services that can move more data in less time, and a gadget called a *cable modem* which takes advantage of the capacity of your cable TV hookup to speed Internet information to you in record time. Although the ability to use these new services isn't completely built into your iMac, the process of adding them is still quite simple.

As you can surely guess, this chapter covers the ins and outs of making the connections you need to become a citizen of our hooked-up world, from setting up your telephone connection to sending and receiving faxes. Have fun!

Configuring Your Modem

Your iMac comes with a built-in modem. A modem is a device that translates, sends, and receives data over normal telephone lines. Modems convert the digital data on your computer into analog information that can be sent through the lines, and then convert it back again on the receiving end. The faster your modem can do this, the faster your connection and the happier you are. The speed of a modem is measured by its *baud rate*. Your modem is capable of achieving baud rates up to 56K (pronounced "fifty-six-kay"), which is the fastest modem you can get these days. You aren't likely to actually achieve speeds of 56K, however, because the telephone lines themselves slow transmission speeds with static and noise, and sometimes even telephone cable limitations.

Before you can use your modem, you must attach a telephone cable between your iMac and a wall jack. Alternately, you can connect an optional AirPort Base Station to your phone line, then slip an optional AirPort Card into your iMac (I discuss AirPort in a bit more detail in Chapter 12). Your iMac modem jack is behind the access panel on the right side of your iMac. You can use the telephone cable that came with your iMac, or you can purchase a longer cable if you need one (look for a standard RJ-11 cable at an electronics, office supply, or hardware store). Plug the other end of the telephone cable into the nearest telephone wall jack. If your surge suppressor has telephone jacks, use them. You'll need to connect another telephone cable between the surge suppressor and the wall jack, too. If your wall jack already has a telephone cable plugged into it, purchase a splitter from your local hardware store; it will allow your two cables to share one jack.

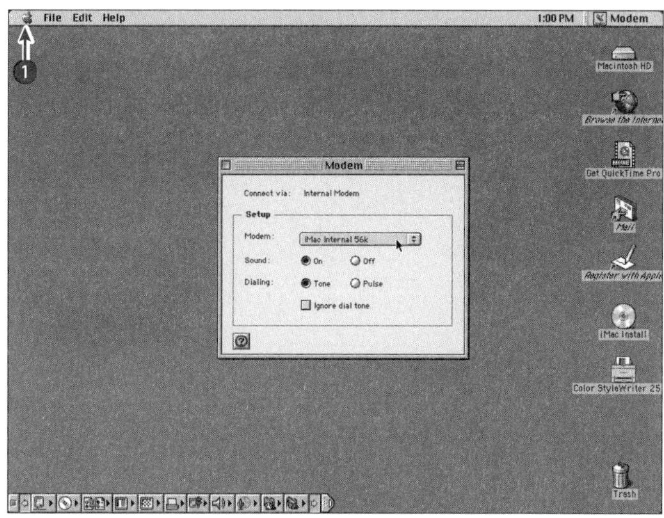

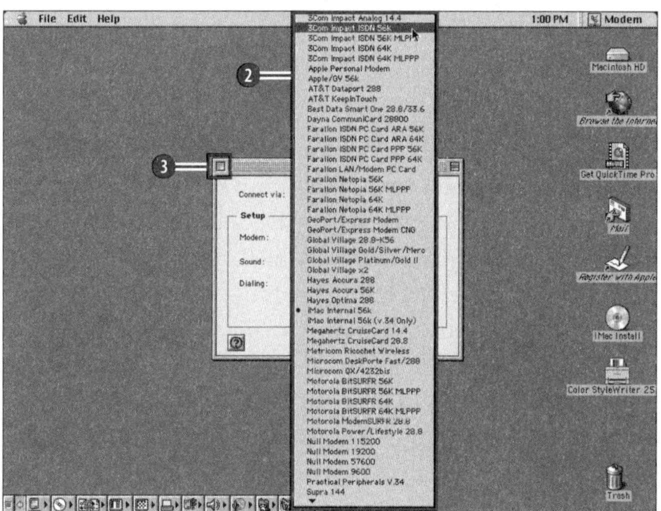

1. *Open the Modem control panel.*

▶ *You probably won't need to change these settings, but they are available if you need to change them.*

2. *Optional: Choose your modem from the drop-down menu if you use a device other than your built-in 56K modem.*
3. *Close the window.*

CROSS-REFERENCE

Refer to Chapter 12 if you want to connect a cable, ISDN, or DSL modem via an Ethernet hub.

Using Your Phone Line

Your phone line is essential to getting connected, and thus deserves some attention before we go much further. First, you need a working phone line — just a regular, garden-variety phone line from your local telephone company. If you want to connect from the office and they use PBX, Merlin, or other proprietary systems, you'll need a phone with a data jack, or to purchase an adapter (try **http://www.hellodirect.com**) or have a regular phone line installed. Second, when your modem is in use, your phone line is also in use. You may want to consider a second phone line for your modem. A second line will leave your first line free for incoming and outgoing calls, plus let you use the first line to talk to someone while you're online (a real boon when you need to call tech support). And if you plan to use your fax software, a dedicated modem line means you can leave your fax software turned on all the time to send and receive faxes. If a second line is out of the question, think about a voice mail service offered by the telephone company. That way, it can take messages for you when your line is busy. If you do opt for a single telephone line, get that line splitter I mentioned earlier. Having to unplug the modem cable so you can plug in your telephone cable is a real drag; keep them both plugged in with the splitter. Plugging a cable in only connects your iMac and/or phone to the line — the line itself isn't in use until you use the modem to make a call.

At this point, your modem configurations are up to the various Internet applications you want to use. They will guide you through the configuration steps, when necessary.

If you want to connect a different modem — perhaps a cable modem or DSL modem — to your iMac, it must either be USB-ready or connected to an AirPort base station (assuming you are using an iMac with an AirPort Card installed). See the Take Note section below for more details.

TAKE NOTE

USING THE MODEM CONTROL PANEL

If you only intend to use your iMac's internal modem, you really don't ever need to use your Modem control panel. If, on the other hand, you connect another modem, you may need to select your modem from the drop-down menu here.

USING CABLE, ISDN, AND DSL MODEMS

If 56K isn't fast enough for you, consider a cable, ISDN, or DSL modem. A cable modem uses your cable company's television signal access to receive data at high speeds. Contact your local cable company to inquire about availability in your area. If your cable modem uses Ethernet, you should be able to use it with your iMac. Internal PCI cable modems probably won't work with your iMac, however. ISDN and DSL are other high-speed data transfer methods offered by local telephone companies. An ISDN or DSL modem can be connected to your iMac through its USB ports, an USB adapter, or with AirPort (if your iMac is AirPort enabled).

FIND IT ONLINE

Visit **http://www.imacworld.com/getconnect.html** for more information on modems and the art of getting connected.

Using Your Fax Software

Faxing is the simplest way to connect your iMac to the rest of the world. Your iMac comes with the FAXstf software (look in the Applications folder), which allows you to send and receive faxes. It works really quite well, though you do need to set it up first.

To begin, open the Fax Browser application inside your FAXstf folder. When you're prompted to register, I recommend you elect to register later, after you've set up your fax software. (Don't forget to register later, however!) Once open, the Fax Browser window appears. Make a beeline for the Edit menu and select Settings near the bottom.

The Settings dialog box is set up a bit different from other settings or preferences you may have seen. Icons along the left side of the window represent the various setting categories. Just click an icon to view a category's options. Start with the Cover Page category. Type your name, and then add a company, school, or organization name. Finally, add voice and fax numbers. This information needs to be displayed on outgoing faxes, so be sure to type in only what you want others to see. Peek at the other category's settings, though you'll probably want to leave them as they are for now. Do pay attention to Fax Menu settings, because they will indicate which keys you should press and hold when you want to fax something from within an application (we'll do this in the next task). Also visit your Fax Modem settings and change your Answer On setting from Never to 1 Ring (if you have a dedicated modem line), or change it to two to three rings (if you use your line for voice, too). Don't go higher than five rings, however, because some fax machines give up after five or six rings.

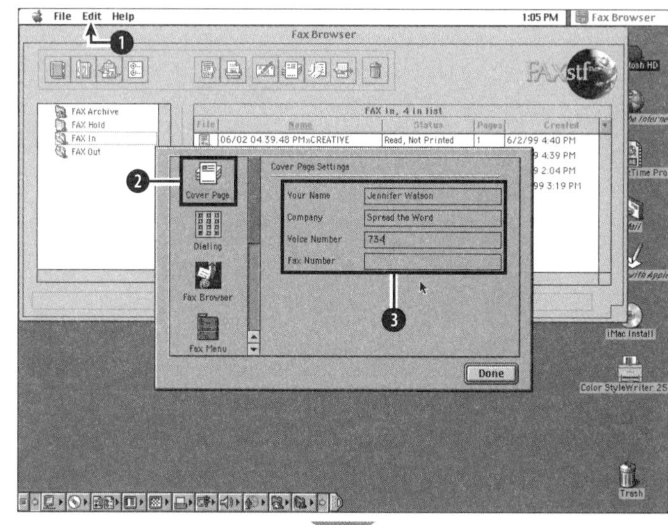

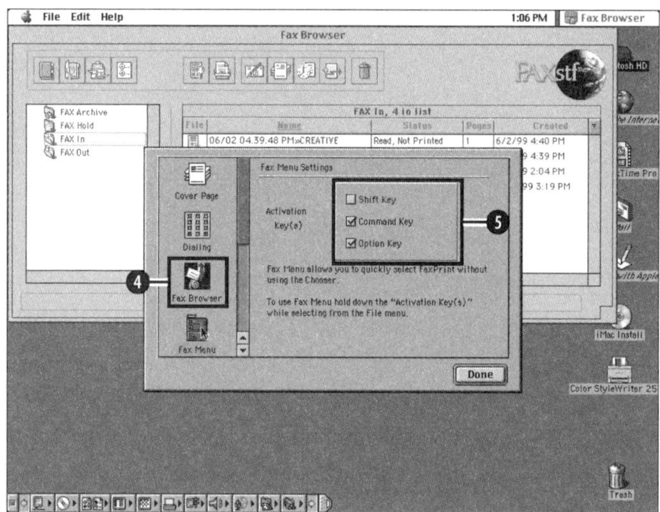

1. Open the Fax Browser and choose Settings from the Edit menu.
2. Click the Cover Page icon.
3. Type your personal information.
4. Click the Fax Menu icon.

▶ Note your activation key.

5. Optional: Change your activation keys.

CROSS-REFERENCE

See "Setting Preferences" in Chapter 8 for additional assistance setting your fax software settings.

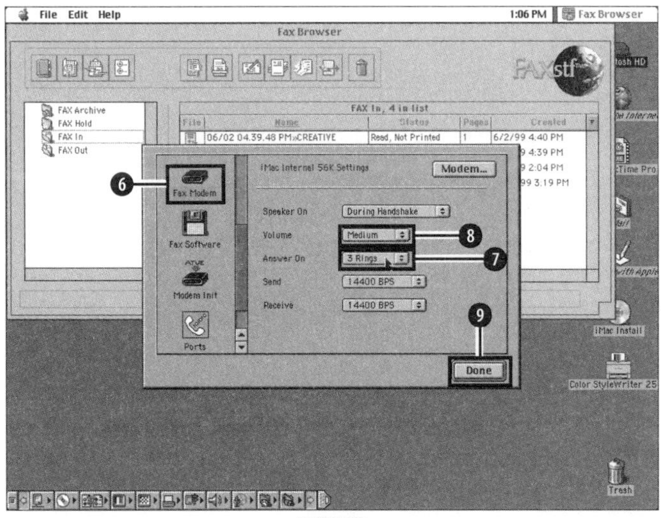

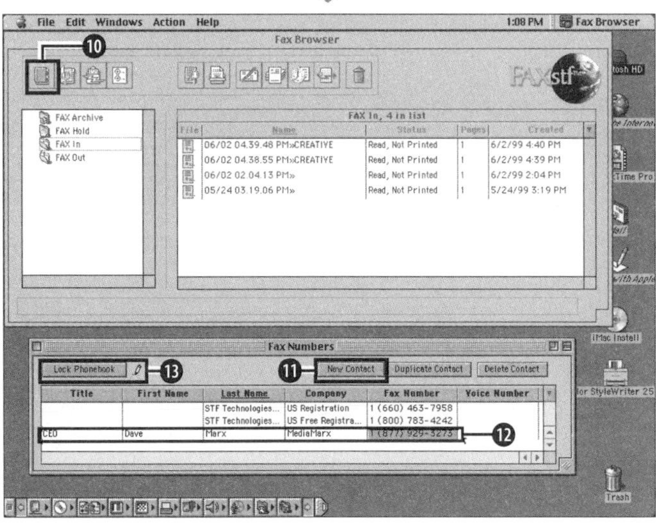

6 *Click the Fax Modem icon.*

7 *Optional: Adjust the number of rings your modem answers on.*

8 *Optional: Adjust the modem volume.*

9 *Click the Done button.*

10 *Click the Phonebook button.*

11 *Click New Contact.*

12 *Type your new contact information.*

13 *Click the Lock Phonebook button when you are finished.*

TAKE NOTE

FILLING IN YOUR PHONE BOOK

This is a good time to add fax numbers to your built-in phone book in FAXstf. You can send faxes without adding phone numbers, but it'll take more time and be much less convenient. To add numbers, choose Fax Numbers from the Windows menu (or click the phone book icon in the Fax Browser window). Now choose New Contact from the Action menu (or click the New Contact button) — a blank line appears in the chart. Type your contact's information, pressing Tab to move to the next column. Be sure to include at least a name and a fax number. Use the Duplicate Contact button if someone has two fax numbers; you'll only need to type the fax number in the duplicate line. When you're finished, click the Lock Phonebook button to protect your data (and allow the numbers to be selected when faxing later). If you forget to click the Lock Phonebook button, closing the window locks it for you automatically. You will need to unlock and lock the Phonebook manually if you intend to keep it open on your screen, however. The phonebook needs to be locked before it can be used by the fax software.

SHORTCUT

Press Command+D to view your Phonebook quickly.

Sending a Fax

You can send faxes two ways. If you just want to dash off a fast fax, the Fax Browser provides a QuickNote feature that lets you send a fax up to 255 characters in length. If, on the other hand, you want to send a longer fax, or one that is formatted or includes graphics, you can send a fax directly from the application you composed it in (such as AppleWorks).

To compose a QuickNote fax, press Command+K in the Fax Browser, enter your contact information, and type your QuickNote. If you've already added the contact information for your fax recipient to your phone book, you can click and drag it from the phone book to the QuickNote window. The Cover Page drop-down menu allows you to select a cover page format (see the Take Note sections for cover page tips). When you're ready, click the Send Fax button to instantly send the fax. You'll hear the modem dial your recipient's fax number and the first couple of squawks of data transfer. When the fax is complete, a dialog box informs you that your fax was sent successfully. FAXstf files a copy of the fax you sent in the FAX Archive section if you should need to check it later.

To fax a document from another application, begin by composing your document as usual, keeping in mind that your font should be no smaller than 12 points for legibility. To send your document as a fax, you need to alert the fax software that your document needs to be sent. Select the Chooser from the Apple menu and then choose FaxPrint. Now, return to your application, display the File menu, and Fax is now available as an option. Select the resolution and page span. If you added

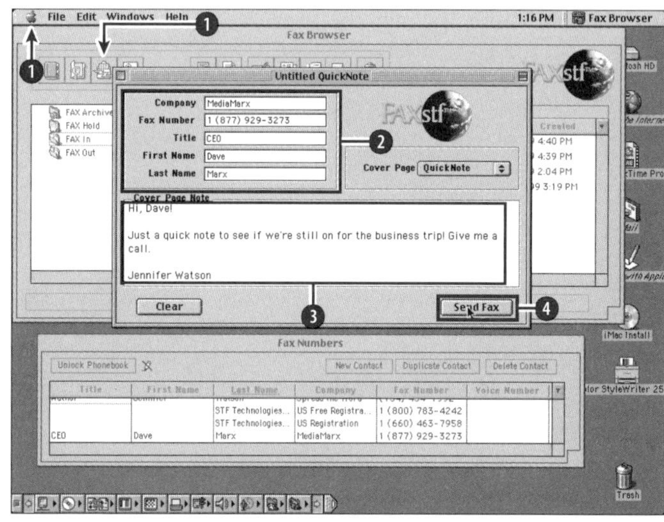

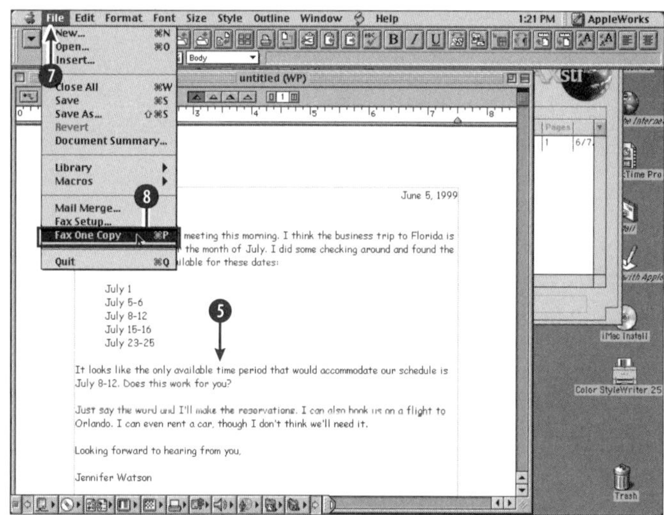

1. *Choose QuickNote from the File menu or click the QuickNote button.*
2. *Address your QuickNote.*
3. *Type your message.*
4. *Click the Send Fax button.*
5. *Compose your fax in another application.*
6. *Hold down your activation keys (Option+Command).*
7. *Pull down the File menu.*
8. *Choose Fax One Copy (or press Command+P).*

CROSS-REFERENCE

Refer to Chapter 6, "Printing Documents," for helpful tips on printing that also relate to faxing.

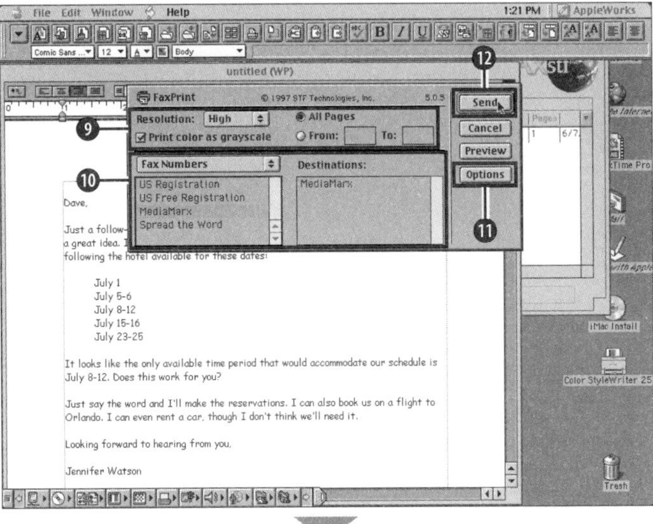

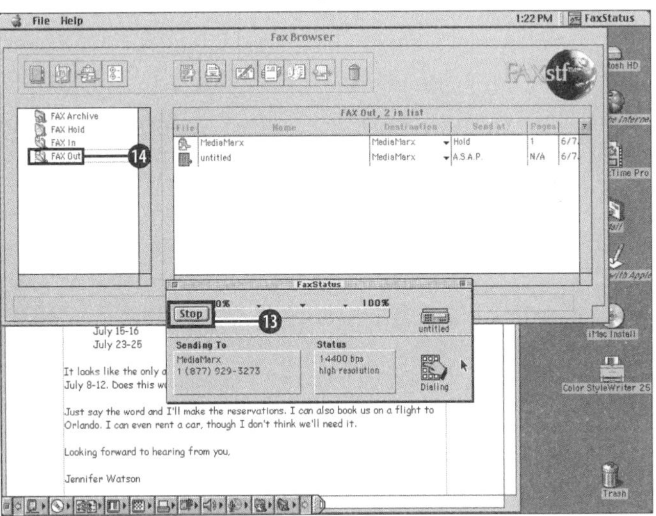

9. *Select your settings in the FaxPrint window.*
10. *Press-and-drag recipients from the left column to the right.*
11. *Click Options to schedule a fax or choose a cover page.*
12. *Click the Send button.*

▶ *The FaxStatus window appears.*

13. *Optional: Click the Stop button to abort the fax transmission.*
14. *The fax is archived in the FAX Out folder in your Fax Browser.*

the necessary information to your Phone Book, you also should see fax numbers in the list box to the left. To address your fax, click and drag a number from the left box to the right box. You can add as many destinations as you like. If your recipient isn't in your phone book, press Command+N to add a temporary address. Click Options to schedule your fax for later, as well as to select a Cover Page. When you are ready, click the Send button to initiate the faxing process.

TAKE NOTE

CREATING COVER PAGES

Cover pages introduce your fax to your recipient(s) and communicate any essential information such as sender name, fax number, fax length, and comments. FAXstf lets you create up to ten different cover pages to use when sending faxes. In the Fax Browser, choose Edit Cover Pages from the Edit menu to see your cover page options. You can edit an existing cover page, or you can create a new one by choosing Empty Cover Page from the drop-down menu and giving it a name. You can even click the Edit Labels Text to change the cover page font and rename the labels it will use. You also can tweak the layout of the cover page by clicking and dragging the elements represented in the window.

SHORTCUT

Press and hold Command+Option while opening the File menu to display the Fax menu option.

Receiving a Fax

Your iMac and the FAXstf software can also receive faxes for you — automatically! In fact, automatically is the only way you can receive faxes. It isn't possible to turn on your fax software after you realize that an incoming call is a fax transmission.

To set up FAXstf to automatically answer your phone, open your Settings and select Fax Modem. Now change Answer On from Never to the number of rings that seems appropriate and click the Done button. When your phone line rings, the FAXstf software will answer your phone with a standard fax tone. If the incoming call is indeed a fax, the software begins receiving it and displays the FaxStatus window during the transmission. You can stop the transmission if you wish (press Stop in the FaxStatus window or press Command+.). After the software successfully receives the fax transmission, you hear a ring (sounds like a phone) and a blinking icon appears over the Apple menu to indicate you have a new fax. To view it, switch to your Fax Browser, click the Fax In button, and double-click your most recent fax. You can scroll through the fax like you would a document. Use the magnifying-glass button in the tool palette to zoom in — press and hold the Option key while clicking to zoom out. Other buttons on the tool palette let you change views and rotate the fax. Use the menu items under the Action menu to see your fax in various ways, including as a continuous roll of paper (like old-fashioned fax machines) or with regular page breaks. Choose Antialiased for the best quality display, or Fast for a rougher view. If you need a hard copy of the fax, you can print it like you would any other page. Just be sure you've selected your printer again in the Chooser before you press Command+P.

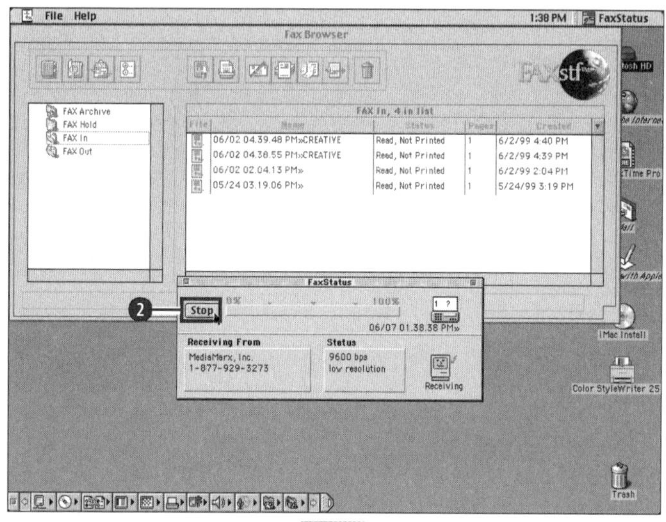

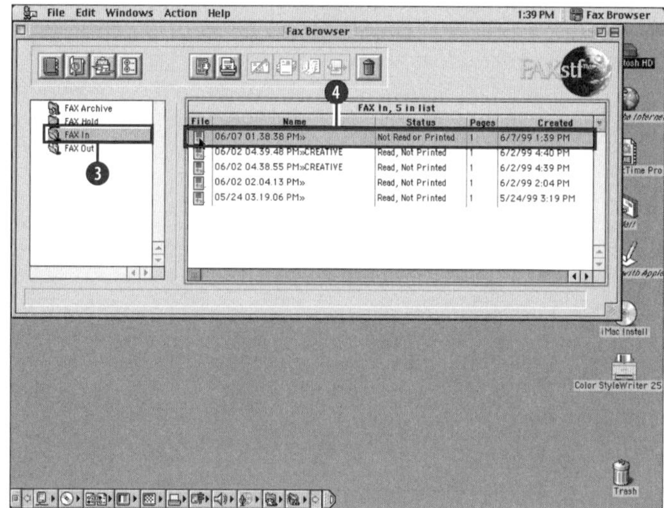

❶ *Confirm that your Fax Modem settings are set to answer on one or more rings.*

▶ *The FaxStatus window appears when a fax comes in.*

❷ *Click the Stop button to abort the transmission.*

❸ *Click the FAX In button to list the faxes you've received.*

❹ *Double-click a fax to view it.*

▶ *Optional: Select a fax and click the View button.*

CROSS-REFERENCE

Refer to the first task in this chapter for tips on managing your phone line.

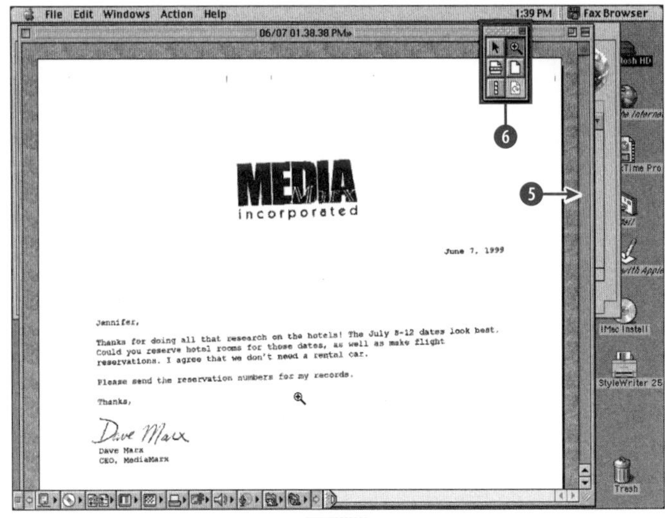

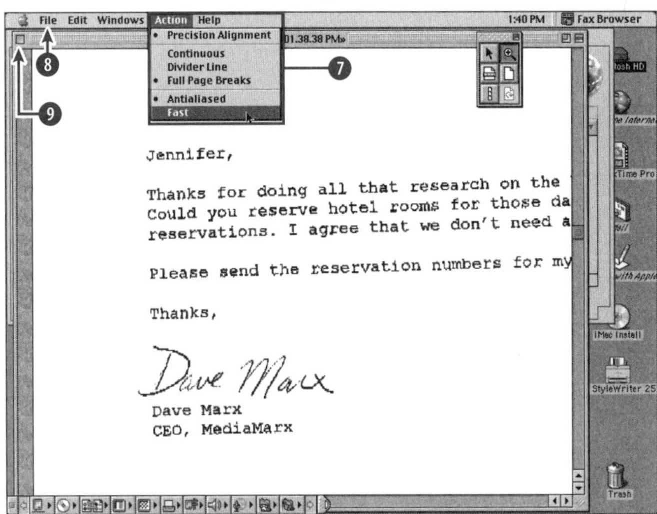

- The Fax Browser displays your fax in a separate window.
- ❺ Use the scroll bars to scroll through your fax.
- ❻ Optional: Use the tool palette to zoom in and out or change your view.
- ❼ Optional: Choose an option from the Action menu.
- ❽ Optional: Choose Print from the File menu.
- ❾ Close the fax window.

All incoming fax transmissions are archived in the FAX In folder in your Fax Browser. Clicking the column names sorts your fax list, which is helpful when you're looking for something specific.

TAKE NOTE

JUGGLING VOICE AND FAX

If you have only one phone line but have elected to let your fax software answer the phone automatically, you may be in for a challenge. If you answer the phone before your fax software does and it turns out to be a fax, there is no way to initiate the fax software to receive the transmission. On the other hand, if the fax software answers the phone first and it turns out to be a voice call, you can pick up your phone and stop the fax software. This often scares away callers, however. The best solution is to have a dedicated line for your modem so no voice calls come in. Alternatively, you can upgrade to FAXstf Pro to get the ability to manually receive faxes (and a whole bunch of other features). Upgrade information is available under the Apple menu.

FIND IT ONLINE

Visit **http://www.stfinc.com** for more information on upgrading to FAXstf Pro.

Personal Workbook

Q&A

1. How do you connect your iMac's internal modem to a phone line?

2. Where do you find your fax software?

3. How do you add a contact to your fax phone book?

4. How do you transfer contact information from your fax phone book to a QuickNote window?

5. How do you send a fax from within another application?

6. How do you create a fax cover page?

7. How do you set your fax software to answer calls automatically?

8. Where do faxes you've received go?

ANSWERS: PAGE 321

EXTRA PRACTICE

1. Purchase a splitter for your telephone wall jack. Plug both your modem line and phone line into it. Try using your modem and your phone at the same time to see what happens. Learn how to manage your fax and phone on the same line so you don't unintentionally interrupt a modem or voice call.
2. Add your contacts to your phone book in your Fax software. Use the Duplicate Contact button to speed up the process when adding an additional fax line for an individual, or additional contacts in the same company.
3. Create cover pages that you can use when sending faxes. Add your logo or clip art to them. Experiment with different fonts. Fax your cover pages to yourself (or to a friend) to see how legible and professional they look.

REAL-WORLD APPLICATIONS

- ✔ Your son is at college and promises you he'll write to you every day if only you connect your iMac to a phone line and sign up for America Online. You do it, and in no time at all you're wondering whether he's forgotten your e-mail address.
- ✔ You're home with the flu and the phone rings. Your assistant just received a critical new proposal from your biggest client and you have to review it today. He pops it in the fax machine. Within minutes you're reading it on the screen of your iMac.
- ✔ A bunch of your friends and neighbors dropped in to help stuff envelopes for an upcoming town council election and they're starving. You open AppleWorks, type in their sandwich orders, and fax the whole thing over to your local deli. What's more, the deli gets everything right!

Visual Quiz

How do you get to this window? What can you do with it?

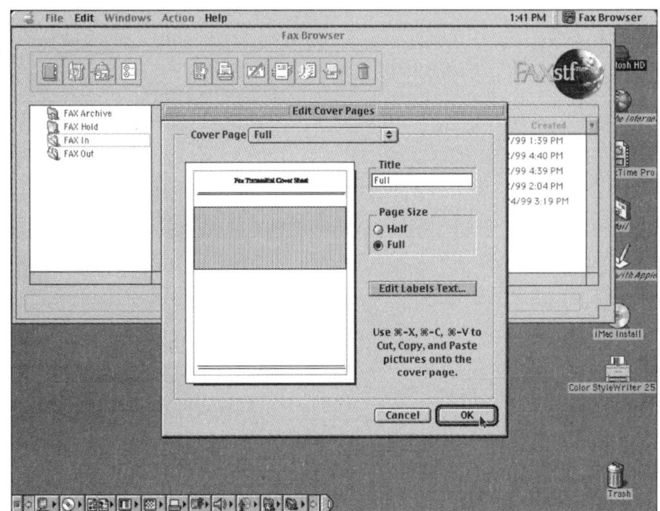

CHAPTER 11

MASTER THESE SKILLS

- Connecting to an Internet Service Provider
- Connecting to America Online
- Sending and Receiving E-mail
- Browsing the World Wide Web
- Finding Information on the Internet (Sherlock)
- Using Internet Applications

Accessing the Internet

In the world of the iMac, *i* stands for *Internet. i* may also stand for *itching*, as in itching to use the Internet. If you've been anxiously waiting for your introduction to the Internet, this is the chapter for you!

In the previous chapter, I discussed how to connect your computer to a telephone line. Now it's time to put that connection to use. If you skipped over that chapter, now's the time to go back and get connected. I'll wait for you here.

The Internet means many things to many people, and it has grown to the point where everyone knows something about it, even if they've never used it or been there themselves. It's a topic that is far larger than any one book has been able to encompass, so if you're a Net neophyte, this small chapter can't hope to do more than point you toward your first, small steps. If you have more experience, count on this chapter to show you how to make use of the software and services that came pre-installed on your iMac. Apple has gone out of its way to make connecting to the Internet easier than ever.

The Internet is the world's largest computer network, where hundreds of millions of people exchange information of all kinds. To prevent everything from turning into unintelligible babble, those who administer the Internet have adopted many technical standards. Regardless of what kind of computer you own, or what company wrote the application software you use, if your computer and the information you seek follows the standards, you're in business. Your iMac comes loaded with software that makes using the Internet a model of simplicity.

To use the Internet, you have to connect to the Internet network itself. For folks at home, this usually means paying for the services of an Internet Service Provider (ISP) such as Earthlink Network or an online service such as America Online (AOL). Using the appropriate application software and your built-in modem, your iMac places a local phone call to your ISP or AOL. Once the call goes through, you're connected to the entire world!

I hope it sounds simple, because it is. Like a walk down to your local public library, the journey itself is easy, but the world of information, com-

Connecting to an Internet Service Provider

The easiest way to get connected is to use Internet Setup Assistant. Start by choosing Internet Setup Assistant from the Internet Access submenu under the Apple menu. The Assistant will guide you through the process step-by-step.

The first question the Assistant asks is if you'd like to set up your iMac to use the Internet. Click the Yes button if, indeed, you do (note that you do not need to use the Internet to use your iMac). Next, you are asked if you have an Internet account. If you already have an account with an ISP (other than the EarthLink Network) or AOL, click the Yes button and jump forward to the Take Note section. If you don't have an Internet account yet (or do have an account with the EarthLink Network), click the No button and the Internet Setup Assistant will display the EarthLink TotalAccess new account window.

The EarthLink Network is a national ISP that you may want to use for your Internet access. EarthLink is not a free service. Its cost is about $20 a month (at the time of this writing), and you also might need to pay an hourly charge of about $5 to use their toll-free access number if there is no local number in your area. EarthLink is a full-service ISP, however, and you could do worse. I recommend that you investigate local ISPs before you decide on EarthLink, however. Look under Internet in your phone book.

If you decide to go with EarthLink, click the Setup button (unless you already have an EarthLink Network account, in which case you should click the Retrieve button instead). You will be asked to enter your new user name and password. Choose these carefully; your

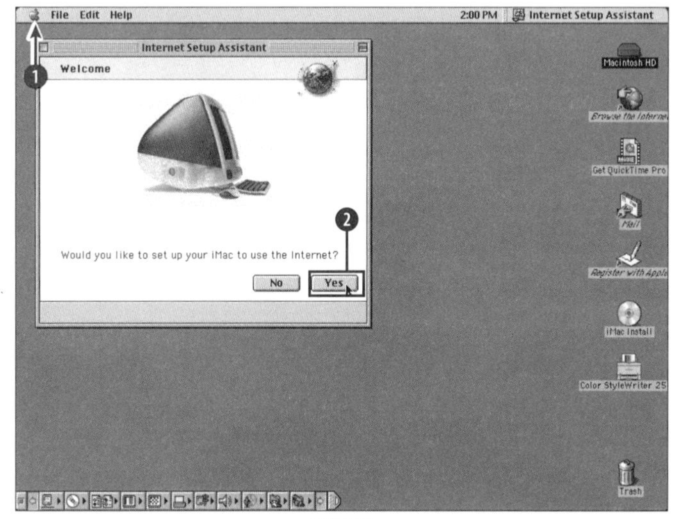

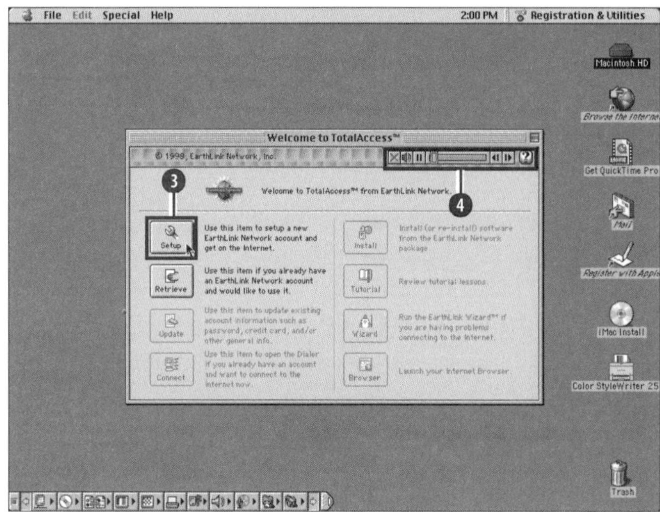

1. Choose Internet Setup Assistant from the Internet Access submenu under the Apple menu.
2. Click the Yes button if you want to use the Internet.

▶ Alternatively, click the No button to cancel or to set up your iMac later.

▶ When you are asked if you already have an Internet account, click the No button if you do not.

3. If you don't have an Earthlink account, click the Setup button.

▶ Alternatively, click the Retrieve button if you already have an EarthLink account.

4. If your iMac starts talking, use these controls to adjust the volume or to stop it.

CROSS-REFERENCE

Refer to the next task in this chapter to learn how to set up a new or existing America Online account.

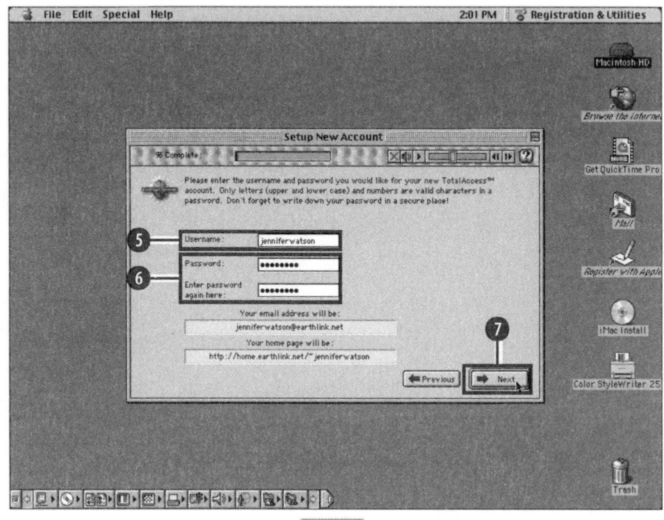

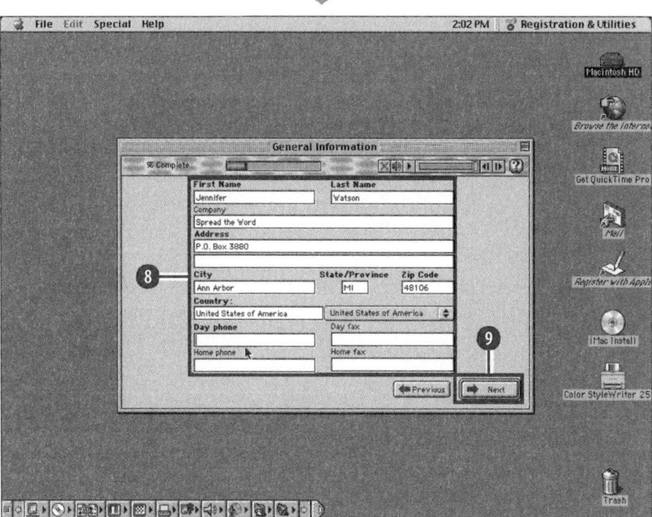

5. *Choose and type a user name.*
6. *Choose and type a password. Type it again for verification. Asterisks will mask your typing for security purposes.*
- *Your future e-mail address and Web site address appears in these boxes.*
7. *Click the Next button (or press Return).*
8. *Type your personal information.*
9. *Click the Next button to continue with the setup and registration process.*

user name will become a part of your e-mail address, and your password will become your first line of defense in protecting your account. Generally, you want a short and simple user name and a long and complicated password. You need to be able to easily remember both. If you have Mac OS 9, you can use your Key Chain control panel to record your password — see Chapter 13 for more information.

Once you've chosen your user name and password, proceed through the setup by clicking the Next button (or pressing Return). Set up your phone and modem, and then select your service. Have your credit card handy; you will need to provide payment information to establish your account.

TAKE NOTE

CONNECTING TO YOUR INTERNET ACCOUNT

If you've already established an Internet account, your setup proceeds along a different path. If you use America Online, turn the page to the next task; otherwise, stay right here. Before you proceed, make sure you have your account information handy, such as domain name service (DNS) and IP addresses, configuration types, access numbers, and your user name and password. If all this seems like a lot of technobabble, or you're unsure of any of this information, call your ISP to obtain it. When you are ready, use the Internet Setup Assistant to enter your account information. When you're finished, you should be ready to connect to the Internet as usual. If it doesn't work, choose Internet from the Control Panels submenu under the Apple menu and modify your information.

SHORTCUT

Hold down the Command key while you press an arrow key to move forward or backward through the Internet Setup Assistant windows.

Connecting to America Online

America Online (AOL) is a special kind of Internet Service Provider (ISP). It provides complete access to the Internet with its fully integrated software, as well as access to its own special online features and content. The cost is about $22 a month for unlimited access (at the time of this writing), or $10 a month if you access AOL through an ISP (yes, you can have both an ISP and AOL if you want).

To set up an AOL account, you use the AOL application program that came on your iMac, rather than the Internet Setup Assistant. You can find the AOL application in the Internet folder on your Macintosh HD. Launching the application starts the setup process. AOL's setup works much like the Internet Setup Assistant — click the Next button to begin.

AOL Setup first searches for a way to connect you and then displays the results of its search. If AOL tells you that the only way you can connect is using *TCP/IP*, have it search again. You want it to find your iMac Internal 56K modem. (You can use TCP/IP if you're planning to connect through your ISP or from a network.) Next comes your Dialing Options. Click the appropriate check boxes, if needed. Click the Next button again, type your area code in the box, and then click the Next button to begin searching for a local access number. Remember that your modem uses the telephone line and then dials one or two local telephone numbers to connect you to AOL. You first connect to AOL through a toll-free number to find local access numbers. (If a dialog box pops up and informs you that you must activate AOL Link, go ahead and click the OK button.)

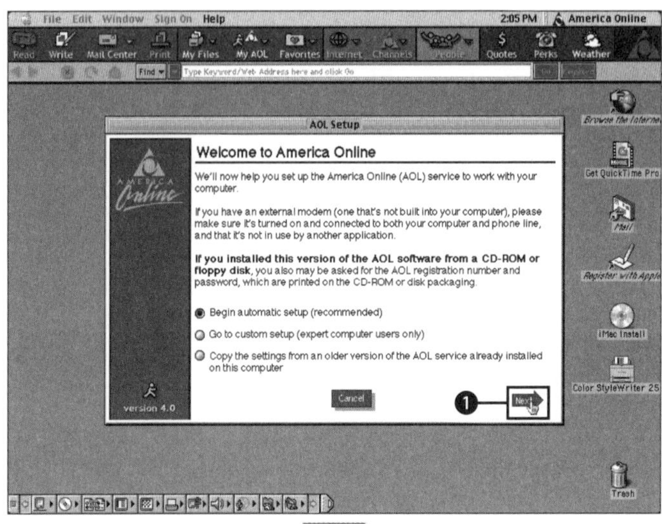

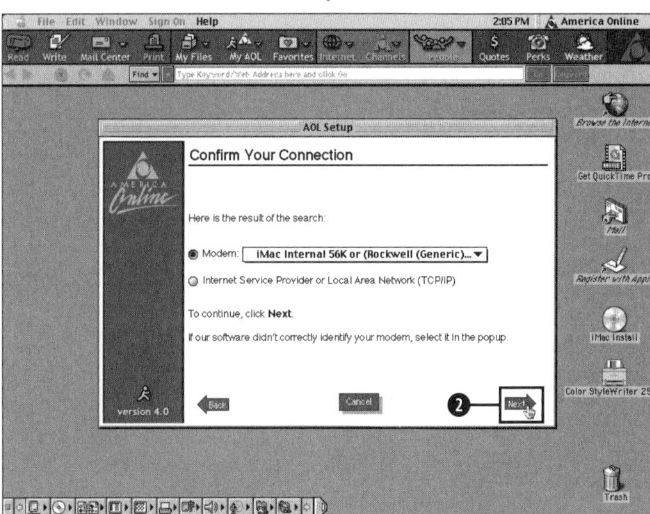

- ▶ *Double-click the America Online icon in your Internet folder.*
- ❶ *Read the information and click the Next button.*
- ▶ *Your modem should appear here. If it doesn't, select it from the drop-down menu.*
- ▶ *If you plan to use an ISP to connect to AOL, select this option.*
- ❷ *Click the Next button to continue.*

CROSS-REFERENCE

If you have no local access number and you want to connect through an ISP, refer to the first task in this chapter for ISP setup.

CHAPTER

11

Accessing the Internet

As AOL connects, it displays a progress box to keep you informed of each step of the connection process. When you connect to AOL later after your account is established, you'll see a similar progress box. AOL then displays the available access numbers. Select a local number and click the Add button. Repeat the process for all of the local numbers that are available. If none of the listed numbers are local calls, you can choose nearby numbers, but you will be responsible for the toll charges. Click the Next button to continue.

AOL uses your new access numbers to dial and connect you to the service. If you already have an AOL account, or you have signed up for the AOL Instant Messenger service, click the appropriate radio button. Otherwise, click the Next button to continue through the new account creation process. Type your name, address, and telephone numbers, and then continue on to provide your billing information (credit cards or checking account withdrawal). The last step is to select your *screen name* and password. If you have any problems, call AOL at 1-888-265-8007 for assistance.

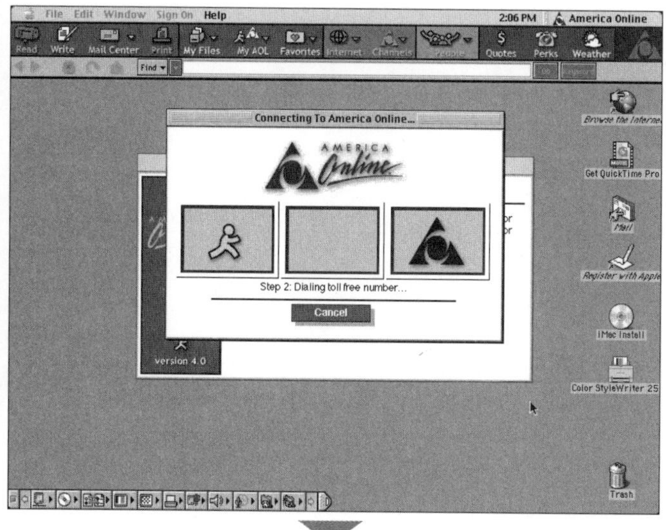

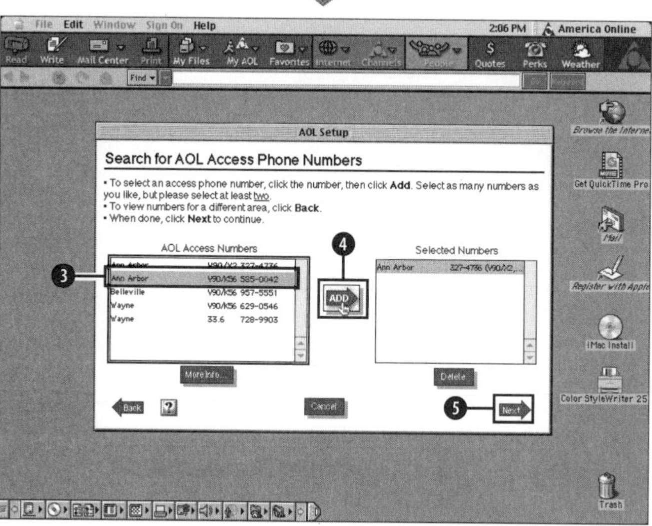

- AOL displays the progress window as it signs on to retrieve local access numbers.
- Click the Cancel button if you need to abort.

3. *Select a local number from the AOL Access Numbers column, if a number is available.*
4. *Click the Add button.*
   - *The number appears in the Selected Numbers column after you confirm its addition.*
5. *Click the Next button to continue your AOL setup and registration.*

TAKE NOTE

CHOOSING A SCREEN NAME AND PASSWORD

Your AOL screen name is also your e-mail address, so choose it wisely. Your screen name can be between 3 and 16 characters. Your password should be a combination of letters and numbers that cannot be easily guessed.

FIND IT ONLINE

Once you are online, press Command+K and type BILLING to select your AOL pricing plan.

Sending and Receiving E-mail

E-mail is the cornerstone of the Internet. It is often what attracts someone to the Internet in the first place. E-mail is fast, convenient, and inexpensive. Your iMac can send and receive e-mail whether you use an ISP or AOL, though the process differs considerably. Let's look at each one individually.

To use e-mail with an ISP, you'll need to use a separate e-mail application. Your iMac came with Outlook Express, and if you used Internet Setup Assistant to connect to the Internet, you're probably already set up to use Outlook Express. Double-click the Mail icon on your Desktop (or select Mail from the Internet Access submenu under the Apple menu) — Outlook Express opens if your Internet settings are configured to do so. (If Outlook Express didn't open, open the Internet control panel, click the E-mail tab, and select Outlook Express from the drop-down menu at the bottom.) Opening Outlook initiates an e-mail check. If any new e-mail is found, Outlook Express displays it in bold in your Inbox. Click a message once to preview it in the lower half of the message window. To reply to an e-mail message, click the Reply button at the top of a message window, type your own message, and click the Send button. Alternatively, you can click the Reply All or Forward icons, or you can click the New icon. For more help using Outlook Express, choose Outlook Express Help from the Help menu.

Reading and sending e-mail on AOL is extremely easy. First, open your AOL application and sign on to the service. If you hear You've Got Mail! when you sign on, click the mailbox icon to display your list of mail.

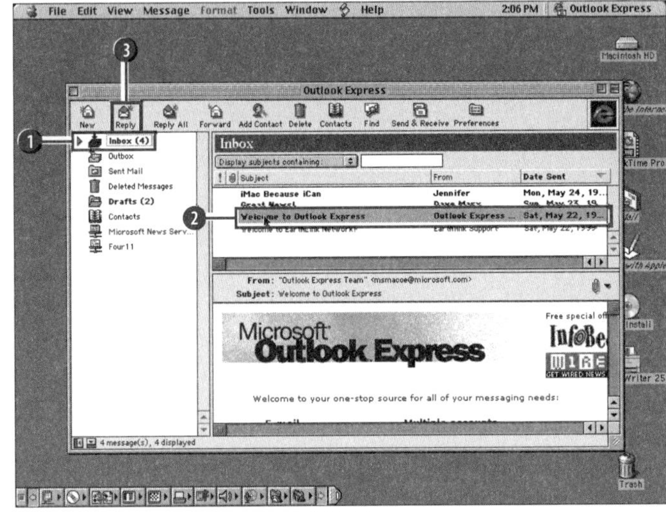

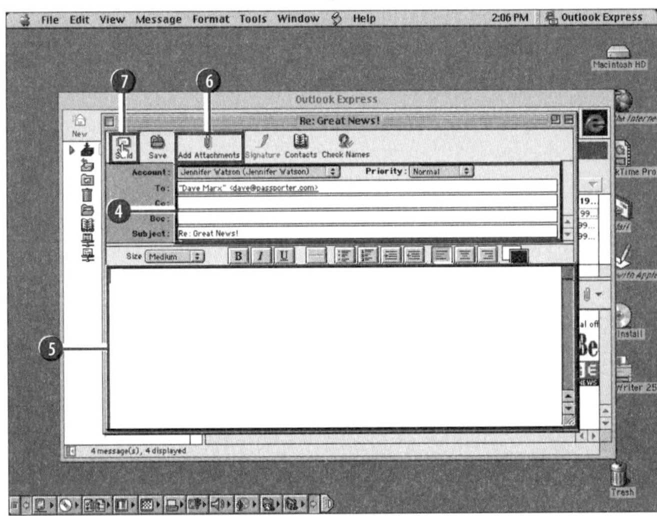

1. Open Outlook Express and click the Inbox icon.
2. Click a piece of unread mail (in boldface) in the top-right pane.

▶ Outlook displays your e-mail.

3. Click Reply on the toolbar to compose a response.
4. Add or modify the address and the subject line.
5. Type your message.
6. Optional: Click Add Attachments icon if you want to attach a file.
7. Click the Send button on the toolbar.

CROSS-REFERENCE

Refer to Chapter 4 for information on working with text to compose your e-mail.

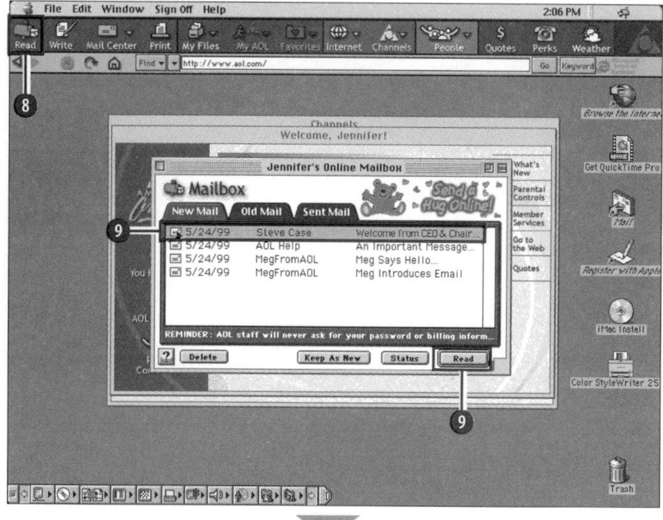

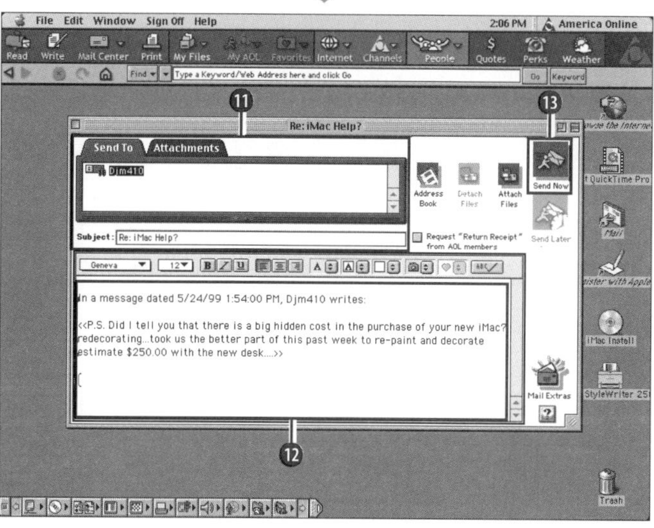

8. *Open AOL and click the mailbox icon.*
   - ▶ *Note that the small mailbox icon blinks when you have mail.*
9. *Select a piece of e-mail and click the Read button.*
   - ▶ *Alternatively, double-click the e-mail message to open and read it.*
10. *Click Reply on the e-mail message.*
11. *Add or modify the address and subject line.*
12. *Type your message.*
13. *Click the Send Now button.*

Now, simply double-click an e-mail name to view the message. You can click the Reply icon to send a response to an e-mail message; just type your message in the new window that appears and click the Send icon. If you want to send a new e-mail message, click the Write icon on the toolbar at the top of the screen, type your recipient's e-mail address, type a subject line, type your message, and then click Send. To learn more about using AOL e-mail, click the Mail Center icon on the toolbar and choose Mail Center. I also authored an entire book on this subject, titled *AOL E-mail* (IDG Books Worldwide, 1999). Look for it wherever you found this book!

TAKE NOTE

UNDERSTANDING E-MAIL ADDRESSES

Like zip codes, it is crucial that you get an e-mail address correct. There is no "close enough" principle in e-mail. An e-mail address has two parts: the user name (everything before the @ symbol) and the domain (everything after the @ symbol). You need to use both, plus the @ symbol, exactly as the e-mail address appears; for example, jennifer@jenuine.net. The exception to this rule is when you're sending e-mail to someone on the same service, such as AOL. In this case, you only need to use the user name. For example, if you're on AOL you can send e-mail to me by typing "Jennifer," which is my screen name.

SHORTCUT

Press Command+N in either Outlook Express or AOL to compose a new e-mail message.

Browsing the World Wide Web

I'll bet you've heard a lot about the World Wide Web (or just *Web,* for short). Well, don't believe everything you hear. It isn't quite as dangerous as it seems, nor is it quite so revolutionary. It is, however, incredibly useful and lots of fun!

To surf the Web you need to use a *Web browser,* an application that is able to display information from the Internet. Your iMac comes with not one, but three, Web browsers! If you're unfamiliar with Web browsers, I recommend you simply double-click the Browse the Internet icon. If you use an ISP, the Internet Explorer Web browser opens on your screen and attempts to connect you to your ISP. If you use AOL, the AOL software opens and waits for you to sign on (unless you're already signed on, in which case AOL's Web browser window is automatically displayed). The third Web browser available on your iMac is Netscape Navigator. If you prefer to use a different browser than the one that opens, open the Internet control panel, click the Web tab, and select your preferred Web browser from the drop-down menu at the bottom.

The first thing you see in a Web browser is your *home page*—the default Web page configured for your browser application. A *page* on the Web is similar to a page in other applications: you can scroll through it with the scroll bars, read information in it, click buttons on it, and so on. The home page is a good place to start if this is your first time on the Web. Take a close look at the Web page. The blue, underlined words are known as *hyperlinks.* You can click these words to move to other pages on the Web. You also can click buttons and icons, or you can select items from drop-down menus in the browser window.

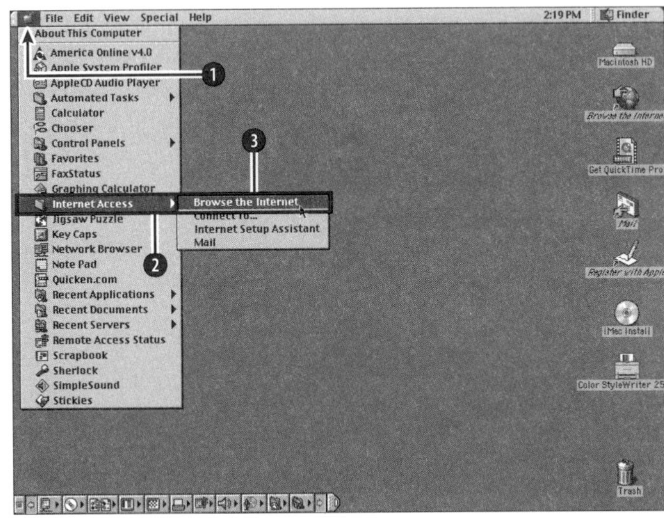

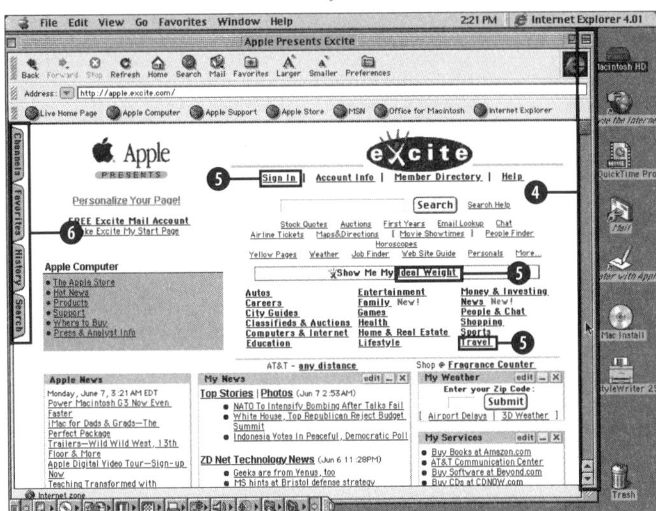

1. Pull down the Apple menu.
2. Display the Internet Access submenu.
3. Choose Browse the Internet.

▶ Alternatively, double-click the Browse the Internet icon on the Desktop.

4. Scroll through a Web page to view it all.
5. Click a hyperlink to move to another page.

▶ The Web address appears in the address box beneath the browser's toolbar.

6. In Internet Explorer, use these tabs for additional navigation.

CROSS-REFERENCE

Refer to the next task in this chapter to learn how to find specific Web pages.

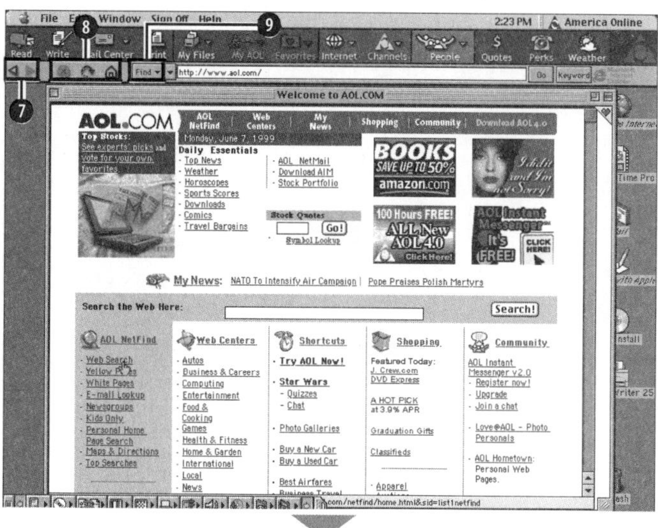

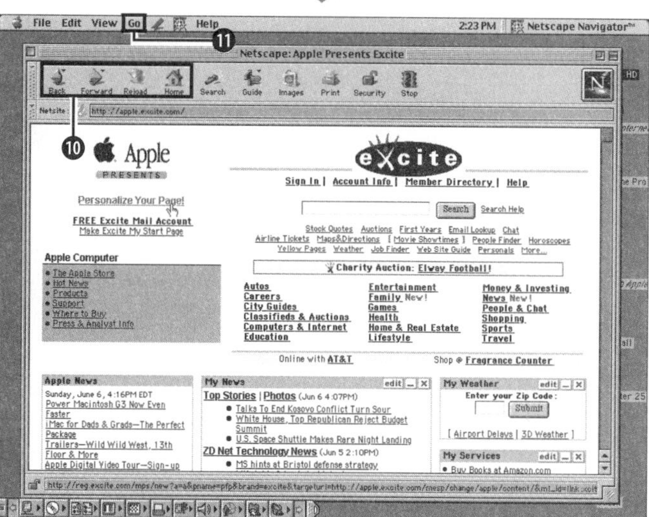

❼ *In AOL's Web browser, use these buttons to move forward and back.*

❽ *Use these buttons to stop, refresh, and return to the home page.*

❾ *Use the Find buttons to find new and old Web pages.*

▶ *The Web address appears in the address box beneath the browser's toolbar.*

❿ *In Netscape Navigator, use the toolbar buttons to navigate between pages.*

⓫ *Use the Go menu for further navigation.*

▶ *The Web address appears in the address box beneath the browser's toolbar.*

TAKE NOTE

NAVIGATING THE WEB

As you move to a new page on the Web, your Web browser refreshes your window to display the new page content. If you want to return to a page you previously visited, click the Back button on the toolbar at the top of your screen (it usually looks like a left arrow) (←). If you want to move forward again, click the Forward button (a right arrow)(→). You also can click the Home button (it usually looks like a small house) to return to your home page. Click the Stop button if you want to cancel the display of a Web page, or click the Refresh button (or the Reload icon) if you want your browser to redraw the page for you.

UNDERSTANDING WEB ADDRESSES

Like e-mail, Web pages have addresses. The string of characters that begins with *http://* near the top of your Web browser is a page's address. You can go directly to a Web page if you know its address. For example, type **http://www.apple.com** (just the way it appears here) to go to Apple Computer's Web page.

SHORTCUT

Click the down arrow next to the Web address field in the AOL and Internet Explorer browser to jump to a Web page you've visited before.

Finding Information on the Internet

The real power of the Internet lies in the vast amount of information it contains. I believe that if it exists, you can find it on the Internet. Finding it, however, is the trick.

Web browsers don't understand telepathic thought yet, so to find something, you need to search for it. Start with your Web browser's default search command. In Internet Explorer or Netscape Navigator, click the Search button on the toolbar at the top of your browser window. In AOL, choose Find it on the Web from the drop-down Find menu on the toolbar. When your Web browser displays the search page, type a word or phrase that describes what you're looking for into the text entry field. Don't be too generic (like "software" or "Mac"). Be sure you spell the word or phrase correctly, too. Click the Search button next to the text entry field to begin your search.

After a few seconds of searching, your browser displays the search results. They are generally listed in the order of relevancy, and you'll need to scroll through your window to see them all. You can click a blue hyperlink to go to a specific page. If none of the results seem right, look near the bottom of the page for a Next or More Results hyperlink to see more matches. If your search returned too many results — or not enough — try a different search using either more specific or more general search words or phrases.

If you don't find what you seek in your Web browser's default search page, try another page. If you're looking for something very specific, visit **http://www.lycos.com** and **http://www.altavista.com.** Both of these Web pages attempt to index everything on the Web, so

Finding Web Pages with Sherlock

Remember Sherlock? You can use it to search the Web, too. Just return to your Desktop (Finder), press Command+F, and click the Search Internet tab (Mac OS 8) or Globe icon (Mac OS 9). Type your word or phrase in the text entry field, check the pages you'd like to search from the list provided, and then click Search or the magnifying class icon. Sherlock takes a few seconds to begin the search and displays matches as it finds them.

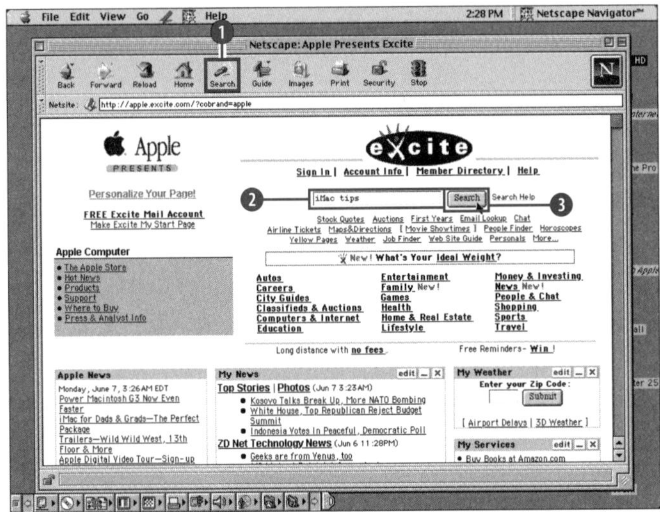

1. *Click the Search button on the toolbar.*
2. *Type your search word or phrase.*
3. *Click the Search button on the Web page.*

CROSS-REFERENCE

See the previous task for more information on navigating through the World Wide Web.

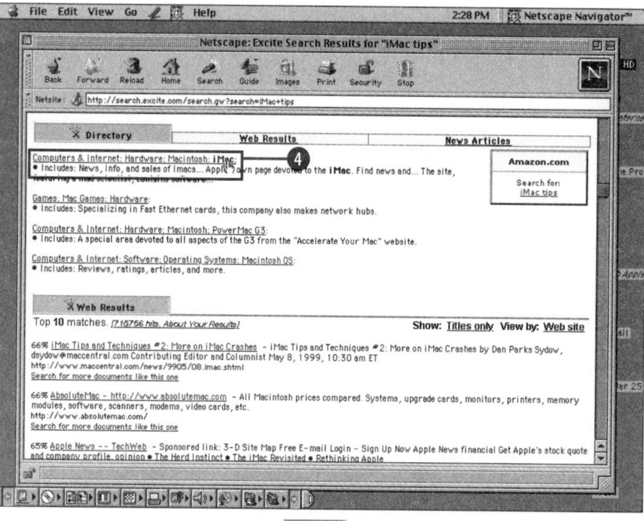

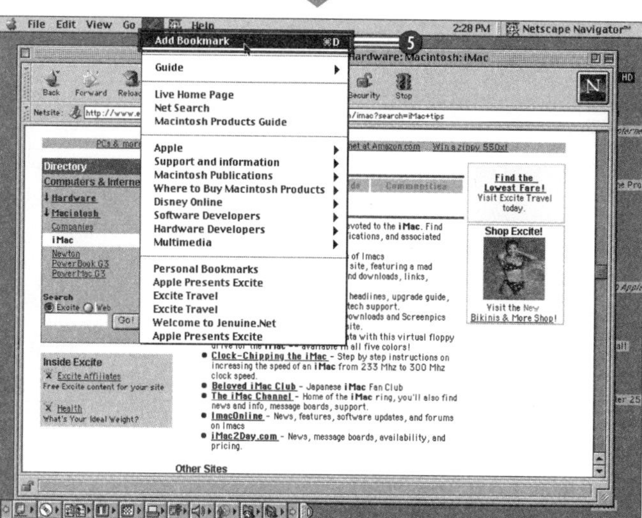

▶ *View your search results, using the scroll bar to see the entire page.*

❹ *Click a hyperlink to go to a Web page.*

▶ *Alternatively, change the sort order of your results.*

❺ *Select Add Bookmark from the Bookmark menu to save a Web page.*

▶ *Alternatively, click the bookmark icon in Netscape Navigator.*

▶ *Your Web site appears here once it is added.*

you should get lots of results. If you're looking for quality pages or categories of pages, try **http://www.yahoo.com.** Yahoo! prides itself on being a directory to the best of the Web. If you're looking for phone numbers, try **http://www.four11.com, http://www.aol.com/netfind/whitepages.adp**, or **http://www.aol.com/netfind/yellowpages.adp**. If you're looking for e-mail addresses, try **http://www.aol.com/netfind/emailfinder.adp**. Many more Web pages exist for finding other pages, people, and places. Try searching for them in your Web browser.

TAKE NOTE

SAVING WEB ADDRESSES

When you search for a Web page and hit pay dirt, you'll want to save it so you can return to it again in the future. To do this in Internet Explorer, choose Add This Page to Favorites on the Favorites menu (or press Command+D). You can access your saved Web pages later by clicking the Favorites icon on the toolbar. In Netscape Navigator, choose Add Bookmark under the green bookmark-like menu (or press Command+D). You can access your bookmarks later in the bookmark menu. In AOL, click the red heart in the upper right corner of a Web page and then click the OK button to save it to your Favorite Places (or just press Command++). You can access your saved Web pages by choosing Favorite Places from the Favorites menu or by choosing the Web page itself from the same menu.

SHORTCUT

If you're looking for a specific word in a Web page, press Command+F, type a word, and press Return.

Using Internet Applications

Your iMac — being an Internet Mac — came with two additional Internet applications: EdView Internet Safety Kit and Adobe PageMill. EdView lets you limit your children's Internet access to a level appropriate to their age level. Adobe PageMill lets you create your own Web pages.

To use EdView, you first need to install it. Insert the Software Install CD-ROM disc into your CD-ROM drive, open the Internet folder in the resulting window, open the EdView Internet Safety Kit folder, and then double-click the Install EdView Family icon. Follow the directions to install it on your hard drive. When you are prompted for a password, go ahead and type one if you want to automatically activate this software; otherwise, leave it blank. After you restart your iMac, connect to the Internet again and launch Microsoft Internet Explorer or Netscape Navigator (EdView doesn't work with AOL's built-in Web browser). If you entered a password, EdView now restricts access to those Web sites available in the EdView Smart Zone. For more information on using EdView, visit **http://www.edview.com.** AOL users are not left out here. Go to keyword: PARENTAL CONTROLS for information on how to control your child's access.

Adobe PageMill is a Web publishing application. All AOL and EarthLink accounts come with Web space so you can create and maintain your own Web pages, and many other ISPs offer Web space, as well (though you'll need to check with them for details). PageMill is located in your Applications folder on your Macintosh HD (if it isn't, install it with the CD-ROM in your disc wallet).

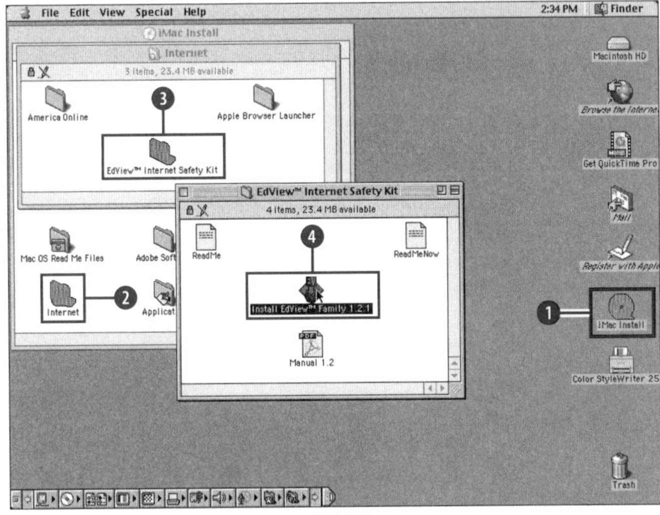

1. *Insert the iMac Install CD.*
2. *Open the Internet folder.*
3. *Open the EdView Internet Safety Kit folder.*
4. *Double-click the installer icon to install the software.*
5. *After you restart your computer, activate the channel lock or set your preferences with this new Finder menu item.*

CROSS-REFERENCE

Refer to "Making the Most of your Applications" in Chapter 8 for more information about using Quicken.

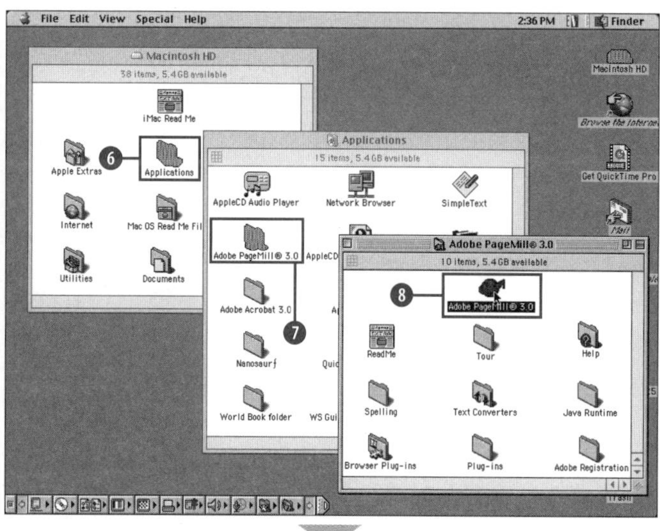

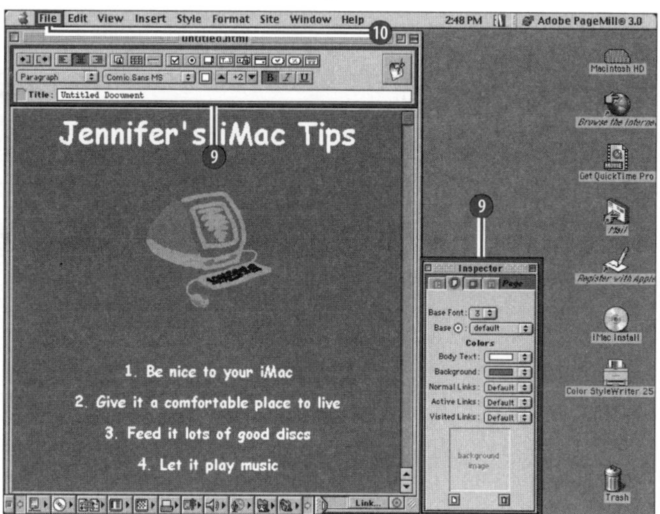

6. *Return to the Desktop and open the Applications folder.*
7. *Open the Adobe PageMill 3.0 folder.*
8. *Double-click the Adobe PageMill 3.0 icon to open the program.*
9. *Design a Web page using the toolbar and tool palette.*
10. *Save and publish your work with the options in the File menu.*

Why would you want to create your own Web page? If you've got something to say or something to show, you've got a reason! Even if your Web page is only for your family and friends, you can have fun and perhaps even save some time by making your information available on the Web. If you're in business, a Web page can make your company more accessible to your customers, as well as put you on the same footing with many of the big companies.

PageMill has far too many features to describe here. I recommend you choose Contents from the Help menu inside the application to learn more about PageMill. Note: PageMill is bundled with the second generation of iMacs (the ones with the fruity colors), which were shipped after November 1998. If you don't have PageMill, other Web publishing options are available. If you're on AOL, try keyword: BHP. If you use an ISP, go to **http://www.netscape.com** and download Netscape Communicator.

TAKE NOTE

FINDING OTHER INTERNET APPLICATIONS

A lot of applications that either work with the Internet, or that take advantage of it, are available these days. For example, did you know you can play games across the Internet? You can even pay bills! Check out the Online menu in Quicken for the appropriate Web pages and information. Check your local computer store, mail-order house, or surf the Web for Internet-savvy software that takes advantage of the Internet.

FIND IT ONLINE

Learn more about Adobe PageMill at **http://www.adobe.com/prodindex/pagemill/main.html.**

Personal Workbook

Q&A

1. What does ISP stand for? What services does an ISP they provide?

2. How do you connect your iMac to AOL if you already have an AOL account?

3. How do you receive e-mail with your ISP or AOL account?

4. How do you reply to an e-mail you received?

5. What are the two components of an e-mail address?

6. What does http:// indicate? How can you use this information on the Web?

7. How can you search several Web sites at a time?

8. How can you set parental controls to limit your children's access to the Internet?

ANSWERS: PAGE 321

Accessing the Internet

CHAPTER 11

EXTRA PRACTICE

1. Visit Yahoo! **(http://www.yahoo.com)** and search for information on your favorite hobby or interest.
2. Explore some of the Web sites that Yahoo! recommends for your hobby or interest, and add the ones you like best to your Favorites List, Favorite Places, or Bookmarks, as appropriate.
3. Use your Favorites List, Favorite Places, or Bookmarks to return to the Web site you liked best.
4. Send yourself some e-mail to practice all the features that interest you. At the least, learn to Forward and Reply to the e-mail you receive and note the difference.
5. Obtain the e-mail addresses of a few of your friends and relatives, and start corresponding with them.

REAL-WORLD APPLICATIONS

✔ Your daughter's school has created a Web site (complete with photos) describing the field trip they are currently taking to Washington, D.C. You take a look at the site to see what the kids are up to today, and find pictures of the kids at the Washington Monument, the White House, and a hot dog stand. You write e-mail to your daughter, telling her to rinse the catsup stain out of her blouse before it sets.

✔ It's Saturday night and you want to know what's happening in your area, but you don't have a newspaper handy. You visit a Web site dedicated to your community and get a listing of every movie, play, and special event in the area. With another few clicks of the mouse, you've read the reviews and made your decision.

Visual Quiz

What do you do at this window? How do you get here?

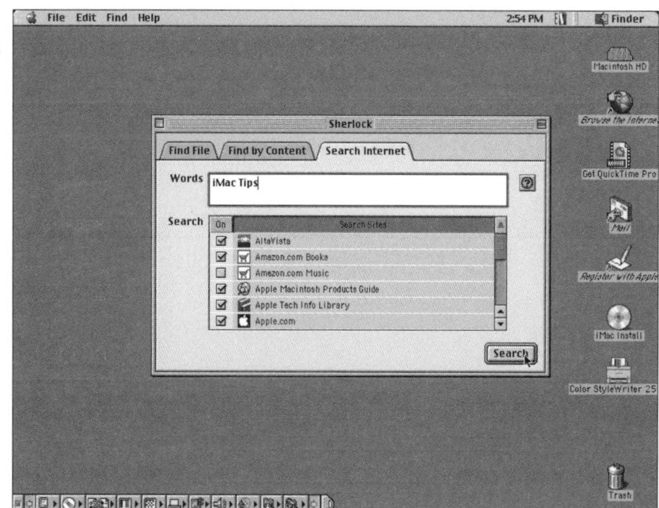

CHAPTER 12

MASTER THESE SKILLS

- Connecting Your iMac
- Configuring File Sharing
- Connecting to Another Computer
- Linking Programs
- Setting Accesses and Privileges
- Identifying Users and Groups
- Monitoring Your Network
- Connecting Remotely via Modem

Networking and File Sharing

In the last chapter, we discussed the Internet, a worldwide network of computers. Now, we're going to discuss a network that's a bit closer to home (or your office).

From the very beginning, Macintosh computers have included built-in networking. If you have two Macs, all you have to do is connect them with the appropriate cable, change a few settings in their software, and start accessing the files and programs stored on both computers. If you're lucky enough to own more than two Macs, they're nearly as easy to connect, but you'll need a bit of extra equipment. If you own an older Mac, you may need a special adapter to connect it to your iMac.

Once you're connected, you can make as much or as little information stored on your computer accessible to the other users of the network as you wish. If necessary, you can require that passwords be used to access the information. Those with access can open a file on your hard disk, make a copy for their own use, or even save it on yet another computer.

Networks do away with *sneakernets* — which is the process of copying files by floppy disk. Instead of copying a file to floppy disk and running to another office, you can just click, click, click with your mouse and have the file you need. In fact, one of the reasons iMacs don't have floppy disk drives is due to the simplicity with which iMacs can be networked.

Networks eliminate other kinds of confusion, too. When many users need the same information or files, it makes sense to keep only one copy of those files on a designated hard disk so that everyone is certain to be using the most recent version.

There are only four essential pieces to the iMac networking puzzle: the Ethernet connection (with cables or AirPort), the network protocol (to talk across the Ethernet), File Sharing (to make a hard disk accessible), and Choosing (to connect you to the shared hard disks). All this can be done with one cable and a few clicks of a mouse. What could be easier?

Unfortunately, networking different kinds of computers (such as IBM-compatible PCs and Macs) can be very complicated. Even though it looks like you can connect your PC and your iMac, don't even try it. It's just not going to work without the help of a highly skilled networking expert.

So, with that all said, let's get networking!

Connecting Your iMac

I can hear it now. "Wait, I thought I *was* connected!" You may be connected to the Internet, but is your iMac directly connected to another computer? No, I don't mean sitting next to another computer on a desk (though that does make things a little easier). Connecting your iMac directly to another computer usually involves at least one cable, which then enables you to transfer files between them, share applications, and expand your computing power. There are other ways to connect your iMac, such as connecting it to an existing network or using Apple's new AirPort technology, but these are a bit beyond the scope of this book. If you want to connect your iMac to an office network, ask your network administrator for assistance. If you want to connect your iMac to another iMac or an older Mac, read on!

Your iMac comes with built-in *10/100Base-T Ethernet*, which is a popular system for connecting computers to networks. There is no question that you can connect your iMac to another iMac, since we know they both have this built-in Ethernet capability. Older Macs may (or may not) have Ethernet. If you're not sure, check the other Mac's specifications or just look at the back of the computer for a port with a symbol that looks like this: <...> It will look like an oversized RJ-11 telephone jack. If your other Mac has it, you're in business! If you don't have an Ethernet port on your other Mac, you will need an adapter or a *bridge* to go from the old-style AppleTalk network connector to Ethernet. Ask for help wherever you purchased your computer.

Once you've established that both Macs you want to connect have Ethernet, you need to purchase an *Ethernet crossover cable*. You can get these inexpensive cables at a computer store, or even at some office supply stores. Get a cable that is long enough to reach from one Mac to the other. Plug one end of the cable into your iMac — your

❶ *Attach one end of your twisted Ethernet cable to your iMac, plugging it into the Ethernet port behind your iMac's access panel.*

❷ *Attach the other end of your cable to your other Mac.*

CROSS-REFERENCE

For information on connecting AppleTalk printers to your Macs, see Chapter 6.

Networking and File Sharing

Naming Your Computer

Connecting your iMac to another Mac requires that you name it. I'll get to how you actually do this later, but now is the time to begin thinking about The Perfect Name. You may want to go with something simple and straightforward, like "Dave's Computer" (assuming your name is Dave, of course). You may even just want to use your name, especially if the other Mac you're connecting to is used by someone else and they use their name, too. On the other hand, you may want to be a bit more descriptive, such as The Tangerine iMac or PowerBook G3. You can even get creative. I've named my computers after characters in Star Trek episodes, William Gibson novels, movie characters (especially sci-fi movies), monsters, places, mythological characters — even cartoon characters. My lime iMac's name is Tinkerbell, and I call her Tink for short. Once I chose that name, I decided to name my PowerMac G3 Wendy and my PowerBook G3 Peter Pan. What you name your computer is entirely up to you. The name you choose might have special meaning to you, or it might just be something you like. I recommend you put some thought into it, however. If you choose a good name, it'll bring a smile to your face each time you see it. And who doesn't need to smile more?

Ethernet port is behind the access door on the right side of your iMac. Plug the other end into your other Mac. You can do this while your Macs are turned on, and there usually is no need for a restart afterward. Do note that an Ethernet crossover cable is good for connecting exactly two Ethernet devices — two Macs, or a Mac and an Ethernet printer. See the Take Note item below if you want to connect more than two devices.

TAKE NOTE

CONNECTING MORE THAN TWO MACS

If you want to connect more than two Macs, a simple Ethernet crossover cable won't do it. You need to purchase an Ethernet hub and plug each Mac into the hub with an Ethernet cable. I network three Macs myself (an iMac, a PowerMac G3, and a PowerBook G3), and using the hub is simple. If you want to network an older Mac without an Ethernet port, you can purchase an adapter or bridge for your hub, too. You can purchase Ethernet hubs and bridges from computer stores and mail-order houses.

USING AIRPORT

AirPort is a Apple's new wireless networking technology, and it comes built-in to newer iMacs (introduced in October 1999). To use it, you need to purchase an AirPort Card and an AirPort Base Station. Install the card in your iMac and plug the base station into your Ethernet network. Once set up, you can share a single Airport Base Station with up to nine other iMacs (or other Airport-enabled Macs) and use it up to 150 feet away. For more information, visit http://www.apple.com/airport/.

FIND IT ONLINE

Visit **http://www.macsonly.com/ethernet.html** for ways to connect your iMac to your old Mac.

Configuring File Sharing

Now that your Macs are connected, its time to fire up the software. Your iMac — and any other Mac running a recent version of the Mac OS — uses a technique called *file sharing* to exchange information with one another. I think the name says it all.

To turn file sharing on, start by opening the File Sharing control panel on your iMac. In the Network Identity field, type your name. (If your name is already there, that just means you ran the Mac OS setup and it inserted your name for you. In this case, you can skip to the next paragraph). If someone else is using the other connected Mac's, you may want to set a password; otherwise, leave the password field blank. In the Computer Name field, type The Perfect Name you came up with earlier (see the previous task for tips). If you're at a loss, just type "iMac" in the Computer Name field.

Now click the Start button under File Sharing (the top Start button). It may take a few moments to start up File Sharing. Once it is finished, the button changes to Stop to indicate that it is on. When it is completed, close the File Sharing window. If you are warned that you didn't type a password, just click the OK button.

Now you need to tell your iMac to use Ethernet to share files. Open the AppleTalk control panel and select Ethernet built-in from the drop-down menu (it may already be selected). Close the AppleTalk window. If you're asked if you want to turn AppleTalk on, click the OK button.

That's it for your iMac. Now, do the same thing with the other connected Macs. Note that if you're using a different version of the Mac OS, your windows may look a bit different. In fact, you may not have an AppleTalk control panel at all. If you don't see one, look for a Network control panel instead. You should be able to select Ethernet from the Network control panel.

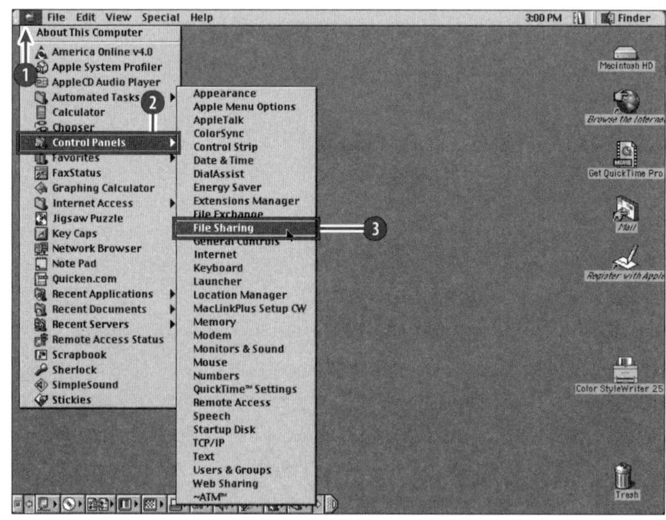

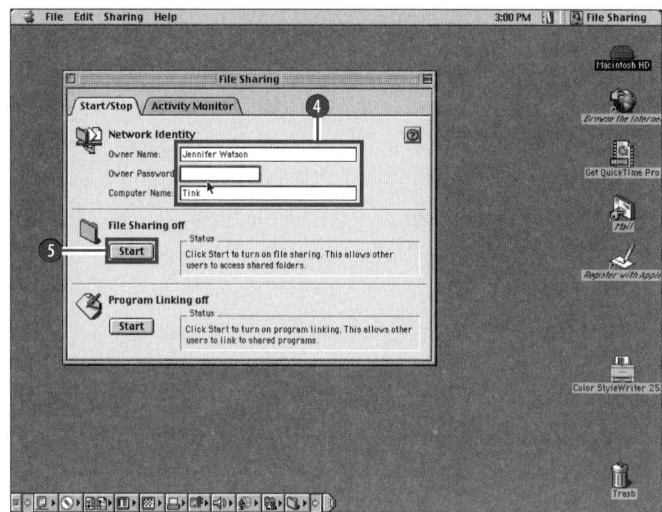

1. *Pull down the Apple menu.*
2. *Display the Control Panels submenu.*
3. *Choose File Sharing.*

▶ *Alternatively, use the Control Strip to open the File Sharing control panel.*

4. *Type your name, a password (optional), and a computer name.*
5. *Click the Start button to initiate file sharing.*

CROSS-REFERENCE

To learn how to control access to your data, see the "Setting Accesses and Privileges" task later in this chapter.

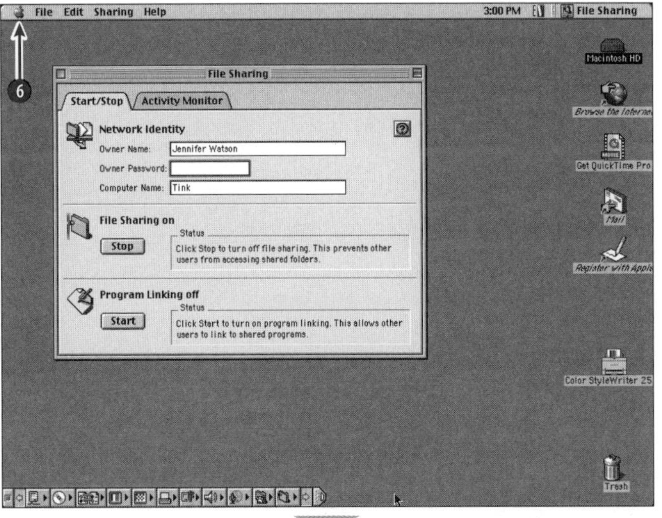

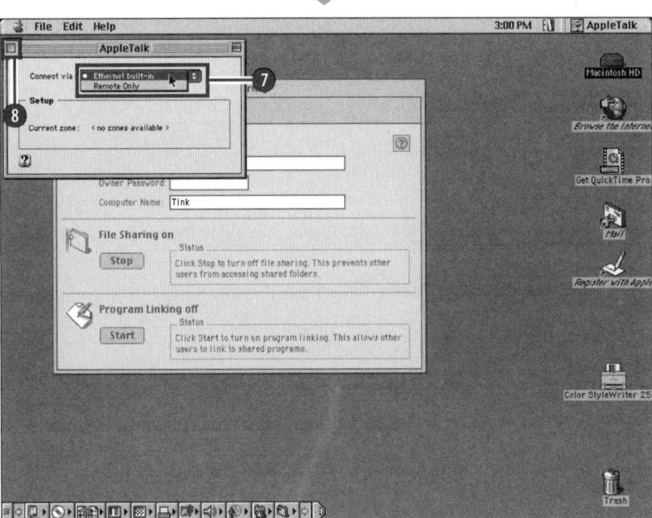

- When File Sharing is on, the Start button changes to a Stop button.
- ❻ Choose the AppleTalk control panel from the Control Panels submenu under the Apple menu.
- ❼ Select Ethernet built-in from the pop-up menu.
- ❽ Close the window.

If this all seems like a lot of work, don't worry — you only need to do this once. After that, you can connect your iMac to the other Macs quickly and easily. You can event set it up to automatically connect each time you turn your computer on. More on that later.

TAKE NOTE

UNDERSTANDING FILE SHARING

Turning on file sharing allows the other Mac's to access the data on your computer. Thus, you need to also turn file sharing on for the other Mac's to access their data. By default, all data is accessible, but if that isn't what you want, you can use the Mac's sophisticated access controls to specifically allow the data you want to share. Another option is to turn file sharing on for only one computer. You don't need file sharing enabled on both (or all) the computers to transfer data.

USING THE CONTROL STRIP

The last button on your Control Strip offers quick and easy File Sharing access. You can see who is connected, open the File Sharing control panel, and turn file sharing on and off.

SHORTCUT

Turn file sharing on and off quickly with the File Sharing button at the far right of the Control Strip.

Connecting to Another Computer

The moment of truth has arrived. Assuming you've attached your Ethernet cables between your Macs (or installed AirPort), turned on file sharing, and selected Ethernet, you're now ready to connect!

To begin, open your Chooser from the Apple menu on your iMac. Select the AppleShare icon in the upper-left corner of the window. You should see your other Mac's computer name appear in the list on the right. If you don't, make sure that the other Mac is powered up, that you've turned file sharing on for that Mac, and that your cables are securely attached. You want AppleTalk to be active on both computers as well. You should see the Active radio button enabled at the bottom of the Chooser on your iMac, as well as on the other Mac.

If the other Mac's computer name does show up in the Chooser, double-click it. A window opens to allow you to connect to the computer as a Guest or as a Registered User. For now, click Registered User (if it isn't already enabled by default) and type the same Owner Name you used on the other computer. Chances are the name will be displayed for you already. If you set a password, type that in, too. Otherwise, click the Connect button to initiate the connection. If you're informed that you are an unknown user, check the Owner Name on your other Mac; this is your Registered User name.

Upon successful connection, you are asked to select the items on the other computer you want to use. You may have only one choice, or you may have several, depending on how the other Mac's hard drive is configured and any removable media present over 2MB in size (such as a CD-ROM disc). If you want to use only one item, select it and click the OK button (or double-click it). Alternatively, you can select multiple items by holding

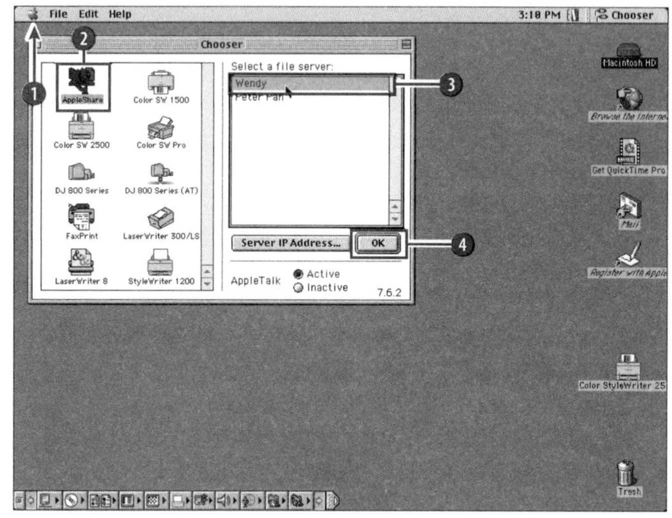

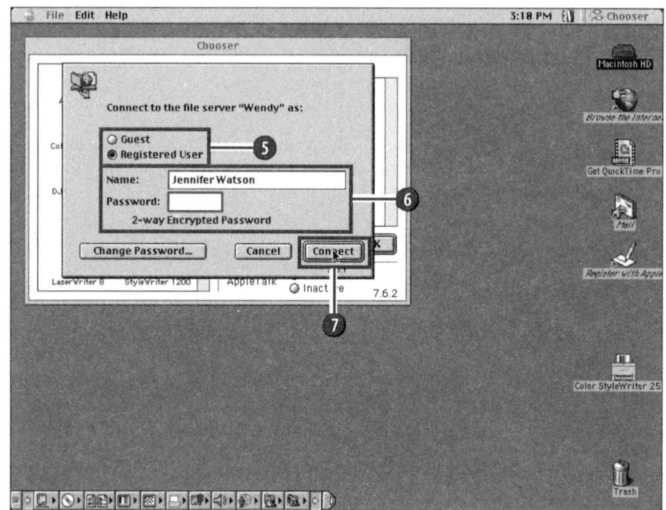

1. *Open the Chooser from the Apple menu.*
2. *Click the AppleShare icon.*
3. *Select the computer to which you want to connect.*
4. *Click the OK button.*
5. *Select Registered User.*
6. *Type your name (if it isn't already entered), plus your password if you set one.*
7. *Click the Connect button.*

CROSS-REFERENCE

Learn how to share programs (applications) as well as files in the next task on "Linking Programs."

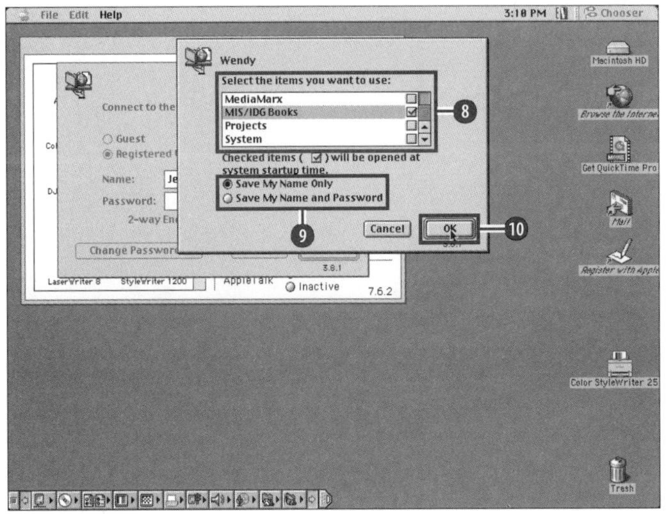

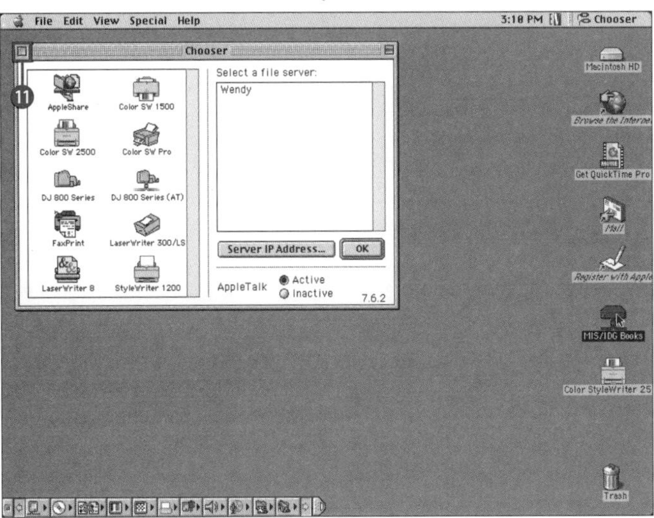

8 *Select the items you want to use. Click the check box if you want them automatically opened on startup.*

9 *Indicate if you'd like your name, or your name and password, stored in the future.*

10 *Click the OK button.*

▶ *An icon representing the item appears on your Desktop. You can double-click it to open it.*

11 *Close the Chooser.*

down the Command key as you click. If you would like to automatically connect to these items on startup, check the boxes to the right. Indicate if you want the software to save your name only or both your name and your password. (I recommend both name and password unless you're concerned about security.) Click the OK button when you're ready.

Any items you selected now appear on your Desktop as *shared disks*. You can spot their names and their icons easily; they look like a hard drive with cables protruding from the bottom. You can now double-click any of the shared disk icons and use them much as you do your own Macintosh HD.

TAKE NOTE

TRANSFERRING FILES

You can copy files to and from the shared disks that you've connected to with your iMac. You also can open files on the shared disk, so long as you have the application that created it on your iMac. Keep in mind, however, that transferring, opening, and using files on the shared disk will seem significantly slower than files on your iMac's hard disk. The Mac does a good job of keeping you up-to-date on transfer progress, however.

SHORTCUT

Watch for two small flashing arrows to the left of your Apple menu for a quick indication that your Mac is transferring data.

Linking Programs

Your iMac can do more than share files. It also can share programs (applications). For example, if the Mac to which you've connected your iMac has an application you want to use, you can actually open it from your iMac and use it there without installing it first. This works best when you don't intend to use the application much or you have limited disk space to install it on your computer. There is a price for this convenience, however. The application will take much longer to get started and can move much slower than usual.

To link application programs, start by opening your File Sharing control panel on the computer that has the application you want to use. Click the Start button below Program Linking to turn linking on. Now close the window and return to the other Mac. Locate the program on the shared disk and open it as usual. Give your Mac a few moments to load the application. You should now be able to use the program!

The biggest catch with program linking is that preferences don't transfer across the network connection. So if you open an application in which you've set preferences, your preferences won't be available. You should be able to set them again, however, and have them accessible the next time you link to this application on this Mac.

If at all possible, avoid launching a program on another computer. Both Macs will slow down significantly, making it hard to accomplish anything on either computer. Instead, install the application on the Mac that doesn't have it and only open data files from the other Mac when necessary.

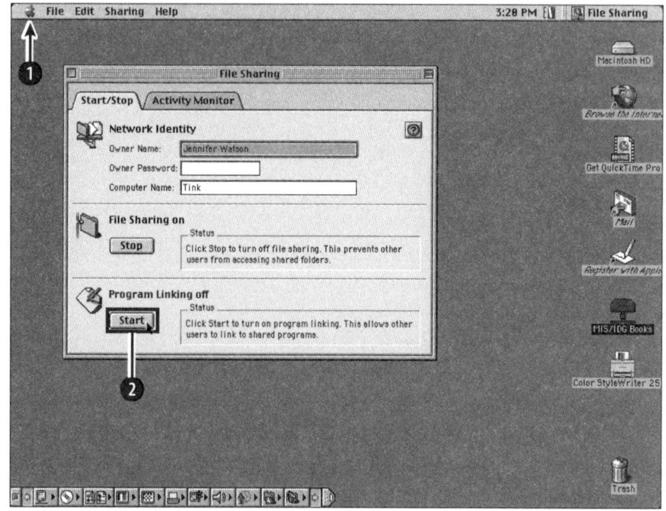

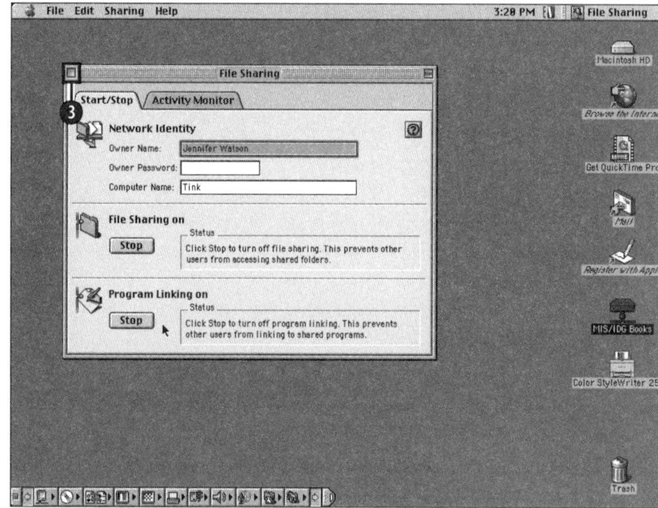

1. *Open the File Sharing Control panel from the Apple menu.*
- *Alternatively, open it from the Control Strip.*
2. *Click the Start button on the bottom.*
- *When Program Linking is on, the Start button changes to Stop.*
3. *Close the window.*

CROSS-REFERENCE

See "Installing Your Bundled Applications" in Chapter 8 for more information about installing applications on other Macs.

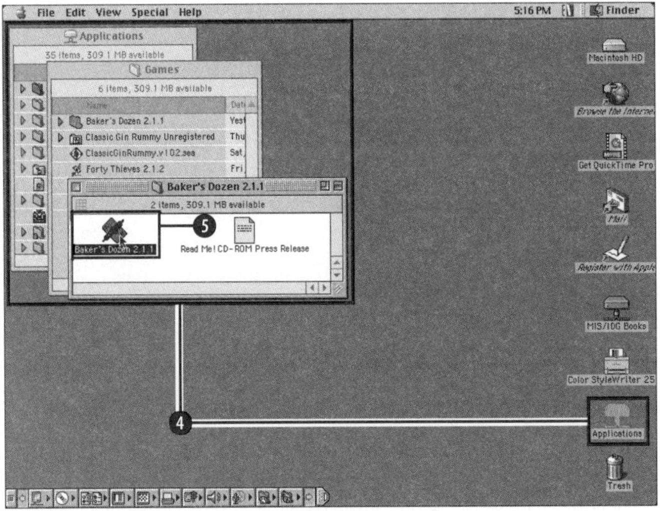

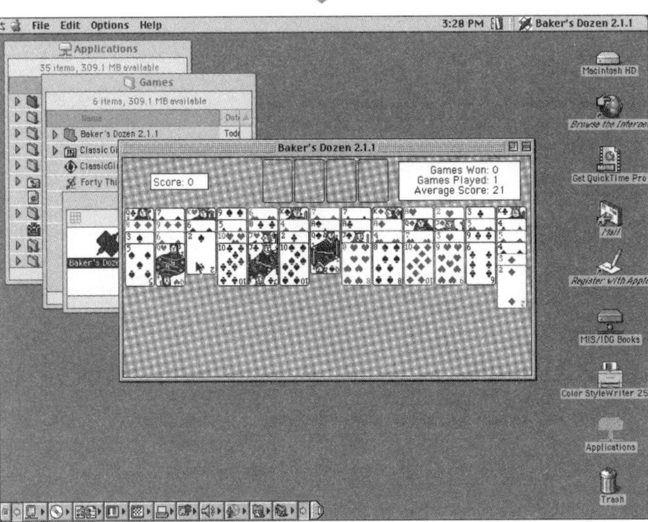

4. *Locate the application you'd like to use on the shared drive.*
5. *Double-click the application as you would any other icon.*

- *The application opens normally.*
- *Watch for the double arrows in the far left side of the menu bar to indicate network activity.*

Something to keep in mind is whether you have a license to open a program on another computer. If you have only a single-user license, you are legally obligated to purchase another copy of the software to install on another computer. You can sometimes purchase group licenses, which allow you to link to the program and sometimes install it on another computer, as well. Check your documentation for details.

TAKE NOTE

CONNECTING APPLICATIONS TO ONE ANOTHER

In addition to sharing programs, it is also possible to open an application on one Mac and connect it to an application on the other Mac. This is most common in head-to-head computer games, where both Macs have a copy of the game installed on the computer and play the game across the network. It's a powerful use of your network (though not terribly productive). Generally, you do need to have two copies of the application you want to link, however. Applications with the ability to connect over a network are usually smart enough to know when you've installed the exact same application on the other computer. And, of course, only a few applications offer this capability. When investigating software for this purpose, look for a Network Edition, or see if it can be used on a network or LAN.

FIND IT ONLINE

Visit **http://www.macgaming.com/** to learn more about the latest games you can play across your network.

Setting Accesses and Privileges

It is possible to share your iMac with others on your network without giving them free run of it. I only recommend you set access privileges if other people will be connecting to your computer on your Ethernet network; however, there's no reason to secure your data if you're the only one using it (well, no logical reason, anyway).

First, it is important to realize that everything on your iMac can be shared until you begin specifying what can and cannot be shared. So if you want everything on your Mac to be shared, do nothing. You don't need to turn sharing on manually.

To share something, begin by selecting its icon on your Desktop. Now press Command+I and select Sharing from the Show drop-down menu. Click the Share this item and its contents check box to enable sharing.

If you want to share an item but you don't want it modified or deleted, click the Can't move, rename, or delete this item (locked) check box. This option is only available on folders within hard drives, not on the hard drives themselves or on CD-ROM discs.

You also can set privileges for those who will be accessing your information (see the next task for more information on this). Use the drop-down menu to choose the level of access for each user and group. If you want to apply the settings to everything within the hard drive or folder, click the Copy button.

If you don't have a drop-down menu with a Sharing option in your Get Info window, look instead for a Sharing option under the File menu.

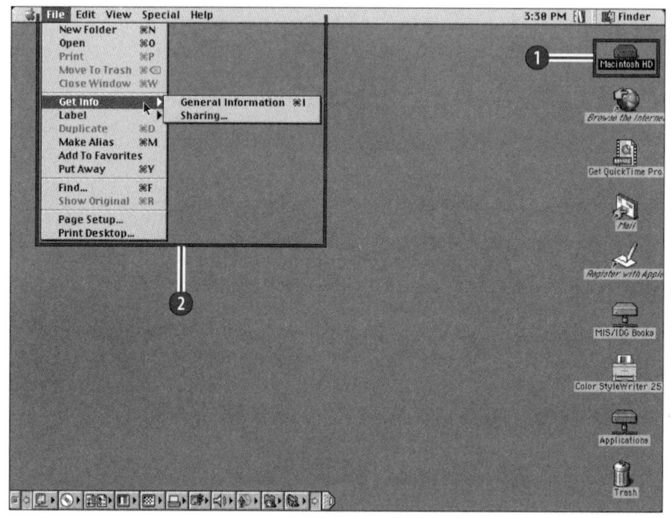

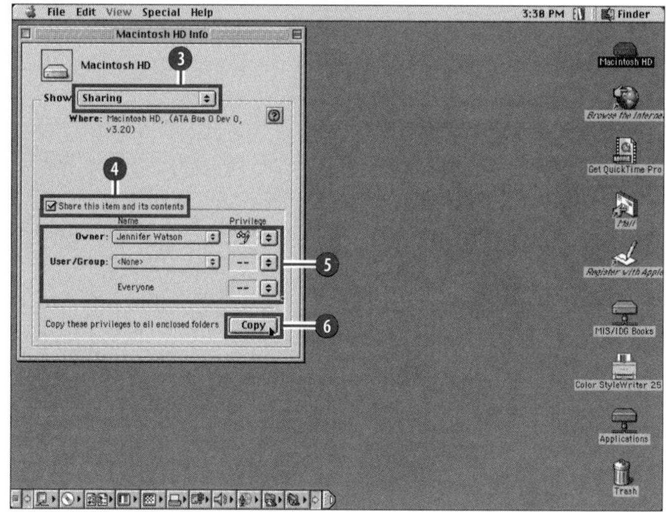

1. *Select an icon.*
2. *Choose Get Info from the File menu (if Sharing is available in the submenu, choose that instead).*
   - ▶ *Alternatively, press Command+I.*
3. *Choose Sharing from the pop-up menu if it isn't selected.*
4. *Optional: Check the box to share the item.*
5. *Optional: Designate users and privileges.*
6. *Optional: Click the Copy button to apply the settings to all enclosed folders.*

CROSS-REFERENCE

See "Aliasing Files" in Chapter 2 for information on how to create an alias.

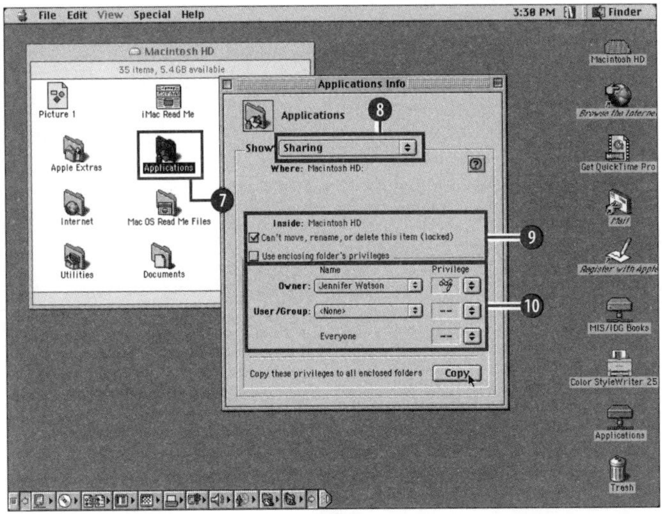

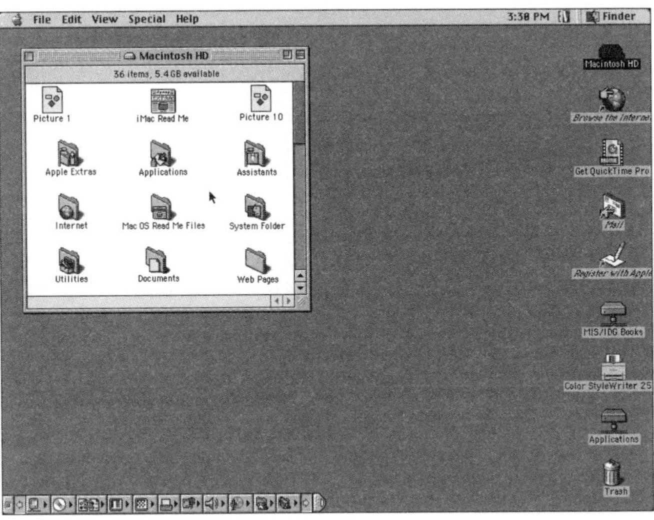

7. *Get Info for a folder.*
8. *Choose Sharing if it isn't selected.*
9. *Optional: Check the box to lock the folder.*
10. *Optional: Set access and privileges for users.*

- *The Apple Extras folder has access enabled (notice the cable on the icon).*
- *The Application folder is locked (notice the padlock on the icon).*

Note that if you allow sharing on a folder within a hard drive, you won't be able to turn on sharing for the hard drive itself. You'll either need to turn on sharing on each folder you want shared on the hard drive, or turn off sharing on any enclosed folder(s) so you can turn it on for the entire hard drive.

TAKE NOTE

VIEWING FOLDERS AND FILES

When you are connected to a Mac with access privileges set, a dimmed folder or file means you do not have access to it. A locked folder or file means you can access it, but you cannot rename, move or delete it. On the other hand, a folder or file with a cable on it means you have full access.

PROTECTING FILES WITH ALIASES

If others access your Mac and have the ability to write to it, you run the risk of having them delete a file you wanted to remain intact. You can turn sharing off for these items, but what if they still need access? Instead of giving them access to the original file, create an alias and give them access to the alias instead. Now, anyone accessing the alias can use it and make changes, but if they try to delete it, they only remove the alias and not the original file.

SHORTCUT

Use the Copy command at the topmost level of your hard drive to apply the same settings to everything on the hard drive.

Identifying Users and Groups

If others access your Mac, it is a good idea to define specific users and groups. Not only does this give you greater control over who accesses your computer, but it also gives you more meaningful information during monitoring.

Open your Users & Groups control panel to make changes. Begin by selecting your name in the list — it was created for you when you typed in your Owner Name in the File Sharing control panel. Double-click it to open it and see its settings. The Identify settings show the name and password, if any. Go ahead and change your name now if you don't like what you typed before. You also can add, modify, or remove your password here. Choose Sharing from the drop-down menu at the top of the window to see and change sharing settings. Because these are your own settings, it is a good idea to enable everything in this window. You want full access to your own computer if you access it from another, after all. Close the window to save any changes.

Now take a closer look at the Guest user. Those who weren't assigned a specific user name and password will use this option. By default, the guest user cannot connect to the computer. Change this if you want to allow access.

To create a new user, click the New User button and type their name and password into the window. If you don't want the user to have the ability to change their own password, disable that option (though generally it is a good idea to allow the user to change their password). Select Sharing from the drop-down menu to configure the user's sharing settings. You may want to create a generic user, and then click the Duplicate button to copy it and add specific user names and passwords.

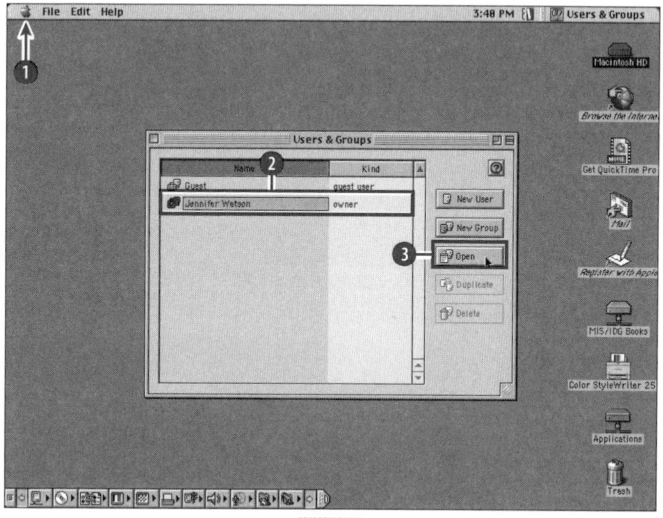

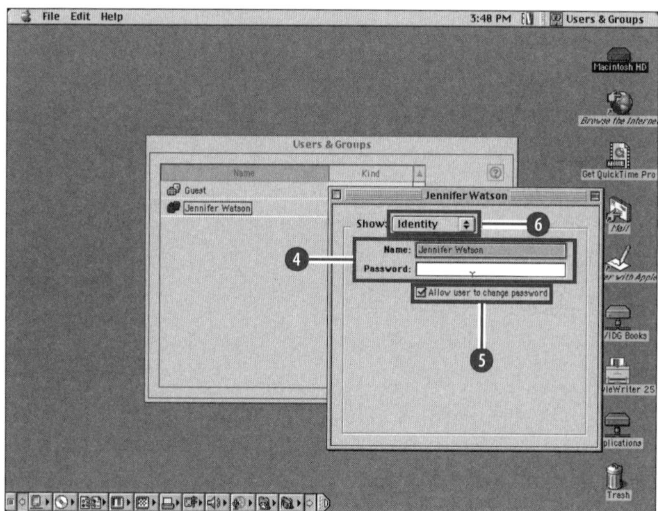

1. *Open the Users & Groups control panel from the Apple menu.*
2. *Select the owner name.*
3. *Click the Open button.*

- *Alternatively, double-click the owner name to open it.*

4. *Optional: Change your name and/or password here.*
5. *Optional: Disable password changing (for high security only)*
6. *Choose Sharing from the pop-up menu.*

CROSS-REFERENCE

Refer to the previous task to set individual user access privileges for a file or folder.

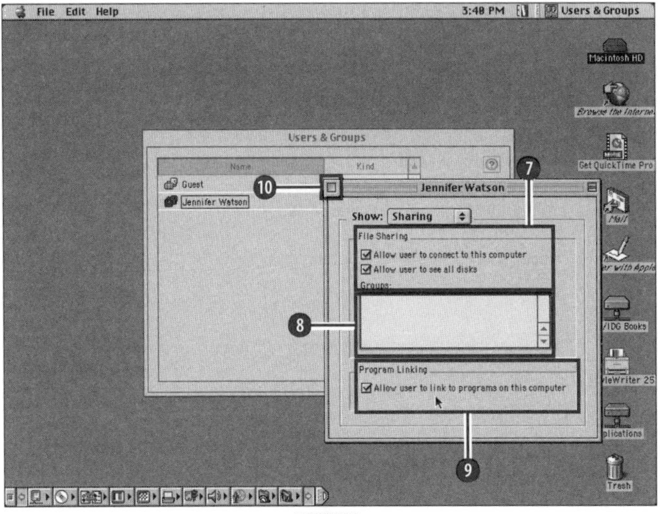

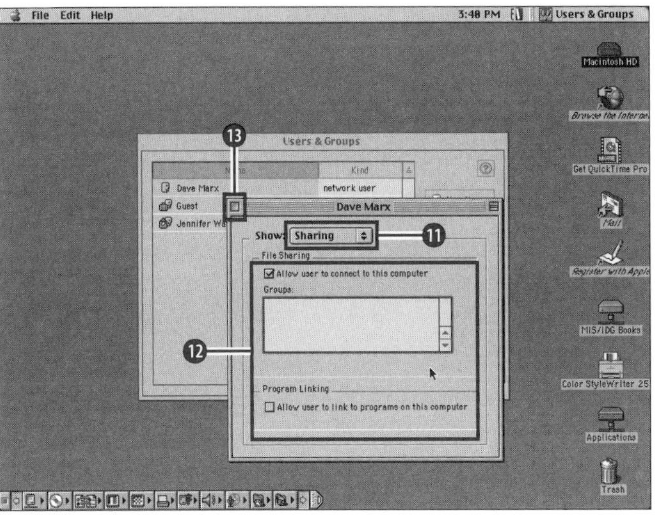

7. *Optional: Set your privileges.*
8. *Optional: Click and drag any groups here.*
9. *Optional: Allow linking to programs.*
10. *Close the window.*
11. *Create a new user, type their name, and choose Sharing.*
12. *Optional: Set the user's privileges.*
13. *Close the window.*

▶ *The user appears in the list.*

If you have a large network, you may want to define groups, too. Just click the New Group button, and click and drag users into it. Members of a group can share files and folders with one another.

TAKE NOTE

FINE-TUNING USER PRIVILEGES

Remember how you enabled sharing for specific folders and files in the previous task? With individual users and groups defined, you can let one user have full access while blocking everyone else out. This could be incredibly time-consuming, of course, but if security is important, this level of detail is crucial. Just select the folder or file you want to set, press Command+I, select Sharing from the drop-down menu, and then choose users/groups and their associated privileges from the menus at the bottom.

LEARNING MORE

I've really only touched the tip of the iceberg in network access, privileges, and permissions. If you plan to use this feature often, I recommend you click the Help button on the Users & Groups window to learn more. Consider investing in a good book about Mac networking, too.

SHORTCUT

Once sharing is set for a folder or file, open the Sharing settings directly by choosing it from the Get Info submenu under the File menu.

Monitoring Your Network

Regardless of the size and complexity of your network, it always helps to monitor it. I don't mean aiming video cameras on your network ports or the other Macs (though I'm sure someone has thought of that, too). Rather, you want to monitor the *activity* of your network.

Open your File Sharing control panel again. This time, click the Activity Monitor tab at the top of the window. This shows you the activity level with a thermometer, a list of the connected users, and a list of the shared items. Clicking a connected user name activates the Disconnect button on the right, which you can use to kick someone off (if you click Disconnect and then change your mind, just click Cancel). Clicking a shared item activates the Privileges button, which you can click to see exactly who and what is allowed to share the item. You can make changes to privileges, too. I recommend you keep this window open on your screen so that you can monitor your network activity. If knowing who and what is connected isn't important, drag the window down and off your screen so only the Sharing Activity thermometer is visible — that will save you some screen real estate.

The Network Browser is another useful tool in monitoring your network, though it is more helpful when it comes to tracking what *you've* connected to over your network. You can open it in your Apple menu or in your Applications folder. The Network Browser lists other computers on the network upon opening it. Double-click a computer name to connect to it and bypass the Chooser altogether. Clicking the small arrow to the left of the computer name connects you, as well. Once you

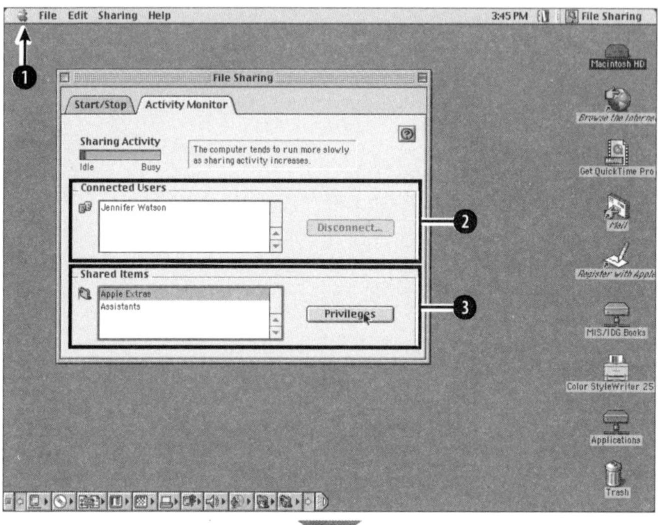

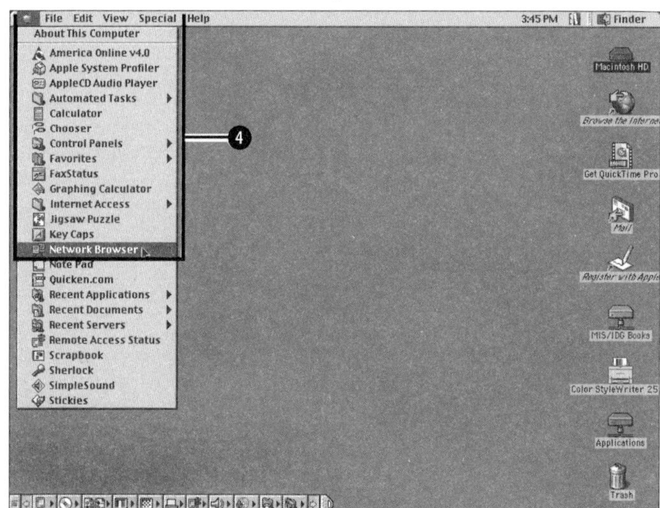

1. Open the File Sharing control panel from the Apple menu.
- Note the activity level.
2. Optional: Disconnect Users.
3. Optional: Set privileges for shared items.
4. Choose Network Browser from the Apple menu.

CROSS-REFERENCE

See "Trashing and Deleting" in Chapter 2 to learn how to trash shared volume and alias icons.

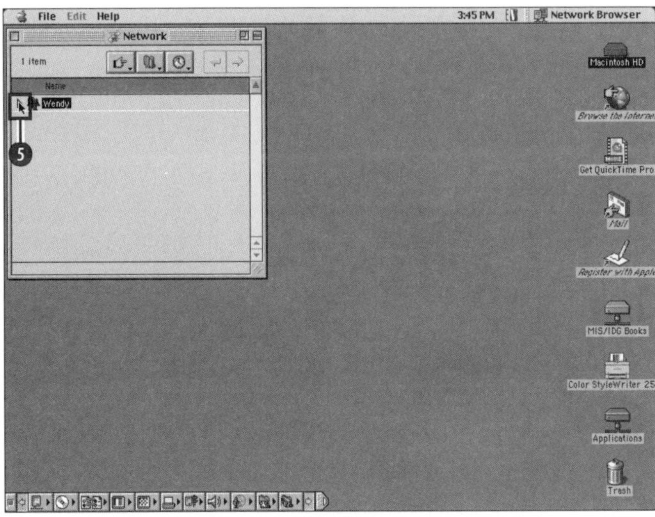

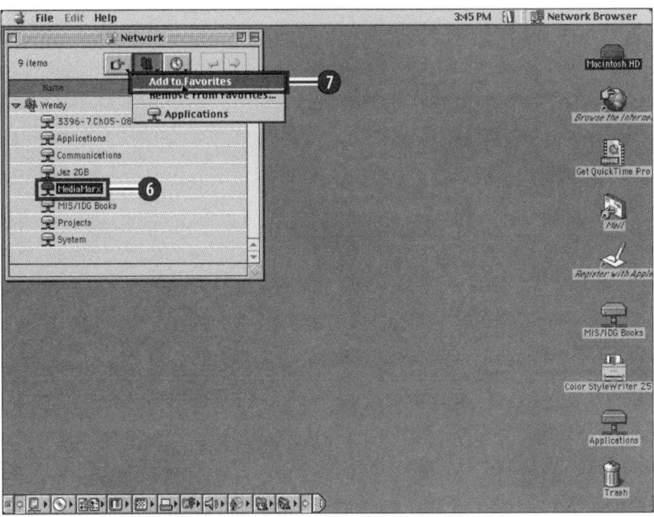

▶ Note the computers to which you are currently connected.

5 Click the small arrow to the left of the computer name to view its shared volumes.

6 Select an item.

7 Choose Add to Favorites.

▶ Its name will appear at the bottom of this menu after you add it.

are connected, the Network Browser lists all the shared items to which you have access. Double-clicking a shared item places its icon on your Desktop and opens its window.

Note that the Network Browser is a new addition to the Mac OS. If you don't see it on your computer and you would like to, consider upgrading to Mac OS 8.5.

TAKE NOTE

ADDING FAVORITES

If you find you're often connecting to one particular item, select it in the Network Browser and choose Add to Favorites under the Favorites button at the top of the window. Now, if you want to connect to that item in the future, you only need to select it from the Favorites button. You also might want to use the History button (the one with a clock on it) to connect to items you've used in the past, or use the forward and back buttons to go forward or back a page, respectively.

MAKING ALIASES

The Network Browser makes it easy to create aliases to a computer or a shared item. Just select it in the Network Browser and choose Make Alias from the File menu.

SHORTCUT

Click and drag an item from your Network Browser to the Desktop to create an alias quickly.

Connecting Remotely via Modem

Not all computers on your network need to be in the same room or building. With Remote Access, it is possible to connect to other computers anywhere in the world and share their items the same way you do with a physical Ethernet connection. There are three catches, however. First, you must have access to that computer (a user name and password). Second, you may need to dial long distance to reach the computer if it isn't local. Third, the remote computer must be compatible with Apple Remote Server (Apple Remote Access Personal Server software must be installed). Your iMac is capable of connecting to a remote computer using Remote Access, but it doesn't include the Personal Server software to allow other computers to connect to you (though you can purchase it separately, if you wish).

To connect to a remote computer, open your Remote Access control panel. Type your user name and password (if any). Type the phone number to reach the computer. If the remote computer isn't within your local calling area, choose User Mode from the Edit menu, click the Advanced radio button, and then click the OK button. Now you can check the Use DialAssist box in the Remote Access window to type an area code and country code for the phone number. You also can click the Options button for more settings, though most are probably okay as they are. Before you connect, visit your RemoteAccess menu and select AppleTalk. Select Remote only from the drop-down menu and close the window. Other related control panels are accessible from the RemoteAccess window; visit them to verify your settings, if necessary.

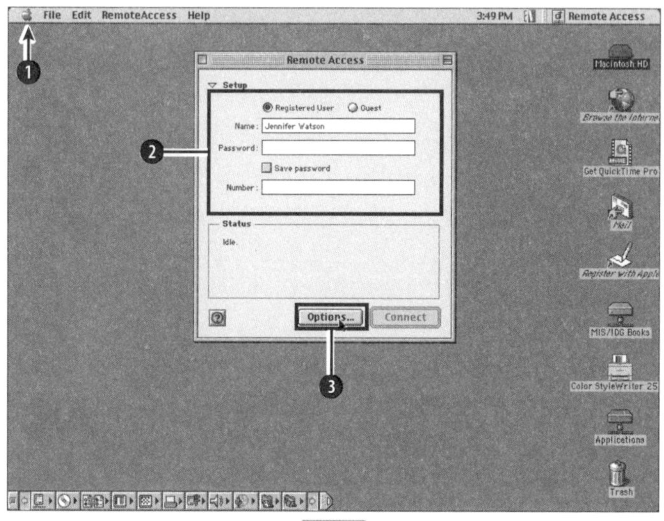

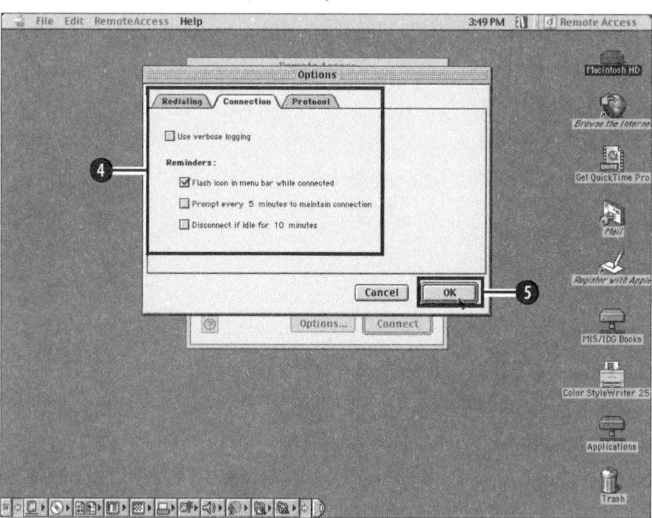

1. *Open the Remote Access control panel from the Apple menu.*
2. *Choose your user status, and then type your name and your password as set on the remote computer.*
3. *Click the Options button.*
4. *Optional: Set your Redialing, Connection, and Protocol options.*
5. *Click the OK button when you are finished.*

CROSS-REFERENCE

Refer to "Configuring Your Modem" in Chapter 10 for assistance using the Modem control panel.

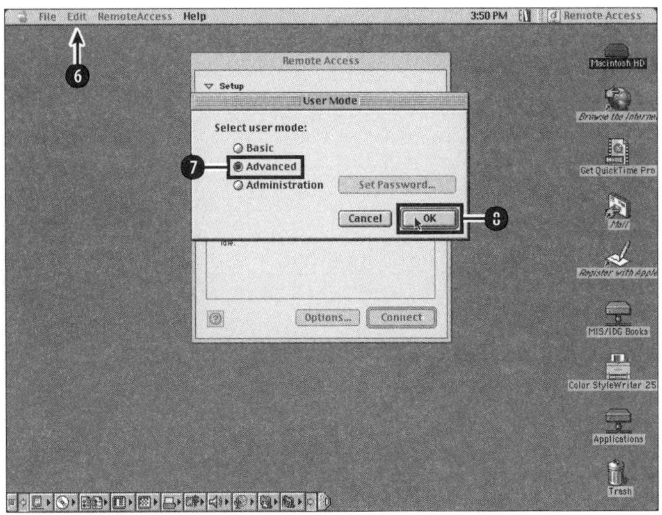

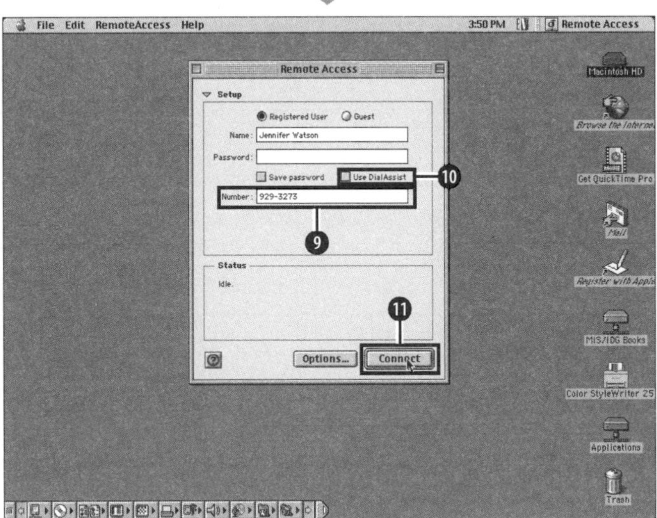

6 *Select User Mode from the Edit menu.*

7 *Click the Advanced radio button.*

8 *Click the OK button.*

9 *Type the remote computer's number.*

10 *Optional: Click the Use DialAssist button to enter area and country codes.*

11 *Click the Connect button.*

When you are ready, click the Connect button to dial the computer. If all goes well, the computer on the other end will answer and begin talking with your iMac through your modem. You may be asked to enter your password (if you didn't already enter it). Successful remote connection will look much like a successful network connection, and you can then use your Network Browser to access the remote computer.

TAKE NOTE

SAVING REMOTE ACCESS CONFIGURATIONS

After typing the information into the Remote Access window, save it for the next time you want to connect to this remote computer. Choose Configurations from the File menu (and click the Save button if you're prompted to save your settings). Now select Default in the list, click the Rename button, and then choose an appropriate name for your settings. In the future, you can choose this configuration to connect quickly. Of course, if this is your only configuration, it automatically becomes your default configuration.

DISCONNECTING FROM A REMOTE COMPUTER

In order to use a remote computer, you need to remain connected through your modem for the duration of use. When you're ready to disconnect and hang up your phone line, select Remote Access Status from the Apple menu and click the Disconnect button.

FIND IT ONLINE

Read the Remote Access User's Manual located on your Software Install CD-ROM disk (use Sherlock to find it).

Personal Workbook

Q&A

1. What kind of cable do you need to connect two Macs?

2. What are the two ways to turn file sharing on?

3. How do you connect to a computer on your network?

4. How do you use a program on another computer to which you're connected?

5. How do you prevent something on your computer from being renamed by someone using it across the network?

6. How do you create a new user name and password?

7. How do you monitor your network activity levels?

8. How can you connect to a remote computer using your modem?

ANSWERS: PAGE 322

Networking and File Sharing

CHAPTER 12

EXTRA PRACTICE

1. Copy an AppleWorks word processing file from your local computer hard disk to the other computer, open AppleWorks on your local computer, and use it to open the file you just stored on the other computer.
2. Set file sharing so that only one folder on your hard disk is accessible to other network users
3. Create an alias on your desktop for a data file stored on a different computer.
4. Set up File Sharing so you can run an application stored on another computer, and create an alias on your desktop to run that application.

REAL-WORLD APPLICATIONS

✔ You're running out of hard disk space on your computer, but the new iMac on your husband's desk has tons of space. You create a folder on his computer and store all your word processing files there.

✔ Your partner has been working on an important proposal and has to leave for the day before you can look at it. She copies it from her hard disk to your computer and shuts down her Mac. It's waiting on your iMac's desktop when you get back to the office.

✔ You bought an external tape backup unit for your iMac to make backups of your hard disk so you won't lose anything in case of disaster. Thanks to the network, you can make backups of every other computer in the office, too.

Visual Quiz

How do you open this window? What do you use it for?

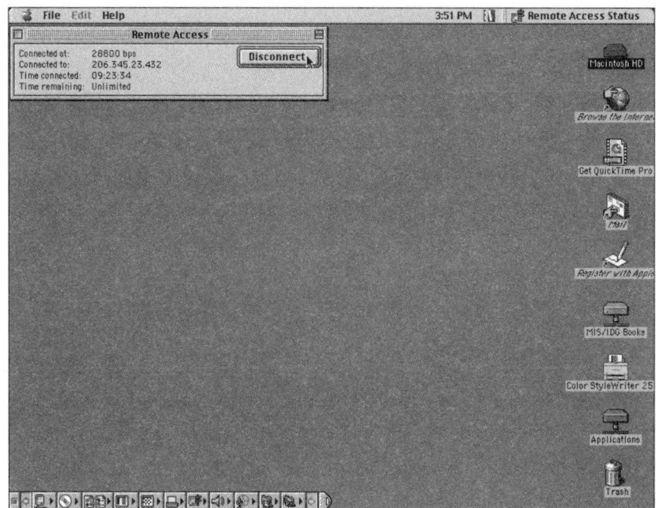

CHAPTER 13

MASTER THESE SKILLS

- Avoiding Crashes and Disasters
- Protecting Your iMac from Viruses
- Locking Your Files and Folders
- Backing Up Your Data
- Optimizing Your iMac

Securing Your iMac

If you fly as often as I do, you've probably become accustomed to all the ways airlines and airports strive to keep their passengers safe and secure. Metal detectors and X-ray machines, bomb-sniffers and air traffic controllers, no-parking zones and emergency exits, preflight safety checks and preventative maintenance schedules, and seat belts, oxygen masks, and life vests — the list seems endless. Some of these safety measures are intended to keep you safe from accidents and normal equipment failure, and others protect you from the acts of people with bad intentions.

Security for your iMac is little different (although the stakes are not nearly so high). At the least, the files saved on your iMac represent hundreds or thousands of hours of hard work, or years of e-mail correspondence. In some cases, your entire livelihood is locked up in your computer. Doesn't it make sense to protect it from accidental damage or intentional harm?

"An ounce of prevention is worth a pound of cure." The phrase rings so true. We all know that eventually *something* will go wrong with your computer. It's just a matter of how and when. There are many ways to delay that day of reckoning, and many other ways to be reduce the damage when it does occur.

Nearly every method described in this chapter is a form of prevention. In some cases, you'll be protecting your iMac from equipment breakdowns and failures through preventative maintenance practices, as well as by making sure it's running at peak performance.

You should also defend against infection — the computer viruses you've heard so much about. Although these malevolent computer programs were created to wreak havoc, simply keeping a watchful eye for shifty characters is not enough. Even your best friend may be an inadvertent carrier, unknowingly spreading the virus through otherwise harmless documents.

Security also extends to protecting the information on your computer from prying eyes, whether it's standing alone in the family room or attached to a corporate network. There's another kind of security as well — the kind that comes from the knowledge that even if your iMac vanished tomorrow, all the information and hard work stored in it has been preserved in a safe place.

So, as bothersome and as tedious as it might seem, let's take a few minutes to learn how to avoid total disaster. A few good habits learned now will pay big dividends in the years to come.

Avoiding Crashes and Disasters

The first step in protecting your iMac is to avoid problems altogether! It isn't always easy, of course, but I do have some suggestions. Think of it as defensive driving for your iMac.

Save your work. Save it regularly. Save it with different names. Save it in different locations. I'm not kidding. Be a compulsive file saver — it'll save you more time than you can imagine!

As irresistible as it may seem, try not to load up your iMac with fancy utilities and cool add-ons. The more extra things you add to your iMac, the more likely you are to have a conflict between them (or with your OS or one of the applications you use). Stick to two or three utilities that really enhance your iMac. Pay attention after you install something new. If your iMac begins to behave oddly, consider disabling your new addition to see if things return to normal. Either use the utility's uninstall function to remove or disable the utility in the Extension Manager control panel (see the next chapter for help on using this powerful tool).

Keep an eye on your available disk space. Your iMac needs at least a few megabytes of free space (preferably much more) to operate well. You can check available space on your Macintosh HD in two ways. Select the icon in the Finder and press Command+I. Or double-click the hard drive's icon and check its window.

As far as your hardware goes, keep your iMac in a room where the temperature and humidity are controlled. Your iMac prefers normal room temperature and moderate humidity. Use a surge protector, and turn your iMac off during electrical storms or during periods of possible power outage. Don't move your iMac while its power is on — it doesn't like vibration and shock. Give your iMac plenty of ventilation space around the outside of the case. Avoid dusty, dirty places whenever possible — coal mines

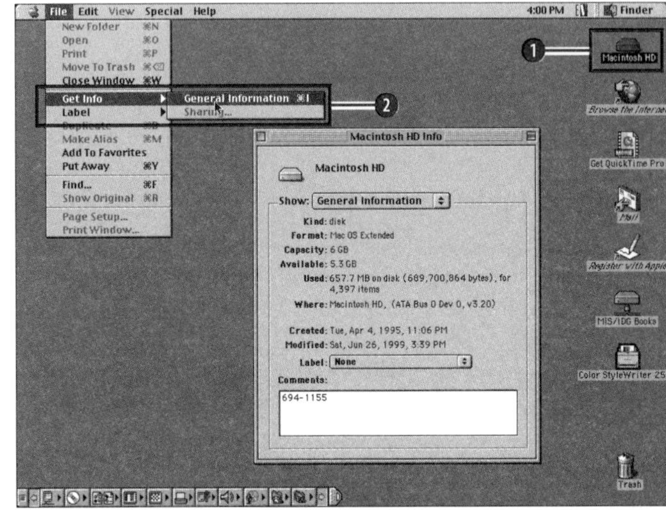

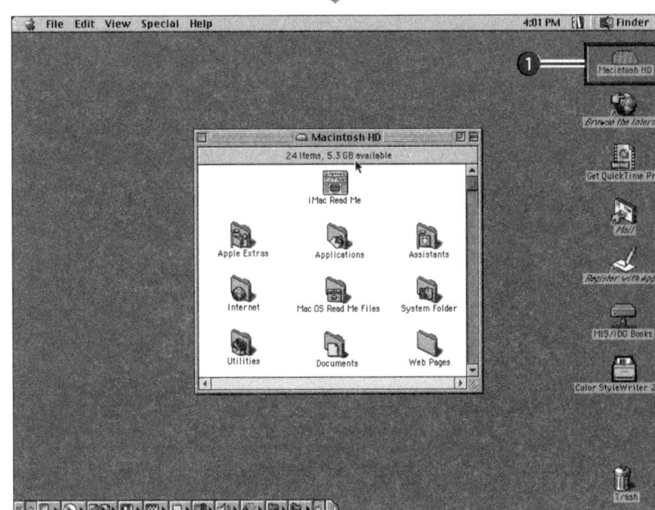

❶ *Select your Macintosh HD icon.*

❷ *Choose General Information from the Get Info submenu under the File menu.*

▶ *Note the available space on your hard drive.*

❸ *Double-click the Macintosh HD icon.*

▶ *Note the available space on your hard drive.*

CROSS-REFERENCE

Refer to Chapter 1 for more information on protecting your iMac with a surge protector.

Keeping Your iMac Up-to-Date

One of the best things you can do to keep your iMac happy and healthy is make sure it is up-to-date! No, I'm not suggesting you buy a new iMac every six months — that wouldn't keep you happy and healthy!. Rather, I'm referring to the software on your iMac, most of which is frequently updated over the course of time. If you register the software that came with your iMac and any software you purchase, most companies will keep you up-to-date on new versions that become available. Some of the new versions (often called "upgrades") may be complimentary, while others may entail separate purchases. If you don't hear from the company itself, but suspect an update may be available, you have two ways to find out. If you have Mac OS 9 on your iMac, open your Software Update control panel and click Update — your iMac will connect to the Internet and begin searching for updates. If updates are found, click the checkbox next to them and then click Install. If you don't have this control panel, try simply searching for the company that created your software on the Web yourself. I also recommend you visit **http://www.versiontracker.com** to get a comprehensive listing of the latest versions available for all your applications. Just compare the latest version to your current version to find out if it has been updated. An application's version number is generally offered in its name, in the Get Info window, or in the application itself (look in About This Application under the Apple menu). Don't forget that your system software is updated often, too! You can get incremental upgrades from Apple at **http://www.apple.com/**. More substantial upgrades may come at an extra charge.

and steel mills probably aren't well suited for an iMac. Turn off your iMac when you aren't using it. Unplug it when you go away for an extended period of time.

If your iMac is at risk from vandalism and theft, protect it with one of the several security devices available on the market. At the very least, insure your iMac. Even insurance won't bring your valuable data back if a thief or a natural disaster takes your iMac away, however. Be sure to back up your data regularly and keep the backup set in a safe place (see the task on backing up later in this chapter).

TAKE NOTE

REBUILDING YOUR DESKTOP

A little preventative maintenance is a good thing. Here's one quick and easy fix: rebuild your iMac's Desktop once a month. This simple process resynchronizes files and their icons, making your iMac run a little faster. Specific directions on how to rebuild your Desktop are in the task "Speeding Up a Slowdown" in Chapter 17. Occasionally, your iMac may want to rebuild the Desktop on its own — which you should let it do.

FIND IT ONLINE

Some iMac-compatible anti-theft devices can be found at **http://www.anchorpad.com**.

Protecting Your iMac from Viruses

No doubt, you've heard of all those terribly dangerous viruses lying in wait for you in the big, bad world. For the uninitiated, a virus is a self-replicating program written and distributed with the sole purpose of messing with your computer. Viruses range from silly pranks to outright catastrophes. However, there aren't quite as many as the media imply, particularly not for the Mac (PC users have a much harder time of it). Nonetheless, you can and should protect yourself from viruses. If nothing else, it will give you peace of mind.

Viruses spread when you exchange computer files with other computers, Your first line of defense from viruses is to use common sense when installing or downloading new files. Ask yourself these questions: Does this file come from a person or company I know and can trust? Did I request or download the file on my own (rather than receive it unsolicited via e-mail)? Is the file too good to be true (a free, full-featured application)? Is the file unsolicited adult software? If you answered no to any of these questions, carefully consider whether the file is legitimate, and avoid using it if at all possible. If you answered yes to any or all of these questions, it still pays to use antivirus software on your iMac to catch potential problem files. After all, you aren't a superhero with the ability to see through files.

Unfortunately, the iMac doesn't come with antivirus software pre-installed, so you'll need to find this software on your own. I recommend you purchase one of two applications: Virex by Network Associates, or Norton AntiVirus for Macintosh by Symantec. You can obtain either package on the Internet, through mail order, and possibly even in a local computer or office supply store (if they carry Mac software titles). On the Internet, look for Virex at **http://www.drsolomon.com/**

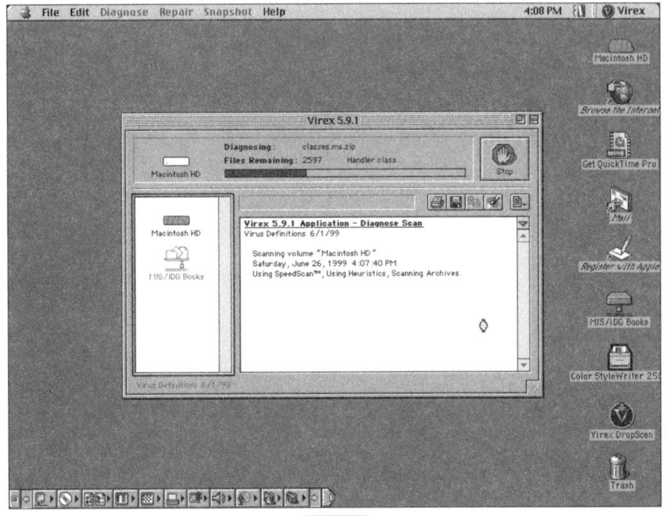

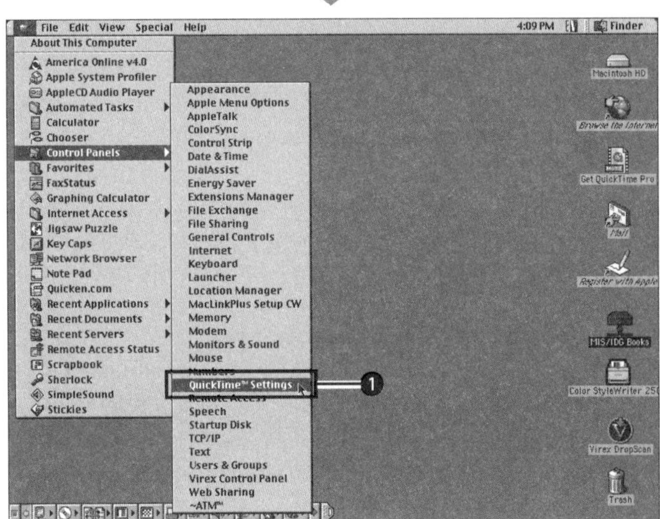

▶ *Virex scans your hard drive and displays a progress meter.*

▶ *Your virus scan results appear here.*

❶ *Open the QuickTime Settings control panel.*

CROSS-REFERENCE

Most viruses are spread via the Internet. Learn how to connect to the Internet in Chapter 11, and be careful out there!

Guarding Against the AutoStart Virus

One particularly nasty virus, called the AutoStart virus, can infect your iMac when you run something on a CD-ROM disc. If your iMac gets infected, the virus will destroy data on your hard drive. Ouch! To protect yourself against this, open your QuickTime Settings control panel, select AutoPlay from the drop-down menu, and clear the two check boxes for Enable Audio CD AutoPlay and Enable CD-ROM AutoPlay.

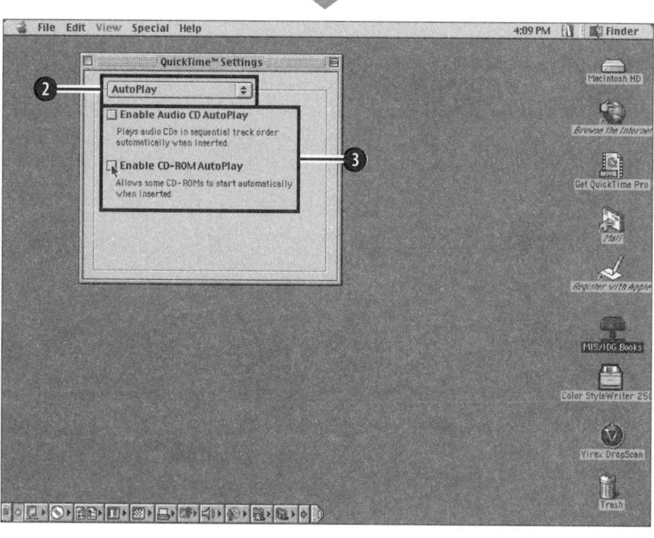

❷ *Select AutoPlay from the drop-down menu.*

❸ *Click the two check boxes to clear the check marks and disable the options.*

and Norton AntiVirus for the Macintosh at **http://www.sarc.com/**.

I won't make an argument for which of these two antivirus software packages is better. Both have their charms. I recommend you pick the one that seems best to you and use it. The key word here is *use*, because the software can't help you if it sits in the box. What I do recommend is that you visit the Mac Virus Web site at **http://www.macvirus.com/**. It offers answers to frequently asked questions, news, descriptions and screen shots of the antiviral software packages, articles, and plenty of information about viruses on the Mac.

TAKE NOTE

IDENTIFYING VIRUS HOAXES

You've just checked your e-mail and it screams "Beware of Good Times Virus!" Before you do anything drastic, consider that it may be a hoax. More people like to worry you with virus scares than actually take the time to program and deploy real viruses. Be suspicious of any virus announcements filled with techno-babble or that claims to be from the FCC (the FCC does not disseminate virus warnings). Check the Internet at (**http://www.macvirus.com/reference/hoax.html**) to see if it shows up on a virus hoax list, too.

FIND IT ONLINE

If you're on America Online, visit the keyword: VIRUS for more links and information.

Locking Your Files and Folders

Another simple thing you can do to protect your iMac is to lock your files and folders. How does locking help? A locked file can't be altered — no accidental deletions, renames, or virus attacks — can affect a file. Of course, a locked file is also barred from updates and other necessary changes, so locking isn't the answer to all your problems. But it is a quick and easy way to protect your most valuable files from user errors.

The best way to lock a file is to select it in your Finder, choose Get Info from the File menu, and check the Locked box in the lower-left corner of the resulting window. The file's icon changes to show a small padlock in the lower-left corner, providing a visual clue that it is locked. You and anyone else with access to your computer can open and view the file, but you cannot make changes to it (the Save button won't be available). You can, however, save changes to a copy of the file. Lock those files that you don't expect to change frequently or those that you intend to copy before making changes.

What about locking a file, or an entire folder, from prying eyes? This is possible, but not without installing extra software. MacLockSmith by Rocco Moliterno can lock files and folders with a strong encryption method, keeping sensitive content away from those who should not see it. You will need to set a password and — more important — remember it. You can download a copy of this shareware utility at **http://users.iol.it/yellowsoft/**.

If you're interested in locking your entire iMac hard drive from snoopers, another shareware utility called LockOut by Maui Software does the trick. LockOut also requires that you enter a password to protect your iMac. Use this when you want to lock your iMac from nosy colleague, friends who like to play pranks, and the innocent eyes of children. Do note, however, that it probably won't stop experienced Mac hacks who are determined

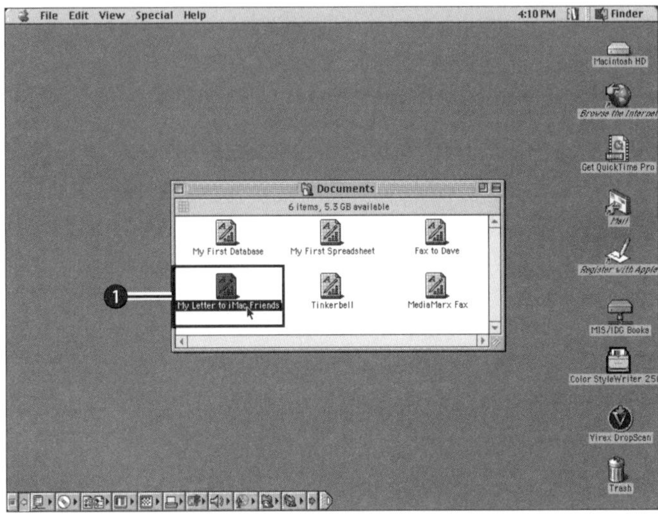

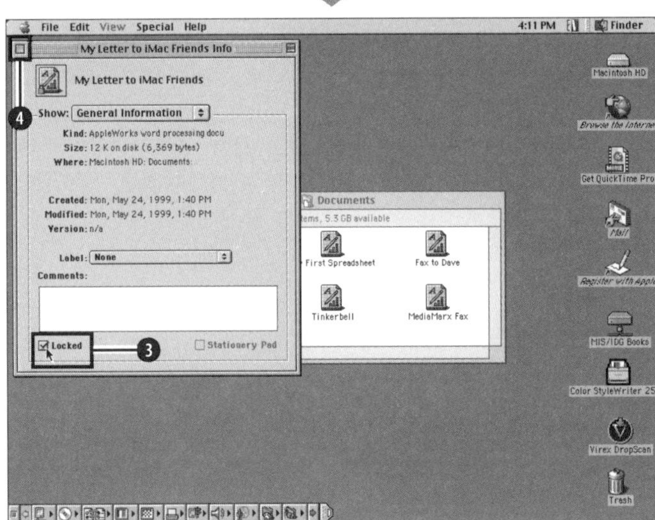

1. *Select the icon of the file you want to lock.*
2. *Press Command+I to get information about the file.*
3. *Click the Locked check box to lock the file.*
4. *Close the window.*

CROSS-REFERENCE

See Chapter 12 for information on locking files on a network.

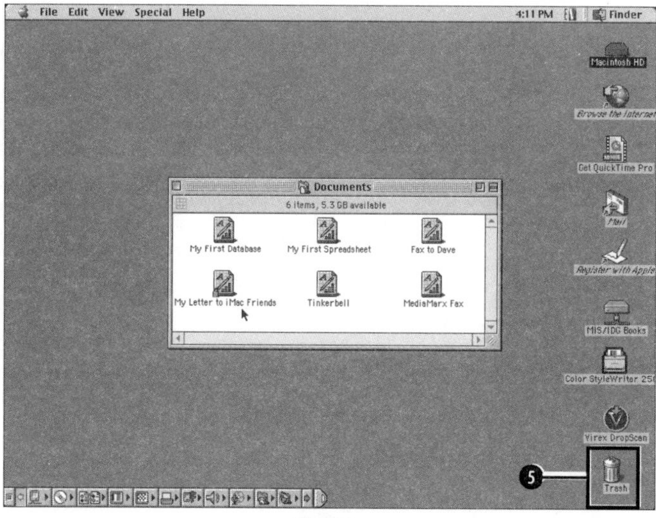

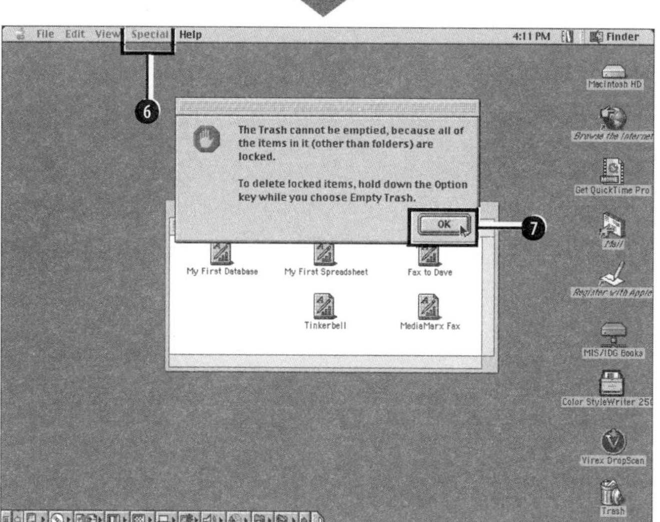

- ▶ *Note the file icon now has a padlock on it, indicating it is locked.*
- 5 *Drag the file to the trash.*
- 6 *Choose Empty Trash from the Special menu.*
- ▶ *Note that your iMac doesn't let you delete a locked item.*
- 7 *Click the OK button to dismiss the window.*
- 8 *Optional: Hold down the Option key while selecting Empty Trash to delete a locked file.*

to get into your computer. You can obtain a copy of this program at **http://www.mauisoftware.com/**.

For serious security, protect your files with passwords. If you have Mac OS 9, you can use the new Encrypt feature to protect your files. Just select the file you want to protect in the Finder and choose Encrypt from the File menu. You will need to type a passphrase of at least five characters as protection — choose something you will be able to remember. You also have the option of adding the passphrase to your Key Chain (a new feature of Mac OS 9), which I highly recommend. Then, if you forget your passphrase, you can open your Key Chain control panel to find it. Note that you must choose a password for your Key Chain control panel, and this one you'll need to memorize. Once a file is encrypted, a small padlock symbol appears on its icon and the passphrase must be input before it is opened. If you don't have Mac OS 9, you can purchase a program called FileGuard from ASD Software, which allows you to password-protect both files and applications — learn more at **http://www.asdsoft.com/**.

SHORTCUT

Press Command+I to bring up the Get Info window (and lock a file) quickly.

Backing Up Your Data

Imagine this scenario: Your boss asks you to write a proposal for that promotion you want so badly. You carefully write the proposal, you include bar charts, and you make it look professional with fonts and formatting. You carefully check it, double-check it, tweak it, and proofread it. This proposal is your pride and joy, the culmination of weeks of effort. Just as you're about to save the final changes and e-mail it to your boss, your Mac inexplicably crashes. Upon restarting, you discover your proposal file was corrupted. Your mouth goes dry. Your hands start to sweat. You *did* make a backup, right?

To avoid this scenario, back up your data regularly. If you've yet to experience this mind-numbing experience, a *backup* is simply a copy of your file (or files) stored in a safe spot. You can back up files in many ways, and some ways work better than others, but you should employ some sort of backup routine. You won't have to restore a file from a backup very often, but when you do, you'll be overjoyed to have it available. Please don't wait until disaster strikes to learn the benefits of backing up your files.

A simple way to back up important files is to save them in another folder on your hard drive. Just choose Save As (when you're editing the document itself) or hold down the Option key and click and drag the file in the Finder. This won't protect your data if your hard drive totally flakes out, but it should protect you from file corruption or accidental deletion. I think of this as the poor person's backup method. You get what you pay for, after all.

Another backup method employs e-mail. If you have an e-mail account, send yourself e-mail with that all-important file attached to it. It won't stay in your mailbox forever (usually only about a month, in fact), but it does provide some short-term protection. Note: You will need to keep the e-mail with the attached file on your server (AOL users need to click the Keep As New button

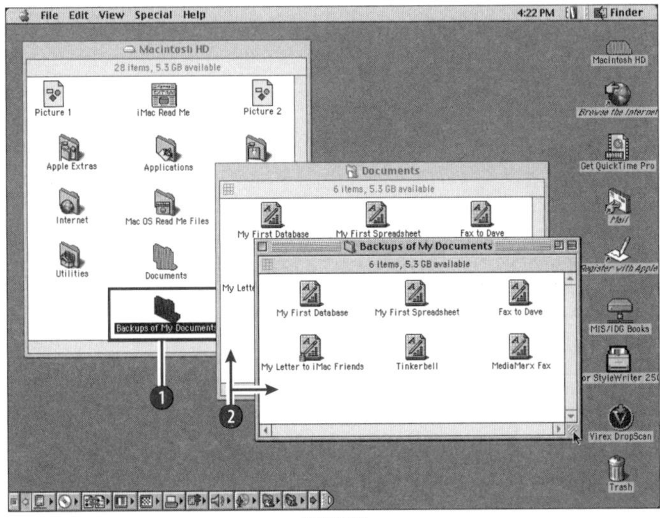

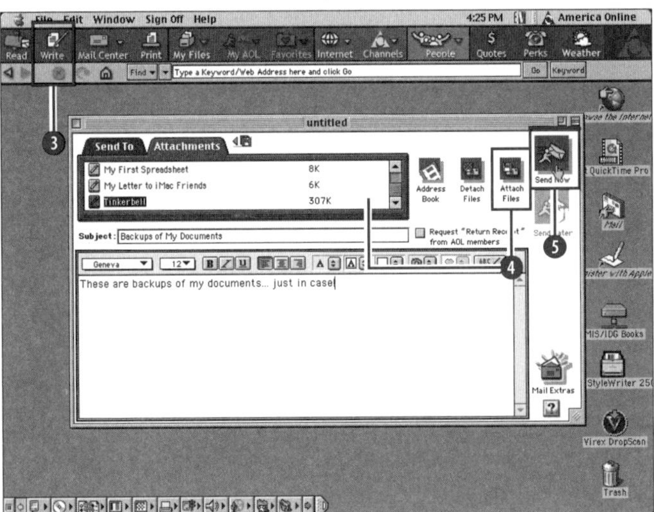

1. *Create a new folder titled "Backups of My Documents."*
2. *Copy the contents of your Documents folder into your Backups folder.*

▶ *If you are an AOL member, sign on to the service.*

3. *Click the Write icon to compose a new e-mail to yourself.*
4. *Click the Attach Files icon and choose a file. The file appear in the Attachments window. Repeat as necessary.*
5. *Click the SendNow icon.*

CROSS-REFERENCE

Read more about connecting and using removable media in Chapter 3.

Make a Backup Date with Your iMac

In order for your backups to be effective, they need to be frequent. After all, what good is a backup if it is over six months old? Restoring an old backup is like going back in time, before you balanced your checkbook, finished your taxes, and finished the novel you'd been meaning to write for years. Yuck! Instead, make a date to back up regularly: once a day, once a week, or once a month.

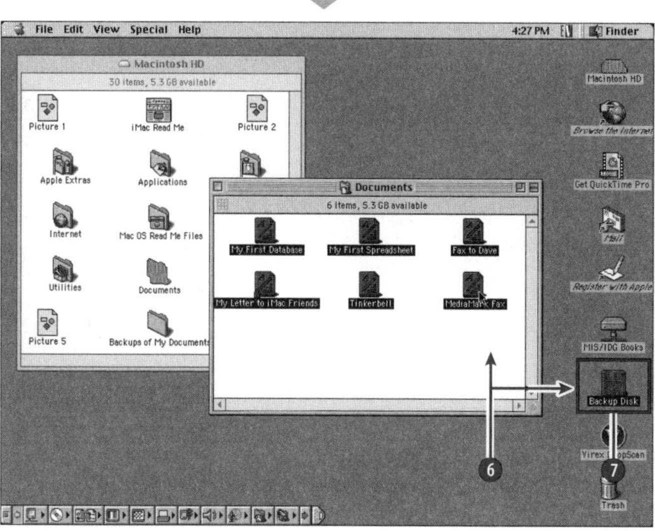

6 *If you installed an external floppy drive, insert a blank floppy disk and name it "Backup Disk."*

7 *Select the files you want to back up and drag them on top of the floppy to copy them to it.*

on the e-mail message). You also might want to investigate file backup services on the Internet, such as iMacBackup.com, which saves copies of your important files to another computer for safekeeping.

If you connected a removable media drive to your iMac, such as a floppy drive, Zip drive, or CD-R drive, save your files to the appropriate disk and store the disk in a safe place. I use CD-R discs myself, backing up my entire hard drive in one step (I have less than 650MB of data on my iMac and that is the CD-R limit).

When you're ready to get serious about your backup routine (probably about the time you lose that important file), you can purchase commercial programs that take the guesswork out of backing up. Retrospect by Dantz and Personal Backup by ASD Software are two good choices.

TAKE NOTE

DECIDING WHAT TO BACK UP

The majority of your applications can be reinstalled from your iMac Install CD-ROM disc if they are lost. Thus, you may only want to back up your document files. Or only those document files that have changed since the last time you did a backup.

FIND IT ONLINE

Find backup software on the Internet at **http://www.dantz.com/** and **http://www.asdsoft.com/**.

Optimizing Your iMac

When you save a file to your hard drive, your iMac places it in the next available space on the drive itself, even if it's too small to hold the entire file. That may mean that the first half of the file goes in one spot and the rest is continued elsewhere. Your iMac seamlessly keeps track of these *fragmented* file locations—you don't need to know exactly where a file resides on your hard drive, so long as you know where it is on your Desktop. Your iMac's efficiency at saving files in this manner means that, after a while, you may have hundreds of files scattered all over your drive in various degrees of fragmentation. This is particularly true if you save and trash files a lot. Too many of these fragmented files can cause your iMac slow down. And in the worst case, an extremely fragmented drive can really mess up your iMac. What do you do? Optimize it!

You'll need to purchase a disk utility program, such as Norton Utilities (by Symantec) or TechTool Pro (by MicroMat Computer Systems). Both offer hard drive optimization features. These programs go through the entire contents of your hard drive, rearranging and rejoining all the fragmented files and organizing the files into a logical order. The process can take a long time, and you won't be able to do anything else while you're optimizing your hard drive. Additionally, the optimization process is a tricky one: if your iMac crashes or loses power during the optimization process, you risk losing data. Always do a backup before you optimize, just to be on the safe side.

With both Norton Utilities and TechTool Pro, you can actually watch a graphic representation of your hard drive as it is optimized. Watching the process can teach you a lot about how your hard drive stores data.

You should only need to optimize your hard drive once every few months. If you save and trash a lot of files, you may need to optimize as often as once a month. I get away with optimizing once every three months myself.

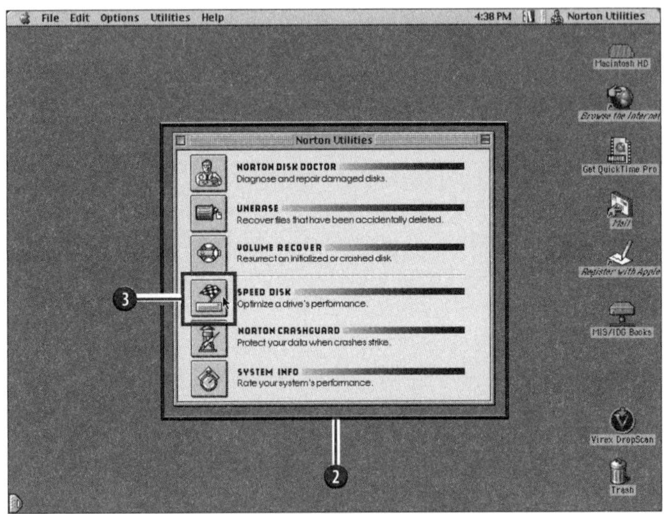

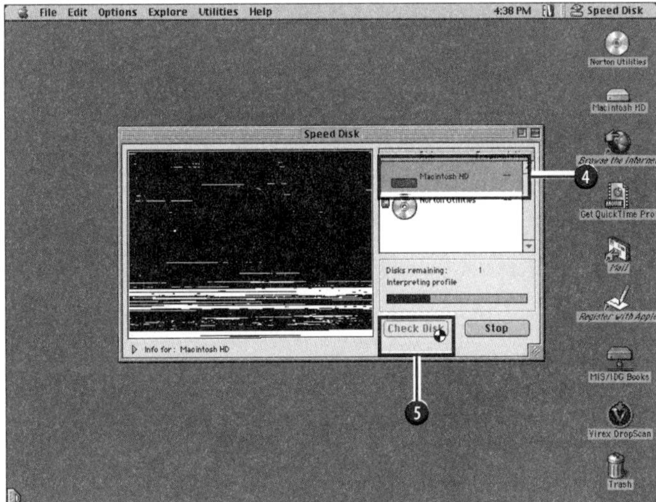

1. If you have Norton Utilities, insert its CD into the CD-ROM drive, restart your iMac, and hold down the C key to start from the CD.
2. Run Norton Utilities.
3. Click the Speed Disk icon to optimize your hard disk.
4. Select your hard drive.
- Note the visual representation of your hard drive.
5. Click the Check Disk button.
- A progress meter is displayed as your disk is checked.

CROSS-REFERENCE

Refer to Chapter 15 for more information about your RAM.

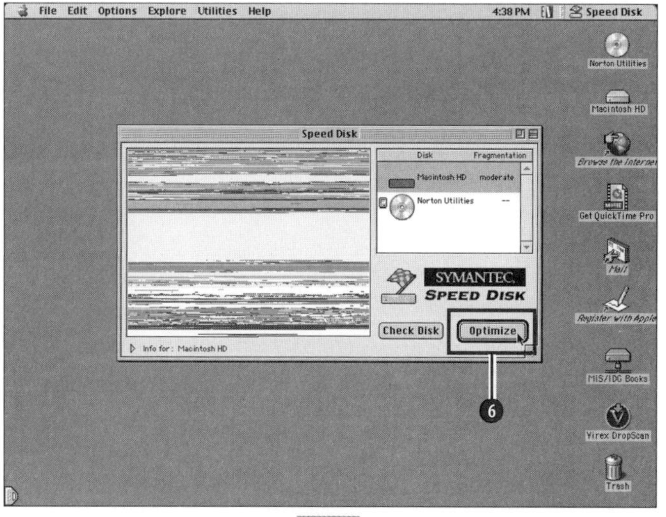

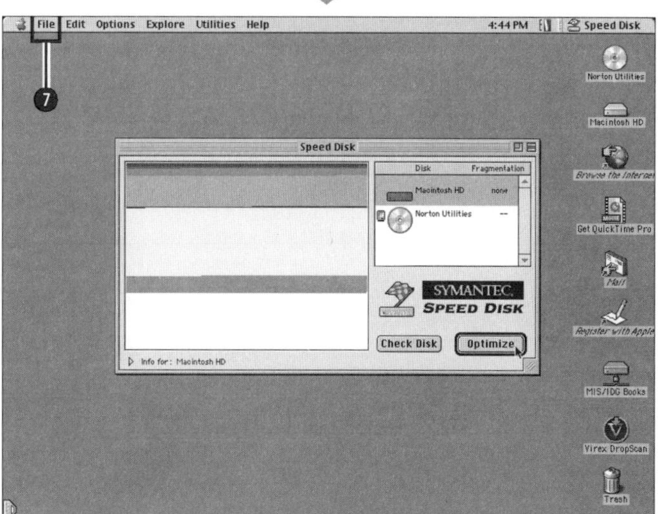

- *Note the more detailed representation of your hard drive, displayed after the disk check. The color blocks you see represent different kinds of files on your drive.*

6. *Click the Optimize button.*

- *Note how the files have been rearranged so that similar files are all together.*

7. *When you are finished, choose Quit and then restart your iMac.*

TAKE NOTE

USING NORTON UTILITIES

Norton Utilities is a full-featured hard drive maintenance and repair software package. Besides its ability to diagnose and repair damaged disks, recover files that have been accidentally lost, and so on, Norton offers a module called Speed Disk for optimization. Speed Disk lets you optimize your entire drive, or just selected files. Look for Norton Utilities 4.0 or higher for compatibility with your iMac.

USING TECHTOOL PRO

TechTool Pro offers File Optimization features similar to those found in Norton. Its other routines focus on testing and repairing various aspects of your system and hardware (including your RAM). Look for TechTool Pro version 2.1.1 or higher for compatibility with your iMac. Note that a free version of TechTool exists, but it doesn't offer disk optimization (or many other features).

FIND IT ONLINE

Norton Utilities is available online at **http://www.symantec.com** and TechTool Pro is at **http://www.micromat.com**.

Personal Workbook

Q&A

1. Why should you avoid adding lots of fancy utilities to your iMac?

2. How do you rebuild your Desktop?

3. What is your first line of defense against viruses on your iMac?

4. How can you protect yourself from the AutoStart Virus?

5. How do you lock a file on your iMac?

6. What are two simple ways to back up your important data?

7. Do you need to back up all your files regularly?

8. Why is it important to occasionally optimize your iMac's hard drive?

ANSWERS: PAGE 323

CHAPTER 13

Securing Your iMac

EXTRA PRACTICE

1. If you haven't already done so earlier in the chapter, rebuild your iMac Desktop, note today's date, and then make yourself a reminder to rebuild it again next month.
2. Disable Audio CD and CD-ROM AutoPlay. If you wish, leave it disabled. If not, re-enable it, and keep this feature in mind if you receive any home-made CD-ROMs.
3. Protect a favorite image or text file from accidental erasure or modification by using file locking.
4. Protect your System Folder and Applications folder using your General Controls control panel.
5. Create a Backups folder on your hard disk and save copies of your most valuable files in that folder.

REAL-WORLD APPLICATIONS

- ✔ A fearsome thunderstorm is approaching. Quickly, you save your work, shut down your iMac, and unplug its power cord. Moments later a lightning bolt shatters the utility pole in front of your house. Your computer is safe, but you wish you had protected your TV the same way.
- ✔ Your six-year-old is an absolute whiz with your iMac. The only trouble is, she loves to fill the trash can and watch it expand. While you always double-check the trash before you empty it, you protect the System Folder and Applications folder, just in case.
- ✔ It's been taking your iMac longer and longer to open and save the files you use every day. You run your disk utility software and discover your hard drive is 25% fragmented. You defragment the drive, bringing your computer back to its old, zippy self.

Visual Quiz

How do you get this window? What can you do here to help secure your iMac?

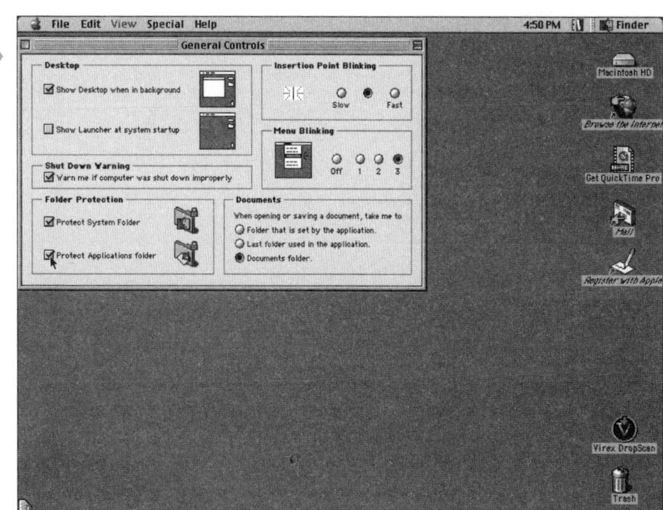

PART IV

Polishing Your iMac

By now, we've covered the basics — and the details — of the many ways you can use your iMac for work and pleasure. Are you ready to start putting your personal imprint on your iMac? Macs have always been fun to decorate and personalize, and your colorful iMac has been waiting *very* patiently for this section.

Of course, personalizing isn't just about good looks. After all, your iMac is a computing machine, and like a finely-tuned sports car, a bit of extra attention under the hood can have you racing through your tasks in record time.

When it comes down to it, a race isn't always won with raw speed. If you know the right shortcuts, you can arrive at the finish line far ahead of the pack. There are ways to automate routine iMac tasks that will knock your socks off, and I'll show you how to get started.

Finally, like any complex, finely-tuned machine, your iMac is going to crash. It's not a pretty thought, but it's true. A little knowledge about getting your iMac back on the road will make you a much happier driver, so I hope you stick around all the way to the end.

CHAPTER 14

MASTER THESE SKILLS

- Setting Your General Controls
- Changing Your iMac's Appearance
- Navigating Your Own Way
- Customizing Your Keyboard and Monitor
- Making the Most of Your Apple Menu
- Setting Your Startup/Shutdown Options
- Using Other Control Panels
- Managing System Extensions
- Enhancing with Utilities

Customizing Your iMac

One of the great benefits of using a Macintosh is the consistent way in which the computer behaves, regardless of which application program you may be using. Unlike the rules of English spelling and grammar, once you learn the basics of menus, mice, folders, and files, you won't be burdened with countless little exceptions and gotchas. Still, the quirkiness and variety of the English language also bestows wordsmiths like me with countless opportunities for personal expression. How do you balance the need for consistency *and* creativity?

Although Shakespeare and Milton never got a crack at enriching the Macintosh OS language, the folks at Apple Computer have gone out of their way to ensure you can say iMac in many different ways. Whether you're changing superficial items such as the look of your iMac desktop, making productivity-related adjustments to your mouse and menus, or tweaking the color monitor to suit the needs of the professional graphic artist in you, your iMac is a marvel of modifiability and adaptability.

You can express your individuality by changing the graphic you see at startup, adding sounds to herald startup and shutdown, replacing the wallpaper on your desktop, substituting new and fun icons for the old familiar ones, and respecifying the fonts and colors of your windows, menus, and folders.

Do you love your Apple menu? Make it even more useful and efficient by adding your most-needed applications and files, removing seldom-used items, and organizing it to suit your own personal logic.

Do you always start your computing day the same way? Rather than go through the rigamarole of manually opening all the applications and files you need, why not have your iMac automatically open them for you?

Of course, all that tweaking may leave you with an iMac that you love, but that the rest of the family can't stand. Once you have your iMac's appearance adjusted just the way you like it, why not save your appearance settings and still let everyone else create their own personal settings?

All this should come as no surprise to you — after all, what other computer comes in five scrumptuous decorator flavors? With just a bit of work (and play) on your part, you can have an iMac that looks fabulous and fits you like a custom-fitted kid glove. I can see everyone oohing and ahhing now!

Setting Your General Controls

Before you begin really customizing your iMac, visit your General Controls. I consider these the equivalent of setting the thermostat in a house. You need to establish basic living conditions before you worry about which shade of green to paint the walls.

Your General Controls control panel is conveniently located in your Control Panels folder (as is most everything else in this chapter). Six categories of options are available. Let's look at each one in detail.

Desktop controls offer two options. The first is to show the Desktop when in background, which means that your Desktop and contents are visible behind any open windows when you're in an application. It also means you can switch to the Desktop simply by clicking whatever little bit of desktop is visible behind the active application. On the other hand, if the Desktop distracts you, or you find yourself switching to the Desktop each time you accidentally click it, go ahead and disable this option.

The second Desktop option shows the Launcher at system startup. The Launcher is a special window with icons leading to applications all over your hard drive. With it, you can use it to quickly open an application. You can see it now by selecting Launcher from the Control Panels. If you find the Launcher helpful, go ahead and enable it to show at startup.

The Shut Down Warning option is straightforward: your iMac will warn you on startup if your computer was not shut down properly. When enabled, your iMac also automatically runs Disk First Aid at startup whenever it detects that it wasn't shut down properly. I recommend you keep this option enabled.

The Folder Protection option lets you safeguard your System Folder and Applications folder from accidental deletion. Note that these options will not be available if you have enabled File Sharing.

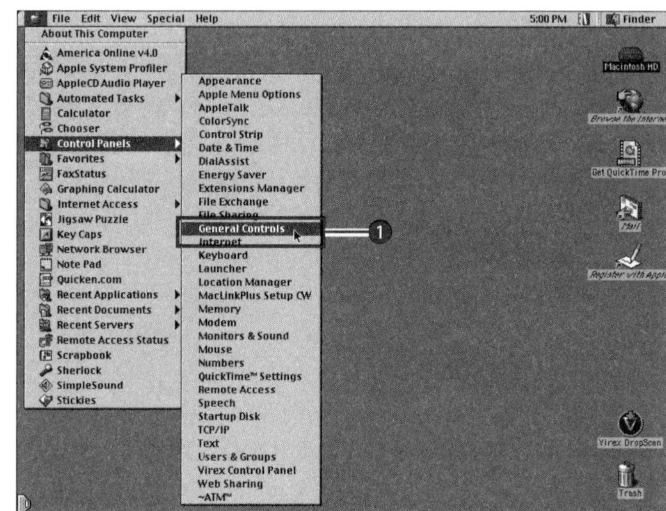

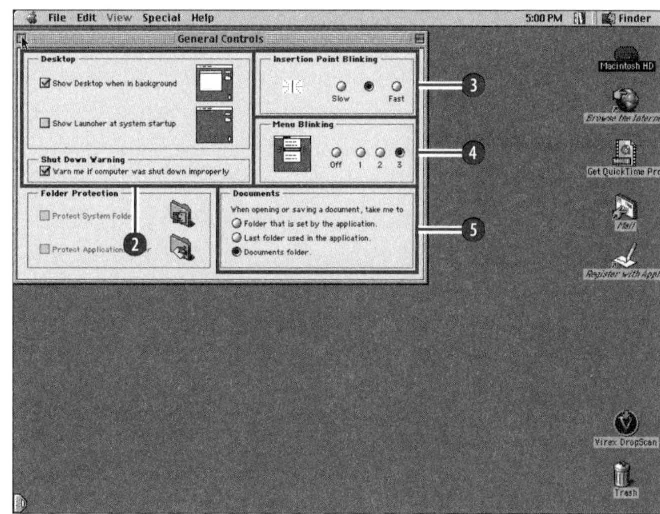

❶ *Open your General Controls.*

❷ *Optional: Set your Desktop settings or Shut Down Warning settings.*

❸ *Optional: Set your Insertion Point Blinking rate.*

❹ *Optional: Set your Menu Blinking rate.*

❺ *Optional: Set your preferred folder for documents.*

CROSS-REFERENCE

See "Locking Your Files and Folders" in Chapter 13 for other ways to protect your System Folder, Application folder, and other folders.

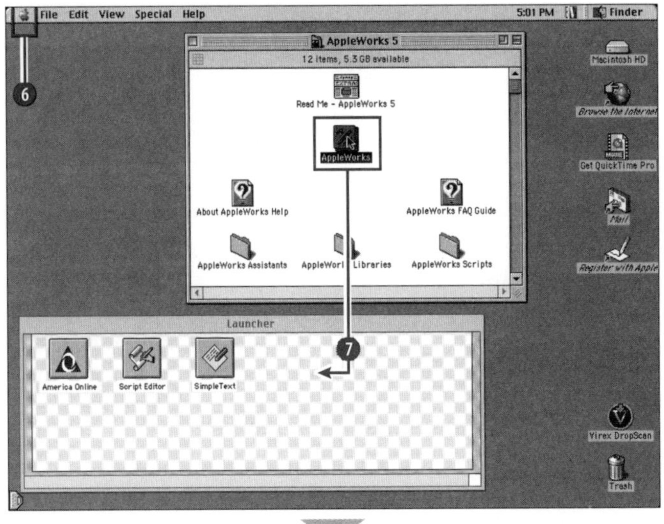

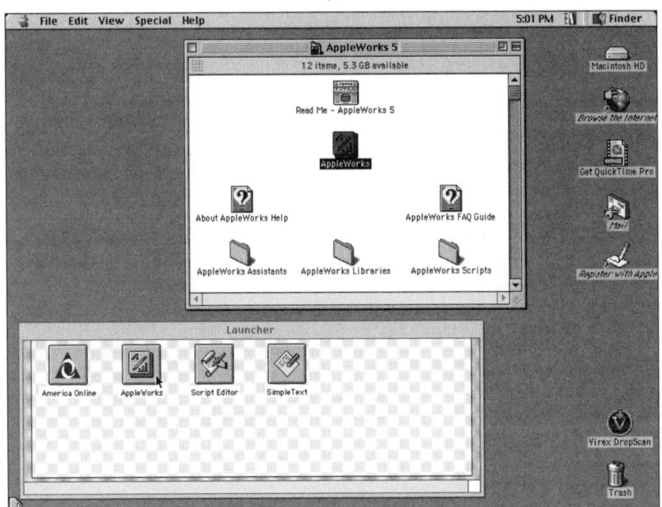

6 *Choose Launcher from the Control Panels submenu under the Apple menu.*

▶ *Note the Launcher window with its icons.*

7 *Drag an icon from elsewhere on your Desktop to the Launcher window and drop it.*

▶ *Note the new icon that appears in the Launcher. You can click it to open it if you wish.*

The Insertion Point Blinking option simply controls the rate at which the insertion point blinks. Slow it down or speed it up if you like. The Menu Blinking option controls the number of blinks you see when you choose a menu item.

The Documents option lets you designate the default folder that is available from within a given application. This is purely a matter of choice, though if you want to save all your documents in the same folder, you might want to choose the Documents folder. I myself prefer to use the setting of last folder used by the application.

TAKE NOTE

▶ **USING THE LAUNCHER**

Before you decide whether the Launcher is for you, it may help to know that you can add icons to it yourself. Just click and drag an application's icon on top of the Launcher window, and then release the mouse button. Your iMac automatically creates an alias for you and places it in the Launcher window in alphabetical order. Change the size of the icons by holding down the Command key, clicking in the window, and selecting a new size from the drop-down menu. If you want to remove an icon from the Launcher window, hold down the Option key, and then click and drag it to the Trash.

SHORTCUT

Enable Show Launcher at startup if you want to open an application quickly.

Changing Your iMac's Appearance

Don't worry — I'm not going to suggest that you change your iMac's appearance by painting it a midnight blue. I am, however, going to recommend what some may consider radical. It's what I like to think of as *virtual decorating,* and it's something I do often with my own Macs. Why? It makes my Mac seem a bit less like a machine and a bit more like a favorite room in my house, which helps me to feel more at home with my Mac. If you're planning to spend any amount of time on your iMac, I strongly recommend you take a few minutes and decorate!

You'll find your virtual wallpaper samples and paint supplies in the Appearance control panel. Open it and click the Themes tab in the upper-left corner. Themes are a bit like hiring a decorator to come in and do all the work — all you need to do is choose the theme you like and let your iMac decorate for you. Each theme offers a different Desktop background (the image or pattern visible behind the icons), highlight colors (the colors that are visible when you select an icon), fonts (the fonts that are shown in both the menu bar and the menus), and so on. To try on a theme for size, just click it.

If you're not the hire-a-decorator type and prefer to choose everything yourself, the Appearance control panels lets you do that, too. Click the Appearance tab at the top of the window to choose your Appearance (overall look of menus, icons, etc.), highlight color, and variation highlight color. You probably have only one Appearance option (Apple platinum), but it's a good choice anyway. Keep in mind when selecting a highlight color that you don't want it to be too dark, or you won't be able to see your highlighted text.

Your Fonts tab lets you choose a system font (two sizes) and a views font. Feel free to play around with your fonts — you can always change them back. If you're

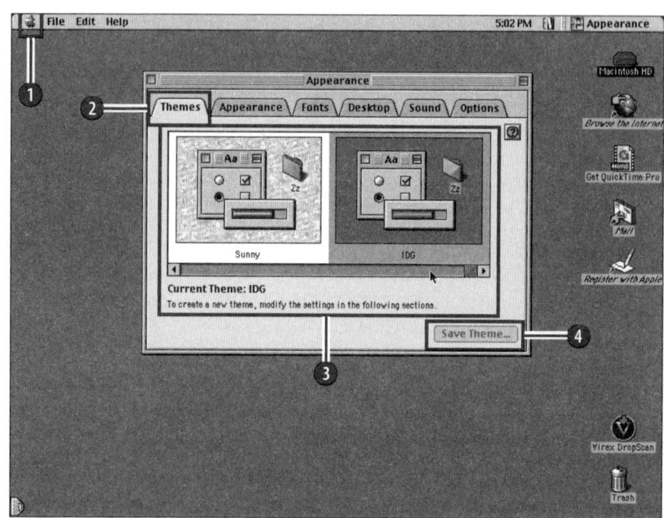

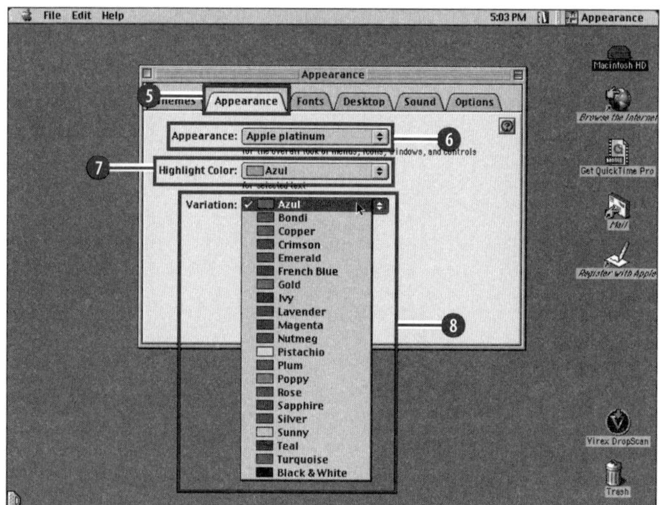

1. *Open the Appearance control panel.*
2. *Click the Themes tab.*
3. *Scroll through the available themes and click one to select it.*
4. *Optional: Click the Save Theme button to create a custom theme.*
5. *Click the Appearance tab.*
6. *Optional: Choose Apple platinum from the Appearance drop-down menu.*
7. *Optional: Choose a new highlight color for selected text.*
8. *Optional: Choose a new variation highlight color for menus and controls.*

CROSS-REFERENCE

See Chapter 9 for more information about Sound options in the Appearance control panel.

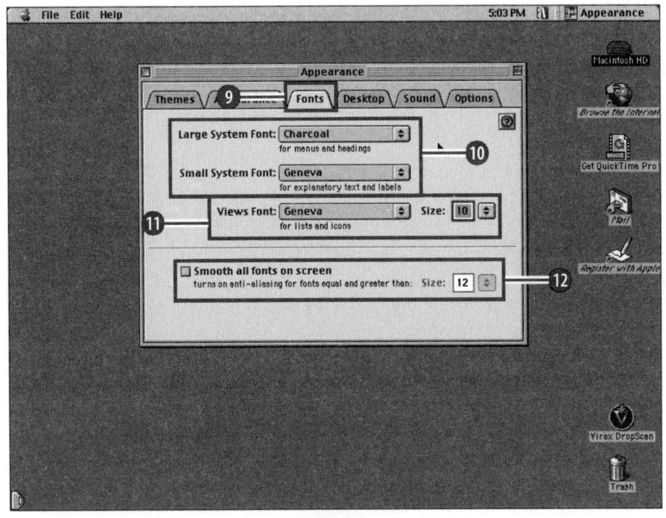

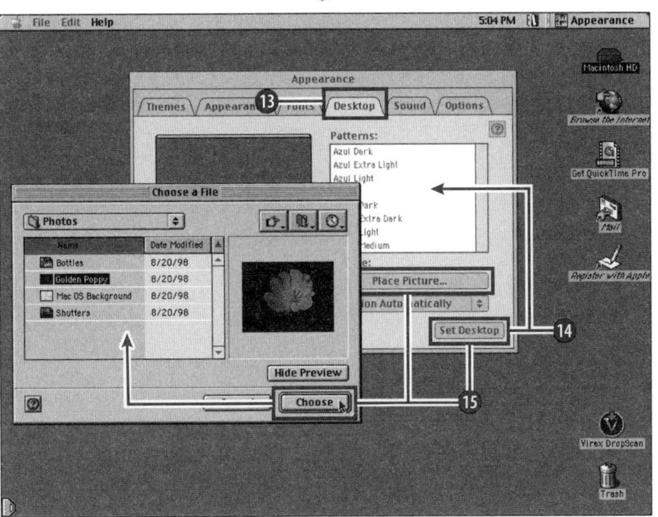

9. *Click the Fonts tab.*
10. *Optional: Choose a new System font (large or small).*
11. *Optional: Choose a new Views font and modify its size.*
12. *Optional: Enable font smoothing and modify its minimum size.*
13. *Click the Desktop tab.*
14. *Optional: Choose a pattern and click Set Desktop.*
15. *Optional: Click the Place Picture button, choose a picture, click Choose, and then click the Set Desktop button.*

looking for optimal readability, or just the classic Mac look, go for the Chicago typeface. The Smooth all fonts on screen option should remain enabled if you want your fonts to look their best.

The Desktop tab lets you choose a Desktop background pattern or image. Set a background pattern by selecting an item from the list, and then click the Set Desktop button. Set a background image by clicking the Place Picture button, choosing an image, and then clicking the Set Desktop button. You'll find some fun images in your Desktop Pictures folder, which is located in your Appearance folder inside your System Folder.

TAKE NOTE

MINIMIZING WINDOWS

You may remember that you can minimize a window when you need more room. Just click the minimize window button in the upper-right corner of most windows. If you minimize your windows often, you may like this shortcut: you can double-click the title bar to minimize — or collapse — your window. You must turn this shortcut on first, however. Click the Options tab in your Appearance control panel to enable the Double-click title bar to collapse windows option.

SHORTCUT

Save your decorating efforts with the Save Theme button available under the Themes tab in the Appearance control panel.

Navigating Your Own Way

Your trusty mouse is always at hand for navigation, but did you know there are several other ways to get around your iMac? You may prefer your mouse, but it pays to learn about other navigation methods, too. Some save time, others save finger and wrist strain, and some are just fun.

The Tab key can become your best friend! Use it to move from icon to icon on the Desktop or in a window (it moves in alphabetical order). You also can use it to move from object to object in a dialog box, or from field to field or cell to cell in a database or spreadsheet, respectively. Try holding down the Shift key while you press the Tab key — it moves you *backward*. If you hold down the Command key while you press the Tab key, you'll cycle through your open applications without ever having to touch your mouse!

If you don't like the way the Tab key moves in alphabetical order through icons, try the up-arrow and down-arrow keys instead. The arrow keys also move you through menus, lists, and documents. Holding down the Shift key as you press an arrow key cycles you between open windows in an application, though this function depends on the application you are using.

In dialog boxes, you can usually type the first letter of a button to activate it. For example, when you close a window, you might be asked if you want to save any changes. If you don't want to save any changes, press the N key (*N* for *No*). If that doesn't work, try holding down the Command key — do you see keyboard shortcuts appear beside the buttons? If you do, you can use those shortcuts to activate various buttons using the keyboard. Remember, also, that the OK button — or any button with a dark border around it — can be activated using the Return key.

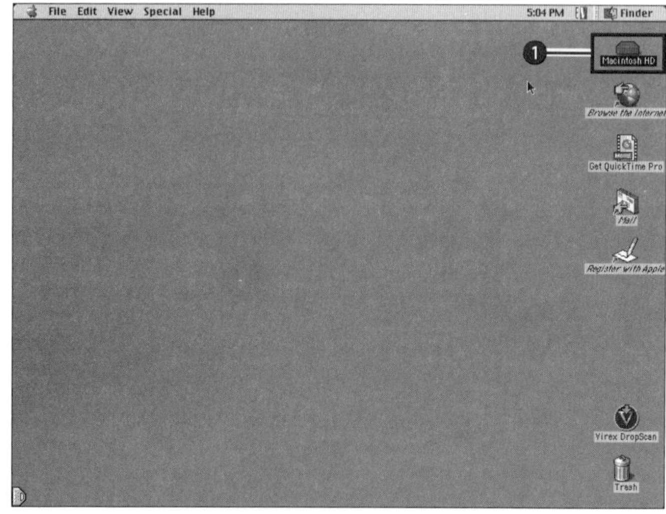

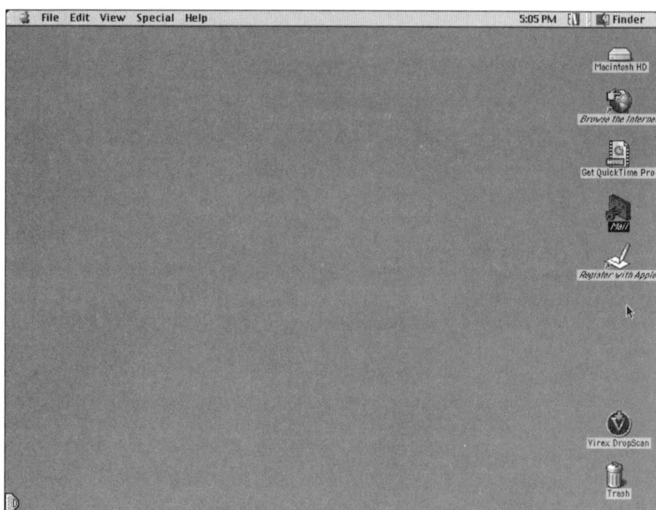

❶ Select your Macintosh HD icon.

❷ Press the Tab key.

▶ Note that the Mail icon becomes selected. Mail comes after Macintosh HD in alphabetical order.

CROSS-REFERENCE

See the Take Note item "Using Keyboard Shortcuts" in Chapter 2 for more information on using keyboard shortcuts.

Customizing Your iMac

CHAPTER 14

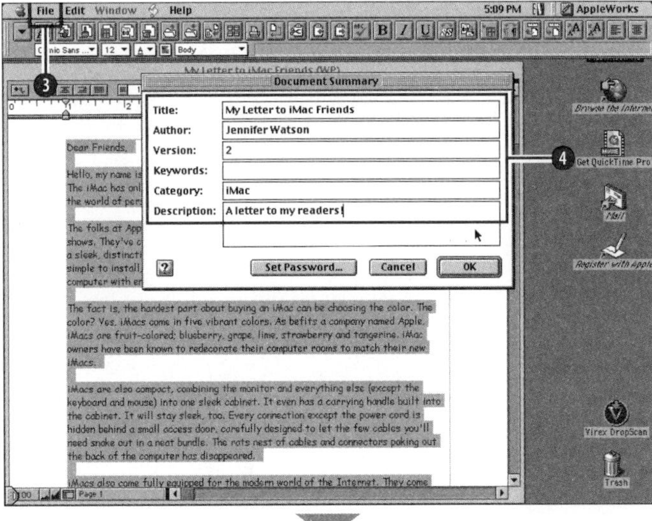

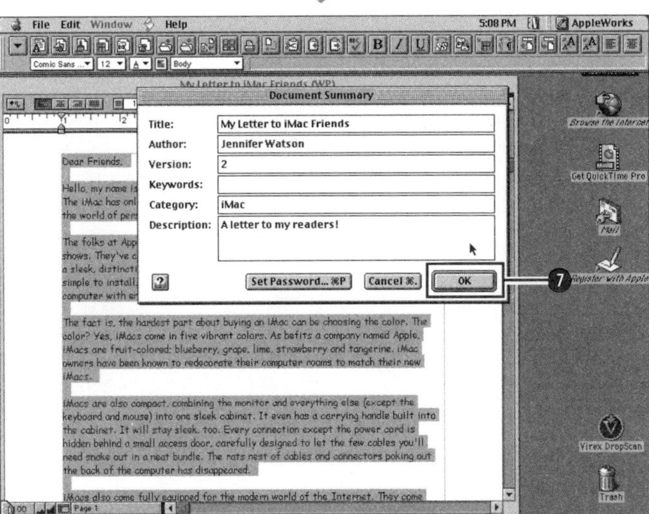

❸ *Open AppleWorks and select Document Summary from the File menu.*

❹ *Press the Tab key.*

▶ *Notice how your cursor jumps to the next field.*

❺ *Hold down the Command key for several seconds.*

▶ *Note the keyboard shortcuts that appear in the buttons.*

❻ *Optional: Press Command+P to set a password.*

❼ *Press Return to activate the OK button.*

Your *F-Keys*—the row of function keys at the top of your keyboard—also can perform tricks for you. For example, in AppleWorks, you can press the F1 key to Undo, the F2 key to Cut, the F3 key to Copy, and the F4 key to Paste. Other applications might use these differently, or they might provide other uses for the other keys. Check your manual or help documentation.

Don't forget those old reliable keyboard shortcuts, either! Watch for keyboard shortcut combinations in menus and windows. Experiment with different combinations. You might even stumble across an undocumented keyboard shortcut. For example, did you know you can switch to a new application and hide everything else in one fell swoop? Just hold down the Option key as you choose an item from the Application menu.

TAKE NOTE

USING EASY ACCESS

Your iMac offers a nifty control panel called Easy Access to help users with physical disabilities use and navigate their iMac more easily. You'll find the control panel on your iMac Install CD-ROM disc. Use Sherlock to locate it, and then click and drag it on top of your System Folder. Once it has been installed, it lets you use the keyboard to move the mouse pointer, among other things.

SHORTCUT

You can use the Page Up and Page Down keys to scroll through a window on your Desktop.

Customizing Your Keyboard and Monitor

If you're the type who spends hours arranging the furniture just so, you're going to love what you can do with your keyboard and monitor! Sure, you can arrange them like you do furniture. You can even adjust their angle with their respective foot stands (flip out the translucent bars under the keyboard and the monitor). But did you know you could customize the way you use and view them, too?

To customize your keyboard, start by opening your Keyboard control panel. Depending on the country in which you purchased your iMac, you can select different keyboard layouts. Chances are good your iMac is already configured to the layout that works best for you. If not, this is where you can change it. You can see the differences another layout makes by selecting it and then opening Key Caps from the Apple menu. The Options button in the lower-right corner of the Keyboard control panel lets you set the keyboard shortcut to rotate to the next keyboard layout (if you selected more than one). Note that a Keyboard menu appears next to your Application menu when you select more than one keyboard layout, too.

You also can adjust your key repeat rate (the speed at which a key you're holding down repeats its letter, number, or symbol). You may want to slow this down if you're a slower typist (or have lead fingers). The Delay Until Repeat option lets you adjust the amount of time before a key begins to repeat — slide the control to Off if you don't think you'll ever want to repeat a character.

Customize your monitor (display) through the Monitors & Sound control panel. Your main Monitor options display first when you open the control panel. You can change the color depth (which is the number of colors displayed). I recommend you use Millions — or at least Thousands — of colors for the best effect. Use

Let Your Fingers Do Less Walking

You may have heard of a way to rearrange your keyboard so that the more frequently used keys are easier to reach. This layout is called *Dvorak* (after the guy who came up with it), whereas your iMac's default layout is called *Qwerty* (after the first six letters on the upper-left side of the keyboard). In an average eight-hour day, your hands travel 16 miles on a Qwerty keyboard, but they only travel 1 mile on a Dvorak keyboard. Look on the Internet for more information; specifically, the Official Dvorak page at **http://www.dvorakint.org**.

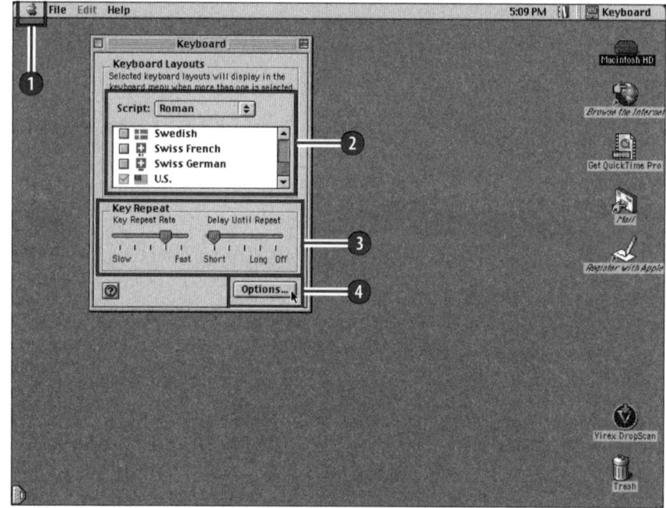

1. *Open the Keyboard control panel.*
2. *Optional: Modify your keyboard layout.*
3. *Optional: Adjust your key repeat rates.*
4. *Optional: Click the Options button to change your keyboard layout shortcuts.*

CROSS-REFERENCE

For more tips on managing memory (RAM), see Chapter 15.

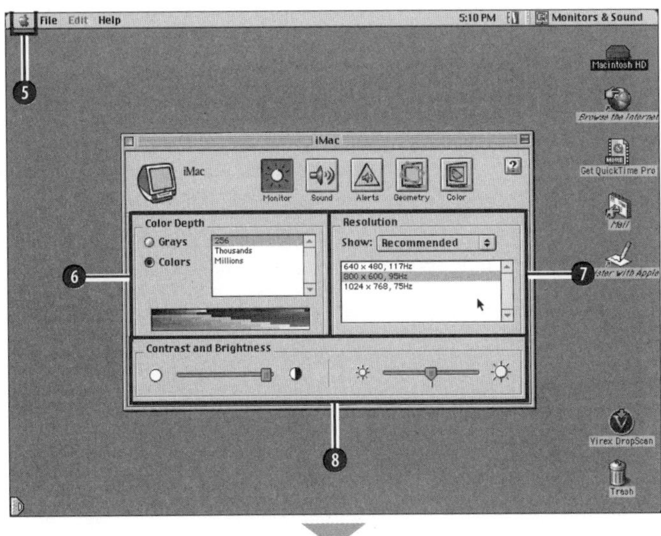

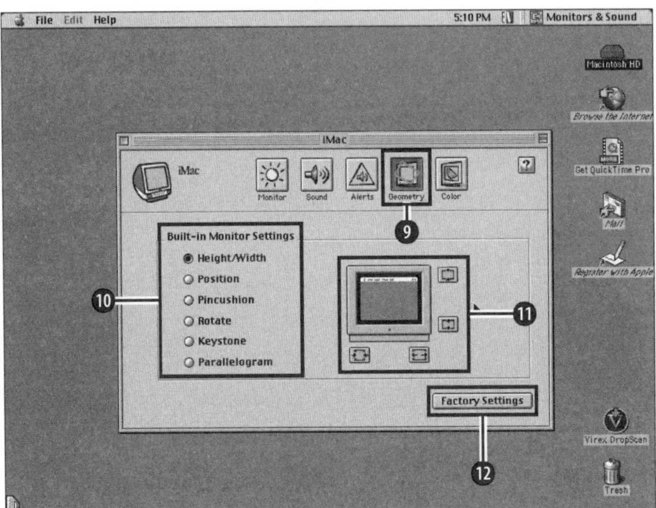

5 *Open the Monitors & Sounds control panel.*

6 *Optional: Adjust your color depth.*

7 *Optional: Choose a new resolution.*

8 *Optional: Adjust your contrast and brightness.*

9 *Click the Geometry button.*

10 *Optional: Choose a setting to adjust.*

11 *Optional: Adjust a setting.*

12 *Optional: Click the Factory Settings button to restore the default settings.*

the 256 colors setting when you want to conserve as much memory (RAM) as possible. Resolution changes the size of the screen: the lower the number, the bigger everything will be, and the less room you'll have to work in. I recommend you use 800 x 600 — it is a good compromise between available real estate and readability. Contrast and Brightness controls let you adjust the monitor for optimal viewing.

Click the Geometry icon near the top of the Monitors & Sound control panel to adjust the display's position on the monitor. Click the Color icon next to the Geometry button to set your ColorSync profile, which is used in desktop publishing and graphics programs to produce the best visual results. The Calibrate button at the bottom guides you through the color adjustment process, if you're so inclined.

TAKE NOTE

ADJUSTING YOUR MOUSE

The Mouse control panel can make you a very happy mouser! Mouse Tracking adjusts how far the mouse travels to move the pointer around the screen. The Faster setting equates to shorter hand movements. Has double-clicking been a hit-or-miss proposition? Then change the Double-Click Speed to match your natural rhythm — from click-click to click-pause-click!

SHORTCUT

Use your Control Strip to adjust color depth and resolution without opening your Monitors & Sound control panel.

Making the Most of Your Apple Menu

By now, you've come to realize the importance of your Apple menu. It's probably the most frequently visited menu on your iMac (though I hope you visit the File menu to save often, too). If you find you use your Apple menu often, take a few minutes to customize and organize it. Your mouse will thank you for it!

To add a new item to your Apple menu, select it in your Finder and choose Automated Tasks ➪ Add Alias to Apple Menu. Alternatively, you can open the Apple Menu Items folder (in your System Folder) and add, rename, and remove items. Before you trash an item, be sure it is either an alias (look for the italic typestyle) or something you really don't think you'll need again. Not everything in the Apple Menu Items folder is an alias.

Another option is to select an item and choose Add to Favorites from the File menu. Now your item is available in the Favorites submenu in your Apple menu.

One thing I highly recommend you add to your Apple menu is an alias of your hard drive (Macintosh HD). With your submenus enabled (from the Apple Menu Options control panel), a hard drive alias in your Apple menu lets you navigate to and open items much quicker. You can add aliases of folders for the same effect. Try it!

If you start adding many items, you'll notice how disorganized your Apple menu becomes. Sure, items are in alphabetical order, but they're not in a *logical* order. You can organize your Apple menu in whatever manner you like with a little patience and few tricks. Start by taking a good look at your Apple menu. Would you prefer to have your hard drive alias at the top of the menu, or perhaps your less frequently used items at the bottom? Decide on an order that works best for you.

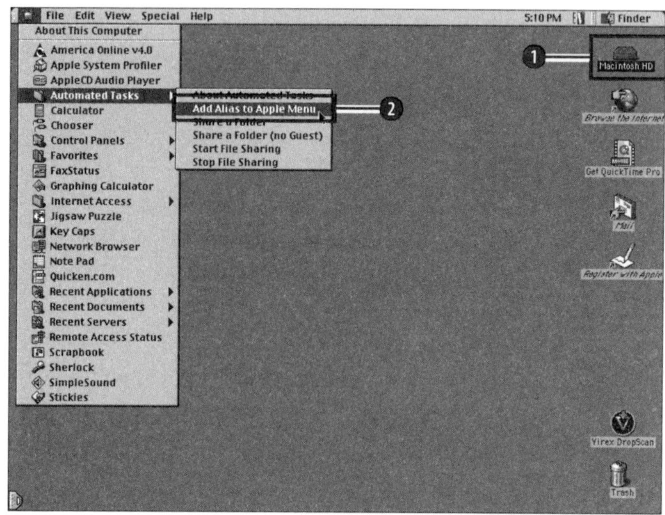

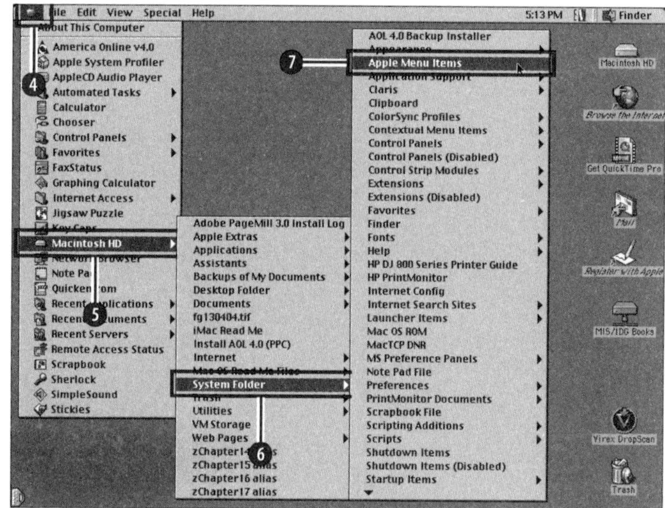

1. Select your Macintosh HD icon.
2. Pull down your Apple menu and choose Add Alias to Apple Menu from the Automated Tasks submenu.
3. Restart your computer.
4. Pull down the Apple menu again.
5. Select the Macintosh HD item.
6. Select the System Folder item.
7. Choose the Apple Menu Items item.

CROSS-REFERENCE

Learn more about submenus in Chapter 1.

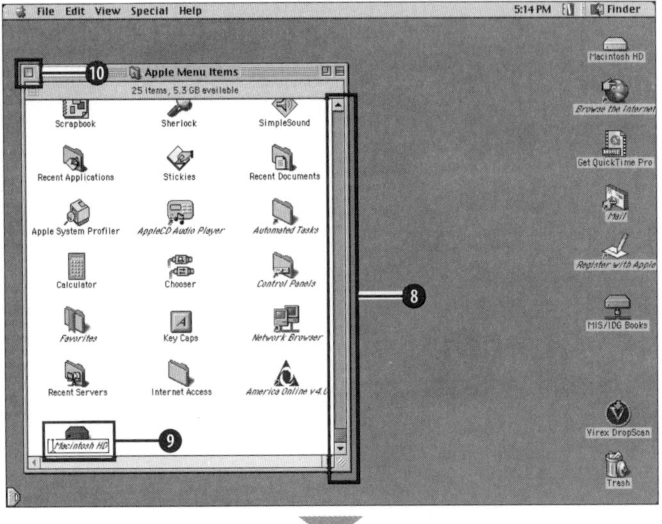

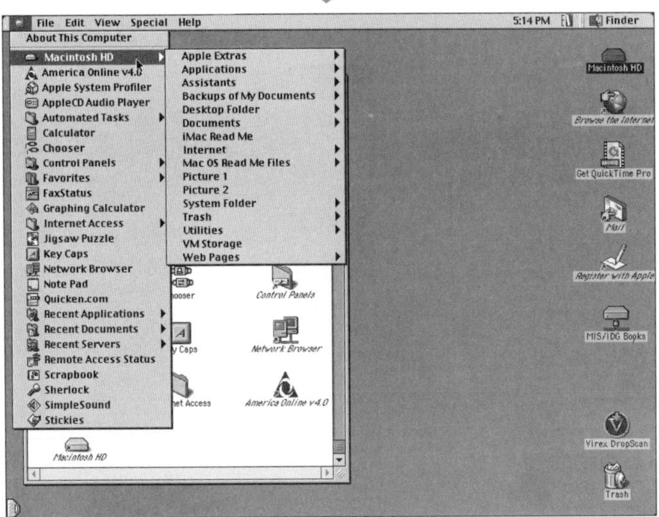

8 *Scroll down in the resulting window.*

9 *Select the Macintosh HD icon, click its name, position your pointer at the start of its name, and then type a space.*

10 *Close the window.*

▶ *Note how the Macintosh HD item now appears at the top of your Apple menu.*

To actually reorder your Apple menu, begin by opening your Apple Menu Items folder and finding the item you want to appear at the top of your menu. Click once on the item's name, wait a moment for it to highlight, click again in front of the first letter in the name, type a space, and then press the Return key. Adding a space at the beginning of a file or folder name forces it to appear at the top of the menu — a space comes before anything else in standard alphanumeric sort order. If you want more than one item to appear at the top, go ahead and put spaces in front of those items' names, too. To organize the items at the top, use multiple spaces — three spaces for the item at the very top, two spaces for the item below that, and so on. You also might want to group items in folders (to shorten your Apple menu). Do note that a filename is limited to 31 characters, including spaces.

TAKE NOTE

TUNNELING THROUGH YOUR APPLE MENU

Placing an alias to your hard drive or folders works great for navigation, up to a point. Generally, you can only use submenus to tunnel down four levels. If your hard drive levels are deeper than this, add folder aliases to your Apple menu instead.

SHORTCUT

Keep an alias of the Apple Menu Items folder on your desktop for quicker customization.

Setting Your Startup/Shutdown Options

Did you know you can tell your iMac to open something immediately on startup or each time you shut down? This can be very useful, or just downright fun, depending on how you implement it. The trick is to place the items you want opened on startup or shutdown in the Startup Items folder or Shutdown Items folder, respectively, inside your System folder.

If you look in your Startup Items folder, you'll probably find it empty or holding only the AOL Scheduler (if you elected to use AOL). What else might you want to put in here? Do you work on a project every day? Add an alias to that file in your Startup Items folder. Do you like to check your mail first thing in the morning? Add an alias to AOL or Outlook Express. Do you keep a journal in AppleWorks? Put an alias to your journal file in the folder. Do you send a report regularly? Create a report template and place the template in the folder. Now, a new report file automatically opens for you, ready to fill out. How about adding an alias to your Applications folder or your Documents folder, so it always opens on startup? You could even add a sound you discovered or created to your Startup Items folder and your iMac will play it (though it will not replace the traditional startup chord you hear immediately after you press the power button). The possibilities are endless.

The Shutdown Items folder isn't quite so useful. After all, when you shut down, you probably don't want any new applications launching! Most folks just use this folder to play a good-bye sound. I recorded a custom sound with my iMac's built-in microphone and placed it in my Shutdown Items folder. Now my iMac says sadly, "Leaving me already, Jennifer?" when I shut down. Silly, huh? Hey, a little silliness is good for your soul.

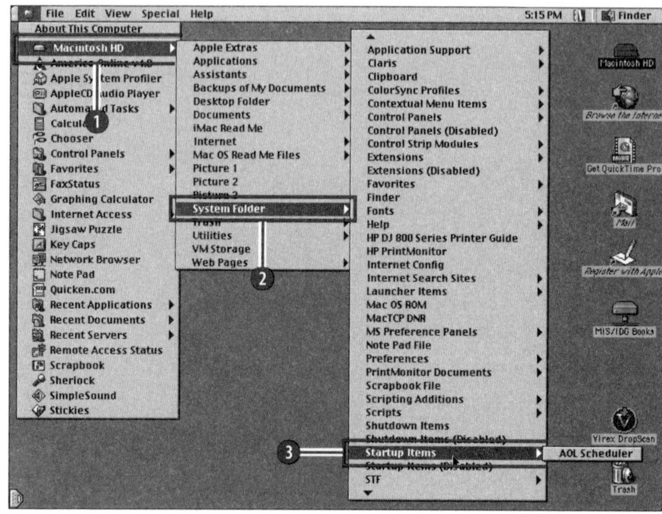

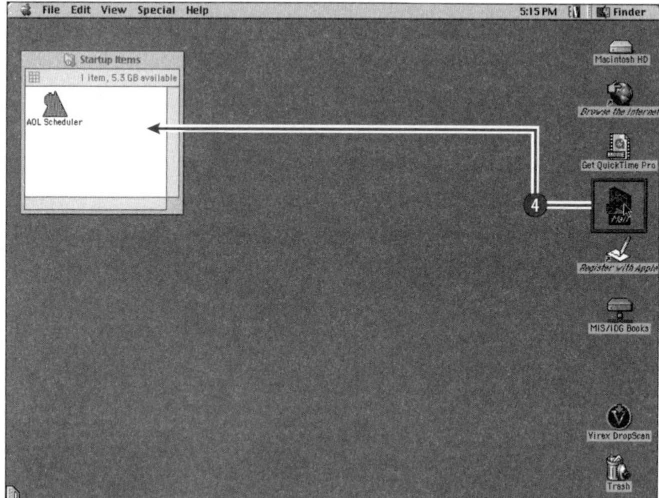

1. *Pull down the Apple menu and select Macintosh HD.*
2. *Select System Folder.*
3. *Choose Startup Items.*

▶ *The Startup Items window opens.*

4. *Select an icon on your Desktop, hold down the Option and Command keys, and click and drag it into the Startup Items window.*

CROSS-REFERENCE

See Chapter 9 on creating custom sounds with your iMac.

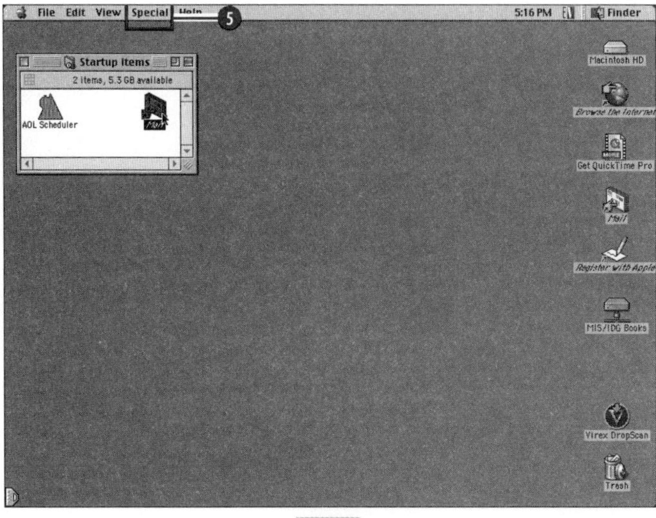

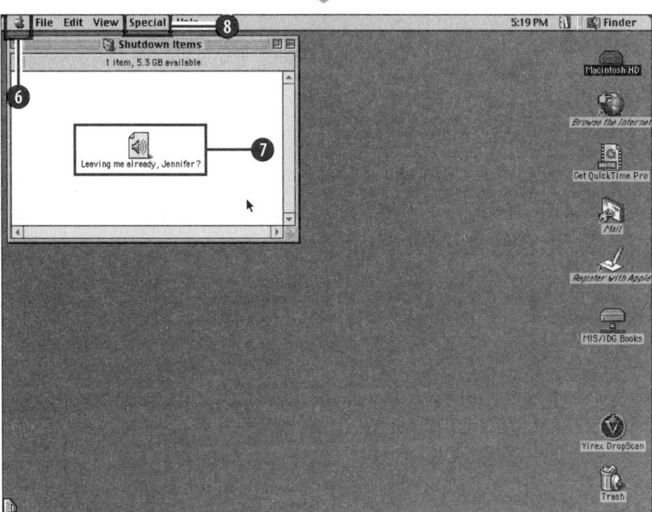

- Note the alias of the item you dragged into the Startup Items window.

5. *Optional: Choose Restart from the Special menu so you can try out your Startup Item.*

6. *Open the Shutdown Items folder.*

7. *Optional: Place an item in the folder.*

8. *Optional: Choose Shut Down from the Special menu to try out your Shutdown Item.*

If you're really into customization, you can place an AppleScript automated task in your Startup or Shutdown Items folder. Read more about these in Chapter 16.

TAKE NOTE

CHANGE YOUR STARTUP SCREEN

If you're feeling adventurous, you can change the image you see at startup and initialization. You can download pre-made startup images on AOL (go to keyword: FILESEARCH and search on the term startupscreen) or on the Internet (try a search for startupscreen in Sherlock). Once you find one, download it and click and drag it to your System Folder (do not put it in your Startup Items folder). You should see your new startup image the next time you power up your iMac!

MAKE A STARTUP SCREEN

Yes, you can make your own startup images! Create an image in AppleWorks, save it in PICT file format, and use another application to convert it to the necessary format. Try GraphicConverter (a shareware program you can download from the Internet or AOL) and save your image in the Startup Screen format.

FIND IT ONLINE

You can download GraphicConverter at **http://www.lemkesoft.de/**.

Using Other Control Panels

I've introduced you to many control panels throughout the book, but a few have managed to slip by. If you've been wondering what that control panel with the funky name does, look no further!

The Energy Saver control panel is the bit of software responsible for turning your monitor and hard drive off when the computer is inactive (also called *sleep* mode). If the sleep rate — or the fact that it sleeps at all — bothers you, open Energy Saver and click the Specify Settings button. You can reduce the sleep rate (actually increase the amount of time the iMac is allowed to be inactive before it sleeps), or you can turn off sleep mode altogether. I recommend you let your iMac go to sleep — it does conserve energy and it is better for your computer. If you click the Show Details button, you can set separate sleep rates for the display (monitor) and hard drive. Hard drives are usually set to go to sleep sooner than monitors, so if you're always waiting for it to rouse itself, readjust! Note that you can schedule startup and shutdown times in Energy Saver. This feature might be useful for allotting iMac time to the kids ("No, Johnny, you can't play Nanosaur before you go to school.").

The Location Manager control panel is really an application (note that it has its own menus in the menu bar). Location Manager organizes your preferences for various settings and controls and saves them, allowing you to restore them quickly or to switch between different ones. This was originally designed for the PowerBook folks, but it is useful when you have more than one person using the iMac. To create a new Location, choose New Location from the File menu. You can learn more about Location Manager by clicking the ? button.

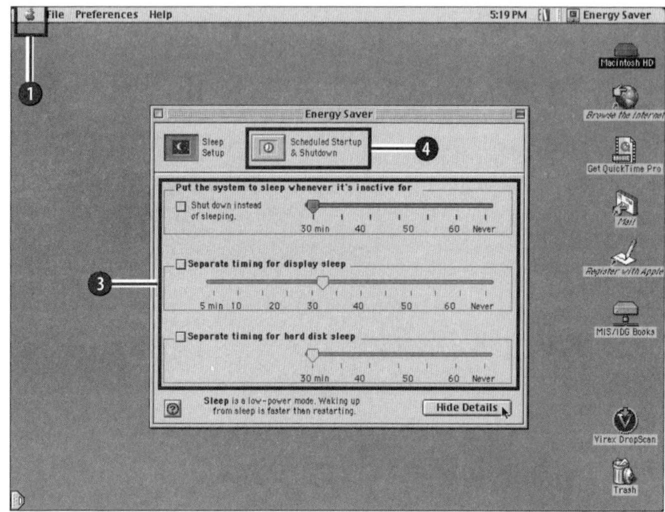

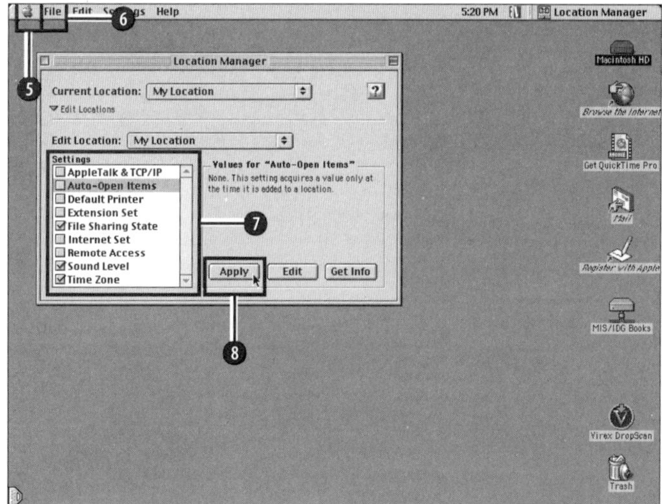

1. Open the Energy Saver control panel.
2. Click the Show Details button.
3. Optional: Adjust your sleep settings.
4. Optional: Click the Scheduled Startup & Shutdown icon to set your scheduled startups and shutdowns.
5. Open the Location Manager.
6. Optional: Choose New Location from the File menu.
7. Optional: Choose your settings.
8. Optional: Click the Apply button to save your settings.

CROSS-REFERENCE

Refer to Chapter 3 to learn more about hard drives and CD-ROM discs.

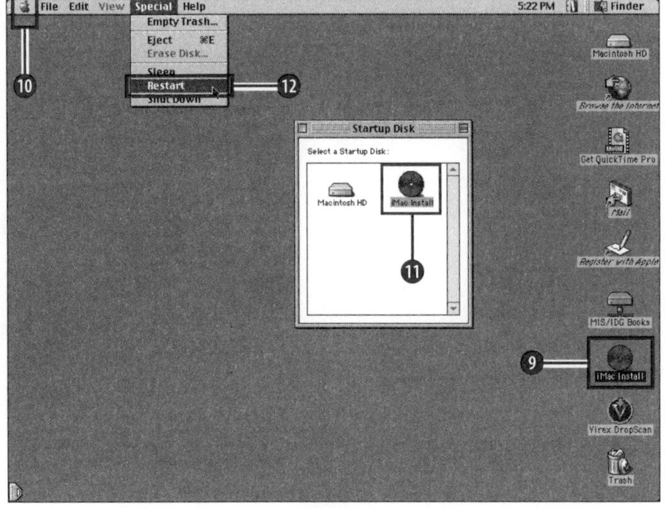

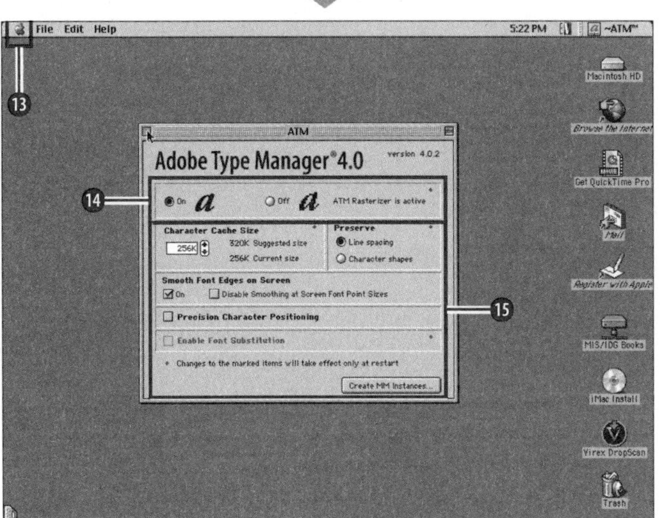

9 *Insert your iMac Install CD-ROM disc.*

10 *Open the Startup Disk control panel.*

11 *Optional: Select the iMac Install icon.*

12 *Optional: Choose Restart from the Special menu.*

13 *Open your ATM control panel (at the bottom of the Control Panels submenu).*

14 *Optional: Enable or disable ATM.*

15 *Optional: Choose your ATM settings.*

Numbers is a small control panel that lets you set your number format preferences. Most likely, you'll want to keep it exactly as it is, but feel free to tinker with it if you know you need something different.

Startup Disk is a very simple control panel that lets you choose which hard drive or disc you want to start from the next time you power up. If you have only one hard drive, chances are you'll just want to keep that selected. If you have an external hard drive with a System Folder on it, select that icon in this control panel; the next time you start your iMac, you'll be running the operating system from the external hard drive you selected. You also can start from a CD-ROM disc if the disc has a System Folder on it (as your iMac Install disc does).

TAKE NOTE

DEMYSTIFYING ATM

ATM, located at the bottom of the Control Panels submenu, is easy to miss. ATM stands for Adobe Type Manager, and it is what makes your fonts look smooth and neat, both onscreen and on paper.

USING MULTIPLE ACCESS

If you have Mac OS 9 on your iMac, take a closer look at the Multiple Access control panel. This is a new feature which allows you to create unique environments for each person that uses your iMac (or for you yourself if you prefer different environments for different tasks). For detailed directions on how to use this new control panel, choose Mac Help from the Help menu in the Finder and search for "Multiple Users control panel."

SHORTCUT

You can open Location Manager, and change between locations, with the Control Strip.

Managing System Extensions

I won't lie to you: managing system extensions isn't always easy. Some people can make a living out of navigating the system extensions sea without crashing or sinking. This topic is worthy of a book, and much ink has already been devoted to it. If you're looking for ways to resolve a possible extension conflict, I've written an entire task on it in Chapter 17. If, on the other hand, you want to know more about system extensions (and how you can manage them), read this task.

System extensions are your ticket to true customization of your iMac. Extensions are essentially small programs that work behind the scenes with your operating system, often in conjunction with a particular application program. Because they work hand-in-hand with the Mac OS, they can be tricky little buggers. Any customization programs you buy or download are likely to be — or to include — system extensions. Instructions will vary on how to install them in your system. Eventually, all system extensions wind up in the Extensions folder in your System folder. You can't open extensions directly, though they may have a corresponding control panel with which you can explore.

Enter the Extensions Manager control panel. This powerhouse control panel is your key to managing and controlling your system extensions. You can turn individual extensions on and off here, as well as control panels, startup items, shutdown items, and system folder items. Note the Selected Set drop-down menu at the top of the window, which lets you choose a set to use or modify. You can't mess with the locked sets at all.

I must give you just a tiny warning — I don't recommend you experiment too much with Extensions Manager until you understand your iMac a bit better. You can really mess up your iMac if you turn off the wrong extension. If you do accidentally turn something

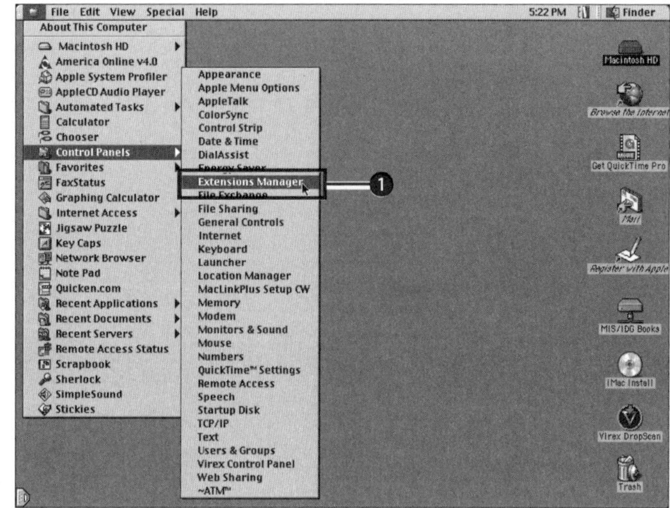

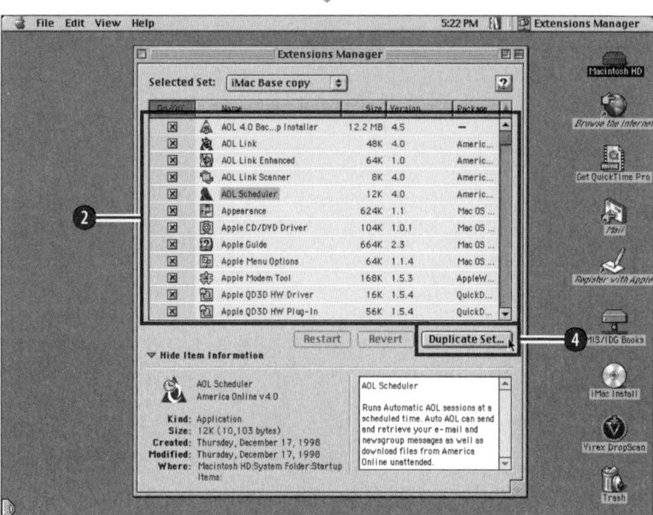

1. *Open the Extensions Manager control panel.*
2. *Check your extensions and select one.*
3. *Click the Show Item Information arrow.*

▶ *Note the information about the item.*

4. *Optional: Click the Duplicate Set button and choose a name for your new set.*

CROSS-REFERENCE

See Chapter 17 for assistance with system extension conflicts.

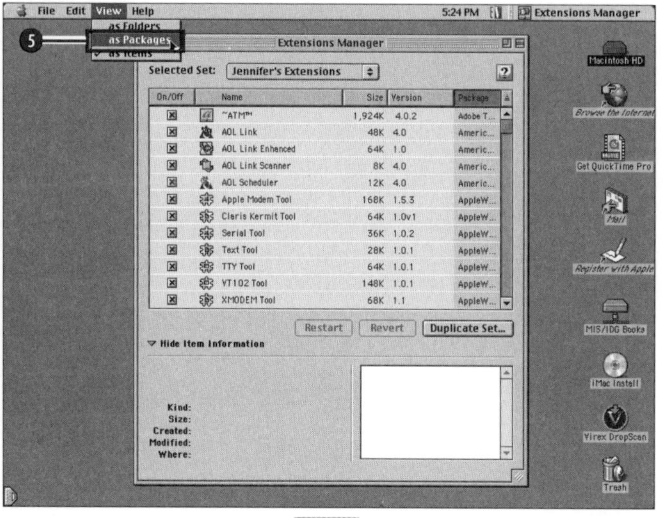

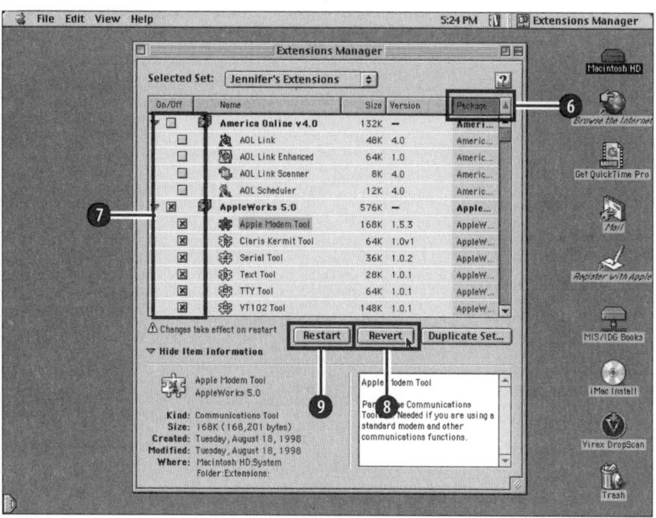

- Note your new extension set name appears in the drop-down menu.

5. Choose As Packages from the View menu.

6. Click the Packages column heading to resort the extensions by package.

7. Optional: Click a checked box to disable an extension.

8. Optional: Click the Revert button to return to the last saved settings of your extension set.

9. Optional: Click the Restart button to put your new extension into effect.

off, don't worry too much — just select iMac Base from the Selected Set drop-down menu and your iMac will be back to the way it was when you bought it.

With that said, its best to turn off a system extension with Extension Manager rather than drag it to the Trash, or to another location on your hard drive. The Extensions Manager is also the best place to learn more about a given extension — just select it in the list and toggle the Show Item Information arrow to see details about it at the bottom of the window.

To learn more about Extension Manager, click the ? button in the upper-right corner of the window.

TAKE NOTE

VIEWING YOUR EXTENSIONS

Finding the extension you're seeking is often easier if you change your view. Use the Views menu to select a new view. Folder view shows you everything sorted by the folders they are located in (Control Panels, Extensions, and so on). Package view shows you related items (for example, all the America Online-related items). Item view shows everything, regardless of the folder or package.

SHORTCUT

Hold down the spacebar while your iMac is starting to access the Extensions Manager.

Enhancing with Utilities

You can customize your iMac beyond the basics with utilities. I can't possibly cover all the options here, but I can pass along some of my favorites. Keep in mind that these may be commercial programs, shareware programs (try for free and pay if you like it), or freeware (no charge at all).

If you like the concept of the Launcher but not its implementation, check out DragThing by James Thomson. This nifty little shareware utility offers the convenience of Launcher, plus the ability to layer groups of icons and then have them float on your screen so that they are always accessible. You can try out DragThing at **http://www.dragthing.com/**.

An alternative to your Scrapbook (under the Apple menu) is ScrapIt Pro by John Holder. This utility lets you store anything you can copy to the clipboard. Better yet, it lets you sort, import and export, search, and edit. The ScrapIt Pro shareware utility is available at **http://www.northcoast.com/~jvholder/**.

Another shareware utility from John Holder is TakeABreak. This control panel can be set up to remind you to take periodic breaks from your iMac, promoting a well-balanced computing life. You can get it in the same place as ScrapIt Pro.

Dumpster is an icon replacement utility to spruce up your Desktop. It allows you to select from hundreds of icons to use on folders — even your Trash (hence the name Dumpster). This is a great way to customize the look of your Desktop without spending a lot of effort. One fun feature lets you choose a different trash icon each time you start up. You can download a demo version of this shareware utility at **http://www.thewc.com/dumpster.html**.

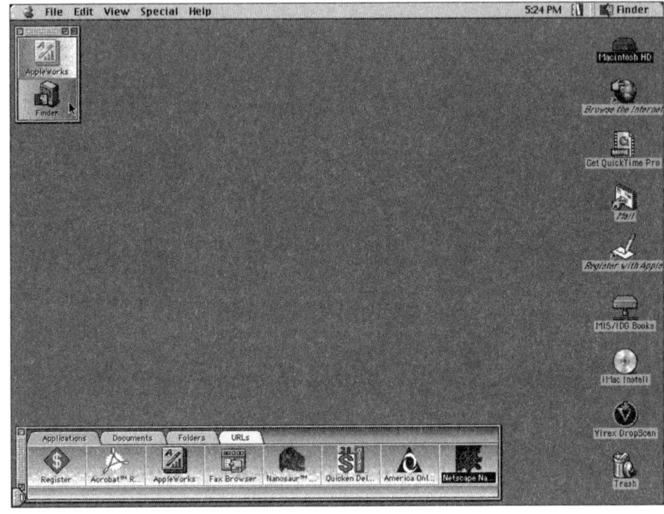

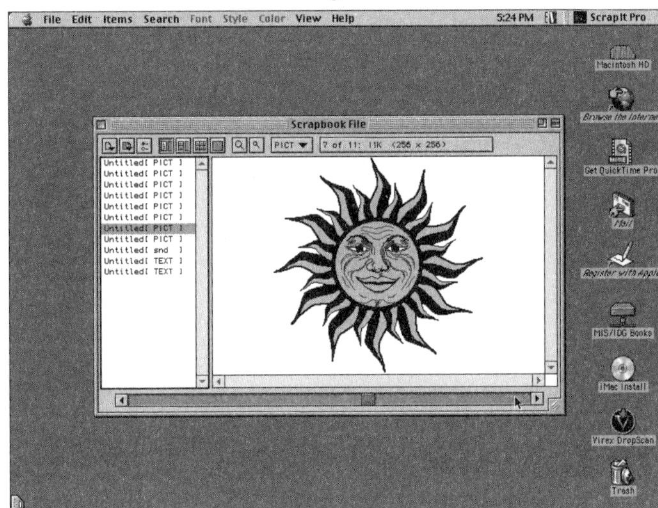

- *With DragThing installed and running, a floating palette for your open applications appears.*
- *DragThing also offers a Launcher-replacement window. Note the tabs along the top.*
- *With ScrapIt Pro installed and running, you can select an item from the list on the left.*
- *You also can search the contents of your scrapbook.*

CROSS-REFERENCE

For more information on installing software, see Chapter 3.

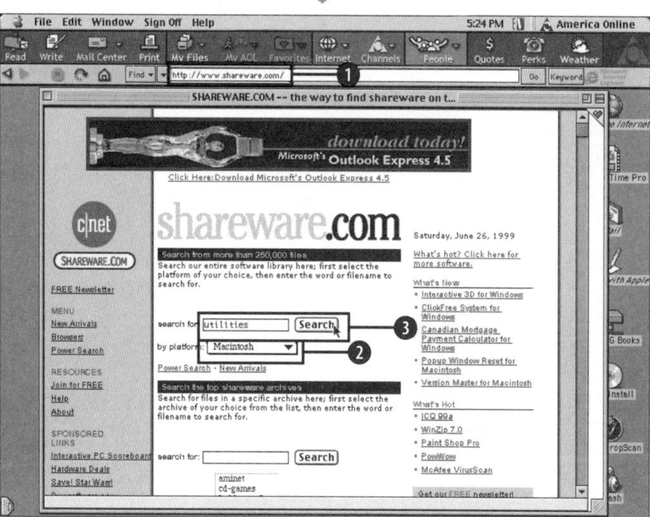

- With the SETI at Home program running, the screen saver kicks in and displays lots of fun, technical statistics.
- The window graphs the radio signal strength.

1. *To find more utilities, point your browser to* ***http://www.shareware.com/***.
2. *Choose Macintosh from the drop-down menu.*
3. *Type your searchword(s) and click the Search button.*

This is only a sampling of the kinds of utilities you can use with your iMac. To find more, I recommend you visit **http://www.shareware.com**, type the search word utilities, select Macintosh from the drop-down menu, and then click the Search button.

TAKE NOTE

SEARCH FOR EXTRATERRESTRIAL INTELLIGENCE

What's a discussion of utilities without mentioning a fun one? How about a utility that lets your iMac analyze outer space radio signals recorded by radio telescopes around the world? With the help of this utility, your iMac downloads the radio signal data from the Internet, analyzes it in the background or during idle times, and sends the results to the observatory. Besides its noble purpose, this utility has a practical function — it works as a screen saver that you can use in place of Energy Saver. If you have Internet access, point your browser to **http://setiathome.ssl.berkeley.edu/mac.html** and click the Macintosh link. Read the instructions to download and install the utility.

INSTALLING UTILITIES

Installation will differ from utility to utility, but you'll usually need to restart after installation. Read the instructions that came with the utility for more details. If your iMac doesn't behave as expected, use your Extensions Manager to disable the new utility. Then restart your computer.

FIND IT ONLINE

Another source of utilities is on America Online at keyword: DOWNLOAD SOFTWARE (click the Utilities & Tools option near the bottom).

Personal Workbook

Q&A

1. What is the benefit of having your Desktop visible in the background? The drawback?

2. How do you change the image or pattern on your Desktop?

3. How do you view keyboard shortcuts in dialog boxes?

4. How do you increase your screen resolution?

5. How can you organize your Apple Menu?

6. How do you get your iMac to greet you on startup?

7. What does Energy Saver do? How do you turn it off?

8. Where can you find utilities for your iMac?

ANSWERS: PAGE 324

Customizing Your iMac

CHAPTER 14

EXTRA PRACTICE

1. Enable the Launcher, restart your iMac, and see if the launcher suits your needs.
2. Go to the Appearance control panel and change the Large System Font, Views Font, and Highlight color. Make sure your choices suit your taste and still leave your iMac easy to view.
3. Save your new Appearance settings as a Theme, and switch between Themes to see which one you like best.
4. Visit the Monitors & Sound control panel and try all available Monitor Resolution settings. Note the relative merits of each setting, and select the setting that best suits your needs.
5. Add the Startup Items folder to your Apple menu.

REAL-WORLD APPLICATIONS

✔ Your uncle is having trouble reading the text on your computer screen. You modify the screen resolution and change the font for icons to a larger size. He calls his attorney and instructs her to double your inheritance.

✔ You have trouble remembering everything you need to do, so you create a ToDo list using the AppleWorks word processor. You save the file and add it to your Startup Items folder so you can review and modify the list at the beginning of each day.

✔ Your mouse starts to misbehave. You finish and save the document you're working on using navigation keys and keyboard shortcuts. You then turn your attention to getting your mouse working again.

Visual Quiz

Where do you find this control panel? What does it do?

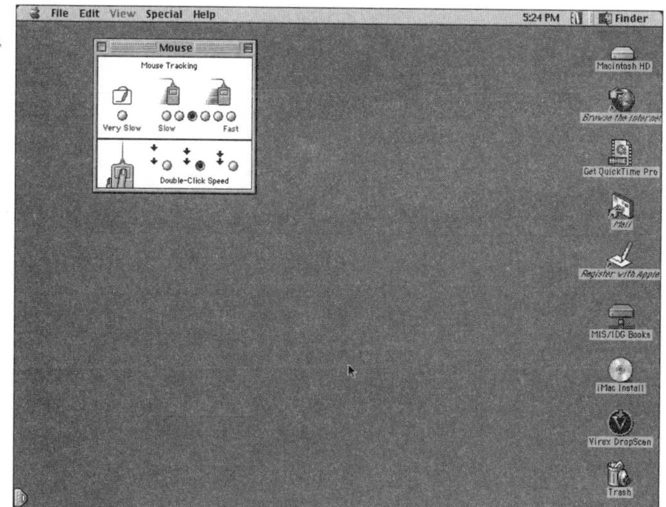

CHAPTER 15

MASTER THESE SKILLS

- Understanding Your iMac's Memory
- Setting an Application's Memory
- Using Your Disk Cache
- Making the Most of Virtual Memory
- Using a RAM Disk
- Expanding Your Memory

Managing Memory

Memory. Where would humans be without it? When it works right, our minds clicks along a mile-a-minute, finding facts, making associations, and reaching decisions. Without memory, we'd keep getting burned by a hot stove, lose our way to Grandmother's house, or forget we have heads attached to our bodies. When our memory doesn't work properly, we're slow and confused, and we can easily be brought to a puzzled standstill.

Computers are no different. Without memory, there's nothing constructive they can do. Memory holds the instructions (programs) a computer needs to perform its assigned tasks, and the information (data) that makes up its raw materials (and its finished product). Computers need memory for long-term storage of infrequently needed information — cheap, slow storage for huge programs and data files. Computers also need fast, expensive, short-term memory that functions as a scratch pad and a blackboard for the active processes of computing. A computer also has to be told how best to use its memory so that its processes can be as fast as possible, while still leaving computers inexpensive to buy.

Is this cost factor really that important? The two principle kinds of memory in your iMac, hard drive and RAM, make up a significant part of the cost of your iMac. At mid-1999 replacement part prices, the standard iMac's 32MB of RAM cost around $100, and its 6GB hard drive cost around $150.

At those prices, it would cost nearly $20,000 to replace that relatively slow, 6GB hard drive with an equal amount of RAM. Of course, a research lab on a government grant will gladly pay that price, and much more. In the case of your not-so-humble iMac, consumers would find the price staggering.

In fact, even if you wanted to pay the price, the likelihood that anyone would want to is so slim that the design of the iMac (and any other Mac, for that matter) doesn't allow for it. Currently, you can install a maximum of 256MB of RAM into older iMacs and up to 512MB of RAM into newer iMacs (introduced in October 1999). While that's a whole lot, it's no replacement for a 6,000MB (6GB) hard disk.

Well, I hope I haven't burdened you with too many numbers to remember. In fact, you don't have to remember any of them. Just remember that there's a fine balancing act between memory cost and speed. With a bit of skill, you can squeeze a good bit of extra speed and performance out of your iMac.

Understanding Your iMac's Memory

Computer memory isn't the easiest concept to understand. After all, we barely know how our own brains work, and we use them 24 hours a day, seven days a week.

The slow, cheap memory in your iMac can be found on your hard drive, CD-ROM drive, and the various removable media drives you can add to your iMac as accessories. Most of these storage devices save your files onto spinning disks or even tape, so it can take considerable time to retrieve a particular piece of information. These are your data storage warehouses, where unused files wait until you need them. Just as with any storage warehouse, it takes time to retrieve the needed information and deliver a copy back to you. Another advantage of this kind of memory is that information stored here isn't lost if your computer crashes or loses power.

The fast, expensive memory in your iMac is called RAM. It's all electronic, contained in integrated circuit chips that are directly adjacent to the microprocessor brain of your computer. The information stored in RAM is constantly changing, based on your immediate computing needs, and the information will be lost in the case of a crash or power failure. But because it's completely electronic, it's also incredibly fast.

For the best performance, all the application program files and data files you need to perform a task should be loaded in RAM. However, since your iMac allows you to have several applications running at the same time, you can easily run out of real RAM and rely more on your slower, hard disk memory than you might prefer. This is where *virtual memory* comes in. A portion of your hard drive can be set aside to provide overflow services for your computer's RAM.

A big part of the job of the Mac OS is to efficiently manage all this information shuffling, and your iMac

CROSS-REFERENCE

See Chapter 3 for information on hard drives and removable media.

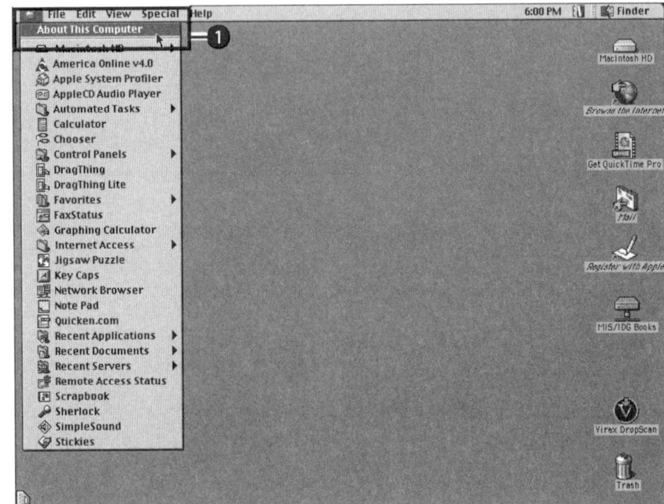

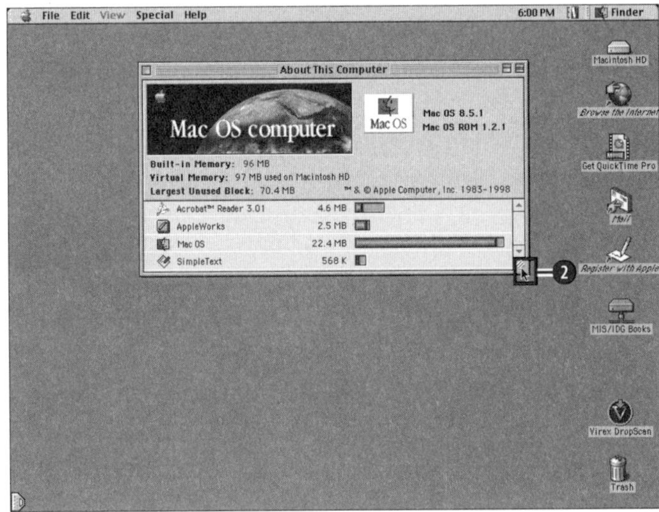

1. *Choose About This Computer from the Apple menu.*

- *Note the amount of built-in memory (RAM), virtual memory, and your largest unused memory block.*
- *Note your open applications and their memory allocations and requirements.*

2. *Resize the window, if necessary.*

does most of it automatically. Still, it can take a bit of human intelligence to make some of the harder decisions, and that's a big part of what we cover in this chapter. To improve computing performance, you can modify the amount of RAM used by an application, set aside hard disk space for use as temporary *cache* memory, and reserve additional hard drive space for virtual memory. If you have lots of RAM, you also can set some of it aside to do work that would normally be assigned to your slower hard drive.

Using Apple System Profiler

Apple System Profiler is a powerful tool for checking memory use, among other things. The System Profile section includes a Memory overview that covers Disk cache, Virtual memory, and Built-in memory. Perhaps even more interesting, the Applications section catalogs every installed application. Of special interest right now are the Memory Size and File Size columns. Memory Size reports the application's Preferred Size — the amount of RAM the application can occupy when it is open. File Size lists the space the application file occupies on your hard drive.

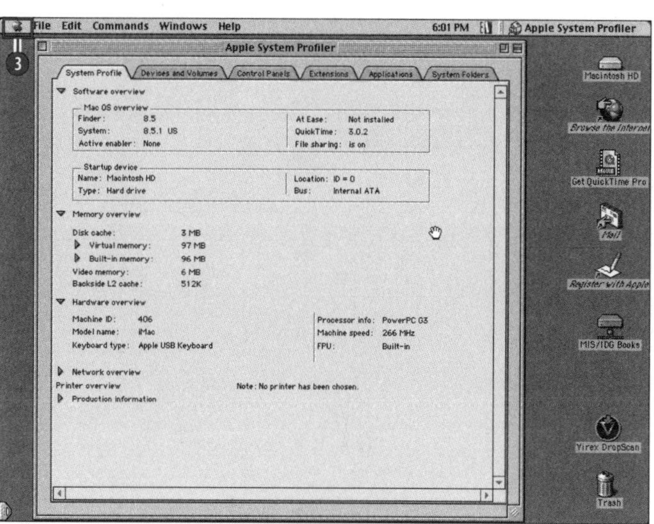

❸ *Choose the Apple System Profiler from the Apple menu.*

▶ *Note the various memory sizes.*

TAKE NOTE

UNDERSTANDING A MEMORY BLOCK

As you start to check your memory settings, you will come across the term *Largest Unused Block*. As the name implies, a *block* is a single chunk of memory. When it's time to open an application and load it into RAM, it's nice to have a good-sized block ready and waiting. If you open About This Computer in your Apple menu, you can see how your various applications use memory, and what their effect is on that Largest Unused Block.

SHORTCUT

Check About This Computer (under your Apple menu in the Desktop) for an overview of your memory capacity and usage.

Setting an Application's Memory

Each application on your iMac has a certain amount of memory allocated to it. Think of it as the amount of space the stuff on your desk needs (like a stapler, a lamp, or a fax machine). Small things may only need a few inches, while the big stuff needs a foot or more. The same applies to your applications. Small applications like AppleCD Audio Player require only a few hundred kilobytes, while larger applications like AppleWorks require a few megabytes. Each application tells your iMac how much memory it needs when it is started.

Occasionally, some of your applications may need more memory than was originally allocated on startup. It works the same way with the stuff on your desk — the stapler may only occupy several square inches on your desk, but you'll need more room than that to really make the most of it. If you try to use your stapler while it is crammed between the pencil holder and the in basket, you're likely to get staples jammed. Likewise, you'll crash more often in applications that are squeezed into a minimum memory allocation. Thankfully, you can give your applications more elbow room and save yourself from more than a few problems!

To increase an application's memory allocation (also called the *application heap*), first quit the application if it is currently running. Then, select the application's icon (not its alias — this technique doesn't work with aliases) in the Finder and choose Memory from the Get Info submenu under the File menu. The resulting window shows the memory requirements of your application, including its suggested, minimum, and preferred sizes.

To change allocation sizes, click in one of the appropriate fields, select the number, and then type a new allocation amount. Never allocate less memory than the suggested size. I recommend you increase the preferred

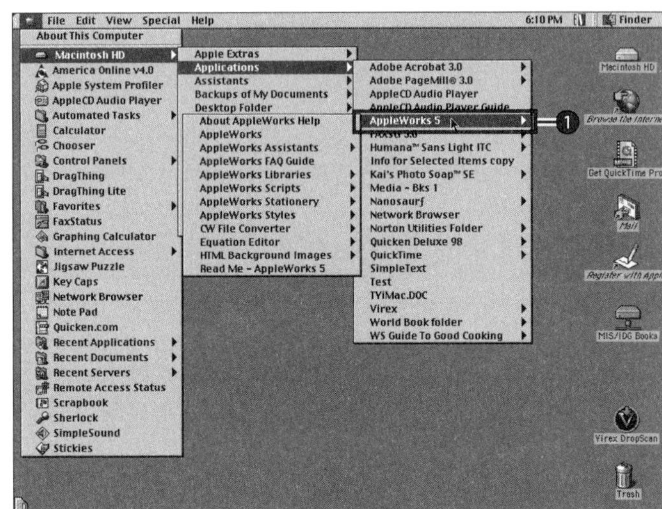

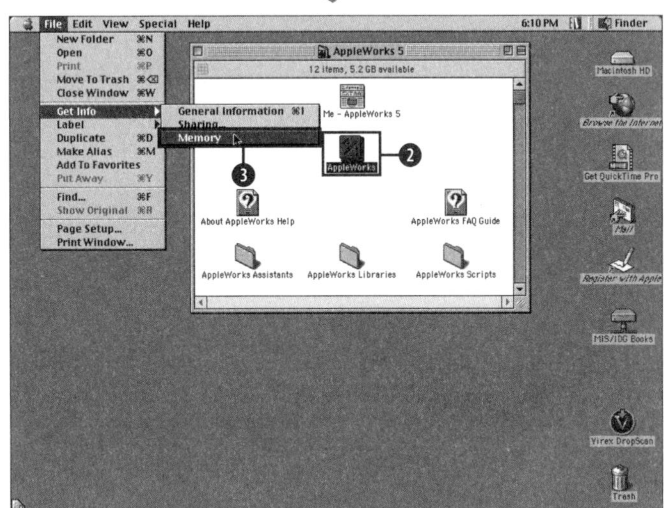

1. *Open the AppleWorks folder (not the application).*
2. *Select an application icon (quit the application first, if it is running).*
3. *Choose Memory from the Get Info submenu under the File menu.*
4. *Alternatively, press Command+I.*

CROSS-REFERENCE

See the last two tasks in this chapter for information on virtual memory and adding RAM.

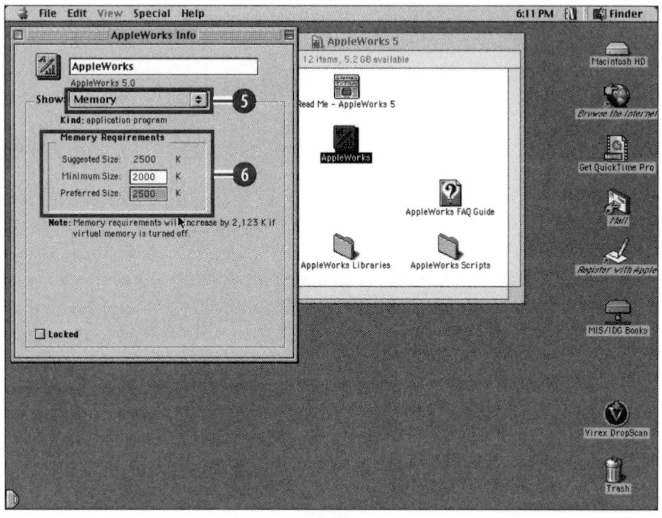

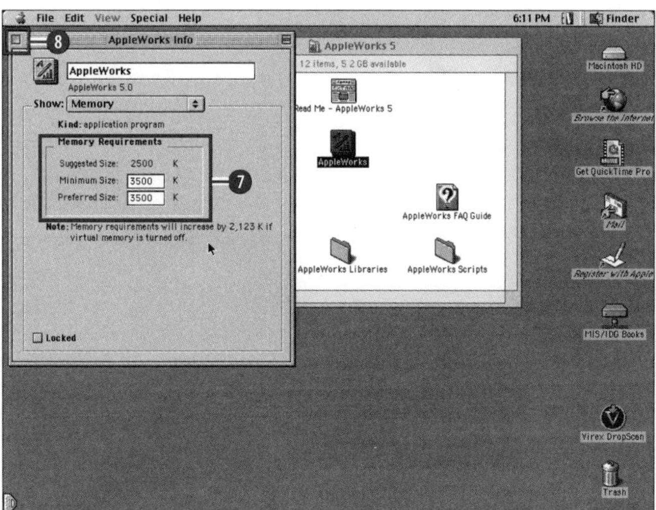

5 *Select Memory from the drop-down menu if it isn't already selected.*

6 *Select the Preferred Size field and type a new amount that is 25 to 50 percent higher.*

7 *Optional: Modify the Minimum Size field to match the Preferred Size field.*

8 *Close the window.*

size amount from 25 to 50 percent over the suggested size. You don't want to give an application more memory than it needs, however — your iMac needs memory for other things, after all. Any memory you allocate to an application is devoted exclusively to it while it is running, and the memory won't be available to any other applications that may need it. If you've got plenty of RAM (more than 64 MB), you also might want to change your minimum size to the same amount. Then close the Get Info window. Your changes take effect the next time you launch the application.

TAKE NOTE

KNOWING WHEN TO ALLOCATE MORE

If an application slows down as you use it, or just seems to crash a lot, chances are good that more memory will help. While the application is running, go to the Finder and choose About This Computer from the Apple menu. Note how much of the application's memory allocation bar is filled. If the application is using most of its allocated memory, you almost assuredly need to assign more memory to the application. While you're here, also check the largest unused block of memory. If this number is small (under 3MB or so), you're low on memory and should reexamine your application memory allocations, increase your virtual memory, or install more RAM.

SHORTCUT

Press Command+I to get information about an application, and then select Memory from the drop-down menu.

Using Your Disk Cache

Let's revisit that desktop analogy again. If setting an application's memory allocation is like making room for stuff on your desk, then setting a disk cache is like making room on the desktop for the papers you're currently using. If your desk is cluttered with stuff and there's no room to write a note, stuff will either start falling off the desk, or you'll have to find some place else to work (been there — done that). Thus, it's always wise to leave some room to work on your desk. Applying this principle to your iMac, it's always wise to allocate some room on your computer to hold information about the most recent things you've done. Your iMac can do this by setting up a disk cache. Using a disk cache speeds up your iMac because there's not as much need to shuffle things around. The disk cache is temporary and its contents are erased when you restart, shut down, or crash.

Your iMac comes with the disk cache already enabled. To increase or decrease the amount of memory set aside for your disk cache, begin by opening your Memory control panel. The disk cache is set in the top of the Memory window. Chances are the Default setting is already enabled. If you aren't sure how to set your disk cache, I recommend you keep the Default setting. On the other hand, you might be instructed to modify your disk cache setting, or you might just want to try out a new setting. To do this, select the Custom radio button, click the Custom button if you're warned of the dangers of independent thinking, and then adjust the cache size by clicking the up or down arrows on the right side of the sizing box. Note that if you have a RAM disk (see the task later on this subject), the percentage of total available RAM needed for it increases as you increase your disk cache. That's because your disk cache uses RAM, too.

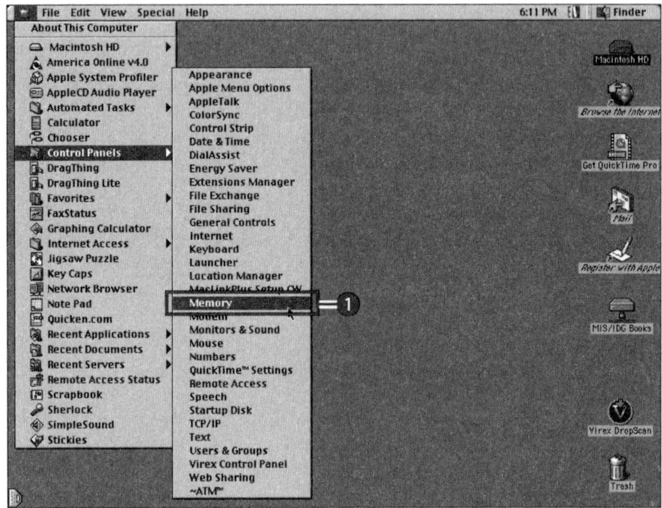

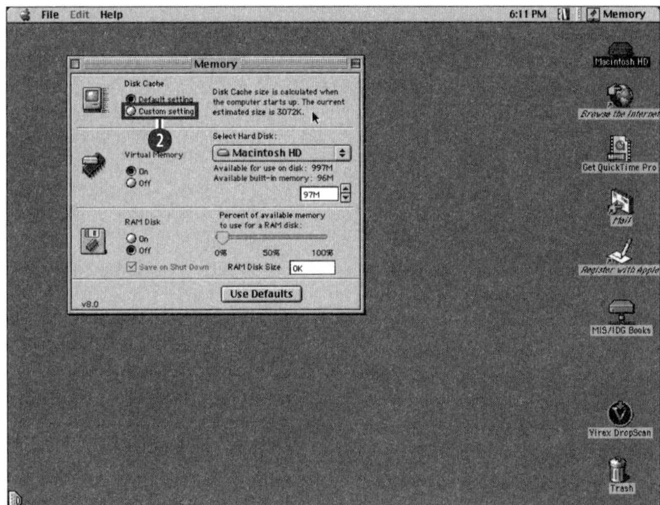

1. *Open the Memory control panel.*

- ▶ *Note your disk cache settings.*
- 2 *Optional: Click the Custom radio button.*

CROSS-REFERENCE

See Chapter 11 for more information about Netscape Navigator.

Managing Memory

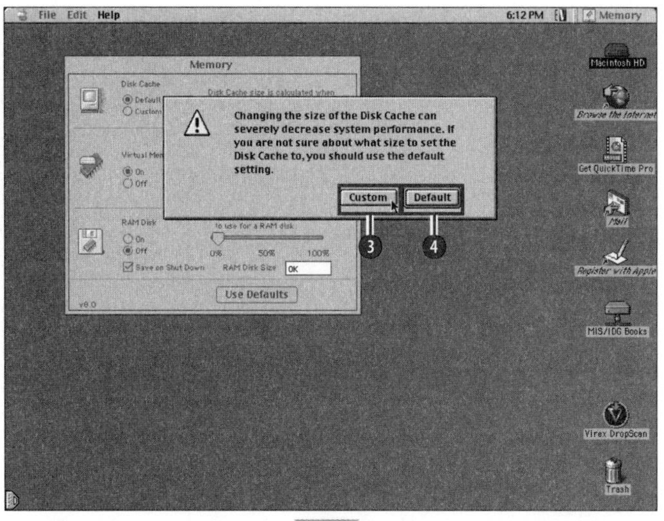

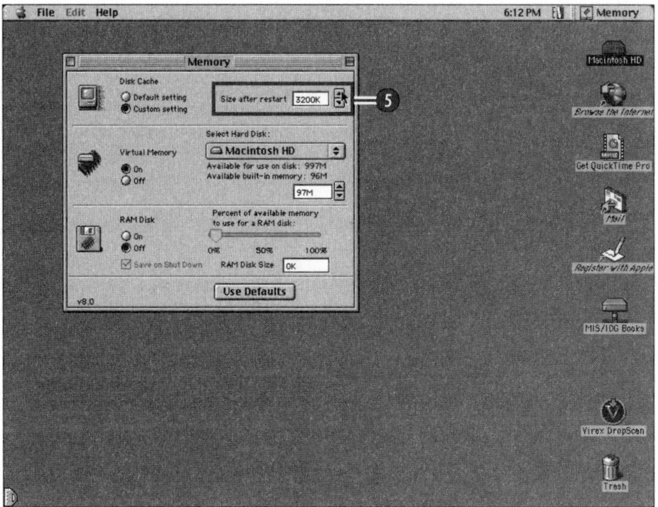

3. *Click the Custom button if you want to create a custom setting.*
4. *Alternatively, click the Default button if you want to use the default setting.*
5. *Increase or decrease your disk cache setting by clicking the up and down arrows.*

TAKE NOTE

REDUCING THE DISK CACHE

You may want to reduce the disk cache if you find you need more memory for an application to run. I recommend that you try increasing your virtual memory first, however (see "Making the Most of Virtual Memory" later in this chapter).

INCREASING THE DISK CACHE

Some applications, like Netscape Navigator, seem to work better with a larger disk cache. The problem with a large disk cache is that it holds on to information longer than usual. This is a problem if you crash, because data you recently added or modified might not have been saved to your hard drive yet. If this is a concern, check out CacheSaver, a shareware utility that saves the contents of your cache to your hard drive periodically in the event of a crash. You can download it at **http://mac.simplenet.com/system/cachesaver/**.

FIND IT ONLINE

Get more information about your disk cache at **http://til.info.apple.com** (search on the term *disk cache*).

Making the Most of Virtual Memory

What do you do if you don't have as much RAM as you (or your iMac) would like? One solution is to buy and install more RAM, which I discuss in the last task in this chapter. A more immediate solution, which costs nothing extra, is *virtual memory*, which is built into your iMac. With it, you can designate a certain amount of your hard disk space to act as RAM. It is a lot slower than real RAM, and you'll have to set aside a good chunk of your hard drive memory for it, but it can work wonders when you need it.

Your iMac comes with virtual memory already enabled. You could turn it off, though I don't recommend it unless you're specifically instructed to do so. Your iMac and its applications work best when virtual memory is enabled. You'll probably want to increase the hard disk space dedicated to virtual memory, however. Your Memory control panel is the key to controlling your virtual memory.

Open your Memory control panel and verify that it is enabled (if isn't, enable it). Now, click the up or down arrows to increase or decrease the total amount of memory you'd like to have available; 1MB of virtual memory is the bare minimum. For example, if you have 32MB of RAM, you can have 33MB or more of combined RAM and virtual memory. You can go higher than double the amount of built-in memory; any more than that and your iMac may slow down to a crawl. When you've completed your virtual memory setup, restart your iMac — your virtual memory won't be available until you do.

When your iMac finishes restarting, check About This Computer under the Apple menu. The Virtual Memory field indicates the total amount of memory you now have, thanks to the wonders of virtual memory. You might want to increase some of your application's memory allocations now to take advantage of your newfound memory.

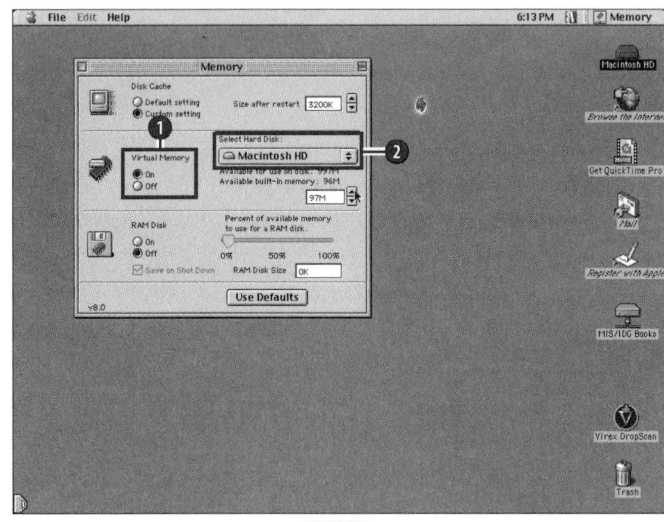

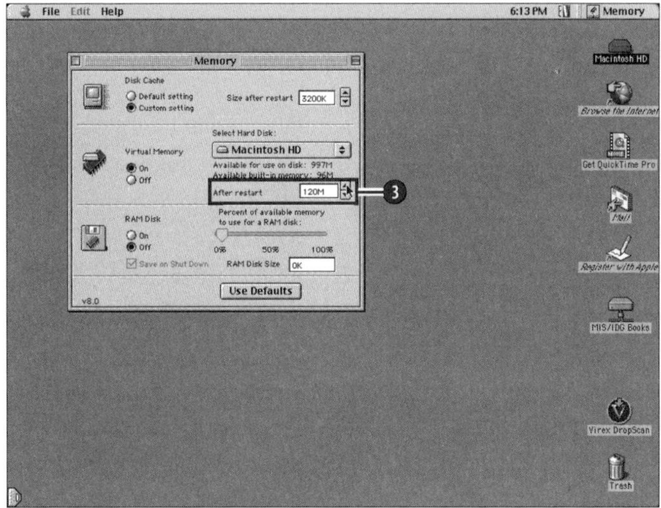

1. *Turn on your virtual memory if it is disabled.*
2. *Optional: Choose another hard drive (if connected) from which to use virtual memory.*

▶ *Note your current built-in and virtual memory sizes.*

3. *Click the up arrow to increase your virtual memory allocation. Note that changes take place after you restart.*

CROSS-REFERENCE

See "Setting an Application's Memory" earlier in this chapter for more information on maximizing your memory capacity.

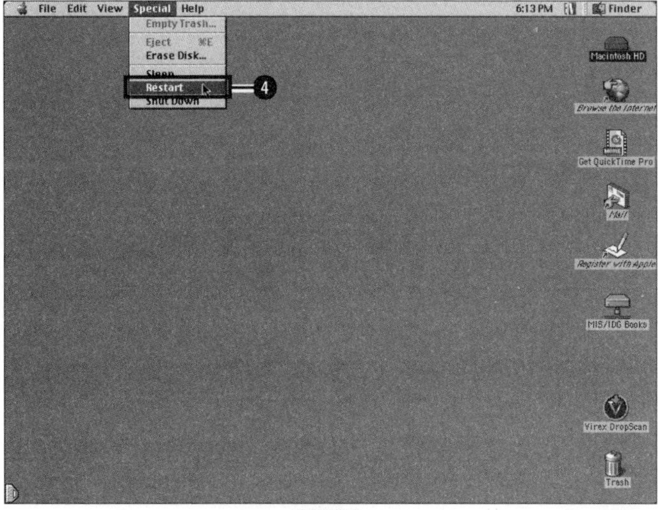

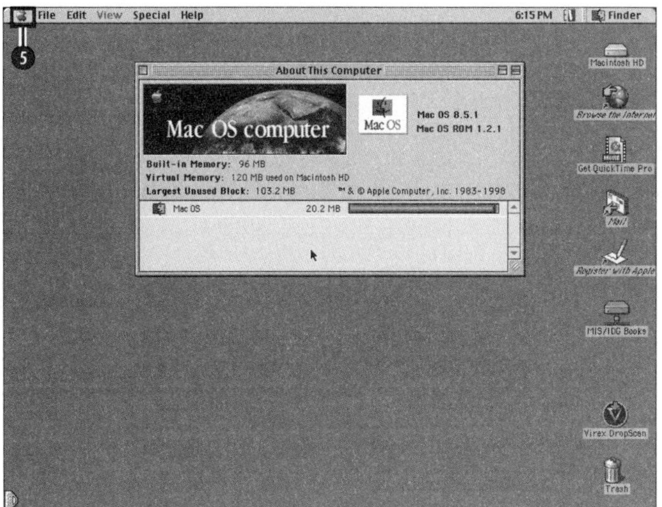

4 *Choose Restart from the Special menu.*

5 *Choose About This Computer from the Apple menu.*

▶ *Note your new Virtual Memory setting.*

TAKE NOTE

USING HARD DRIVE SPACE FOR VIRTUAL MEMORY

If you're low on hard drive space, keep in mind that the iMac reserves more space for virtual memory than you may think. Virtual memory requires space for the amount you designate, plus the amount of built-in memory. For example, if you designated 10MB of virtual memory and your iMac has 32MB of built-in memory, your iMac will actually use 42MB for virtual memory.

USING RAM DOUBLER

An alternative to Virtual Memory is RAM Doubler by Connectix. Contrary to its name, RAM Doubler can actually double or triple your available memory for running applications — up to 256MB. RAM Doubler works best when you are running several applications simultaneously, rather than one really huge application. On the down side, RAM Doubler is commercial software and costs about $60 (at the time of this writing). You can purchase and download it online.

FIND IT ONLINE

Visit **http://www.connectix.com** for more information about RAM Doubler.

Using a RAM Disk

If your hard drive can pretend to be RAM, why shouldn't your RAM pretend to be a hard drive? It can, and it's known as a RAM disk, appropriately enough. RAM disks are as fast as they are fleeting. Anything you put on a RAM disk will be speedy, but it won't be permanent. A RAM disk will disappear when you crash or lose power for any reason (though it will remain if you specifically restart or shut down your iMac). You won't want to use a RAM disk for storage of important files. Rather, RAM disks are most useful when you want to speed up an application you're using intensively.

To create a RAM disk, open your Memory control panel and click the On radio button under RAM disk. Now slide the adjustment control to indicate how much of your RAM you want to use as a RAM disk. Note that as you slide the control, the Disk Cache size and Available Built-In Memory amounts change accordingly. The actual size of the RAM disk displays below the sliding adjustment. Note also the Save on Shut Down check box—make sure this is checked to preserve your RAM disk (and contents) when you shut down your iMac. Restart your iMac after you've set up your RAM disk.

After you restart the computer, your RAM disk appears on your Desktop as an icon that looks like a floppy disk with a RAM chip on it. Double-click the icon to open it as you would your hard drive, and then copy items into it. Try copying an application you use frequently into it. I installed another copy of AOL on my RAM disk and it was delightfully fast!

When your restart or shut down the iMac, it saves a copy of everything on the RAM disk. This process takes a few moments—your iMac changes your mouse pointer to a miniature version of the RAM disk icon as a visual clue that it is saving this information. When the process is complete, your iMac restarts or shuts down as you requested. When your iMac powers back up again, your RAM disk is intact, along with all its contents.

CROSS-REFERENCE

See Chapter 3 for alternative drives and discs you can use.

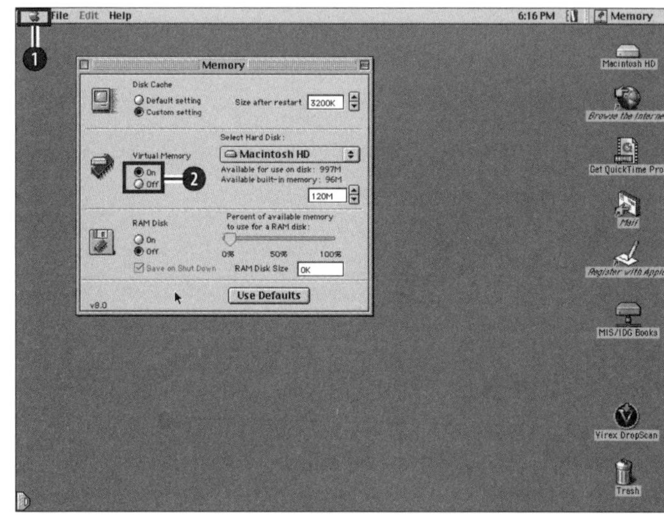

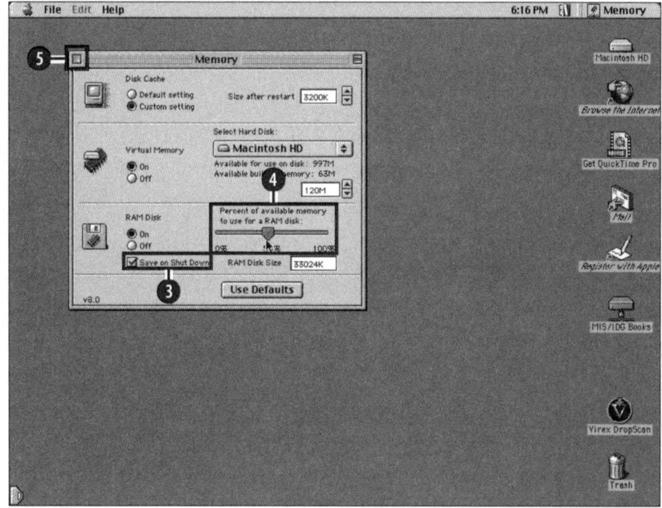

1. *Open the Memory control panel.*
2. *Optional: Click the On radio button to create a RAM disk.*
3. *Optional: Clear this box if you don't want your RAM disk preserved on restart or shut down.*
4. *Optional: Adjust the size of your RAM disk.*

▶ *Note the exact size of your RAM disk.*

5. *Close the window.*

When Not to RAM Disk

RAM disks borrow from Peter to pay Paul, so be careful about how much RAM Peter can lend out. If you have very little real RAM, you'll end up using slower virtual memory to run your applications, instead of the real thing. What good is speedy access to a data file when the application using it is running slower than usual? Consider your memory capacity and requirements carefully before you bang heads with a RAM disk.

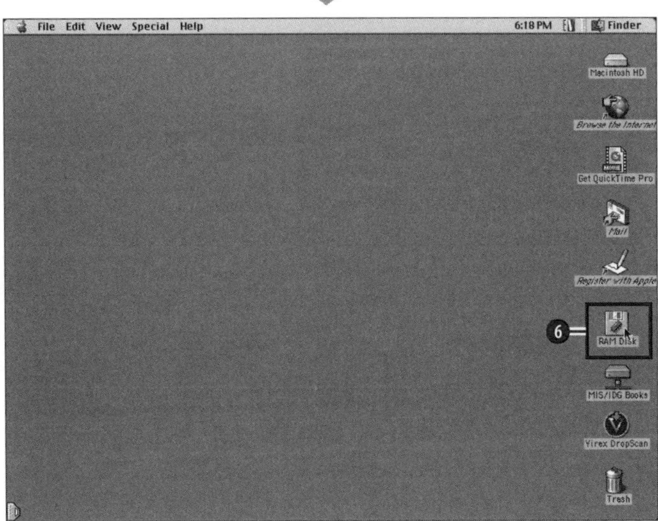

6 *Double-click your RAM disk icon like any other disk.*

TAKE NOTE

RESIZING A RAM DISK

If you discover you need more space on your RAM disk or that you need more RAM to run applications, you can increase or decrease the size of your RAM disk. Unfortunately, you'll need to recreate the RAM disk to do so. Erase the RAM disk (copy anything you need first), adjust the RAM disk size in your Memory control panel, and then restart the computer.

REMOVING A RAM DISK

Getting rid of a RAM disk isn't a simple as dragging it to the trash. If you try, it just bounces back! The best method to remove a RAM disk is to trash everything on the RAM disk, disable file sharing if it is on, and then turn off the RAM disk in your Memory control panel.

FIND IT ONLINE

Check out the shareware utility ramBunctious at **http://mac.org/utilities/rambunctious/** to increase your RAM disk functionality.

Expanding Your Memory

Virtual memory works most of the time, but it isn't the solution to all your memory needs. If you find you just can't get away without more memory in your iMac, don't worry — you can install a maximum of 256MB of RAM in older iMacs and up to 512MB in newer iMacs. You can purchase iMac memory chips (also called DIMM modules) from Apple and from mail-order houses. You must be specific about the kind of memory you want when you order, however. Your iMac is very picky about its memory — use anything else and not only won't it work, but you could damage your iMac.

Your iMac has two RAM slots. One slot is already occupied with the RAM that came with your iMac, and the other may be empty. Note that if you ordered additional RAM with your iMac, the extra RAM is probably occupying that second slot. How do you know? If your iMac has more than 32MB (older iMac) or 64MB (newer iMac) of built-in RAM, then you probably have both slots occupied. To find out for sure, open Apple System Profiler and click the arrow next to Built-in memory. The window changes to show the locations and sizes of your built-in RAM. You will probably see 32MB DIMM in the bottom location. If you also see a DIMM in the top location, then you know both slots are full.

You can still increase your iMac memory, even if both slots are full. However, you will need to replace one or both of the installed DIMM modules with new modules sporting higher capacities. Any combination of DIMM sizes is acceptable. If you paid for a RAM upgrade when you ordered your iMac, this may seem like a waste of money. Give the old DIMM to a friend or family member with an iMac and it won't seem so bad.

Installing memory in your iMac can be an adventure. First, you should know that Apple says you need to have

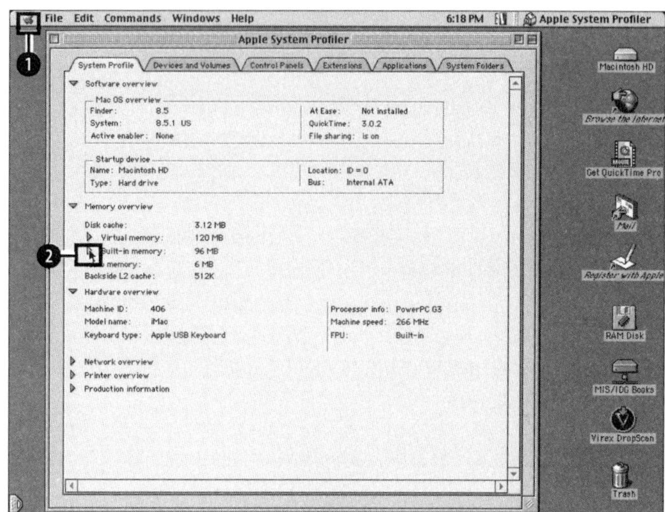

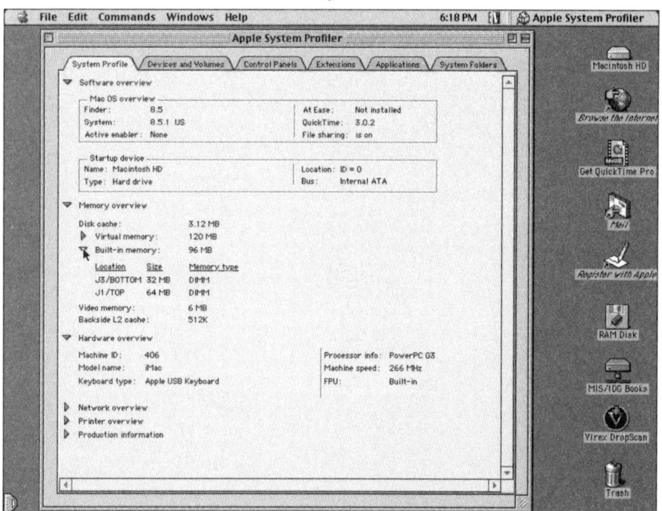

❶ *Open your Apple System Profiler.*

❷ *Click the arrow next to Built-in memory.*

▶ *Note the location(s) of your RAM. If more than one appears here, you do not have a vacant slot for another RAM chip and will need to remove one to increase your memory.*

CROSS-REFERENCE

If you're considering more memory because your iMac seems sluggish, refer to "Speeding up a Slowdown" in Chapter 17 first.

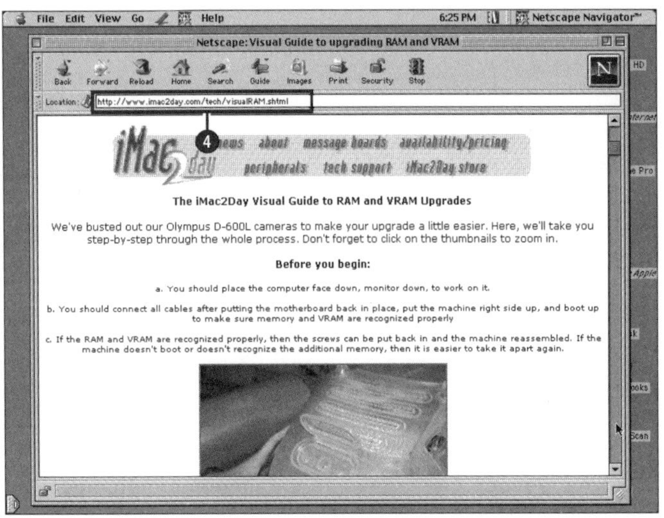

3. *Open your Web browser of choice.*
4. *Go to* ***http://www.imac2day.com/tech/visualRAM.shtml****.*

► *Note the instructions and photos for installing RAM on your own.*

5. *Point your browser to* ***http://www.apple.com/support/****.*
6. *Choose iMac support from the drop-down menu.*

an authorized service provider install your new memory. If you're not mechanically inclined, this is probably your best bet. On the other hand, it is possible to install the memory in your iMac yourself. If this interests you, I recommend you point your browser to **http://www.imac2day.com/tech/visualRAM.shtml** for photos and systematic instructions on how to install more memory.

Once your iMac has its new memory, revisit your Memory control panel and click the Use Defaults button in the lower right corner. Also access the Get Info window for key applications (select the icon and press Command+I) and increase their allocated memory sizes.

TAKE NOTE

CHOOSING YOUR MEMORY

When deciding how much extra memory to install in your iMac, I recommend you get as much as you can afford. You can never have too many Macs or too much memory.

VOIDING YOUR WARRANTY

If you're worried about voiding your warranty by installing new memory in your iMac, you shouldn't. If you damage your iMac while installing memory, however, Apple cannot be held responsible, naturally. If in doubt, have your dealer install the memory.

FIND IT ONLINE

Apple offers information on adding more memory to your iMac at **http://www.apple.com/support/** (choose iMac Support, then Adding RAM).

Personal Workbook

Q&A

1. What are the three differences between your hard drive memory and your RAM memory?

2. What is a memory block? Where do you find your largest unused memory block?

3. How do you increase an application's memory allocation? By what percentages should you increase it?

4. What is the keyboard shortcut to get more information about an application?

5. What is your disk cache? How do you increase or decrease it?

6. How do you increase your virtual memory? How much hard disk space does virtual memory require?

7. What is the benefit of using a RAM disk? The drawback?

8. How much RAM do you have? How much more can you add?

ANSWERS: PAGE 325

Managing Memory

CHAPTER 15

EXTRA PRACTICE

1. Open About This Computer from the Apple menu while you're in the Finder. Note the amount of memory used by the Mac OS.
2. Leave About This Computer open, and then open a few applications. Observe how the display changes as you open and then close those applications.
3. Check the current memory allocation for AppleWorks.
4. Note the current settings in the Memory control panel.
5. Open Apple System Profiler and review the Built-in memory information. Do you have room for more RAM?

REAL-WORLD APPLICATIONS

✔ You've begun to use your iMac for creating computer graphics. Life gets frustrating as you keep waiting and waiting for your graphics to render onscreen. You make adjustments to your graphics program's memory allocation and your productivity soars.

✔ You've adjusted memory allocations, increased your Virtual Memory, increased your cache, and it still didn't completely solve your memory problem. You check Apple System Profiler for built-in memory and see that you have a 32MB DIMM module in the bottom slot, but nothing in the top slot. You have your dealer install an additional 128MB of RAM and life is grand!

Visual Quiz

How do you produce this window? What information does this window convey?

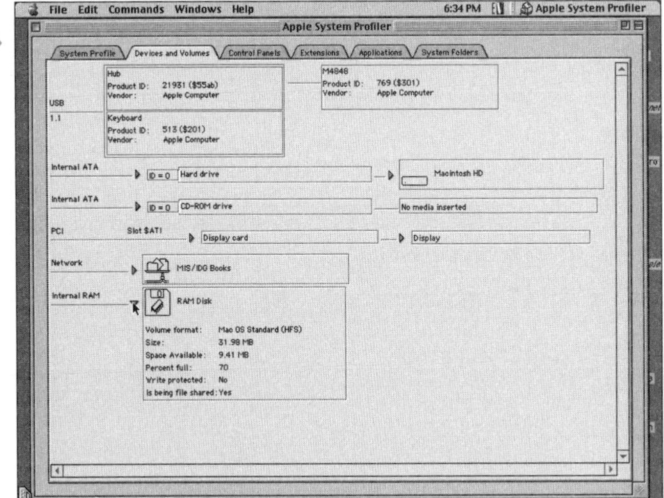

CHAPTER 16

MASTER THESE SKILLS

- Learning to Use AppleScript
- Understanding an Automation Script
- Writing Your Own Automation Scripts
- Using Other Automation Applications

Automating Your iMac

Ah, the promise of automation! Find a mundane, repetitive task, and then teach a machine to do it for you! Why then does it seem like half of what you do on your iMac is still a series of repetitive, mundane actions? Click this, open that, select this, do that. There must be a better way, and there is!

Twenty years ago, the solution to this problem was to write your own computer program! Of course, computers were far simpler, programs were far less complex, and everyone's expectations were much lower. For that matter, in the early days of home computing, there was very little in the way of prepackaged consumer software. Home computers were hobbies, and home computer users were expected to tinker around with homemade software.

Today, computer programming is almost exclusively performed by professionals or young people on their way to careers in computer programming. Even so, the need to custom-automate your personal tasks still exists. There are more computer users yearning to automate their tasks than ever before.

The solution for Macintosh users is something called AppleScript. AppleScript is what's called a *scripting language*. To be perfectly honest, scripting is another way of saying programming, but scripts are far simpler than most programs and programming languages.

Much of what scripts can do is limited to a series of actions that you'd normally perform with mouse clicks and perhaps some words typed on a keyboard. In fact, in the case of AppleScript, you don't even have to know a programming language or a single programming command to get started. All you have to do is use the AppleScript recorder to memorize your actions as you go about the task you want to automate. When you're finished, you can play back the script just as if it was an audiotape. If you performed the task correctly, you now have a finished script that will flawlessly perform that mundane task from now on.

Now, the folks at Apple who created AppleScript love to create computer programs, so if you want to dig deeper into AppleScript, you'll find that they have created ways to do far more than save a few clicks of a mouse. But for now, know that if you keep doing the same thing over and over again, there's a good chance you can save your mouse finger a lot of wear and tear.

Learning to Use AppleScript

If you got your iMac to save time, you're going to love AppleScript! In essence, AppleScript is the ultimate timesaver for your iMac, automating the most mundane routines and complicated functions, too.

You can use AppleScript in two ways. The first way is to simply take advantage of the premade scripts. These scripts automate a variety of normally mundane tasks to save you time. You don't need to know anything about how AppleScript works to use them. The second way is to create your own AppleScripts using the AppleScript Editor that comes with your iMac. This takes a bit more time and effort to learn, but you will be well rewarded. I discuss creating your own scripts in the next task.

Your iMac comes with a number of scripts that are ready to use. You can find five of them in the Apple menu under Automated Tasks. Each does exactly what it says, and they are really quite convenient if you find yourself doing these tasks often. I use Add Alias to Apple Menu frequently, as well as Start/Stop File Sharing. The most popular task — Add Alias to Apple Menu — requires that you first select an appropriate item in the Finder and then choose it from the Automated Tasks submenu. Share a Folder and Share a Folder (No Guest) both create a folder named Shared Folder on your hard drive and allow others to access it across a network — this is useful for exchanging files. There's no trick to Start File Sharing and Stop File Sharing — just use them when you need to turn file sharing on and off.

Does your iMac offer any more pre-made AppleScripts? Yes, though they're hiding for some reason. You can find three more scripts inside the More Automated Tasks folder, which is located in the AppleScript folder inside the Apple Extras folder on your Macintosh HD. You can get details on how each of the scripts work in the About More Automated Tasks

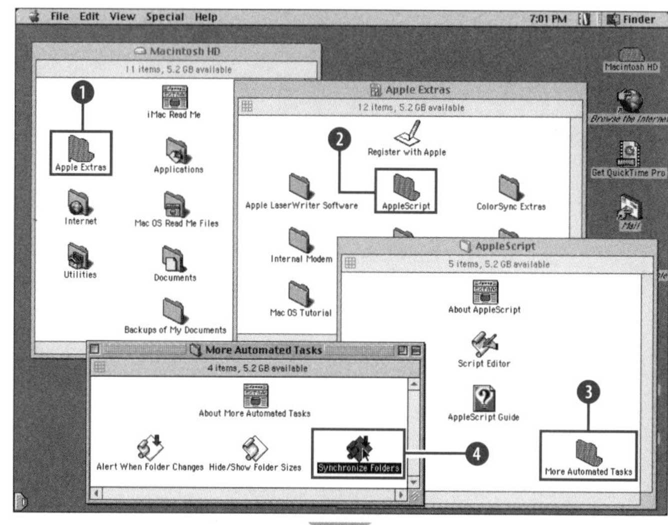

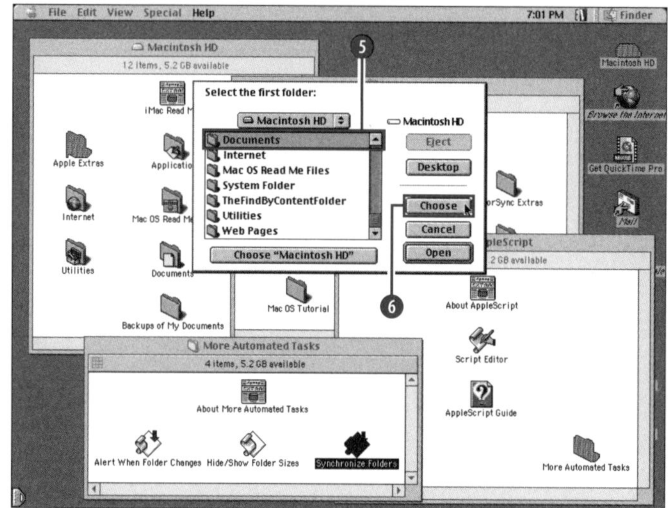

1. *Open the Apple Extras folder on the Macintosh HD.*
2. *Open the AppleScript folder.*
3. *Open the More Automated Tasks folder.*
4. *Open the Synchronize Folders script.*
5. *Navigate to and select the folder whose files you want to synchronize.*
6. *Click the Choose button.*

CROSS-REFERENCE

See Chapter 15 for more information on setting your startup and shutdown routines.

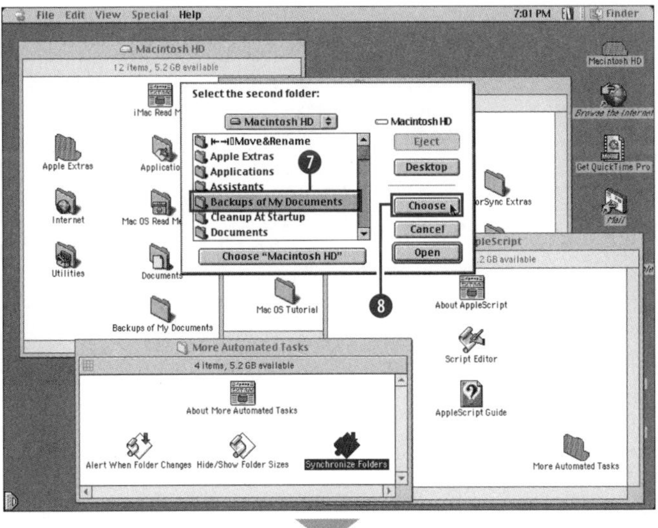

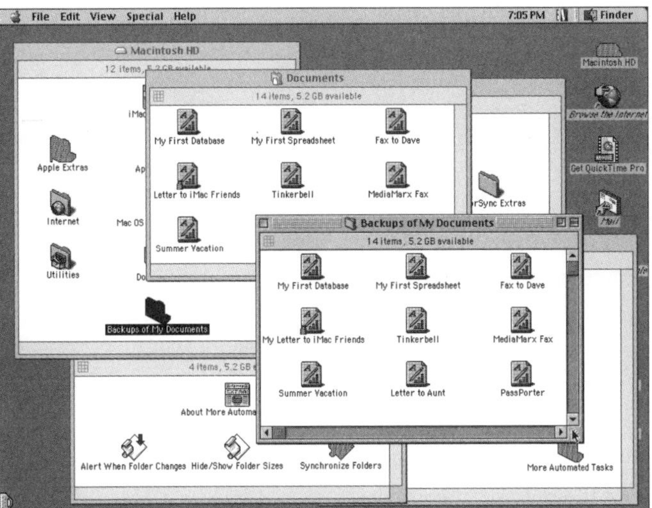

- ❼ *Navigate to and select the folder to which you want to synchronize files.*
- ❽ *Click Choose.*

- ▶ *Watch as the script synchronizes your files. It may take some time, depending on how many files you have.*
- ▶ *Note your first folder and its contents.*
- ▶ *Note your second folder and its contents, synchronized with the first folder.*

document. Synchronize Folders is a particularly intriguing script, comparing the contents of two folders and synchronizing the contents. You could even use this script to help you back up your files!

Over 20 more sample scripts are lurking on your iMac Install CD-ROM disc. To find them, insert the disc in the drive, open the CD Extras folder, the AppleScript Extras folder, and then the More Sample Scripts folder. Read the AppleScript Read Me file to learn more about each script, its purpose, and how to install it. There's even a handy utility called OSA Menu which, when installed, places an icon at the top right of your menu bar. Click the icon for a drop-down menu of your available scripts.

TAKE NOTE

RUNNING SCRIPTS AT STARTUP AND SHUTDOWN

Let's say you want to run the Synchronize Folders script each time you shut down your iMac to keep a backup copy of an important folder synchronized. To do this, just place the script in your Shutdown Items folder. Any script you want run automatically at startup should go in your Startup Items folder.

SHORTCUT

Use the OSA Menu utility (on your iMac Install CD-ROM) to quickly and easily run scripts.

Understanding an Automation Script

The AppleScript language is generally easy to understand and use. You don't need to be a programmer or to have any knowledge of programming to gain a basic understanding of how an automation script works. Understanding a script, however, is the first step in creating your own!

To begin, open the Script Editor application on your iMac. You'll find it in your AppleScript folder inside your Apple Extras folder. Now choose Open from the File menu, navigate to your Automated Tasks folder (also in your AppleScript folder), and then open a script. I recommend you open the Turn File Sharing On script, but any script will do. Once the script file is open, a simple description of the script appears in the top pane, while the actual code of the script appears in the bottom pane.

Take a good look at the script's code. Try not to be intimidated by the abbreviations. Look beyond them and you'll see that the code reads like plain-English instructions. The script tells an application to do something here, beep there, display a dialog box over here, and so on. You'll notice that much of a script consists of sending dialog boxes to the user (you), along with some basic error-checking code designed to avoid problems. Notice any comments in the code — you can spot them by the italic text and double hyphens in front of the text.

If learning to write in the AppleScript language intrigues you, pay a visit to the Help menu and select AppleScript Help. You'll find plenty of good information on scripting, as well as links to AppleScript on the Web. The Web site offers tutorials, resources, and scripts, scripts, scripts! I also encourage you to peek at each of the pre-made scripts on your hard drive and the iMac Install CD. You can learn a lot by examining the way the other scripts are structured.

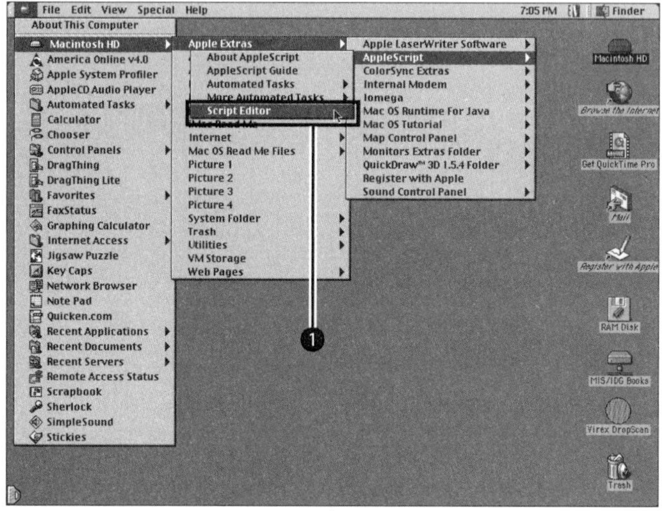

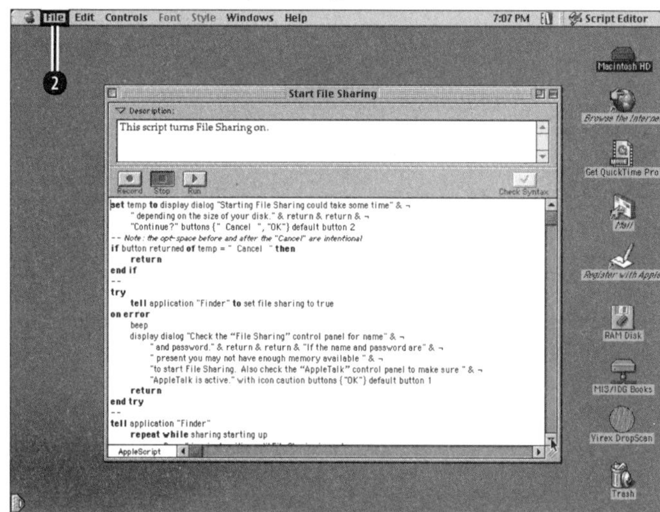

❶ *Open the Script Editor.*

❷ *Open the Start File Sharing Script.*

▶ *Note the script description.*

▶ *Examine the script.*

CROSS-REFERENCE

Refer to the previous task in this chapter for locations of other scripts you can peek at.

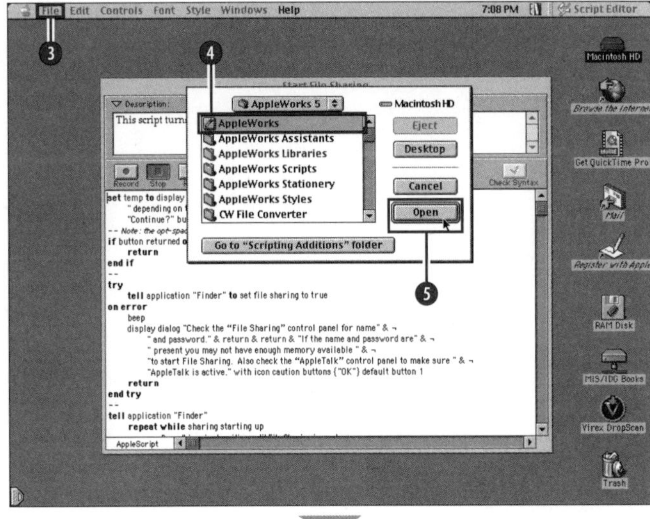

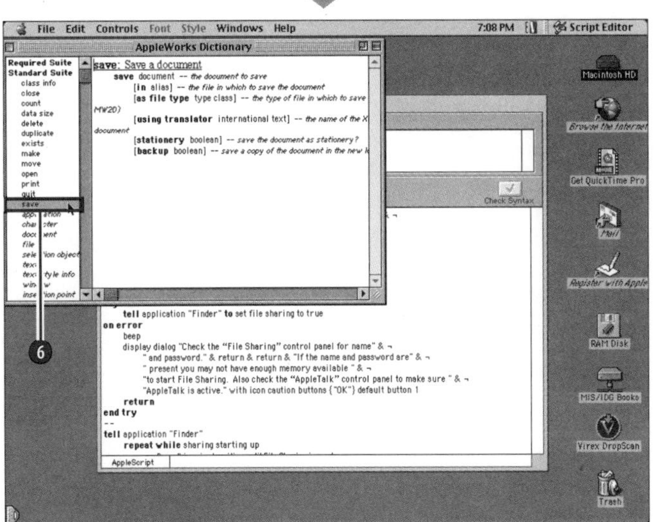

3. *Choose Open Dictionary from the File menu.*
4. *Navigate to the AppleWorks application.*
5. *Click the Open button.*

▶ *The dictionary of AppleScript definitions opens.*

6. *Select a definition.*

▶ *Note the parameters.*

If you like the idea of AppleScript but don't have the time or inclination to invest in learning the language, you can still create your own automation scripts. The Script Editor also functions as a script recorder, monitoring your actions and saving them as a script. I'll show you how to create a basic automation script in the next task.

TAKE NOTE

SCRIPTING COMPATIBILITY

AppleScript works with your Finder and many — but not all — applications. Happily, AppleWorks does support AppleScripts. In fact, AppleWorks offers its own pre-made scripts — look in the AppleWorks Scripts folder inside the AppleWorks folder in your Applications folder. When in doubt about whether an application supports AppleScript, click and drag the icon of the application over the Script Editor icon. If the Script Editor highlights as the icon you're dragging passes over it, you know it is compatible with AppleScript! Here's another way: If AppleScript is already open, choose Open Dictionary from the File menu and navigate to the application in question. If the application appears in the list of files that can be opened, it is compatible.

FIND IT ONLINE

Visit **http://www.apple.com/applescript/** for more information on AppleScript.

Creating Your Own Automation Scripts

While teaching you the AppleScript language is beyond the scope of this book, you can still create your own automation script today. The simplest way to create basic scripts without any knowledge of the script language is through the Script Editor's recording feature. I'll show you how to create an easy script to turn on smart scrolling for those times when you're doing intensive scrolling in a document.

To begin, open Script Editor if it isn't already running. Click the Record button. Open the Appearance control panel from the Apple menu. Click the Options tab. Click the Smart Scrolling check box. Close the Appearance control panel window. Return to the Script Editor window and click the Stop button. Voila! The code for your new script automatically appears in Script Editor. You didn't have to type a thing.

To check your script to see how well it works, first return to the Appearance control panel and turn off Smart Scrolling. Now return to Script Editor and click the Run button. Watch closely now — you should see your iMac open your Appearance control panel and enable Smart Scrolling. It all happens very quickly, which is the beauty of it. If it worked, your Script Editor window should now have the scroll arrows at one end of the scrollbar, as it should when Smart Scrolling is enabled.

If your script works, give it a description. Just type a descriptive sentence in the top pane of the Script Editor window, such as "Turns on Smart Scrolling in the Appearance control panel." To save your script, choose Save from the File menu and name your script ("Turn On Smart Scrolling Script" is a good choice). Choose Application from the Kind drop-down menu before you click the Save button. Alternatively, you could save your script by choosing Save As Run-Only from the File

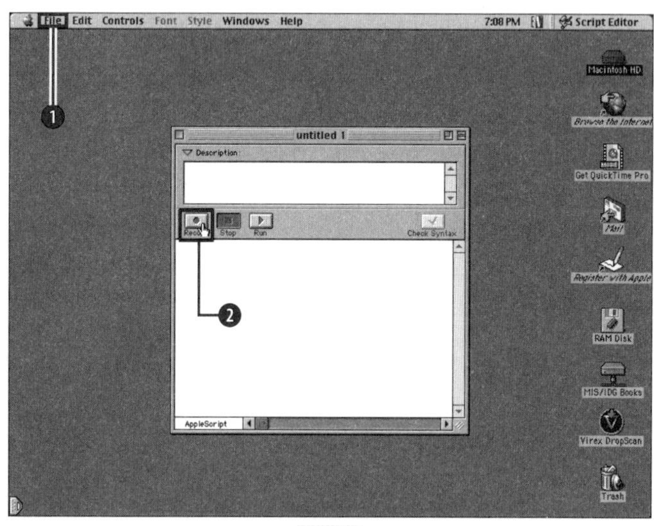

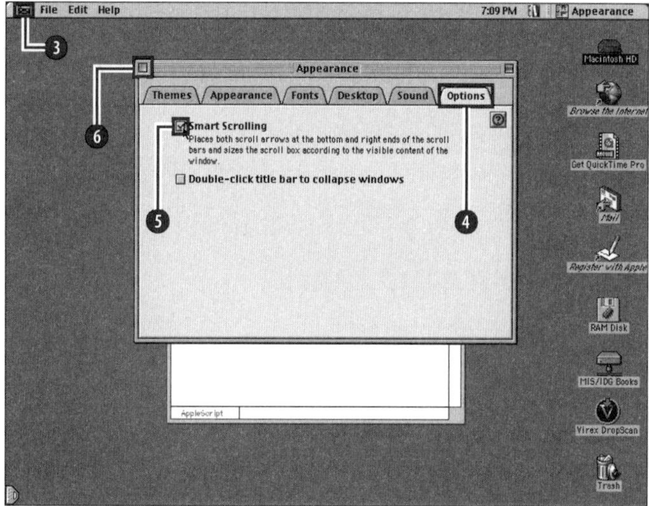

1. *Choose New Script from the File menu, if a new script window isn't already open.*
2. *Click the Record button.*
3. *Open the Appearance control panel (note that a tape flashes over the Apple menu to indicate that it is recording).*
4. *Click the Options button.*
5. *Enable Smart Scrolling.*
6. *Close the Appearance control panel.*

CROSS-REFERENCE

Learn more about Smart Scrolling in Chapter 5.

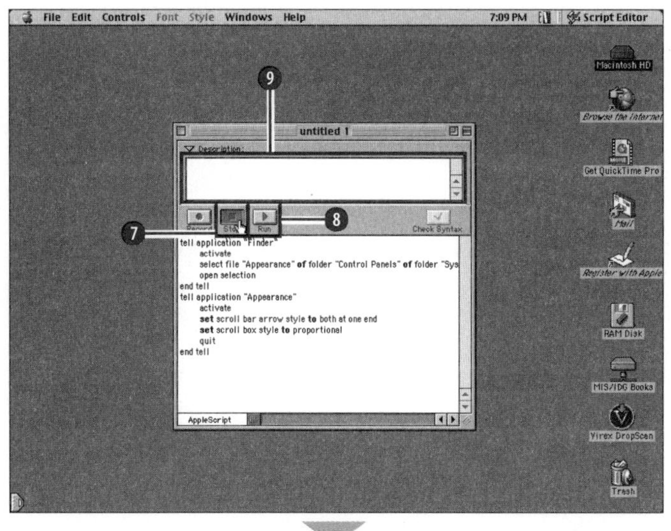

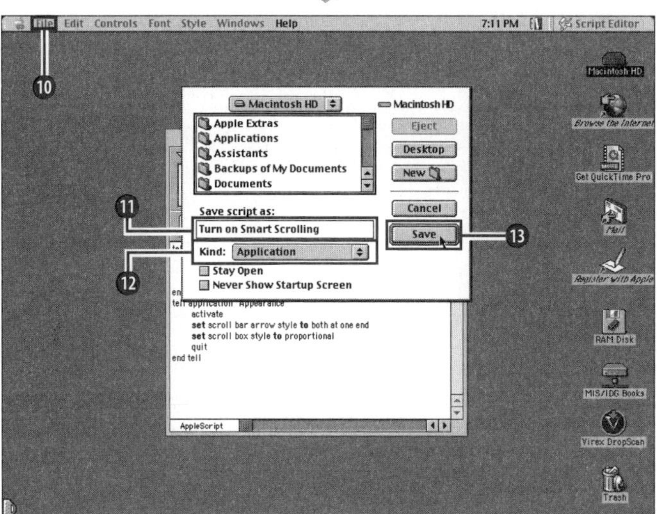

7 *Return to the Script Editor and click Stop.*

8 *Click Run to try out your script.*

9 *Type a description of your script.*

10 *Return to Script Editor and choose Save from the File menu.*

11 *Type a name for your new script.*

12 *Choose Application from the drop-down menu.*

13 *Click the Save button.*

menu. This does the same thing, but it protects the script from being edited.

Return to the Finder and navigate to your saved script. Double-click your script to run it. A dialog box pops up, shows you the description of your script, and offers you the choice to Run the script or Quit. If you prefer not to see this dialog box in the future, open the script again in Script Editor, choose Save As from the File menu, and this time, click the Never Show Startup Screen option before you save it.

If you find the Turn On Smart Scrolling script useful, make a script to turn it off, too! Place them both in your Apple Menu Items folder for quick access and you're all set.

TAKE NOTE

RECORDING COMPATIBILITY

Simply establishing that an application is compatible with AppleScript doesn't ensure it is also capable of *recording* scripts. For example, while you can create scripts to work AppleWorks, you cannot record them with ScriptEditor. If you want to create scripts for applications such as AppleWorks, you'll need to write them manually.

SHORTCUT

Press Command+D to start recording and Command+. to stop while the ScriptEditor is running.

Using Other Automation Applications

Beyond AppleScript, there are several other ways to automate tasks on your iMac. All involve downloading or purchasing other applications, some of which are specifically designed for automation, while others incorporate automation features. I can't list all the possibilities in the Mac universe, but I can list my favorites here!

KeyQuencer Lite by Binary Software is a shareware macro program that lets you program and perform various tasks on your iMac. A *macro* is a set of actions that you can perform with a single keystroke. I've used KeyQuencer with much success over the years and highly recommend it. It's a great introductory macro program at a reasonable price. Visit **http://www.binarysoft.com/** for more information and to download a demo.

QuicKeys by CE Software is another macro program that's been around for over ten years. (I cut my teeth on QuicKeys!) It offers a bit more oomph at a slightly higher price. For example, QuicKeys can watch what you do and automatically record a macro. QuicKeys is also a commercial software package. You can download a demo, and you can order it online at **http://www.cesoft.com/**.

OneClick by WestCode Software is a fun and creative program that features floating palettes of macro buttons. I say fun and creative because you can create cool-looking, customized palettes, in addition to saving time and effort with your macros. If you're not into palettes, you can use keyboard shortcuts, too. OneClick has a strong following, and many of its users create and share their palettes online. Visit their Web site for more information and to access their palette libraries at **http://www.westcodesoft.com/**.

In addition to these macro programs, several applications offer built-in scripting features. Microsoft Word (a word processing application) has macros that you can

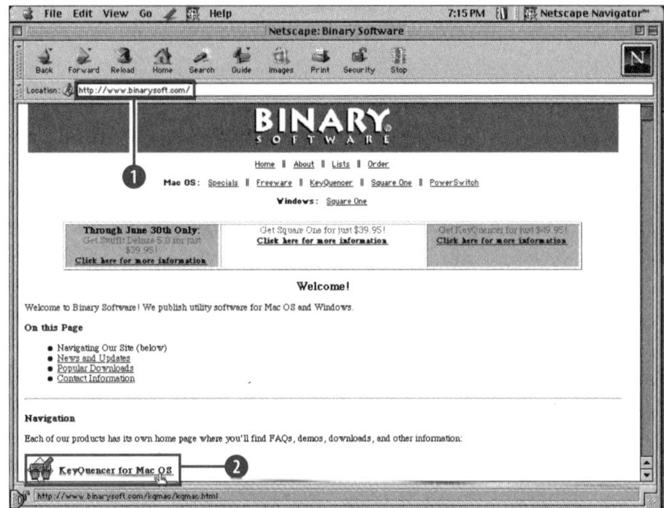

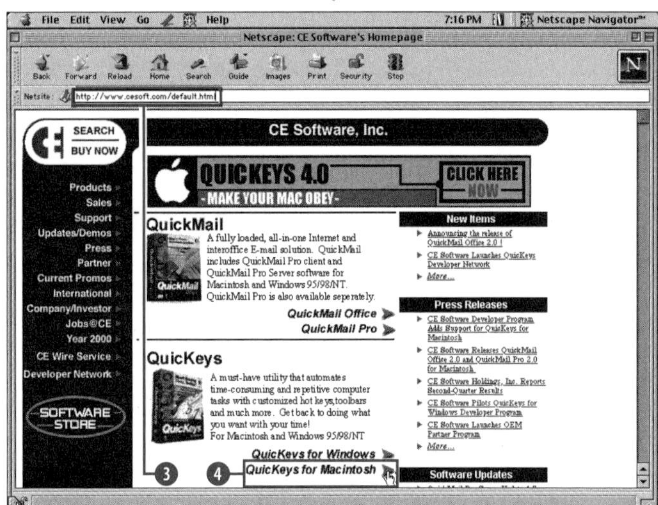

1. Sign on the Internet and point your browser to **http://www.binarysoft.com**.
2. Click here for more information about KeyQuencer.
3. Point your browser to **http://www.cesoft.com/**.
4. Click here for more information about QuicKeys.

CROSS-REFERENCE

Refer to task "Navigating Your Own Way" in Chapter 14 for more information on f-keys.

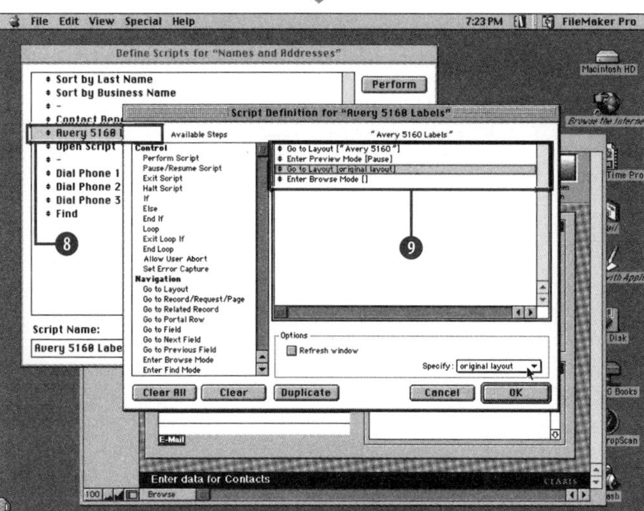

5 Point your browser to ***http://www.westcodesoft.com***.

6 Click here for more information about OneClick.

7 If you have FileMaker Pro, open a database and choose ScriptMaker from the Script menu.

8 Select a script and click the Edit button.

9 Optional: Edit a script. Note the scripting choices along the left side of the window.

program to help with word processing tasks. Adobe Photoshop (a graphic editing application) offers actions — another word for scripts — that save time in performing repetitive or complex tasks. FileMaker Pro (a database application) offers scripts that let you manipulate and use your data easier and faster. This is just a sampling. Be on the lookout for automation features in your favorite applications, whether they call it scripts, macros, or actions.

TAKE NOTE

REPROGRAMMING YOUR FUNCTION KEYS

The keys at the very top of your keyboard, known as *function keys* (or F-keys, for short) are often the key to performing macros and scripts. As I mentioned in Chapter 15, some applications use these keys for shortcuts even without specifically programming them. Keep this in mind when designating them for use in a macro program.

USING MACROS IN MICROSOFT WORD

Regrettably, a number of viruses are associated with the use of macros in Microsoft Word. Before you enable the use of macros in Word, install some anti-viral software to keep your iMac happy and healthy. Although you won't get a virus from a macro you create, documents you receive from others may include macro viruses.

FIND IT ONLINE

Visit **http://www.shareware.com** for more macro applications and utilities.

Personal Workbook

Q&A

1. How do you execute a ready-made AppleScript (automated task)?

2. Where can you find additional AppleScript automated tasks?

3. Where is the Script Editor? What does it do?

4. Where can you learn more about the AppleScript scripting language?

5. How can you create your own script without knowing the scripting language?

6. Can you record a script for anything you want to do on your iMac? Why or why not?

7. What is a macro? How do you create one?

8. What is an action?

ANSWERS: PAGE 326

Automating Your iMac

EXTRA PRACTICE

1. Use a pre-made AppleScript (automated task) to add an alias to the Apple menu. Check the Apple menu to see if your alias appeared.
2. Run the Alert When Folder Changes script, choose your Applications folder, and keep the script running. Make some changes to your Applications folder.
3. Find out which applications are compatible with AppleScript. To do this, open Script Editor, choose Open Dictionary from the File menu, and browse your hard drive. Specifically, find out if your Apple Menu Options control panel is compatible.
4. Record a script to open your Apple Menu Items and turn your submenus off. Test the script. Save it if it works.

REAL-WORLD APPLICATIONS

✔ You have your iMac on a network at the office. You find you are constantly turning file sharing on and off. You discover the Start/Stop File Sharing automated tasks under the Apple menu and begin using them instead.

✔ You purchased and installed an optional Zip drive and want to use it for backup. You create two folders: one on your hard drive for your important letters and one on your Zip drive for backups of those important letters. At the end of each day, you run the Synchronize Folders script on the two folders, effectively backing up your important letters on your hard drive to the Zip drive.

Visual Quiz

How do you navigate to this window? What does it offer?

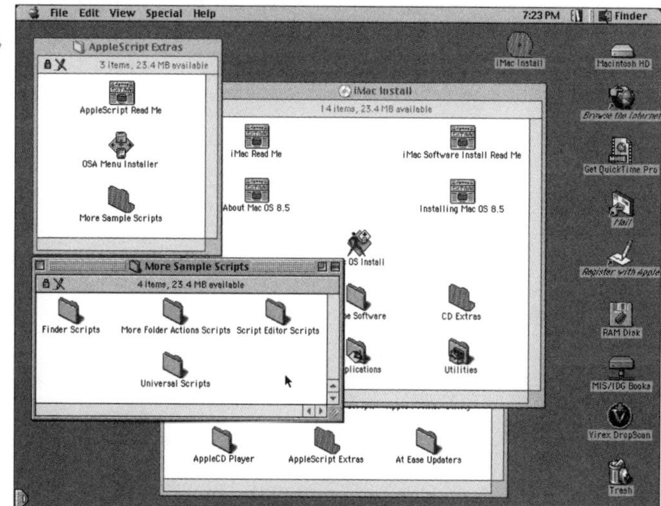

CHAPTER 17

MASTER THESE SKILLS

- Resolving a Startup Problem
- Surviving a Freeze or a Crash
- Finding a Lost File or Application
- Fixing a Printing Problem
- Clearing Your Desktop
- Speeding Up a Slowdown
- Resolving Extension Conflicts
- Finding More Help

Troubleshooting Your iMac

"Oops!" "Grrrrr, grumble, grouch, curse..." "Oh, (expletive deleted)!" If you're anything like me, at least one of these phrases will escape your lips during your otherwise happy relationship with your iMac. It's inevitable. The more you depend on your iMac and the closer your relationship with your iMac becomes, the more likely your iMac will let you down. It's the law: Anything that can go wrong will go wrong, and at the worst possible moment.

Now, when Murphy's Law rears its less-than-pretty head, restrain yourself. Please don't invoke Hammurabi's "eye-for-an-eye" Law — your iMac's screen is *very* expensive to replace. Instead, take a deep breath and regain your composure. Your iMac is a very complex piece of equipment, and figuring out what went wrong may take some careful thought.

Troubleshooting a problem is as much an art as it is a science, but a bit of logic goes a long way. As you try to resolve a problem, think of the *gozinta's* — this *goes into* that, and that *goes into* the next thing — the logical chain of events your computer follows as it does its work. Where along the line did the process break down? As you trace through the steps, keep track of what fixes you tried, and whether they helped, hurt, or had no effect.

It helps to know exactly what was happening before everything went kaflooey. If you get an error message or a warning from your iMac, write it down immediately so that if you need help from tech support, they'll have some extra clues to go on. If things were acting funny, jot that down, too.

It's also important to know what changes you (and anyone else) have recently made to your iMac — new software, new hardware, new control panel settings, and so on. This information is critical if you need to undo the damage.

Finally, know your limits. If you have no clue, changes blindly made can create even more troubles. If you're in over your head, get help. Call a Mac-wise friend, reach out to technical support resources, and look for answers in a book like this one. Many times, the answer will turn out to be very simple, if only you had known it.

So, do yourself a big favor and read this chapter now. You'll be a bit more prepared for the day when Murphy comes knocking on your door.

Resolving a Startup Problem

Sometimes things just don't go as planned. Take the power button, for example. You press it and expect that your iMac will power up, your icons will march along the bottom of the screen, and your Desktop will appear. You take this for granted, as well you should. So what happens if you power up your iMac one day and things don't go as planned? Here are some common problems and — more importantly — possible solutions:

You press the power button and nothing happens. No chime, no lights, no nothing. First, check that your iMac is actually plugged into a wall outlet. If you use a surge protector, verify that it is turned on and plugged in, too. Be sure your power cord is pushed all the way into your iMac, too. Second, if you pressed the power button the keyboard, verify that the keyboard is plugged into the iMac — if it is, try the power button on the iMac instead.

You press the power button, the monitor comes to life, but you don't hear the customary chime. First, check that your sound is on (in the Monitors & Sound control panel). Second, remove any headphones you may have plugged into your headphone jacks. Third, verify that any external speakers you may have installed are on and that the volume is turned up.

You press the power button and see only a flashing question mark icon. This icon means that your iMac is having a problem locating the software it needs to power up. First, try restarting your iMac (see the Take Note section to learn how to do this). If that doesn't work, dig out your iMac Install CD-ROM disc, insert it in your iMac, restart, and hold down the C key while your iMac powers up. The C key tells your iMac to use the software on the CD-ROM disc, rather than the software on your hard drive to start up. If this works, locate Disk First Aid in your Utilities folder and run it — it corrects most hard drive problems. If that isn't successful, consider reinstalling your

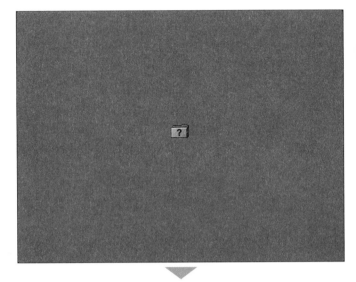

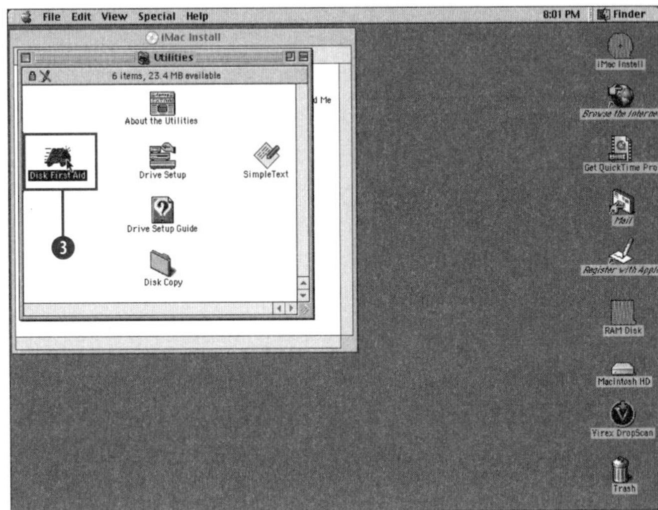

1. *If you see this flashing icon when you power up your iMac, restart your iMac.*
2. *If a restart isn't successful, insert your iMac Install CD-ROM disc, restart again, and hold down the C key until you see the happy Mac icon.*

▶ *Your iMac started up from the CD-ROM disc.*

3. *Open Disk First Aid in the Utilities folder on your iMac Install CD-ROM disc.*

CROSS-REFERENCE

See "Setting Your Startup/Shutdown" in Chapter 14 if an unwanted application launches every time you power up your iMac.

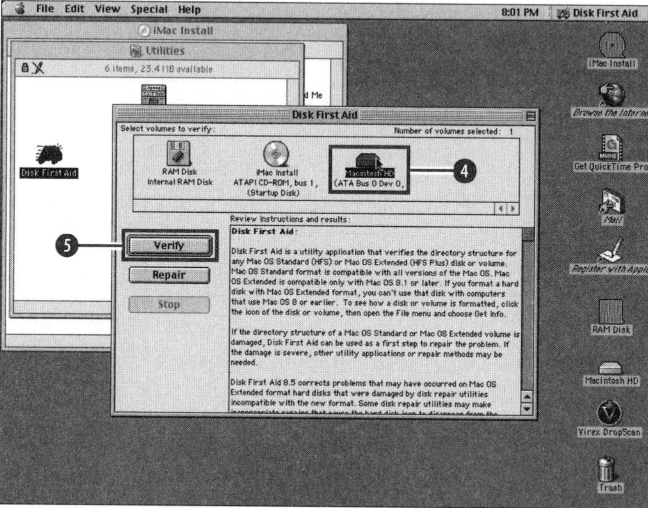

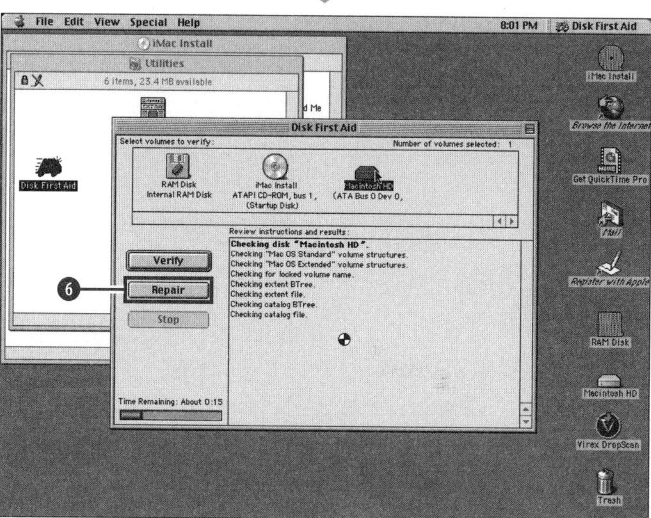

4 *Select your hard drive.*

5 *Click the Verify button to check your drive.*

▶ *A progress meter is displayed as your drive is verified.*

▶ *Information regarding your drive is displayed here.*

6 *Click the Repair button if problems are found.*

operating system using the installation program on the CD-ROM disc. If all else fails, call up your trusty dealer or service shop for assistance.

You press the power button, your iMac begins its normal startup sequence, and then informs you that a system error has occurred, or something along those lines. See the task on "Resolving Extension Conflicts," later in this chapter.

TAKE NOTE

RESTARTING YOUR IMAC

Most of the time you can — and should — use the Restart command under the Special menu. If the Special menu is unavailable, however, that becomes a bit difficult. Another way to restart your iMac is by pressing Control+Command+ the power button. If that doesn't work, look behind the access panel. Do you see a very small access hole — the one with the small arrow above it — between the phone jack and the Ethernet jack? This is the restart access hole. Straighten out a paper clip and insert one end it into this hole, pushing firmly (but not forcing it) until your iMac restarts. Elegant? No. Effective? Yes.

SHORTCUT

Unplugging your iMac when it has a problem is *not* a shortcut, as it can cause even more problems.

Surviving a Freeze or a Crash

Inevitably, your iMac will freeze or crash. It happens to all of us — usually more often than we like. If you're new to the concept of a freeze or crash, let me explain: A *freeze* occurs when everything on your iMac comes to a complete standstill. Your mouse might move, or it might appear to be inoperative, but it can't select anything. A *crash,* on the other hand, is when your iMac has the decency to announce that something has gone wrong. It may inform you that an application has unexpectedly quit or simply that a system error has occurred. Rarely are either of these problems fatal — you usually can recover quickly and get right back to work. You may lose whatever you were working on, however (you did save your work recently, right?)

If you encounter a freeze or a crash, try this: press Option+Command+Esc (the key in upper-left corner of your keyboard), all at the same time. A dialog box should pop up asking you if you want to force quit the application. You could click the Cancel button, but it probably won't matter at this point. Go ahead and click the Force Quit button. About half the time, the application actually quits and dumps you back to the Finder. If this happens, I recommend you swiftly save any work that is open in other applications, quit those applications, and then restart your iMac. Why? Because a force quit action, as this technique is called, generally leaves your iMac's resources precariously hanging, and you're more likely to freeze or crash again.

If a force quit isn't successful, you'll need to be more forceful and restart your iMac. Alas, a restart will mean losing any unsaved work, but at least you can get your iMac up and running and quickly return to work. To restart your iMac without access to the Special menu, try one of these three techniques (in this order): First, press the power button on your keyboard. If you're

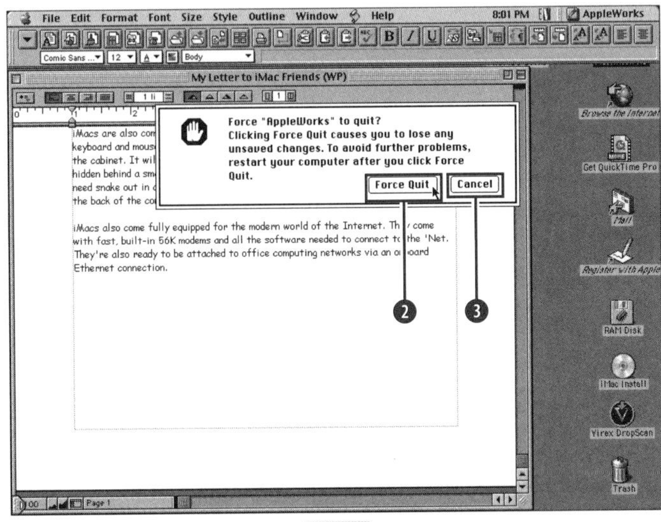

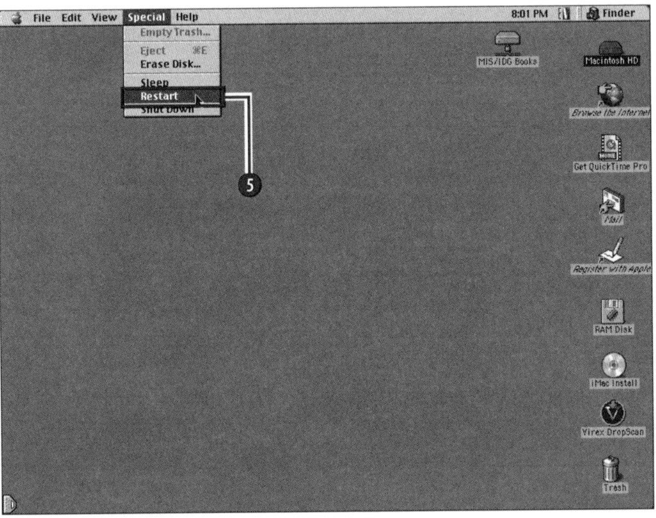

1. If your iMac freezes, press the Option+Command+Esc keys.
   - ▶ The force quit dialog box appears.
2. Click the Force Quit button.
3. Alternatively, click the Cancel button.
4. Save your work in any open applications and exit them.
5. Restart your iMac.

CROSS-REFERENCE

If you should you need to disable the self-diagnosis, see Chapter 14 on setting your General Controls.

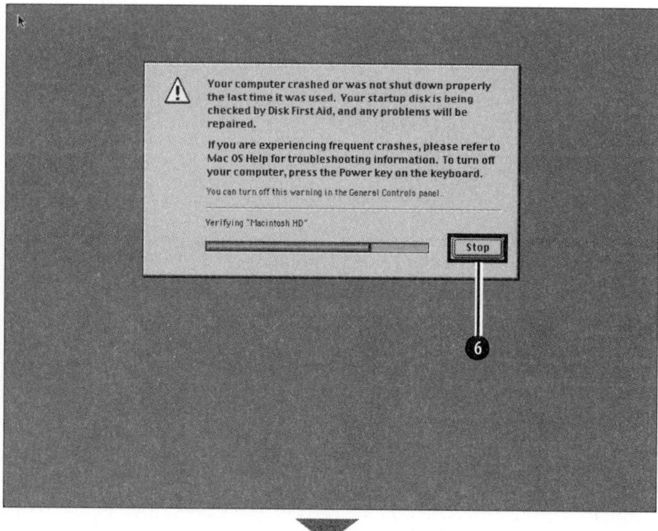

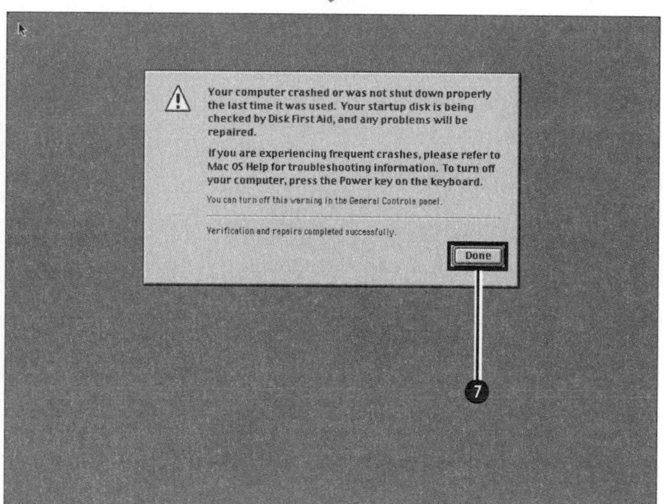

- *Your iMac automatically checks your hard drive when it restarts.*

6 *Optional: Click the Stop button if you need to start up quickly for some reason.*

7 *Click the Done button to continue when the check is complete.*

lucky, you'll get the dialog box asking if you want to restart, sleep, cancel, or shut down — click the Restart button. Second, try pressing Control+Command+ the power button on your keyboard. This is known as the *three-finger salute,* and it should restart your iMac. If that doesn't work, get out that paper clip and insert it into the restart access hole as described previously.

TAKE NOTE

SELF-DIAGNOSING AND SELF-REPAIRING

If you were unable to restart your iMac the normal way, your iMac automatically performs a self-diagnosis routine the next time it powers up (unless you disabled this option in your General Controls control panel). A large dialog box appears, offering an explanation of what's going on and displaying a progress bar. If any problems are detected, the iMac repairs them. Once the process is complete, you'll need to click the Done button to continue restarting your iMac. If you don't click the Done button, the iMac assumes you want to continue anyway after a few minutes and clicks it for you (so it's okay to go get a cup of coffee).

FIND IT ONLINE

Visit **http://www.zplace.com/crashtips/** for mounds of information on surviving crashes.

Finding a Lost File or Application

You finally worked up the motivation to send your Aunt Betty a letter. You power up your iMac and look for the letter you wrote to Aunt Ann last week — you figure you can make a few changes and effectively recycle it. You look in your Documents folder. No luck. You look in a few other likely places. The letter isn't there either. What do you do now?

Enter Sherlock, your iMac's trusty searching assistant. If you can't find it, Sherlock probably can. Open Sherlock, click the Find File tab (if it isn't already displayed), and type in the filename you think you may have used. For example, if your letter was to Aunt Ann, it seems likely your filename has "Ann" in it somewhere. Click the Find button. If that produces too many results (you may find files with names like annual report or scanner), click the More Choices button at the bottom. Choose the date modified option from the second drop-down menu on the left, choose the is after option from the drop-down menu beside it, and then type a date from the previous week. Click the Find button again. This time, you should find all files with "Ann" in them that were modified in the past week. If that doesn't produce any results, try removing "Ann" from the top field (just select it and press the Delete key) and the search again. This time, you'll find all the files you modified in the last week. Your file is bound to be in that list somewhere — probably with a name you wouldn't expect.

If Sherlock doesn't turn up your missing file, try opening the application itself and looking near the bottom of the File menu. Some applications list recent documents there, and you may find your missing file in the list. Alternatively, choose Open from the File menu and see where it takes you — it might open to the folder you saved your last document in (if you've set your General Controls to do so).

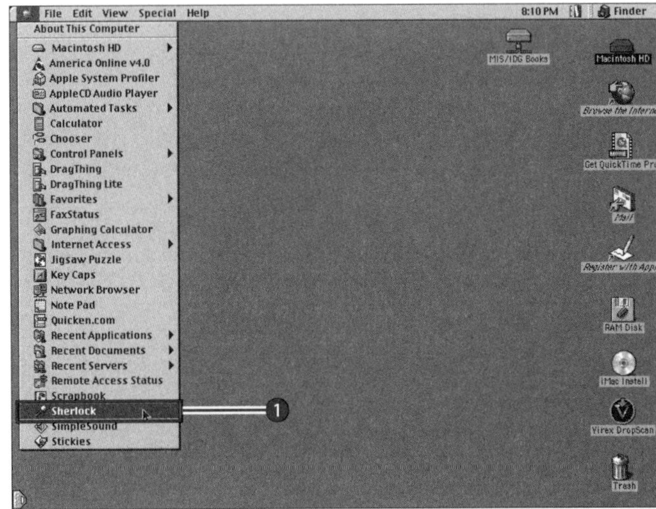

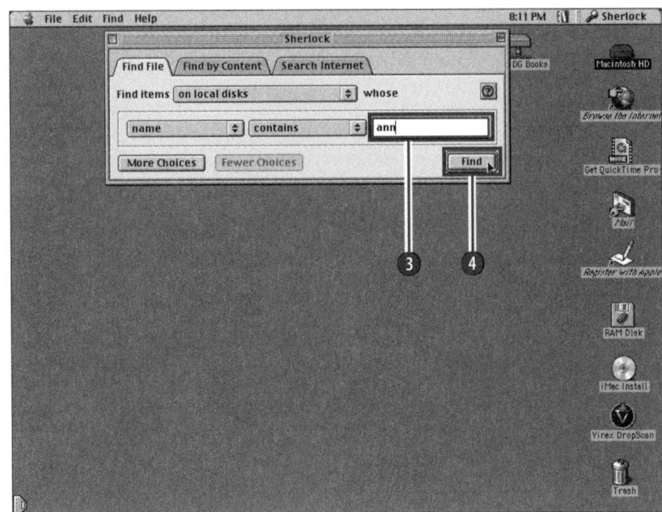

❶ *Choose Sherlock from the Apple menu.*

❷ *Alternatively, press Command+F.*

❸ *Type in a search word.*

❹ *Click the Find button.*

CROSS-REFERENCE

See "Finding Files" in Chapter 2 for more details on using Sherlock.

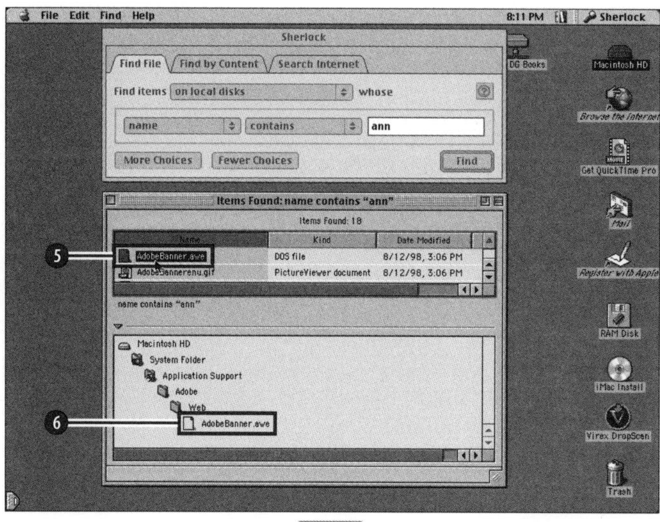

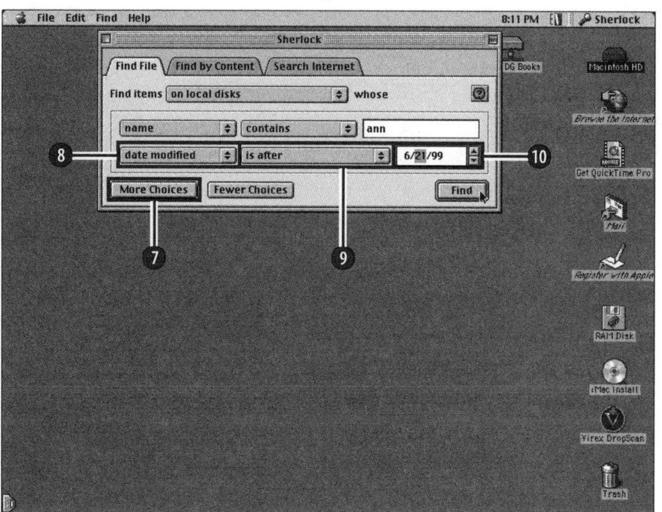

- *Check your search results.*
- ❺ *If you find a likely file, click a result for the location of the file.*
- ❻ *Optional: Double-click the file to open it.*
- ❼ *If you didn't find your file, click the More Choices button.*
- ❽ *Choose Date Modified.*
- ❾ *Choose the is after option.*
- ❿ *Select a date in the past, and then click the Find button again.*

TAKE NOTE

FINDING MISSING APPLICATIONS

If you double-click a file and a dialog box tells you the application could not be found, here's what to do. First, find out what application created the file in question by selecting its icon and pressing Command+I (check the Kind field). If you know you have this application, try opening the document from within the application. If the application itself won't open, it may be damaged — try reinstalling it. If you aren't sure if you have the file's application, use Sherlock to look for it on your hard drive. If you don't have the application that created the file, you can try to open it from within a similar application. As a last resort, try rebuilding your desktop (see "Speeding Up a Slowdown," later in this chapter, for details).

USING FILE EXCHANGE

File Exchange is a control panel that gives you the capability of opening PC documents on your iMac. You also can use it to automatically translate files created by applications you don't have into files readable by applications you do have. Click the ? button for more details.

SHORTCUT

Remember to use Command+F to quickly bring up Sherlock.

Fixing a Printing Problem

Let's assume you found that letter you wrote to Aunt Ann last week. You changed a few things here and there and readdressed it to Aunt Betty. Now you're ready to print it (Aunt Betty doesn't have e-mail — yet!) and mail it. Yet, when you attempt to print, nothing happens. Or, if it does, it doesn't behave as expected.

If your iMac tells you that your printer could not be opened (or found), first make sure that your printer is turned on and that it is properly connected to your iMac. (Don't feel bad if it wasn't — I've made that mistake a lot!) If that wasn't the problem, be sure that you have selected your printer in the Chooser. If you're using a laser printer, or you have your inkjet printer connected via a network, be sure that AppleTalk is turned on and that your network is functioning. You might need to turn your network hub or bridge on and then off again, which usually means unplugging and replugging its power cord.

If you successfully send a file to the printer but nothing happens, make sure you haven't paused or stopped printing. To check this, double-click the printer icon on your Desktop, pull down the Printing menu, and verify that there is a checkmark next to Start Print Queue. If it isn't there, choose Start Print Queue to enable it. If you don't have a printer icon on your Desktop, look under the Applications menu for a PrintMonitor application (or something similar). Confirm that printing is enabled in your PrintMonitor and that data is being sent to your printer. Sometimes a document takes a while to send to your printer, and you simply need to give it some more time. Long files, or those with complex graphics, can take five or more minutes.

If nothing else works, zap your PRAM. I explain this in the task in "Speeding up a Slowdown."

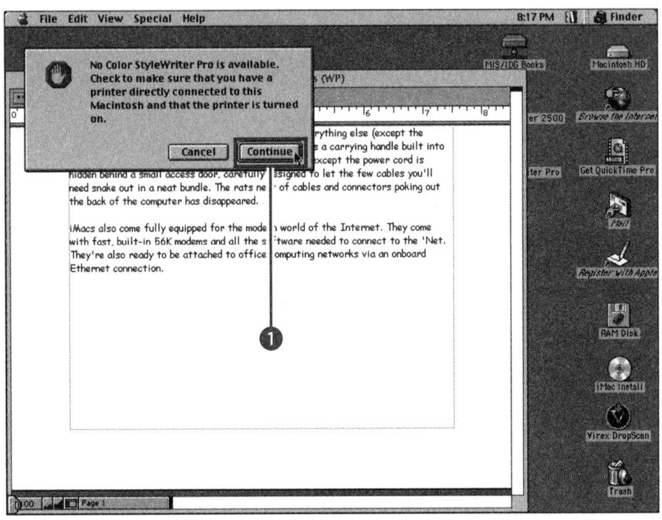

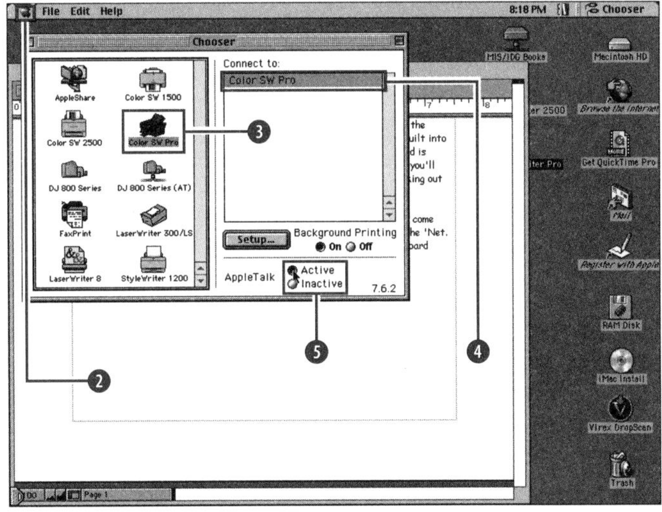

1. If you receive a printing error, try to print again by clicking the Continue button.
2. If printing is still unsuccessful, open the Chooser.
3. Select your printer icon.
4. Select your printer name.
5. Click the Active radio button if AppleTalk isn't already active.

CROSS-REFERENCE

See Chapter 6 for more details on printing.

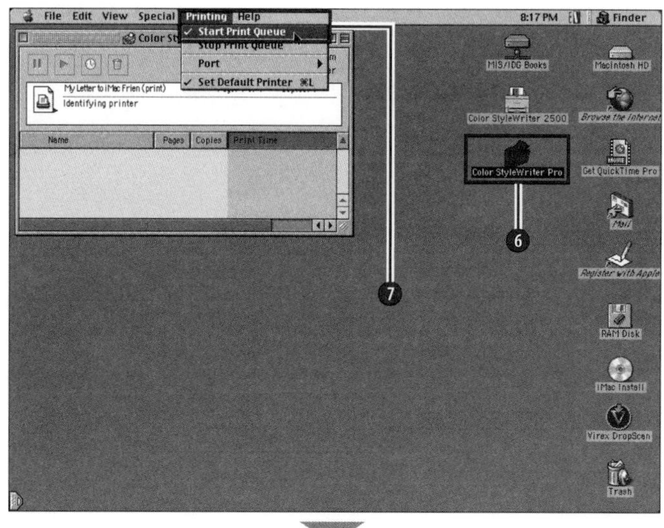

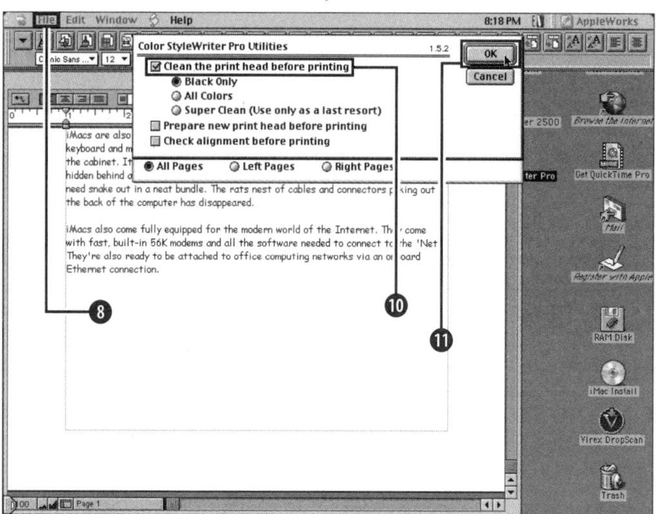

6. *If printing is still unsuccessful, double-click your desktop printer icon.*
7. *Choose Start Print Queue from the Printing menu (if it is not already selected).*
8. *If pages come out blank on your inkjet printer, choose Print.*
9. *Click the Utilities button or the Options button in the Print window.*
10. *Select the option Clean the print head before printing.*
11. *Click the OK button.*

TAKE NOTE

GETTING POSTSCRIPT ERRORS

Sometimes your iMac may report that a file could not be printed due to PostScript errors. This may happen fairly frequently on a laser printer. You may have the option to try printing again (it can't hurt), but chances are, you will need to cancel the print job and try again. Before you send your document to the printer again, turn your printer off and on again, wait a few minutes, and then try another print. If printing is still unsuccessful, try turning off background printing. If all else fails, you may need to update your printer driver software or even your printer.

PRINTING BLANK PAGES

If your printer outputs blank pages, it may be low or empty on toner or ink. Check your cartridge and replace if it necessary. Alternatively, you may need to clean your inkjet nozzles (look for a function to do this under the Options or Service buttons in the Print dialog box). Also consider that you may need to update your printer drivers to work with your iMac (the Epson color inkjet printer is a good example).

FIND IT ONLINE

Visit **http://www.epson.com** if you're experiencing problems with an Epson color printer.

Clearing Your Desktop

Is your iMac Desktop becoming as cluttered as your real desktop? If yours looks anything like mine, you probably have icons everywhere! I'm notorious for saving files on my Desktop when I'm in a hurry. Over time, my icons can entirely cover my Desktop and even begin to overlap. Terrible, isn't it? If you also suffer from iconitis, or if you just want things a bit tidier on your Desktop, read on!

The best solution for an untidy Desktop is to save your files in folders. It pays to take a few minutes and create folders for the types of files you generate or collect, sweep your existing files into them, and save files to them in the future. It takes a bit of discipline, but it really makes a difference in the long run. This is my preferred method of file management when I have the luxury of time to be organized.

If you can't resist saving items to your Desktop, make it a point to do a weekly Desktop cleaning. If this isn't possible, you may find it helpful to at least drag your Desktop items (though not your hard drive icon, trash icon, or printer icons) to a new, dated folder. This will clean off your desktop, though it may make finding files difficult. You could write an AppleScript to clean off your Desktop on a daily or weekly basis, if you're really pressed for time.

If you enjoy having files at your fingertips on your Desktop, but hate having them scattered about, consider using the Launcher to organize them. You could even use your Apple Menu to store aliases to frequently used files and keep them close at hand. Another option is to set your Desktop View Options to Always snap to grid or Keep arranged by and select by Name, by Date, and so forth.

If you simply must keep all those files on your Desktop and your icons are overlapping, you can do two things. Reduce your icon size (in View Options under the View menu) or increase your monitor resolution (in the Monitors & Sound control panel). If you do both, you may need to get yourself a magnifying glass!

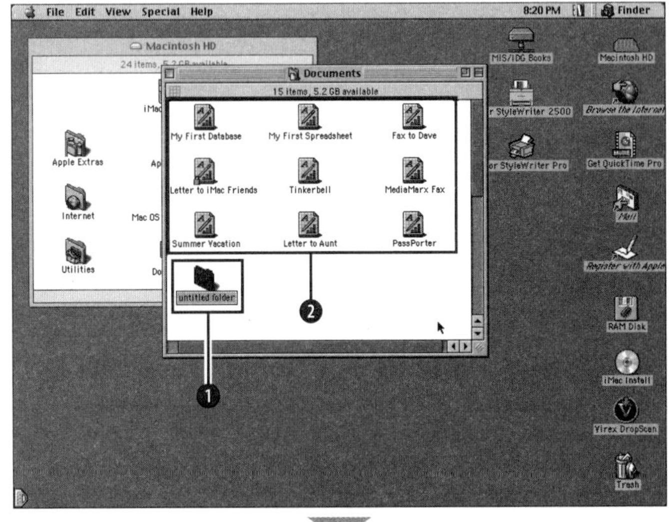

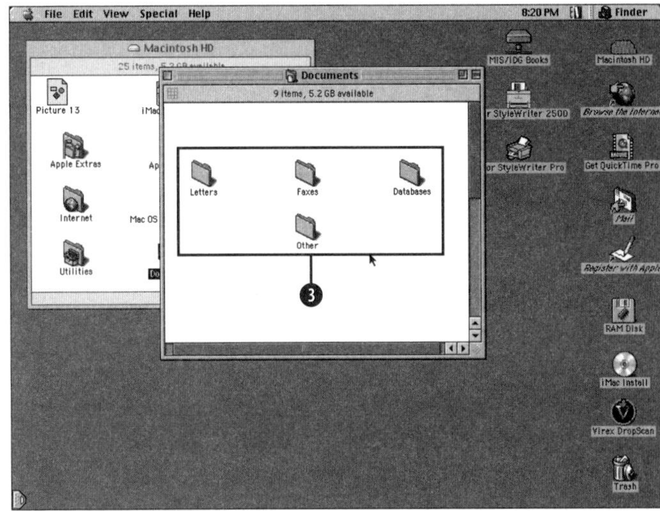

1. *Locate several unorganized files in a folder on your Desktop.*
2. *Create a new folder and give it a descriptive name.*
3. *Create several more folders, also with descriptive names.*
4. *Move your files into the folders as appropriate.*

CROSS-REFERENCE

See Chapter 13 to learn how to unlock a file.

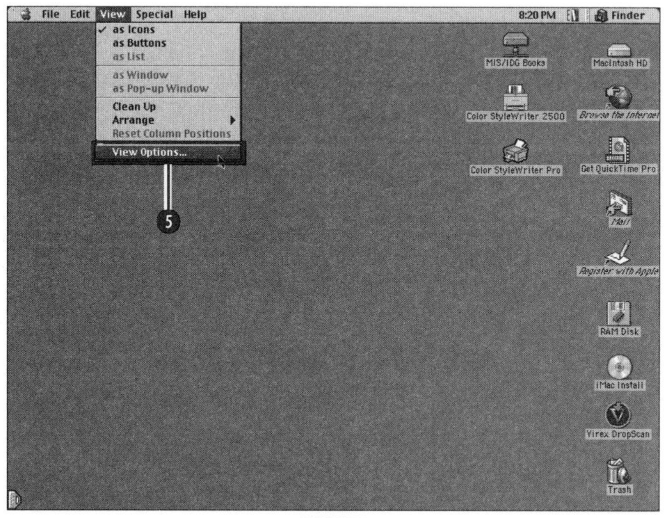

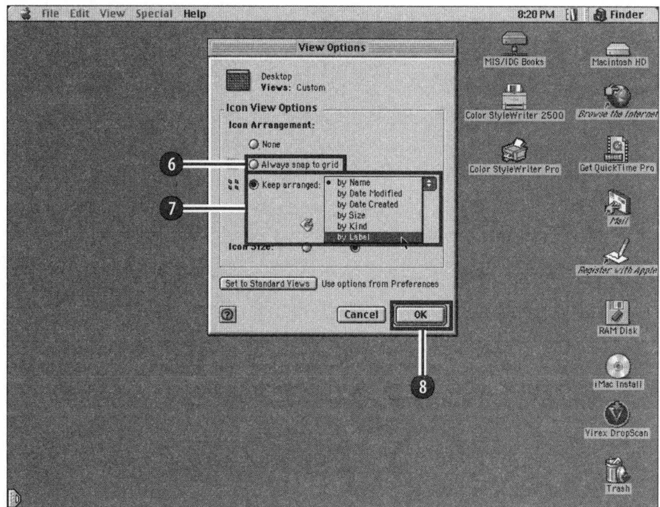

5. *To arrange your Desktop icons neatly, choose Options from the View menu.*
6. *Select Always snap to grid.*
7. *Alternatively, select Keep arranged and choose a sort order.*
8. *Click the OK button.*

TAKE NOTE

RENAMING FILES

If you can't rename a file, you (or someone else) may have locked it. Remember that all files on CD-ROM discs are locked and cannot be unlocked.

VIEWING ICONS

If your icons show up as default icons that look like blank sheets of paper, you'll need to rebuild your Desktop to set them right. See the next task for assistance.

RESETTING CLOCKS

If your iMac's date is wrong, verify it is set correctly in your Date & Time control panel. If your clock won't stay set (and insists on it being 1904), your clock battery may be dead (they last around 2 to 3 years). Call your local dealer and have them replace it.

SHORTCUT

You can select every item on your Desktop by pressing Command+A.

Speeding Up a Slowdown

It is a truth universally acknowledged that an iMac in possession of a large hard disk will eventually slow down, especially if your hard disk is filled with copies of novels by Jane Austen. Seriously though, your iMac is bound to slow down sooner or later. You don't need to let that slow you down, however.

If your iMac slows down suddenly, you may be on the verge of a crash or freeze. Examples of such a slow down include a sluggish or jerky mouse, the sound of your hard drive or CD-ROM chugging away for longer than seems necessary, or everything stopping until you click your mouse (when everything lurches forward again). If you notice any of these signs, immediately save your work, quit all your applications, and restart your iMac. If you're unable to restart right now, save your work, quit as many applications as possible, and keep working. Just be sure to save your work frequently and restart as soon as possible.

If you notice a gradual slow down over the weeks and months that you use it, you can do some simple maintenance to speed it up. One option is to rebuild your desktop, which simply means to resynchronize the icons with their respective files and applications. The invisible file that keeps the Desktop organized can become unwieldy over time, causing your iMac to slow down, or to cause icon or application problems. To rebuild the Desktop file, restart your iMac (or power it up if it is off) and hold down the Option+Command keys until you're asked if you want to rebuild your desktop. Click the OK button and sit back while your iMac rebuilds it (which can take a while if you have lots of files).

Another way to potentially speed up your iMac is to optimize your hard drive. See Chapter 15 for details on how to do this. Also consider allocating more memory to an application that seems particularly sluggish, which I also discuss in Chapter 15.

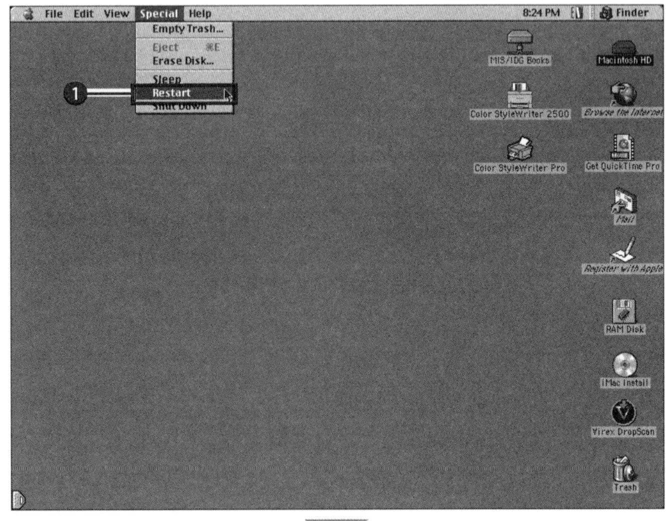

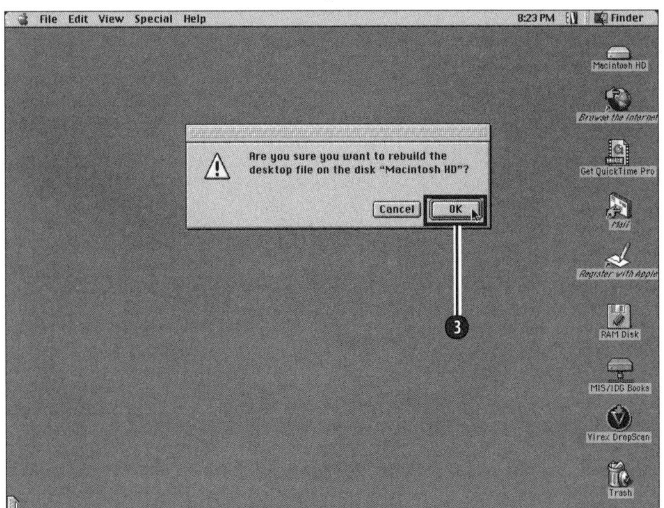

1. *To rebuild your Desktop, quit all open applications and choose Restart from the Special menu.*
2. *Hold down the Option+Command keys while your iMac starts up.*
3. *Click the OK button when you are asked if you're sure you want to rebuild the Desktop.*

CROSS-REFERENCE

Refer to Chapter 15 for more memory management tips.

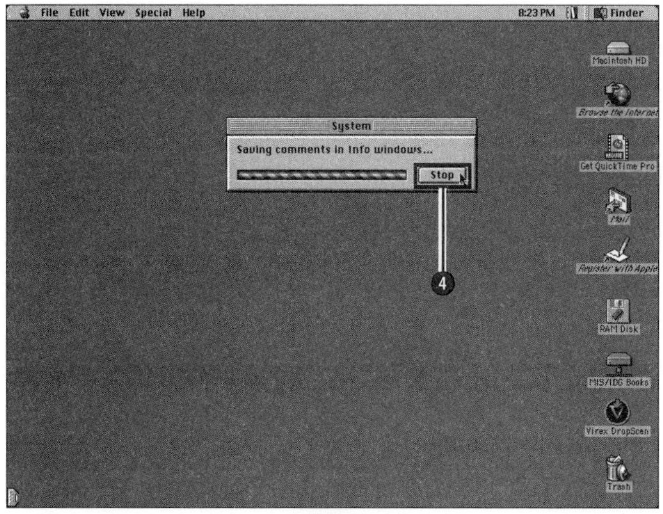

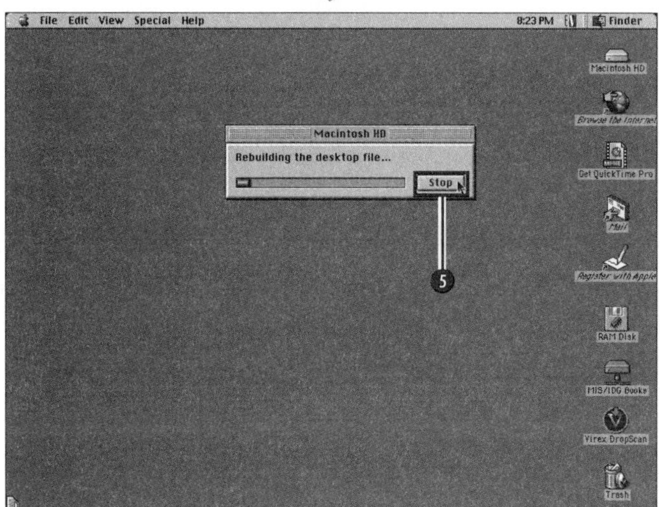

- ▶ *Any comments in Get Info windows are saved.*
- ❹ *Optional: Click the Stop button if you want to abort the process.*

- ▶ *A progress meter is displayed as your Desktop is rebuilt.*
- ❺ *Optional: Click the Stop button if you want to abort the process.*

TAKE NOTE

ZAPPING YOUR PRAM

Your PRAM (pronounced "p-ram") is a special form of memory powered by your iMac's battery — this is where the current date and time are stored. Sometimes your PRAM can get confused and cause problems with settings, printing, networking, and so on. You can reset this memory by restarting your iMac and holding down Command+Option+P+R while it starts — release the keys when you hear the second chord. You will need to reset control panels, printers, and networked computers afterward.

REINSTALLING YOUR SYSTEM

Occasionally your Mac OS gets corrupted, damaged, or confused, resulting in slower performance. If nothing else seems to speed up your iMac, consider reinstalling your system software using the Mac OS Install program on your iMac Install the CD-ROM disc into the drive, and be sure to do a Clean Install. You will also need to restore your printer drivers, fonts, settings, preferences, and so on after installation.

SHORTCUT

If your iMac is slowing down and you can't restart immediately, save your work every few minutes by pressing Command+S.

Resolving Extension Conflicts

As you may recall from our discussion in Chapter 14, extensions are those small programs that work hand-in-hand with your iMac operating system. Your iMac comes with a bunch already installed (and which are necessary to the proper functioning of your iMac). Other applications may also install them, and some are related to control panels and various other utilities. All these different extensions flying about can cause conflict, and I deliberately use the word *conflict.* Two disparate extensions can get into a knock-down, drag-out fight and crash your entire system. It's ugly.

Most extension conflicts happen on startup, when your iMac rudely announces that a system error has occurred and everything locks up. Don't panic. Instead, calmly restart your iMac using the restart techniques described in the first task in this chapter. As your iMac is starting, hold down the Shift key until you see the message Extensions Off. Your iMac should be able to continue starting up, but it won't be particularly useful — all your extensions will be disabled, which means no faxes, no e-mail, no CD-ROM discs, and so on.

At this point, you can do two things. You can figure out which extensions are conflicting using the Extensions Manager control panel to disable the offending extension, or you can purchase a program called Conflict Catcher (by Casady and Greene) which can locate the extensions that are causing problems. You can download a demo version of Conflict Catcher at **http://www.casadyg.com**, and you also can buy it online, from mail-order houses, and from computer stores.

Even if you decide to purchase Conflict Catcher, you may need to get your iMac back up and running *now.* To resolve your own extension conflicts, open Extensions Manager and turn off half of your extensions. Just click the checked boxes to clear them. Now, restart your iMac

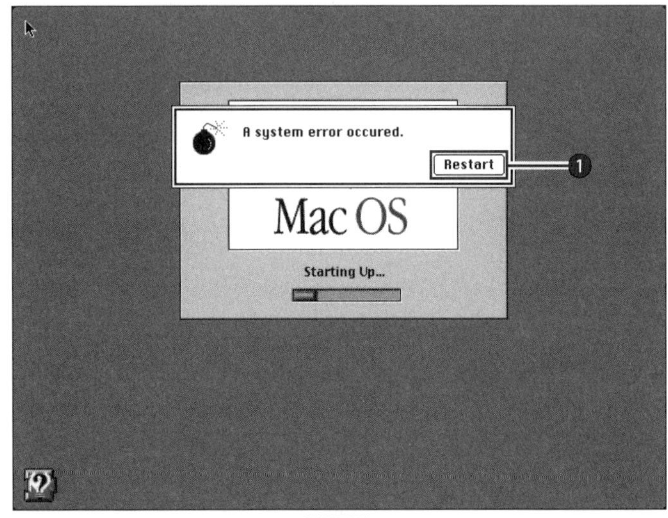

▶ *You may see this dialog box, or one like it, during an extension conflict at startup.*

❶ *Select Restart from the Special menu, and then hold down the Shift key as you start up.*

❷ *Release the Shift key when you see this message.*

CROSS-REFERENCE

See Chapter 3 for more details on installing applications.

Resolving the Williams Sonoma Error

Did you install the Williams-Sonoma Guide to Good Cooking, only to get a system error? In fact, the conflict is between the Williams-Sonoma Guide and file sharing. The solution is to turn off file sharing when you want to use the Williams-Sonoma Guide. Alas, Extensions Manager isn't what led me to the answer. Instead, the solution was unearthed on the Broderbund Web site (**http://support.broderbund.com**). Checking a product's Web site, if available, is always a good idea if you get stuck!

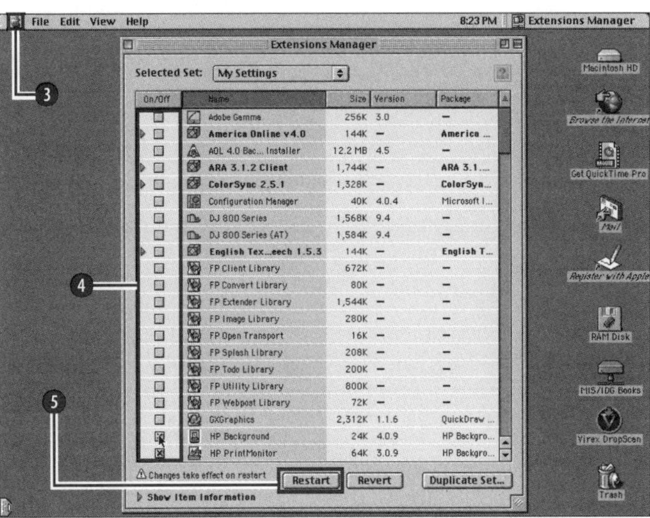

3 *Open your Extensions Manager.*

4 *Disable about half of your extensions.*

5 *Restart your iMac.*

6 *Continue doing this until you discover the problem extension.*

normally. If everything goes smoothly, you know that your problem resides with at least one of the extensions you turned off. If it doesn't, turn off some more extensions and restart again. Return to your Extensions Manager and turn half of those you turned off back on again, and restart again. Keep doing this until you hone in on your problem extension. Keep in mind that your problem may be between two extensions, but at least you'll find one of the problem extensions this way and can then repeat the procedure to find the second one.

Once you find the conflicting extensions, turn off the one you don't need. Now save your extension set.

TAKE NOTE

UNINSTALLING APPLICATIONS

An extension conflict often occurs immediately after you've installed a new application or utility. Thus, you could try uninstalling it to see if it also uninstalls the problem extension. If that doesn't work, open your Extensions Manager and click the Package column label to sort the extensions by their related applications. Now look for extensions related to an application you recently installed. One of these may be your culprit.

SHORTCUT

Hold down the spacebar while powering up the iMac to open Extensions Manager.

Finding More Help

As much as I'd like to, I can't possibly cover all the problems you may encounter during your iMac career. There are simply too many variables. More to the point, your world (and thus your iMac's environment) is changing and evolving daily. I can't foresee the applications you'll install on your iMac which, at the moment, are nothing more than a gleam in their programmer's eye. Besides, the likelihood that you'd encounter even 10 percent of all the possible problems is very slim. Instead, it makes the most sense to point you in the direction of more help. And help is bountiful!

First, your purchase of an iMac entitles you to 90 days of free technical support from Apple. It begins on the date of your computer purchase. Phone numbers and additional Apple support options are available on the Apple Service and Support Guide that came with your iMac.

I've hinted throughout the book about Apple's Web site (at **http://www.apple.com**). This isn't your typical glossy company brochure-style Web site. You can find software updates, an extensive technical information library, peer-to-peer assistance, and lots of articles and tips for making the most of your iMac. Visit it often.

Apple isn't the only source of iMac help on the Web. Virtually every application and utility has some form of technical support (or at least information) on the Web. If you don't know the company's name, search for the product name in Sherlock's Internet search feature.

In addition to company sites, hundreds of Mac sites created and maintained by fans offer some of the best guru-style help around. To find a good list of them, try searching for iMac at **http://www.yahoo.com/**. I also recommend **http://www.macfixit.com/** for wonderful peer assistance.

You are also welcome to ask me! While I may not always know the answer to your problem, I may have some ideas about where you can look! I would enjoy

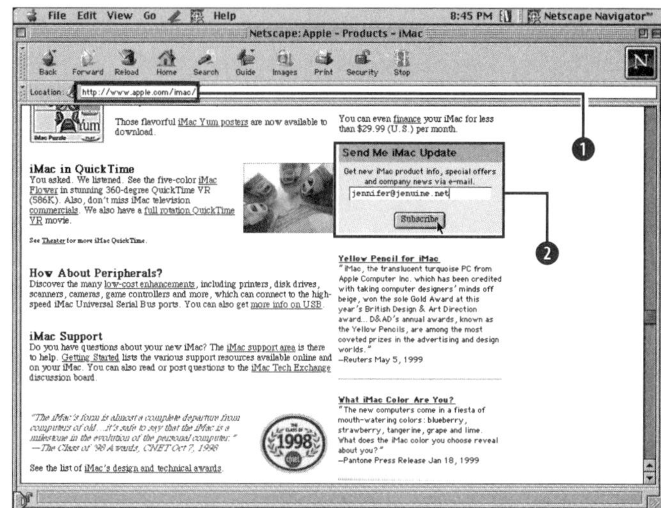

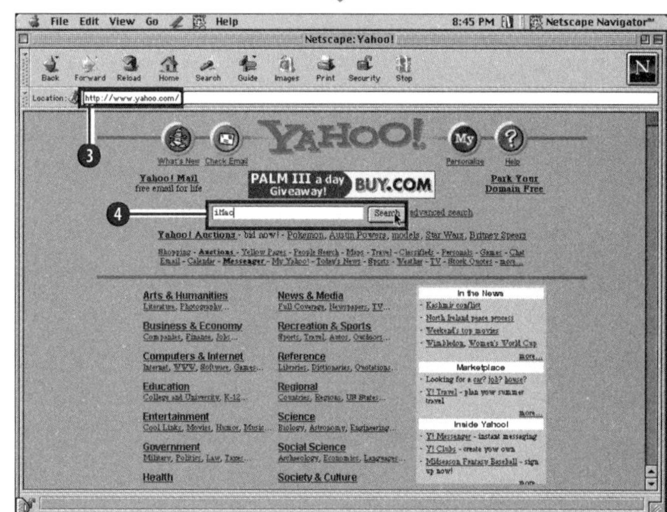

❶ *Sign on to the Internet, and point your Web browser to **http://www.apple.com/imac**.*

❷ *Sign up for the iMac update, if you want.*

❸ *Point your browser to **http://www.yahoo.com**.*

❹ *Type iMac and click the Search button.*

CROSS-REFERENCE

Review Chapter 11 to access the Internet, which is your richest source of iMac help.

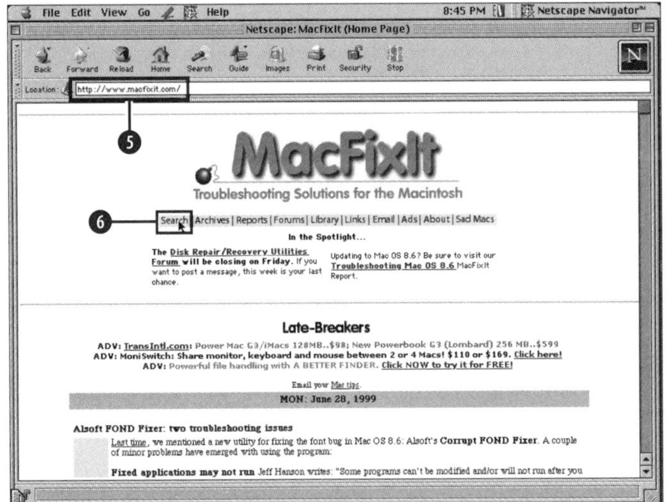

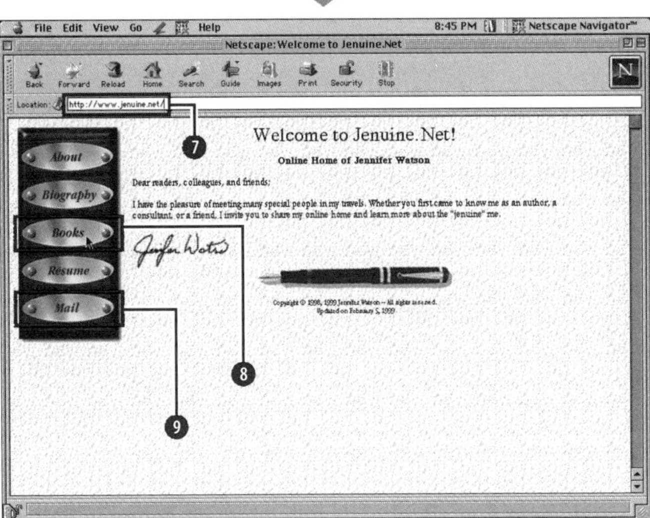

5 *Point your browser to* ***http://www.macfixit.com****.*

6 *Click the Search button.*

7 *Point your browser to* ***http://www.jenuine.net****.*

8 *Click Books to learn more about this book and others.*

9 *Click the Mail hyperlink to send me e-mail.*

meeting you, either way. Send me e-mail at jennifer@jenuine.net and visit me at **http://www.jenuine.net/**. You don't need to have a problem to e-mail me, either! I love hearing from my readers!

TAKE NOTE

BUY A BOOK

While this book is pretty darned good (in my humble opinion, of course), it is only intended to give you an introduction to your iMac. Many other wonderful books are available on specific applications and tasks you may want to explore further.

JOIN A USER GROUP

Mac users are a particularly loyal bunch and like to band together in what are known as *user groups.* Not only are they are great way to meet people who love their iMac as much as you do, but they can be incredible sources of help. I found them invaluable during my early Mac years. Most large communities have a Mac user group. Call 800-538-9696 to find one near you.

SHORTCUT

Don't' forget your onboard help, which is virtually always accessible by pressing Command+?.

Personal Workbook

Q&A

1. How do you restart your iMac if you can't choose Restart from the Special menu?

2. How do your force quit your iMac?

3. If you can't locate a file, what keyboard shortcut can you use to search for it on your hard drive?

4. If your iMac complains that it cannot open or find your printer, what should you do?

5. How do you set your Desktop to display all its icons in neat rows and columns?

6. If all your icons now look like blank sheets of paper, how do you restore them to normal?

7. What are two ways to resolve extension conflicts?

8. What is Apple's Web site address?

ANSWERS: PAGE 326

Troubleshooting Your iMac

CHAPTER 17

EXTRA PRACTICE

1. Visit Apple's Web site (**http://www.apple.com**) and get familiar with all the kinds of help available there.
2. Search your home (or office) for all the literature and CD-ROMs that came with your iMac, along with the installation discs for your application programs. Keep them all together, in a safe place.
3. It's time to clean up your Desktop. Put stray files in appropriate folders, remove seldom-used aliases, and rebuild the Desktop.
4. Do a safety inspection. Make sure all external wires and cables are securely connected, that they aren't stretched tightly, and that they aren't routed where they can be tripped over. Consider obtaining a surge protector if you don't already have one.

REAL-WORLD APPLICATIONS

✔ While using your iMac to type up a travel report on your business trip, it begins to slow down. Sensing that a crash is near, you save your report. Two minutes later, your iMac freezes. You press Option+Command+Esc to force quit. You then save the spreadsheet you were creating in another application, quit that application, and restart your iMac.

✔ You power up your iMac the next day and the same system error returns. A simple restart makes no improvement. You restart again, this time holding down the Shift key while restarting. Your iMac successfully powers up without extensions. You use Extensions Manager to track down the offending extension and disable it.

Visual Quiz

What does this dialog box signify?

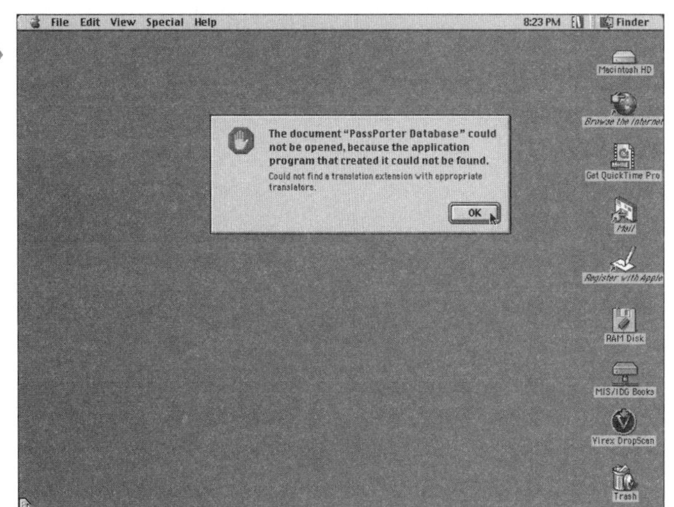

Personal Workbook Answers

Chapter 1

See page 5

1. **What can a surge protector do for you?**

A: Protect your iMac from most power surges caused by lightning storms and brownouts. A surge protector also may provide similar protection for your phone lines. Additionally, a surge protector may act as an extension cord if your wall outlet is more than several feet from your iMac.

2. **Where do the cables go when you close the access door?**

A: Contrary to popular belief, your cables snake out through the two bottom corner cutouts of your access panel door. They do not thread through the round hole, which is intended as a door pull.

3. **What is the Finder and what is another term for it?**

A: The Finder is your home base on the iMac. Another term for Finder is Desktop.

4. **What does a gray menu item indicate?**

A: A menu item in gray is an indication that it is not available (it cannot be selected or chosen).

5. **What are the two ways to open (activate) an icon on the Desktop?**

A: Select the icon with your pointer (click once) and choose Open from the File menu (or press Command+O). Another way is to double-click the icon. Alternatively, you can press Control while clicking an icon, and then select Open from the drop-down contextual menu which appears.

6. **What are submenus, how do you use them, and how do you enable or disable them?**

A: Submenus are nested, hierarchical menus found in the Apple menu and in applications that offer additional options. You can enable and disable those that appear in your Apple Menu Options control panel.

7. **What is the difference between collapsing a window and closing it?**

A: Collapsing a window only minimizes it on your screen; the titlebar remains. Closing a window dismisses it completely.

8. **What are the two proper ways to shut down your iMac?**

A: Choose Shut Down from the Special menu. Alternatively, press the Power button on your keyboard and click the Shut Down button (or press Return).

Personal Workbook Answers

Visual Quiz

Q: What is missing from this Apple menu? How would you get it back?

A: The submenus are missing. To restore your submenus, choose Control Panels from the Apple menu, double-click the Apple Menu Options in the Control Panels window, click the On radio button under Submenus, and close the Apple Menu Options window.

Chapter 2

See page 29

1 What is the Application menu and how does it work?

A: The Application menu is at the far right of your menu bar and lists all open applications. Choose an application to switch to it. A check mark next to an application indicates the active program. If no applications are open, only the Finder (Desktop) is listed.

2 How do you view the items in a window as a list?

A: Open the window and select as List from the View menu.

3 How do you change the name of a folder?

A: Click the name of the folder once. The folder's name is highlighted, indicating that you can start typing a new name. When you are done typing, click an empty space on the Desktop once and the highlight will disappear, indicating that the name has been changed.

4 How do you move a file from one folder to another?

A: Click and drag the file's icon directly into the new folder's window (find an empty spot) and release the mouse button. If the new folder isn't open, click and drag the file's icon directly on top of the icon representing the folder; when the folder icon darkens (highlights), let go of the mouse button.

5 How do you copy a file or folder without selecting Duplicate from the File menu?

A: Hold down the Option key, press and drag the file or folder icon to a blank spot on the Desktop or in its window, and release the mouse button. A copy is automatically created in the exact spot where you released the mouse button (unless you have your icons set to Snap to Grid view).

6 How can you tell the difference between an alias and an original?

A: The alias's icon includes a small arrow in its lower-left corner and the alias's title appears in italics. The alias's title may also include the word alias, but it can be renamed to eliminate that word.

7 How do you remove an item from the Trash?

A: Double-click the Trash icon to open the Trash window and click and drag the item to another folder or the Desktop, or choose Put Away from the File menu (Command+Y) to return it to the location from which it was located before being sent to the Trash.

8 How do you find a file on your hard drive without opening a single folder?

A: Use Sherlock to search for the file. Sherlock is a utility found in the Apple menu.

Visual Quiz

Q: What kind of menu is this, and how do you access it?

A: This is a Contextual menu. Hold down the Control key, click on the desired item on the Desktop, and then release the Control key.

Chapter 3

See page 51

1 What is the difference between a hard drive and RAM?

A: A hard drive provides long-term storage. It is a mechanical device that stores data on a magnetically-coated platter. Information on a hard drive is preserved if the power is turned off. RAM is short-term memory. It is at least 10 times faster than a hard drive, and 60 times more expensive for an equivalent amount of hard disk space. Information in RAM is lost if the power fails or the computer crashes.

2 How many bytes is a kilobyte? A megabyte? A gigabyte?

A: There are 1,024 bytes in a kilobyte, 1,048,576 bytes in a megabyte, and 1,073,741,824 bytes in a gigabyte.

3 How do you determine the size of a file or folder?

A: Select the item in question and press Command+I to access the Get Info window. Alternatively, you can hold down the Control key while clicking an item, and then choose Get Info from the drop-down menu that appears. Another option is to change the view of the item's folder to as List under the Views menu, and then choose View Options and enable the Calculate Folder Size option.

4 How do you mount a CD-ROM disc? How do you dismount it?

A: To mount the disc on a newer iMac, insert the disc into the slot and gently push it in until it is flush with the slot. On an older iMac, open the CD-ROM tray, place the disc in the tray and press down until it clicks in place, and then gently push the tray back into the computer. The disc's icon will appear on the Desktop. To dismount the disc, close all open files and programs that are associated with the disc, and then click and drag the disc's icon to the Trash. Alternatively, you can select Eject from the Special menu or Put Away from the File menu.

5 How do you play a music CD on your iMac?

A: Open the CD-ROM drawer and insert the CD the same way you do an application CD-ROM. Your iMac automatically recognizes the disc as an audio CD (unless you've disabled AutoPlay settings in the QuickTime Settings control panel) and begins playing the disc. Double-click the CD's icon to view the track list. Double-click an item in the track list to open the Audio Player, which contains controls like play, stop, pause, fast forward, and reverse.

6 How do you tell your iMac where you want it to install a new piece of software?

A: The main Installer window — where you actually click the Install button — allows you to choose a location for your new software to be installed. You can use either the hard drive drop-down menu or the Switch Disk button. To choose a specific folder on the hard drive (strongly recommended), choose Select Folder from the drop-down menu, select a folder in the dialog box, and then click the Select button.

7 What is the best way to remove installed software from your iMac?

A: Open the application's folder (on its CD-ROM disc or on your hard drive) and run the Installer. Look for a remove or uninstall feature.

8 What is the difference between a CD-ROM disc and a removable media disk?

A: You can write (record) data to a removable media disk, as well as read data from it. CD-ROMs are read-only.

Visual Quiz

Q: What does this dialog box mean and why would you see it?

A: You tried to copy something to a locked volume.

Personal Workbook Answers

Chapter 4

See page 65

1. **How do you open a document file?**

A: Double-click the file's icon, or its alias, or use the Open command in the File menu of the active application or the Finder or the contextual menu.

2. **What is the difference between the Caps Lock key and the Shift key?**

A: The Caps Lock key turns all letters you type into capital letters, but does not affect the numbers and punctuation marks. The key has a light to indicate when the Caps Lock is active. Once active, it remains active until the next time you press the key. The Shift key will capitalize all letters and produce punctuation marks as well, but only when the Shift key is pressed.

3. **What is an I-beam and what is its significance?**

A: The mouse pointer turns into the I-beam when the mouse is positioned over a document window or text entry field. It indicates that, wherever you next click, the text insertion point will be placed. The I-beam's shape makes it easy to precisely position the text insertion mark.

4. **What is the quickest way to move a block of text from one part of a document to another?**

A: Select the text, click and drag the text to the desired location, and then release the mouse button.

5. **What is the Clipboard? How do you view it?**

A: The Clipboard holds text or other data that has been selected and copied, so that the information can be pasted elsewhere. You can view the current contents of the Clipboard by selecting Show Clipboard from the Edit menu. If the application you're using doesn't have a Show Clipboard command, switch to the Finder and use the Edit menu there.

6. **What is the difference between the Delete key and the Space key?**

A: The Delete key can be used to backspace and delete one character at a time. When a block of text has been highlighted, the Delete key will erase the text. The Space key inserts a blank space between characters. If a block of text has been highlighted, the Space key will replace that text with a single blank space.

7. **What is the keyboard shortcut for Undo?**

A: Command+Z.

8. **Why is it important to save early and often?**

A: Your iMac holds all unsaved information in temporary memory (RAM), which means you could lose it in the blink of an eye. To protect your data, you must save it to store your data in permanent memory on your hard drive.

Visual Quiz

Q: Why would you see this dialog box? When would you click Cancel? When would you click Replace?

A: You see this dialog box when you try to save something with the same name as another item in the same folder. You click the Cancel button when you don't want to replace the existing item. You click the Replace button when you do want to replace the existing item.

Chapter 5

See page 87

1. **In addition to the Fonts menu, where else might you find a menu of available fonts?**

A: On an application's toolbar. Also look in Key Caps, which is found in the Apple menu.

2 How do you install a new font on your iMac?

A: To install a font, click and drag the font suitcase (or font files, if there is no font suitcase) on top of your System Folder icon. Once you release the mouse button, your iMac informs you that the item needs to be stored in the Fonts folder. Click the OK button to authorize the iMac to place it where it belongs. If you had an application program running when you did this, quit and re-open the application to make the new font available to that program.

3 What is the difference between the styles Superscript and Subscript?

A: Superscript shifts text ^{above} the line, Subscript moves text $_{\text{below}}$ the line.

4 Ideally, what is the maximum number of fonts and/or styles you should use in a single document?

A: Two fonts and two styles.

5 How do you find a specific word or phrase in a document? How do you replace it?

A: Select the Find (or Find/Replace) command from the File menu. Type the word or phrase you wish to find in the text entry box and click the Find button. To replace that word, type the new word or phrase in the Change text entry box and click the Change button to replace the original text.

6 How do you zoom in (enlarge your view) or zoom out (shrink your view)?

A: On the lower-left corner of your document window in AppleWorks, you will see two buttons: the decrease and increase scale buttons (they look like mountains). Use these buttons to expand or shrink your page view.

7 What is smart scrolling and how do you enable it on your iMac?

A: Smart scrolling places both scroll arrows at the lower end and far right edge of the scrollbars so your mouse has less distance to travel. To enable smart scrolling, go to the Apple menu, select the Control Panels submenu, and then choose the Appearance tab. Click the Options tab at the top of the resulting window and select the Smart Scrolling box.

8 Where can you find a collection of stationary template files for AppleWorks?

A: These ready-made templates are stored in the AppleWorks Stationery folder.

Visual Quiz

Q: Where would you find this file on your hard drive? What can you do with it?

A: This file is located in your Stationery folder in your AppleWorks folder. You can use it to browse and open the pre-made stationery for AppleWorks.

Chapter 6

See page 107

1 Where do you find the Chooser?

A: The Chooser can be found in the Apple menu.

2 Why is it necessary to align ink cartridges in an inkjet printer?

A: If a cartridge isn't aligned, everything you print will be offset a bit on the page. Color inkjet printers commonly have two cartridges: one with black ink, one with colored inks. If the cartridges aren't aligned, the various colors can overlap, giving everything a funky light/dark shadow or a muddy, imprecise image.

3 **What is the difference between portrait and landscape view? How does this relate to page setup?**

A: In portrait view, the page is taller than it is wide, while in landscape view, the page is wider than it is tall. The margins in your page setup should be consistent with the orientation of the paper.

4 **How do you tell your iMac that you want to print a range of pages in a document?**

A: When you execute the Print command, the Printing Options window will open. Find the option for setting the range of pages to be printed. The specific location of this setting in the software varies with the printer you're using.

5 **How do you print while previewing a page?**

A: The Print Preview window includes a Print button. You also can cancel Print Preview, and then select the Print command as you normally do.

6 **What is the keyboard shortcut to print?**

A: Command+P.

7 **How do you enable background printing?**

A: Open Chooser in the Apple menu. Select the icon for your printer from the box on the left, and then click the Background Printing radio button on the right side of the Chooser window.

8 **How do you schedule a print job for four hours from now?**

A: Send the print job to your printer in the usual manner. Double-click the printer's icon on the Desktop and select the print job you wish to schedule. Click the clock button, and then schedule the print job for the desired time.

Visual Quiz

Q: **What does this window do? How would you get to it?**

A: This window lets you configure a laser printer. You get to it by opening the Chooser, selecting a laser printer icon, selecting a laser printer name, and then clicking the Setup button.

Chapter 7

See page 127

1 **Why is it a good idea to use separate First Name and Last Name fields in a database?**

A: It is always a good idea to separate first and last names so you can properly sort the names later.

2 **What constitutes a record in a database?**

A: If you think of an old-fashioned card index file, the information you write on the card is the data, and each card is a record.

3 **How do you create a new record?**

A: Choose New Record from the Edit menu, press Command+R, or click the Create Record button on the toolbar.

4 **How do you view the information in your database as a list?**

A: To view your data in list form, select List from the Layout menu (or press Shift+Command+L).

5 **How do you increase (or decrease) the size of a column or row?**

A: Move your pointer to the line separating two column headings (or row numbers), and then click and drag to the left, right, up, or down, as appropriate.

6 **How do you format a cell in a spreadsheet so it shows a full dollar amount?**

A: Select the cell in question and choose Number from the Format menu. Select Currency from the choices on the left.

7 **How do you add two cells together in a spreadsheet?**

A: Select the cell where you would like to display the results. Choose Paste Function from the Edit menu, select SUM(number1, number2,...) from the list, click the OK button, and then select and delete everything in between the parentheses in the formula displayed in the formula entry field at the top of the screen. (You also can type =SUM() in the entry field and press the left-arrow key once.) Now, with your insertion point between the two parentheses in your formula, click the first cell you want to add to your formula, click the second cell, and then press the Enter key.

8 **What symbol do you type first when creating your own formula?**

A: Type an equal (=) sign.

Visual Quiz

Q: Where would you see this window? What is its purpose?

A: You would see this window when you create fields in a database, and then click the Options button. The Options window lets you require information for a given field, as well as set information to be added automatically to that field.

Chapter 8

See page 143

1 **How do you recognize an application program on your iMac?**

A: You can tell if a file is an application program by selecting its icon and pressing Command+I. The Get Info window displays the kind of file near the top of the window.

2 **Where can you find the CD-ROM installation discs that came with your iMac?**

A: You can find the installation discs in the iMac CD-ROM wallet that came packaged with your iMac accessory kit.

3 **What is the keyboard shortcut to quit a running application?**

A: Command+Q.

4 **How do you close an open file window without quitting the application?**

A: To close an open file without quitting the application altogether, choose Close from the File menu. You also can click the close box in the upper-right corner of the window, or type Command+W.

5 **Under what menus are you likely to find the Preferences command in an application?**

A: The most likely places to find an application's preferences are under the File, Edit, Tools, or Help.

6 **How do you expand or collapse the application menu's heading?**

A: To expand or collapse the heading of the application menu, click and drag the dotted bar to the left of it.

Personal Workbook Answers

7 What is the keyboard shortcut to cycle through open applications?

A: Press Command+Tab to cycle through each open application until you reach the one you want.

8 Where would you look for an instruction manual?

A: Most applications come with a Read Me file, which you should always read. Look for a separate instruction manual file either in the application's folder, within the application itself, or on the application's CD. You might find a printed manual in the packaging the application came in. Explore the Help menu inside the application, and look under the Apple menu for an About command, too.

Visual Quiz

Q: How do you get this window and what can you do there?

A: You choose About Quicken from the Apple menu. You can read a tip and learn more about the tip.

Chapter 9

See page 161

1 How do you adjust the volume of only your system alerts?

A: Click the Alerts button at the top of the Monitors & Sounds (or Sound) control panel and adjust the slider control.

2 How do you set an audio CD to endlessly play or loop?

A: Open the AppleCD Audio Player. Click the arrow button next to the Prog (Program) button and it changes to a looped arrow.

3 Where are your iMac's headphone jacks? How many are there?

A: The headphone jacks are on the front of the computer. There are two jacks.

4 How do you turn on your iMac's soundtrack?

A: Pull down the Apple Menu and choose Appearance from the Control Panels submenu. Click the Sound tab near the top of the window, and then select a soundtrack from the drop-down menu.

5 Where is your built-in microphone and how do you turn it on?

A: The small rectangle above the iMac screen is a microphone. To turn the microphone on, open the Monitors & Sounds (or Sound) control panel and select Built-in Mic from the Sound Monitoring Source drop-down menu.

6 How do you give your iMac a new voice?

A: Open the Speech control panel and select Voice from the Options drop-down menu. Select a voice from the Voice drop-down menu.

7 How do you turn off the Talking Alerts you hear when you don't dismiss a dialog box right away?

A: Open the Speech control panel, select Talking Alerts from the Options drop-down menu, and then clear the Speak the alert text check box.

8 What is the difference between a QuickTime video and a QuickTime virtual reality movie?

A: QuickTime videos are two-dimensional multimedia presentations. QuickTime virtual reality movies give you the ability to view an object or setting from all vantage points, and even move through them in some cases.

Visual Quiz

Q: When would you see these windows? What do they accomplish?

A: When you open the Speech control panel, select Talking Alerts, choose Edit Phrase List from the drop-down menu, and then click the Add button. These windows let you create your own talking alert for dialog boxes.

Chapter 10

See page 179

1. **How do you connect your iMac's internal modem to a phone line?**

A: Find the iMac modem jack behind the access panel on the right side of your iMac. Attach a telephone cable between your iMac and a telephone wall jack. If you have a newer iMac, you have another option: You can purchase an AirPort Card, install it in your iMac, purchase an AirPort base station, and connect it to your wall jack with a phone cable.

2. **Where do you find your fax software?**

A: Your iMac comes with FAXstf software, which can be found in the Applications folder.

3. **How do you add a contact to your fax phonebook?**

A: Choose New Contact from the FAXstf Action menu, or click the New Contact button.

4. **How do you transfer contact information from your fax phone book to a QuickNote window?**

A: Click and drag it from the phone book to the QuickNote window.

5. **How do you send a fax from within another application?**

A: Open the Chooser from the Apple menu and select FaxPrint. Return to your application, open the File menu, and then select Fax.

6. **How do you create a fax cover page?**

A: In the FAXstf Fax Browser, choose Edit Cover Pages from the Edit menu. You can edit an existing cover page, or create a new one by choosing Empty Cover Page from the drop-down menu and giving it a name.

7. **How do you set your fax software to answer calls automatically?**

A: To set up FAXstf to automatically answer your phone, open your FAXstf Settings and select Fax Modem. Now, change Answer On from Never to the number of rings that seems appropriate, and then click the Done button.

8. **Where do faxes you've received go?**

A: All incoming fax transmission are archived in the FAX In folder in the FAXstf Fax Browser.

Visual Quiz

Q: How do you get to this window? What can you do with it?

A: Open your Fax Browser and choose Edit Cover Pages from the Edit menu. You can create and modify fax cover pages here.

Chapter 11

See page 191

1. **What does ISP stand for? What services do they provide?**

A: ISP stands for Internet Service Provider. ISPs provide connections to the World Wide Web, e-mail accounts, and access to other Internet functions, such as file downloads.

Personal Workbook Answers

2 How do you connect your iMac to AOL if you already have an AOL account?

A: Install the AOL software by double-clicking the America Online icon in the Internet folder. Once it is installed and you've selected your access numbers, click the appropriate radio button that indicates you're a current member. You'll be asked for your screen name and password.

3 How do you receive e-mail with your ISP or AOL account?

A: With an ISP: Double-click the Mail icon on your Desktop, or select Mail from the Internet Access submenu in the Apple menu. With AOL: Sign on to AOL. If you have e-mail you'll hear the famous You've Got Mail! alert. Click the mailbox icon on the AOL toolbar or on the Welcome screen.

4 How do you reply to an e-mail you received?

A: Click the Reply button on the e-mail you received. A new e-mail composition window will open. Type your reply, and then click the Send button.

5 What are the two components of an e-mail address?

A: An e-mail address consists of the user name (to the left of the @ symbol) and the domain name (everything to the right of the @ symbol.)

6 What does http:// indicate? How can you use this information on the Web?

A: The string of characters that begins with "http://" in the address bar of your Web browser is a page's address. You can go directly to a Web page if you know its address.

7 How can you search several Web sites at one time?

A: Use a search resource — either the search page available on your browser or a search engine such as Lycos or AltaVista. Another good option is to use Sherlock's Search Internet feature.

8 How can you set parental controls to limit your children's access to the Internet?

A: If you use an ISP, install EdView using the CD-ROM that came with your iMac. If you use AOL, sign on to AOL and go to the keyword: PARENTAL CONTROLS.

Visual Quiz

Q: What do you do at this window? How do you get here?

A: You can search the Internet (assuming you are currently connected to the Internet). Choose Sherlock from the Apple menu, or press Command+F while you are in the Finder.

Chapter 12

See page 207

1 What kind of cable do you need to connect two iMacs?

A: An Ethernet crossover cable.

2 What are two ways to turn file sharing on?

A: From the File Sharing control panel and from the File Sharing button on the Control Strip. A third alternative is to choose Start File Sharing from the Automated Tasks submenu under the Apple menu.

3 How do you connect to a computer on your network?

A: Open Chooser, select AppleTalk on the left side, double-click the computer name on the right side, connect to the computer, indicate which item(s) you want to use, and click the OK button.

4. **How do you use a program on another computer to which you're connected?**

A: Connect to the computer through the Chooser, locate the program on the computer's disk, and then open it normally. If it doesn't allow you to open it, verify that Program Linking is enabled on the other computer.

5. **How do you prevent something on your computer from being renamed by someone using it across the network?**

A: Select the item in the Finder, press Command+I, choose Sharing from the drop-down menu, and then select the option Can't move, rename, or delete this item.

6. **How do you create a new user name and password?**

A: Open the Users & Groups control panel, click New User, and then type their name and password.

7. **How do you monitor your network activity levels?**

A: Open the File Sharing control panel and click the Activity Monitor tab at the top of the window.

8. **How can you connect to a remote computer using your modem?**

A: Open the Remote Access control panel, type your user name and password, type the phone number of the computer to which you want to connect, select AppleTalk from the Remote Access menu and choose Remote Only, and then click the Connect button.

Visual Quiz

Q: How do you open this window? What do you use it for?

A: Choose Remote Access Status from the Apple menu. This window is used for the connecting to, monitoring, and disconnecting from a remote location.

Chapter 13

See page 227

1. **Why should you avoid adding lots of fancy utilities to your iMac?**

A: You increase the chances of creating conflicts when you add utilities to your iMac, and conflicts can lead to crashes.

2. **How do you rebuild your Desktop?**

A: Power up your iMac, and then hold down the Option and Command keys until you're asked if you want to rebuild your Desktop. Then click the OK button.

3. **What is your first line of defense against viruses on your iMac?**

A: Use common sense, and don't accept files from strangers or disreputable companies.

4. **How can you protect yourself from the AutoStart Virus?**

A: Disable the AutoPlay features in your QuickTime Settings control panel.

5. **How do you lock a file on your iMac?**

A: Select the file in the Finder, press Command+I, and select the Locked box in the lower-left corner of the General Information pane.

6. **What are some simple ways to back up your important data?**

A: Save another copy (or two, or three, or ten) in another spot on your hard drive, send yourself a copy of the file in e-mail, or save a copy of the file on removable media.

7. **Do you need to back up all your files regularly?**

A: The safe answer is yes. You can never be too careful. On the other hand, you can choose to save only your documents (if you have the installation discs for all your applications).

Personal Workbook Answers

8 **Why is it important to occasionally optimize your iMac's hard drive?**

A: Because your hard drive becomes fragmented over time, which results in slower performance and more disk problems.

Visual Quiz

Q: **How do you get this window? What can you do here to help secure your iMac?**

A: Choose General Controls from the Control Panels submenu under the Apple menu. The Folder Protection option (in the lower-left corner of the window) allows you to safeguard your System Folder and your Applications folder.

Chapter 14

See page 243

1 **What is the benefit of having your Desktop visible in the background? The drawback?**

A: The benefit is that you can change to the Finder by simply clicking the Desktop in the background. The drawback is that you may accidentally click it when you attempt to click the scroll bar. If you find that you frequently click it accidentally, you can disable the feature in General Controls.

2 **How do you change the image or pattern on your Desktop?**

A: Open the Appearance control panel, click the Desktop tab, select a pattern from the list, and then click the Set Desktop button. Alternatively, you can click the Place Picture button to locate, and then choose an image for your Desktop.

3 **How do you view keyboard shortcuts in dialog boxes?**

A: Hold down the Command key to see keyboard shortcuts (if any exist). You can use them by continuing to hold down the Command key and typing the shortcut key.

4 **How do you increase your screen resolution?**

A: Open the Monitors & Sound (or Sound) control panel and select a new resolution size from the list on the right. Alternatively, you can choose a new resolution from the Resolution menu on the Control Strip.

5 **How can you organize your Apple Menu?**

A: Open your Apple Menu Items folder inside your System folder, locate the items you want to move to the top of your menu, and type a space (or two, or three) before their titles. Alternatively, you can create folders and place items in folders.

6 **How do you get your iMac to greet you on startup?**

A: Move a sound file that you found or created to your Startup Items folder within your System folder and restart your iMac.

7 **What does Energy Saver do? How do you turn it off?**

A: Energy Saver puts your iMac in sleep mode after a set amount of idle (inactive) time, among other things. You can disable Energy Saver's automatic sleep mode by opening the Energy Saver control panel and sliding the adjustment control to the Never setting.

8 **Where are some places you can find utilities for your iMac?**

A: On the Internet at **http://www.shareware.com** or on AOL at the keyword: DOWNLOAD SOFTWARE.

Visual Quiz

Q: Where do you find this control panel? What does it do?

A: Pull down the Apple menu, select Control Panels, and choose Mouse. The Mouse control panel adjusts your mouse tracking speed and double-click rate.

Chapter 15

See page 265

1 What are the three differences between your hard drive memory and your RAM memory?

A: Size, speed, and permanence. Your hard drive's memory is larger, slower, and permanent, while your RAM memory is smaller, faster, and temporary.

2 What is a memory block? Where do you find your largest unused memory block?

A: A memory block is a single chunk of memory used by your iMac. You can check the size of your largest unused memory block at any time by going to the Finder and choosing About This Computer from the Apple menu.

3 How do you increase an application's memory allocation? By what percentages should you increase it?

A: Quit the application you want to reallocate, select its icon on the Desktop, choose Memory from the Get Info submenu under the File menu, and then type a new amount in the Suggested Size field. A 25 to –50 percent memory allocation increase is a good guideline for most applications.

4 What is the keyboard shortcut to get more information about an application?

A: Command+I.

5 What is your disk cache? How do you increase or decrease it?

A: Your disk cache is a special part of your computer's memory that holds information about the recent things you've done on your iMac. To reallocate memory for your disk cache, open your Memory control panel, click the Custom setting, and adjust the disk cache amount.

6 How do you increase your virtual memory? How much hard disk space does virtual memory require?

A: Open your Memory control panel and click the up or down arrows next to the total amount of memory you'd like to have available as memory. The hard disk space taken up on your hard disk by virtual memory is equivalent to the total amount of memory (built-in RAM plus additional virtual memory).

7 What is the benefit of using a RAM disk? The drawback?

A: The benefit is much faster performance from applications installed on and being run from the RAM disk. The drawbacks are that the RAM disk will be lost if you crash or lose power, and you have that much less of your RAM available for use by applications.

8 How much RAM do you have? How much more can you add?

A: To find out how much RAM you have, open the Apple System Profiler and note the amount next to built-in memory. Subtract this number from 256 to learn how much more memory you can add to your iMac.

Visual Quiz

Q: How do you produce this window? What information does this window convey?

A: Open Apple System Profiler from the Apple menu and click the Devices and Windows tab. This window offers information about your hard drives and other media, including specific information about your RAM disk (if one has been created).

Personal Workbook Answers

Chapter 16

See page 281

1 How do you execute a ready-made AppleScript (automated task)?

A: Double-click the script icon or choose it from a menu. You may also need to click the Run button.

2 Where can you find additional AppleScript automated tasks?

A: Additional scripts are located in the AppleScript folder on your hard drive (look in the More Automated Tasks folder) and on your iMac Install CD-ROM disc (look in the AppleScript Extras folder in your CD Extras folder). You will also find scripts with some applications — do a search in Sherlock to find all scripts on your hard drive.

3 Where is the Script Editor? What does it do?

A: The Script Editor is located in your AppleScript folder inside your Apple Extras folder on your hard drive. The Script Editor allows you to write, record, test, and record AppleScript tasks.

4 Where can you learn more about the AppleScript scripting language?

A: Under the Help menu within the Script Editor, and on the Internet at **http://www.apple.com/applescript/**.

5 How can you create your own script without knowing the scripting language?

A: Use Script Editor's record function and then perform the task for which you want to create a script.

6 Can you record a script for anything you want to do on your iMac? Why or why not?

A: No. Not all applications support AppleScript recording with the Script Editor.

7 What is a macro? How do you create one?

A: A macro is a set of actions which you can perform with a single keystroke (or the click of a mouse button).

8 What is an action?

A: An action is a discrete operation, such as selecting an icon, choosing a menu item, and so on. Scripts generally incorporate one or more actions. Action is also another word for a script in some applications.

Visual Quiz

Q: How do you navigate to this window? What does it offer?

A: Insert your iMac Install CD-ROM disc, open the CD Extras folder, open the AppleScript Extras folder, and then open the More Sample Scripts folder. Additional pre-made AppleScripts are located here.

Chapter 17

See page 293

1 How do you restart your iMac if you can't choose Restart from the Special menu?

A: Two ways. Either Press Control+Command+ the power button or, if that doesn't work, press a straightened paper clip into the restart access hole behind the access panel until your iMac restarts.

2 How do your force quit an application on your iMac?

A: Press Option+Command+Esc.

3 If you can't locate a file, what keyboard shortcut can you use to search for it on your hard drive?

A: Press Command+F to open Sherlock.

4 If your iMac complains that it cannot open or find your printer, what should you do?

A: First verify that your printer is turned on and connected to your iMac. Next verify that your printer is selected in the Chooser. Then verify that AppleTalk (and your network, if you have one) is turned on. If you have a network, you also may want to reset your network hub or bridge.

5 How do you set your Desktop to display all its icons in neat rows and columns?

A: Click the Desktop, choose View Options from the View menu, and then select Always snap to grid.

6 If all your icons now look like blank sheets of paper, how do you restore them to normal?

A: Rebuild your Desktop by restarting your iMac and holding down the Option+Command keys until you're asked if you want to rebuild the Desktop. Click the OK button.

7 What are two ways to resolve extension conflicts?

A: Use Extensions Manager to home in on and disable the problem extensions, or purchase and install Conflict Catcher 8 (or later).

8 What is Apple's Web site address?

A: **http://www.apple.com.** The iMac-specific address is **http://www.apple.com/imac**.

Visual Quiz

Q: What does this dialog box signify?

A: This dialog box appears when you try to open a file and the application that created it cannot be found.

Glossary

10Base-T A kind of Ethernet connection. It describes a network with 10 megabit per second capacity that uses 4-twisted-pair cable and RJ-45 connectors.

100Base-T 100 megabit per second Ethernet, otherwise identical to 10Base-T.

Active application On the Macintosh, a running application that is on top — its window(s) and menu items are available for immediate use. *See background application.*

Adobe PostScript System for describing type fonts so that font size, shape, and other attributes can be changed without distorting the appearance of the font. A proprietary technology of Adobe Corp.

Adobe Type Manager (ATM) Application program found in the iMac Control Panels for improving the appearance of fonts on a computer screen. It can also smooth fonts printed on a non-PostScript printer. A proprietary technology of Adobe Corp.

Air Port A wireless network technology enabled in newer iMacs (those introduced in October 1999).

Alias An icon or menu item that points to a file, folder, or application located elsewhere on the computer. Selecting an alias has the same effect as selecting the actual item it represents.

America Online (AOL) The world's largest Internet Online Service. AOL provides news, information, entertainment, e-mail, chat, and Internet access services to nearly 20 million subscribers worldwide.

AOL *See America Online.*

Appearance Control Panel that allows iMac users to change the cosmetic appearance of Macintosh onscreen items such as windows, menus, backgrounds, sounds, and wallpaper, and the fonts used in menus, title bars, dialog boxes, and icons.

Apple Computer Designer and manufacturer of the iMac computer and the Macintosh Operating System.

Apple key *See Command key.*

Apple menu Menu item represented by a multicolored apple icon, ever-present on the far left of the iMac menu bar. The Apple menu provides access to Control Panels and many other important applications and utilities.

AppleScript Application included with the Macintosh OS which permits the user to automate certain tasks involving the Macintosh OS and some other application programs. Also refers to the individual applications created with AppleScript.

AppleShare A network protocol built into the Macintosh OS that permits the sharing of files between computers on the network. Also an icon in Chooser used to connect an iMac to other computers on an Apple network.

AppleTalk A network protocol used by Macintosh computers for basic communication between those computers.

AppleWorks Previously called ClarisWorks. An application program combining word processor, spreadsheet, database, communications, drawing, and painting.

Glossary

Application A computer program (or set of instructions) designed to perform a task or series of tasks unrelated to the fundamental operation of the computer. Common applications include word processors, spreadsheets, databases, Web browsers, and games.

Application switching An aspect of multitasking. The ability to switch from one running application to another without closing either application.

ASCII American Standard Code for Information Interchange. The ASCII code defines 128 text characters (upper- and lowercase), numbers, and symbols, much like Morse Code did in the days of the telegraph. The common use of ASCII for e-mail, Web pages, and many other kinds of computer generated files promotes worldwide communication via computers.

B

Background application A running application which is not on top. It may be performing tasks, but another application is currently on top.

Backup A copy of individual computer files or the contents of an entire computer disk, created to preserve the information in case of equipment failure or other loss.

Baud A unit of measure common to data communication via modem. Equivalent to a rate of one data bit per second.

Binary The common system used to encode information for manipulation by a computer. All information is represented by a combination of ones and zeros (the base 2 number system). The zeros and ones of binary code can be represented by an on or off condition of a switch or other electronic device.

Bit The smallest unit of computer information, representing either a single one or zero of binary code.

Boot To start up (power up) a computer. *See boot sequence.*

Boot sequence The steps a computer goes through during startup. Commonly, a boot sequence includes testing the computer's critical components and loading its operating system.

Bridge Electronic device intended to connect incompatible computer networks. Bridges are commonly used to connect older AppleTalk networks to the Ethernet networks that are used by iMacs and other more recent Apple computers.

Browser Application program used to view information posted on the Internet's World Wide Web. Browsers fetch, assemble, and display Web pages from the many individual files that can make up a single page. The iMac comes with three browsers: Microsoft Internet Explorer, Netscape Navigator, and the AOL browser.

Button An onscreen representation of a push button which can be pressed when the mouse pointer is brought over the button and the mouse button is clicked.

Byte A group of 8 data bits which, together, carry encoded computer information. A byte in ASCII code represents a single character of text. A series of bytes may be combined into a single binary word. *See also ASCII, Binary, and Bit.*

C

Cache Literally, to store. In a computer, a cache is a section of memory in RAM or on disk set aside for temporary storage of data that may be needed in the near future.

CD-R drive A compact disk drive that can record CD-ROMs, as well as play them. Normally available as a peripheral device in an iMac. Special laser-sensitive blank CDs are required; once recorded, they cannot be erased and re-recorded.

CD-ROM Compact Disk-Read Only Memory. CDs that contain computer programs and data, rather than music.

Glossary

CD-ROM drive A compact disc player intended for use in a computer. Despite the name, CD-ROM drives can play nearly any kind of CD, provided the correct software is loaded in the computer.

Chooser A utility found in the Apple menu. Used to specify and select the printers (and networks) attached to an iMac.

Click A single press-and-release of the button on a mouse.

Click and Drag The mouse gesture used to highlight text and to move selected text or other objects across the screen to another location. The user selects the object, positions the mouse pointer above that object, clicks and holds down the mouse button, moves the mouse so that the object is in the desired position, and then releases the mouse button.

Client/Server network A computer networking arrangement where centralized server computers provide services and facilities such as data storage, e-mail, and Internet access to individual client computers attached to the network. America Online is an example of a client/server relationship, where AOL's central computers are the servers and each home user is a client.

Clipboard A core facility of the Macintosh OS. The clipboard is a section of memory that stores the most recent data that has been cut or copied, so that it may later be pasted elsewhere. As the clipboard is part of the Mac OS rather than any one application, materials copied in one application can be pasted into another application. The current contents of the clipboard are erased whenever new data is copied, and the information is lost if the computer crashes or is shut down.

Close box A button in the upper-left corner of a window. When clicked, the window closes.

Cold boot Starting a computer from a power-off condition. A cold boot differs from a warm boot in that all power has been removed from the computer prior to starting, positively resetting the condition of all electronic circuits.

Collapse box A button in the upper-right corner of a window. When clicked, the bulk of the window disappears (minimizes), leaving only the title bar. When clicked again, the window reappears.

Command key Also known as the Apple key, for the Apple icon it displays. Normally found to the left of the spacebar on the iMac keyboard, it's used in combination with other keys to perform a variety of keyboard shortcuts and other functions.

Connector Devices used to attach wires and cables to computers and other electrical equipment. Specific connectors are used for specific purposes, and there are generally two complimentary male and female mating connectors known commonly as a plug and socket (or jack).

Control key The Control key is used in combination with other keys to perform a variety of keyboard shortcuts and other functions. Located in the lower-left corner of the iMac keyboard.

Control panel A utility or built-in function of the Macintosh OS used to change settings and features of the computer or specific applications. Control Panels are found in the Control Panels folder inside the System Folder and in the Control Panels submenu in the Apple menu.

Control strip A group of icons found (by default) at the bottom of the iMac Desktop. The control strip supplies shortcuts to certain frequently used features and controls. It can be resized by clicking and dragging the tab on the far right side.

Copy To duplicate computer data. *See Copy file/folder and Copy text/data.*

Copy file/folder To duplicate one or more data files, or the contents of an entire folder or group of folders.

Copy text/data To duplicate text, data, or graphics displayed onscreen so that it can be pasted into another application or document. Copied text or data is stored in the Clipboard.

Glossary

CPU Central Processing Unit. The brain of a computer. In personal computers like the iMac, a single CPU on an integrated circuit chip directly performs or controls all the calculations and manipulations that take place in the computer.

Crash The abrupt, catastrophic failure of a computer program, operating system, or the computer itself. Crashes generally do not involve physical damage to the computer, but rather, the loss of power, or an error or errors in the application or operating system. Commonly, the computer can be successfully restarted following a crash, with only the loss of work that was in process immediately prior to the crash. The failure of component parts such as hard drives can also cause a crash, in which case the computer may need repairs, and all data on the hard drive may be permanently lost.

Cursor *See Mouse pointer.*

Cursor keys A group of four keys that can be used to move the cursor around a computer screen, in lieu of a mouse. The cursor keys are; up-arrow, down-arrow, left-arrow and right-arrow.

Cut To copy data to the clipboard while deleting that data from its current location.

Data Information. Data files contain text, images, numbers, sounds, and so forth.

Database A program designed to store and retrieve data in an organized manner, and to analyze and display that data in useful forms. Also, a data file or group of related data files created by a database program, dedicated to a particular purpose.

D

Delete Erase. Also a key on the iMac keyboard used to delete selected text or items.

Desktop The central workspace of a Macintosh computer, displayed on the computer's monitor. Like an actual desktop, all your work is done on top of the Desktop, and all the facilities, tools, and resources you need are found on the Desktop. Also known as the Finder.

Desktop pattern A color, pattern, or graphic used to decorate your Desktop. May also be called wallpaper.

Dialog box A small window that appears onscreen to request data input or to deliver a message.

Dialup A network connection via a conventional telephone line. The networking application and computer's modem dial a specific phone number in order to be connected to the computer network. Most connections to America Online and other ISPs are via dialup.

DIMM Dual In-line Memory Module. The small electronic circuit boards to which the integrated circuit chips are affixed that, in turn, makes up the RAM in an iMac. An iMac can hold two DIMMs, each of which can have between 32MB and 256MB of RAM (depending on the iMac model).

DNS Domain Name Server. The master address book system of the Internet, and of any other computer network that uses the Internet's TCP/IP networking protocol. Also, a server on a TCP/IP network which stores the address and location of every computer on that network. The Internet has many DNS servers, each of which holds a complete copy of the addresses maintained on the Master DNS server.

Documents Data files that generally hold text, graphics, or similar information.

Domain name A primary address on the Internet, such as Apple.com, AOL.com or Jenuine.net. A domain is roughly equivalent to city and state in a conventional postal address.

Double-click To press and release a mouse button twice, in rapid succession. Double-clicking an icon opens a file or runs an application.

Drag To move a mouse, usually while pressing the mouse button. Dragging can be used to select text or to move objects around onscreen.

Driver A small utility program associated with a particular piece of equipment, such as a printer, modem, or removable media drive. A driver functions as an adapter, so that the equipment will function correctly when connected to the computer. Some drivers come preinstalled with the Macintosh OS, and others are supplied when you purchase a piece of peripheral equipment.

DVD-ROM Digital Video Disc-Read Only Memory. The successor technology to the compact disc. DVD-ROM drives can play older CDs, as well as newer DVDs. DVDs can be used to store video, audio, and data. The iMac DVD models come with built-in DVD-ROM drives.

E

E-mail Electronic Mail. Text messages sent between computers and related devices via a network using a set of standard protocols.

Encryption The encoding of data so it cannot be viewed by others. The Mac OS 9 offers an Encrypt feature for protecting files.

Energy saver A feature of the Macintosh OS which shuts down monitors and hard disks after a predetermined period of inactivity. Energy Saver settings can be adjusted using the Energy Saver control panel.

Error message A dialog box that appears onscreen to warn you of a program failure or other problem. Error messages should be written down to aid in the troubleshooting process.

Escape key Key in the upper-left of the iMac keyboard, marked Esc. Used in conjunction with the Option key and the Command key to abort an application that has frozen.

Ethernet A communications system used for computer networking. Ethernet defines the wiring and electrical characteristics of the network. Ethernet supports the operation of networking protocols such as AppleTalk and TCP/IP, both of which can operate over Ethernet.

Ethernet adapter An electronic circuit built into an iMac (and available as an accessory on other computers) which permits the computer to be attached to an Ethernet network.

Ethernet bridge An electronic device used to connect multiple Ethernet networks, or non-Ethernet networks, to an Ethernet network. Commonly needed to connect older AppleLink/AppleTalk networks or printers to an iMac.

Ethernet hub An electronic device that functions as a central connection point for computers and other equipment attached to a 10Base-T or 100Base-T Ethernet network.

Extensions Manager A utility provided with the Macintosh OS to help users identify extensions and resolve conflicts between extensions that may be having a negative effect on the operation of the computer.

Extensions Additions to the Macintosh OS intended to expand the capabilities of the OS, for the benefit of one or more applications. Extensions are commonly installed during the installation of a new application program.

FAQ Frequently Asked Questions. Help documents at Web sites are often called FAQs.

Field A single category of information within a database record, such as first name, street address, or postal code in an address book. Also, a text entry box in a computer application, where the information will be stored within a particular field in a database. *See Record.*

Glossary

File A unit of storage on a computer. Each file has a unique name, and contains either data or program instructions. Typically, a single document is stored in a file, but some applications consist of many files.

File locking A feature of the Macintosh OS that allows a file to be protected from accidental or intentional erasure.

File sharing A feature of Macintosh networking that makes files on one computer available to the users of other computers on the network.

Finder *See Desktop.*

F-Keys Function Keys. The keys across the top of the keyboard — F1, F2, and so on — which are often assigned special functions by various applications.

Floppy disk A removable storage device once prevalent on personal computers. The iMac does not include a built-in floppy drive.

Folder A method of organizing information and applications in the Macintosh OS, analogous to folders in a filing cabinet. Folders can hold files, as well as other folders.

Font An electronic file that defines a particular style of type with which you can display and print text. Also refers directly to the distinctive style of that type.

FTP File Transfer Protocol. An Internet protocol for transporting data files across that network.

Function keys *See F-Keys.*

G

GIF Graphic Interchange Format. A file format for photographs and other images originally developed by the CompuServe Information Service (CIS). GIF files are commonly used on the Web.

Gigabyte About 1 billion bytes. Typically used as a measure of size in a computer file or memory, as in a 6 Gigabyte hard drive. Abbreviated as GB.

Graphic An image, such as a drawing or photograph.

Graphical User Interface (GUI) A major principle underlying the Macintosh OS. A GUI attempts to make a computer more user-friendly by providing graphical objects such as icons and buttons to represent programs and actions, and pointing devices such as mice, which permit a user to gesture, point, and manipulate the information onscreen in a manner closer to a non-machine environment. GUIs also provide a What You See Is What You Get environment for text and graphics, so that the image onscreen will look like the final printed document.

Grayed-out Buttons, icons, folders, menu items, or windows belonging to running applications that are not currently available for use, or features that are not appropriate for current conditions. Grayed-out folders and icons are already open, or the program they represent is already running. Grayed-out windows belong to background applications, and can be brought on top by clicking the window. This converts the application from a background application to an active (foreground) application.

Hard disk *See hard drive.*

Hard drive A device for the storage of computer files. Every iMac comes equipped with a hard drive, upon which is stored the Macintosh OS, application programs, and data files. Files stored on a hard drive are copied into RAM for use and computation, and the results are recorded back to the hard drive. Information on a hard drive remains intact when the power is turned off.

Hardware Physical computing equipment, including monitors, circuit boards, hard drives, and keyboards.

Highlight To select a block of onscreen text for further manipulation. The computer user clicks and drags the mouse across the desired text, and that text is displayed as light text against a dark background. Once text has been highlighted, it may be dragged to another location, copied, deleted, or reformatted.

Home page The first Web page displayed by a browser when a person accesses the World Wide Web. Users may designate any home page they desire by changing a setting in their browser.

HTML Hypertext Markup Language. The language and formatting codes interpreted by browsers to display Web pages.

http Hypertext Transfer Protocol. The networking protocol of the World Wide Web.

I

Icon A graphical image used to represent an application, file, hard drive, printer, or other object on a computer screen. Double-clicking an icon will perform an action, such as running the application.

Internet An international, public computer network, originally developed by the U.S. Department of Defense to facilitate communications among corporations, as well as educational and research institutions, working on defense projects.

Internet Service Provider A business that connects individual users to the Internet, usually over a dial-up connection.

IP address The unique numeric address of a computer or other resource connected to a TCP/IP network.

ISP *See Internet Service Provider.*

J

JPEG A common file format for graphics and photographs that is very popular on the Web. JPEG stands for Joint Photographic Experts Group, the organization that set the technical standards for this file format. Also abbreviated as JPG.

K

Key caps A utility supplied by the Macintosh OS that displays the characters, accessible from the keyboard, in a selected font.

Keyboard The oblong-shaped input device used to type and navigate.

Keyboard shortcut Two or more keys that, when pressed down together or in prescribed sequence, can execute a command or perform a function that is more commonly accomplished by clicking buttons or selecting menu options with a mouse.

Kilobyte 1,024 bytes. Commonly used as a measure of the size of a computer file. Abbreviated as KB.

L

LAN Local Area Network. A small computer network, generally encompassing an office or a single building.

Load The process of transferring computer data from storage to active memory. When a program is loaded, it is ready to run. When data is loaded, it is ready to be acted upon by a running program.

Glossary

M

Macintosh A computer and operating system developed and manufactured by Apple Computer that employs a graphical user interface. The iMac is a Macintosh.

Megabytes 1,048,576 bytes. Commonly used as a measure of computer memory capacity in RAM and hard drives. Abbreviated as MB.

Memory A song from the Broadway musical, *Cats*, with lyrics adapted from T.S. Eliot, with the music by Andrew Lloyd Webber. Also, various systems for storing data and programs for use by a computer.

Modem A device that converts computer data into a signal that can be sent over a voice-grade telephone line to another computer. The same device also can decode a signal received over a voice-grade phone line.

Monitor A video display screen that provides visual information to a computer user.

Mouse An electromechanical device used as part of the interface between human and computer. Movements of the mouse are represented on the computer screen by a pointer, so that a person's hand gestures can be translated to onscreen actions. The mouse includes a pushbutton so that the user can initiate an action after positioning the mouse pointer over an onscreen simulation of a pushbutton.

Mouse pointer The onscreen representation of the position of a mouse. Depending on circumstances, the pointer may be an arrow, a hand, or a vertical I-shaped bar called an I-beam.

Multitasking The ability of a computer and operating system to run more than one application or task at a time. The Macintosh OS is a multitasking operating system.

Murphy's Law "Anything that can go wrong will go wrong, and at the worst possible moment." The creed of computer users everywhere.

N

Network A method for interconnecting computers so they can share information and resources such as data files and printers.

O

Online To be connected to a network, to the Internet, or to a service such as America Online, where information and communications can be exchanged in a real-time environment.

On top When more than one application is running, the application whose window is active and foremost on the screen. The title bar of a window on top has dark labels and a series of horizontal lines, and its control buttons are both visible and accessible. When an application is on top. the menu bar items will be appropriate to that application.

Operating System (OS) A collection of computer programs that controls the behavior of a computer, including the manner in which memory and data is organized and stored; the way that the computer communicates with hard drives, keyboards, peripheral devices, and networks; and, the onscreen user interface.

P

Paste To insert the data stored on the iMac clipboard into the selected location in a document or application.

Peer-to-peer network A network in which each computer on the network may act as a server to other computers, sharing the contents of hard drives and other resources. Macintosh computers come with built-in support for peer-to-peer networking.

Peripheral An optional computing device connected, but external, to a computer. Peripherals include floppy drives, printers, scanners, network hubs, and removable media drives.

PICT The native graphic file format of the Macintosh. Icons are PICT images. PICT is not compatible with the Microsoft Windows operating system, among others, so PICT images are commonly converted to GIF or JPEG prior to being exchanged with other computer users via the Internet.

Pointer *See Mouse pointer.*

PostScript *See Adobe PostScript.*

PPP A network protocol used for connecting to an ISP via a dial-up connection.

PRAM Parameter Random Access Memory. A section of integrated circuit memory in an iMac which is used to store basic configuration information. The contents of PRAM are preserved during power-off conditions by battery power. The battery must be replaced roughly every 2–3 years, and the configurations saved in PRAM will have to be manually restored after the battery is replaced.

Print queue A procedure for controlling the printing of multiple documents. As each document is prepared for printing, the print data is stored in a file on the hard drive until the printer has completed the printing of the previous document. Once a document has been added to the queue, the computer user is free to proceed with other tasks.

Printer driver *See Driver.*

Program *See Application.*

Protocol A collection of technical standards and procedures specific to a particular system or function. Standardized protocols underlie all computer networking systems, including the Internet.

Q

QuickTime A file format for presenting multimedia content developed by Apple Computer.

R

RAM Random Access Memory. High-speed computer memory utilizing integrated circuits, commonly used for the storage of currently running computer applications and the data files needed by those applications. The contents of RAM are constantly changing and are generally lost if the computer crashes or loses power.

RAM disk A portion of RAM set aside to simulate the behavior of a hard drive or other removable storage. RAM disks are far faster than the disks they simulate, but the contents of a RAM disk will be lost during a crash or loss of power.

Reboot To restart a computer and its operating system. *See Restart.*

Record In a database, a collection of related information. For example, a single name, address, and phone number entry in an address book. A record will contain multiple fields, and every record will have the same fields. *See Field.*

Removable media Devices such as CD-ROM drives, floppy disk drives, Jaz or Syquest drives, and backup tape drives. The removable nature of the disks and tapes allows easy exchange of information with other computer users and off-premises storage of important data. It also can extend the storage capacity of a computer beyond the capacity of its built-in hard disk.

Resize box An area in the lower-right corner of some windows, indicated by a series of diagonal lines. When present, a user can click and drag the resize box to change the dimensions of the window.

Restart To reload a computer's operating system.

ROM Read Only Memory. Computer memory that can be read, but that cannot be erased. Generally, information in ROM will survive during a power failure.

RTFM An acronym sometimes used by frustrated technical support personnel when faced with a person who, unlike you, didn't do their homework. Stands for Read the flipping manual!

Run To load and place a computer program into active use.

Running application An application that is currently loaded in memory and ready for use. Running applications may be either in the background or on top.

S

Save To record the current data or document to a hard drive or other permanent storage media, such as a removable media drive. It is important to save data frequently to avoid data loss.

Scanner A device to convert a photograph, printed document or other graphic into a computer format.

Scroll bars A feature of a window that allows the user to view more information than can be displayed in the window at any one time. When scroll bars are present, the user can click the up-, down-, left-, or right-arrow buttons, or click and drag a slider box, to view information that would otherwise be hidden.

Search engine A program designed to search for information.

Select The act of clicking an icon or menu item, or highlighting text with a mouse.

Server A computer attached to a network that provides centralized services to the users of that network.

Sherlock A utility supplied with the Macintosh OS used for searching the iMac, the network, and the Internet for information.

Shutdown A function of the Macintosh OS that closes all operations of the computer in a systematic manner, so that no information is lost or corrupted. The shutdown command can be found on the Special menu in the Finder.

Shutdown items A folder in the System Folder that contains applications, AppleScripts, sounds, or files that are executed following a Shutdown command but before the computer actually shuts down.

Sign On To connect to a network or online service such as AOL. Generally requires the use of a password.

Sleep A function of the Energy Saver feature, which shuts down the monitor and hard drive without totally shutting down the computer. A user can place a computer in sleep mode from the Special menu on the Desktop. A computer in Sleep mode can be reawakened quickly with the press of a key, far faster than it would take to restart.

SMTP Simple Mail Transfer Protocol. The standard protocol for e-mail on the Internet.

SND The standard Macintosh audio file format. Not compatible with most other operating systems, including Microsoft Windows.

Software Computer applications (programs).

Spreadsheet A type of application optimized to store and manipulate numbers. Spreadsheets display information in an array of rows and columns, much like the ledger paper used by an accountant. Numbers and formulas are entered into cells, and those cells will display the result of a prescribed calculation.

Startup disk A disk that has a System Folder on it. A removable media (i.e., CD-ROM) startup disk can be used to startup a computer in the case of a hard disk or operating system failure. On an iMac, the iMac Install CD-ROM that came with the computer is its startup disk. Don't lose it.

Startup items A folder in the System Folder that contains applications, AppleScripts, sounds, or files that are automatically run at startup.

Storage Permanent memory, such as a hard drive or removable media.

Surge protector An AC outlet box that includes additional electronic components to protect your equipment from power line surges and spikes.

System *See Operating System.*

System clock The clock built into a computer, which maintains day and date information, even when the power is off.

System folder A special folder on the iMac that stores the operating system and other critical applications, utilities, and data files needed by the operating system.

T

Tape drive A kind of removable media commonly used to back up entire hard drives. Backup tape drives are very slow, but the tapes are inexpensive relative to cost of the hard drives they are protecting.

TCP/IP The networking protocol of the Internet.

Telnet An Internet protocol that allows users to access and run programs on other computers via the network. A user with Telnet access to a computer can operate that computer from anywhere in the world.

TIFF A file format used for photographs and other graphics. TIFF files are generally used in the graphic arts when high image quality must be maintained. This added detail makes TIFF files too large for many uses, including display on the Web. Scanners will commonly save a scanned image as a TIFF file to preserve maximum quality, and users then convert the file to a lower-quality format such as GIF or JPG for display on the Web. Also abbreviated as TIF.

Trash A special folder that stores files, folders, and aliases intended for deletion. Indicated by a trashcan icon on your Desktop. Items in the trash are truly deleted only when you empty the trash.

Universal Serial Bus *See USB.*

URL Uniform Resource Locator. The Internet's addressing system. Each document and resource has its own URL, such as **http://www.apple.com/index.html,** Apple Computer's home page on the World Wide Web.

USB Universal Serial Bus. A system for connecting keyboards, mice, and peripheral equipment including printers, scanners, and removable media drives, to computers. iMacs come with four USB ports, two of which are occupied by your keyboard and your mouse.

USB bridge Electronic device for connecting non-USB equipment to a USB-equipped computer.

USB hub Electronic peripheral equipment for connecting multiple USB devices to a computer.

USB port Connection point for Universal Serial Bus equipment.

Utility Program intended to augment or enhance the function of a computer or operating system.

Glossary

V

V.90 Telecommunications protocol for modems communicating at 56,000 baud.

W

Wallpaper *See Desktop pattern.*

WAN Wide Area Network. Computer networks that combine two or more Local Area Networks to encompass more than one building or a larger geographical location.

Warm boot Restarting a computer and operating system without first shutting off the power.

Web *See World Wide Web.*

Web site A location or page contained on a World Wide Web site. A site is typically comprised of many Web pages, generally organized around a central theme or topic.

Window A bounded workspace or visual display on a computer display. In the Macintosh OS, there may be many windows open onscreen at any one time, each displaying a different document or open application. Windows are bordered by a frame and have an identifying title across the top of the window to distinguish one from the other.

Word processor Application for composing, editing, and formatting text documents. AppleWorks contains a word processor.

World Wide Web A subdivision of the Internet that uses the Hypertext Transfer Protocol to present rich, multimedia content, including text, graphics, animation, video, and sound.

WWW *See World Wide Web.*

Z

Zoom box A button in the upper-right corner of a window, to the left of the Collapse Box, visible only when a window is resizable. When clicked, the window alternates in size between its original dimension and the resized dimension. *See Resize box.*

Index

Continued

Index

Index

C

Index

D

Index

E

Index

F

G

Index

Index

Continued

Index

Index

Index

O

P

Index

Index

Index

Index

T

Index

Y

Z